Arctic Ocean

FINLAND
Helsinki ■

■ Tallinn
EST.

Riga ■
LAT.

LITH.
Vilnius ■

■ Minsk

AND

BELARUS

Warsaw ■

VAKIA

atislava

Budapest ■

GARY

a

ROMANIA

Belgrade ■

IA

SLAVIA

Sofia ■

Skopje ■

na ■  FYROM.

ALB.

GREECE

Athens ■

Crete

rranean Sea

UKRAINE

MOLDOVA

■ Kiev

Dnieper R.

■ Chisinau

■ Bucharest

BULGARIA

Black Sea

RUSSIA

Moscow ■

Don R.

Volga R.

KAZAKHSTAN

Caspian Sea

GEORGIA
Tbilisi ■

ARM.          Baku ■
Yerevan ■  AZER.

■ Ankara

TURKEY

CYPRUS

Tigris R.

Euphrates

LEB. ■   SYRIA
Beirut ■   ■ Damascus

ISR.
Jerusalem ■     ■ Amman
JOR.

Cairo ■

EGYPT

Nile R.

Teheran ■

Baghdad
■

IRAN

IRAQ

R.

Kuwait ■
KUWAIT

SAUDI
ARABIA

LIBYA

QATAR

# www.wadsworth.com

*wadsworth.com* is the World Wide Web site for Wadsworth and is your direct source to dozens of online resources.

At *wadsworth.com* you can find out about supplements, demonstration software, and student resources. You can also send email to many of our authors and preview new publications and exciting new technologies.

**wadsworth.com**
Changing the way the world learns®

# Essentials of
# WESTERN CIVILIZATION

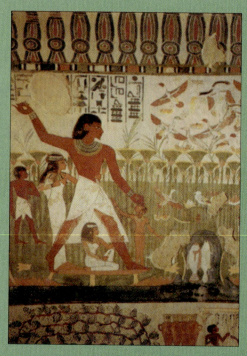

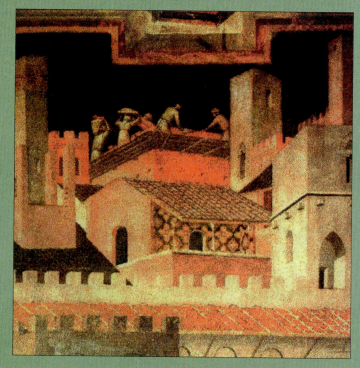

# Essentials of
# WESTERN
# CIVILIZATION

## A HISTORY OF EUROPEAN SOCIETY

*Volume 1: to 1715*

## Steven Hause
University of Missouri–St. Louis

## William Maltby
University of Missouri–St. Louis

**WADSWORTH**

**THOMSON LEARNING**

Australia • Canada • Mexico • Singapore • Spain • United Kingdom • United States

History Publisher: Clark Baxter
Senior Development Editor: Sharon Adams Poore
Assistant Editor: Cherie Hackelberg
Editorial Assistant: Jennifer Ellis
Marketing Manager: Diane McOscar
Marketing Assistant: Kristin Anderson
Print Buyer: Barbara Britton
Production Management: Lori Dalberg, Carlisle Publishers Services
Text Designer: Harry Voigt
Copy Editor: Pat Eichhorst
Maps: MapQuest.com
Cover Designer: Harry Voigt
Cover Image: Scala/Art Resource, N.Y. Master of Frankfort (15th c.). Festival of the Archers, c. 1493. Koninklijk Museum voor Schone.
Compositor: Carlisle Communications
Text and Cover Printer: R.R. Donnelley & Sons, Willard

Wadsworth/Thomson Learning
10 Davis Drive
Belmont, CA 94002-3098
USA

For more information about our products, contact us:
Thomson Learning Academic Resource Center
1-800-423-0563
http://www.wadsworth.com

International Headquarters
Thomson Learning
International Division
290 Harbor Drive, 2nd Floor
Stamford, CT 06902-7477
USA

UK/Europe/Middle East/South Africa
Thomson Learning
Berkshire House
168-173 High Holborn
London WC1V 7AA
United Kingdom

Asia
Thomson Learning
60 Albert Street, #15-01
Albert Complex
Singapore 189969

Canada
Nelson Thomson Learning
1120 Birchmount Road
Toronto, Ontario M1K 5G4
Canada

ISBN: 0-534-57871-3

# ABOUT THE AUTHORS

◆◆◆◆◆◆◆◆◆◆◆◆◆◆◆◆◆◆◆◆

**Steven C. Hause** is Professor of History and Fellow in International Studies at the University of Missouri–St. Louis, where he has won the Chancellor's Award for Excellence in Teaching (1996) and the Pierre Laclede Honors College Teacher of the Year Award (1989). He is the author and co-author of three previous books on the history of the women's rights movement in modern France, which have won four research prizes: *Women's Suffrage and Social Politics in the French Third Republic*, with Anne R. Kenney (Princeton University Press, 1984); *Hubertine Auclert, the French Suffragette* (Yale University Press, 1987); and *Feminisms of the Belle Epoque*, with Jennifer Waelti-Walters (University of Nebraska Press, 1994). His essays have appeared in several journals, including *American Historical Review* and *French Historical Studies*.

**William S. Maltby** is Professor of History Emeritus at the University of Missouri–St. Louis, where he continues to teach on a regular basis. Among his publications are: *The Black Legend in England: The Development of Anti-Spanish Sentiment, 1558–1660.* (Duke University Press, 1971), *Alba: A Biography of Fernando Alvarez de Toledo, Third Duke of Alba, 1507–1582.* (University of California Press, 1983), and articles on various aspects of Early Modern European history. From 1977 to 1997 he also served as Executive Director of the Center for Reformation Research and as editor of several volumes and series of volumes on the history of the Reformation.

# CONTENTS IN BRIEF

♦♦♦♦♦♦♦♦♦♦♦♦♦♦♦♦♦♦♦♦

### ▧ CHAPTER ▧

# CONTENTS IN DETAIL

◆◆◆◆◆◆◆◆◆◆◆◆◆◆◆◆◆◆◆◆◆

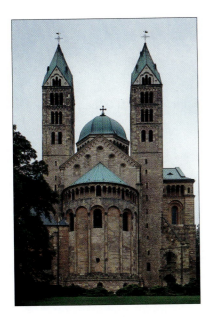

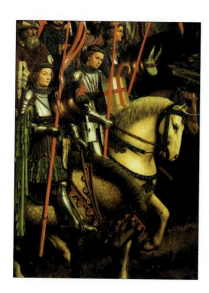

# DOCUMENTS

◆◆◆◆◆◆◆◆◆◆◆◆◆◆◆◆◆◆◆◆◆

# TABLES

◆◆◆◆◆◆◆◆◆◆◆◆◆◆◆◆◆◆◆

# MAPS

◆◆◆◆◆◆◆◆◆◆◆◆◆◆◆◆◆◆◆◆◆◆◆◆

# PREFACE

◆◆◆◆◆◆◆◆◆◆◆◆◆◆◆◆◆◆◆

*E*ssentials of Western Civilization: A History of European Society is a compact introduction to a large subject. Like other Western civilization texts, we have written a text that interweaves into a coherent narrative the development of political institutions; the cultural, religious, and intellectual contributions of the European elite; the military history that shaped the lives of everyone; and the everyday life experiences of ordinary men, women, and children. We have sought to locate that social history in its economic and political context and in relation to other historical issues. Similarly, we have treated war and technology as phenomena that influenced, and were influenced by, social and economic structures, and we have given popular culture its due without sacrificing the special interests of the elites.

## A Brief Text

In the words of Jonson's Volpone, we think the many virtues of this book are too numerous not to mention. But we will emphasize only a few in this preface. First, the book is intentionally briefer than many standard survey texts, including our own recent *Western Civilization: A History of European Society*. We think a briefer text is more useful for those instructors who use a textbook chiefly as the core of a course that includes numerous outside readings or use of other supplementary material. We hope that by omitting a degree of detail that is not central to an understanding of the subject that we have made it easier for students to absorb and understand the broad currents of Western civilization. This less expensive text also makes the purchase of outside readings more affordable. A brief examination of the text itself will reveal that we have not skimped on full-color maps illustrations, which help bring this material to life.

## Learning History Through Primary Source Documents

The second thing we want to bring to the attention of the first-time reader is the boxed inserts we have included. These are of two types. In every chapter we have included written primary source documents similar to the material that most instructors use to supplement their courses. We have chosen a broad range of letters, treaties, poems, broadsides, declarations, and other things that bring to the attention of students the kinds of material that historians have traditionally used in doing their own research. We have enjoyed watching our own students wrestle with these excerpts from primary documents, and we hope other students will find them as stimulating as our students do.

## Learning History Through Tables and Charts

In addition, the book is filled with numerous tables and charts of historical data, involving trade balances, the relative size of various European cities over time, and military expenditures. But the majority of these tables involve the details of everyday life. Until very recently, of course, the great majority of Europeans was illiterate and unable to leave behind a written record of their lives. But the story of these people is, to say the least, an important part of the overall account of Western civilization. This statistical information appears most frequently in those chapters that cover modern times when such records are more reliable and available. They provide us with our best information on life outside the court or castle, and we are delighted to include many of them in this text. These are especially helpful in teaching students about the lives of the millions of ordinary men and women who left behind no written accounts of their lives. By examining parish, municipal, and other records, we are able to piece together such information as wages and prices in ancient Rome, life expectancy in the middle ages, the incidence of abandoned children in major cities, and other telling details of everyday life over time.

## Studying the Past Through Maps, Tables, Charts, and Art

Most historians are more accustomed to explaining the past through prose than with numbers. We are pleased, therefore, that John Soares, a gifted historian and teacher, has written a brief booklet, entitled Studying the Past through Maps, Tables, Charts, and Art, that helps students see the human faces hidden just behind each column of numbers. For example, table 18.3 in chapter 18 shows that 45 percent of a worker's family income in late 18th-century Berlin was spent on bread, 12 percent was spent on other vegetable products, and 15 percent on meat and dairy products. The booklet helps students see that for many centuries bread was the major source of nutrition among peasants and workers, rather than the side dish it has become today. The booklet goes on to help students realize that the recurring bread riots discussed in the text arose out of real deprivation: when the price of bread rose, ordinary people starved. The numbers make these things starkly plain, and this wonderful manual make them easy for the first-time reader to decipher. This manual is free with every student copy of the text.

In Addition to an explication and directed questions about each of the book's tables, the booklet also helps students see the cultural information imbedded in one of the pieces of art in every chapter. For example, an illustration in chapter 18 shows a coach stop in a small 18th-century town. Students will enjoy the picture on their own. But many may need to be prodded to speculate on the time it will take to fix the broken wheel on one of the stage coaches, and to think further about the pace of transportation in 18th-century Europe. This invaluable booklet brings these historically important considerations to the attention of the first-time reader.

## Maps

All of the book's many maps appear in full color, and may include such topographic features as mountains and rivers. Like most historians, we use maps extensively in our teaching. And we know that color can convey more information than can hash marks or degrees of shading. Likewise, we think it essential that a map of archaic Greece, for example, reinforce the text by showing students the mountainous terrain that led to development of independent city-states. The map of archaic Greece in chapter two does this.

## Illustrations

The book includes some 200 illustrations, most of them in color. Each is identified in the text and bears directly on the discussion in the adjoining pages on which they appear. And each includes a caption that adds some additional information that complements the text.

## Ancillaries

The package that accompanies this book is full of print and electronic ancillaries that cost a fortune to produce and sucked the life blood out of the people who prepared and produced them. Among them are the following:

**Instructor's Manual with Test Bank** Prepared by John Soares. Each chapter contains Chapter Outlines, Learning Objectives, Suggested Lecture Topics, Suggested Student Activities, Test Questions (Multiple Choice, True/False, Essay, and Identification), Table, Figure, and Art analysis, Internet resources, and Video Resources.
One volume for all three versions of the text.

**ExamView** Create, deliver, and customize tests and study guides (both print and online) in minutes with this easy-to-use assessment and tutorial system. ExamView offers both a Quick Test Wizard and an Online Test Wizard that guide you step-by-step through the process of creating tests, while its unique "WYSIWYG" capability allows you to see the test you are creating on the screen exactly as it will print or display online. You can build tests of up to 250 questions using up to 12 question types. Using ExamView's complete word processing capabilities, you can enter an unlimited number of new questions or edit existing questions.

**Study Guides** Volume I, Volume II Prepared by John Soares. Contains Chapter Outlines, Learning Objectives, Identifications, Matching, Multiple Choice questions, Fill-in-the Blank questions, Chronologies, Questions for Critical Thought, Analysis of Primary Source Documents, Geography and Map Analysis, and Table, Figure, and Art analysis. Two volumes to correspond with volumes I and II of the main text.

**Map Acetates and Commentary for Western Civilization, 2000 Edition**  This extensive four-color acetate package includes maps from the text and from other sources and includes map commentary prepared by James Harrison, Siena College. The acetates and commentary are 3-hole punched and shrink-wrapped.

**Western Civilization PowerPoint**  Windows and Macintosh Contains all the four-color maps from the map acetate package, described above.

**Document Exercises Workbooks**  Volume I, Volume II Prepared by Donna Van Raaphorst, Cuyahoga Community College is a two-volume collection of exercises based around primary sources, teaching students how to use documents and historiographic methods.

**Map Workbooks**  Volume I, Volume II Prepared by Cynthia Kosso, Northern Arizona University, this two-volume workbook features over 20 map exercises. The exercises are designed to help students understand the relationship between places and people through time. All map exercises incorporate three parts; an introduction, a locations section where students are asked to correctly place a city, site, or boundary, and a question section.

**Sights and Sounds of History**  VHS video Short, focused video clips, photos, artwork, animation's, music, and dramatic readings are used to bring life to historical topics and events which are most difficult for students to appreciate from a textbook alone. For example, students will experience the grandeur of Versailles and the defeat felt by a German soldier at Stalingrad. The video segments, each averaging 4 minutes long, make excellent lecture launchers.

**CNN Today Videos: Western Civilization**  Volume I, Volume II These 3-4 minute introductions to various topics make great lecture launchers.

**History Video Library**  Many new videos for this edition. Available to qualified adoptions.

**Journey of Civilization CD-ROM**  This CD-ROM takes the student on 18 interactive journeys through history. Enhanced with QuickTime movies, animations, sound clips, maps, and more, the journeys allow students to engage in history as active participants rather than as readers of past events.

**Internet Guide for History, Third Edition**  Prepared by John Soares. Provides newly revised and up-to-date internet exercises by topic. Can be found at http://history.wadsworth.com.

**Archer, Documents of Western Civilization, Volume I: To 1715**

**Archer, Documents of Western Civilization, Volume II: Since 1550**  A broad selection of carefully selected documents.

**Magellan World History Atlas**  Available to bundle with any History text contains 44 historical four-color maps.

**Webtutor**  Volume I, Volume II Two volumes to correspond with Volumes I and II of the main text. This content-rich, Web-based teaching and learning tool helps students succeed by taking the course beyond classroom boundaries to an anywhere, anytime environment. *Web Tutor* offers real-time access to a full array of study tools, including flashcards (with audio), practice quizzes, online tutorials, and Web links.

## *Acknowledgments*

We owe our gratitude to all those who helped us in the preparation of *Essentials of Western Civilization: A History of European Society:*

We would also like to thank all those at Wadsworth Publishing who have assisted us in producing this book: Clark Baxter, our editor who suggested the book and carried it into production; Sharon Adams Poore, our developmental editor; Cherie Hackelberg, assistant editor, who put the supplement package together; Hal Humphrey, project editor; Diane McOscar, marketing manager; Jennifer Ellis, editorial assistant, and Lori Dalberg at Carlisle Publishers Services.

## *Reviewers*

Gerald D. Anderson, North Dakota State University; Roz L. Ashby, Yavapai College; David Bartley, Indiana Wesleyan University; Anthony Bedford. Modesto Junior College; Rodney E. Bell, South Dakota University; Richard Camp, California State University–Northridge; Elizabeth Carney, Clemson University; Sherri Cole, Arizona Western College; Jeffrey Cox, University of Iowa; Philip B. Crow; Leslie Derfler, Florida Atlantic University; Marsha L. Frey, University of

Montana; Sarah Gravelle, University of Detroit; Stephen Haliczer, Northern Illinois University; Barry Hankins, Baylor University; William Hartel, Marietta College; Mack Holt, George Mason University; Frank Josserand, Southwest Texas State University; Gary Kates, Trinity University; Paul Leuschen, University of Arkansas; Eleanor Long, Hinds Community College; Olivia H. McIntyre, Eckerd College; David L. Longfellow, Baylor University; Bill Mackey, University of Alaska–Anchorage; Tom McMullen, Georgia Southern University; Paul L. Maier, Western Michigan University; Larry Marvin, St. Louis University; Carol Bresnahan Menning, University of Toledo; Jeffrey Merrick, University of Wisconsin–Milwaukee; Dennis Mihelich, Creighton University; Charles G. Nauert, Jr., University of Missouri–Columbia; Thomas C. Owen, Louisiana State University; William E. Painter, University of North Texas;

Kathleen Paul, University of Southern Florida; Nancy Rachels, Hillsborough Community College; Elsa Rapp, Montgomery County Community College; Miriam Raub Vivian, California State University–Bakersfield; Richard R. Rivers, Macomb Community College; Kenneth W. Rock, Colorado State University; Karl A. Roider, Louisiana State University; Leonard Rosenband, Utah State University; Joyce E. Salisbury, University of Wisconsin–Green Bay; Jerry Sandvick, North Hennepin Community College; Thomas P. Schlunz, University of New Orleans; Donna Simpson, Wheeling Jesuit University; Elisabeth Sommer, Grand Valley State University; Ira Spar, Ramapo College of New Jersey; Jake W. Spidle, University of New Mexico; Roger D. Tate, Somerset Community College; Jackson Taylor, Jr., University of Mississippi; Timothy M. Teeter, Georgia Southern University; Lee Shai Weissbach, University of Louisville

# Essentials of
# WESTERN CIVILIZATION

CHAPTER 1

# THE ANCIENT NEAR EAST: MESOPOTAMIA, EGYPT, PHOENICIA, ISRAEL

## CHAPTER OUTLINE

◆ ◆ ◆ ◆ ◆ ◆ ◆ ◆ ◆ ◆ ◆ ◆ ◆ ◆ ◆ ◆ ◆ ◆

Western civlization rests upon the achievements of far more ancient societies. Long before the Greeks or Romans, the peoples of the ancient Near East had learned to domesticate animals, grow crops, and produce useful articles of pottery and metal. The ancient Mesoptamians and Egyptians developed writing, mathematics, and sophisticated methods of engineering while contributing a rich variety of legal, scientific, and religious ideas to those who would come after them. The Phoenicians invented the alphabet and facilitated cultural borrowing by trading throughout the known world, and ancient Israel gave birth to religious concepts that form the basis of modern Judaism, Christianity, and Islam. Chapter 1 will look briefly at life in the Paleolithic or Old Stone Age before examining the Neolithic revolution and its material consequences, including its impact on diet, demography, and the advent of warfare. It will then describe the development and structure of two great ancient societies, the Mesopotamian and the Egyptian, before concluding with descriptions of the Phoenicians and of the life and religion of ancient Israel.

◆

## The First Europeans: The Paleolithic Era

Few subjects are more controversial than the origins of the human species. During the long series of ice ages, the fringes of the European ice pack were inhabited by a race of tool-making bipeds known conventionally as Neanderthals. Heavier, stronger, and hairier than modern *Homo sapiens*, they hunted the great herding animals of the day: mammoth, bison, wooly rhinoceros, and reindeer. They lived in caves, knew how to make flint tools and weapons, and buried their dead in ways that suggest some form of religious belief.

About thirty thousand years ago the Neanderthals were abruptly superseded by people who were physically identical to modern men and women. Where they came from or whether they somehow evolved within a few generations from a basically Neanderthal stock is unclear, but within a short time the Neanderthals were no more. This development remains a mystery because the first true humans did not have a more advanced culture or technology than their more established neighbors and were by comparison weak and puny. Some have suggested that the Neanderthals fell victim to an epidemic disease or that they could not adapt to warmer weather after the retreat of the glaciers. They may also have found hunting the faster, more solitary animals of modern times difficult after the extinction of their traditional prey, but no one knows.

The new people, like their predecessors, were hunter-gatherers who lived in caves and buried their dead. They, too, used stone tools and weapons that became steadily more sophisticated over time, which is why the period up to about 9000 B.C. is known as the Paleolithic or Old Stone Age. Paleolithic people lived on a healthy diet of game and fish supplemented by fruit, berries, nuts, and wild plants, but little is known about their social structure. If the hunter-gatherer societies of modern times are an indication, they probably lived in extended families that, if they survived and prospered, eventually became tribes. Extended families may contain older surviving relatives—siblings, aunts, uncles, nieces, nephews, and cousins—as opposed to nuclear families of only parents and children. Tribes are composed of several nuclear or extended families that claim common descent. The division of responsibilities probably was straightforward. Men hunted and perhaps made tools; women cared for the children, preserved the fire, and did most of the gathering.

Among the most extraordinary achievements of these paleographic cultures was their art. Caves from Spain to southern Russia are decorated with magnificent wall paintings, usually of animals. Many groups also produced small clay figurines with exaggerated female features. This suggests the widespread worship of a fertility goddess, but Paleolithic religious beliefs remain unclear. Were the cave paintings a form of magic designed to bring game animals under the hunter's power, or were they art for art's sake? The question may sound silly, but articles of personal adornment in caves and grave sites indicate, as do the paintings themselves, that these people had a well-developed sense of aesthetics (see illustration 1.1).

**Illustration 1.1**

🎨 **Paleolithic Cave Paintings of Bison, at Altamira, Spain.** The cave paintings at Altamira in Spain and at Lascaux in France were evidently produced by the same Paleolithic culture and date from c. 15,000 B.C. to 10,000 B.C. The purpose of the paintings is unclear, but the technical skill of the artists was anything but primitive.

## The Neolithic Revolution

Hunting and gathering remained the chief economic activity for a long time, and even today they provide supplementary food for many westerners. The bow and arrow as well as the basic tools still used to hook or net fish or to trap game were developed long before the advent of agriculture, pottery, or writing. The domestication of animals probably began at an early date with the use of dogs in hunting, but was later extended to sheep, goats, and cattle that could be herded to provide a reliable source of protein when game was scarce. Shortly thereafter, about ten thousand years ago, the first efforts were made to cultivate edible plants. The domestication of animals and the invention of agriculture marked one of the great turning points in human history.

Several species of edible grasses are native to the upper reaches of the Tigris and Euphrates valleys in Asia Minor, including wild barley and two varieties of wheat. Of the latter, einkorn (one-corn), with its single row of seeds per stalk, produces only modest yields, but emmer, with multiple rows on each stem, is the ancestor of modern wheat. When people learned to convert these seeds into gruel or bread is unknown, but once they did so the value of systematic cultivation became apparent. By 7000 B.C. farming was well established from Iran to Palestine. It spread into the Nile valley and the Aegean by 5000 B.C. and from the Balkans up the Danube and into central Europe in the years that followed. Radiocarbon dating has established the existence of farming settlements in the Netherlands by 4000 B.C. and in Britain by 3200 B.C.

The diffusion of agricultural techniques came about through borrowing and cultural contact as well as through migration. Farming, in other words, developed in response to local conditions. As the last ice age ended and hunting and fishing techniques improved, a general increase in population upset the Paleolithic ecology. Game became scarcer and more elusive while the human competition for dwindling resources grew more intense. Herding and the cultivation of row crops were soon essential to survival. In time, as the human population continued to grow, herding diminished. It provides fewer calories per unit of land than farming and was increasingly restricted to tracts otherwise unsuitable for cultivation. Though crop raising would always be supplemented to some extent by other sources of food, it gradually emerged as the primary activity wherever land could be tilled.

The invention of agriculture marked the beginning of the Neolithic or New Stone Age. The cultivation of plants, beginning with grains and expanding to include beans, peas, olives, and eventually grapes, made food supplies far more predictable than in a hunting or herding economy. At the same time, it greatly increased the number of calories that could be produced from a given area of land. Efficiency was further enhanced by the invention of the wheel and the wooden plow, both of which came into common use around 3000 B.C. Farming therefore promoted demographic growth both absolutely and in the density of population that a given area could support.

On the negative side, the transition to a farming economy often resulted in diets that were deficient in protein and other important elements. Bread became the staff of life, largely because land supports more people if planted with grain. The nuts, animal proteins, and wild fruits typical of the Paleolithic diet became luxuries to be eaten only on special occasions. As a result, the skeletal remains of Neolithic farmers indicate that they were shorter and less healthy than their Paleolithic ancestors. Though beans, peas, lentils, and other pulses became a valuable source of protein, ordinary people consumed as much as 80 percent of their calories in the form of carbohydrates.

Caloric intake varied widely. An adult male engaged in heavy labor requires a minimum of thirty-seven hundred calories per day. No way exists to measure a normal diet in Neolithic or ancient times, but the average peasant or laborer probably made do on far less, perhaps only twenty-five hundred to twenty-seven hundred calories per day. Grain yields on unfertilized land are relatively inelastic, typically ranging from three to twelve bushels per acre with a probable average of five. Populations expand to meet the availability of resources, and Neolithic communities soon reached their ecological limits. If they could not expand the area under cultivation, they reached a balance that barely sustained life. Moreover, because grain harvests depend upon good weather and are susceptible to destruction by pests, shortfalls were common. In years of famine, caloric intake dropped below the level of sustenance.

The establishment of permanent farming settlements also encouraged the spread of disease. The hunter-gatherers of Paleolithic times had lived in small groups and moved frequently in pursuit of game, a way of life that virtually precluded epidemics. Farming, however, is by definition sedentary. Fields and orchards require constant attention, and the old way of moving about while camping in caves or temporary shelters had to be abandoned. Early farmers built houses of sun-dried brick or of reeds and wood in close proximity to one another for security and to facilitate cooperation. The establishment of such villages encouraged the accumulation of refuse and human waste. Water supplies became contaminated while disease-bearing rats, flies, lice, and cockroaches became the village or town dweller's constant companions.

Inadequate nutrition and susceptibility to epidemic disease created the so-called biological old regime, a demographic pattern that prevailed in Europe until the middle of the nineteenth century. Though few people starved, disease kept death rates high while poor nutrition kept birth rates low. Malnutrition raises the age of first menstruation and can prevent ovulation in mature women, thereby reducing the rate of conception. After conception, poor maternal diet led to a high rate of stillbirths and of complications during pregnancy. If a child were brought to term and survived the primitive obstetrics of the age, it faced the possibility that its mother would be too malnourished to nurse. Statistics are unavailable, but infant mortality probably ranged from 30 to 70 percent in the first two years of life.

The distribution of Neolithic and ancient populations therefore bore little resemblance to that of a modern industrial society. Ancient people were younger and had far shorter working lives than their modern counterparts. Their reproductive lifetimes were also shorter, and in people of mature years (aged thirty to fifty), men may have outnumbered women, primarily because so many women died in childbirth. The life expectancy for either gender may not have been much more than thirty years at birth, but those who survived their fifties had as good a chance as their modern counterparts of reaching an advanced age. This pattern, like the conditions that produced it, would persist until the industrial revolution of modern times.

The invention of agriculture expanded the idea of property to include land and domesticated animals, which were not only personal possessions but also the means of survival. In Paleolithic times the primary measure of individual worth was probably a person's ability as a hunter or gatherer, skills from which the entire tribe presumably benefited. The Neolithic world measured status in terms of flocks, herds, and fields. This change affected the structure of human societies in three important ways. First, because luck and management skills vary widely, certain individuals amassed greater wealth than others. To gain the maximum advantage from their wealth, they found it necessary to utilize, and often to exploit, the labor of their poorer neighbors. Neolithic society was therefore characterized by social stratification, though a measure of cooperation could be found at the village level in the performance of agricultural and construction tasks.

Second, the emergence of property seems to have affected the status of women. Little is known about the lives of women in Paleolithic times, but most theorists agree that, with the development of herds and landed property, controlling female sexuality became necessary in ways that would have been unnecessary in a community of hunter-gatherers. The issue was inheritance. The survival of the family depended upon the preservation and augmentation of its wealth. Women were expected to provide heirs who were the biological children of their partners. The result was the development of a double standard by which women had to be pure and seen to be pure by the entire community. If anthropologists are correct, the subjugation of women and the evolution of characteristically feminine behaviors were an outgrowth of the Neolithic revolution.

Third, the Neolithic age marked the beginning of warfare, the systematic use of force by one community against another. Though Paleolithic hunters may have fought one another on occasion, the development of settled communities provided new incentives for violence because homes, livestock, and cultivated land are property that must be defended against the predatory behavior of neighboring peoples. Dealing with the problems of population growth by annexing the land of others was all too easy. War, in turn, made possible the development of slavery. To a hunter-gatherer, slaves are unnecessary, but to herders and agriculturalists their labor makes possible the expansion of herds and the cultivation of more land because under normal circumstances slaves produce more than they consume.

At first, Neolithic communities seem to have been organized along tribal lines, a structure inherited from their hunting and gathering ancestors when they settled down to till the land. Most inhabitants shared a common ancestor, and chieftainship was probably the dominant form of social organization. The function of the chief in agricultural societies was far more complex than in the days of hunting and gathering, involving not only military leadership but also a primary role in the allocation of goods and labor. Efficiency in operations such as harvesting and sheep shearing requires cooperation and direction. In return, the chief demanded a share of an individual's agricultural surplus, which he then stored against hard times or allocated in other ways.

This function of the chief helps to explain the storehouses that were often constructed by early rulers. As agriculture developed, crops became more varied. Wheat, wine, and olives became the basic triad of products on which society depended in the Mediterranean basin. One farmer might have a grove of olive trees but no land capable of growing wheat, while another would be blessed with well-drained, south-facing hillsides that produce the best grapes. In such cases the chief encouraged a measure of agricultural specialization. He could collect a tribute of oil from one and grapes from another and barter both to a third farmer in return for his surplus wheat. In the north, different commodities were involved, but the principle was the same. Specialization in Neolithic times was rarely complete because prudent farmers knew that diversification offered a measure of security that monoculture, or the growing of only one crop, can never provide. If the major crop fails, something else must be available to fall back upon, but even a modest degree of specialization can increase efficiency and raise a community's standard of living.

Effective systems of distribution can also encourage the development of technology. Pottery was invented soon after the Neolithic revolution, primarily as a means of storing liquids. The first pots were probably made by women working at home and firing their pots in a communal oven, but the invention of the potter's wheel allowed for throwing pots with unprecedented speed and efficiency. Because the new method required great skill, those who mastered it tended to become specialists who were paid for their work in food or other commodities.

**Illustration 1.2**

**Stonehenge.** The greatest of all stone circles, shown here from the north, stands on England's Salisbury Plain. Some believe that Stonehenge served as an astronomical calculator, but the real purpose is as obscure as the culture of its builders. The huge stones were quarried, and perhaps shaped elsewhere, and transported many miles to their present site. The lintels are pegged and fitted into prepared holes in the standing stones or fitted with mortise-and-tenon joints. The stonemasonry as well as the size of the project is remarkable.

The advent of metallurgy provides a more dramatic example of occupational specialization. Pure copper, which is sometimes found in nature, was used for jewelry and personal items before 6000 B.C., but by 4500 B.C. it was being smelted from ores and forged into tools and weapons. These complex processes appear to have evolved separately in the Middle East and in the Balkans, where copper deposits were common. They were based on the development of ovens that could achieve both a controlled air flow and temperatures of more than two thousand degrees Fahrenheit. An analysis of pottery from these areas reveals that such ovens had already been developed to facilitate glazing. By 3500 B.C., bronze—a mixture of copper and tin—was in general use throughout the West for the manufacture of tools and weapons. The Neolithic Age was over, and the Bronze Age had begun. Because the skills involved in working bronze were highly specialized, smiths probably forged their wares almost exclusively for sale or barter. A sophisticated system of trade and governance must have been established. Furthermore, the large-scale production of metal weapons further enhanced the power of chiefs.

Chieftainship might also involve religious duties, though organized priesthoods evolved in some soci-

eties at an early date. Chiefs almost certainly organized the building of communal burying places in the Aegean and along the Atlantic and North Sea coasts from Iberia to Scandinavia. Originally simple dolmens formed of a giant stone or megalith laid upon other stones, these tombs gradually evolved into domed chambers that were entered through long masonry passages.

Graves of this kind are often found in the vicinity of stone circles. Stonehenge, constructed around 3500 B.C. on England's Salisbury Plain, is the largest and best known of these structures (see illustration 1.2). Because the circles are oriented astronomically, many have assumed that they served as giant calendars, but their precise function and the beliefs that mandated their construction are unknown.

The prevalence of these large-scale construction projects, whatever their purpose, indicates that Neolithic societies could achieve high levels of organization and technological sophistication. When survival—as opposed to the demands of ritual—required a major cooperative effort, some societies evolved into civilizations. *Civilization* is a term loaded with subjective meanings. In this case, it refers to the establishment of political and cultural unity over a wide geographic area and the development of elaborate social, commercial,

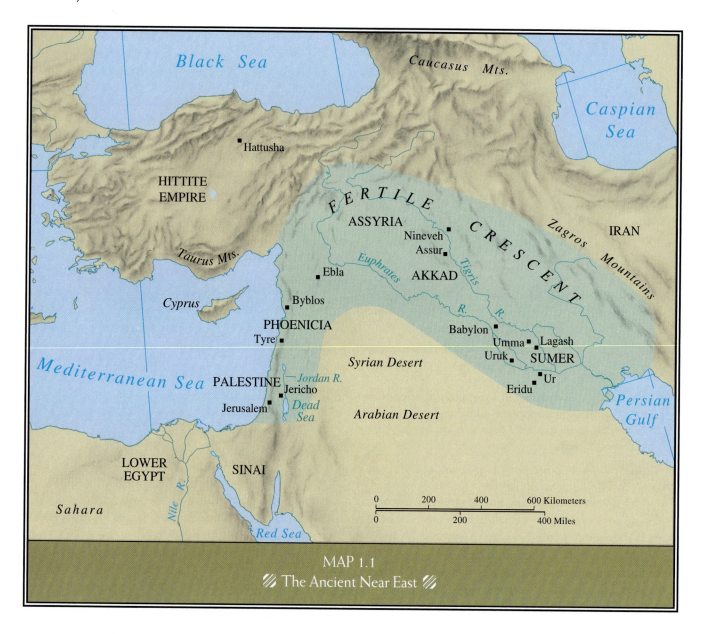

MAP 1.1
《 The Ancient Near East 《

and administrative structures based upon high population densities and the production of substantial wealth.

In most cases, civilization also meant the development of mathematics and written languages. Both were needed for surveying, administration, and the distribution of goods and services in a complex society. As chiefs became kings, the record of taxes and tributes paid, of lands annexed, and of the provisions consumed by their ever-larger armies acquired great significance. The desire to record the ruler's glorious deeds for posterity came slightly later but was nevertheless important. Writing gives names to individuals and permits the dead to speak in their own words. Without it there is no history.

The emergence of societies at this level of complexity affected even those areas that they did not directly control. Great civilizations are magnets that draw other cultures into their orbits. As peoples on the pe-

riphery become involved with the larger market through trade or tribute, cultural borrowing accelerates. Then, as civilizations expand, they come into conflict with one another, a process that brings neighboring peoples into their systems of war and diplomacy as well. By 3000 B.C., at least two such civilizations had begun to emerge, one in the valley of Tigris and Euphrates rivers, the other in the valley of the Nile.

## Mesopotamia: The Social and Economic Structures of Mesopotamian Life

*Mesopotamia*, in Greek, means the land between the rivers, in this case the Tigris and the Euphrates (see map 1.1). It is a hot, fertile flood plain, most of which falls within the borders of modern Iraq. Summer temperatures reach 110 to 120 degrees Fahrenheit, and no rain falls from May to late October. Winters are more moderate, but only Assyria in the north receives enough rainfall to support agriculture without irrigation. In the lower valley, everything depends upon water supplied by the two rivers.

Of the two, the Tigris carries by far the larger volume of water. The Euphrates on the east has fewer tributaries and loses more of its flow to evaporation as it passes through the dry plains of Syria. In April and May the melting of snow in the Zagros Mountains causes massive flooding throughout the region. This provides needed water and deposits a rich layer of alluvial silt, but the inundation presents enormous problems of management. The floods must not only be controlled to protect human settlement, but water also must somehow be preserved to provide irrigation during the rainless summer. To make matters worse, both rivers create natural embankments or levees that inhibit the flow of tributaries and over time have raised the water level above that of the surrounding countryside. If spring floods wash the embankments away, the river changes its course, often with disasterous results. The biblical story of Noah and the Flood originated in Mesopotamia, though there was probably not one flood but many (see document 1.1).

The first known settlements in the region were village cultures possibly speaking a Semitic language distantly related to the more modern Hebrew or Arabic. They grew wheat and barley and were established as far south as Akkad, near modern Baghdad, by 4500 B.C. Other Semitic peoples continued to migrate into the region from the west and southwest until the Arab invasions of the ninth century A.D., but by 3000 B.C. the Sumerians, a non-Semitic people who may have come originally from India, had achieved dominance in the lower valley. They introduced large-scale irrigation and built the first true cities.

Sumerian cities were usually built on a tributary and dominated a territory of perhaps a hundred square miles. Their inhabitants cultivated cereals, especially barley, and had learned the secret of making beer. Sumerian homes, made of sun-baked brick, originally were small and circular like a peasant's hut but gradually expanded to become large one-story structures with square or rectangular rooms built around a central courtyard. Governance seems to have been by elected city councils. Each city also had a king who ruled with the assistance of a palace bureaucracy. The precise division of powers is unknown, but the later Babylonian council had judicial as well as legislative authority.

## ◆ DOCUMENT 1.1 ◆

### The Flood

*The great Mesopotamian epic about Gilgamesh contains an account of the Flood that strongly resembles the biblical account in Genesis, although divine caprice, not human wickedness, brings on the disaster. Here, Utnapashtim, the Mesopotamian equivalent of Noah, tells his story to the hero Gilgamesh.*

In those days the world teemed, the people multiplied, the world bellowed like a wild bull, and the great god was aroused by the clamor. Enlil heard the clamor and said to the gods in council, "the uproar of mankind is intolerable and sleep is no longer possible by reason of the babel." So the gods agreed to exterminate mankind. Enlil did this, but Ea [the god of the waters] because of his oath warned me in a dream . . . "tear down your house and build a boat, abandon possessions and look for life, despise worldly goods and save your soul alive . . . then take up into the boat the seed of all living creatures . . ."

[After Utnapashtim did this] for six days and six nights the winds blew, torrent and tempest and flood overwhelmed the world, tempest and flood raged together like warring hosts. When the seventh day dawned the storm from the south subsided, the sea grew calm, the flood was stilled; I looked at the face of the world and there was silence, all mankind was turned to clay. The surface of the sea stretched as flat as a rooftop; I opened a hatch and the light fell on my face. . . . I looked for land in vain, but fourteen leagues distant there appeared a mountain, and there the boat grounded; on the mountain of Nisir the boat held fast. . . . When the seventh day dawned I loosed a dove and let her go. She flew away, but finding no resting place she returned. Then I loosed a swallow, and she flew away but finding no resting place she returned. I loosed a raven, she saw that the waters had retreated, she ate, she flew around, she cawed, and she did not come back. Then I threw everything open to the four winds, I made a sacrifice and poured out a libation on the mountain top.

*The Epic of Gilgamesh*, trans. N.K. Sandars. Rev. ed. Harmondsworth, England. Penguin Classics, 1964.

An organized priesthood served in the great raised temple or ziggurat that dominated the town. The ziggurat was a stepped pyramidal tower dedicated to the god or goddess who was the patron of the city. The earliest examples were built of packed earth. After about 2000 B.C. most were constructed on a foundation of imported stone and decorated with glazed tiles. The temple and its priests were supported by extensive landholdings. Other large tracts were owned by the royal family and its retainers. Sumerian kings were likely at first war chiefs whose powers became hereditary as their responsibilities for the distribution of goods and labor grew. Like chiefs in other societies, they stood at the center of a system of clientage that involved their families and their servants as well as officials, commoners, and probably priests.

Clientage is best defined as a system of mutual dependency in which a powerful individual protects the interests of others in return for their political or economic support. With or without legal sanction, clientage is the basic form of social organization in many cultures and was destined to become a powerful force in the history of the West. In Sumer, clients formed a separate class of free individuals who were given the use of small parcels of land in return for labor and a share of their produce. Their patrons—kings, noble officials, or temple priests—retained title to the land and a compelling hold on their client's political loyalties. The cities were therefore ruled by a relatively small group. Clients had full rights as citizens, but they could not be expected to vote against those who controlled their economic lives.

The rest of the land was owned by private families that were apparently extended, multigenerational, and organized on patriarchal lines. Though rarely rich, these freeholders enjoyed full civil rights and participated in the city's representative assembly. The greatest threat to their independence was debt, which could lead to enslavement. Other slaves were sometimes acquired for the temple or palace through war, but Sumer was not a slave-based economy. The organization of trade, like that of agriculture, reflected this social structure. For centuries Sumerian business was based on the extended family or what would today be called family corporations. Some firms ran caravans to every part of the Middle East or shipped goods by sea via the Persian Gulf. They exported textiles, copper implements, and other products of Mesopotamian craftsmanship and imported wood, stone, copper ingots, and precious metals. Iron and steel were as yet unknown. Later, in the time of Hammurabi, Babylonian rulers attempted to

**Ilustration 1.3**

🎗 **A Cuneiform Tablet.** This fragment of the eleventh tablet of the *Epic of Gilgamesh* from Ashurbanipal's great library at Nineveh is a superb example of cuneiform text.

bring some of these trading concerns under government regulation.

The organization of Sumerian society was probably much like that of earlier Neolithic communities, and its political institutions reflect the ancient idea of chieftainship. More is known about it only because the Sumerians were the first Western people to create a written language. Their political and economic relationships had reached a level of complexity that required something more than the use of movable clay tokens to record transactions, a practice characteristic of many earlier cultures. Though the Sumerian language was apparently unrelated to any other and was used only for ritual purposes after the second millennium B.C., all later Mesopotamian cultures adopted its cuneiform system of writing.

Cuneiform refers to the wedge-shaped marks left by a stylus when it is pressed into a wet clay tablet. Sumeria was rich in mud, and slabs of clay were perfect for recording taxes, land transfers, and legal agreements. When the document was ready, the tablet could be baked hard and stored for future reference (see illustration 1.3).

## The Sumerians, Akkad, Babylonia, and Assyria

Even with written records, political relations between the Sumerian city-states are difficult to reconstruct. As populations increased, struggles over boundaries and trading rights grew more violent, and by 2300 B.C. inter-city conflicts engulfed all of Mesopotamia. At times, a king would claim to rule over more than one city or over Sumer as a whole. There may therefore have been no Sumerian Empire, or if there was, its existence could have been brief. According to his inscriptions, Lugalzaggeszi of Umma (c. 2375 B.C.) achieved control over the entire region only to have it taken from him by a non-Sumerian, Sargon of Akkad (reigned c. 2350–2300 B.C.).

The Akkadian triumph marked the beginning of a new imperial age. The unification of southern and central Mesopotamia provided Sargon with the means to conquer the north together with Syria. Though Akkadian rule was brief, it transmitted elements of Mesopotamian culture throughout the Middle East, and Akkadian, a Semitic language, became standard throughout the Tigris and Euphrates valleys. But the brevity of Sargon's triumph set a pattern for the political future. For a millennium and a half, the rulers of different regions in succession achieved hegemony over all or part of Mesopotamia. This was normally achieved by force combined with the careful manipulation of alliances and ended when the ruling dynasty fell prey either to the divisive forces that had created it or to invasions by people from the surrounding highlands. Throughout its history, Mesopotamia's wealth and lack of natural defenses made it a tempting prize for conquerors.

After the overthrow of Sargon's descendents by a desert people known as the Guti and a brief revival of Sumerian power under the Third Dynasty of Ur, Babylon became the chief political and cultural center of the region. Under Hammurabi (ruled c. 1792–1750 B.C.) the Babylonians achieved hegemony over all of Mesopotamia, but a series of invasions after 1600 B.C. led to a long period of political disorder. The invaders, the most important of whom were Hittites, an Indo-European people from central Asia Minor. Their influence was otherwise impermanent, but a rivalry soon developed between Babylon and Assyria, a kingdom in the northern part of the valley centered first on the city of Ashur and later on Nineveh.

The Assyrians, a fierce people who spoke a dialect of Akkadian, may have been the first people to coordinate the use of cavalry, infantry, and missile weapons. Not only were their armies well organized, but their grasp of logistics also appears to have surpassed that of other ancient empires. Though in other respects a highly civilized people whose literary and artistic achievements continued the traditions of Sumer and Babylon, they waged psychological warfare by cultivating a reputation for horrific cruelty. They eventually defeated the Babylonians and after 933 restored the achievements of Sargon by establishing an empire that stretched from Egypt to Persia. In spite of these violent political alterations, Mesopotamia remained culturally homogeneous for nearly three thousand years.

## Mesopotamian Culture, Law, and Religion

Though capitals and dynasties rose and fell, the land between the rivers remained captive to the annual floods and to the consequent need for cooperation, superlative engineering, and frequent redistribution of land. The Mesopotamians' highest intellectual achievements were therefore practical rather than speculative. The development of writing is a prime example of their talents. The Mesopotamians were also the first great mathematicians. Using a numerical system based on sixty instead of the modern ten, they produced reference tables for multiplication, division, square roots, cube roots, and other functions. Their greatest achievement, however, was the place-value system of notation in which the value of each digit is determined by its position after the base instead of by a separate name. This makes describing large numbers possible and is the basis of all modern numeral systems.

The Babylonians also created one of the first comprehensive legal codes. Named after Hammurabi, it is almost certainly a compendium of existing laws rather than new legislation and reflects a legal tradition that had been developing for centuries. Its basic principles were retribution in kind and the sanctity of contracts. In criminal cases this meant literally "an eye for an eye, a tooth for a tooth," if the social status of the parties was equal. If not, a defendant of higher status could usually escape by paying a fine. Blood feuds, private retribution, and other features of tribal law were, however, forbidden. This same sense of retributive justice extended to the punishment of fraud and negligence. A builder whose house collapsed and killed its occupants could be executed; tavern keepers who watered their drinks were drowned. Craftsmen were required to replace poor workmanship at their own expense, and farmers who failed to keep their ditches and levees in good repair were sold into slavery if they could not compensate the victims of their

**Illustration 1.4**

Sumerians Worshipping Abu, God of Vegetation.  This group of marble votive statues (the largest is thirty inches high and probably represents the local king) was carved at Eshnunna in southern Mesopotamia between 2700 and 2500 B.C. The figures were placed around the altar and were expected to serve as perpetual stand-ins for their donors. The huge, staring eyes reflect the rapt attention expected by the god.

carelessness. Contracts governed everything from marriage to interest rates and could not be broken without paying a heavy fine.

Hammurabi's Code was driven by an almost oppressive sense of social responsibility. The ecology of Mesopotamia was both fragile and highly artificial. Only elaborate regulation could prevent disaster, and the law is explicit on many aspects of trade, agriculture, and manufacturing. Courts and town councils took an interest in matters that other cultures have regarded as private. Furthermore, because there were no lawyers, the parties to a dispute were expected to plead their own cases.

Marriage, as in most ancient cultures, was arranged by parents. The bride received a dowry, which she was entitled to keep in the event of widowhood or divorce. Husbands could demand a divorce at any time but had to pay maintenance and child support unless they could demonstrate that the wife had failed in her duties. These duties, like all other aspects of the marriage arrangement, were spelled out in a detailed contract that in effect made the couple a single person, responsible before the law for their actions and their debts. The latter was an important point, for husbands had the right to sell wives and children into servitude, usually for no more than two or three years, to satisfy their creditors.

The system was patriarchal, but wives could sue for divorce on grounds of cruelty or neglect, or if their husband falsely accused them of adultery. If adultery were proved, the guilty couple would be tied together and drowned; if the aggrieved husband forgave his wife, her lover would be pardoned as well. All of these family issues were heard before the city councils, which demonstrates the continuing importance of local government even after the establishment of an empire. Women, like men, were expected to plead their own cases—a right often denied them in more modern legal systems—but recourse to the law had its perils. To reduce litigation, Hammurabi's Code decreed the death penalty for those who brought false accusations or frivolous suits.

Hammurabi, like most lawgivers, claimed divine sanction for his code, but Mesopotamian religion was not legalistic. The Sumerians had worshipped more than three thousand deities, most of whom represented natural forces or the spirit of a particular locality. In time many of them acquired human form, and a rich mythology developed around their adventures. Babylon made its city god, Marduk, its chief, while the Assyrians accorded similar honors to Ashur. Both were thought of as creators who had brought the universe out of primal chaos. Other gods and goddesses were still worshipped, but in an apparent step toward monotheism, they were increasingly described as agents of Marduk or Ashur and eventually as manifestations of a single god.

The power of the gods was absolute. Humans were dependent on their whims and could hope only to propitiate them through the ceremonies of the priests (see illustration 1.4). The problem of the righteous sufferer

## ◈ DOCUMENT 1.2 ◈

### A Mesopotamian Prayer

*This fragment from a longer prayer displays the characteristic Mesopotamian attitude toward the gods, who are seen as hostile, demanding, and inscrutable.*

The sin, which I have committed, I know not.
The iniquity, which I have done, I know not.
The offence, which I committed, I know not.
The transgression I have done, I know not.
The lord, in the anger of his heart, hath looked
    upon me.
The god, in the wrath of his heart, hath visited me.
The goddess hath become angry with me, and
    hath grievously stricken me.
The known or unknown god hath straightened
    me.
The known or unknown goddess hath brought af-
    fliction upon me.
I sought for help, but no one taketh my hand.
I wept, but no one came to my side.
May the known and unknown god be pacified!
May the known and unknown goddess be pacified!

"Penitential Psalms." In *Assyrian and Babylonian Literature,* trans. R. F. Harper. New York: D. Appleton, 1901.

was therefore a recurring theme in Babylonian literature. Even death offered no hope of relief. In the greatest of all Babylonian epics, the hero Gilgamesh is inspired by the death of his friend Enkidu to wrestle with the problem of the hereafter. His discoveries are not reassuring. The nether world is portrayed as a grim place, and neither the mythical Gilgamesh nor any other Mesopotamian could apparently imagine the idea of personal salvation. If their extensive literature is an indication, the peoples of ancient Mesopotamia knew how to enjoy life, but their enjoyment was tempered by a grim fatalism (see document 1.2). In the land between the rivers, with its terrible inundations and vulnerability to invaders, it could hardly have been otherwise.

## Ancient Egypt

While the Sumerians were establishing themselves in Mesopotamia, another great civilization was develop-

ing in the valley of the Nile. In central Africa, more than three thousand miles from the shores of the Mediterranean, streams running from a cluster of great lakes merge their waters to form the White Nile. The lakes serve as a reservoir, and the river's volume remains constant with the seasons as it flows north to meet the Blue Nile at Khartoum. The Blue Nile is smaller than the White, but its sources are in the Ethiopian highlands where the monsoon rains of June and the melting mountain snow become a torrent. This annual flood, which reaches the lower Nile valley in July or August, provides both the moisture and the rich layer of black silt that support Egyptian life.

From the confluence of the two rivers, the Nile makes a wide sweep to the west before flowing northward through a valley more than 350 miles long but rarely more than ten miles wide. The historic land of Egypt is a narrow well-watered passageway between the Mediterranean and the heart of Africa. To the west lies the vast emptiness of the Libyan desert; to the east, a line of parched and rugged hills mark the shores of the Red Sea. Open country is found only near the river's mouth, a vast alluvial delta through which, in antiquity at least, seven main channels provided access to the Mediterranean. Summer temperatures in the valley are not as hot as those of Mesopotamia, but little or no rain falls and, without the river, life would be insupportable.

As in Mesopotamia, the key to Egyptian agriculture was the proper management of the annual flood. The Nile is more predictable and less violent than the Tigris or Euphrates, but the construction of levees, catchments, and an extensive network of ditches, was essential both to protect settlements and to preserve water after the flood subsided in the fall. The high level of organization needed for such tasks and for the preservation and distribution of grain during the dry months may have been responsible for the centralized, hierarchical character of ancient Egyptian society, but the point is arguable. Little is known of politics before the advent of the First Dynasty around 3100 B.C. At that time, the kings of the First Dynasty or their immediate predecessors united the two lands of Upper (southern) and Lower (northern) Egypt and laid the foundations of a political culture that would endure for nearly three millennia. The essential characteristics of Egyptian society were in place when the Third Dynasty assumed power in 2686 B.C. and began the Old Kingdom.

The history of ancient Egypt is conventionally divided into three kingdoms and no fewer than twenty-six dynasties: the Old Kingdom (2686–2181 B.C.), the Middle Kingdom (2133–1786 B.C.), and the New

Kingdom (1567–525 B.C.). The terms *old, middle,* and *new* do not necessarily reflect progress. Some of Egypt's greatest achievements came during the predynastic period and the Old Kingdom. The Intermediate Periods between these kingdoms were troubled times during which provincial governors, known to the Greeks as nomarchs, increased their power at the expense of the central government. Eventually one would gain ascendancy over the others and establish a dynasty that served as the cornerstone of a new kingdom.

The Old Kingdom ended when massive crop failures coincided with the political collapse of the Sixth Dynasty. After an anarchic Intermediate Period of more than one-hundred years, Amenemhet I, the ruler of Thebes in Upper Egypt, reunited the country and established the Middle Kingdom. During the Twelfth Dynasty (c. 1991–1786 B.C.), Egypt found itself under military pressure in both the north and south and, for the first time in its history, created a standing army. Expeditions into Palestine, Syria, and Libya helped to stabilize the north, while massive fortresses were built in Upper Egypt as protection against the growing power of Kerma, an expansionist state in what is now Sudan. The Middle Kingdom dissolved when a series of foreign dynasties known as the Hyksos supplanted the native Egyptian rulers. From the late eighteenth century B.C., Egypt's wealth attracted an influx of immigrants from Palestine and other parts of the Middle East. They came to power by infiltrating high office instead of by invasion, but their success was deeply resented.

The restoration of a native dynasty in 1567 B.C. marked the beginning of the New Kingdom. A series of warlike pharaohs destroyed the capital of Kerma and briefly extended their authority to the banks of the Euphrates. Ramses II (1279–1213 B.C.), the ruler associated with the Hebrew exodus, fought the Hittite empire to a truce. Ramses III remained strong enough to protect Egypt against the great population movements of the early twelfth century B.C. Thereafter, the power of the monarchy declined, perhaps because the imports of gold and silver that sustained its armies began to shrink. After 525 B.C. Egypt fell first to the Persians and then to the Macedonians of Alexander the Great.

The society that survived these changes bore little resemblance to that of Mesopotamia. Its most unusual feature was the absolute power it accorded to the king, or pharaoh, a Middle Kingdom title meaning "great house." His authority in life was absolute, though in practice he presumably would always act according to *ma'at,* a concept of justice or social order based on the balance or reconciliation of conflicting principles. The

king could not therefore appear arbitrary or irresponsible, and his actions were further limited by precedent, for Egyptian society was conservative. If *ma'at* were not preserved, dynasties could fall, but the historical circumstances in which this took place are generally unknown.

When the king died, his spirit or *ka* would take its place in the divine pantheon and become one with Osiris, god of the dead. This was the purpose of the pyramids, the largest of which were built at Giza by the Fourth Dynasty (2613–2494 B.C.) monarchs—Khufu (Cheops), Khafre, and Menkaure. Constructed of between eighty million and one hundred million cubic feet of cut and fitted stone, these vast funeral monuments held the deceased ruler's mortal remains and served as the center of a temple complex dedicated to his worship.

Projects on this scale were a measure of the king's wealth and power. Scholars believe that the taming of the Nile was achieved by workers conscripted and directed by early rulers in the common interest. This right to labor services was retained by later kings, and conscript labor rather than slaves probably built the pyramids as well as the massive fortifications constructed in Upper Egypt to protect the kingdom from Nubian invasions. Similar works in the delta have been obliterated by shifts in the course of the river.

Bureaucrats, with multiple titles and responsibilities, supervised the construction of pyramids and other public projects. Many of these people combined priestly, secular, and military offices, which suggests that managerial competence was valued above specialized skills. The establishment of a standing army during the Middle Kingdom encouraged the emergence of professional soldiers, but no military aristocracy existed. Some high officials were royal relatives, while others were drawn from what may have been a hereditary caste of scribes and civil servants. All, like the laborers, were paid in food, drink, and various commodities including gold, for the Egyptians did not coin money until long after the end of the New Kingdom.

Pyramids after the Fourth Dynasty grew smaller and less expensive, but the Egyptian penchant for public works, temples, and funerary monuments continued until the Hellenistic era. The Egyptians were superior craftsmen in stone and could convert even the hardest granites into works of art. As architects they seem to have invented post-and-lintel construction in masonry. Their temples, whether cut into the limestone cliffs of the Nile valley or freestanding, are graced with magnificent galleries and porticoes supported by stone columns, many of which were decorated or inscribed with writing. The Egyptians also built spacious palaces for the kings and their officials, but few palaces survived the centuries intact.

These projects could be seen as an appalling waste of resources, but they may have served a vital economic and social purpose. They certainly provided sustenance for thousands of workers, especially during the months of flood from July to November when the fields could not be worked. As such, they were an important mechanism for the distribution and redistribution of wealth. Furthermore, by centralizing the direction of arts and crafts under royal patronage, the projects improved the quality of both and led to technological advances that might not otherwise have occurred.

## The Social and Economic Structures of Ancient Egypt

The character of Egyptian society is difficult to reconstruct, in part because no legal code comparable to that of Hammurabi has been found. Little is known about land tenure, though vast tracts were held by the king and by pious foundations set up to support temples and those who served them. As many temples were small and as the priests and accolytes supported by their foundations were also farmers, it appears that the tax exemptions enjoyed by the trusts were a primary reason for their establishment. The owners of land held privately, which was abundant, had to pay an annual tribute in kind to the ruler. The king may also have been able to confiscate private property on the theory that, as a god, he owned the entire country. The remaining records of assessment are detailed and reveal a competent and often ruthless bureaucracy at work in even the humblest of villages.

Slaves, most of whom had been captured in war, were found in the fields and households of the rich. They belonged by law to the pharaoh who granted them in turn to private individuals or to the great trusts that managed the temples. They could hold property in their own right and were frequently manumitted, or freed, through a simple declaration by their owners. They were neither numerous nor central to the workings of the economy except perhaps in the expansionist period when the New Kingdom pharaohs conquered much of Phoenicia and Syria (c. 1560–1299 B.C.). The vast majority of Egyptians were humble farmers whose life probably resembled that of today's *fellahin*. They lived in small villages built of mud bricks and spent their days working in the fields and drawing precious

water by means of the *shaduf*, a bucket swung from a counterbalanced beam. They were subject to the payment of taxes as well as to labor services and perhaps to conscripted service in the army. The idea of conscription was so pervasive that people expected to labor in the fields of Osiris after death and placed small clay figurines of slaves in their tombs to help them with the work.

Crops were remarkably varied. Barley and wheat were the staples, and the average person's diet included large quantities of bread and beer with broad or fava beans for protein and the tender stalks of the young papyrus plant for an occasional salad. Papyrus was primarily valued because its fibers could be formed into a kind of paper, an Egyptian invention that takes its name from the plant, though modern paper is derived from a process developed originally in China. Wines for consumption by the upper classes were produced in the delta and painstakingly classified according to source and quality. Beef, too, was a delta product and formed an important part of a wealthy person's diet along with game birds, mutton, and pork. Poultry was common, as were many different kinds of fruit and, above all, onions. Cotton, so closely associated with the Egyptian economy in modern times, was not introduced until about 500 B.C., and most Egyptians wore simple linen garments made from locally grown flax.

Famines and epidemics were rare, but the life expectancy of ancient Egyptians was no more than thirty-five or thirty-six years, a figure comparable to that for most other societies before the industrial revolution. In spite of their belief in an afterlife, the Egyptians seemed unwilling to accept these harsh demographic realities. An extensive medical literature reflects their reputation as the greatest doctors of antiquity. Rules for diagnosis and treatment, lists of remedies, and careful instructions for surgical operations on every part of the body have been preserved. The Egyptian practice of embalming the dead and removing their organs contributed to a knowledge of anatomy unequaled by any other ancient culture.

Egypt was not a heavily urbanized society like Mesopotamia. The major cities, including Thebes, the capital of Upper Egypt, and Memphis, near the present site of Cairo, were centers of government and ceremony. Commerce, though important, was conducted mainly by royal officials. Traders operating at the village level served the modest needs of the countryside. Official expeditions collected the gold and copper that were among Egypt's most important exports. Copper was also used domestically for tools and weapons, but the Egyptians did not adopt the use of bronze until about 1500 B.C., long after it was common elsewhere.

Wood was the chief import. Egypt was self-sufficient in most other commodities, but the Nile valley contained few trees and those that existed were of species unsuitable for boat building or for the exquisite cabinetry favored by the royal court. Long before the First Dynasty, ships were sailing to Byblos on the coast of Lebanon and returning with cargos of rare timber. This trade probably was the primary vehicle for cultural and demographic contacts with Asia.

The role of Egypt as a connecting link between Asia and Africa was reflected in the appearance of its people. In Upper Egypt, the predominant physical type was slender with dark skin and African features. The people of the delta were heavier, with broad skulls and lighter complexions that betrayed Asian or European origins. But representatives of both types were found everywhere, and the Egyptians as a whole seem to have been indifferent to racial or ethnic classifications. No apparent connection was made between rank and skin color. Immigrants from Palestine to the north and Nubia in the south were found in the army as well as in civilian society and often achieved high office. The Egyptian language, too, contained a mixture of African and Semitic elements.

Women enjoyed considerable status. In art they were often, though not always, portrayed as equal to their husbands (see illustration 1.5). They could hold property, initiate divorce, and undertake contractual obligations in their own right. The women of the royal family owned vast estates and seem to have exerted an influence on politics. At least one queen ruled Old Kingdom Egypt in her own name, and two women ruled in the New Kingdom—Hatshepsut (c. 1503–1482 B.C.), who devoted her reign to the development of commerce and commissioned some of the finest monuments of Egyptian architecture, and Tawosre. But no evidence exists that women served as scribes or as officials in the royal administration.

The absence of a legal code and the shortage of court records makes evaluating the true status of women in Egyptian society difficult, but several factors seem to have operated in their behalf. The identity of a child's mother, not its father, established heredity, and the matrilineal inheritance of private property, a practice dating from predynastic times, was far more common in Egypt than in other parts of the ancient Near East. Attitudes may also have been affected by the respect accorded to women of the royal family.

**Illustration 1.5**

**The Pharaoh Menkaure and His Queen.** This statue from the Old Kingdom (Fourth Dynasty) is remarkable, not only for its artistic skill, but also for its intimacy. The couple is portrayed as affectionate equals, something that would have been virtually unthinkable in other ancient societies where the place of women was openly inferior.

## Egyptian Culture, Science, and Religion

Writing evolved in Egypt and in Mesopotamia at about the same time, but the two systems were different. Egyptian writing is known as hieroglyphics and in its earliest form consisted of lifelike pictures representing specific objects or actions. By a process similar to word association certain hieroglyphs acquired additional meanings, and by about 2700 B.C., seventy-eight of them were being used phonetically to represent consonants or groups of consonants. As in the Semitic languages, Egyptian writing had no vowels. Symbols representing both the object or idea and its pronunciation were often used simultaneously to avoid confusion, and spelling was not standardized. Though Egyptian can be read vertically or horizontally in any direction, the hieroglyphic figures always face the beginning of the line.

Hieroglyphics were used primarily for inscriptions and were typically inscribed on stone. Correspondence, contracts, and other everyday documents were produced by professional scribes writing with reed pens on a paper made from papyrus fiber. The written script, known as hieratic, was based on hieroglyphics but became more cursive over time. Most of Egyptian literature, including poems and popular romances as well as learned treatises, was circulated in this form.

Egyptian mathematics were in general less sophisticated than those of Mesopotamia. The need for land surveys after each annual flood forced the Egyptians to become skilled measurers and the construction of the pyramids reveals an impressive grasp of geometry. The Egyptians never developed a place-value system of notation, so a bewildering combination of symbols was needed to express numbers that were not multiples of ten. Ancient Egyptians could multiply and divide only by doubling, but this appears to have been sufficient for their needs. They understood squares and square roots, and they knew, at an early date, the approximate value of $\pi$. The Greeks adopted, and passed on to other European peoples, the Egyptians' use of ten as the numerical base.

Though few cultures have devoted more attention to religion and philosophy or produced a larger body of speculative literature, the ancient Egyptians maintained ideas that are difficult to describe. This is in part because they saw no need to demonstrate the logical connection between different statements. Asserting principles or retelling illustrative myths was enough; analysis was left to the wit or imagination of the reader. If an oral tradition supplemented these utterances or provided a methodological guide to their interpretation, it has been lost. The surviving literature is therefore rich, complex, and allusive, but to literal-minded moderns, full of contradictions.

The earliest Egyptian gods and goddesses were nature spirits peculiar to a village or region. They were usually portrayed as animals, such as the vulture goddess Nekhbet who became the patroness of Upper Egypt and her Lower Egyptian counterpart, the cobra goddess Buto. The effigies of both adorned the

pharaoh's crown as a symbol of imperial unity. This animal imagery may reflect totemic beliefs of great antiquity, but in time the deities acquired human bodies while retaining their animal heads.

Eventually, new deities emerged who personified abstract qualities. *Ma'at*, the principle of justice and equilibrium, became the goddess of good order; Sia was the god of intelligence. None of this involved the displacement of other gods; the Egyptians, like other societies with polytheistic religions, sought to include and revere every conceivable aspect of the divine.

The Egyptians long resisted monotheism. Perhaps they felt that it was too simple a concept to account for the complexity of the universe. When the New Kingdom pharaoh Akhenaton (reigned c. 1379–1362 B.C.) banned all cults save that of Aton, the Sun disk (formerly an aspect of Re-Horus), his ideas were rejected as heretical and abandoned soon after his death. Akhenaton has been seen by some writers as an early pioneer of monotheism, but little reason can be found to believe that his views had much influence either in Egypt or elsewhere. Akhenaton's greatest legacy was probably artistic, for he and his queen, Nefertiti, were great patrons, and the art of the Amarna Age, named after the new capital he constructed at Tell el-Amarna, was magnificent.

Of the many facets of Egyptian religion, the one that most intrigued outsiders was its concern with eternal life. The funerary cults of the pharaohs, the practice of embalming, and the adoption of similar practices by men and women of lesser status have been noted, but a full description of Egyptian lore about the hereafter would require volumes. Broadly speaking, the Egyptians thought of eternal life as a continuation of life on Earth, spent somewhere beyond the "roads of the west" (see document 1.3). They also believed that, like the pharaoh, the virtuous dead would merge their identities with Osiris. This was possible because the human soul had many aspects or manifestations, including the *akh*, which emerged only after death. The fate of the wicked was not reassuring. Their sins were weighed in a scale against the feather of *ma'at*, and if the scale tipped, their souls were thrown to the monstrous, crocodile-like "devourer of hearts" (see illustration 1.6).

The richness and complexity of Egyptian belief extended beyond religion to astronomy, astrology, and natural magic. The works attributed by Greek scholars to Hermes Trismegistus (Hermes the Thrice-Great, or Thoth) may be a compilation of ancient Egyptian sources on these subjects, though their origins remain the subject of controversy. Indisputable, however, is

## ◆ DOCUMENT 1.3 ◆

### An Egyptian Mortuary Text

*This prayer or incantation was found on coffins during the Middle Kingdom. It provides not only a vision of the here-after, but also a sample of Egyptian religious imagery. The Eastern Doors mark the entry into paradise. Re is the Sun god, and Shu is the god of air who raised Heaven above the Earth and planted trees to support it. A cubit measures between seventeen and twenty-one inches.*

Going in and Out of the Eastern Doors of Heaven among the Followers of Re. I know the Eastern Souls.

I know the central door from which Re issues in the east. Its south is the pool of *kha*-birds, in the place where Re sails with the breeze; its north is the waters of *ro*-fowl, in the place where Re sails with rowing. I am the keeper of the halyard of the boat of the god; I am the oarsman who does not weary in the barque of Re.

I know those two sycamores of turquoise between which Re comes forth, the two which came from the sowing of Shu at every eastern door at which Re rises.

I know the Field of Reeds of Re. The wall which is around it is of metal. The height of its barley is four cubits; its beard is one cubit; and its stalk is three cubits. Its emmer is seven cubits; its beard is two cubits, and its stalk is five cubits. It is the horizon dwellers, nine cubits in height, who reap it by the side of the Eastern Souls.

I know the Eastern Souls. They are Har-akhti, The *Khurrer*-Calf, and the Morning Star.

Pritchard, James B. *Ancient Near Eastern Texts Related to the Old Testament*, vol. 1, 2d ed. Princeton, NJ: Princeton University Press, 1955.

that the Greeks admired the Egyptians for their wisdom and would borrow heavily from them, especially after the establishment of a Greco-Egyptian dynasty by Ptolemy in 323 B.C.

Yet Egyptian culture, for all its concern with the unseen world, was at another level deeply practical. Its institutions, like its engineering, held up well. Conservative, inward-looking, and less aggressive than many empires, it served as a bridge not only between Africa and Europe, but also between historic times and an al-most unimaginably distant past. Growing involvement with the outside world after about 900 B.C. was in some ways a tragedy for the Egyptians. The country fell to a succession of foreign rulers, but most of them, whether Persian, Greek, or Roman, were content to preserve Egyptian institutions. Only the triumph of Islam in the the seventh century A.D. brought fundamental change. By this time much of the Egyptian achievement had been incorporated, often unconsciously, into the development of the West.

◆

## Canaan, Phoenicia, and Philistia

The eastern shore of the Mediterranean has been inhabited since earliest times. Neanderthal and Cro-Magnon remains are found in close proximity to one another in the caves of Mt. Carmel, and agriculture was established on the eastern shore before it was introduced to Egypt or Mesopotamia. The climate is benign, with mild winters and enough rainfall to support the Mediterranean triad of crops—wheat, olives, and grapes. The Bible calls it "the land of milk and honey," but it was also a corridor and at times a disputed frontier between the civilizations of Mesopotamia and Egypt. Its inhabitants never enjoyed the political stability of the great river empires. The eastern shore of the Mediterranean was from the beginning a world of small, aggressive city-states whose wealth and strategic position attracted the unwelcome attention of stronger powers.

The first Canaanites or Phoenicians, as they were known to the Greeks, spoke a variety of Semitic dialects and moved into the region during the fourth millennium, superseding or blending with an earlier Neolithic population (see map 1.2). Their first urban foundations, at Sidon, Byblos, and Ras Shamra (Ugarit), date from around 3000 B.C. From the beginning, these and a host of other cities traded actively with both Egypt and Sumer. Their inhabitants were sailors, shipbuilders, and merchants who played a vital role in the process of cultural exchange.

They were also skilled craftsmen. Carved furniture of wood and ivory was an obvious speciality, but metalworking was equally important. The Phoenicians exported fine gold and copper jewelry, bronze tools, and weapons over a wide area. Around 1500 B.C. they seem to have invented the process of casting glass around a core of sand. Decorative glassware remained an important export throughout antiquity, and glassblowing likely was invented by their descendants in Roman

**Illustration 1.6**

🎐 **Egyptian Beliefs about the Afterlife.** In this papyrus from the Theban *Book of the Dead,* the dead man and his wife watch as the god Anubis weighs his heart against a feather and Thoth records the results. The Devourer of Hearts waits at the far right. The writing in the background provides a good example of New Kingdom hieroglyphics.

MAP 1.2
🎐 Ancient Palestine 🎐

times. The women of Sidon were known for their remarkable textiles, and Sidon and Tyre were the primary source of the purple dye that symbolized royalty throughout the ancient world. It was extracted with great difficulty from the shell of the *murex* snail, a creature abundant in the harbors of Lebanon.

Politically, Phoenician towns were governed by a hereditary king assisted by a council of elders. In practice, they were probably oligarchies in which policy was decided by the wealthy merchants who served on the council. Little is known of their civic life or even of their religious practices. The Phoenicians are credited with inventing the first true alphabet, a phonetic script with twenty-two abstract symbols representing the consonants. Vowels, as in the other Semitic languages, were omitted. Their system is regarded as the greatest of all Phoenician contributions to Western culture because it could be mastered without the kind of extensive education given to professional scribes in Egypt or Mesopotamia. Literacy was now available to nearly everyone, but because the Phoenicians normally wrote with ink on papyrus, most of their records have perished.

Political crises were common. Phoenicia was invaded and at times ruled by both Egypt and the Hittites of Asia Minor. In 1190 B.C. a mysterious group known as the Sea Peoples attacked the Egyptian delta. They were driven out but eventually established themselves along the coast south of Jaffa. They appear to have come from somewhere in the Aegean or western Asia Minor and to have brought with them the use of iron weapons. Little of their language has survived. Their gods appear to have been Canaanite deities adopted on arrival. The Sea People were great fighters and iron-smiths who dominated the iron trade in the Middle East for many years. Politically, their towns of Gaza, Ashkelon, Ashdod, Gath, and Eglon formed a powerful league known as Philistia or the Philistine confederacy. The Bible calls these people Philistines, and the Romans used Palestine, a term derived from that name, to describe the entire region.

While the Philistines annexed the southern coast, the Hebrews, recently escaped from Egypt, invaded the Canaanite highlands. They fought bitterly with the Philistines, but after establishing a united kingdom of Israel that stretched from the Negev to Galilee, they formed an alliance of sorts with the Phoenicians of Tyre. Both of these incursions were related to broader population movements in the eastern Mediterranean. They coincide roughly with the displacement of the Ionians in Greece and a successful assault on the western portion of the Hittite empire by the Phrygians, a people who may have come from the same region as the Philistines. In Canaan proper, both Philistines and Hebrews were forced to contend with other peoples pushing in from the Arabian desert and the country beyond the Jordan.

Canaan was becoming crowded. The newcomers encountered a land that may already have been reaching its ecological limits after several millennia of human settlement. The Phoenician cities, already closely spaced, now saw their hinterlands greatly reduced, and with that their ability to feed their people. Led by Tyre, the Phoenicians began planting colonies from one end of the Mediterranean to the other. The first was at Utica in North Africa, supposedly founded by 1101 B.C. In the next three centuries, dozens of others were established in Cyprus, Sicily, Sardinia, and Spain. At least twenty-six such communities were in North Africa, the most important of which was Carthage, founded about 800 B.C. near the present site of Tunis.

Like the colonies later established by the Greeks, those of the Phoenicians retained commercial and perhaps sentimental ties to their founding city but were for all practical purposes independent city-states. They did not normally try to establish control over large territories. They served as commercial stations that extracted wealth from the interior in return for goods from the civilizations of the eastern Mediterranean. They were also useful as safe harbors for Phoenician traders.

By the seventh century B.C., Phoenician ships had reached Britain in search of precious tin, and Phoenician caravan routes based on the African colonies had penetrated the regions south of the Sahara. The Carthaginians later claimed to have circumnavigated Africa, and, at the very beginnings of the age of colonization, Hiram I of Tyre and his ally Solomon of Israel sent triennial expeditions to Ophir, a place now thought to have been on the coast of India. Wherever they went, the Phoenicians carried their system of writing together with the ideas and products of a dozen other cultures. Though their history was all too often neglected or written by their enemies, they played a vital role in the establishment of Mediterranean civilization.

## The Historical Development of Ancient Israel

The *Hapiru* who entered Canaan around 1200 B.C. came from Egypt. The name is thought to mean outsider or marauder and is the probable root of the term *Hebrew*. The invaders were a Semitic group of mixed ancestry whose forebears had left Mesopotamia some six hundred years earlier during the conquest of Sumeria by Babylon. According to tradition, their patriarch Abraham came from Ur. They lived for several generations as pastoralists in the trans–Jordan highlands and then emigrated to Egypt, probably at about the time of the Hyksos domination. With the revival of the New Kingdom under native Egyptian dynasties, the situation of the Semitic immigrants became more difficult. Oppressed by a pharaoh (or pharaohs) whose identity remains the subject of controversy, a group of them fled to Sinai under the leadership of Moses. Moses, whose Egyptian name helps to confirm the biblical story of his origins, molded the refugees into the people of Israel and transmitted to them the Ten Commandments, the ethical code that forms the basis of Judaism, Christianity, and Islam.

The Israelites conquered their new homeland with great difficulty. The period between 1200 and 1020 B.C. appears to have been one of constant struggle. As described in the Book of Judges, the people of Israel were at this time a loose confederacy of tribes united by a common religion and by military necessity. Saul (reigned c. 1020–1000 B.C.) established a monarchy of sorts in response to the Philistine threat, but it was not until after his death that David (ruled 1000–961 B.C.)

consolidated the territories between Beersheba and the Galilee into the kingdom of Israel.

Under David's son Solomon (reigned 961–922 B.C.), Israel became a major regional power. Commerce flourished, and the king used his wealth to construct a lavish palace as well as the First Temple at Jerusalem, a structure heavily influenced by Phoenician models. But Solomon's glory came at a price. Heavy taxation and religious disputes led to rebellion after his death, and Israel divided into two kingdoms: Israel in the north and Judah in the south. Israel was a loosely knit, aristocratic monarchy occupying the land later known as Samaria. Judah, with its walled capital of Jerusalem, was poorer but more cohesive. Both, in the end, would fall prey to more powerful neighbors.

The danger came from the north. In what is now Syria, remnants of the Hittite empire had survived as petty states. Many of them were annexed in the twelfth century by the Arameans, a Semitic people whose most important center was Damascus. The Aramaic language would become the vernacular of the Middle East—it was the language, for example, in which Jesus preached. However, Syria remained politically unstable. Assyria, once more in an expansionist phase and enriched by the conquest of Mesopotamia, filled the vacuum. The ministates of the region could not long expect to resist such a juggernaut. For a time, an alliance between Israel and Damascus held the Assyrians at bay, but by 722 B.C., both had fallen to the armies of the Assyrian conquerors Tiglath-pileser and Sargon II. Sennacherib (ruled 705–682 B.C.) annexed Philistia and Phoenicia, after which Esarhaddon (ruled 680–689 B.C.) and Assurbanipal (reigned 669–c.627 B.C.), the greatest and most cultivated of the Assyrian emperors, conquered Egypt. The tiny kingdom of Judah survived only by allying itself with the conquerors.

The end came in 587 B.C. A resurgent Babylonia had destroyed Assyria by allying itself with the Medes and adopting Assyrian military tactics. In a general settling of scores the Babylonian king Nebuchadrezzar II then sacked Jerusalem, destroyed the temple, and carried the Judaean leadership off to captivity in Babylon. Many of these people returned after Babylon was conquered by the Persians in 539 B.C., but the Israelites or Jews, a name derived from the kingdom of Judah, did not establish another independent state until 142 B.C. Judaea and Samaria would be ruled for four hundred years by Persians and by Hellenistic Greeks, while thousands of Jews, faced with the desolation of their homeland, dispersed to the corners of the known world.

## The Origins of Judaism

Ancient Israel was not, in other words, a material success. Its people were never numerous or rich, and it was only briefly a regional power. Its contributions to art and technology were negligible, yet few societies have had a greater influence on those that followed. The reason for this paradox is that the Jews developed a religion that was unlike anything else in the ancient world. It was not wholly without precedent, for ideas were borrowed from Mesopotamian and perhaps from Egyptian sources. Moreover, though inspired by revelations that can be dated with some accuracy, its basic practices evolved over time. But if the history of the beliefs themselves can be traced like those of any other religion, the Jewish concept of the divine was nevertheless revolutionary.

Its central feature was a vision of one God who was indivisible and who could not be represented or understood in visual terms. Yahweh, the God of the Jews, could not be described. The name is formed from the Hebrew word *YHWH* and appears to be a derivative of the verb "to be," indicating that the deity is eternal and changeless. Creator of the universe and absolute in power, the God of Israel was at the same time a personal god who acted in history and who took an interest in the lives of individual Jews.

Above all, the worship of Yahweh demanded ethical behavior on the part of the worshipper. This was extraordinary, because though the Mesopotamians had emphasized the helplessness of humans and Akhenaton had thought of a single, all-powerful god, the idea that a god might be served by good deeds as well as by ritual and sacrifice was new. The concept was founded on the idea of a covenant or agreement made first between God and Abraham and reaffirmed at the time of the exodus from Egypt (see document 1.4).

The people of Israel formally reaffirmed the covenant on several occasions, but failure to observe it could bring terrible punishment. The fall of Jerusalem to Nebuchedrezzar was thought to be an example of what could happen if the Jews lapsed in their devotion, and a rich prophetic tradition developed that called upon the people of Israel to avoid God's wrath by behaving in an ethical manner. The Jews thus became the first people to write long narratives of human events as opposed to mere chronologies and king lists. Much of the Jewish Bible is devoted to the interaction between God and the children of Israel and is intended to provide a record of God's judgments on Earth to discern the divine will. Therefore, while not history as the

## ◆ DOCUMENT 1.4 ◆

### The Covenant

*This passage (Exod. 19:1–9) describes the making of the covenant between the Hebrews and their God that forms the basis of the Jewish religion and the concept of the Jews as a chosen people.*

On the third new moon after the Israelites had gone out of the land of Egypt, on that very day, they came into the wilderness of Sinai. . . . Israel camped there in front of the mountain. Then Moses went up to God, the LORD called to him from the mountain, saying, "Thus you shall say to the house of Jacob, and tell the Israelites: You have seen what I did to the Egyptians, and how I bore you on eagle's wings and brought you to myself. Now, therefore, if you obey my voice and keep my covenant, you shall be my treasured possession out of all the peoples. Indeed, the whole earth is mine, but you shall be for me a priestly kingdom and a holy nation. These are the words that you shall speak to the Israelites." So Moses came, summoned the elders of the people, and set before them all these words that the LORD had commanded him. The people all answered as one: "Everything that the LORD has spoken we will do." Moses reported the words of the people to the LORD. Then the LORD said to Moses, "I am going to come to you in a dense cloud, in order that the people may hear when I speak to you and so trust you ever after.

## ◆ DOCUMENT 1.5 ◆

### The Prophet Isaiah: Social Justice

*This passage (Isa. 1:11–17), attributed to Isaiah of Jerusalem in the mid-eighth century B.C., demonstrates the increasing emphasis on social justice in Hebrew religious thought.*

What to me is the multitude of your sacrifices? says the LORD. I have had enough of burnt offerings of rams and the fat of fed beasts; I do not delight in the blood of bulls, or of lambs, or of he-goats. When you come to appear before me, who requires of you this trampling of my courts? Bring no more vain offerings; incense is an abomination to me. New moon and sabbath and the calling of assemblies—I cannot endure iniquity and solemn assembly. Your new moons and your appointed feasts my soul hates; they have become a burden to me, I am weary of bearing them. When you spread forth your hands I will hide my eyes from you; even though you make many prayers, I will not listen; your hands are full of blood. Wash yourselves; make yourselves clean; remove the evil of your doings from before my eyes; cease to do evil, learn to do good; seek justice, correct oppression; defend the fatherless, plead for the widow.

Greeks would write it, it remains the first attempt to provide a coherent account of past events.

The primary expression of Yahweh's will is found, however, in the Ten Commandments and in the subsequent elaboration of the Mosaic Law. The Ten Commandments, brought down by Moses from Mt. Sinai and delivered to the people of Israel before their entry into Canaan, formed the basis of an elaborate legal and moral code that governed virtually every aspect of life and conduct. Like the concept of God, the law evolved over time. Refined and amplified by generations of priests, prophets, and teachers, it remains to this day the foundation of Jewish life.

Certain features of Mosaic Law—such as the principle of an eye for an eye, a tooth for a tooth—recall Babylonian precedents, but it went much further by seeking to govern private as well as public behavior. Dietary regulations were set forth in great detail along with rules for sexual conduct and the proper form of religious observances. Though legalistic in form, the Mosaic Law offered a comprehensive guide to ethical behavior whose force transcended social or political sanctions (see document 1.5). It was intended not only as legislation but also as a prescription for the godly life. God could mete out terrible punishment; but the commandments were to be kept, not in brute fear or from a sense of grudging duty, but in awe of God's majesty and holiness, and in gratitude for God's blessings. This concept of righteousness as an essential duty, together with many of the specific ethical principles enshrined in the Torah, or first five books of the Jewish Bible, would later be adopted by both Christianity and Islam. The influence of Mosaic Law on Western thought and society has therefore been incalculable.

## The Social and Economic Structures of Ancient Israel

The society that produced these revolutionary concepts was not in other respects much different from its neighbors. From a federation of nomadic herdsmen initially organized into twelve tribes, the earliest Jews evolved into settled agriculturalists after their arrival in Canaan. Tribal survivals such as the communal ownership of resources gave way to a system of private property in which land and water were generally owned by families. Inevitably, some families were more successful than others, and many became substantial landholders with tenants and perhaps a few slaves. As in Mesopotamia, these families were often extended and always patriarchal in organization. A gradual process of urbanization increased the importance of crafts and trade, but the basic family structure remained.

In earliest times, fathers held absolute authority over wives and children. As ethical standards evolved, patriarchy was increasingly tempered by a sense of responsibility and mercy. However, the status of women was lower in ancient Israel than among the Hittites, the Egyptians, or the Mesopotamians. Under the Judges who ruled Israel from the invasion of Canaan to the emergence of the monarchy, women presided as priestesses over certain festivals. As interpretation of the Mosaic Law evolved, their participation in religious life was restricted (see document 1.6). The worship of Yahweh demanded purity as well as holiness, and women were regarded as ritually impure during menstruation and after childbirth. They were also exempted from regular prayer and other rituals on the theory that they should not be distracted from child care. In effect, they were excluded from direct participation in all public rites and were segregated from men even as observers because their presence was thought to be distracting. The proper role of women was in the home.

The home, however, was central to religious life. Marriages were arranged between families and sealed by contract as in Babylon, but only men could initiate

### ◈ DOCUMENT 1.6 ◈

# Leviticus: The Impurity of Women

*These passages of the Mosaic Law are part of a much longer section concerned with impurity, that is, those conditions under which performing religious rituals is not permissible. Note that, although men, too, could be impure, the purification of women took longer and the amount of time required for purification after the birth of a girl was twice as long as that for a boy.*

12:2–5. If a woman conceives and bears a male child, she shall be ceremonially unclean seven days; as at the time of her menstruation she shall be unclean. On the eighth day the flesh of his foreskin shall be circumcised. Her time of blood purification shall be thirty-three days; she shall not touch any holy thing, or come into the sanctuary, until the days of her purification are completed. If she bears a female child, she shall be unclean two weeks, as in her menstruation; her time of blood purification shall be sixty-six days.

15:12–22. If a man has an emission of semen, he shall bathe his whole body in water, and be unclean until the evening. Everything made of cloth or skin on which the semen falls shall be washed with water and be unclean until the evening. If a man lies with a woman and has an emission of semen, both of them shall bathe in water and be unclean until the evening. When a woman has a discharge of blood that is her regular discharge from her body, she shall be in her impurity for seven days, and whoever touches her shall be unclean until the evening. Everything on which she lies during her impurity shall be unclean; everything also on which she sits shall be unclean. Whoever touches her bed shall wash his clothes, and bathe in water, and be unclean until the evening. Whoever touches anything on which she sits shall wash his clothes and bathe in water, and be unclean until the evening.

divorce and no provision was made for a dowry, which usually meant that a man could divorce his wife without financial loss. Divorces were nevertheless uncommon because Mosaic Law and Jewish custom placed a premium on the family. Polygyny and concubinage, though permitted, were rare for economic reasons, and adultery was punishable by death.

Within the home, women were more respected than their legal position might indicate. They had the right to name the children and were responsible for their early instruction in moral and practical matters. Theory aside, they often controlled the everyday life of the household. Furthermore, Jewish literature reveals none of the contempt for women and their capacities sometimes found in the writings of ancient Greece. The Bible abounds in heroic women such as Esther, Rachel, and Deborah, and the Book of Proverbs holds the value of a good woman as "beyond rubies." But the patriarchal nature of Jewish society coupled with the divine origin of the Mosaic Law would have a profound impact on subsequent history. Christianity, Islam, and modern Judaism absorbed from the Bible the idea that women's exclusion from many aspects of public and religious life was ordained by God.

The Mosaic emphasis on family placed a high value on children. Infanticide, a practice common in other ancient cultures, was forbidden, and child-raising practices, like every other aspect of life, were prescribed by

law. On the eighth day after birth, male children were circumcised as a sign of their covenant with God. They received religious instruction from their fathers and at age thirteen assumed the full religious responsibilities of an adult. Eldest sons, who were especially honored, had extra responsibilities. Both boys and girls were expected to help in the fields and in the home, but gender roles were carefully preserved. Boys learned their father's trade or cared for the livestock. Girls were responsible for gleaning the fields after harvest and for keeping the house supplied with water from wells that, in town at least, were usually communal. What remained in the fields after gleaning was left for the poor.

The obligation to assist the poor and helpless—symbolized by this minor, yet divinely established, injunction—was central to the Jewish conception of righteousness. A comprehensive ideal of charity and communal responsibility gradually evolved from such precepts and, like monotheism itself, spread to Western society as a whole long after Israel as a political entity had ceased to exist.

The central features of the Jewish faith were well established at the time of the Babylonian exile. The subsequent history of the Jewish people and the transmission of their religious and ethical concepts to other cultures are important to consider, for the interaction of the Jewish, Christian, and Islamic faiths continues to this day.

CHAPTER 2

# ANCIENT GREECE TO THE END OF THE PELOPONNESIAN WARS

## CHAPTER OUTLINE

◆◆◆◆◆◆◆◆◆◆◆◆◆◆◆◆◆◆◆◆◆

Ancient Greece was part of the larger Mediterranean world. The eastern Mediterranean in particular may be likened to a great lake that facilitated trade, communication, and cultural borrowing. Phoenicians, Egyptians, Greeks, and many others shared a similar diet as well as some ideas and institutions, but each synthesized their borrowings in different ways. The Greeks, for example, took their alphabet from the Phoenicians and some of their scientific and philosophical ideas from Egypt, while their social organization resembled that of the Phoenician city-states. Greek civilization nevertheless remained unique. Its aesthetic ideals and its commitment to human self-development, competition, and linear thought transformed everything it touched and laid the foundations of a characteristically Western culture.

◆

## Geography, the Aegean, and Crete

Mainland Greece is an extension of the Balkan Peninsula. It is, as it was in antiquity, a rugged land—mountainous, rocky, and dry, with much of the rainfall coming in the autumn and winter months. Large areas suitable for cultivation are rare, and deforestation, largely the result of overgrazing, was well advanced by the fifth century B.C. The Aegean Sea, with its innumerable islands, separates European Greece from Asia Minor. It has been a crossroads of trade and communication since the first sailors ventured forth in boats. At its northern end stood Troy, the earliest of whose nine cities, each one built upon the ruins of its predecessors, dates from before 3000 B.C. The town was built upon a ridge overlooking the southern entry to the Dardanelles, the long narrow strait through which ships must pass to enter the Sea of Marmara, the Bosporus, and the Black Sea. The current in the strait runs southward at about three knots and the prevailing winds are from the north, making it passable to early ships only under the most favorable of conditions. Fortunately, a small harbor just inside its mouth allowed goods to be transshipped from the Aegean and ships to lie at anchor while awaiting a favorable wind. That harbor was held by Troy, as was the best crossing point on the land route from Europe and Asia a few miles to the north. The city had great strategic importance, and its wealth was founded on tolls.

Far to the south is Crete, in ancient times the navigational center of the eastern Mediterranean. Approximately 150 miles long and no more than 35 miles wide, it lies across the southern end of the Aegean Sea, about 60 miles from the southernmost extremity of the Greek mainland and not more than 120 miles from the coast of Asia Minor. Africa is only 200 miles to the south. The importance of Crete was determined less by raw distances than by wind and current. Ships westbound from Egypt had to follow the currents north along the Phoenician coast and then west to Crete before proceeding to the ports of Italy or North Africa. Phoenicians on the way to Carthage or the Strait of Gibraltar did the same. They could pass either to the north or to the south of the island. Most preferred the northern shore because it offered more sandy inlets where their ships could be anchored for the night or hauled ashore for repairs and cleaning. Crete was therefore a natural waystation as well as a convenient point for the transshipment of Egyptian and Phoenician goods. The same harbors offered easy access to the Greek mainland, the Ionian islands, and Troy.

## The Society of Minoan Crete (3000–1400 B.C.)

The first inhabitants of Crete arrived before 4000 B.C. They found not only a strategic location, but also land that was well suited for Neolithic agriculture. Crete's mountains rise to more than eight thousand feet, but the island has rich valleys and coastal plains that provide abundant grain. The climate is generally mild. Perfection is marred only by summer droughts, winter gales, and devastating earthquakes that are perhaps the most conspicuous feature of the island's history.

The civilization that had developed on Crete by 3000 B.C. is usually called Minoan, after Minos, a legendary ruler who became part of later Greek mythology. Its chief characteristics were the early manufacture of bronze and the construction of enormous palaces that combined political, religious, and economic functions. Four main complexes were constructed—at Knossos (see illustration 2.1), Phaistos, Zakros, and

Mallia—though the ruins of other large houses are found throughout the island. All are built around large rectangular courts that were apparently used for religious and public ceremonies. The upper levels of the palaces had decorative staircases and colonnades that resemble those of Egyptian temples. The walls were covered with thin layers of shiny gypsum or decorated with naturalistic wall paintings. Below were innumerable storerooms and a system of drains for the removal of wastes and rainwater. So elaborate was the floor plan that the Greek name for the palace at Knossos (the Labyrinth, after the heraldic labrys or two-headed axe of the Minoan royal house) became the common word for a maze.

The presence of such vast storage facilities indicates that Minoan rulers played an important part in the distribution of goods, but little is known of Minoan social or political life. The early language of Crete has not yet been deciphered. It was written at first in hieroglyphic characters derived from Egyptian models. A later linear script is equally unreadable, and only Linear B, dating from the last period of Minoan history, has been translated. The language revealed is an early form of Greek, probably introduced by a new ruling dynasty from the mainland around 1400 B.C.

Minoan religious beliefs are equally obscure. Wall paintings portray women in priestly roles, and the dominant cult was almost certainly that of the Earth Mother, the fertility goddess whose worship in the Mediterranean basin dates from Paleolithic times. Other paintings show young women and men vaulting over the heads of bulls and doing gymnastic routines on their backs (see illustration 2.2). This dangerous sport probably had religious significance and was performed in the palace courtyards, but its exact purpose is unknown. In any case, the prominence of women in Minoan art and the range of activities in which they were portrayed indicate a measure of equality rare in the ancient world.

## The Mycenean Greeks

The people who seem to have conquered Crete around 1450 B.C. are known as Myceneans, though Mycenae was only one of their many cities. They spoke an early form of Greek and may have occupied Macedonia or Thessaly before establishing themselves along the western shores of the Aegean. Their chief centers—apart from Mycenae and its companion fortress, Tiryns—were Athens on its rich peninsula and Thebes in the Boetian plain. All were flourishing by 2000 B.C.

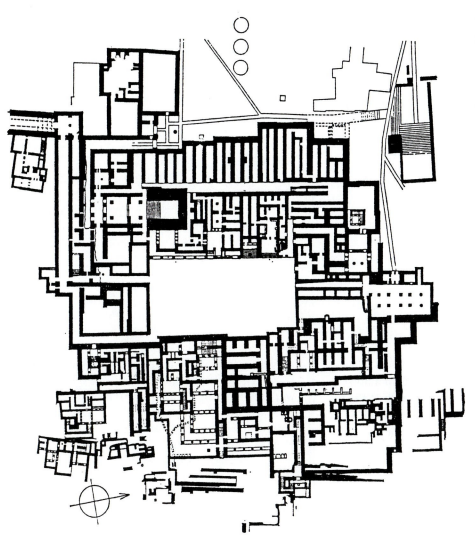

Illustration 2.1

▓ **Plan of the Palace at Knossos.** This partial plan of the great palace at Knossos shows the central courtyard, private apartments, and what are probably storerooms.

Illustration 2.2

▓ **Bull Leaping at Knossos.** This fresco from the east wing of the palace at Knossos portrays a man and two women somersaulting over the back of a charging bull. Whether this was a sport, a religious ritual, or both is not known.

Kings or chieftains ruled each of the Mycenean communities and apparently distributed commodities in the traditional way. They built vast palaces and tombs using cut stones of as much as one hundred tons apiece and carried on an extensive trade with Crete and Egypt. The palaces, though similar in function to those on Crete, were more symmetrical in design, with spacious apartments and colonnaded porches on the upper levels and storerooms below. Olive oil was a major export, and some of the storage spaces were heated to keep it from congealing in the winter cold.

The earliest tombs were shaft graves of the sort found throughout Europe; later, vast corbeled vaults became common. The dead were buried with magnificent treasures, for the Myceneans collected art and luxury goods from other cultures as well as from their own. They were also skilled metalworkers. Their bronze armor and weapons, like their gold jewelry and face masks, were among the finest ever produced in the ancient world.

But aside from their material culture, these precursors of the ancient Greeks remain something of a mystery. Homer, the semimythical poet who stands at the beginnings of Greek culture, made them the heroes of his *The Iliad* (see document 2.1). This great epic describes their successful siege of Troy, an event partially supported by archaeological evidence, but the society he describes is unlike that revealed by the ruins of Mycenean cities. Homer's Myceneans cremate their dead and fight as individual champions. No mention is made of the tombs, the vast storerooms, the voluminous accounts, and the careful, hardheaded organization of vast enterprises that created them. Homer likely was describing a much later world—perhaps the one in which he lived—and attributing its values to its predecessors. Only the violence and the lack of political unity are the same.

## Early Greek Society

Homer, or whoever created *The Iliad* and its companion piece *The Odyssey*, from an existing body of oral traditions, probably lived in the ninth century B.C. By this time the Aegean world had changed almost beyond recognition. The population movements of the thirteenth century B.C. inaugurated a kind of dark age about which little is known. The Homeric poems probably refer to this era but provide only fragmentary information about actual events. Greeks of the classical age believed that the Dorians, a Greek-speaking people from the north, swept into the peninsula and estab-

---

◈ DOCUMENT 2.1 ◈

### The Iliad

*Homer's great epic of the Trojan War—The Iliad—in many ways defined Greek values and ideals for later generations. Those values are humanistic in the sense that its heroes strive for excellence in human instead of religious terms, but underlying everything is a sense that even the greatest of mortals live within a universal order. This passage, in which the aging Priam of Troy comes to ask Achilles for the body of his son, Hector, who has been killed by Achilles, reflects the tragic side of Greek consciousness.*

Priam had set Achilles thinking about his own father and brought him to the verge of tears. Taking the old man's hand, he gently put him from him; and overcome by their memories, they both broke down. Priam, crouching at Achilles's feet, wept bitterly for man-slaying Hector, and Achilles wept for his father, and then again for Patroclus. The house was filled with the sounds of their lamentation. But presently when he had had enough of tears and recovered his composure, the excellent Achilles leapt from his chair, and in compassion for the man's grey head and grey beard, took him by the arm and raised him. Then he spoke to him from his heart: "You are indeed a man of sorrows and have suffered much. How could you dare to come by yourself to the Achaean ships into the presence of a man who has killed so many of your gallant sons? You have a heart of iron. But pray be seated now, here on this chair, and let us leave our sorrows, bitter though they are, locked up in our own hearts, for weeping is cold comfort and does little good. We men are wretched things, and the gods, who have no cares themselves, have woven sorrow into the very pattern of our lives."

Homer. *The Iliad*, trans. E. V. Rieu. Harmondsworth, England: Penguin books, 1950.

---

lished themselves in the Peloponnese and other Mycenean centers. Mycenae was destroyed, but the lore is that the invaders bypassed Athens, which became the conduit for a vast eastward migration. Thousands of refugees, their lands taken by newcomers, fled to Attica. From there they colonized the islands of the Aegean and the western coast of Asia Minor. The migration of these Ionian Greeks displaced others who flowed eastward into Asia Minor. The Phrygians who toppled the weakened fragments of the Hittite Empire and the Philistines who descended on the Canaanite coast were almost certainly among them, for all of these events occurred at about the same time.

Recent scholarship casts doubt on the theory of a Dorian invasion, but by the ninth century B.C. the Greek world was divided into two major subgroups, the Dorians, who dominated most of the peninsula, and the Ionians, who inhabited Attica, Euboia, and the east. They spoke different dialects but shared many aspects of a common culture. Both groups thought of the Greek-speaking world as Hellas and referred to themselves as Hellenes.

The religion of the Greeks was based on an extended family of twelve gods who were supposed to inhabit Mt. Olympus in northeastern Greece. The greatest were Zeus, the father of the Gods; his consort, Hera; and his brother Poseidon, the god of the sea and of earthquakes. Hestia, the goddess of hearths, and Demeter, often associated with the earlier Earth Mother, were his sisters. His children were Aphrodite, goddess of love; Apollo, god of the Sun, music, and poetry; Ares, god of war; Athena, goddess of wisdom and the fine arts; Hephaestus, god of fire and metallurgy; and Hermes, their messenger, who was also god of commerce and other matters that involved cleverness or trickery. Perhaps the most popular was Artemis, the virgin nature goddess who symbolized chastity and to whom women prayed for help in childbirth.

The Greeks conceived of these deities in human terms, though the gods were immortal and possessed superhuman powers. Because Olympian behavior was often capricious and immoral, Greek ethical principles in the Archaic Period were derived not from divine precepts but from commonsense notions of how to get along with one's neighbors. Worship meant offering prayers and sacrifices in return for divine protection or to secure the goodwill of the spirits who ruled over particular localities. Little or no hope of personal immortality seemed to exist. By the eighth century B.C., centers of worship open to all Greeks had been established at several locations. Olympia, dedicated to Zeus, and the shrine of Poseidon at Corinth were famous for athletic contests held annually in the god's honor. The shrine of Apollo at Delphi was home to the Delphic oracle, whose cryptic predictions were widely sought until Roman times.

Common shrines, and above all the Olympic games, provided unifying elements in a culture that would for centuries remain politically fragmented. The

---

### ◈ DOCUMENT 2.2 ◈

## Pindar: Ode to an Athlete

*Pindar (c. 518–c. 438 b.c.) was a native of Thebes and one of the greatest lyric poets of ancient Greece. He is best known for odes composed in honor of successful athletes. Many— such as* Isthmian V: For Phylakidas of Aegina, Winner in the Trial of Strength, *presented here—were commissioned by the athlete's native cities. Pindar often included a brief warning against* hubris, *the fatal pride that leads men to challenge the gods.*

In the struggle of the games he has won
The glory of his desire,
Whose hair is tied with thick garlands
For victory with his hands
Or swiftness of foot.
Men's valor is judged by their fates,
But two things alone
Look after the sweetest grace of life
Among the fine flowers of wealth.

If a man fares well and hears his good name
    spoken,
Seek not to become a Zeus!
You have everything, if a share
Of those beautiful things come to you.

Mortal ends befit mortal men.
For you Phylakidas, at the Isthmus
A double success is planted and thrives,
And at Nemea for you and your brother Pytheas
In the Trial of Strength. My heart tastes song.

Pindar. *The Odes of Pindar,* p. 47, trans. C. M. Bowra. Harmondsworth, England: Penguin Books, 1969. Copyright © The Estate of C. M. Bowra, 1969. Reproduced by permission of Penguin Books Ltd.

---

games drew men (women were not permitted to compete) from every part of the Greek world and provided a peaceful arena for the competitive spirit that was a great part of ancient Greek life. Winners were praised by poets (see document 2.2) and showered with gifts by their grateful communities. All Greek men participated in sports, for they saw athletics as an essential component of the good life. Physical fitness prepared them for war, but competition lay at the heart of their concept of personal worth, and athletic success was seen as almost godlike.

## The Development of the Polis

The Dorians tended to settle in fortified high places that could be defended against their enemies, expelling some of the existing population and subjugating others. Each one of these communities—and there were scores of them—claimed full sovereign rights and vigorously defended its independence against all comers. On the rugged Greek peninsula, most of the arable land is found in valleys isolated from one another by mountains, but three or four of these ministates might be found in the same area with no geographical barriers between them. Many did not possess enough land to support their populations. The men organized themselves into war bands that, like those of Homer's heroes, might ally with the warriors of another community in the pursuit of a major objective, but cooperation was always fragile and warfare endemic.

Ionic settlements in the Aegean were similar. Some of the islands had been Cretan colonies, and most were inhabited when the Ionian refugees arrived. Like their Doric enemies, the Ionians established themselves in fortifiable places and sometimes imposed their rule on existing populations. Although a few smaller islands formed political units, others were divided into many settlements. These early communities were the precursors of the *polis*, the basis of Greek political and social life. Each, whether Doric or Ionic, claimed the primary loyalties of its inhabitants. To Greeks of the classical period, the polis was far more than a city-state; it was the only form of social organization in which the individual's full potential could be achieved. Composed in theory at least of those who shared common ancestors and worshipped the same gods, it molded the character of its inhabitants and provided a focus for their lives. To live apart from the polis was to live as a beast.

Security from outside threats made this political decentralization possible. The Greek city-states developed after the Hittites had fallen and when Egypt was in decline. The great Asian empires were not yet a threat. Conflict, and there was much of it, involved other cities whose population and resources were often minuscule. Many were little more than villages whose armies might number no more than eighty or one hundred men. Even the largest, including Athens and Corinth, were small by modern standards, but military resources could be augmented through the formation of temporary alliances.

In the beginning, the government of these communities was aristocractic. Kings might be hereditary or elected, but they ruled with the assistance of a council composed of warriors from the more distinguished families. Warfare, aimed largely at seizing or destroying a neighbor's crops, reflected the organization of society. Individual champions fought one another with sword, lance, and shield, while tactics in the larger sense were unknown.

This period of aristocratic dominance came to an end with the adoption of the hoplite phalanx, a formation of trained spearmen who fought shoulder to shoulder in a rectangle that was normally eight ranks deep (see illustration 2.3). As long as no one broke ranks, the phalanx was almost invincible against a frontal attack by horse or foot and could clear the field of traditional infantry at will. Only another band of hoplites could stand against them. Flanking attacks by cavalry were prevented by grounding the sides of the formation against natural or man-made obstacles, an easy task in the rugged Greek countryside. Missile weapons were only a minor threat because the hoplite's bronze armor was heavy and enemy archers usually had to fight in the open. After the first volley, the phalanx could cover the distance of a bowshot in the time it took to fire a second or third arrow, and the archers would be forced to flee in disorder. The major weakness of the formation was its immobility. Maneuvering was difficult and pursuit impossible without breaking ranks. This tended to reduce the number of casualties but made achieving decisive results difficult.

The hoplite phalanx gave birth to the polis in its classical form. The new tactics required the participation of every able-bodied freeman who could afford arms and armor, and men who fought for the city could not be denied a say in its governance. Those too poor to equip themselves as hoplites were expected to serve as support troops or to row in the city's galleys, for most Greek cities maintained a navy as well. Though wealth and heredity still counted, the eventual effect of the new warfare was to increase the number of those who participated in government. Slaves, women, and foreigners—meaning those who had been born in another polis—were excluded from public life, but all male citizens were expected to participate in matters of justice and public policy.

The growth of democracy, however, was slow, for the aristocrats resisted change. Efforts to maintain their traditional privileges caused disorder in every polis, and the late eighth and early seventh centuries B.C. were times of conflict. Tyrants or dictators who promised to resolve these struggles found achieving power easy. Though their rule was condemned by later theorists, they developed administrative structures and tried to

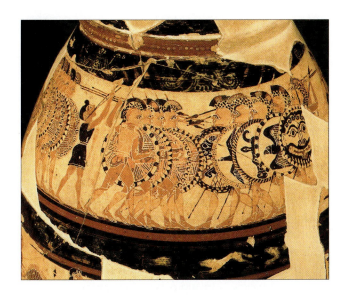

Illustration 2.3

Hoplite Warfare. This vase painting from the seventh century B.C. is one of the few surviving portrayals of hoplites at war. The piper on the left is leading another phalanx into the battle.

establish a broader patriotism by weakening the old loyalties based on tribe or district. Most of the tyrants were also great builders whose temples and public works gave form to the cities of the classical age.

Greek towns were usually built around an *acropolis*, the high point selected as a place of refuge by the original inhabitants. Here the first rude temples were established in honor of the city's gods. Under the tyrants, new and more magnificent structures replaced them, and private buildings were banished to the area around the base of the hill. With rare exceptions, Greek homes were simple, and much of daily life was lived in the streets or in the *agora*, an open space that served as the economic and social center of the town. This, perhaps as much as any other factor, accounts for the vitality of Greek politics and intellectual life; the life of the citizen was one of constant interaction with his fellows.

The more ambitious tyrants not only built temples, but also remodeled such public spaces as the agora. They strengthened the defensive walls that surrounded their cities and worked to improve the quality and quantity of the water supply. Some went even further. Corinth, one of the wealthiest Greek cities, bestrides the narrow isthmus that separates the Saronic Gulf from the Gulf of Corinth. The Corinthian tyrant Periander built a stone trackway across the isthmus, allowing entire ships to be hauled from the Aegean to the Adriatic. Merchants willing to pay a substantial toll could thereby save a voyage of several hundred miles.

The troubled years that gave birth to the tyrants were also the great age of Greek colonization. Greece was by any standards a poor country with little room for internal growth, but it had an extensive coastline with good harbors and it was inhabited by a seafaring people. The limits of agricultural expansion were reached by the beginning of the eighth century B.C., and like the Phoenicians of a century before, Greek cities were forced to establish colonies in other parts of the Mediterranean world as an outlet for surplus population. Though some of the colonists were merchants or political exiles, most sought only enough land to feed their families.

The process seems to have begun around 750 B.C. with the establishment of a trading community in the Bay of Naples. It was intended to provide access to the copper of Etruria, but the colonies established during the next fifty years in eastern Sicily were almost purely agrarian. Settlements then spread throughout southern Italy and westward into France, where Massalia, the future Marseilles, was founded around 600 B.C. by the Ionic town of Phocaea. Others were founded around the shores of the Black Sea, and those in what is now the southern Ukraine would one day play an important role by supplying the Greek peninsula with grain.

Some Italian colonies, such as Sybaris on the Gulf of Taranto, became wealthy through trade. Though originally founded to exploit a rich agricultural plain, Sybaris became a point of transshipment for goods from the Adriatic to the Tyrrhenian Sea, thereby avoiding the treacherous Strait of Messina. Others, such as Syracuse in Sicily, owed their wealth to agriculture, but Syracuse grew as large as its parent Corinth and became a major regional power in the fifth century B.C. Virtually all of these towns came into conflict with the Phoenicians and Carthaginians who had settled in Spain, Africa, and western Sicily. By the beginning of the sixth century B.C. at least five hundred Greek *poleis* were in existence from Spain to the Crimea.

The use of the term *polis* is technically correct in this case, for these were not colonies but fully independent states. They venerated the divine patron of their founding city and sometimes extended special privileges to its citizens. "Mother" cities competed with their "colonies" for trade and on occasion fought them. All, however, were regarded as part of Hellas. Governing institutions paralleled those in the older Greek cities, and the colonies, too, were forced to confront the problem of tyranny. Some failed to eject their tyrants; others were able to achieve a measure of democracy in the course of the sixth century B.C.

Tyrants had been accepted for the most part out of necessity, but the Greeks had regarded their rule as an aberration, a temporary suspension of the laws instead of a permanent institution. Most were eventually overthrown and replaced by some form of representative government. This might be a narrowly based oligarchy, as at Corinth, or a true democracy of the kind that gradually evolved at Athens.

## Life in the Polis: The Early History of Athens

Though Athens, on the Attic Peninsula north of the Saronic Gulf, would become the cultural center of classical Greece, its initial development was slow. Until 594 B.C. it was governed by an aristocratic council known as the Areopagus, which elected nine magistrates or archons on an annual basis. Membership in the Areopagus was hereditary, and there was no written law. The archons, who were always aristocrats, interpreted legal issues to suit themselves.

Aristocratic dominance and the gradual depletion of the soil eventually produced an agrarian crisis. Most Athenians—and most Greeks—were small farmers who grew wheat and barley and tried to maintain a few vines and olive trees (see document 2.3). Wheat yields probably averaged about five bushels per acre; barley, ten. Such yields are normal for unfertilized, unirrigated soils in almost any region. This was generally enough to guarantee subsistence but little more. When yields began declining in the early seventh century B.C., Attic farmers were forced to borrow from the aristocrats to survive. Inevitably, harvests failed to improve, and citizens who defaulted were enslaved and sometimes sold abroad.

Dissatisfaction with this state of affairs and with the endless blood feuds among aristocratic clans led to an abortive tyranny in 632 B.C. Eleven years later, a semilegendary figure named Draco passed laws against aristocratic violence so harsh that *draconian* has become a

byword for severity. However, the agrarian problem remained. Political tensions remained high until the election of Solon as the only archon in 594 B.C.

Solon was in effect a tyrant, though he had no intention of serving for life and retired when he had completed his reforms. He canceled outstanding debts, freed many slaves, and forbade the use of a citizen's person as collateral. Solon also broadened the social base of the Athenian government by creating a popularly elected Council of 400 as a check on the powers of the Areopagus. His economic ideas were less successful. Though he tried to encourage commerce and industry, Solon prohibited the export of wheat and encouraged that of olive oil. The larger landholders, seeing profit in olives and other cash crops, took wheat land out of production and Athens became permanently dependent upon imported food. Most of its grain would eventually come from the rich plains north of the Black Sea. This meant that, in later years, Athenian survival required control of the Hellespont, the narrow strait that separates Europe from Asia and provided access to the Greek ports of the Crimea.

These measures, though popular, failed to prevent the emergence of Pisistratus as tyrant, briefly in 560 B.C. and then from 546 B.C. to his death in 527 B.C. The constitution was unchanged, and Pisistratus ruled through his mastery of electoral politics, but like the tyrants of other cities, he worked tirelessly to break the remaining power of the aristocratic families. Taxation and subscriptions for more and more public festivals weakened them financially while magistrates were sent into the countryside to interfere in their legal disputes. Public works flourished, and such projects as temple construction and the remodeling of the agora provided work for thousands.

Pisistratus was succeeded by his son Hippias, but Hippias became a tyrant in the more conventional sense of the word. He was overthrown with Spartan assistance in 510 B.C. and replaced by Cleisthenes, who laid the foundations of the democratic system that lasted throughout the classical age.

Cleisthenes expanded the number of demes, or wards, which served as the primary units of local government, and divided them into ten tribes instead of four. A Council of 500 was elected with fifty members from each tribe. This body prepared legislation and supervised finances and foreign affairs. Final authority in all matters now rested with an assembly of all citizens that met at least forty times a year. Dangerous or unpopular politicians could be ostracized, a process by which the citizens voted to exile an individual from the

### ◆ DOCUMENT 2.3 ◆

## The Life of a Greek Landowner

*Hesiod (fl. late eighth century B.C.) was one of the first Greek poets and a landowner from Boeotia. His* Works and Days *is a long didactic poem addressed to his ne'er-do-well brother, Perses. It provides an unforgettable description of rural life in an age when farmers still went to sea to sell their goods abroad.*

When the thistle blooms and the chirping cicada
sits on trees and pours down shrill song
from frenziedly quivering wings in the toilsome summer
then goats are fatter than ever and wine is at its best
women's lust knows no bounds and men are all dried up,
because the dog star parches their heads and knees
and the heat sears their skin. Then, ah then,
I wish you a shady ledge and your choice wine,
bread baked in the dusk and mid-August goat milk
and meat from a free-roving heifer that has never calved—
and from firstling kids. Drink sparkling wine,
sitting in the shade with your appetite sated,
and face Zephyr's breeze as it blows from mountain peaks.
Pour three measures of water fetched from a clear spring,
One that flows unchecked, and a fourth of wine.
As soon as mighty Orion rises above the horizon
exhort your slaves to thresh Demeter's holy grain
in a windy, well-rounded threshing floor.
Measure it first and then store it in bins.
But when your grain is tightly stored inside the house
then hire an unmarried worker and look for a female
servant with no children—nursing women are a burden.
Keep a dog with sharp teeth and feed it well,
wary of the day-sleepers who might rob you.

Bring in a lasting supply of hay and fodder
for your oxen and your mules. Once this is done let your
slaves rest their weary knees and unyoke the oxen.
When Orion and the dog star rise to the middle of the
sky and rosy-fingered dawn looks upon Arcturus,
then Perses, gather your grapes and bring them home
and leave them in the sun for ten days and nights,
in the shade for five, and on the sixth day
draw the gift of joyous Dionysos into your vats.
When the Pleiades, the Hyades, and mighty Orion set,
remember the time has come to plow again—
and may the earth nurse for you a full year's supply,
And if longing seizes you for sailing the stormy seas,
when the Pleiades flee mighty Orion
and plunge into the misty deep
and all the gusty winds are raging,
then do not take your ship on the wine-dark sea
but, as I bid you, remember to work the land.
Haul your ship onto land and secure it to the ground
with stones on all sides to stay the blast of rain and wind,
and pull the plug to avoid rotting caused by rain water.
Store up the tackle compactly inside your house
and neatly fold the sails, the wings of a seafaring ship.
Hang your rudder above the fireplace
and wait until the time to sail comes again.

Hesiod. *Theogony, Works and Days, Shield,* ed. and trans. A. N. Athanassakis. Baltimore: John Hopkins University Press, 1983. Copyright © 1983 Johns Hopkins University Press. Used by permission.

city for ten years without a formal trial. Magistrates were chosen by lot, though the city's military commander or *strategos* continued to be elected, presumably on the basis of merit. Plato and others who sympathized with aristocracy found this system, which was liberalized even further after 461 B.C., absurd, but competence was at least partially ensured because candidates had to volunteer and were subjected to a stringent review of their actions at the end of the year.

Athens represented an extreme of democratic government, but its level of public participation was not unique. The system worked remarkably well for almost two hundred years and provided the basis for local government even after the city lost its freedom to the Macedonians. At the very least, it guaranteed intense involvement by the entire population of male citizens in the life of the polis, any one of whom could be part of its political, military, and judicial processes. Democratic theorists have held that this level of participation helps to account for the extraordinary intellectual and artistic achievements of the Athenians. Furthermore, Athens, its institutions, and its way of life became an inspiration to many throughout the later history of the West. While it fostered slavery and excluded women from public life, Athens was the first and perhaps the greatest of the early democracies.

## The Social and Economic Structures of Athenian Society

In material terms, the Athenian way of life was remarkably simple. Athenians, like other Greeks, lived on bread, wine, and oil, often garnished with onions or garlic. Beans and various fruits supplemented this otherwise meager diet. Meat was expensive and normally consumed in small quantities. Even the largest houses were small by Egyptian or Mesopotamian standards, though their arrangement was similar. Square or rectangular rooms were grouped around a central courtyard, which might contain a private well. Some houses had second stories. Merchants and artisans often conducted their business from rooms on the street side of their dwellings. Housing for the poor, being more cheaply built, has not been well preserved.

The poor were numerous. Population estimates vary, but classical Athens probably had between forty thousand and fifty thousand male citizens in both town and country and at least an equal number of slaves. Most of the latter were either domestic servants and laborers of both sexes or artisans. A large number worked in the mines. As in the rest of the ancient world, slavery among the Greeks had begun with the taking of captives in war, but by the classical age most slaves were barbarians (that is, non-Greeks) purchased from itinerant traders. No great slave-worked estates existed, and even the richest citizens seem to have owned only a few. Slave artisans who toiled outside their master's home were normally paid wages, a fixed portion of which was returned to their owner. This practice tended to depress the pay rates of free workers and ensured that many citizens lived no better than the slaves. As in Mesopotamia, killing a slave was a crime, and slaves were guaranteed their freedom (manumission) if they could raise their price of purchase.

In addition to slaves and free citizens, Athens boasted a large population of foreigners. The city was a commercial center that, though located a few miles from the coast, had a bustling port at Piraeus. Unlike some Greeks, the Athenians welcomed foreign ideas— and capital. Though they could not participate in public life or own real estate, foreign residents were well treated and many became wealthy. They controlled many aspects of the city's commerce.

The situation of Athenian women, however, is a matter of some controversy. Even women who were citizens had no political rights, and their judicial rights had to be exercised for them by others, because their status was that of permanent legal minors. They did have dowries, which protected them to some extent if they were divorced or widowed. But divorce seems to have been rare. As in other Mediterranean societies, wives usually controlled the management of their husband's household and avoided public life. The Athenians, like most ancient Greeks, made extraordinary efforts to segregate the sexes. Respectable women of the citizen class stayed at home except for occasional attendance at festivals, sacrifices, or the theater. Even then they were accompanied by male relatives, and it is thought that men also did the shopping to keep their wives and daughters from coming into contact with strangers. Furthermore, women were expected to avoid certain areas within the home. The *andron*, a room where men received their male guests, was strictly off-limits to women, and in many Greek houses it had a separate entrance to the street (see illustration 2.4).

Underlying these practices was the conviction, voiced frequently by Greek writers, that women were incapable of controlling their sexuality. A woman suspected of having a child by someone other than her lawful husband endangered the status of her other children, who might lose their citizenship if challenged in court by an enemy. For this reason, the head of a family had the right to kill any man who seduced his wife, daughter, or any other female relative under his protection. Being nonconsensual, rape was considered less serious. As one offended husband said in a famous case: "The lawgiver prescribed death for adultery because he who achieves his ends by persuasion thereby corrupts the mind as well as the body of the woman . . . gains access to all a man's possessions, and casts doubt on his children's parentage." The adulterous woman could not be killed because she was legally and morally irresponsible. If married, she could be divorced; if single, she ruined her prospects for finding a husband and spent the rest of her life as a virtual prisoner in the house of her father or guardian. In spite of these sanctions, adultery may not have been as uncommon as scholars once believed.

By modern standards, the women of middle-and upper-class families were virtual prisoners in any case (see document 2.4). They married early, often at fourteen or fifteen, to men chosen by their families who were usually far older than themselves, and they almost never received a formal education. Much of their time was spent in spinning and sewing because Greek clothing was simple and could easily be manufactured at home. There were, however, exceptions. As in other societies, a propertied widow might enjoy considerable influence and a few upper-class women, such as the sis-

**Illustration 2.4**

🟨 **Plan of a Typical Greek House.** This house was part of a residential block on the south slope of the Areopagus in Athens. Drawing A shows its location; drawing B, the probable function of the rooms. In drawing C the shaded area was used by men only. Note that the men's and women's areas of the house had separate street entrances (arrows) and that no interior access appears between them.

ter of the statesman Cimon, were well educated. From a modern perspective, poor and alien women had more interesting lives. Many worked or sold goods in the marketplace, activities essential to the survival of their families that guaranteed them a freedom of movement unknown to their wealthier sisters. The price of that freedom was extreme economic and physical vulnerability.

Segregation of the sexes led to an acceptance of male extramarital relations with slave and alien women. Prostitution was common, and at the higher levels of society, courtesans or *betairai* were highly valued as companions at banquets and other social occasions from which respectable women were excluded. Courtesans were often highly educated. Some—such as Aspasia, the mistress of the fifth-century statesman Pericles—achieved considerable fame and could hold their own in intellectual discourse, but they were still regarded as prostitutes. Aspasia ended her days as the madam of an Athens brothel.

Homosexuality, too, was regarded by many Greeks as normal, and in some cases praiseworthy

## ◈ DOCUMENT 2.4 ◈

## The Role of the Athenian Wife

*In this excerpt from Xenophon's Oeconomicus (Household Management), Ischomachus tells Socrates how he began to train his fifteen-year-old bride. His views reflect conventional Athenian wisdom.*

Well Socrates, as soon as I had tamed her and she was relaxed enough to talk, I asked her the following question: "Tell me, my dear," said I, "do you understand why I married you and why your parents gave you to me? You know as well as I do that neither of us would have had trouble finding someone else to share our beds. But after thinking about it carefully, it was you I chose and me your parents chose as the best partners we could find for our home and children. Now if God sends us children, we shall think about how best to raise them, for we share an interest in securing the best allies and support for our old age."

My wife answered, "But how can I help? What am I capable of doing? It is on you that everything depends. My duty, my mother said, is to be well-behaved."

"Oh, by Zeus," said I, "my father said the same to me. But the best behavior in a man and woman is that which will keep up their property and increase it as far as may be done by honest and legal means. . . ."

"It seems to me that God adapted women's nature to indoor and man's to outdoor work. . . . As Nature has entrusted woman with guarding the household supplies, and a timid nature is no disadvantage in such a job, it has endowed women with more fear than man. It is more proper for a woman to stay in the house than out of doors and less so for a man to be indoors instead of out. . . . You must stay indoors and send out the servants whose work is outside and supervise those who work indoors, receive what is brought in, give out what is to be spent, plan ahead for what is to be stored and ensure that provisions for a year are not used up in a month. . . . Many of your duties will give you pleasure: for instance, if you teach spinning and weaving to a slave who did not know how to do this when you got her, you double your usefulness to yourself."

Xenophon. "*Oeconomicus.*" In Julia O'Faolain and Lauro Martines, *Not in God's Image: Women in History from the Greeks to the Victorians.* London: Temple Smith, 1973.

(see document 2.5). Soldiers, for example, were thought to fight more bravely when accompanied by their male lovers. Many of these relationships were formed in the gymnasia where men of the citizen class trained for war or athletics. It was not uncommon for a youth to become sexually involved with an older man who then served as his mentor in intellectual as well as athletic matters. Such arrangements were widely accepted. The Greeks, however, did not view homosexuality as an orientation that precluded sexual relations with women or a conventional family life. Furthermore, homosexual promiscuity could ruin a man's reputation or lead to exile, and many regarded it as inferior to married love.

As in many other cultures, Greek men and women may have belonged in effect to separate societies that met only in bed. If true, this would also account for the widespread acceptance of lesbianism. Greek men may not have cared about sex between women because it did not raise the issue of inheritance. The term *lesbian* is derived from the Ionic island of Lesbos, home of Sappho (c. 610–c. 580 B.C.), a woman and the greatest of Greek lyric poets. Europeans of a later age found her erotic poems to other women scandalous, and their renown has perhaps unfairly eclipsed the much wider range of her work in the minds of all but the most determined classicists.

Though Athenians, like other Greeks, were remarkably open about sexual matters, the assumption should not be made that they abandoned themselves to debauchery. Self-control remained the essence of the ideal citizen, and sexual restraint was admired along with physical fitness and moderation in the consumption of food and drink. A man who wasted his wealth and corrupted his body was of no value to the polis, for the polis was always at risk and demanded nothing less than excellence in those who would defend it.

### Sparta: A Conservative Garrison State

To moderns, Athens represents the model Greek polis—free, cultivated, and inquiring—but to the ancients, and to many Athenians, an alternative existed. Far away to the south, in a remote valley of the Peloponnese, lay Sparta. Sparta produced few poets and no philosophers. Its unwalled capital, built on a raised mound to keep it from the floodwaters of the river Eurotas, was said to resemble an overgrown village. There was no commerce to speak of, and long after other Greeks had adopted money, Spartans continued to use iron bars as their only currency. Because the Spartans

### ◆ DOCUMENT 2.5 ◆

## Plutarch: Dialogue on Love

*Debates over the relative merits of homosexual and heterosexual love were commonplace. Plutarch, the author of this one, lived in the first century A.D. He was an avid propagandist for Hellenic values, and his works are thought to reflect the attitudes of an age long past. Here Protogenes, who believes that women are incapable of true feeling or intellect, argues that love is almost by definition homosexual. His friend Daphnaeus, who seems to represent Plutarch, vehemently disagrees.*

"Do you call marriage and the union of man and wife shameful?" interposed Daphnaeus, "there can be no bond more sacred."

"Such unions are necessary for the propagation of the race," said Protogenes, "and so our lawgivers have been careful to endow them with sanctity and exalt them before the populace. But of true Love the women's apartment has no shred. For my part I deny that the word "love" can be applied to the sentiment you feel for women and girls, no more than flies can be said to 'love' milk, or bees honey, or victualers and cooks can be said to have amorous feelings for the beeves and fowl they fatten in the dark. . . ." A noble love which attaches to a youthful [male] spirit issues in excellence upon the path of friendship. From these desires for women, even if they turn out well, one may enjoy only physical pleasure and the satisfaction of a ripe body."

[After much argument, Daphnaeus responds:] "If we examine the truth of the matter, Protogenes, the passion for boys and for women derives from one and the same Love, but if you insist on distinguishing between them for argument's sake, you will find that the Love of boys does not comport himself decently; he is like a late issue, born unseasonably, illegitimate, and shady, who drives out the elder and legitimate love. It was only yesterday, my friend, or the day before, after lads began to strip and bare themselves for exercise that it crept surreptitiously into the gymnasia with its allurements and embraces, and then, little by little, when it had fledged its wings full in the palaestras, it could no longer be held in check; now it abuses and befouls that noble conjugal Love which assures immortality to our mortal kind, for by procreation it rekindles our nature when it is extinguished.

"Protogenes denies there is pleasure in the Love of boys: he does so out of shame and fear. He must have some decent pretext for attachment to his young beauties, and so he speaks of friendship and excellence. He covers himself with athlete's dust, takes cold baths, raises his eyebrows, and declares he is chastely philosophizing—to outward view and because of the law. But when night falls and all is quiet then 'sweet is the fruit when the keeper is gone.'"

Plutarch. "Dialogue on Love," trans. Moses Hadas. In Moses Hadas, ed., *On Love, the Family, and the Good Life: Selected Essays of Plutarch*, pp. 307–308. Mentor books, 1957.

wrote little, they are chiefly known through the writings of foreign political theorists. By all accounts, Sparta was a grim place: poor, rigidly conservative, and distinguished only by its magnificent army and by the single-minded discipline of its citizens.

Sparta was an aristocratic garrison state. The first Spartans were probably a band of Doric invaders who established their polis on the ruins of an earlier society. They displaced an earlier ruling class that was probably Dorian as well, allowing these *perioikoi* to retain property and personal freedom within their own communities. The original pre-Dorian inhabitants became serfs, or in Spartan terms, helots. This was not unusual, but around 725 B.C. Sparta conquered the neighboring polis of Messenia and reduced its inhabitants to serfdom as well. Helots outnumbered Spartans by a probable ratio of ten-to-one. In the Second Messenian War (c. 650 B.C.) the helots of both communities rose against their masters and, with the help of some neighboring cities, came close to destroying the Spartan state. Unless the Spartans were prepared to give up Messenia, survival would require complete social reorganization.

The Spartans attributed their reorganization to the legendary figure of Lycurgus, but the new practices almost certainly evolved over time. The Spartan government had long been a dual monarchy in which two hereditary kings exerted equal powers in war and in religious matters. Their influence, however, was severely limited. A Council of Elders, composed of twenty-eight men over the age of sixty, advised them and served as a kind of appellate court in reviewing their legal decisions. The ephors, a committee of five, ran the

## ◆ DOCUMENT 2.6 ◆

# A Spartan Childhood

*This is one of several descriptions of Spartan values as perceived by other Greeks, many of whom were both attracted and repelled by them. It is taken from Xenophon's* The Constitution of the Lacedaemonians.

In other Greek cities, parents who profess to give their sons the best education place their boys under the care and control of a moral tutor as soon as they can understand what is said to them, and send them to a school to learn letters, music, and the exercises of the wrestling ground. Moreover, they soften the children's feet by giving them sandals, and pamper their bodies with changes of clothing; and it is customary to allow them as much food as they can eat.

Lycurgus, on the contrary, instead of leaving each father to appoint a slave to act as tutor, gave the duty of controlling the boys to a member of the class from which the highest offices are filled, in fact to the "Warden" as he is called. He gave this person authority to punish them severely in case of misconduct. He also assigned to him a staff of youths provided with whips to chastise them when necessary. . . . [I]nstead of softening their feet with sandals he required them to harden their feet by going without shoes. He believed that if this habit were cultivated it would enable them to climb hills more easily and descend steep slopes with less danger. [A]nd instead of letting them be pampered in the matter of clothing, he introduced the custom of wearing one garment throughout the year, believing that they would thus be better prepared to face changes of heat and cold. As to the food, he required the prefect to bring with him such a moderate amount of it that the boys would never suffer from repletion and would know what it was to go with their hunger unsatisfied; for he believed that those who underwent this training would be better able to continue working on an empty stomach if necessary, and would be capable of carrying on longer without extra food. . . .

[H]e allowed them to alleviate their hunger by stealing something. It was not on account of a difficulty in providing for them that he encouraged them to get their food by cunning. . . . [O]bviously, a man who intends to take to thieving must spend sleepless nights and play the deceiver and lie in ambush by day, and moreover, if he means to make a capture, he must have spies ready. There can be no doubt then, that all this education was planned by him in order to make the boys more resourceful in getting supplies and be better fighting men.

Xenophon. "The Constitution of the Lacedemonians." in *Scripta Minora*. Loeb Classical Library. Cambridge, MA: Harvard University Press, 1925.

government. They conducted foreign policy, watched over the helots, and could, if necessary, override the military decisions of the kings. Both groups were elected by an assembly composed of all Spartan males over the age of thirty, the ephors for one-year terms, the councillors for life. Though the assembly voted by acclamation on all important matters, decisions were usually negotiated in advance and presented at meetings by the ephors.

The system struck other Greeks as old-fashioned, but they admired its effectiveness and stability. The social system over which it presided was far stranger. From the sixth century B.C. onward, everything in the Spartan's life was subordinated to the security of the polis (see document 2.6). Infants who appeared physically unfit were killed. At seven, males were taken from their mothers and trained to fight, endure pain, and survive without supplies in a hostile countryside. At twenty, they entered a *phiditia*, a kind of barracks where they would live for most of their lives, taking their meals in common. Though allowed to marry, younger Spartans could visit their wives only in secret, and family life in the ordinary sense was discouraged. Their military obligation ended only at the age of sixty. To the Spartan, eternal vigilance was the price of survival. Foreigners were periodically expelled. Trade and agricultural work were forbidden; fitness, discipline, and courage were prized.

The Spartan warrior paid dues to his *phiditia* from the proceeds of land worked by the helots. That work was supervised to some extent by the Spartan women, who were renowned throughout Greece for their independence and assertiveness. Though not expected to fight, they received extensive physical training on the theory that a strong mother produces strong children. Spartan women dressed simply and wore no jewelry.

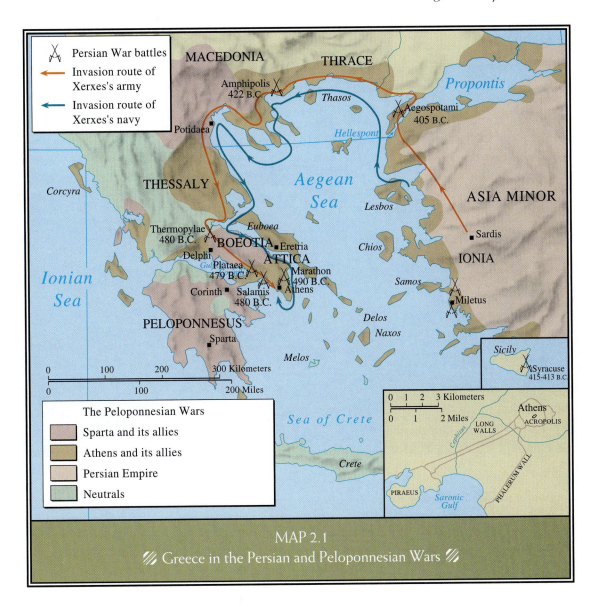

MAP 2.1

⫸ Greece in the Persian and Peloponnesian Wars ⫷

They could hold land in their own right and were capable of dealing with hostile and rebellious helots. Their courage, like that of the Spartan men, was legendary.

In spite of their military virtues, the Spartans were not an aggressive power until late in their history. The constant threat of helot insurrection made them wary of foreign entanglements, and Spartan policy was traditionally defensive and inward-looking. This changed in the course of the fifth century B.C. when the Persian invasion and the subsequent expansion of Athens forced them to take a more active role. They would eventually be drawn into a fatal rivalry with the Athenians, whose army was inferior but whose superior navy and greater wealth made them formidable antagonists. The story of those struggles forms the political background of the Greek classical age.

## The Persian War

The Greeks developed their unique civilization in large part because for centuries they were isolated from the turbulent politics of the Asian land mass. That isolation came to an abrupt end in the Persian War of 499–479 B.C. (see map 2.1). The tiny states whose competition with one another had long since become traditional now faced the greatest military power the world had yet known.

The Persians were an Indo-European people from the Iranian highlands who emerged in the sixth century B.C. as the dominant power in the vast region between Mesopotamia and India. By the end of the sixth century B.C. the ruling elite had adopted Zoroastrianism, a religion preached by the prophet and reformer Zoroaster

**Illustration 2.5**

⧅ **Reconstruction of a Greek Trireme from the Persian Wars.** The *Olympias*, shown here coming into port, was constructed on the basis of ancient evidence and commissioned into the Greek navy in 1987. Like the triremes of Themistocle's day, it is propelled by 170 rowers arranged on three decks. Sup-

plemental power is provided by square sails rigged on two masts. In this photo the stern where the triarch or commander sat is shown at left. The bow with its formidable ram is visible on the right.

(sometimes called Zarathustra). A dualistic system in which Ahura Mazda, the god of light, truth, and goodness contends eternally with Ahriman, the god of darkness and evil, Zoroastrianism condemned graven images and maintained the highest of ethical precepts. Its radical distinction between good and evil would influence early Christianity, and Ahriman has been seen by some as a prototype of the Christian Satan.

Under Cyrus I "the Great" (c. 585–c. 529 B.C.) the Persians conquered Babylon, together with Egypt, Syria, Palestine, and most of Asia Minor. Persian success was based largely upon imitating Assyrian military tactics while reversing the Assyrian policy toward conquered peoples. Like the Assyrians, the Persians used cavalry, many of them armed with bows, to pin down the enemy's infantry until their own infantry could destroy them. But Persian government was generally benign. It avoided atrocities, except in cases of outright

rebellion, and asked only that new subjects pay tribute and provide troops for the army. Because local institutions were typically preserved, many parts of the former Assyrian Empire welcomed the Persians as liberators.

Greek involvement with the Persian Empire began when Cyrus the Great conquered the kingdom of Lydia in 546 B.C. Located in western Asia Minor, Lydia was heavily influenced by Greek culture and famous for its wealth. The Lydians are credited with the invention of modern coinage. Under the fabulously wealthy king Croesus they established a loose dominance over the Ionic communities of the western Aegean. When Lydia fell, the Persians assumed control of its Greek dependencies. In 499 B.C. several Ionian states rebelled against local rulers backed by Persia and asked mainland Greeks to help. Sparta, worried about the internal threat of helot rebellion, refused, but Athens and the

Euboean city of Eretria sent twenty-five ships. Athenian rhetoric stressed the city's ancient and sentimental ties to Ionia, but the Athenians also feared that if the Persians gained control over the approaches to the Black Sea their vital supply of imported grain might be threatened.

In a short-lived triumph, the Ionians and their allies managed to burn Sardis, the Lydian capital. Persia soon reestablished control over western Asia Minor and in 490 B.C. dispatched a retaliatory expedition against Eretria and Athens. The Persians destroyed Eretria, but Athens fought and defeated them at Marathon. The marathon as a modern Olympic event commemorates the achievement of a courier who brought the news to Athens, twenty-two miles away. This victory, achieved in the absence of the feared Persian cavalry, was important because the Greeks gained confidence in their ability to defeat an enemy who until then had been regarded as invincible.

That confidence was tested in 480 B.C. when the new Persian emperor, Xerxes, launched a full-scale invasion of Greece by land and sea. It is a measure of Greek disunity that only thirty-one cities were prepared to resist. Sparta and Athens took the lead. Athenian politics were dominated by Themistocles, an advocate of seapower who used his influence to build a fleet of two hundred triremes in anticipation of a Persian attack. The trireme was a large, complex warship with three ranks of oarsmen and a metal prow for ramming (see illustration 2.5). Though far superior to earlier galleys, triremes were expensive, and only the discovery of new silver deposits at Laureion in Attica made their construction possible.

The ships were needed because Greek defensive strategy was essentially naval. The main Persian army was marching south along the European shore after crossing the Hellespont from Asia Minor. It was dependent for its supplies on a fleet of perhaps three hundred triremes manned by Persia's Phoenician and Ionian allies. Themistocles hoped to delay the Persian land forces at the narrow pass of Thermopylae while weather and a proposed naval action at nearby Artemisium depleted the Persian fleet (see document 2.7).

In spite of a heroic defense coordinated by the Spartans under their king Leonidas, Thermopylae fell when the invaders found a way to flank the Spartan position. Offshore, the Greeks fought an indecisive naval battle with a Persian force that, as Themistocles predicted, had been weakened by a series of earlier storms. These actions provided time for the evacuation of Athens and for the Greek fleet to take up a position

## ◆ DOCUMENT 2.7 ◆

# The Spartans at Thermopylae

*The doomed defense of the pass at Thermopylae by a handful of Spartans and their Thespian allies captured the imagination of the Greeks and has remained an archetypal story of heroism in the face of great odds. To the Greeks, it also showed, in dramatic terms, the difference between free Greeks fighting for their native soil and what they saw as servile Asians who had to be driven into battle with whips. This account is from Herodotus, the great historian of the Persian War.*

As the Persian army advanced to the assault, the Greeks under Leonidas, knowing that the fight would be their last, pressed forward into the wider part of the pass. . . . Many of the invaders fell; behind them their company commanders plied their whips, driving the men remorselessly on. Many fell into the sea and were drowned, and still more were trampled to death by their friends. No one could count the number of the dead. The Greeks, who knew that the enemy were on their way round by the mountain track and that death was inevitable, fought with reckless desperation. . . . By this time most of their spears were broken, and they were killing Persians with their swords.

In the course of that fight Leonidas fell, having fought like a man indeed. Many distinguished Spartans were killed at his side. . . . There was a bitter struggle over the body of Leonidas; four times the Greeks drove the enemy off, and at last by their valor succeeded in dragging it away. So it went until the fresh troops with Ephialtes [the Greek who had revealed the secret track to the Persians] were close at hand; and then when the Greeks knew that they had come, the character of the fighting changed. They withdrew again into the narrow neck of the pass, behind the walls, and took up a position in a single compact body . . . on the little hill at the entrance to the pass, where the stone lion in memory of Leonidas stands today. Here they resisted to the last, with their swords if they had them, and if not, with their hands and teeth, until the Persians coming on in front over the ruins of the wall and closing in from behind, finally overwhelmed them.

Herodotus. *The Histories*, pp. 492–493, trans. Aubrey de Sélincourt. Baltimore: Penguin Books, 1954.

some miles to the east near the island of Salamis. The Athenians and their allies hoped that by forcing a sea battle in the narrow waters between the island and the mainland they could compensate for the greater speed and maneuverability of the Persian fleet.

Xerxes's army entered the deserted city and burned it. Shortly thereafter half of his fleet was destroyed by the Greek triremes in the battle of Salamis, one of the greatest naval engagements in history. As Themistocles had foreseen, the Persians crowded into the narrow strait and could not maneuver properly. The Greek ships, though slower, carried more fighting men and found it easy to ram and overwhelm their opponents as they came in. Salamis was the turning point of the war. Without the support of his fleet, Xerxes returned to Persia, leaving a portion of his army to winter in Greece. The garrison was defeated at Plataea in the summer of 479 B.C. and fled, never to return. At the same time, a fleet under Spartan command dislodged the enemy from the Ionian coast in the battle of Mycale.

## The Peloponnesian Wars

The Persian threat had been repelled but not extinguished. Under the direction of Themistocles, the Athenians began to rebuild their city, fortifying its port at Piraeus, and constructing the Long Walls that protected the road connecting the two. After Themistocles was ostracized in 472 B.C. (the great enemy of the Persians ended his life as a Persian governor in Asia Minor), the work was continued by his successor, Cimon. Then, in the winter of 478–477 B.C. Athens, as the leading Greek naval power, joined with a number of its allies to form the Delian League, an association dedicated to protecting the cities of the Aegean from Persians and pirates. Sparta, though it had led the war on land, did not join, preferring instead to concentrate on the helot problem and on strengthening its own Peloponnesian League. By 467 B.C. the Athenian navy and its Delian allies had secured the coasts of Asia Minor and achieved unquestioned dominance at sea. Greece was now divided into two increasingly competitive alliance systems.

The size of its fleet made Athens the dominant partner in the Delian League, and though at first the Athenians maintained the rhetoric of friendship, they used the alliance to further their own purposes. Under Cimon's leadership, Athens sought to control grain supplies in the Aegean and to improve its access to ship's timber and precious metals by seizing new territory.

Heavy tributes swelled the Athenian treasury. Some of the conquered land was distributed to poor citizens, and wealthier Athenians acquired property in allied cities without regard for local law. The true nature of the league was revealed when the island of Thasos tried to withdraw from it in 465 B.C. Athens treated the matter as a rebellion and laid siege to the place for two years. Corinth, Athen's chief commercial rival and an ally of Sparta, had long argued against what it saw as Athenian imperialism. Now both Delians and Peloponnesians began to fear that Athens sought nothing less than political hegemony over the Greek world. As long as Cimon, an admirer of Sparta, controlled Athenian policy, every effort was made to avoid open conflict with the Peloponnesian League. But he, too, was ostracized in 461 B.C.

The removal of Cimon coincided with a further democratization of Athenian government under the leadership of Ephialtes and his younger colleague Pericles (c. 495–429 B.C.). The Persian War and its aftermath had for the first time involved large numbers of poor citizens in combat, especially in the navy. Their claims to full participation in civic life could no longer be ignored, and Pericles, who would play a dominant role in Athenian politics for more than thirty years, built his career on changes that further liberalized the constitution of Cleisthenes.

Realizing that most people could not afford to serve the polis, the reformers adopted the novel policy of paying men for public service, including jury duty, a measure paid for by the wealth accumulated in Cimon's day. Citizenship, which now became more valuable than ever, was restricted for the first time to men with two citizen parents, but by 450 B.C. Athens had become a participatory democracy in which every male citizen could play a role. Some have held that this democratization contributed to the tremendous flowering of high culture in the classical or Periclean age (see chapter 3); others that it fueled the increasingly aggressive and reckless character of Athenian policy. The two arguments are not incompatible, but war followed almost immediately upon the downfall of Cimon.

In the First Peloponnesian War (460–445 B.C.) the Delian league defeated both the Peloponnesians and the Persians, but when several allies rebelled against the arrogance of Athenian leadership Pericles agreed to a thirty years' peace. His skills as an orator and popular leader were balanced with prudence. The peace, which enabled Athens to recover its strength and reorganize its empire, lasted only fourteen years. In 435 B.C. war broke out between Corinth and Corcyra. Corcyra was a former

Corinthian colony in the Adriatic that had long been neutral. The Athenians feared that if its powerful fleet fell into Corinthian hands, their own naval dominance would be lost. When they allied themselves with the Corcyrans, Corinth protested to the Peloponnesian League, claiming again that the Athenians wanted total hegemony over all the Greeks. Attempts at negotiation failed, and in 431 B.C. the Spartans invaded Attica (see map 2.1).

Realizing that the Spartans could not be defeated on land, Pericles allowed them to occupy the Athenian countryside. People from the rural demes crowded into the city. Though the Athenians mounted cavalry raids against Spartan garrisons, the major thrust of their policy was to launch amphibious expeditions against Sparta's allies. Pericles reasoned that because Athens was wealthy and its fleet controlled the seas, the city could survive on imports for up to five years before further tribute had to be demanded from the empire. Sparta's Peloponnesian allies were more vulnerable and would, he thought, sue for peace within three years.

Unfortunately, a great plague struck Athens in the second year of the war and killed a third of its population. Pericles was driven from office. He was recalled briefly only to die of the pestilence, and his defensive policies were eventually abandoned. The more aggressive strategy advocated by Cleon, who followed Pericles as leader of the popular faction, at first succeeded. The Athenians fomented popular revolutions in a number of cities and supported democratic factions within them, while the Spartans predictably backed their opponents. The Athenians then fortified Pylos on the western coast of Messenia and defeated a Spartan fleet that had been sent to drive them out. More than four hundred Spartans were isolated on a nearby island. This was a significant portion of Sparta's fighting elite. Without a navy and facing yet another helot revolt, the Spartans were desperate to recover their men and sued for peace.

Once again, the Athenians were undone by overconfidence. Dreaming of total victory, they refused to negotiate, but their attempts to recapture Megara and Boeotia failed. The Spartan general Brasidas easily detached a number of cities from their allegiance and ended by capturing Amphipolis, the most important Athenian base in the northwestern Aegean. When relief efforts failed, it was the Athenian's turn to ask for a truce.

The peace of Nicias (421 B.C.) accomplished little, in part because several important cities on both sides of the dispute refused to accept it. Hostilities continued, though Athens and Sparta remained only indirectly involved. Both sides attempted through diplomacy to lure

away each other's allies. Athens was hampered in its efforts by internal factions and instability. Cleon died in the attempted relief of Amphipolis. Alcibiades, an unscrupulous young aristocrat who had been a pupil of Socrates, succeeded him as the dominant voice in Athenian politics. Under his guidance, Athens supported a Persian governor and his son in their revolt against the king. Persia, which had remained neutral, now had reason to back Sparta if hostilities resumed. Then in 415 B.C., Alcibiades convinced the Athenians to mount a great expedition against Sicily. It was a brazen attempt to acquire new resources by broadening the scope of the war, and it failed. Syracuse alone proved to be the equal of Athens in wealth, population, and naval preparedness, and the rest of Sicily backed Syracuse. The Sicilians, with their superior cavalry, disrupted the Athenian siege and defeated their army on land. In 413 B.C. they destroyed the Athenian fleet in the city's harbor. All told, the Athenians lost two hundred ships, more than forty-five hundred of their own men, and perhaps twenty thousand of their allies.

Though Athens rebuilt its fleet and continued the struggle, its allies deserted one by one. The Spartans, under the command of Lysander and backed by Persian money, launched a series of naval campaigns against them. Most were unsuccessful, but in 405 B.C. the Athenian fleet was destroyed at Aegospotami and Lysander cut off his enemy's grain supplies by seizing the Hellespont. Faced with starvation, the Athenians surrendered unconditionally in 404 B.C.

The Peloponnesian Wars revealed the tragic flaw at the heart of Greek society, a flaw that had been obscured by the successful war against Persia. The independent, competitive psychology of the polis made it difficult, if not impossible, for the Greeks to unite or to live at peace with one another. They had driven off the Persians, but even then much of the Greek world had sided with the enemy out of rivalry with either Athens or Sparta or, in some cases, with one of their allies. The failure of Athens—or Sparta—to forge an effective Panhellenic alliance created a power vacuum that would eventually be filled by the Macedonians, a people who, though related to the Greeks, did not share in the culture of the polis. As a result, the independence of the polis would be gravely compromised. Athens fell under the control of the Thirty Tyrants, a group of collaborators who ruled with Spartan support. The city's empire disintegrated and its trade diminished, though it remained the cultural heart of the Greek world for centuries to come. The great struggles of the fifth century B.C. may be regarded as the high-water mark of classical Greek civilization.

CHAPTER 3

# GREEK CULTURE AND ITS HELLENISTIC DIFFUSION

## CHAPTER OUTLINE

For all its violence and insecurity, the age of the Persian and Peloponnesian wars was for the Greeks, and in particular for Athens, a time of unparalleled creativity. The intensity of life in the midst of almost perpetual crisis called forth their best efforts, not only in war and politics, but also in art, literature, and philosophy.

The conquests of Alexander spread Greek culture and values to the limits of the known world, but the process was one of diffusion rather than imposition. The peoples of the Middle East retained their own identities while adopting Greek ideas, and the Greeks changed through contacts with ancient civilizations whose cultural norms differed radically from their own. The result was a rich and cosmopolitan fusion that is usually referred to as the Hellenistic Age.

### Art and Literature in Classical Greece

Greek literary and artistic inspiration stemmed from two basic sources: the Homeric poems and the mythology that had grown up around the adventures of the gods. Together, these wellsprings of the Greek tradition provided a rich fund of themes and motifs that illustrated in graphic terms what it meant to be Greek. The influence of that tradition had little to do with religious teachings as they are now understood. The behavior of the gods—and of Homer's heroes—was often highly improper, and Greek religion offered few ethical prescriptions. The ancient tales did not preach, but even when they taught by bad example, they offered a precious guide to values, social attitudes, and conduct. For this reason, each polis sought to encourage the arts to the best of its financial ability. They were the means by which citizens were created and common values reaffirmed.

Nowhere was this concern more evident than in the drama. Plays, like athletic contests, accompanied many religious festivals. They were performed in open-air amphitheaters constructed at public expense, and the actors were usually paid by the state. In fifth-century Athens, as many as thirty thousand people might attend a single performance. The first plays were tragedies, a dramatic form probably invented by the Athenians. The themes of Attic tragedy came with rare exceptions from mythology and drew their dramatic power from irreconcilable conflicts. The hero, who might be a man or woman, is faced with a conflict, not always between right and wrong, but sometimes between right and right. He or she is undone either by an unsuspected personal flaw or by *hubris*, the pride born of overconfidence.

Among the greatest of the Greek dramatists were Aeschylus (c. 525–456 B.C.), who may have invented the tragedy as a dramatic form, and Sophocles (c. 495–406 B.C.), whose *Antigone, Oedipus Rex, Electra,* and other works continue to inspire modern authors. Euripides (c. 484–406 B.C.) was more popular in the fourth century B.C. than in his own time. His later plays diluted the original tragic formula and led the way to more personal and unheroic themes. A similar progression is seen in comedy. The plays of Aristophanes (c. 450–c. 388 B.C.) and his contemporaries, usually known as the Old Comedy, were political satire with a razor's edge. As the third century B.C. progressed, comedy lost its public focus and turned to love stories and domestic situations.

The Greeks may also be said to have created history. Earlier peoples preserved king lists and inscriptions that record the doings of royalty. The Hebrews had chronicled their history to illuminate God's purposes, but the Greeks made history a branch of literature. The first writer to do this was Herodotus, whose history of the Persian War was written specifically "to preserve the memory of the past by putting on record the astonishing achievements both of our own and of the Asiatic peoples; secondly, and more particularly, to show how the two races came into conflict." The result is both history and anthropology—an entertaining tour of the ancient world, its cultures, and its myths. The story of the war itself comes only toward the end of the book. However, his portraits of individual leaders are unforgettable, and he probably deserves his title, "the father of history."

The history of the Peloponnesian Wars by the Athenian Thucydides (c. 460–c. 404 B.C.) is different (see document 3.1). Exiled for his role as a naval commander in the ill-fated attempt to relieve Amphipolis, Thucydides was determined to understand the past be-

---

### ◆ DOCUMENT 3.1 ◆

## Thucydides: The Practice of History

*In this famous passage, from* The Peloponnesian War, *Thucydides lays the foundation for history as a serious intellectual discipline. Few historians today believe that history repeats itself in any predictable way, but they appreciate Thucydides's critical approach to his sources.*

And with regard to my factual reporting of the events of the war I have made it a principle not to write down the first story that came my way, and not even to be guided by my own general impressions; either I was present myself at the events which I described or else I heard of them from eyewitnesses whose reports I have checked with as much thoroughness as possible. Not that even so the truth was easy to discover: different eyewitnesses have different accounts of the same events, speaking out of partiality for one side or the other or else from imperfect memories. And it may well be that my history will seem less easy to read because of the absence in it of romantic elements. It will be enough for me, however, if these words of mine are judged useful by those who want to understand clearly the events which happened in the past and which (human nature being what it is) will at some time or other and in much the same ways, be repeated in the future. My work is not a piece of writing designed to meet the taste of an immediate public, but was done to last forever.

Thucydides. The Peloponnesian War, trans. Rex Warner. Baltimore: Penguin Books, 1954. Copyright © Rex Warner, 1954. Reproduced by permission of Penguin Books Ltd.

---

cause he believed that human nature was constant and that history therefore repeats itself. If one knows the past, it should be possible to avoid similar mistakes in the future. Other cultures had believed that history moves in cycles and that, as the biblical author of Ecclesiastes said in a notable departure from Jewish tradition, "there is no new thing under the sun." But the Greeks, beginning with Thucydides, used this ancient notion to justify the systematic study of history. It was among the most original of their achievements. Many of the better Roman historians studied history to avoid the mistakes of the past,

Corinthian
capital

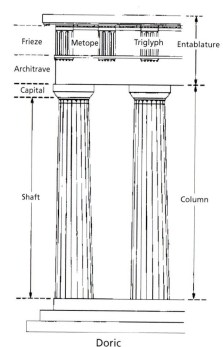

Doric

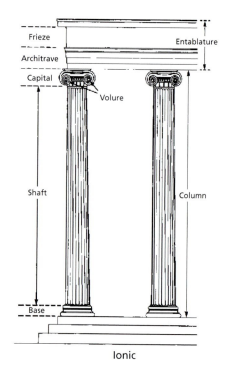

Ionic

**Illustration 3.1**

🖋 **Architectural Orders.** The architectural orders were an important part of Greek temple architecture and were used by the Romans as well as by European architects from the Renaissance to the present day. The Corinthian order was similar to the Ionic but featured a leaf motif in its capitals.

and the idea, revived during the Renaissance, remained influential until well into the twentieth century.

Greek art, too, served public purposes. Though a fine aesthetic sense extended to everyday objects such as jewelry, armor, and decorated pottery, the greatest artistic achievement of ancient Greece was its monumental sculpture and architecture. The Greeks built temples to the gods who protected the polis or to house the oracles who were consulted on all important occasions. These structures, whose function was as much civic as religious, were subtle adaptations of earlier Egyptian or Minoan ideas.

Construction was basic post-and-lintel; the genius lay in the proportions and the details. The heart of the temple was an inner sanctuary that housed the statue of the deity. It was surrounded by a colonnade supporting a sloped roof with triangular pediments at each end. The columns, which might or might not have decorated capitals (see illustration 3.1), were wider at the middle and tapered gently toward the top to counteract the optical illusion known as parallax and make them appear straight. The frieze, the entablature, and the pediments were decorated with sculptured reliefs of gods, goddesses, and heroes.

Greek sculpture was concerned almost exclusively with the lifelike portrayal of the human figure (see illustration 3.2). Early statues had a formal, abstract

quality, with power and dignity that reflected their subjects: gods, goddesses, heroes, and athletes. Male figures were almost invariably nude, a preference that reflected the Greek willingness to appear naked in games and on the battlefield and that non-Greeks found shocking. Female figures were invariably clothed. Gradually, during the sixth century B.C., sculptors began to work toward a more lifelike image. By the fifth century B.C. sculptors such as Phidias had achieved a level of skill that has never been surpassed, but realism was not their goal. Faces and figures reflect an idealized vision of human beauty rarely seen in nature. Female nudes, reflecting a sensuality hitherto seen only in the portrayal of men, became common. The aesthetic conventions developed by Phidias and the fourth-century B.C. master Praxiteles became the basis of later Hellenistic and Roman tastes. Like the conventions of Greek architecture, they have been restored to temporary dominance by classic revivals in more modern times and remain an underlying part of the Western visual tradition.

Unfortunately, that vision may be historically misleading. Most of Greek art was destroyed by the early Christians, who saw it as idolatrous if not obscene, and modern taste has been formed largely by Roman copies. Painting, which to many ancient Greeks was more important than sculpture, has been lost entirely. The Greeks loved color, and statues preserved only in

 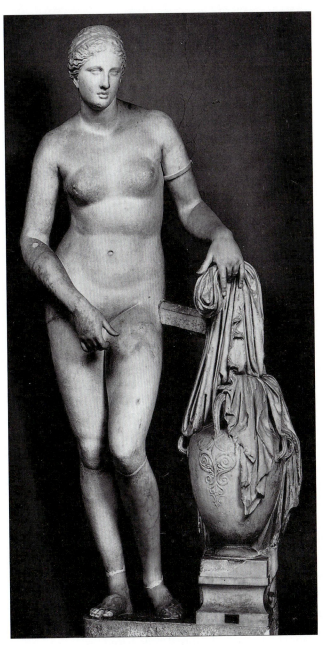

**Illustration 3.2**

 **The Evolution of Greek Sculpture.** The figure on the left is a *kore* (masc. *koros*) from the Athenian acropolis, c. 520 B.C. Figures of this kind were used as tomb markers or votive statues and are one of the most common forms of early Greek sculpture. Though more delicately modeled than most, this piece is still for-

mal, two-dimensional, and somewhat abstract. On the right is a Roman copy of the famous Aphrodite by Praxiteles. Though the statue reflects a certain classical serenity, the sensuality is, by earlier Greek standards, remarkable. In archaic times, only male figures were portrayed in the nude.

their undecorated state were once brilliantly painted. Some had precious stones for eyes. The overall impression must have been unlike the serene appearance that later generations associated with classicism, and the more refined modern critics of the eighteenth and nineteenth centuries would probably have found the statues tasteless.

## Greek Thought from the Pre-Socratics to Aristotle

The earliest Greek thought concerned the nature of the physical universe and was formulated in terms that suggest Egyptian or Mesopotamian influence. According to tradition, the sixth-century B.C. philosopher Thales of Miletus introduced geometry and astronomy to Greece after visiting Egypt. He may also have encountered there the idea that the universe was based ultimately upon water. But Greek thought was unlike that of the Egyptians in several important respects. Perhaps because of the structure of their language, the Greeks sought from the beginning to demonstrate the logical connection between statements in the clearest possible way. This in turn forced them to confront the problem of epistemology, or how what is known is known. These two issues, epistemology and the nature of the physical universe, have remained among the central concerns of Western thought.

Most Greek thinkers believed that the impressions produced by the senses are deceptive. To be truly knowable, something must be both permanent and accessible to thought. Thales, like most early philosophers, assumed the essential unity and permanence of all matter. The view of Heraclitus (c. 500 B.C.) that the universe was in a state of perpetual movement at first found little support, and much effort was expended on determining the fundamental element or elements upon which the universe was based. Eventually, Empedocles of Acragas (c. 490–c. 430 B.C.) declared that four existed: earth, air, fire, and water. His theory was later accepted by Aristotle and formed the basis of most physical speculation until the scientific revolution of modern times. An alternative, proposed by Leucippus of Miletus and his pupil Democritus, seemed less persuasive. It held that everything was composed of atoms, invisible particles that combined and separated to produce the various forms of matter.

If these early philosophers speculated on ethical matters, their writings on the subject have been lost, but the proper conduct of life was vitally important to people who lacked a moral code based on divine revelation. Pythagoras, who founded a school at Croton in Italy around the year 500 B.C., taught ethics based in part on the cult of Orpheus. In the process he discovered the mathematical basis of musical harmony and decided that the fundamental organizing principle of the universe was number. This idea, like his theory that the Earth revolved around the Sun, would prove interesting to later thinkers.

By the fifth century B.C., however, most people learned their ethics and the practical arts of rhetoric and persuasion from the Sophists. These itinerant teachers charged high fees for their services but offered nothing less than a prescription for success in private and public life. Their teachings varied, but most were subjectivists. As Protagoras, the most famous of them,

said: "Man is the measure." He meant that the individual's experience, however imperfect in an absolute sense, is the only conceivable basis for knowledge or judgment. Everything is relative.

The implications of such a view were profoundly disturbing. Extreme Sophists held that truth was objectively unknowable. Law and even the polis were based on convention and mutual agreement, not fundamental principles. Some went so far as to claim that justice was merely the interest of the strong and that the gods had been invented by clever men as a means of social control. The teachings of Socrates and of his pupil Plato were intended in part to refute these ideas.

Socrates (c. 470–399 B.C.) wrote nothing. He wandered about the streets of Athens asking questions that revealed the underlying assumptions behind human values and institutions. Using logic and irony, he would then question the validity of those assumptions. His purpose, unlike that of the Sophists whom he otherwise resembled, was to find an objective basis for ethical and political behavior. He made no promises and took no fees, but his questions were rarely open-ended and made people feel foolish.

The patience of the Athenians was severely tried. In 399 B.C. they executed him for corrupting the youth of Athens and inventing new gods. The charges were largely specious, but they reflected something more than public irritation. Socrates, though himself of humble origins, favored aristocracy as the ideal form of government and mocked the democratic notions then in favor.

His views on other subjects are unknown, but Plato (428–347 B.C.) made him the leading character in his dialogues. As a young man from an aristocratic Athenian family, Plato toyed with the idea of a political career until the aftermath of the Sicilian expedition and the execution of Socrates convinced him that politics was incompatible with a good conscience. Around the year 387 B.C. he founded the Academy, a kind of institute for advanced studies in mathematics, the physical sciences, and philosophy.

Plato's dialogues present philosophical arguments in dramatic form. The Socrates character reflects the author's views. With the exception of the *Timaeus*, a later dialogue that deals with cosmology and mathematics, most explore questions of ethics, education, government, and religion. The *Republic* describes the ideal state, while the *Protagoras* argues against the Sophists.

Their underlying principle is the theory of forms. Plato argued that the form of a thing has an objective reality of its own. It is a "universal" or "idea" that can be understood only by the intellect and that exists apart from any object perceived by the senses. Because the senses are deceptive, understanding can be achieved only through the knowledge of forms. When extended to such universal qualities as justice or beauty, the theory of forms becomes the basis for absolute standards that can be applied to human conduct, both public and private. To Plato, the relativism of the Sophists was an illusion (see document 3.2).

Platonic Idealism (also known as Realism, because it affirms the reality of ideas) was one pole of the epistemological debate that would occupy Western philosophy for centuries. Subjectivism in its various forms was the other. Because the argument dealt with what was real and what was knowable, the position of philosophers on epistemology influenced and in some cases determined their view of everything else.

Aristotle (384–322 B.C.) was the most famous of Plato's pupils. After studying at Plato's Academy until Plato's death, Aristotle served as tutor to the future conqueror Alexander the Great. In 336 B.C. Aristotle established his own school at Athens called the Lyceum. His followers were known in later years as the Peripatetics after the covered walkway or *peripatos* under which they met. Most of the enormous body of work attributed to him appears to be derived from lecture notes and other materials collected by the Peripatetics in the course of their studies.

Though he accepted Plato's theory of forms, Aristotle rejected the notion that they were wholly separate from empirical reality. He relied heavily upon observation, especially in his scientific work. His basic viewpoint, however, remained, like Plato's, teleological. Both thinkers believed that things could be understood only in relation to their end or purpose. To Aristotle, for example, actions must be judged in terms of the result they produce, an ethical principle that in medieval times would form the basis of natural law. In politics, this led him to an impassioned defense of the polis as the best form of social organization. Although these contributions to ethics and politics were enormously important, Aristotle's greatest influence lay elsewhere.

Logic, or the process by which statements are formed and relate to one another, was central to Greek discourse. Aristotle was the first to analyze this process and, in so doing, codified a logical method that dominated formal thought until the twentieth century. Its basis is the syllogism, an argument that in its simplest form says that if all A is B and all C is A, then all C must be B. Aristotle went far beyond this, and his six treatises on logic, known collectively as the *Organon*, describe many types of syllogisms, the formation and

## DOCUMENT 3.2

### Plato: The Parable of the Cave

*The parable of the cave appears in* The Republic *by Plato. It describes in graphic terms the difference between sense perceptions and reality, which can only be perceived through thought. The cave is a metaphor for the world of sense impressions in which nothing is as it appears, and to Plato all people are prisoners within it. The author is speaking to his friend Glaucon.*

"Picture men dwelling in a sort of subterranean cavern with a long entrance open to the light on its entire width. Conceive of them as having their legs and necks fettered from childhood, so that they remain in the same spot, able to look forward only, and prevented by the fetters from turning their heads. Picture further the light from a fire burning higher up and at a distance behind them, and between the fire and the prisoners and above them a road along which a low wall has been built, as the exhibitors of puppet-shows have partitions before the men themselves above which they show the puppets." "All that I see," he said. "See also, then, men carrying past the wall implements of all kinds that rise above the wall, and human images and shapes of animals as well, wrought in stone and wood and every material, some of these bearers presumably speaking and others silent." "A strange image you speak of," he said, "and strange prisoners." "Like to us," I said: "for, to begin with, tell me do you think that these men would have seen anything of themselves or of one another except the shadows cast from the fire on the wall of the cave that fronted them?" "How could they," he said, "if they were compelled to hold their heads unmoved through life." "And again, would not the same be true of the objects carried past them?" . . . "Then in every way such prisoners would deem reality to be nothing else than the shadows of artificial objects."

Plato. *The Republic*, trans. Paul Shorey. Cambridge, MA: Harvard University Press, 1963.

categorization of statements, and the nature of language itself.

In the physical sciences, Aristotle's influence dominated thought until the scientific revolution of the sixteenth and seventeenth centuries. He wrote extensively on biology, physics, and human psychology and was responsible for collecting and transmitting much of what is known about the early Greek philosophers. His method was to observe natural phenomena and to understand them in terms of what he called the "four causes." These were not causes in the modern sense, but aspects of a problem that had to be considered in its solution. The four causes are the matter out of which a thing is made (material cause), its form or shape (formal cause), the purpose it is intended to fulfill (final cause), and the force that brings it into being (efficient cause).

These causes are discovered by logical inference from empirical observations. Aristotle made no effort to create predictive mathematical models based upon these inferences and did not attempt to verify them by experiment. His method was therefore unlike that of modern science and produced different results. Scientists no longer believe that the process by which a physical change occurs can be fully explained by its final cause or teleological purpose. Since the seventeenth century they have asked different questions and have rejected most of Aristotle's conclusions about the behavior of matter. But even if the scientific theories of this ancient philosopher are no longer accepted, his work is still of great importance. Aristotle's observations and hypotheses set the agenda for more than a thousand years of speculation, while his teleological bias and preoccupation with qualitative descriptions (the material and formal causes) was a compelling if not always productive influence on later thought. His insistence on careful observation and logically constructed argument remains a part of the scientific tradition today. No other thinker has had such a powerful impact on later generations.

## The Macedonian Conquests

Aristotle lived in the twilight of classical Greek civilization. Though he probably did little to inspire them, the exploits of his pupil Alexander of Macedon changed the political structure of the Greek world and spread Greek values and ideas throughout the Middle East. Inevitably, those values were changed and diluted in the process, and the culture that emerged from the Macedonian con-

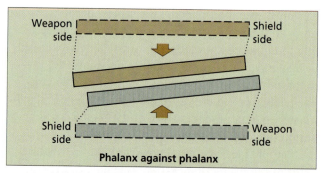

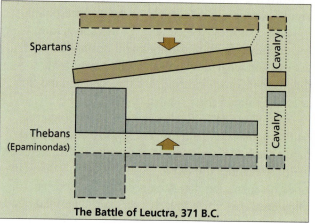

Illustration 3.3

The Theban Formation.  The top drawing shows the traditional pattern of hoplite warfare with the shield side of each formation slowly giving way as the battle develops. The bottom drawing shows how Epaminondas weighted his formation at Leuctra to crush the Spartans at their strongest point (the "weapon side" or right).

quests was at the same time more cosmopolitan and less intense than that of the ancient polis.

The end of the Peloponnesian Wars had left the Greek states under the political influence of Sparta. The Spartans, like the Athenians before them, soon made themselves hated by interfering with the internal policies of their allies. Athens and Thebes combined against them, and in 371 B.C. the Spartans were defeated at Leuctra by a Theban army under the command of Epaminondas (c. 410–362 B.C.). Sparta's role as a major power ended, and a new era of military innovation began. Epaminondas had given careful thought to a peculiarity of hoplite warfare (see illustration 3.3). Hoplites carried their shields on the left. In combat they shifted toward the right, away from the point of impact. This threw the phalanx out of balance, but the consequent strengthening of its right side meant that the right frequently won the battle. Epaminondas took advantage of this oddity and weighted his phalanx heavily to the left and held back the right. This unbalanced formation, supported by cavalry on his right flank, enabled him to crush the Spartans at their strongest point and envelop them. The use of deep formations, effectively supported for the first time by cavalry, would be greatly expanded by the Macedonians.

Though supported by the relative wealth of Boeotia, Theban hegemony lasted no longer than that of the Spartans. The Athenians had revived their alliance system in the years immediately before Leuctra and, fearing Theban ambition, soon turned it against Epaminondas. By 362 B.C. the Peloponnesians had also reconstituted their confederacy, and though Epaminondas defeated the combined forces of Athens and Sparta at Mantinea, he died in the battle. Deprived of his leadership, Theban military power declined. Without the stimulus of threats from Thebes or Sparta, the "second" Athenian Empire collapsed, and Greece reverted to its traditional state of disorganization.

A century of warfare had brought economic decline and social tension to the Greek cities. The Carthaginians encroached upon their overseas markets while the Greek colonies in Italy became, of necessity, more self-sufficient. As exports diminished, thousands of Greeks sought employment as mercenaries. One such group found itself stranded in Mesopotamia when the schemes of their Persian employer miscarried. A leader of the expedition, the Athenian writer and military theorist Xenophon (c. 431–c. 350 B.C.) left a vivid account of their march to the Black Sea coast and safety. Xenophon and the career of Epaminondas show that Greek fighting men had lost nothing of their skill and valor. The artistic and intellectual achievements of the fourth century B.C. demonstrate that the culture was alive and well. But for all its evident vigor, Greece had become a political vacuum.

That vacuum was filled by the Macedonians. Ancient Macedonia occupied the broad plain at the head of the Thermaic Gulf in northeastern Greece. Its people spoke a dialect of Greek, but their social and political institutions were different from those of the *poleis*. The population was almost entirely rural and, by Greek standards, widely scattered. Rich pastures encouraged the raising of horses. Macedonian society was therefore dominated by a landholding aristocracy that fought on horseback, usually against the neighboring hill tribes whose raids posed a constant threat to the country's borders. Hereditary kings tried to rule, with or without cooperation from the aristocracy, and internal strife was common. To other Greeks, the Macedonians seemed primitive, but their homeland was rich in timber, minerals, and agricultural resources. Many believed that if Macedon could achieve stability it would one day become a major power.

That goal was achieved by Philip II (382–336 B.C.). Philip was a younger son of the Macedonian royal family who, while hostage at Thebes, had observed the military reforms of Epaminondas. His brother died in 359 B.C. and left Philip as regent for the youthful heir, Amyntas IV. Cunning and energetic, Philip used his position to remove political rivals and suppress the local hill tribes. In 357–356 B.C. he seized Amphipolis and then Mt. Pangaeus with its rich deposits of gold and silver. At about this time he also took control of his nephew's throne.

With his political base secure, and fortified by the wealth of Mt. Pangaeus, Philip moved to extend his power over Greece as a whole. Through warfare, bribery, and skilled diplomacy, Philip played upon the disunity of the Greeks until it was too late for them to mount an effective resistance. In 338 B.C. he defeated a poorly organized army of Thebans and Athenians at Chaeronea and became master of the Greek world. For the most part, Philip wore his new authority lightly. He secured a measure of acceptance by not interfering in local politics, but his plan to lead the united Greeks against Persia did not materialize in his lifetime.

Philip II left a formidable legacy. Not only did he unite the Greeks, but he also created the army with which his son Alexander III, "the Great," would conquer most of the known world (see illustration 3.4). The heart of the Macedonian army remained the companions of the king, some two thousand cavalry armed with sword and spear. They were supported by infantry drawn up in the Macedonian phalanx, a formation that differed substantially from that of the hoplites. The peasants of Macedonia could not afford hoplite equipment, and their geographic isolation made intensive training difficult. Philip solved these problems by arranging his men into deep formations and arming them with spears longer than those used by the hoplites. By fighting in tightly closed ranks, the Macedonians could thereby present an almost impenetrable front without the need for highly specialized combat skills.

Hoplites were added to the Macedonian ranks as Philip's system of alliances grew. He also recruited mercenary horsemen from Thessaly and supplemented his infantry with slingers, bowmen, and javelin throwers. The genius of Philip (and Alexander) lay in the ability to coordinate these varied elements and to make even the cavalry fight as a disciplined tactical unit instead of as individual champions. But the Macedonians were

**Illustration 3.4**

*///* **Alexander the Great.** This bust of Alexander the Great is a Roman copy of the lost original. It closely resembles literary descriptions of the conqueror's appearance by Plutarch and Appian.

in India were brilliant cavalry actions in which the infantry played only a secondary role. His sieges were consistently successful, and his ability to hold a multiethnic army together on hard campaigns in unfamiliar territory attest to an extraordinary capacity for leadership. In the end, the Macedonians mutinied and demanded to return home, but even then he preserved their loyalty by officially making them his kinsmen.

His purposes, however, are not entirely clear. Many of his contemporaries saw only personal ambition. Arrian, the chronicler of his campaigns, said that "if he had found no one else to strive with he would have striven with himself." Others, including Plutarch, detected more noble motives (see document 3.3). Alexander's publicists encouraged the notion of a vast state based upon universal brotherhood. He proclaimed the equality of all subjects regardless of religion or ethnicity and gave this policy tangible form by marrying Roxana, a princess from Bactria in central Asia.

He may also have hoped to spread the benefits of Hellenic culture, but he seems to have stressed this only in dealing with Greeks. Not all Greeks were convinced. They resented his acceptance of foreign customs and his tendency to claim divine attributes when dealing with easterners. His idealism, if such it was, was accompanied by utter ruthlessness and by a casual brutality aggravated by heavy drinking. When he died in 323 B.C. at the age of thirty-two, he left no successors and only the most general plan for the governance of his realms.

equally attentive to the problems of siegecraft. Philip introduced to the Aegean world the techniques and siege engines developed by Dionysius, the Tyrant of Syracuse, and used them successfully against Perinthus and Byzantium. His son would employ them against the more distant cities of Tyre, Halicarnassus, and Gaza.

In ten years (334–324 B.C.) Alexander used this formidable army to conquer the Persian Empire and extend his authority from Greece to Egypt and from Egypt to India (see map 3.1). His exploits caught the imagination of his contemporaries and of historians ever since, but his character remains something of a mystery.

He was clearly an outstanding general. His great battles on the Granicus in Asia Minor, at Issus in Syria, at Gaugamela on the upper Tigris, and on the Hydaspes

## The Hellenistic Kingdoms

Alexander's death led to a prolonged struggle among the Macedonian generals. Though Roxana was pregnant when he died, there was no immediate successor. The commanders at first divided the empire into governorships with the intention of preserving it for the conqueror's unborn heir, but they soon fell to fighting among themselves. In the civil wars that followed, Roxana and her son, together with several of the generals, were murdered. Three main successor states emerged from the shambles. Macedon, much of Asia Minor, and a dominant position in the Greek alliance fell to Antigonus (382–301 B.C.). The descendants of Ptolemy (d. 283 B.C.) ruled Egypt as its thirty-third Dynasty until the death of Cleopatra in 30 B.C., while Seleucus (d. 281 B.C.) established an empire based on Syria and Mesopotamia (see map 3.1).

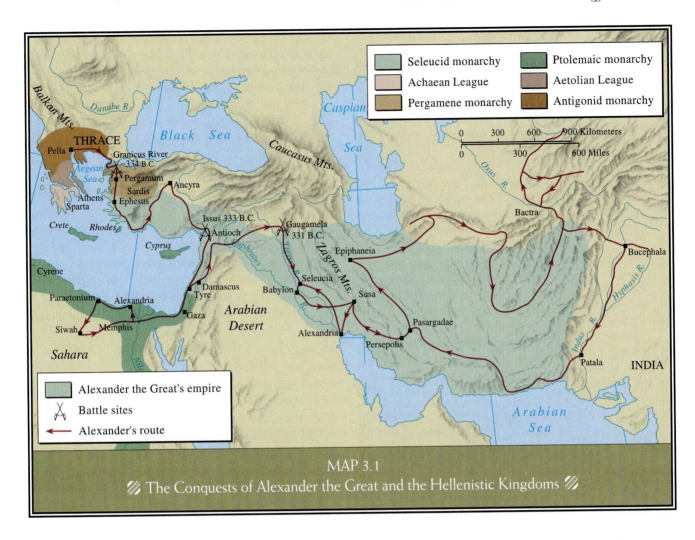

**Legend:**
- Seleucid monarchy
- Achaean League
- Pergamene monarchy
- Ptolemaic monarchy
- Aetolian League
- Antigonid monarchy

0   300   600   900 Kilometers
0   300   600 Miles

THRACE
Pella
Granicus River 334 B.C.
Pergamum
Aegean Sea
Sardis
Athens
Sparta
Ephesus
Crete
Rhodes
Cyprus
Cyrene
Ancyra
Issus 333 B.C.
Antioch
Gaugamela 331 B.C.
Epiphaneia
Seleucia
Babylon
Susa
Damascus
Tyre
Gaza
Paraetonium
Alexandria
Arabian Desert
Alexandria
Persepolis
Pasargadae
Siwah
Memphis
Sahara
Bactra
Bucephala
Patala
INDIA
Balkan Mts.
Danube R.
Black Sea
Caucasus Mts.
Caspian Sea
Zagros Mts.
Oxus R.
Hyphasis R.
Indus R.
Arabian Sea

- Alexander the Great's empire
- Battle sites
- Alexander's route

MAP 3.1
The Conquests of Alexander the Great and the Hellenistic Kingdoms

All three dynasties, the Antigonids, the Ptolemies, and the Seleucids are called Hellenistic, presumably because their Hellenism was less pure than that of the polis, but the term is unduly patronizing. The Hellenistic period was one of unprecedented cultural borrowing and transmission. Ideas, religions, and artistic motifs from Egypt and the Middle East fused with those of the Greeks and spread throughout the Mediterranean world. Science, philosophy, and the arts flourished. But the term is unfortunate for another reason. It implies a uniformity that did not exist. Politically and socially, the successor kingdoms differed widely from one another. If they shared a certain veneer of Greek culture, their problems were unique and for more than a century they maintained a rivalry that sometimes degenerated into open war.

The chief foreign policy goal of the Ptolemies was to protect the Nile delta from foreign invasion. This required the maintenance of a large navy and, from the Egyptian point of view, control over Phoenicia and the Syrian coast, which supplied the fleet with timber and

naval stores. The Seleucids resisted Ptolemaic claims to Syria because they needed the Mediterranean ports to maintain their trade with the west. After a series of wars, the Seleucids ultimately gained control of both Syria and Palestine, but not before the Antigonids, too, became entangled in the web of Ptolemaic diplomacy. Fearing an alliance between the Seleucids and the Antigonids, the Ptolemies supported the growth of Pergamum as a buffer state between the two kingdoms and, whenever possible, stirred up anti-Macedonian sentiment in Greece. This usually meant support for one of the two leagues of city-states that formed in third-century Greece: the Aetolian League in the west-central part of the peninsula and the Achaean League, headed by Corinth, in the northern Peloponnese. Egyptian policy collapsed when, in about 230 B.C., the Ptolemies also formed an alliance with Sparta. The frightened Achaeans turned to the Antigonids for help, and the Ptolemies, under attack by the Seleucid king, Antiochus III, "the Great," could do nothing to protect the Aetolians. In the end Antiochus conquered Syria,

## ◆ DOCUMENT 3.3 ◆

### Plutarch: A Positive View of Alexander's Conquests

*Plutarch, who wrote the important* Life of Alexander, *believed in the conqueror's "civilizing" mission and dedication to the universal brotherhood of humankind. In this oration he makes the best possible case for his hero's motives.*

Alexander did not follow Aristotle's advice to treat the Greeks as a leader, the barbarians as a master, cultivating the former as friends and kinsmen, and treating the latter as animals or plants. Had he done so his kingdom would have been filled with warfare, banishments and secret plots, but he regarded himself as divinely sent to mediate and govern the world. And those whom he failed to win over by persuasion he overpowered in arms, bringing them together from every land, combining, as it were in a loving cup, their lives, customs, marriages, and manners of living. . . .

For he did not cross Asia like a robber, nor did he have it in mind to ravage and despoil it for the booty and loot presented by such an unheard-of stroke of fortune. . . . Instead he conducted himself as he did out of a desire to subject all the races in the world to one rule and one form of government, making all mankind a single people. Had not the divinity that sent Alexander recalled his soul so soon, there would have been a single law, as it were, watching over all mankind, and all men would have looked to one form of justice as their common source of light. But now, that portion of the world that never beheld Alexander has remained as if deprived of the sun.

Plutarch. "De Alexandri Magni Fortuna ast Virtute, Oratio I." In *Sources in Western Civilization: Ancient Greece,* pp. 199–200, ed. and trans. Truesdell S. Brown. New York: The Free Press (Simon & Schuster), 1965.

Phoenicia, and Palestine, and the Aetolians allied themselves with a new power then emerging in the west: Rome.

The struggles between the Hellenistic kingdoms, though occasionally dramatic, seem to have had little impact on everyday life. The most important social and economic effect was a periodic influx of slaves into the labor market as one side or the other succeeded in tak-

ing large numbers of captives. As a result, slavery became increasingly important to the Hellenistic economy, forcing free laborers into marginal occupations or outright unemployment. By the end of the third century B.C., the cities of all three kingdoms were struggling with the social problems created by poverty.

Otherwise, in the Antigonid kingdom, life went on largely as before, though without the endless warfare of Greek against Greek that had characterized the classical period. Under Macedonian rule the states retained their separate identities, but loss of control over foreign and military affairs blunted the intensity of their political life. Not even the formation of the Achaean and Aetolian leagues could restore it. Economic decline continued. Poor yields as a result of erosion and soil exhaustion forced landowners to compensate by experimenting with fertilizers and new agricultural techniques. These methods were modestly successful, but for small farmers their cost was prohibitive. Large estates, many of them worked by slaves, became more common. For thousands of Greeks, service as mercenaries or as administrators in the other Hellenistic kingdoms remained the most promising route to success.

Most of these ambitious folk were absorbed by the Seleucid kingdom. Alexander had established almost seventy Greek cities in what had been the Persian Empire. He sought to provide homes for his veterans and for those fleeing overpopulation in their native land. He also hoped to establish trustworthy centers of administration in a vast region populated by dozens of different ethnic and religious groups. This policy was greatly expanded by the Seleucids. The new cities tried to duplicate as far as possible the life of the polis. In the years after Alexander's death, the wealth extracted from his conquests paid for the construction of temples, theaters, and other public buildings in the Greek style. Greek law and Greek political institutions were imposed, but these cities, for all their magnificence, remained cultural hybrids thronged with people of many cultures. Unlike the citizens of a polis, they had neither gods nor ancestors in common.

The Seleucids respected the cultural and religious sensibilities of their subjects but preferred to rely on Greek or Macedonian soldiers and administrators for the day-to-day business of governing. The Greek population of the cities, reinforced until the second century B.C. by emigration from Greece, formed a dominant though not especially cohesive elite. Their own origins were diverse and their perspective was essentially careerist. They formed few emotional ties to their new homes and were usually prepared to go elsewhere if opportunity knocked. The Syrians, Persians, and Babylonians who made up the bulk of the population adopted a few Greek ideas and customs while retaining their own cultural identities.

The result was a cosmopolitan society held together largely by military force. The cities were unstable amalgams of contending ethnic and religious groups. They had their own administrations and popular assemblies but were legally the possessions of the king and had to deal with him through emissaries to protect their interests. Riots were common. *Koine*, a universal Greek dialect, evolved as the language of trade and administration but never fully displaced Aramaic or the other tongues of the ancient Middle East. In the countryside Greek influence remained negligible. Village societies retained their traditional structure even when they were regarded as part of the royal domain and paid taxes directly to the crown. Some were allotted to the cities by royal grant, while others were legally subject to a variety of private landholders. The forms of land tenure, taxation, and provincial administration were diverse.

The Seleucid Empire survived for nearly three hundred years largely because its cities and provinces had no common basis for resistance to the crown and because—until the coming of the Romans—it faced no serious outside threats. The conflicts with the Ptolemies over Palestine and Syria and with the Antigonids over portions of Asia Minor were largely settled by the early second century B.C. Border provinces, especially in the east and in Asia Minor, sometimes broke away, but the royal administration was generally competent. If the empire failed to attract the loyalty of its subjects, its cosmopolitanism offered at least some of them increased opportunities for profit.

Until the disorders of the first century B.C., the eastern empire enjoyed a relative prosperity. No internal trade barriers were established, and the Seleucids guaranteed the safety of caravans as a matter of policy. Even when its leaders were fighting over Alexander's inheritance, the entire Hellenistic world had been open to commerce. A merchant in Damascus or Babylon could trade unimpeded with Greece or Egypt. The more adventurous sent their goods into India or traded with Carthaginians and Romans in the west. Perhaps the most enduring of Alexander's legacies was the creation of a great world market in goods and ideas. It was this, more than anything else, that led to what traditionalists called a dilution of Greek values. Under the influence of Syria and Egypt, Greek legal traditions and even the status of women began to change (see document 3.4).

### DOCUMENT 3.4

## A Hellenistic Marriage Contract

*This marriage contract, dated 311 b.c., between Heracleides and Demetria, a Greek couple from the island of Cos on the shores of Asia Minor, demonstrates how the status of women had improved since the days of classical Attic Law. It not only mentions Demetria's mother, but also takes the infidelities of the husband as seriously as those of his wife.*

Heracleides takes Demetria of Cos as his lawful wife. He receives her from her father, Leptines of Cos, and from her mother, Philotis. He is a free man and she a free woman. She brings with her clothes and jewels worth 1000 drachmas. Heracleides will provide Demetria with all the requirements of a free woman. They shall live in whatever place seems best to Leptines and Heracleides.

If Demetria is found to have done something which disgraces her husband, she shall lose everything she brought with her. And Heracleides shall accuse her before three men chosen by the pair of them. Heracleides shall not be permitted to wrong Demetria by keeping another woman or having children by another woman, nor to harm Demetria in any way under any pretext. If Heracleides is found to have done such a thing, Demetria shall accuse him before three men whom they shall have selected together. Heracleides shall then pay Demetria back the 1000 drachmas she brought as dowry and a further 1000 drachmas in Alexandrian silver as recompense.

Préaux, Claire. "Le Statut de la femme à l'époque hellénistique, principalment en Egypte." In Julia O'Faolain and Lauro Martines, *Not in God's Image: Women in History from the Greeks to the Victorians.* London: Temple Smith.

Egypt under the Ptolemies contrasted vividly with the decentralized empire of the Seleucids. Egypt was a far more homogeneous society than that of the old Persian Empire, and Ptolemy I (d. c. 282 B.C.) had little difficulty in substituting his own rule for that of the pharaohs. After reaching an accommodation with the country's religious leaders, he established a royal despotism that reached into every corner of Egyptian life. With the exception of three Greek cities, only one of which was established by the Ptolemies, all of the country's land was regarded as the property of the king.

A large and efficient bureaucracy managed royal monopolies in essential goods and collected more than two hundred different taxes. The most important of these monopolies was in grain. Royal officials distributed seed to the peasants in return for a substantial percentage of their yields. The grain was then stored and released to the export market when prices were high. Grain was Egypt's leading export, and the profits from this trade were immense. The crown also held a complete monopoly on the production of vegetable oils, which it protected with a 50 percent duty on imported olive oil, and partial monopolies on virtually every other commodity from meat to papyrus. Policy was based on extracting the maximum amount of wealth from the country. By the middle of the second century B.C. many peasants were desperate. But being in a narrow valley surrounded by desert, they had nowhere to flee. The Ptolemies continued to pile up a great treasury until the fall of the dynasty in 30 B.C.

Much of that wealth was lavished on their capital at Alexandria. The city had been founded on the shores of the Mediterranean by Alexander. The narrow offshore island of Pharos was connected to the mainland by a causeway forming two spacious harbors, one of which was linked to Lake Mareotis by a canal. A second canal connected the lake with the western branch of the Nile. This enormous port soon formed the nucleus of the Mediterranean's largest city. Under the first and second Ptolemies, the population of Alexandria grew to nearly 500,000 Greeks, Macedonians, Egyptians, and Jews. Its people drew their water supply from vast cisterns built beneath the city, and a lighthouse, said to have been more than four hundred feet in height, was constructed on Pharos.

The cosmopolitan nature of its population and the patronage of the Ptolemies made Alexandria the cultural and intellectual center of the Hellenistic world. Its center was the Museum, which was a kind of research institute, and a library that collected materials from every literate culture known to the Greeks. The crown used some of its vast revenues to subsidize these institutions as well as the scholars who attended them, and the learned flocked to Alexandria from all over the Mediterranean basin.

## Hellenistic Science, Philosophy, and Religion

The encouragement of the Ptolemies and the intellectual foundations laid down by Aristotle made the third century B.C. a period of extraordinary achievement in science, mathematics, engineering, and navigation.

Nothing like it would be seen again until the scientific revolution of the sixteenth and seventeenth centuries.

Some of the work done at Alexandria was scholarship—the compilation and transmission of earlier ideas. Euclid's *Elements of Geometry*, composed early in the century, contained little that was completely new but became the basis of geometric instruction until the present day. Hellenistic speculations on cosmography and physics were more original. Aristarchus of Samos (c. 310–230 B.C.) disputed Aristotle's theory that the Earth was the center of the universe. He reasoned, without benefit of telescopes or other instruments, that the Sun was larger than the Earth and that the planets were far more distant from one another than Aristotle had imagined. The Sun was therefore the center around which the Earth and planets revolved. Eratosthenes of Cyrene (c. 276–c. 194 B.C.), a mathematician who spent most of his life as head of the Library at Alexandria, founded mathematical geography. Among other things, he calculated the circumference of the Earth to within fifty miles of modern estimates and devised a calendar that used leap years.

Like much of Hellenistic science, these theories bore little fruit until they were revived by scholars in the sixteenth century. The authority of Aristotle was too great to permit their acceptance without independent proof, and the telescopes and navigational instruments needed to support them were not yet invented.

In physics, the work of Archimedes of Syracuse (c. 287–c. 212 B.C.) encountered no such resistance. Archimedes, who studied at Alexandria and was a friend of Eratosthenes, spent most of his life in his native city. A close associate and perhaps a relative of the ruling dynasty, he was valued for his work on catapults; compound pulleys; and the screw of Archimedes, a helical device for lifting water out of wells, mineshafts, and the hulls of ships. Most of these devices had both military and civilian applications, but Archimedes regarded them as little better than toys. He is best known for his work *On Plane Equilibriums*, which describes the basic principle of levers, and for his discovery that solids can be weighed by measuring the amount of liquid they displace. These achievements stand at the beginning of modern physics. In physics, cosmology, and biology, where Theophrastus (d. c. 287 B.C.) used the methods of Aristotle to classify plants and animals discovered in the east, the inspiration of Hellenistic science was largely Greek. In medicine, however, two ancient traditions merged. The Greek Hippocratic tradition was based on the teachings of Hippocrates, a semimythical figure who is supposed to have lived on the island of Cos in the fifth century B.C. (see document 3.5). Its main feature was the theory of the humors. Until late in the eighteenth century, most doctors believed that the human body contained four humors: blood, black bile, yellow bile, and phlegm. Good health depended upon keeping these humors in perfect balance, and medication was typically prescribed if one or more of them was either deficient or present in excess. An excess of blood, for example, could be reduced by bleeding.

The Alexandrians added Egyptian surgery and anatomy to the Hippocratic tradition and passed their findings on to the Romans.

Greeks of the classical era derived much of their identity from the polis and assumed that the good life could be lived only within its social framework. In the great empires of Hellenistic times, that framework no longer existed. For the Greco-Macedonian elite, cut off from their homelands and living essentially as mercenaries, the gratifications of private life gradually replaced those of the organic community. For the non-Greek masses with their long history of subjection to alien empires, there was no issue: The individual and the family were all that mattered.

The arts reflected this new individualism. Hellenistic drama abandoned the great themes of tragic conflict in favor of domestic comedies and tragedies that dealt with pathetic events on the personal level. The works of Menander (c. 300 B.C.) are typical of this genre.

Painting and sculpture flourished as never before. Painting especially is said to have reached unprecedented levels of excellence. However, owing to the perishable nature of the colors, all of it has been lost. In sculpture, much of which has been preserved in Roman copies, many of the best artists abandoned the serene classicism of Phidias and Praxiteles and sought to express emotion through the dramatic arrangement of their figures, agonized facial expressions, and exaggerated muscular tension. The famous statue of Laocoön and his sons is an outstanding example (see illustration 3.5). Others chose humble figures from everyday life and portrayed them in sympathetic detail (see illustration 3.6). Whatever their subject, the artists of the Hellenistic age achieved new heights of technical virtuosity that would astonish and at times dismay the critics of a later age.

Hellenistic philosophy, too, reflected this shift in values, abandoning political theory in favor of individualistic prescriptions for the good life. The philosophic school known as the Cynics carried this tendency further than anyone else. They argued that the best life

## ◆ DOCUMENT 3.5 ◆

# The Hippocratic Oath

*The origins of the Hippocratic oath are unclear. Hippocrates was supposed to have imposed the oath upon his students, but it may have appeared at any time between the fifth century B.C. and the first century A.D. Latin and Arabic versions appear throughout the Middle Ages. The text more closely resembles an indenture between master and apprentice than a pure statement of medical ethics.*

I swear by Apollo Physician, by Asclepius, by Health, by Panacea, and by all the gods and goddesses, making them by witnesses, that I will carry out, according to my ability and judgment, this oath and this indenture. To hold my teacher in this art equal to my own parents; to make him partner in my livelihood; when he is in need of money to share mine with him; to consider his family as my own brothers, and to teach them this art, if they want to learn it, without fee or indenture; to impart precept, oral instruction, and all other instruction to my own sons, the sons of my teacher, and to indentured pupils who have taken the physician's oath, but to nobody else. I will use treatment to help the sick according to my ability and judgment, but never with a view to injury and wrongdoing. Neither will I administer a poison to anybody when asked to do so, nor will I suggest such a course. Similarly I will not give a woman a pessary to cause abortion. But I will keep pure and holy both my life and my art. I will not use the knife, not even, verily, on sufferers from stone, but I will give place to such as are craftsmen therein. Into whatsoever houses I enter, I will enter to help the sick, and I will abstain from all intentional wrong-doing and harm, especially from abusing the bodies of man or woman, bond or free. And whatsoever I shall see or hear in the course of my profession, as well as outside my profession in my intercourse with men, if it be what should be published abroad, I will never divulge, holding such things to be holy secrets. Now if I carry out this oath, and break it not, may I gain for ever reputation among all men for my life and for my art; but if I forswear myself, may the opposite befall me.

"The Hippocratic Oath." In Logan Clendening, ed., *Source-Book of Medical History.* pp. 14–15. New York: Dover, 1960.

**Illustration 3.5**

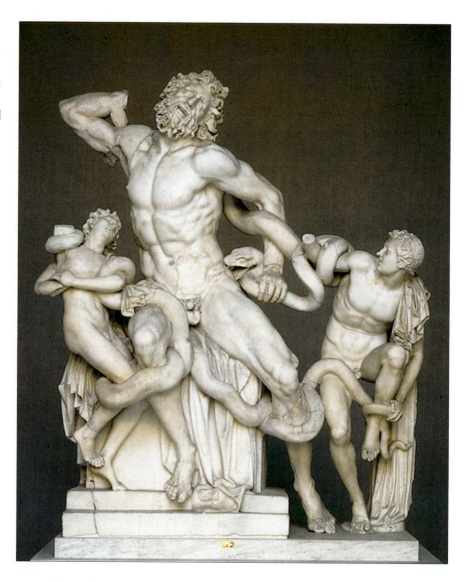

*Laocoön and His Sons.* This monumental sculpture from Pergamon is an example of the way in which Hellenistic artists used formal arrangement, exaggerated musculature, and agonized facial expressions to portray emotion. The serene classicism of Praxiteles and his contemporaries has been abandoned. Even the theme, an episode from *The Iliad* in which the gods sent serpents to destroy the Trojan priest Laocoön and his children, is chosen for its emotional impact. The work as shown is probably a Roman copy.

was lived closest to nature and that wisdom lay in abandoning worldly goods and ambition. Diogenes (d. 320 B.C.), their most effective spokesman, delighted in exposing the folly and vanity of others. Popular legend has it that he lived in a tub and carried a lantern with which he hoped—unsuccessfully—to find an honest man.

Among those attracted to the teachings of the Cynics was Zeno (c. 335–c. 263 B.C.). A native of Phoenician Cyprus, he established a school at Athens named the Stoa after the portico in the Agora where his disciples met. The Stoics, as they were called, believed that living in harmony with nature was essential. They identified nature with the divine principle or *logos*. Each human being and each object had the *logos* within it and acted according to a divine, predetermined plan. This plan, though good in itself, might not always work in the best interests of a particular individual. Sickness,

death, and misfortune were all part of a providential order that could not be escaped but only endured.

The implications of this theory were liberating. Moral qualities such as prudence, courage, folly, and intemperance were good or bad. Wealth, pleasure, beauty, and health were morally indifferent because they were essentially states of mind—the products of feeling or passion. The wise person, regardless of condition, should realize that it is not what happens but how one reacts to it that determines the good life. The goal of wisdom is therefore *apatheia*, or indifference to that which is morally neutral, coupled with ethical behavior and the cultivation of personal qualities that are morally good. According to the Stoics, anyone could achieve this goal. Men and women, slaves and princes, all possessed the same divine spark. Though the conditions of their lives might differ, they were all inherently equal.

**Illustration 3.6**

🏛 **Hellenistic Realism.** This life-size statue of a poor shepherdess is part of an important Hellenistic genre that portrayed the life of the poor, and particularly of poor women, with a sympathetic but unflinching eye.

terns. Growth and dissolution were inevitable, but no providential order existed of the sort claimed by the Stoics. In the absence of such an order, the greatest good from the human point of view was pleasure, and the search for pleasure should be the philosopher's primary goal. By pleasure, Epicurus meant peace of mind and the absence of pain, not the active pursuit of dissipation. He sought a quiet life, removed from the troubles of the world and governed by the principle of moderation in all things. Even the gods were not to be feared but emulated in their Olympian detachment from the things of this world. Epicureanism, too, had its followers, but detachment from the world did not always recommend itself to those with practical responsibilities.

Like all philosophical schools, Stoicism and Epicureanism appealed primarily to the educated. The mass of people in the Hellenistic world found solace in religion. This in itself was a relatively new development, at least among the Greeks, for the gods of Olympus had offered little to their worshipers beyond a conditional protection from their wrath. In the classical age, while the learned took refuge in philosophy, ordinary men and women had resorted to superstition and a helpless resignation to *tyche*, or fate.

Hellenistic religions were different. Many, though not all, had Eastern or Egyptian roots, and most were what are called mystery religions. That is, they claimed to guarantee personal immortality, often through the intervention of a god or goddess who came to Earth in human form and suffered for the sins of humankind. Among the more important were the cult of Serapis, encouraged by Ptolemy I, and the far more ancient veneration of Isis.

## The Jews in the Hellenistic World

Hellenistic culture, for all its richness and sophistication, was not universally admired. Among those who resisted it most persistently were the Jews. The dispersions of the sixth century B.C. had created a vast Jewish exile population. The largest of these communities were in Egypt and Babylon, but virtually every city in the ancient world had Jewish residents. Most were artisans or small tradesmen. While some were eventually submerged in the local population, others gathered together in close-knit communities to preserve their religious and cultural identity.

In Palestine, a remnant of impoverished peasants held on, reinforced after the Persian conquest of Babylon by small numbers of the devout who sought to re-

Unlike the teachings of the Cynics, Stoicism was rooted in physical and epistemological principles derived at some distance from Aristotle. It offered not only an ethical code but also a means of understanding and accepting an often hostile universe. Of all the philosophical schools of late antiquity, it was the most popular among educated people. It became the dominant belief among the Roman upper classes and would strongly influence the development of Christianity.

Stoicism's chief rival was Epicureanism. Epicurus (341–270 B.C.) was born to an Athenian family on the island of Samos and established a school at Athens that was notable among other things for being open to women. He argued, as Leucippus and Democritus had done, that the universe was composed of atoms that combined and recombined in an infinite variety of pat-

## ◆ DOCUMENT 3.6 ◆

## The Jewish Struggle Against Hellenism

*The First and Second Book of Maccabees tells the story of the struggle against the hellenizing policies of Antiochus Epiphanes from the standpoint of observant Jews. Not all Jews opposed Greek tendencies, and the struggle waged by the Maccabees was not only against Antiochus, but also against his local supporters.*

Jason obtained the high priesthood by corruption, promising the king in his petition 360 talents of silver and 80 talents from other revenues. When the king had consented and he had taken office, he immediately brought his countrymen over to the Greek way of living. He set aside the royal ordinances especially favoring the Jews . . . and abrogating the lawful ways of living he introduced new customs contrary to the Law. For he willingly established a gymnasium right under the citadel, and he made the finest of the young men wear the Greek hat. And to such a pitch did the cultivation of Greek fashions and the coming-in of foreign customs rise . . . that the priests were no longer earnest about the services of the altar, but disdaining the sacrifices, they hurried to take part in the unlawful exercises of the wrestling school, after the summons to the discus throwing, regarding as worthless the things their forefathers valued, and thinking Greek standards the finest. [2 Macc. 2:23–27]

The Apocrypha. First Maccabees 2:23–27, 42–48. trans. Edgar J. Goodspeed. New York: Random House, 1959.

turn to their homeland. In 516 B.C. they rebuilt the Temple at Jerusalem. Not so grand as the Temple of Solomon, it served as the center of Jewish faith and aspirations until its destruction by the Romans in A.D. 70.

The glue that held the many Jewish communities together was the teaching of prophets and devotion to the Law, as symbolized by the gradual evolution of the Talmud from the fifth century B.C. onward. The Prophets, many of whose writings have been preserved in the Bible, exhorted the Jews to remain faithful. The Talmud was the product of scribes who sought to uncover the full meaning of the Mosaic Law and apply it to every conceivable circumstance. This process of commentary, which continues today, was central to the development of mature Judaism, but certain aspects of it were not unopposed. The biblical books of Jonah and of Ruth are veiled protests against what many saw as an increasingly narrow and overly proscriptive faith.

This struggle between a Judaism based firmly upon the Law and a broader tolerance of the non-Jewish world reached its greatest intensity in the Hellenistic era (see document 3.6). The conflict between Hellenism and Hebraism was fundamental. A life lived according to divinely revealed law was incompatible with the Greek love of speculation and with aesthetic standards based upon the beauties of nature and the perfection of the human body. In spite of this, many Jews were clearly attracted to Greek thought and customs.

The excesses of the Seleucid monarch Antiochus IV Epiphanes (c. 215–164 B.C.) turned the tide decisively against them. When he introduced the worship of Zeus to the temple at Jerusalem, a revolt led by the Maccabees, the five sons of the priest Mattathias, resulted in the restoration of an independent Jewish state.

In later years the dynasty founded by the Maccabees embarked upon a policy of expansion and forced conversions to Judaism. This was opposed by the Pharisees, who sought a return to the Law and to traditional Jewish values. A bloody civil war between the Pharisees and the Sadducees, as the supporters of the dynasty were known, ended only with Roman intervention in 64 B.C. and the abolition of the monarchy in the following year. Though political independence was lost, the danger of Hellenism had been avoided. The Romans made no effort to interfere with the Jewish faith, and the Pharisees emerged as the dominant faction in religious life—both at home and in the scattered communities of the dispersion.

Unlike that of the Jews, the culture of ancient Greece was profoundly humanistic in the sense that Greek thinkers emphasized the cultivation of virtue and the good life within a social instead of a religious framework. Greek artists concentrated almost exclusively on the human form, while poets found inspiration in the heroic dignity of men and women in the face of tragedy. This intense concentration on the human experience was coupled with an extraordinary spirit of inquiry. Other ancient societies, notably the Egyptians and Mesopotamians, had rich speculative traditions, but the Greeks were unique in insisting upon a rigorous form of logic in which the connections between each part of a statement had to be made perfectly clear.

These habits of thought, together with a mass of learning and speculation drawn from the most diverse sources, were the Greek legacy to Western society. From the beginning the Greeks were borrowers. They had a rare ability to absorb the ideas and beliefs of oth-

ers without threatening their own sense of what it meant to be Greek. When, in the Hellenistic age, they penetrated to the edges of the known world, this tendency accelerated. Elements from every ancient culture were adopted and transformed according to their own needs and preconceptions. In so doing they imposed a kind of intellectual unity that, if it distorted some things and neglected others, was passed on intact to the Romans and from the Romans to the modern Western world. For good or ill, the ancient world is viewed through Greek eyes.

CHAPTER 4

# THE RISE OF THE ROMAN REPUBLIC

## CHAPTER OUTLINE

◆ ◆ ◆ ◆ ◆ ◆ ◆ ◆ ◆ ◆ ◆ ◆ ◆ ◆ ◆ ◆ ◆ ◆ ◆

Rome united the ancient Mediterranean and joined it to western Europe. In the process, the Romans created an amalgam of ideas and institutions that would become the basis of later European life. This achievement, while enormous, was not especially original. The Romans excelled in the practical arts of war, law, engineering, and administration. They possessed in Latin a language of great richness and flexibility that would become the mother of many other tongues, but they borrowed virtually everything else from the Greeks, the Etruscans, the Egyptians, and other ancient cultures of the Near East. This was not simple mimicry but creative assimilation, for Roman culture had a coherence and integrity of its own. The Romans borrowed selectively, taking only what they found useful and transforming it according to their own traditions and social norms.

In the years when Greek civilization was at its height, Rome was still a modest settlement in central Italy. Poor and surrounded by powerful enemies, it survived by developing a superb army and a political system that, though authoritarian enough to be effective in times of crisis, was based upon the active participation of its citizens and the rule of law. By the middle of the third century B.C. Rome controlled the Italian peninsula. By 133 B.C. it had defeated both Carthage and Macedon and acquired an empire that stretched from Spain to Greece.

The creation of this empire was, at least in the beginning, a response to adversity rather than the product of deliberate intent. Surrounded by more powerful enemies, it developed a culture that stressed the military values of courage, discipline, and endurance. The early history of Rome is therefore one of harsh adaptations followed by explosive growth—the tale of how a poor, often beleaguered community developed political and military institutions capable of ruling an empire.

MAP 4.1

Ancient Italy and the City of Rome

## Ancient Italy

The long, boot-shaped Italian peninsula bisects the Mediterranean (see map 4.1). At first glance it seems especially favored by nature. Its central location lends it strategic and commercial importance while its climate is generally milder and wetter than that of Greece. Agricultural yields are higher, and some of the upland regions, which in Greece have become a moonscape of rocks and dry scrub, can support grazing. These advantages, however, are relative. The development of prehistoric Italy was at first hindered by natural obstacles of every kind. For most of its length the Italian peninsula is dominated by the Appenines, a mountain range that in its central portions reaches nearly ten thousand

feet in height. On the east, the mountains drop precipitously to the Adriatic Sea. Few good harbors can be found on the Italian shore of the Adriatic, and arable land is scarce except in Apulia, the region immediately southeast of Mt. Garganus, which protrudes like a spur into the Adriatic.

The western coast, also lacking in good harbors, is more hospitable. The valleys of the Arno and the Tiber are suitable for agriculture and open out onto an extensive coastal plain that, though potentially fertile, was in early times marshy and subject to floods. Further south, around the Bay of Naples, is the rich plain of Campania whose soil is the gift of volcanic deposits from Mt. Vesuvius. Another active volcano, Mt. Etna, dominates the eastern part of Sicily, the large, wedge-shaped is-

Illustration 4.1

⚡ **An Etruscan Tomb.** Wealthy Etruscans often buried the dead in replicas of their homes. In this example of a domestic interior from the third century B.C., the household goods are portrayed in stucco relief.

land immediately southwest of the mainland. As a consequence of climatic change, Sicily today is dry and relatively poor, but until the sixteenth century A.D. it supplied much of Italy with grain.

At the opposite end of the peninsula, between the westward curve of the Appenines and the great northern barrier of the Alps, is the valley of the Po. Flowing eastward into the Adriatic, it is now among the world's richest agricultural and industrial regions, but its wealth is largely the fruit of human effort. As recently as the fourth century B.C. it was a wild marshland, not yet tamed by two millennia of canalization and levee building.

Beginning in the eighth century B.C., Greek colonists had established themselves in the richest of the southern coastal lands. Eastern Sicily, Apulia, and Campania, as well as Calabria (the heel of the boot) and the shores of the Gulf of Taranto (its arch), were soon dominated by *poleis* of the Aegean type, rich and vigorous, but as combative and incapable of unified action as their models. At the same time, the Carthaginians colonized western Sicily and contended violently with their Greek neighbors for land and trade. Of the original inhabitants of these areas, some became slaves or tenants of the colonists, while others retreated to the interior and retained their tribal cultures.

A variety of tribes, Latins, Umbrians, and Samnites—each speaking its own Italic or other Indo-European language—inhabited Latium, the central part of the peninsula. The Etruscans dominated the region between the Tiber and the Arno. Their language can be only partially deciphered, but their alphabet was similar

to that of the Greeks and their art seems also to have been derived from Greek models. Most of what is known about the Etruscans comes from archaeology, and little has survived from the days when Etruscan power was at its height (see illustration 4.1). Above all, the Etruscans were city dwellers. Their economy was based heavily on trade and manufacturing, and though they were also accomplished farmers, they preferred whenever possible to live in town. They constructed their twelve main cities according to engineering and religious principles that would profoundly influence the Romans. Where terrain permitted, the Etruscans favored a symmetrical and axial city plan that was unlike anything devised by the Greeks. Elaborate tunnels of dressed stone drained low-lying areas or brought fresh water for the consumption of the townspeople, while the buildings featured arches and vaulted ceilings, construction techniques that appear to have been invented by Etruscans.

This sophistication did not extend to political arrangements. Etruscan society was rigidly stratified. A handful of wealthy families dominated each of the twelve cities through legally enforceable clientage and the ownership of many slaves. In war, the rich fought on horseback under a king who may have been elective. By the fifth century B.C. the Etruscans had adopted the hoplite tactics of the Greeks and replaced their kings with aristocratic magistrates. No movement toward democracy is evident. But if the political evolution of the Etruscans differed from that of the Greeks, in another respect they closely resembled them: The twelve cities were almost incapable of united action. At an early date they formed a league, which was chiefly religious and athletic in purpose. The cities also celebrated certain religious festivals in common, but otherwise they fought incessantly and their merchants competed for each other's markets as well as for those of the Greek and Carthaginian colonies to the south.

## The Origins of Rome

The Tiber is the largest river in central Italy. Its valley, running roughly from north to south, is strategically important because it provides the easiest land route for travelers—and armies—moving between the Po valley and southern Italy. The last point at which the river can be easily crossed lies about fifteen miles from its mouth, where the valley is broad and marshy. Seven low hills in the immediate area provide a refuge from floods and invaders alike. In the eighth century B.C. one hill, the Palatine, was occupied by a tribe of people who spoke an early version of Latin. Shortly afterward, a related group took up residence on the nearby Aventine hill. These two settlements formed the nucleus of ancient Rome. They were part of a larger group of Italic communities that formed themselves into the Latin League for political and religious purposes, but their common ties did not prevent them from fighting among themselves.

Blessed with rich land and abundant water, the early Romans were nevertheless too few to preserve full autonomy in the face of Etruscan influence. The nearest of the Etruscan cities was Veii, only twelve miles away, and almost from the first, the Romans found themselves under the influence of their more powerful neighbors. Some of the first kings of Rome bore Etruscan names, and reportedly the last of them was not deposed and replaced by a Roman republic ruled by two magistrates until 509 B.C. (although it could have been a generation later).

In any event, Etruscan influence contributed greatly to Roman civilization. The Romans adopted the Etruscan alphabet, though not the language itself, and learned most of what they knew about metalworking, civic planning, and architecture from their northern neighbors. Many religious customs described by Livy, together with a number of Roman political institutions, have Etruscan roots as well.

Under the kings, Rome used its dominant position in the Latin League to subdue the Sabines and other Italic communities along the lower Tiber, absorbing their populations and granting citizenship to the lead-

ing families. This enlightened policy, a marked contrast to the exclusiveness of the Greek *poleis*, was largely responsible for Rome's successful expansion. The prospect of fair treatment discouraged fanatic resistance among the city's enemies and made accepting Roman hegemony far easier for its neighbors.

The policy was continued after the formation of the republic. The Romans expelled the Etruscans as part of a larger movement that involved Rome's Greek and Latin neighbors. The Etruscan city of Veii was taken after an extensive siege in 396 B.C., almost doubling Roman territory. Nine years later, however, disaster struck. The Gauls, a Celtic people from central Europe, descended on the peninsula and burned Rome in 387 B.C. The action was a tremendous psychological blow, for the Gauls, with their vast numbers and sheer ferocity, appalled the Romans. They sometimes fought naked and seemed to live exclusively on meat and alcohol. Fortunately, they made no effort to consolidate their victory and retired to the sparsely inhabited valley of the Po. They settled down to a more-or-less ordered agricultural life and began the long process of clearing and draining the region, which in later times would be known as Cisalpine Gaul.

Among the more serious consequences of the Gallic invasion was that it undermined the loyalty of Rome's Latin allies. The Latin League rebelled against Roman hegemony, but the Romans recovered quickly. By 338 B.C. all of Latium was again subdued. Once more, the Romans showed a restraint and a grasp of political realities that were all too rare in the ancient world. The towns nearest Rome received full citizenship. Others, farther away, were granted municipal status, which meant that their citizens could marry or trade with Romans but had no voting rights outside their own communities. The specific provisions of these agreements were tailored to individual circumstances and were open-ended in the sense that Rome always held out the prospect of new privileges in return for good behavior. Some towns were merely enrolled as allies, but all save those that received citizenship retained self-government. The one universally enforced rule was that none of the federated communities could make similar agreements with each other.

To ensure communication and provide for the common defense, the first of a series of paved, all-weather roads were built linking Rome with her allies (see illustration 4.2). A policy that would be followed until the end of the empire was thus begun. Because all roads led to Rome, these highways had the effect of separating the allies from one another while allowing Rome to intervene militarily in case of rebellion or some other

**Illustration 4.2**

🏛 **A Section of the Appian Way.** Begun about 312 B.C., the Appian Way was the first of the great paved highways built to link Rome with its allies and eventually with the farthest reaches of its empire. As this modern photo demonstrates, Roman engineering was built to last.

threat. Surfaced in stone and often lined with trees, a few of the roads are still in use today.

These arrangements proved effective in the next great crisis. The consolidation of Latium threatened the Samnites, a warlike people who inhabited the uplands between Rome and the Greek settlements around the Bay of Naples. Joined by the Gauls and by the Etruscans, whose power was greatly reduced, they launched a series of bitter struggles that ended with the Roman victory at Sentinium in 295 B.C. Though a few of Rome's Latin allies deserted, the coalition as a whole held firm.

The Roman military system achieved maturity during the Samnite wars. Under the monarchy, the Romans had learned to use hoplites flanked by cavalry from the Etruscans. Their greater success resulted largely from a superior discipline rooted ultimately in cultural values. The Romans prized self-discipline, de-

termination, and a sense of duty to the community above all else, but they were not indifferent to practical concerns. After about 400 B.C. they paid their troops while on duty. The Samnites, who were as tough as the Romans and who enjoyed the defensive advantage of a rugged, mountainous terrain, forced them to change tactics. To achieve greater maneuverability, the Romans abandoned the phalanx in favor of smaller units known as maniples. A maniple contained 100 to 120 foot soldiers and was commanded by an officer known in later days as a centurion. Thirty maniples, plus five in reserve, made up a legion. In battle, the maniples were arranged in three lines, with a space between each unit large enough to permit the forward ranks to move back or the rear ranks to move forward as needed. Such a formation required discipline and control, while permitting an almost infinite number of tactical combinations regardless of the terrain. The new system, which in its basic outlines lasted until the end of the fourth century A.D., was badly needed in the years after it brought success in the battle of Sentinium. The Romans had to defend themselves against a series of powerful neighbors, but each victory made them new enemies (see document 4.1). The defeat of the Samnites and their allies awakened the Greek cities of the south. The Romans now controlled all of Italy from the borders of Campania to the Po, and the Greeks feared that such a concentration of power would lead to their downfall. Bickering and complaining to the last, they nevertheless united enough to hire the greatest mercenary of the age to defend their interests.

Pyrrhus of Epirus was ruler of a small state in what is now Albania. Backed by Greek wealth and supported by a contingent of war elephants, he twice defeated the Romans but suffered such heavy casualties that he retreated to Sicily in 278 B.C., saying that if he won another such victory he would be ruined. Nevertheless, he returned again in 275 B.C. only to be defeated. These wars gave rise to the term *Pyrrhic victory* and marked the end of Greek independence on the Italian mainland. The Greek cities, too, were incorporated into the Roman system, and the Roman republic thus ruled all Italy south of the Po.

## The Economic and Social Structures of Early Rome

The city that conquered Italy was similar in its social arrangements to the classical Greek polis. A majority of early Romans were small farmers. Though their plots

## ◆ DOCUMENT 4.1 ◆

# Livy: Roman Tactics at the Time of the Samnite Wars

*Titus Livius (59 B.C.–A.D. 17), known as Livy, was the greatest historian of ancient Rome. Writing with the patronage of the Emperor Augustus, Livy compiled a history of Rome from its origins to 9 B.C. This work, known as The Annals of the Roman People, consisted of 142 books; only 35 of these (plus fragments) have survived. Livy was a conservative analyst who stressed the traditional strengths of Rome, such as the citizen army. The following excerpt from Livy's history explains the organization of the army during the Samnite Wars (343–341 B.C.) of the early republic.*

The foremost line consisted of the *hastati*, forming 15 maniples [companies] stationed a short distance from each other. This front line . . . consisted of the flower of the young men who were growing ripe for service. Behind them were stationed an equal number of maniples, called *principes*, made up of men of a more stalwart age. . . . This body of 30 maniples was called the *antepilani* because behind the standards there were stationed 15 other companies, each of which was divided into three sections, the first section being called the *pilus*. The company consisted of three *vexilla* [banners]. A single *vexillum* had 60 soldiers, two centurions, and one *vexillarius*, or color-bearer; the company numbered 186 men. The first *vexillum* led the *triarii*, veterans of proven courage; the second, the *rorarii*, or skirmishers, younger and less distinguished men; the third, the *accensi*, who were least to be depended upon and were therefore assigned to the rearmost line.

When an army had been drawn up in these ranks, the *hastati* were the first of all to engage. If the *hastati* failed to repulse the enemy, they slowly retired through the intervals between the companies of the *principes*, who then took up the fight, the *hastati* following in their rear. The *triarii*, meanwhile, were kneeling under their standards with left leg advanced, their shields leaning against their shoulders, and their spears planted in the ground with points obliquely upward, as if their battle line were fortified by a bristling palisade. If the *principes* were also unsuccessful, they slowly retired from the battle line to the *triarii* (which has given rise to the proverbial saying, when people are in great trouble, "matters have come down to the *triarii*"). When the *triarii* had admitted the *hastati* and *principes* through the intervals between their companies, they rose up and, instantly closing their companies up, blocked the lanes, as it were, and in one compact mass fell on the enemy, there being no more reserves left behind them. The enemy, who had pursued the others as though they had defeated them, saw with the greatest dread a new line suddenly rising up with increased numbers.

Livy. "History of Rome," book 8, from *Roman Civilization: Third Edition: 2. Vol. Set.* Naphtali and Meyer Rheinhold, eds. Copyright © 1990, Columbia University Press. Reprinted with permission of the publisher.

probably averaged no more than two or three acres—twenty acres was regarded as a substantial estate—the intensive cultivation of many different crops provided them with a measure of self-sufficiency (see illustration 4.3). Wherever possible, grain was planted between rows of vines or olive trees and replaced with beans or other legumes in alternate years, for the Romans practiced crop rotation and were careful to enrich the soil through composting and animal fertilizers. Because grazing land was scarce, there was never enough manure. Sheep were raised for their wool and for milk, while cattle were used mainly as draft animals. Everyone tried to maintain a miniature orchard of apples, pears, or figs.

This kind of farming required skill and a great deal of effort in virtually every month of the year. Fields had to be plowed at least three times, then hoed frequently during the growing season to reduce soil temperature

and preserve moisture. Water was always a problem in the hot, dry Italian summer and often had to be carried from some distance to irrigate the garden vegetables. Compost piles, which used every bit of organic matter available, needed water as well as frequent turning with the pitchfork. The successful cultivation of vineyards and fruit trees demanded clever techniques for grafting and pruning.

Heroic efforts produced a balanced but simple diet: wheat or barley gruel supplemented by olives, cabbage, and beans. Milk, cheese, fruit, and baked bread provided variety, but meat—usually pork—was reserved for special occasions. Sheep, goats, and cattle were too valuable to be slaughtered for their meat but sometimes found their way to the table after serving as burnt offerings to the gods. Hogs, which could root in the oak forests or in other waste spaces, provided not only

**Illustration 4.3**

Roman Agriculture. These mosaics from Saint Roman-en-Gal, France, show Roman farmers engaged in gathering grapes, picking apples, and bundling straw.

hams and sausages but also that greatest of all Roman delicacies: roast suckling pig.

Roman farms were usually worked by the owner and his *familia*—the legal definition of which, though precise, was remarkably inclusive. It meant the nuclear family as well as the entire household including dependent relatives and slaves. Most plots could support only the owner, his wife, and his children, but the labor-intensive character of Italian agriculture favored the growth of extended families whenever sufficient land was available. It also encouraged slavery, even on properties that seem small by modern standards. No great slave-worked estates existed of the kind that be-

came common in the second century B.C., but many families found that owning a few extra workers was a good investment.

Some slaves were war captives, but most were Romans subjugated for debt. As in Mesopotamia or early Greece, those unable to satisfy their creditors were forced to sell themselves or their children to discharge their obligation. Under the early republic, slavery was not as harsh as it would later become. The term of debt servitude was usually limited, with freedom guaranteed after a fixed period of years. Dehumanization was further reduced by the fact that most slaves lived under their master's roof and shared his table. Marcus Porcius

Cato (234–149 B.C.), the author, general, and statesman from whom much information is derived about rural society under the republic (see document 4.2), reported that his wife sometimes nursed the children of slaves. But slaves were still property and could be sold, beaten, or killed without recourse to law.

In this, slaves were little different from the other members of the *familia*. Theoretically and legally, the father, or *paterfamilias*, had absolute power of life and death over his children and slaves. His wife, too, was subject to his will, but he could neither kill nor sell her. In practice, affection and the need for domestic tranquility diluted the brutality of the law. By the second century B.C. women had, through court decisions and senatorial decrees, gained a much larger measure of control over their persons and dowries than they had enjoyed in the early years of the republic.

In much the same way, the sale or execution of a child rarely took place without the approval of the entire family, and public opinion had to be considered as well. Rome, like ancient Greece, was a "shame" society that exercised social control primarily through community pressure. Reputation was vitally important, and the mistreatment of women and children was regarded as shameful.

Women guarded their reputations and were generally respected. Like their Greek counterparts, they managed the day-to-day life of the household. Women, no less than men, were expected to conform to the ideals of *dignitas*, *fides*, and *pietas* (dignity, faithfulness, and piety) and to exhibit physical and moral courage of the highest order. They were also expected to remind their menfolk when they failed to honor those ancient virtues. In many ways, the Roman model of feminine behavior was more Spartan than Athenian.

Roman families were part of larger social groupings that influenced their conduct. The importance of clans, tribes, and other survivals from an earlier time has been much debated, but clientage, the system of mutual dependency in which a powerful individual protects the interests of others in return for their political or economic support, was legally enforceable and even more highly developed than in Mesopotamia.

All of these arrangements were sanctioned by religion. The Roman pantheon of gods was superficially like that of the Greeks, with Jupiter corresponding to Zeus, Juno to Hera, Venus to Aphrodite, and so on. However, in the early days at least, the gods do not seem to have had clearly defined human forms. No myths sprung up about them, and no suggestion was made that they engaged in the kind of sexual antics

## ◆ DOCUMENT 4.2 ◆
### Cato: Farm Management

*Marcus Porcius Cato (234–149 B.C.) was the first Latin writer of prose. Though he wrote in the second century B.C., his fervent traditionalism led him to value the social ideals of a far earlier time, and much of his political career was devoted to a vigorous attack on luxury and the importation of foreign ideas. His De agri cultura, the first of many Roman tracts on farming, was directed to men like himself who had farmed modest acreage with the help of an overseer and a few slaves, not toward the owners of opulent estates. It includes a wealth of technical information on every aspect of farming as well as advice on management. The following passages reflect a hard-bitten attitude that must have been common among Romans in the earliest days of the republic.*

Sell worn-out oxen, blemished cattle, blemished sheep, wool, hides, an old slave, a sickly slave, and whatever else is superfluous. The master should be in the selling habit, not the buying habit. . . .

[O]n feast days, old ditches might have been cleaned, road work done, brambles cut, the garden spaded, a meadow cleared, faggots bundled, thorns rooted out, spelt ground, and general cleaning done. When the slaves were sick, such large rations should not have been issued.

When the weather is bad and no other work can be done, clear out manure for the compost heap; clean thoroughly the ox stalls, sheep pens, barnyard, and farmstead; and mend wine-jars with lead, or hoop them with thoroughly dried oak wood. . . . In rainy weather try to find something to do indoors. Clean up rather than be idle. Remember that even though work stops, expenses run on none the less.

Cato. *De agricultura*, trans. W. D. Hooper and H. D. Ash. Loeb Classical Library. Cambridge, MA: Harvard University Press, 1934.

common among the Olympians. When Greek culture became fashionable in the second half of the third century B.C., such distinctions tended to vanish. Greek myths were adapted to the Roman pantheon, and the Roman gods and goddesses were portrayed according to the conventions of Greek art. The Romans also believed in a host of spirits that governed places and natural processes (see document 4.3). They consulted the

## ◆ DOCUMENT 4.3 ◆

# St. Augustine: Animistic Spirits in Roman Religion

*St. Augustine (A.D. 354–430) was born Aurelius Augustinus in the Roman province of Numidia in north Africa, the son of a Christian mother and pagan father. Augustine moved to Rome, where he taught rhetoric and continued to accept traditional Roman religious practice. He converted to Christianity in his thirties and became a priest, returning to Africa, where he served as bishop of Hippo. His writings, especially his autobiographical* Confessions *and* The City of God, *were extremely influential in shaping early Christianity. The following excerpt from* The City of God *describes the polytheistic Roman religion of his youth.*

But how is it possible to mention in one part of this book all the names of gods or goddesses, which the Romans scarcely could comprise in great volumes, distributing among these divine powers their peculiar functions concerning separate things? They did not even think that the care of their lands should be entrusted to any one god; but they entrusted their farms to the goddess Rumina, and the ridges of the mountains to the god Jugatinus; over the hills they placed the goddess Collatina, over the valleys, Vallonia. Nor could they even find one Segetia so potent that they could commend their cereal crops entirely to her care; but so long as their seed grain was still under the ground, they desired to have the goddess Seia watch over

it; then, when it was already above ground and formed standing grain, they set over it the goddess Segetia; and when the grain was collected and stored, they entrusted it to the goddess Tutilina, that it might be kept safe. Who would not have thought the goddess Segetia sufficient to protect the standing grain until it had passed from the first green blades to the dry ears? Yet she was not enough for men who loved a multitude of gods. . . . Therefore they set Proserpina over the germinating seeds; over the joints and knobs of the stems, the god Nodutus; over the sheaths enfolding the ears, the goddess Volutina; when the sheaths opened and the spikes emerged, it was ascribed to the goddess Patelana; when the stems were of the same height as new ears, because the ancients described this equalizing by the term *hostire*, it was ascribed to the goddess Hostilina; when the grain was in flower, it was dedicated to the goddess Flora; when full of milk, to the god Lacturnus; when maturing, to the goddess Matuta; when the crop was "runcated"—that is, removed from the soil—to the goddess Runcina.

omens before virtually every act, public or private, and performed sacrifices to assure its success. The sacrifices might involve the burnt offering of an animal, which was usually then eaten, or a libation of wine or oil. Gods and spirits alike had to be appeased. The Romans were not, however, a priest-ridden people. Priests of both sexes specialized in the care of temples or in foretelling the future. They were never a separate caste. At home, the father presided over religious rites and was responsible for making sure that the family did not offend the gods. No concept of personal salvation is evident, and ethical concepts were largely unrelated to divine will.

Some Romans were richer than others. The source or extent of their greater wealth is hard to determine, but at an early date the Etruscan kings identified one hundred men of substance and appointed them to an advisory body known as the Senate. The senators represented families that owned land, held slaves, and

could afford to fight on horseback instead of on foot. Like their Etruscan counterparts, they presided over elaborate networks of clientage in which mutual obligation was enforced by religious and legal sanctions. When the monarchy fell, the Senate remained to advise the two governing magistrates, who would eventually be known as *consuls*, and the senatorial families became the core of the patrician order.

The patricians were the hereditary aristocracy of the Roman republic. While other citizens could vote, only the patricians could hold office as magistrates or serve in the Senate. The plebeians, who were free citizens even though many of them were bound by ties of clientage, resisted this situation from the start. Some of them had grown rich during the years of expansion under the monarchy and resented being excluded from public life.

The majority of plebeians had grown poorer. Their farms, which had never been large, were divided and divided again by inheritance until many citizens were virtually landless. Roman law insisted on partible inheritance, the more-or-less equal division of property among heirs. The practice persists today wherever the Roman legal tradition remains. It is a major obstacle to the preservation of a family's wealth. The only solution to the problems it created, apart from demographic catastrophe, was territorial growth. New lands acquired through conquest were distributed to Roman citizens, with those who commanded the legions taking the lion's share. Poor plebeians, faced with imminent bankruptcy, wanted a fairer division of this public land and an end to debt slavery.

These aims were not incompatible. Rich and poor knew that both could be achieved by combining forces against the patriciate. As a result, plebeian efforts to develop institutions and win for themselves a place in government were the dominant theme of Roman politics from the beginnings of the republic until the third century B.C. This Struggle of the Orders forged the basic institutions of the Roman state.

## The Evolution of Roman Government

The power of the patricians was deeply rooted in law and custom, but even before the fall of the monarchy it was in one sense an anachronism. The heart of the Roman army was infantry, and Roman survival depended upon the swords and spears of plebeians, not horse-mounted aristocrats. In Rome, as in the Greek polis, political rights would grow from military service.

The plebeians began their struggle in 494 B.C. when they answered a senatorial call to arms by leaving the city and refusing to fight against the Volscians, a neighboring people who threatened to invade Roman territory. This dramatic gesture won them the right to elect *tribunes*, who could represent their interests and defend them against unjust decrees by the magistrates. In the following year they erected a temple on the Aventine to Ceres, the Roman variant of the Earth Mother. Ceres, unlike the sky-gods favored by the patricians, had long been associated with peasants and artisans. The temple, along with its *aediles*, or wardens, gave sacred status to the plebeian cause and placed its tribunes under divine protection. It also provided the basis for a political organization. The meetings of the cult, which were open only to plebeians, issued decrees or *plebiscites* in opposition to the public assembly. This body soon evolved into an assembly that was regarded by plebeians as a kind of alternative government.

Pressure from the plebeian assembly bore fruit more than a generation later in the publication of the Twelve Tables (c. 451–450 B.C.). They were the first body of written law in Roman history, and Livy called them, with some exaggeration, "the fountainhead of all public and private laws." The codified laws reinforced the privileges of the patricians, recognized the plebeians as a distinct order, and indirectly offered them a measure of legal protection. Laws that were written down could not be altered at will by patrician judges who often acted out of self-interest or class prejudice. The tables also introduced the principle of equality before the law (*aequatio iuris*) because these laws applied to patricians and plebeians alike. The Twelve Tables themselves were destroyed during the Gallic sack of Rome in 387 B.C., and their provisions are known today primarily through the commentaries of later jurists (see document 4.4). Seen through the eyes of these commentators, the tables seem harsh and regressive. The principle of *patria potestas*, for example, gave the husband the powers of "head of the family" and instructed him to kill a deformed baby. Another table stated that women were perpetual minors under the guardianship of their fathers or husbands, a legal principle that persisted in European law for more than two thousand years. But if the Twelve Tables seem conservative in many respects, they were also an important step in the establishment of plebeian rights and the rule of law.

Among the more revolutionary features of the Twelve Tables was their recognition of wealth, in addition to birth, as a measure of social stratification. This may not seem like an advance, but it reflected an important part of the plebeian agenda. By 443 B.C. all citizens were ranked by property qualifications, which determined not only their military role but also their right to participate in the public or centuriate assembly that elected the magistrates. A new official, the *censor*, was elected to determine the rankings on an ongoing basis, and the census became an important civic and religious ritual (see illustration 4.4).

The entire body of male citizens was divided into centuries, roughly corresponding to the size of a maniple, the military unit that, in its original form, had probably contained about one hundred troops (see table 4.1). The centuries were in turn divided into classes ranging from the first class of heavily armed hoplites to a fifth class armed only with slings. The patrician *equites*, or cavalry, and the *proletarii*, who owned only their children and could afford no weapons, were technically outside the class system, but this was little more than a convenient social fiction. The important point

## ◈ DOCUMENT 4.4 ◈

### Ulpian: Roman Law

*The Roman jurist Ulpian was born at Tyre in Phoenicia and died in A.D. 225. His writings on the law comprise almost a third of Justinian's Digest of the Laws. (see chapter 6). In this selection he describes the moral and intellectual basis of Roman law and, in so doing, demonstrates its importance in Roman thought and practice. Note in particular Ulpian's understanding of natural law, which was to have a great influence on Western jurisprudence down to the present day.*

When a man means to give his attention to law, he ought first to know whence the term law (*ius*) is derived. Now it is so called from justice (*iustitita*). In fact, as Celsus neatly defines it, *ius* is the art of the good and fair. Of this art we may deservedly be called the priests; we cherish justice and profess the knowledge of the good and the fair, separating the fair from the unfair, discriminating between the permitted and the forbidden, desiring to make men good, not only by the feat of penalties, but also by the incentives of rewards, affecting, if I mistake not, a true and not a simulated philosophy.

This subject comprises two categories, public law and private law. Public law is that which regards the constitution of the Roman state, private law that which looks to the interest of individuals; for some things are beneficial from the point of view of the state, and some with reference to private persons. Public law is concerned with sacred rites, with priests, with public officers. Private law is tripartite, being derived from the rules of natural law, or of the law of nations, or of civil law. Natural law is that which all animals are taught by nature; this law is not peculiar to the human race, but is common to animals which are produced on land or sea, and to the birds as well. From it comes the union of male and female, which we call matrimony, and the procreation and bearing of children; we find in fact that animals in general, even the wild beasts, are marked by acquaintance with this law. The law of nations is that which the various people of mankind observe. It is easy to see that it falls short of natural law, because the latter is common to all living creatures, whereas the former is common only to human beings in their mutual relations.

Justinian. *Digest of the Laws* I: 3–4, from *Roman Civilization: Third Edition: 2 Vol. Set,* Naphtali Lewis and Meyer Rheinhold, eds. Copyright © 1990, Columbia University Press. Reprinted with permission of the publisher.

was that the *equites* and the hoplite class had enough votes between them to outnumber everyone else. This protected the wealthy of both orders and, on property issues at least, made them allies. Wealth rather than birth was becoming the chief source of political power.

Property issues came to a head after the Gallic invasion of 387 B.C. Many poor Romans lost their property and were forced into debt slavery. Popular rebellions in 385 B.C. and 375 B.C., though unsuccessful, led to a series of reforms. Under the Licinian-Sextian Laws of 367 B.C., plebeians were admitted to the highest offices of the state, and the popular assembly was allowed to pass laws, subject to senatorial approval. The result was a century of reforms. New laws abolished debt slavery and expanded the distribution of public land to poor citizens. Implementation was made easier by rapid territorial expansion during the second half of the fourth century B.C. The rich were prevented from seizing all of the gains. Finally, in 312 B.C., the Senate admitted plebeians to membership for the first time, and in 287 B.C. it lost its veto power over the popular assembly. The Struggle of the Orders had ended.

The government that emerged from this prolonged controversy was, in theory at least, carefully balanced to represent the interests of all Roman citizens and was for this reason of great interest to the theorists who, two thousand years later, framed the U.S. Constitution. Legislative authority rested in the centuriate and plebeian assemblies, though the decrees of the latter may not have been binding upon all citizens and the most important function of the centuriate assembly was to elect the consuls and other magistrates. Leadership of the state, including command of the army, was vested in two consuls who served one-year terms and could succeed themselves only after a ten-year interval. In theory, the consuls inherited the full *imperium* or authority of the old monarchy, and their edicts had the force of law. In practice, they consulted closely with the Senate and could veto each other's measures if necessary. In war, one consul normally commanded the legions while the other remained at home to govern, but it was not uncommon for both consuls to take the field and command the army on alternate days. In moments of extreme crisis, the consuls could also appoint a *dictator*, subject to senatorial approval. The dictator, who was always an experienced general, held absolute power for six months and could mobilize the resources of the state without legal interference.

These arrangements met the defensive needs of a small community, but as Rome expanded, campaigns grew longer. Armies had to be maintained in distant ar-

**Illustration 4.4**

💯 **A Census.** A census was taken every five years by the consuls of the republic to ensure that citizens were properly assigned to their classes and to facilitate recruitment into the army. On the right, citizens make their declarations to a scribe and an assessor in the presence of soldiers. On the left, a bull, a sheep, and a pig are offered in sacrifice. Like most civic rituals in the Republic, the census had a religious dimension as well. The reliefs probably date from 115 B.C. to 97 B.C.

---

### ⟡ TABLE 4.1 ⟡
### The 'Servian' Classification of Male Citizens

The classification of troops by the first census after the Servian reforms of 444 B.C. provides a measure of Roman wealth and population in the early republic. The classifications of wealth in terms of *asses*, a coin introduced in the third century B.C. when about thirty-three of them were needed to purchase a bushel of wheat, are therefore approximate, but scholars believe that they provide a fair estimate of the citizen population and its relative poverty.

| Class | Number of centuries | Number of men | Property qualification (in *asses*) |
|---|---|---|---|
| Cavalry | 18 | 1,800 | |
| I | 80 | 8,000 | 100,000 |
| II | 20 | 2,000 | 75,000 |
| III | 20 | 2,000 | 50,000 |
| IV | 20 | 2,000 | 25,000 |
| V | 30 | 3,000 | 12,500 |
| Engineers | 2 | 200 | Ranked with class I |
| Musicians, proletarians, and others | 3 | 300 | None |
| Total | 193 | 19,300 | |

Source: Adapted from T. Frank, ed., *An Economic Survey of Ancient Rome,* vol. 1 (Paterson, N.J.: Pageant Books, 1959), p. 20.

---

Other magistrates called *praetors* administered justice, though they, too, might serve as generals in time of war. Upon taking office they made a public declaration of the principles by which they would interpret the law, and these statements became landmarks in the development of Roman jurisprudence. The most respected office in the Roman state was that of *censor.* There were two of them, and they registered citizens as well as supervised morals and guaranteed public contracts. They could also remove senators from office on financial or ethical grounds. Other offices included the *quaestors* who assisted the consuls, especially on financial matters, and four *aediles,* who supervised markets and other public services. All were subject to interference from the tribunes, whose persons were still sacrosanct and who served as spokesmen for those who felt oppressed by the magistrates.

But the Senate, in theory no more than an advisory body, remained the most powerful institution of the Roman state (see document 4.5). Its members were originally appointed by the consuls; after 312 B.C. that right was given to the censors. Most senators were former consuls, which meant that they were men of great wealth and experience—the leading citizens of Rome. Few consuls dared to ignore their advice, and the quaestors, who were mostly young men ambitious for higher office, followed them without hesitation. Because the quaestors administered public expenditures, this gave the Senate *de facto* control over finance.

The Senate was also responsible for provincial affairs, including the distribution of newly acquired public lands and of income derived from provincial sources. This enormous source of patronage supplemented the vast resources already available to the rich and powerful. Whether patrician or plebeian, the senators were all *nobiles* and patrons who could count on the support of clients in the assemblies and at every level of the administration. They could therefore influence legislation

---

eas for years at a time. In 325 B.C., the office of *proconsul* was created by extending a consul's field command for the duration of the campaign even though his term as consul had expired. This institution, even more than the dictatorship, became a threat to the survival of the republic in later years, for it allowed the proconsul to develop an independent geographic and military base.

## ◆ DOCUMENT 4.5 ◆

### The Roman Constitution

*Polybius (c. 200–c. 118 B.C.) was a Greek who wrote the history of Rome's wars with Carthage and Macedon. He was also fascinated by the Roman system of government. The following is an excerpt from* The Histories *describing it as a mixed constitution with monarchic, aristocratic, and democratic elements.*

The consuls, before leading out the legions, remain in Rome and are supreme masters of the administration. All other magistrates, except the Tribunes, are under them and take their orders. They introduce foreign ambassadors to the Senate; bring matters requiring deliberation before it; and see to the execution of its decrees. If, again, there are any matters of state which require the authorization of the people, it is their business to see to them, to summon the popular meetings, to bring the proposals before them, and to carry out the decrees of the majority. . . .

The Senate has control of the treasury and regulates receipts and disbursements alike. . . . Similarly, all crimes committed in Italy requiring a public investigation such as treason, conspiracy, poisoning, or willful murder, are in the hands of the Senate. Besides, if any individual or state among the Italian allies requires a controversy to be settled, a penalty to be assessed, help or protection to be afforded,—all this is the province of the Senate. Or again, outside Italy, if it is necessary to send an embassy to reconcile warring communities, or to remind them of their duty, or sometimes to impose requisitions upon them, or to receive their submission, or finally to proclaim war upon them, this too is the business of the Senate.

After this, one would naturally be inclined to ask what part is left for the people. . . . Again, it is the people who bestow offices upon the deserving, which are the most honorable rewards of virtue. It also has the absolute power of passing laws; and, most important of all, it is the people who deliberate on the question of peace and war.

Polybius. "The Histories." In *The Histories of Polybius*, vol. 1, trans. Evelyn S. Shuckburgh. London: Macmillan, 1889.

in a dozen ways and affect its implementation by the magistrates when it passed.

The power of such networks was augmented by their tendency to combine within the Senate. There were no political parties as such, but the senators grouped themselves into factions or cliques associated with five great historic clans—the Fabii, Claudii, Cornelii, Aemelii, and the Valerii. At this level, cohesion was maintained in large part through friendship or agreement on policy. Able men of relatively humble parentage might also attach themselves to a senatorial clan and be carried by this informal sort of clientage to the highest levels of the state. In many ways, the organization of senatorial cliques mirrored that of society as a whole.

Factions of this sort could wield enormous power at every level of society. When they could agree on a policy, which was not unusual because they all came from the same social and economic group, their combined influence was overwhelming. The Senate's constitutional role as a mere advisory body was therefore an illusion. By controlling the informal mechanisms through which business was done, the Senate remained the heart of the Roman state.

◆

## The Wars with Carthage

The new constitutional order was put to the test in less than a generation. In 264 B.C. Rome embarked upon a mortal struggle with Carthage that threatened its existence and ended only after more than a century of bitter conflict (see document 4.6). The former Phoenician colony had become the dominant naval power in the western Mediterranean. Like their ancestors, the Carthaginians were great merchants and colonizers, but unlike them, they gradually assumed direct control of the colonies they had planted in western Sicily, Spain, Sardinia, Corsica, and the Balearic islands. Theirs was a true empire, financed by trade with three continents and defended by a magnificent fleet. Because Rome was still an agrarian state with few commercial interests, the Carthaginians did not regard it as a threat. For centuries the two powers had enjoyed a cordial if somewhat distant relationship.

The conflict known as the First Punic War (*punic* is the adjectival form of the Roman word for Phoenician) started in Sicily. A nest of pirates and mercenaries, the Mamertines, had established themselves at Messana

◆ DOCUMENT 4.6 ◆

## Polybius: Rome Compared with Carthage

*This comparison of the rivals Rome and Carthage is conditioned by the author's suspicion of democracy, but it remains a useful measure of their strengths and weaknesses.*

The constitution of Carthage seems to me to have been originally well contrived as regards its most distinctive points. For there were kings [sic] [the chief officials were annually elected *shofetim*, or judges] and the house of elders was an aristocratic force, and the people were supreme in matters appropriate to them, the entire frame of the state much resembling that of Rome or Sparta. But at the time when they entered on the Hannabalic War, the Carthaginian constitution had degenerated, and that of Rome was better. . . . [T]he multitude of Carthage had already acquired the chief voice in deliberations; while at Rome the senate still retained this, as in the one case the masses deliberated and in the other the most eminent men, the Roman decisions on public affairs were superior. . . .

But to pass to differences of detail . . . the Carthaginians are naturally superior at sea, both in efficiency and equipment, because seamanship has long been their natural craft, and they busy themselves with the sea more than any other people; but as regards infantry services, the Romans are much more efficient. They indeed devote their whole energies to this matter, whereas the Carthaginians wholly neglect their infantry, though they do pay some slight attention to their cavalry. The reason for this is that the troops they employ are foreign and mercenary, whereas those of the Romans are natives of the soil and citizens. So that in this respect also we must pronounce the political system of Rome to be superior to that of Carthage, the Carthaginians continuing to depend for the maintenance of their freedom on the courage of a mercenary force but the Romans on their own valor and that of their allies.

Adapted from Polybius, *Histories*, books 4: 2–3, trans. W. R. Paton. Loeb Classical Library. Cambridge, MA: Harvard University Press, 1960–1968.

(Messina), which controls the strait between Sicily and the Italian mainland. The Syracusans sent an army to root them out, whereupon one faction among the Mamertines appealed to Carthage, the traditional enemy of the Sicilian Greeks. When the Carthaginians gained control of the city, the other faction appealed to Rome. After long debate, the Senate agreed to help. The majority apparently felt that, if Carthage conquered Sicily, it could threaten the basis of Roman power in the south. No real evidence existed of Carthaginian interest in the mainland, however.

The resulting war was a long, drawn-out affair in which the Romans tried to besiege the Carthaginian towns in western Sicily. Though the Roman army won consistently in the field, it could do nothing to prevent the Carthaginians from bringing in supplies by sea. The Romans soon realized that only seapower could defeat Carthage and, for the first time in their history, constructed a navy (see illustration 4.5). After some remarkable victories and one catastrophic defeat, they destroyed the main Carthaginian fleet in an epic battle off Drepanum (Trapani) in March 241 B.C. Knowing that it could no longer hold Sicily, Carthage sued for peace.

Rome was now a major naval power and the ruler of Sicily, but peace did not last, for the attitude of Rome's political elite was changing. After the First Punic War, Rome's intentions became more openly aggressive and expansionist when the possibility of achieving vast wealth through conquest began to dawn on even the most honorable of men.

Sicily became the first Roman province. Its people were granted neither citizenship nor allied status. Roman governors exercised full powers unlimited by local custom—or by interference from the capital. They raised taxes to ruinous levels and distributed large tracts of land to wealthy Romans who worked them with slaves captured in the war. When Carthage's army, composed largely of mercenaries, rebelled in 238 B.C., the Romans took advantage of the situation and annexed the islands of Corsica and Sardinia. The Carthaginians saw that Roman imperialism had to be stopped.

Fortunately for Carthage, Rome was distracted for some years by a new war with the Gauls. Hamilcar Barca, a prominent Carthaginian who had waged guerrilla warfare against the Roman army in Sicily, used this respite to consolidate the Carthaginian hold on Spain. The Spanish interior was inhabited by a variety of Celtiberian tribes whose common characteristics included an aptitude for war. Hamilcar and his son-in-law

Ilustration 4.5

*A Roman Warship of the Late Republic.* The wars with Carthage forced the Romans to become a maritime power for the first time in their history. This segment of a frieze in the Vatican Museum shows troops disembarking from a galley of the type used during the Punic Wars.

and successor, Hasdrubal, bound them to Carthage by force or negotiation, creating in the process the nucleus of a formidable army. The Second Punic War (218–202 B.C.) grew out of Roman attempts to interfere with this process and nearly ended in the destruction of Rome. Rome demanded a treaty limiting Carthaginian expansion to the region south of the river Ebro but then formed an alliance with Saguntum, a city within the Carthaginian sphere of influence. The new Carthaginian commander, Hamilcar's son Hannibal (247–c. 183 B.C.), had long dreamed of avenging his country's defeat in the First Punic War. Knowing that the Romans would retaliate, he took Saguntum by siege. Then, while the Romans raised an army to invade Spain, he took the war to Italy, threatening Rome and forcing the Romans to divide their forces.

With his Spanish army, his African mercenaries, and a famous contingent of war elephants, Hannibal crossed the Alps and allied himself with the Gauls, whose hatred for Rome had in no way diminished. He knew that Rome was too large and well fortified to be conquered, but he hoped by a show of force to disengage the Italian allies from their allegiance. In spite of tireless diplomacy and exquisite care for the lives and property of the Italians, this effort was largely a failure.

Success in battle was easier to achieve. Hannibal defeated the Romans on the banks of the river Trebbia and then crossed the Appenines to defeat them again at Lake Trasimeno. The Romans adopted a mobile defense under the leadership of the dictator Quintus Fabius Maximus (known as Cunctator, or the delayer). Realizing that he could not defeat the Carthaginians in the

field, Fabius drew them into southern Italy, maintaining contact with the enemy but avoiding a battle. Many Romans felt that this strategy was for cowards, but when the successors of Fabius reversed his policies and sought a battle at Cannae in 216 B.C., the Roman legions were virtually annihilated. Hannibal had uncovered the tactical weakness of the Roman legions: They were trained only to move forward and were therefore vulnerable to cavalry attacks from the sides and rear. His Spanish and African infantry fell back before the Roman assault but did not break; his Carthaginian cavalry enveloped the Romans, leaving them surrounded. As many as forty-eight thousand were slain on the spot.

Cannae was the worst defeat in the history of the Roman republic and one of the great military disasters of all time. It led to the defection of Capua, the largest city in Campania, and indirectly to a revolt in Syracuse that threatened Roman control over Sicily. The Romans were forced to besiege both cities while reverting to Fabian tactics in Apulia where Hannibal remained at large. Rome was approaching the end of its agricultural and financial resources. Nearly 200,000 men were under arms in Spain, Italy, and Sicily. Italian agriculture had been devastated by the campaigns, and Rome was increasingly dependent upon imports of grain from Sicily and Sardinia. The Carthaginians, who understood the economic dimensions of war better than most, attacked the latter in 215 B.C. while forming an alliance with Philip V of Macedon, who harassed Rome's allies on the eastern shore of the Adriatic. Rome was engaged on no fewer than five fronts.

The turning point came in 207 B.C. when Hannibal's younger brother, who was in command of the Carthaginian garrisons in Spain, decided to reinforce him. A second Carthaginian army crossed the Alps, but the Romans, who had remedied the tactical deficiencies that had plagued them at Cannae, destroyed it before it could join forces with Hannibal. Hannibal's brother was killed, leaving Spain helpless in the face of a new Roman offensive. The Roman commander Publius Cornelius Scipio (236–c. 183 B.C.) was not yet twenty-five years old when he assumed the proconsulship, but he proved to be Hannibal's equal and the greatest Roman general of the age. By the end of 206 B.C. he had driven the Carthaginians from Spain (see illustration 4.6).

The loss of Spain meant that Carthage was deprived of its chief source of wealth and manpower. In 204 B.C. Scipio landed in Africa with a powerful army. Hannibal was recalled from Italy, and in 202 B.C. he fought his last battle against the Romans at Zama. Hannibal's North African allies deserted him, and Scipio won the title Africanus by defeating Hannibal with tactics similar to those used by Hannibal at Cannae. With their army destroyed, the Carthaginians agreed to peace terms that included the surrender of Spain and the islands and the dismantling of their war fleet. Rome was the undisputed master of the western Mediterranean.

## The Establishment of Roman Hegemony

Rome's victory over Carthage had been in doubt almost until the end. It was purchased with enormous expenditures of wealth and manpower. The ink on the treaty had scarcely dried when the Senate called for yet another war, this time in Greece. The motives for Roman intervention in that troubled region are unclear. The power of Macedon had waned during the third century B.C., and Greek politics was dominated by two loose and turbulent federations: the more aggressive Aetolian League in central Greece, and the Achaean League in the south. The result was constant warfare. This suited the purposes of three neighboring states with vested interests in the area. Rhodes, a commercial center with a fine navy, and Pergamum, a growing kingdom in western Asia Minor, feared the revival of Macedonian power and saw Rome as a potential ally. The third state, Ptolemaic Egypt, had since its founding attempted to undermine both Macedon and the Seleucid kingdom in Syria (see chapter 3). By 202 B.C. the balance of power among the three Hellenistic monarchies had been upset

Illlustration 4.6

Scipio Africanus. The Roman commander who defeated the Carthaginians was also the head of the aristocratic Scipio clan and a leading advocate of Greek culture. This bust from Herculaneum was carved after his death and is thought to be an accurate likeness.

by the accession of a child to the throne of the Ptolemies. Freed from the restraining influence of Egypt, Philip V of Macedon (238–179 B.C.) hoped to regain control over Greece and made common cause with the Seleucid monarch Antiochus III. Antiochus was not interested in Europe, seeking only to annex Palestine and those parts of Asia Minor that were under Egyptian rule. Though the situation was unstable, it did not appear to endanger Rome.

Many senators pretended to feel otherwise. On the eve of the Second Punic War, Rome had sent a naval expedition to suppress piracy along the eastern shore of the Adriatic. Philip V felt threatened by the navy's presence and, in the dark days after the battle of Cannae, declared war against Rome in alliance with Carthage. His action had little effect on the outcome of the war, but it was remembered. Many prominent Romans had grown enamored of Greek culture. Rome was still in many ways a crude place. It had yet to develop a literature of its own, and wealthy families relied upon Greek tutors to educate their sons. Some of these boys, including Scipio Africanus and most of his extended family, grew up to become ardent Grecophiles. Even hard-bitten traditionalists such as Cato spoke Greek and were familiar with Greek literature. The appeals of Rhodes and other Greek communities for protection against Philip therefore fell upon sympathetic ears.

In the war that followed, seapower gave Rome a decisive advantage, while the Roman maniples outmaneuvered the Macedonian phalanx at the battle of Cynoscephalae (197 B.C.). Philip was forced to retreat within his borders. He became a staunch ally of Rome and for the remainder of his reign concentrated on rebuilding the shattered Macedonian economy. The Greek leagues were left intact.

The Romans then turned their attention to Antiochus III. The Seleucid monarch had by this time achieved his goals in Palestine and Asia Minor. Egged on by Hannibal, who had taken refuge at his court, and by the Aetolian League, which had turned against Rome as soon as it was delivered from Philip, he took advantage of Macedonian weakness to cross the Hellespont and annex Thrace. This time, the Senate was less eager for war. Efforts to remove Antiochus from Europe by negotiation failed. He was routed in 191 B.C. at the historic site of Thermopylae by a Roman force under Cato. In the winter of 190–189 B.C. a second Roman army marched into Asia to defeat him again near Sardis. Antiochus abandoned all thought of Europe and surrendered most of his lands in Asia Minor to Rome's ally, Pergamon. The Romans kept nothing, but in 133 B.C. the childless Attalus III of Pergamum bequeathed the entire kingdom to Rome in his will.

The defeat of the two Hellenistic kingdoms proved that Rome was the dominant power in the Mediterranean world. Greece, meanwhile, remained unstable. Rome was forced to intervene repeatedly in Greek affairs, and with each new intervention, the Senate's impatience grew. Two main factions emerged. The Grecophile Scipios and their allies still hoped to achieve a settlement based on friendship with the Greek leagues. Their views have been preserved by Polybius (c. 200–c. 118 B.C.), an Achaean Greek who wrote the history of Rome's wars in Greece and with

**Illustration 4.7**

*⁄⁄* **Marcus Porcius Cato.** This bust, like that of Scipio Africanus, was carved after its subject's death. It captures the power of the great orator's personality and agrees with literary descriptions of his appearance. As a defender of traditional Roman values, Cato was the mortal enemy of the hellenizing Scipios and ultimately triumphed over them in the Senate. He failed, however, in his efforts to restrict the spread of Greek ideas.

Carthage and who was an important example of Greek influence on Roman thinking. The opposing faction was headed by Cato (see illustration 4.7), who was immune to any form of sentimentality and wanted an end to adventures in the east. He thought that contact with Greeks was corroding the traditional Roman values that he had extolled in his writings and, though he had no desire to annex Greek territory, was prepared to end their mischief-making by any means possible.

Cato's views gradually prevailed. Philip V's son, Perseus, allowed Pergamum to maneuver him into another disastrous war with Rome. The Romans defeated him at Pydna in 168 B.C. and divided Macedon into four parts, but their patience was wearing thin. They destroyed seventy towns in Epirus, which had supported Macedon, and sold 150,000 of its inhabitants into slavery. Troops were then sent to bolster the pro-Roman party in the Aetolian League, while one thousand hostages were taken from Achaea even though the Achaeans had supported Rome. One of them was Polybius, who used his exile to form a connection with the Scipios. The others were not so fortunate. Most were dispersed among the Italian provincial towns. Those who survived were returned in 151 B.C. after seventeen years in exile.

Meanwhile, a revolt had broken out in Macedonia under the leadership of a man who claimed to be Perseus's son. The Romans easily suppressed it and annexed Macedon as a Roman province, but the Achaeans, still angry over the hostage issue, decided to challenge Roman authority on several fronts. The response was devastating. In 146 B.C. the Achaean League suffered its last defeat on the battlefield. The Romans, thoroughly exasperated, destroyed the ancient city of Corinth in reprisal. They killed the men, enslaved the women and children, and carried away the city's priceless art treasures. They then abolished the Greek leagues and replaced democratic governments in several cities with oligarchies responsive to Rome. Years later the terms of settlement were loosened, but Greece remained a Roman protectorate with no independent policy of its own.

It is a measure of Rome's enormous power that, while annexing Macedon, defeating Antiochus, and re-ordering the affairs of Greece, the republic abandoned none of its ambitions in the west. Between 201 B.C. and 183 B.C. the Romans annexed Liguria, the area around modern Genoa, and settled their old score with the Gauls. The Gallic tribes south of the Po were defeated, and many fled beyond the Alps to be replaced by Italian colonists.

At the same time, the Romans embarked upon a bitter struggle for the Iberian Peninsula. After Carthage surrendered, Roman magistrates seized its Spanish colonies and extracted a fortune in tribute that came ultimately from mines in the interior. The towns, supported by a number of Celtiberian tribes, rebelled in 197 B.C., and Cato was sent to suppress them. Cato believed that "war supports itself." He insisted that his troops live off the country, and though modestly successful in military terms, his campaign of atrocity and confiscation ensured that the war would continue.

The Celtiberians resorted to guerrilla warfare. Other communities became involved, and it was not until 133 B.C. that Numantia, the last center of Span-

ish resistance, fell to the Romans after a lengthy siege. Scipio Aemilianus, the Roman commander and adopted grandson of Africanus, ordered it burned to the ground without waiting to consult the Senate. The siege of Numantia, like the war itself, had been conducted with unparalleled savagery on both sides. Whole tribes had been massacred even when they surrendered to the Romans on terms, but Spain, too, was now Roman territory.

Meanwhile, Carthage had been observing the terms of the peace treaty. Its military power and much of its wealth were gone, but the Roman faction headed by Cato wanted nothing less than the total destruction of its old rival. For years Cato had ended every speech in the Senate, regardless of the subject, by saying *"Ceterum censeo delendam esse Carthaginem"* ("Moreover, I think Carthage must be destroyed"). In 151 B.C. he and his followers saw their chance.

Since joining the Romans at the battle of Zama, the able and ambitious Masinissa, king of Numidia, had built a powerful North African state at Carthage's expense. When the Carthaginians tried to stop him, his Roman allies saw their action as a breach of the treaty. In a series of cunning diplomatic moves, the Romans demanded ever greater concessions, ending with a demand for the destruction of the city and the removal of its population. Surprisingly, the Carthaginians, who had been deprived of most of their weapons, refused. After a long and bitter siege, the city fell in 146 B.C. Carthage was destroyed as promised, and a furrow plowed through it that was then sown to salt to indicate that the land would never be occupied again.

By 133 B.C. Rome had acquired seven overseas provinces. Carthaginian territory was incorporated into the province of Africa and protected by an alliance with the Numidians. Spain, though technically a single province, had been divided in two by Scipio Africanus: Nearer Spain (*Hispania Citerior*), comprising the east coast from the Ebro valley to Cartagena, and Further Spain (*Hispania Ulterior*) to the south and west in what is now Andalusia. Macedon was protected by alliances with the Illyrians and by the utter dependency of the Greeks, while Sicily, Corsica, and Sardinia were islands in a sea commanded by the Roman fleet. Pergamum became the Roman province of Asia Minor.

The Romans had not planned to create a world empire and were at first unprepared to govern it. Their political institutions, though sophisticated, were those of a city-state. Financial structures remained primitive. The Senate would not extend ally status to the newly conquered regions and was at first reluctant to organize them into provinces or to maintain armies

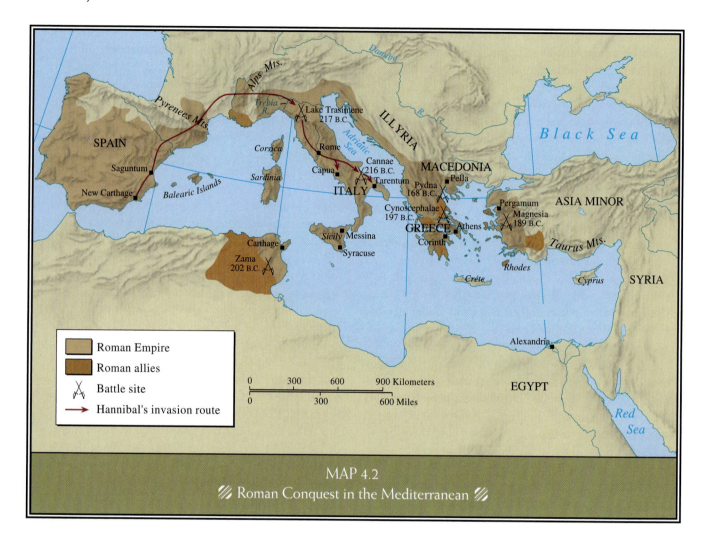

MAP 4.2

🍂 Roman Conquest in the Mediterranean 🍂

for their defense. Among other things, the senators feared that the creation of new magistrates and proconsuls might dilute their own membership and weaken their power as individuals.

Provincial charters varied widely. Different provinces were taxed at different rates and certain towns paid no taxes at all. In some places overtaxation caused widespread poverty, but whatever the rates, collection was almost always inefficient. Private contractors extracted cash, bullion, or agricultural commodities from taxpayers and kept a portion of the yield for themselves, a system that bred corruption and led to interminable complaints. The governors were at first admired for their honesty, but Roman virtue soon crumbled in the face of older, more cynical traditions. Bribes and extortion could make a magistrate rich beyond imagining. No imperial bureaucracy provided effective oversight and, for many, the temptation proved irresistible. Provincial government under the republic was not, in other words, as efficient or capable as it

would eventually become. It could be brutal and even extortionate, but for most of those who found themselves under Roman rule, it was probably no worse than the governments to which they had long been accustomed. The majority offered no resistance to the new order and in time accepted it as preferable to any conceivable alternative.

From humble beginnings, Rome had first conquered Italy and then an empire. In the mid-second century B.C. the Mediterranean world was politically united for the first time. Roman provinces stretched from the Atlantic to Asia Minor (see map 4.2), and those peoples who were not under Roman rule were Roman allies or dependents.

The Romans had not set out, like Alexander, to conquer new worlds, but neither had they acquired their empire in a fit of absentmindedness. They understood from the beginning that security depended upon controlling the activities of their neighbors. Gradually, "fear of the enemy," as Polybius put it, gave way to larger ambitions. Though hard evidence could come only from a transcript of Senate debates, Rome's elite seems to have adopted the goal of imposing order upon the world as they knew it. The Second Punic War was the turning point. After that narrow brush with catastrophe, a combination of greed and impatience led the Romans onward. But if the Senate was willing to shoulder new massive responsibilities, it refused to follow that willingness to its logical conclusion. Many years would pass before Rome learned to govern its new possessions effectively, and in the meantime, Rome had itself changed almost beyond recognition.

# CHAPTER 5

# SOCIAL, POLITICAL, AND ECONOMIC STRUCTURES OF IMPERIAL ROME

## CHAPTER OUTLINE

◆ ◆ ◆ ◆ ◆ ◆ ◆ ◆ ◆ ◆ ◆ ◆ ◆ ◆ ◆ ◆ ◆ ◆ ◆ ◆ ◆

The acquisition of an empire changed the basic fabric of Roman society and created tensions that could not be resolved by the existing political system. Civil strife produced by these tensions, and by the emergence of a professional army whose members had no stake in the preservation of traditional society, led in turn to the breakdown of republican institutions. Rival commanders struggled for control of the state until, in 31 B.C., Octavian, known as Augustus, emerged supreme and imposed a new system of government. Though he retained the outward forms of republicanism, Augustus was an autocrat. During the first century A.D. his successors gradually abandoned republican pretense and adopted the ceremonial trappings of the Hellenistic monarchies. The Roman world, governed by a quasi-divine emperor, was far larger than it had been under the republic and increasingly less "Roman."

◆

## The Transformation of Roman Society

Ordinary Romans gained little from the acquisition of an empire. Thousands found only an unmarked grave in some remote corner of Spain or the Balkans. Those who returned often discovered that their ancestral farms had been devastated by neglect or—after the Second Punic War—by the passage of armies. All faced a burden of wartime taxation that would have made economic survival difficult in any circumstances. The great senatorial families, meanwhile, profited enormously. Roman military commanders came almost exclusively from this class, and they took most of the loot from captured provinces. This included not only gold, silver, and commodities of every sort, but also tens of thousands of slaves. In addition, the Senate granted vast provincial estates to those whose leadership it regarded as outstanding.

The recipients of this new wealth invested much of it in Italy. Small farmers, impoverished by war and taxes, sold their plots to former officers who incorporated them into large, slave-worked plantations. Whenever possible, investors purchased land in different parts of the peninsula so that each property could be devoted to a specialized crop. This allowed owners to take maximum advantage of soil and climate while minimizing the risks of a bad harvest, for it was unlikely that every part of Italy would be hit simultaneously by drought or other catastrophes. Specialization also permitted economies of scale. Owners devoted careful thought to the optimum size for a vineyard, an olive plantation, or a ranch. Slaves may have been cheap in the aftermath of the wars, but feeding more of them than necessary was pointless.

Ideally, in addition to its cash crop, an estate produced just enough to support its labor force. Self-sufficiency reduced costs and was relatively easy to achieve, in part because slaves were no longer regarded as part of the family. In the past, most slaves had been Italian. Now they were foreign captives and therefore harder to fit into the fabric of Roman life. Conditions on some of the estates were appalling. In the Sicilian grain lands, slaves worked on chain gangs and were locked up at night. To be sold to the Spanish mines was a death sentence. Elsewhere, conditions were better, but even the most enlightened owners viewed slaves as an investment, and slave revolts were common (see document 5.1).

In this way wealthy families developed networks of specialized properties that brought in huge profits and insured them against risk through diversification (see illustration 5.1). Ordinary farmers could not compete. Their small plots were inherently inefficient, and they lacked the capital either to expand or to make improvements. If they tried to do so, they had to borrow from their wealthier neighbors, and though debt slavery had long been abolished, many lost their land through foreclosures. Others were forced out of business by unfair competition. Someone with a half-dozen great estates could easily sell below cost if by so doing he or she could drive out a competitor and pick up his land at distress-sale prices.

Citizens by the thousands gave up their land and migrated to the cities, but opportunities were limited. Imperialism had concentrated wealth in the hands of a few while doing little to increase the overall rate of economic activity. The rich developed habits of conspicuous consumption that horrified traditionalists such as Cato, but their most extravagant wants could be met by a handful of artisans, many of whom were skilled slaves

## DOCUMENT 5.1

### A Slave Revolt in Sicily

*The habitual mistreatment of slaves under the late republic provoked a series of terrifying slave revolts. The one described below by Diodorus of Sicily lasted from 134 to 131 B.C. and involved an army of more than seventy thousand slaves. Another great uprising occurred in Sicily in 104–100 B.C., and yet another in Italy under the gladiator Spartacus (73–71 B.C.) in which 100,000 slaves were said to have been killed.*

The Servile War broke out from the following cause. The Sicilians, being grown very rich and elegant in their manner of living, bought up large numbers of slaves . . . and immediately branded them with marks on their bodies. Oppressed by the grinding toil and beatings, maltreated for the most part beyond all reason, the slaves could endure it no longer.

The whole revolt began in the following manner. There was a man in Enna named Damophilus, magnanimous in his wealth but arrogant in disposition. This man was exceedingly cruel to his slaves, and his wife Megallis strove to outdo her husband in torture and general inhumanity toward them. As a result, those who were thus cruelly abused were enraged like wild beasts and plotted together to rise in arms and kill their masters. They applied to Eunus [a slave from Syria who was also a well-known magician] and asked whether the gods would speed them in their design. Performing some of his usual mumbo-jumbo, he concluded that the gods granted it, and urged them to begin at once. Thereupon they forthwith collected 400 of their fellow slaves and, when the opportunity presented itself, they burst fully armed into the city of Enna with Eunus leading them and performing tricks with flames of fire for them. They stole into the houses and wrought great slaughter. They spared not even the suckling babes, but tore them from the breast and dashed them to the ground. It cannot be expressed with what wanton outrage they treated wives before the very eyes of their husbands. They were joined by a large throng of the slaves in the city, who first visited the extreme penalty upon their masters and then turned to murdering others.

**Illustration 5.1**

Plan of a Typical Villa. This villa at Boscoreale near Pompeii was the headquarters of a typical working estate. Wealthy Romans spread their financial risks by investing in several such properties during the later republic. Worked by slaves, this one produced wine. The existence of a threshing floor (T) indicates that it was more diversified in its products than some other farms. Though comfortable enough by the standards of the time, the primary emphasis is on efficiency and practicality.

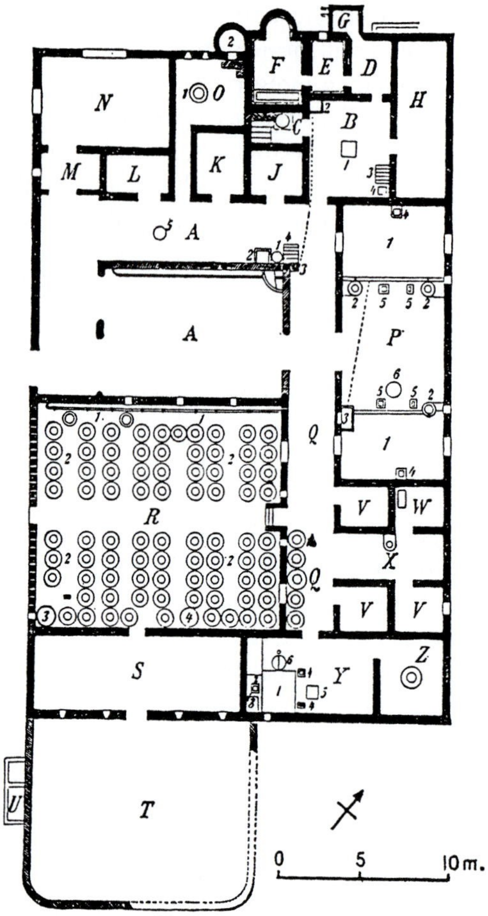

Villa no. 13 at Boscoreale. A, court: 1, 5, cistern curbs; 2, wash basin; 3, lead reservoir; 4, steps. B, kitchen: 1, hearth; 2, reservoir; 3, stairway; 4, entrance to cellar. C–G, bath complex. H, stable. J, tool room. K, L, sleeping rooms. M, anteroom. N, dining room. O, bakery: 1, mill; 2, oven. P, two wine presses: 1, foundations of the presses; 2, receptacles for the grape juice; 3, receptacle for the product of the second pressing; 4, holes for the standards of the press beams; 5, holes for the posts of the windlasses for raising and lowering the beams; 6, access pit to the windlass framework. Q, corridor: 1, wine vats. R, court for fermentation of wine: 1, channel; 2, fermentation vats; 3, lead kettle; 4, cistern curb. S, use unknown. T, threshing floor. U, cistern for water falling on the threshing floor. V, sleeping rooms. W, entrance to cellar. X, hand mill. Y, oil press: 1, foundations of the press; 2, hole for the standard of the press beam; 3, entrance to cellar; 4, holes for windlass posts; 5, access to windlass framework; 6, receptacle for oil. Z, olive-crusher

from the east. Slaves, whether in town or country, consumed little, and citizens who had been driven from the land consumed less. Most of the latter were destitute. After 213 B.C., senatorial factions began to distribute charity among them in return for votes.

Aside from the senatorial elite, only one other group appears to have benefited from the wars—the merchants, purveyors, and military contractors who organized the logistics of imperial expansion. Most were men of humble origin, often manumitted slaves who used knowledge and connections gained from their former masters to win contracts. They amassed great wealth in shipbuilding, arms manufacture, and commodity speculation and made an effort to acquire estates because land remained the most secure and prestigious source of income. Others followed the lead of certain senators and invested their surplus capital in urban real estate—ramshackle five-story tenements built to house the growing masses of urban poor. In later years these people would be known as equestrians, a separate class with a political agenda of its own.

Roman society had changed beyond recognition in little more than a century. Though pockets of traditional life remained, most small independent farmers who were the backbone of the republic had been reduced to dependency. Production was largely in the hands of slaves, while a few families lived in luxury that seemed more oriental than Roman. The situation could lead only to civil strife.

## Social Conflict: The Reforms of the Gracchi

In 133 B.C., the same year in which Numantia fell and Pergamum was ceded to Rome, a newly elected tribune, Tiberius Sempronius Gracchus, initiated reform legislation. A member of the aristocracy and a descendant of Scipio Africanus, he hoped to improve the condition of landless Romans by redistributing public lands acquired through conquest. Such properties were to have been allocated among the citizens as a whole, but families like his own often had seized them illegally through the use of political influence. His motives included both moral outrage and personal ambition; his most persuasive argument was practical. From the beginning of the republic, land ownership was a prerequisite for military service. An absolute decline in the number of free citizens caused by the wars, coupled with a loss of property by thousands of others, threatened the security of the state by shrinking its base of recruitment. Only by restoring land to Roman citizens could the legions be preserved.

A number of powerful senators agreed. The dislocations of the past century threatened to undermine recruitment as well as the moral fiber of society. Moreover, Tiberius tried to couch the proposal in terms acceptable to the landowners. Up to one thousand *iugera* (about six hundred acres) of land per family could be excluded from the distribution even if it had been taken illegally, and only Romans would receive the proceeds of the confiscations. This was not enough. Some senators balked at giving up land held by their families for three or four generations. They were backed by a tremendous outcry from the Italian allies. Wealthy Italians, too, had received public lands. They would be forced to surrender them, not to other Italians, but to Romans. To them, the reform was clearly discriminatory.

Faced with an uncertain outcome in the Senate, Tiberius decided to bypass it altogether. He went to the plebeian assembly, which rapidly authorized the necessary legislation. When another tribune vetoed the bill, he convinced the plebeians to vote the man out of office. Ignoring the Senate was bad politics, but deposing a tribune was unconstitutional. Then, to make matters worse, Tiberius left himself open to charges of corruption by entrusting the redistribution of lands to a committee composed of himself, his brother Gaius, and his father-in-law.

The Senate began to close ranks against Tiberius. While allowing the committee to proceed with its work, the senators refused to appropriate money for its support. This was critical, because land reform proved more difficult than Tiberius had expected. Establishing clear title to many public lands was nearly impossible, and virtually every decision aroused protest. Desperate for funds, he asked that revenues from the newly acquired kingdom of Pergamum be devoted to the task. The Senate saw this as an assault on its traditional dominance in the areas of finance and provincial policy. In its view, Tiberius and his reforms had become a threat to the constitution.

Knowing that, if he left the tribuneship, he would lose judicial immunity and be charged with treason by his enemies, Tiberius decided to run for a second term.

This, too, was unprecedented, if not unconstitutional. A group of senators claimed that he was trying to establish himself as a tyrant and instigated riots in which they and their clients killed Tiberius and three hundred of his followers. It was the first outbreak of civil violence in the history of the Roman republic, but it would not be the last. The divisions in Roman society were too great to be resolved without constitutional change, and ambitious politicians had learned from Tiberius Gracchus that they could ride to power on the shoulders of the multitude. Such people were called *populares*. Their opponents, who supported the traditional role of the Senate, were known as *optimates*.

Among the *populares* was Gaius Gracchus, the younger brother of Tiberius. When elected tribune in 123 B.C. he prepared to implement reforms more far-reaching than those favored by his brother (see document 5.2). Gaius realized that the agrarian problem was only one of many created by the transformation of Roman society. First he reenacted his brother's agrarian law, which had been repealed in 129 B.C. Then, knowing that not everyone could receive land in Italy, he guaranteed annual grain rations to every poor Roman at a fixed price and tried to set up overseas colonies for those willing to emigrate in return for land. The first of the new settlements was to be established on the site of Carthage.

To prevent the reversal of these policies by the Senate, he allied himself with the equestrians to weaken its power. The assemblies were given the sole right to establish capital courts, and he replaced senators with equestrians as jurors in cases of extortion. A more important attack on senatorial prerogatives came in the area of provincial administration. The Senate had for years influenced the behavior of consuls by waiting until after their election to designate which provinces they would control. By forcing them to make their appointments before the election, Gaius deprived the senators of an important source of political leverage. From the senatorial point of view this was even worse than another new policy by which he allowed syndicates of rich equestrians or *publicani* (the biblical publicans) to bid at auction for the right to collect provincial taxes. In later years this practice became a fertile source of corruption.

The issue of whether a tribune could succeed himself had apparently been resolved since Tiberius Gracchus's death, and Gaius was reelected tribune in 122 B.C. Having addressed the grievances of the poor and satisfied the equestrians in his first term, he turned to the problem of the Italian allies, who remained angry over agrarian reform and a host of other slights. His

## The Reform Program of Gaius Gracchus

*Here Plutarch summarizes Gaius Gracchus's plan for reforming Roman society as presented in 123–121 B.C. It is easy to see why the senators felt that he must be destroyed.*

Of the laws which he now proposed with the object of gratifying the people and destroying the power of the senate, the first concerned public lands, which were to be divided among the poor citizens; another provided that the common soldiers should be clothed at public expense without any reduction in pay, and that no one under seventeen years of age should be conscripted for military service; another concerned the allies, giving the Italians equal suffrage rights with the citizens of Rome; a fourth related to grain, lowering the market price for the poor; a fifth, dealing with the courts of justice, was the greatest blow to the power of the senators, for hitherto they alone could sit on the juries, and they were therefore much dreaded by the plebs and *equites*. But Gaius joined 300 citizens of equestrian rank with the senators, who were also 300 in number, and made jury service the common prerogative of the 600. . . . When the people not only ratified this law but gave him power to select those of the *equites* who were to serve as jurors, he was invested with almost kingly power, and even the senate submitted to receiving his counsel. . . .

He also proposed measures for sending out colonies, for constructing roads, and for building public granaries. He himself undertook the management and superintendence of these works and was never too busy to attend to the execution of all these different and great undertakings.

Plutarch. "Life of Gaius Gracchus," from *Roman Civilization: Third Edition: 2 Vol. Set,* Naphtali Lewis and Meyer Rheinhold, eds. Copyright © 1990, Columbia University Press. Reprinted with permission of the publisher.

for reelection in 121 B.C. When the assembly began to repeal its earlier reforms, rioting began. Gaius and a band of followers fortified themselves on the Aventine hill. The Senate declared martial law for the first time in its history, and the reformers were slaughtered. The violence was committed by Roman troops, not by members of the senatorial opposition and their clients.

### The Fall of the Republic

The Gracchi had tried to address Rome's fundamental problems and failed. Though the Senate's view of the constitution triumphed, at least for the moment, that failure led ultimately to the collapse of the republic. Equestrians and Italian allies felt excluded from their rightful place in the political system, and far too many citizens remained landless and dependent upon what amounted to welfare. The army, deprived of an adequate number of recruits, grew steadily weaker. Although not the time for foreign adventures, in 111 B.C. the Senate reluctantly declared war on Numidia. The African kingdom had been engulfed by a succession struggle during which the Romans backed the losing candidate. The winner, Jugurtha, celebrated his victory by murdering a number of Roman businessmen. Because most of the victims were equestrians, a tremendous outcry arose in the plebeian assembly, and the Senate was forced to give way.

For nearly four years the war went badly. The plebeian assembly and its equestrian allies knew that the senators disliked the war and began to suspect that some of them were taking Numidian bribes. In 107 B.C. they elected Gaius Marius consul. Like Cato before him, Marius (c. 157–86 B.C.) was a "new man" who came to politics with the support of an old senatorial family. To gain the votes of the assembly, he turned against his patrons. If his ethics were questionable, his military abilities were not. He defeated Jugurtha without capturing him and then turned his attention to the north where two Germanic tribes, the Cimbri and the Teutones, threatened the Roman settlements in Gaul. His lieutenant, the quaestor Lucius Cornelius Sulla (138–78 B.C.), was left to track down the Numidian and destroy him in a hard-fought guerrilla campaign that made his reputation and infuriated Marius, who thought that the younger man had taken too much credit for the victory.

War on two fronts when social dislocation had reduced the pool of eligible recruits made keeping the legions up to strength virtually impossible. Marius felt that he had no choice but to reform the army by admit-

proposal, though not original, was straightforward: Admit them to Roman citizenship. Had this been done, Rome might have been spared a bloody war, but the plebeian assembly had no desire to share its privileges. A conservative reaction set in, and Gaius was defeated

ting volunteers even if they owned no land. Recruits
were to be paid in cash as they had always been. Marius
also promised them a plot of land in Gaul or Africa
when they retired.

To thousands of slum dwellers and landless peasants, the Marian reforms offered an escape from grinding poverty, but the recruitment of proletarians created a
new danger for the state. Lacking property of their own,
the men became wholly dependent upon their commander for pay and, more important, for the security of their
old age. Though land and money came ultimately from
the Senate, neither could be obtained without the influence of the consul or proconsul who requested them.
The troops, in short, became the clients of their general
who could use military force to threaten the government. Rome was at the mercy of its own armies.

The implications of this change became evident after the Italian wars of 90–88 B.C. For decades the Italian
allies had sought Roman citizenship to no avail (see
table 5.1). Their patience exhausted, they abandoned
Rome and decided to form an independent confederation. Belatedly, the Romans extended citizenship to all
who returned to their allegiance, but two years of fighting were required to reach a final settlement.

Sulla, whose reputation as a soldier had grown
greater during the Italian wars, was elected consul in 88
B.C. with the support of the Senate. His services were
needed in the east, where Mithradates, King of Pontus,
had annexed parts of Asia Minor and invaded Greece.
The aged Marius came out of retirement and convinced
the plebeian assembly to appoint him commander instead. His action, based in part on personal resentment
of Sulla, provoked a lengthy crisis. Sulla, ostensibly to
defend the Senate, marched on Rome and drove out
Marius. When Sulla left for Asia, Marius returned with
his own army and conducted a bloody purge of his opponent's senatorial friends. Finally, in 83 B.C. Sulla returned and established a dictatorship. To do so he had
to conclude a compromise peace with Mithradates and
fight a civil war on Italian soil against the followers of
Marius, who had died of a stroke three years before.

Sulla's dictatorship was unlike any that had yet
been declared. It lasted four years and was intended to
reform the state from within, not to protect the state
from outside enemies. To do this, Sulla launched a
reign of terror by proscribing or outlawing his opponents, his personal enemies, and the rich, whose only
crime was that their property was needed to pay his
troops. He then passed a series of laws intended to
strengthen senatorial power and improve the criminal
justice system. Some of these changes survived his re-

## TABLE 5.1
### Citizenship in the Roman Republic, 264–70 B.C.

These census estimates refer only to adult male citizens
and are taken primarily from Livy. The lower figure for
208 B.C. seems to reflect the defection of Capua and
other allies after the defeat at Cannae as well as war
losses. The major increases after 204 B.C. and 115 B.C. reflect the expansion of citizenship rather than a change in
underlying demographics.

| Year | Census total | Year | Census total |
|---|---|---|---|
| 264 B.C. | 292,234 | 147 B.C. | 322,000 |
| 251 B.C. | 297,797 | 142 B.C. | 328,442 |
| 246 B.C. | 241,212 | 136 B.C. | 317,933 |
| 240 B.C. | 260,000 | 131 B.C. | 318,823 |
| 233 B.C. | 270,713 | 125 B.C. | 394,736 |
| 208 B.C. | 137,108 | 115 B.C. | 394,436 |
| 204 B.C. | 214,000 | 86 B.C. | 463,000 |
| 154 B.C. | 324,000 | 70 B.C. | 910,000 |

Source: Data from Tenney Frank, ed., *An Economic Survey of Ancient Rome*, vol. 1 (New York, N.Y.: Pageant Books, 1959), pp. 56, 216–17.

tirement in 79 B.C. Although Sulla was in theory a conservative who sought only to preserve the traditional
system, his career marked the end of constitutional
government. For almost a decade Roman soldiers had
been used repeatedly against Roman citizens and
against each other. Power now rested with the legions
and those who commmanded them, not with the Senate or the assemblies.

Sulla's departure created a political vacuum. Generals, including his former lieutenants Pompey and Crassus, vied for preeminence using the wealth and power
generated by proconsular commands. Such commands
proliferated mainly because the perception of disorder
encouraged Rome's enemies. Roman politicians welcomed the commands because they wanted armies of
their own as protection against their domestic rivals.
Spain rebelled under a former ally of Marius and had to
be suppressed by Pompey. At the same time, Italy was
threatened by a massive slave rebellion led by Spartacus, a Thracian gladiator. A direct result of the brutality
and greed of the slaveowners, it was put down with
great difficulty by Crassus, who crucified six thousand
of the rebels along the Appian Way between Rome and

Capua. To the east, Mithradates of Pontus resumed his aggression, while in the Mediterranean as a whole, widespread piracy threatened trade and communications throughout the empire.

The Senate responded to each crisis by granting extraordinary appointments, often in violation of the constitution, and then refusing full honors to the victors when they returned. The Senate was especially stingy in denying them the great ceremonial processions known as triumphs. Grants to veterans were also delayed. The senators thought that in this way they could weaken the authority of successful commanders, but their policy served only to irritate them. Although Pompey and Crassus feared and disliked each other, in 60 B.C. they made common cause with another popular politician, Gaius Julius Caesar (100–44 B.C.), to dominate the elections and create a kind of governing committee known as the First Triumvirate.

Pompey and Crassus had disbanded their legions when they returned to Rome. They either were loyal to republican institutions or failed to understand that Marius and Sulla had changed the political rules. Caesar's vision was clearer. He knew that talent alone was useless without an army, and he used the power of the triumvirate to grant him proconsular authority over Cisalpine Gaul. From 58 to 50 B.C. he conquered Gaul, an area roughly equivalent to modern France, and raided Britain. A master of public relations, he offered a selective account of these exploits in the *Commentaries*, a classic that remains the first book read by most students of Latin.

The Gallic campaign brought Caesar enormous wealth, an army of hardened veterans, and a reputation. The other triumvirs were less fortunate. Crassus died in 53 B.C. while fighting in Asia. At Rome, an inactive Pompey grew fearful of Caesar's ambitions, and the Senate, sharing his distrust, ordered Caesar to return home as a private citizen. Knowing that to do so would end his career and perhaps his life, Caesar crossed the Rubicon, the small river that divided Cisalpine Gaul from Italy, and marched on Rome in 49 B.C.

The civil war that followed lasted three years. Because legions loyal to either Pompey or Caesar could be found from Spain to Syria, it involved almost every part of the empire. Pompey was murdered at Alexandria in 48 B.C., but his friends continued the struggle until 46 B.C. when Caesar returned to Rome in triumph as sole consul. Caesar's power, like Sulla's before him, was based on control of a professional army whose ties to the political order had been broken by the Marian reforms. Unlike Sulla, Caesar did not in-

tend to retire. Though Caesar's rule was destined to be brief, the Roman republic had fallen, never to be revived.

## The Rise of Augustus and the Augustan Principate

Caesar's rule was generally benign and devoted to reform, including the proclamation of a new calendar that remained standard in Europe until the sixteenth century, but it was autocratic and clearly unconstitutional. On the ides of March (March 15) in 44 B.C. he was assassinated as he entered the Senate house. The conspiracy involved sixty senators under the leadership of G. Cassius Longinus and Marcus Junius Brutus, who believed that his death would restore the powers of the senatorial class. The murder led to thirteen more years of war and the establishment of what amounted to an autocratic state. The violent and dramatic events of this period have fired the imagination of writers and artists down to the present day and have been analyzed by a host of political theorists.

Caesar's heirs were his close associate Marcus Antonius (Mark Antony) and his grandnephew Gaius Octavius (63 B.C.–A.D. 14), then a boy of eighteen. Antony, in a famous funeral oration, turned the mob against Caesar's assassins and forced them to flee the city. Those senators who were not assassins but who favored the restoration of the republic feared that Antony, or Antony in combination with Octavius, would seize control of the state. Their leader was Marcus Tullius Cicero (106–43 B.C.), the brilliant lawyer, writer, and philosopher whose works are among the finest monuments of Latin literature. Cicero's political career had been blocked only by his failure to achieve military command. He was the finest orator of the age. He easily persuaded the Senate that Antony was unprincipled and a potential tyrant and that a consular army should be sent against him. He then tried to drive a wedge between Octavius and Antony, who resented that most of Caesar's enormous wealth had been left to the younger man.

Caesar's heirs disliked one another, but the policy misfired. When the consuls of 43 B.C. died fighting against Antony in Cisalpine Gaul, the Senate, on Cicero's advice, gave Octavius command of the armies but refused him the consulship because he was still only nineteen years old. The future Augustus, who now called himself Julius Caesar Octavianus, went to Rome with his legions and took the office by force.

Octavian, though young, understood the need for overwhelming military power. He made peace with those who commanded the remaining legions—Antony and a former Caesarian governor named Lepidus—and together they formed the Second Triumvirate. To consolidate their position and, above all to pay their legions, they launched a proscription that led to the death of more than three hundred senators, including Cicero, and two thousand equestrians who had, by definition, no part in politics. Octavian then turned his army against Brutus, who had taken refuge in Macedon, while Antony defeated Cassius in Syria. In the course of these actions, both of Caesar's assassins were killed in battle.

Octavian and Antony were the dominant figures of the triumvirate. With the removal of Lepidus in 36 B.C., they divided the empire between them. Octavian took the west; Antony, the east. Realizing that conflict with Octavian was inevitable, Antony turned for assistance to the Egyptian queen Cleopatra VII (69–30 B.C.). A woman of great charm and intelligence, Cleopatra was determined not only to revive the power of the Ptolemies, but also to play a part in Roman affairs (see illustration 5.2). To that end she had become Julius Caesar's mistress and traveled to Rome where she bore him a son. When Caesar died, she returned to Alexandria and arranged for the murder of her brother, who was also her husband and coruler according to the Egyptian custom. Now sole ruler of Egypt, she hoped that through Antony she could preserve the empire of the Ptolemies for herself and her children.

For his part, Antony needed the immense wealth of the Ptolemies to defeat Octavian. The alliance of Antony and Cleopatra resulted in the birth of twins as well as in a formidable conjunction of military and financial power. Octavian, in a skillful propaganda campaign, portrayed himself as the champion of Rome and the west against the decadent east as symbolized by the Egyptian queen. In 31 B.C. he defeated Antony and Cleopatra at the naval battle of Actium and followed them to Alexandria where, in the summer of A.D. 30, they both committed suicide.

Octavian became the undisputed ruler of the western world. With characteristic subtlety, he asked only that he be called *princeps*, or first citizen, and moved over the next seven years to consolidate his influence in ways that would not offend the Senate or other traditionalists. He treated the senators with courtesy, expanding their numbers and increasing their legislative power, but his much vaunted partnership with the Senate was a sham. The real basis of his power was proconsular authority over Spain, Gaul, and Syria, the border provinces that contained a majority of the legions. After 23 B.C. his proconsular authority was extended to Rome, and he was awarded the powers of a tribune, to

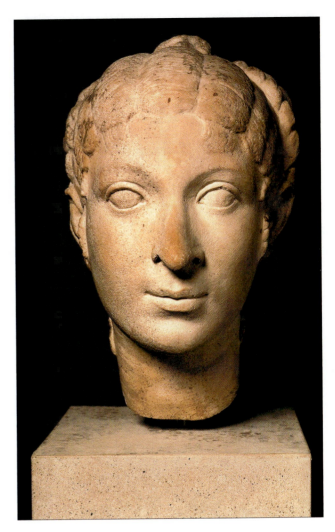

**Illustration 5.2**

⚜ **Portrait Bust of Cleopatra.** Cleopatra, the last of the Ptolemaic dynasty, failed to preserve Egypt's independence from Rome. Her defeat at Actium in 31 B.C. and subsequent suicide paved the way for Octavian's triumph.

be renewed annually for the remainder of his life. This enabled him to participate in the assemblies and gave him veto power over their legislation. As tribune, his person was also sacrosanct, though the Senate, in 27 B.C., had already granted him the semidivine title Augustus (see illustration 5.3). After 23 B.C. he left consular authority to others, accepting the office only on occasion.

In person, the new Augustus tried to appear modest and unassuming (see document 5.3). As an administrator, he was without equal. By controlling the electoral apparatus, Augustus made certain that magistracies went to men of ability with little regard for their origins. Provincial administration, a disgrace under the later republic, was greatly improved. Wherever possi-

**Illustration 5.3**

🖉 **Augustus as Princeps.** An idealized but recognizable statue of Augustus from Prima Porta.

ble, Augustus and his successors encouraged provincial cities to adopt Roman institutions and granted Roman citizenship to their leaders. Where this was impossible, they encouraged similar developments on a tribal level, often with considerable success.

The improvement of provincial government was essential in part because the empire continued to expand. The defeat of Antony and Cleopatra resulted in the annexation of Egypt. Augustus added several provinces in Asia, including Judaea, and extended the northern borders of the empire to the Danube and the Rhine. His successors would add Britain and Mauretania (Morocco), Armenia, Assyria, Dacia (Romania), and Mesopotamia (see map 5.1).

In Rome, Augustus embarked upon an ambitious program that replaced many of the city's old wooden tenements, established rudimentary fire and police ser-

vices, and improved the city's water supply. Much of this was accomplished by using the vast resources of Egypt, which he had appropriated, not by taxing the Romans. When Augustus died in A.D. 14, he had established a legacy of sound administration and what has been called the *pax romana,* an era of peace and prosperity that later ages would look upon with envy (see document 5.4).

### The First Emperors

Augustus's successors, the Julio-Claudian emperors, continued his administrative policies, though none of them was his equal as statesmen. His adopted son,

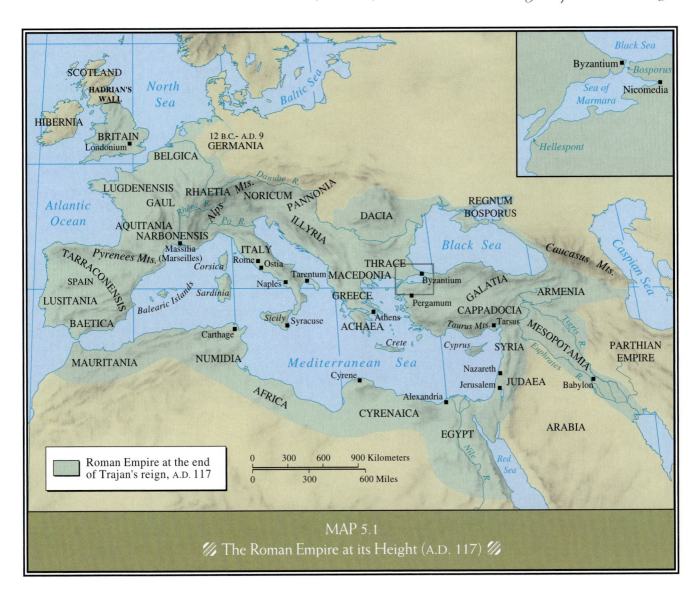

MAP 5.1

〃 The Roman Empire at its Height (A.D. 117) 〃

Tiberius, succeeded him by inheritance; Tiberius ruled A.D. 14–37. Caligula, Claudius, and Nero abandoned republican formalities, expanded the imperial bureaucracy, and sometimes treated the Senate with open contempt. Caligula so scorned the republican tradition that he designated his horse, Incitatus, as his coconsul. Augustus's successors institutionalized the powers that had been granted personally to Augustus and gradually appropriated semidivine status (see illustration 5.4). The Roman Empire became a hereditary monarchy, though as always, real power rested with the army. Claudius, thought wrongly by the Senate to be an incompetent figurehead, was placed on the throne by the Praetorian guard, an elite unit established by Augustus for the protection of the *princeps*. In spite of a speech defect and physical disabilities, Claudius astonished everyone by ruling capably and conscientiously. He took the first steps toward

establishing a regular imperial civil service staffed by members of the equestrian order.

Nero, whose tutor and chief adviser at the beginning of his reign was the Stoic philosopher Seneca, showed early promise. He neither was responsible for the great fire that consumed much of Rome in A.D. 64, nor did he fiddle while it burned, but his behavior grew increasingly more erratic with the passage of time. In A.D. 68, the legions began a series of revolts that ended with the emperor's suicide. The next year saw no fewer than four separate emperors, each a commander supported by his troops in the hope of securing their retirements by seizing the *imperium*. The last of them, Vespasian (ruled A.D. 69–79), established the Flavian dynasty, which lasted until A.D. 96, and formally adopted the title *imperator* or emperor. When his descendant, Domitian, left no successor, the Senate revived sufficiently to appoint another general in his

### ◈ DOCUMENT 5.4 ◈

## Plutarch: The *Pax Romana*

*The* pax romana *referred to the peace within the empire that had been established by Augustus. Though it did not preclude a number of regional revolts, it was a remarkable achievement and, as this sensible if unheroic passage from* Precepts of Statecraft *makes clear, the primary justification for Roman rule.*

The greatest blessings that cities can enjoy are peace, prosperity, populousness, and concord. As far as peace is concerned, the people have no need of political activity, for all war, both Greek and foreign, has been banished and has disappeared from among us. Of liberty the people enjoy as much as our rulers allot them, and perhaps more would not be better. A bounteous productiveness of soil; a mild, temperate climate; wives bearing "children like their sires" [a quotation from Hesiod] and security for their offspring—these are the things that a wise man will ask for his fellow citizens in his prayers to the gods.

place named Nerva, who ushered in the age of the five good emperors. Neither Nerva nor the three emperors who followed him (Trajan, Hadrian, and Antoninus Pius) had sons, and each appointed a successor who was acceptable to both the Senate and the legions. (The fifth emperor of the period was Marcus Aurelius.)

The age of the five good emperors (A.D. 96–180) was later remembered as one of exceptional happiness. The *pax romana* or Roman Peace described by Plutarch seemed to be a permanent condition, and trade flourished. Trajan and Hadrian sponsored lavish building programs, and Trajan introduced the *alimenta*, a subsidy to help poor parents in raising their children. All five emperors refined and strengthened imperial administration, but the possibility of military intervention remained. The Stoic philosopher Marcus Aurelius (ruled A.D. 161–180) broke the tradition of appointment by merit, not only by having a son, but also by having the poor judgment to leave him the throne. The reign of Commodus, from A.D. 180 to 192, was a disaster that ended in yet another military revolt. But by this time the empire was experiencing difficulties that had little to do with the personality of its rulers.

◈

## Art, Literature, and Thought in Imperial Rome

Throughout the late republic and early empire, the culture of Rome's elite remained heavily dependent upon Greek models. Painting and sculpture were an integral

**Illlustration 5.4**

▧ **Base of the Column of Antoninus Pius.** This scene shows the apotheosis of the emperor Antoninus (reigned A.D. 138–161) and his wife, Faustina; that is, the imperial pair are in the process of becoming gods after their death. Based on the symbolism of the eagles, they are about to become the new Jupiter and Juno, an indication of how the imperial office had become deified.

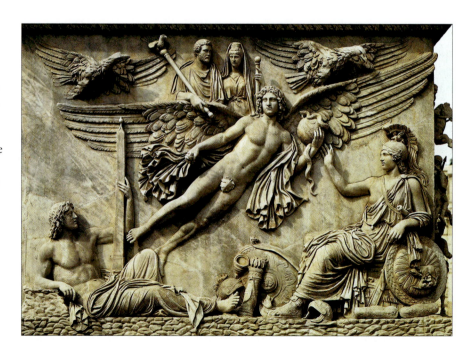

**Ilustration 5.5**

🟊 **A Roman Family.** This relief probably came from a tomb on the outskirts of Rome. It shows L. Vibius, his wife, and what appears to be the death mask of a son who died in childhood. Based on the woman's hairdo, the work has been attributed to the time of Augustus.

part of most public places and adorned the luxurious palaces of the rich. Reliefs on public buildings featured mythological subjects or idealized versions of historic events. Private collectors bought reproductions of famous Greek statues from Roman workshops, and a thriving trade existed in bronzes from Greece. In some cases these skillful copies provide the only access to lost originals. Only in portrait statuary did the Romans break with established tradition. Ignoring the Greek tendency to idealize the human form, they produced busts whose photographic realism is a monument to individual men and women (see illustration 5.5).

Architecture, too, abandoned Greek precedent. Temples and theaters recalled Hellenistic models, while other public buildings used the arch and vault construction favored by the Etruscans. Augustus and his successors built baths, aqueducts, warehouses, and stadia for games and chariot races whose scale virtually precluded the post-and-lintel construction of the Greeks. Some structures, such as the Mausoleum built by Augustus for his family and the Pantheon constructed by Hadrian, featured domes that spanned enormous spaces. Increasingly, columns, friezes, and pediments evolved into decorative elements without structural purpose. Engineering and an imperial taste for grandeur triumphed over the aesthetics of simplicity.

In philosophy as in art, the Romans tended to borrow Greek conventions and adapt them to their own

purposes. The dominant current in Roman thought was Stoicism. Cicero, Seneca (4 B.C.?–A.D. 65), and the emperor Marcus Aurelius wrote extensively on Stoic themes, in part because, as men of affairs, they appreciated the philosophy's moral activism and the comfort it offered a politician in difficult times (see document 5.5). Their emphasis, however, was on the practical application of Stoic principles, and their writings added little or nothing to the speculative tradition.

The same might be said of Roman writings on science. Alexandria remained the center of scientific and philosophical inquiry, and Greek the primary language of scientific publication. The most important scientific work in Latin, the *Natural History* of Pliny the Elder (A.D. 23–79), was little more than a vast compendium of information, much of it false, gleaned by the author from nearly 500 sources—327 of them Greek. The work is important primarily because it summarized ancient knowledge and transmitted it to a later age.

Roman literature was more original than Roman thought. By ancient standards, literacy was widespread in the late republic and early empire (perhaps 15 percent of the population), and books were produced in large numbers. As many as thirty copies at a time could be produced by having a reader dictate to slaves who wrote the words on papyrus scrolls. A more modern form of the book, the codex, made its appearance in the first century B.C. Written on vellum or parchment and bound in leather, it was preferred by lawyers and, later, by Christian scholars who needed to compare several texts at a time and found codices more convenient to handle than scrolls.

The Romans favored practical treatises on agriculture, the mechanical arts, law, and rhetoric. Cicero, as the most successful litigator of his day, was especially valued for his attempt to reconcile traditional jurisprudence with the Stoic idea of natural law and for his writings on oratory. His work, together with that of Quintilian (c. A.D. 35–c. 100), elevated rhetoric to a science and had a profound impact on educational theory. Another literary form unique to Rome was the publication of personal correspondence, with Cicero and Pliny the Younger providing the best and most interesting examples. History, too, was popular, though it was rarely studied in a spirit of objective inquiry. Caesar wrote to advance his political career, while Livy (see chapter 3) sought to revive republican virtue. Tacitus (c. A.D. 56–c. 120) produced a history of the early emperors from a similar point of view, while his younger contemporary, Suetonius, provided a background of scandalous personal gossip in his *Lives of the Caesars*. The vices he attributes to the Julio-Claudian emperors transcend normal human capacities. Plutarch (c. A.D. 46–after 119), a Greek whose popular *Lives* included famous Romans as well as Greeks, pursued a less sensational approach to biography and wrote extensively on ethics.

These contributions, however great, pale by comparison with the poetry that made the Augustan age synonymous with Rome's highest literary achievement. The greatest of the Augustan poets, Virgil (70–19 B.C.), was responsible for the *Eclogues*, a series of pastoral poems based loosely on Hesiod, and for his masterpiece, *The Aeneid*, the national epic about the founding of Rome. Both were gratefully received by Augustus as expressions of the civic virtue he was trying to encourage. The *Odes* and *Satires* of Horace (65–8 B.C.) were equally acceptable, but the works of Ovid (43 B.C.–A.D. 17) were not. Augustus was sufficiently offended by his *Ars Amatoria*, a poetic manual of seduction, to exile the poet to a remote town on the Black Sea.

Surprisingly, drama, the most public and political of all art forms, never achieved greater importance in

Rome. Greek tragedies aroused enthusiasm among Roman intellectuals, but the public preferred comedy. Plautus, in the late third century B.C., and Terence in the second century B.C., produced works that, though based heavily upon the Greek New Comedy, had a ribald vigor. In later years, public taste turned toward mime and simpleminded farce, while theater attendance declined as gladiatorial combats and similar entertainments became more popular. The nine tragedies of Seneca, so inspiring to the great dramatists of the late Renaissance, were apparently written to be read, not performed.

## The Social and Economic Structures of the Early Empire

The age of Augustus and the century that followed were a time of relative prosperity. Italy and the regions affected by the civil wars recovered quickly, and neither Augustus nor his successors afflicted their subjects with excessive taxation. Their policies were conducive to economic growth, because the *pax romana*, by uniting the western world under a single government, limited warfare to the periphery of the empire and created a market of unprecedented size. Tariffs on the transfer of goods between provinces generated revenue but were too low to inhibit trade. For the first and last time in its history, the west had uniform coinage and systems of banking and credit that transcended national boundaries.

The policy of settling veterans on land of their own, though it sometimes dispossessed existing farmers, may also have temporarily improved the well-being of the peasant class. The initial effect of these resettlements was to reduce the number of *latifundia*, or great slave-worked estates. Many regions saw a resurgence of the small independent farm, while middling properties of the kind described by Cato prospered. The number of slaves declined, in part because the annexations of Augustus did not involve the large-scale enslavement of new subjects, and in part because manumission was common. On the estates that remained, the treatment of slaves appears to have improved. Slaves grew more valuable as the supply dwindled, and owners found that they could best be replaced by encouraging them to reproduce. The Augustan age did not see a resumption of the three Servile Wars, such as the slave rebellion led by the gladiator Spartacus, fought during the last century of the republic.

In time, however, the economies of scale that had doomed the small farmers of the republic reasserted themselves. Not every veteran understood agriculture; those who did could not always compete with their larger neighbors. Eventually, these men or their descendants sold their farms and returned to the city, or they became tenants (*coloni*) of the great estates. In the early empire, *coloni* remained technically free, leasing their land and returning a portion of the yield to the estate owner. This was thought to be less efficient than slavery, but it became increasingly common as slaves grew scarcer. Once again the average size of properties began to grow and peasant income resumed its decline. By the end of the first century A.D. half of the land in the province of Africa was owned by six men.

Changes in the distribution of wealth were therefore both temporary and relative. If veterans benefited from the distribution of land and from cash payments derived from booty, the wealthy gained even more from imperial gifts. Townspeople, too, received payments from the emperors as a kind of bribe for good behavior and sometimes found work on the construction projects funded by Augustus from the spoils of Egypt. Another burst of prosperity seems to have followed the great fire of A.D. 67, which destroyed much of Rome; Nero financed a massive reconstruction that gave work to thousands. Temporary benefits of this kind may have improved the lives of ordinary people, especially in Italy, but the amounts involved were too small to expand significantly their role as consumers or to change the basic distribution of wealth.

The economic polarization that had characterized Roman society since the second century B.C. continued to influence the development of trade (see table 5.2). Though Julius Caesar had attempted to limit the number of Romans eligible for the grain dole, it remained available to all Roman citizens under Augustus. This, together with the policy of urbanization in the provinces, ensured the continuation of a massive trade in bulk agricultural commodities (see map 5.2). Spain, Africa, Sicily, and, above all, Egypt exported vast quantities of grain to the growing cities of the empire. Italy produced wine and oil, but it had many competitors and probably lost in relative economic importance as the first century B.C. progressed.

Meanwhile, the lack of an adequate consumer base limited manufacturing. Something like a mass market existed for metal tools and weapons, and several Italian towns produced red-glazed pottery for export to every corner of the empire. Some potteries may have employed more than fifty workers, most of them slaves.

## TABLE 5.2
## Roman Wages and Prices in the Late Republic

These figures regarding wages and prices are estimates for central Italy c. 150 B.C. Prices of wheat in particular fluctuated wildly during the civil wars, but the numbers listed below are a fair estimate of those in the early years of Augustus. Prices were lower in the Po valley and in other areas remote from Rome. There were sixteen copper asses or four sesterces in a silver denarius. The difference in wages between a slave hired for the day and a free laborer demonstrates why so many of the latter were unemployed.

| Service or product | Average cost |
| --- | --- |
| Unskilled slave laborer | 2 sesterces per diem |
| Free laborer | 3 sesterces per diem |
| Soldier | 120 denarius per annum |
| Wheat (enough for 20 lbs. of bread) | 3 sesterces per *modius* |
| Barley | 2 sesterces per *modius* |
| Wine (average grade Italian) | 3–4 *asses* per liter |
| Wine (best imported) | 1–4 denarius per liter |
| Olive oil | 6–8 *asses* per liter |
| Beef | 4–5 *asses* per lb. |
| Pork | 2–3 *asses* per lb. |
| Clothing (Cato's toga, tunic, and shoes) | 100 denarius |
| A farm slave | 500 denarius |
| An ox for plowing | 60–80 denarius |
| A sheep | 6–8 denarius |
| A cavalry horse | 500 denarius |

Source: Data from Tenney Frank, ed., *An Economic Survey of Ancient Rome*, vol. 1 (New York, N.Y.: Pageant Books, 1959), p. 200.

Woolen cloth, once processed in the home, was more commonly manufactured for sale. The size of this trade is difficult to estimate, and it, too, probably employed mostly slaves. Generally speaking, the availability of slave labor, though declining, continued to hold down the wages of free workers and to restrict the development of technology. Perhaps the greatest innovation of the period was the development of glassblowing at Sidon.

Most commodities were more limited in their distribution. Egypt retained its monopoly on papyrus, and the cities of what had once been Phoenicia produced glass and the expensive dyes and textiles for which they

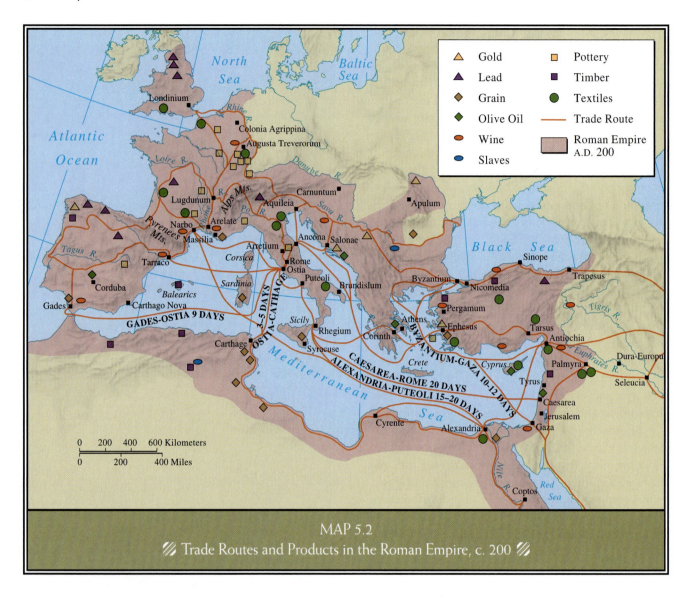

Gold △
Lead ▲
Grain ◆
Olive Oil ◆
Wine ⬭
Slaves ⬭
Pottery ▨
Timber ◼
Textiles ●
— Trade Route
Roman Empire
A.D. 200

GADES-OSTIA 9 DAYS
3–5 DAYS
OSTIA-CARTHAGE
CAESAREA-ROME 20 DAYS
ALEXANDRIA-PUTEOLI 15–20 DAYS
BYZANTIUM-GAZA 10–12 DAYS

MAP 5.2
⧗ Trade Routes and Products in the Roman Empire, c. 200 ⧗

had long been famous. Linens, drugs, perfumes, precious stones, and such delicacies as dried fruit and pickled fish came from various sources within the empire. Other luxuries came from far away. The Silk Road across central Asia connected Syria with China. More than a hundred ships sailed annually from the Red Sea ports to India for cargoes of spice, and Africa continued as it had for centuries to provide the Mediterranean world with gold, ivory, palm oil, and those hardy perennials, frankincense and rhinoceros horn.

Almost without exception, these were low-volume, high-profit trades that entailed a substantial element of risk. They made a few people, mostly equestrians or freedmen who eventually merged with the equestrian class, enormously rich, but the prosperity they generated was not widely shared. Aristocrats, too, sometimes invested in such ventures or speculated on the com-

modities market. They usually did so through agents because the old prejudice against trade died hard. Overall, the economy of the empire remained agrarian, and mercantile activities were restricted to a few.

In the first century A.D. a million people may have lived in the city of Rome, a nearly incredible total given the limits of ancient technology and systems of distribution. As in any community, their lives were constrained by an elaborate social structure. While most were desperately poor, few would have chosen to live anywhere else. Rome was, to the Romans, the center of the world.

About one-third of the city's land area was occupied by the palaces of the rich, the most spectacular of which were clustered on the Palatine Hill. Some of these structures, with their courtyards, galleries, baths, and gardens, covered several acres and employed hun-

**Illlustration 5.6**

**Central Courtyard of a Roman Villa (First Century A.D.)**
The homes of wealthy Romans were normally one story in
height and built around a series of courtyards. This one, from
the House of the Vettii in Pompeii, is unusually graceful. It was
preserved in 79 A.D. when the volcano Mt. Vesuvius buried Pompeii in volcanic ash, killing most of the city's twenty thousand
inhabitants.

dreds of domestic slaves. Because Romans believed, or
pretended to believe, that the pursuit of wealth and luxury for their own sake was dishonorable, such homes
were meant to fulfill a public function. The atrium, or
courtyard, and the rooms that surrounded it were devoted to entertaining and conducting business (see illustration 5.6). The rear of the house with its garden or
gardens provided a retreat for the family.

The senatorial or equestrian families that lived
within derived their wealth primarily from land, though
virtually all engaged in some form of trade or speculation as well. Most therefore owned country villas in addition to their city property. Cicero, who was not
particularly wealthy, owned eight such residences in
various parts of Italy and visited them according to the
season.

The life of such a man began at dawn, when he was
visited by his clients who came to show their respect,
request favors, or receive his instructions. Most of the
day was devoted to politics, business, or the law courts,
but like Romans of every class, the rich found time for
physical exercise and an elaborate bath before the main
meal of the day. In imperial times, this was usually
taken in the evening and might involve a banquet of
epic proportions. Women sat upright, while the male
guests reclined on couches around a central table and
consumed delicacies brought from specialized farms in
the area around the city. Songbirds, exotic fruits, and
fish grown in special ponds were extremely popular, as
were vintage wines such as the famous Falernian. Excess
was common. Afterward, the guests would return
home, sometimes in coaches or litters, but always accompanied by a small army of bodyguards. After dark,
the Roman streets were dangerous.

Moralists seeking a return to the more restrained
attitudes of an earlier time objected to this behavior.
Their complaints had little effect until Augustus began
to support reform as a matter of official policy. Romans
of the late republic and early empire believed in physical fitness, but they had long since lost Cato's taste for
simplicity and their attitude toward sex had become remarkably casual. Homosexuality and bisexuality,
though perhaps not as common as among the Greeks,
were mocked but tolerated even in public figures such
as Julius Caesar. Casual sex of every kind was encouraged by the institution of slavery.

Roman women, too, had achieved a level of sexual
and personal freedom that has rarely been equaled before or since. In the first century B.C. they acquired the
legal right to own and manage their property apart
from that of their husbands. The women of the upper
classes therefore owned slaves and managed estates of
their own. Many were successful businesswomen, and
not a few involved themselves in politics.

Economic independence freed such women from
marital tyranny, and in some cases encouraged both
sexes to seek divorce for political or financial advantage. Among the more prominent families, four or five
marriages in succession were not uncommon, and extramarital affairs were frequent. No real penalty was
meted out for such behavior, because divorce was regarded as a private matter under the laws of the republic and could be concluded by simple agreement.
Wives in such cases retained their dowries. Tradition
held that adultery was punishable by death, but the
law in question was confusing and had not been enforced for generations.

Augustus believed that this situation undermined
traditional Roman virtues and deterred men from marrying, at least in part because they could not control
their wives. Other reasons existed for a precipitous decline in marriage rates among the Roman upper class.
An increasing number of both sexes regarded children
as an expensive nuisance and preferred to remain single,
believing that they could guarantee a far more pleasant
life by surrounding themselves with legacy hunters who
hoped to be included in their wills. Beginning in 18 B.C.

Augustus tried to legislate against these abuses by demanding seven witnesses to a divorce and making it possible for a man—though not a woman—to sue for adultery thereafter. Legacy hunters were restrained by limiting the bequests that could be received by widowed or unmarried persons. Augustus's efforts aroused intense opposition and seem to have had little immediate effect beyond enriching the treasury with the estates of those whose heirs had been disqualified, but they mark a turning point of sorts in the history of Roman morals. Others shared his distaste for sexual license and their attitudes, later reflected in those of Christianity, gained ground with the passage of time.

Augustus may have been right in thinking that divorce and sexual misconduct led to social instability, but their prevalence did not imply that all of the men and women of the Roman upper class were irresponsible pleasure seekers. A high level of education, secured largely by private tutors, was common to both sexes, and magnificent private libraries were a status symbol. Moreover, a measure of debauchery did not seem to interfere with the effective management of complex enterprises. In the Roman system of values, the ability when necessary to control the passions, not the vice, mattered.

Slaves were the constant companions of the rich, and even poor households might own one or two. They may at various times have numbered as much as a third of the city's population, but their role in Roman society defies easy categorization. The lot of the urban slave was in some ways preferable to that of the poor citizen.

Domestic slaves lived as part of their master's household and were sometimes friends or lovers. Others were highly skilled professionals: teachers, physicians, librarians, or entertainers who might have homes of their own in the city and earn additional fees by offering their services to the general public. Craftsmen and industrial workers generally lived apart and returned a portion of their earnings to their owners, keeping the rest for themselves. Though slaves, their daily lives were similar to those of ordinary citizens.

Roman slavery was a legal and personal relationship that had little to do with lifestyle. Simply put, slaves were not persons under the law. The only virtue required of them was loyalty to their master, and they could neither serve in the army nor participate in public life. Though slaves could testify in court, it was customary to torture them first on the theory that this released them from their obligation of loyalty. Corporal punishment was sometimes inflicted by owners as well, but the emperors introduced legislation against the worst

excesses. Claudius forbade the exposure of slaves who were old or sick. Domitian prohibited castration, and Hadrian abolished private executions, even for criminal behavior.

As is often the case with legislation, these acts lagged far behind practice. Most owners knew that the system worked only if the loyalty of the slaves were genuine. No one would want to be shaved by a malcontent or protected by untrustworthy bodyguards. Slaves who rebelled might expect the fate of Spartacus. Those who were merely difficult might be threatened with being sent to the farm, a fate that for most of them must have seemed worse than death.

Though kindness was important, the prospect of manumission was a better guarantor of personal and public safety. Urban slaves of either sex could look forward to being freed, usually by the time they reached age thirty. This was about the average life expectancy in ancient Rome, but many lived far longer, and, as in all preindustrial societies, the percentage of very old people in the population was probably not much less than it is today. To know with reasonable certainty that one would be freed mitigated despair, but it also made economic sense for the owners.

The Roman system allowed slaves to purchase their freedom as soon as they could accumulate their purchase price. Those who worked outside the household could do this easily. Domestics, too, were often encouraged to develop private sources of income. The owner could then use the most productive years of a slave's life and recover his or her purchase price before sickness and old age diminished the total profit. As an added incentive to manumission, the freed slave became the owner's client, a relationship that might work to the advantage of both.

After the third century B.C. nearly all slaves were foreigners, with Gauls, Syrians, and Africans being perhaps the most numerous. Rome was therefore a multi-hued city of immigrants in which people from every corner of the known world mingled without apparent racial tension. Consciously or not, slavery was the means by which they were turned into Romans. The owner purchased them, introduced them to Roman ways, and in many cases provided them with the training and education needed to survive. Once free, their lives were often more prosperous than those of citizens who had nothing but a monthly allotment of grain.

Most of Rome's free citizens were officially categorized as poor. Some found work, often in jobs so hazardous or unhealthy that they could not be given to valuable slaves. Those who ran small shops faced intense competition from slaves and freedmen who were

Illustration 5.7

/// Reconstruction of a Typical *Insula* or Apartment House, Ostia. These strikingly modern-looking apartment blocks were based on design codes established during Nero's reconstruction of Rome. By the second century A.D., when the one depicted here was built at Rome's port of Ostia, they had become the standard form of urban housing in Italy.

better connected than themselves, while a few managed, for a time at least, to hang on to whatever money they had realized from the sale of their country farms. The majority lived in near destitution, kept alive only by occasional labor, the grain dole, and contributions from the rich. Nearly everyone, however, belonged to mutual aid societies that helped their members in time of need and guaranteed them a decent burial.

Like most of the urban slaves and freedmen, the poor inhabited a room or two in one of the innumerable *insulae* or tenements that packed the lower regions of the city (see illustration 5.7). After the rebuilding projects of Augustus and the fire of A.D. 64, these structures were usually of brick with concrete grills instead of windows. Though an improvement over the makeshift buildings of the republic, the new *insulae* were not safe. Wooden floors, stairs, and roofs kept the fire companies busy, while excessive height and cheap construction sometimes caused them to collapse and kill their inhabitants (see document 5.6). Individual apartments must have been dark and smoky with poor ventilation and no heat beyond that provided by a charcoal brazier for cooking.

Fortunately, the Romans spent little time at home. They met their friends in the street or in the Forum, where they would gather to pick up gossip and make their views known by rowdy demonstrations. Wealthy Romans affected to despise the mob, but no politician, not even the emperor, could afford to ignore it. Great efforts were made to distract and amuse the citizenry, for the stability of the state depended upon "bread and circuses." Those with political ambitions funded theatrical presentations, circuses, gladiatorial combats, chariot races, and huge public feasts in which the en-

tire body of Roman citizens ate and drank itself into oblivion. Only the enormous cost of such entertainments could justify the wealth amassed by the Roman aristocracy.

Whatever their political function, such spectacles did little to elevate public taste. Circuses involved the slaughter of exotic animals by men, or of men by animals. The Romans enjoyed seeing convicted criminals mauled by bears or lions almost as much as the gladiatorial contests in which specially trained slaves fought to the death. Chariot racing, too, was a blood sport in which fatal accidents were common. Various teams represented political factions and betting was heavy.

After the games—or a hard day's work—Romans headed for the public baths. These massive facilities, which could be enjoyed by anyone, provided exercise rooms, steambaths, and hot and cold pools for bathing. Separate areas were reserved for men and women, though the women were given no place to exercise. Because the Romans had no soap, the bathing ritual began with a steambath. They then scraped their bodies with an instrument called a *strigel* and immersed themselves successively in hot and cold water. The whole process was lengthy enough to provide further opportunity for socializing.

Amenities provided at little or no cost made life in the city tolerable, even for the poor. The streets were noisy—even at night—and the crime rate was relatively high, but those who had neither jobs nor possessions could ignore such problems. The city was clean by all but twentieth-century standards. Massive aqueducts brought pure water into every neighborhood where it bubbled up in innumerable fountains, and even the meanest apartment had a terrace garden or a few potted

## ◆ DOCUMENT 5.6 ◆

# City Life in the Roman Empire

*In his* Third Satire, *the poet Juvenal (c. A.D. 60—after 128) congratulates a friend on his decision to leave Rome for a small country town by cataloging the hazards of urban life.*

Who, on Tivoli's heights, or a small town like Gabii, say,
Fears the collapse of his house? But Rome is supported on pipestems,
Matchsticks; it's cheaper, so, for the landlord to shore up his ruins,
Patch up the old cracked walls, and notify all the tenants
They can sleep secure, though the beams are in ruins above them.
No, the place to live is out there, where no cry of *Fire!*
Sounds the alarm of the night, with a neighbor yelling for water,
Moving his chattels and goods, and the whole third story is smoking.
This you'll never know: for if the ground floor is scared first,
You are the first to burn, up where the eaves of the attic
Keep off the rain, and the doves are brooding over their nest eggs.

Look at the other things, the various dangers of nighttime. . . .
You are a thoughtless fool, unmindful of sudden disaster,
If you don't make your will before you go out to have dinner.
There are as many deaths in the night as there are open windows
Where you pass by; if you're wise, you will pray in your wretched devotions,
People may be content with no more than emptying slop jars.

The Satires of Juvenal, *pp. 40, 43, trans. Rolfe Humphries. Bloomington: Indiana University Press, 1958. Used by permission.*

plants, for the Romans, though thoroughly urbanized, never lost their taste for growing things.

Yet by modern standards, the lives of ordinary Romans must have been largely without root or purpose. Marriage was rare, and people tended to contract casual relationships with little regard for the social standing of their partners. The birthrate remained correspondingly low, and children born to these unions were sometimes left to be found by slave traders. The population of the city would have declined had it not been for the steady influx of slaves and of refugees fleeing from the hard life of the countryside.

The Romans made little effort to impose their culture on the peoples of the empire, asking only that taxes be paid and peace maintained. Areas such as Egypt or Judea whose cultures were long established and fundamentally alien to Greco-Roman values therefore remained unassimilated. Tribal societies, or those in which the ideal of civic life had native roots, were more likely to imitate Roman models. By the end of the principate, Italy, Spain, Africa, and much of Gaul had been thoroughly Romanized, while Greece, Syria, and the Greek-speaking communities of Asia Minor, though they retained their native cultures, were drawing closer to the Roman orbit.

In general, the social structure and daily life of western cities resembled that of Rome. Eastern towns were different. Slavery was much less widespread, and the bulk of the artisans and laborers were citizens. Most of the latter, though poor, appear to have been self-supporting. In general, craft production in the eastern cities was far more important than in the more agrarian west, and their average size was probably greater. Alexandria, still more Greek than Egyptian, was almost as large as Rome, while places such as Pergamum and Antioch probably had close to a half million inhabitants.

Country life also differed. In the west, large farms and latifundia, worked either by slaves or *coloni*, were common. In the east, wealthy townsmen and city governments owned tracts that they rented to tenant farmers in return for cash payments or a portion of the yield. In both regions, independent farmers worked freehold plots with varying degrees of success. Egypt remained as it had been under the Ptolemies—a world of impoverished peasants laboring for the state under an appalling burden of taxation.

The age of Augustus and the early emperors has been called the peak of Roman civilization and its achievements were great, but beneath the surface, social polarization continued to limit economic growth and lay the foundation for future crises. The *pax romana* was something of an illusion. Roman rule masked, but did not resolve, underlying political and economic tensions in many parts of the empire. Riots and revolts were common and became more so with the passage of time. The empire, in short, was barely sustainable even in the absence of external threats, and it had become obvious even in the reign of Augustus that a threat of monumental proportions was developing in the north. Masses of Germanic tribesmen had begun to press against the Rhine and Danube frontiers. Unprecedented efforts were needed to contain them, and, as time would tell, the social and economic structures of the empire proved unequal to the task.

## CHAPTER 6

# THE ORIGINS OF CHRISTIANITY AND THE DECLINE OF THE ROMAN EMPIRE

## CHAPTER OUTLINE

T he triumphal expansion of the early Roman Empire brought with it the seeds of change. Judaea, one of the poorer, more remote places annexed by the Romans, gave birth to Christianity, a religion that, after three centuries of sporadic persecution and relative obscurity, became the empire's dominant faith. Meanwhile, as Christianity grew, the empire fell into decline. The cause of that decline was not Christianity but a generalized crisis whose basic outlines had become apparent by the end of the second century. Put simply, the empire had expanded beyond the limits imposed by its economic resources. The emperors of the third and fourth centuries tried in various ways to reverse the process of economic and social decay, but gradually, the western and eastern halves of the empire grew further apart. The west, pressured by Germanic invaders and weakened by a stagnant economy, disintegrated. The Greek-speaking east, richer and untroubled by Germans, survived until 1453.

## The Origins of Christianity: Rome and the Jews

The breakup of the Hasmonaean dynasty, as the descendants of the Maccabees were known, resulted in a protracted, messy civil war in which the various contenders were supported by outside forces. Rome, in the person of Pompey, became involved in 66–64 B.C. as part of the effort to defeat Mithridates and capitalize on the collapse of the Seleucid Empire. The consequent spread of Roman influence in the Middle East alarmed Parthia, the successor of the Persian Empire, and aroused the interest of Cleopatra, who opposed Roman policy in the region even as she seduced Caesar and Antony. The situation was further complicated by the religious struggle between Jewish Sadducees and Pharisees (see chapter 3).

Eventually, a Roman client, Herod "the Great" (73–4 B.C.), emerged supreme and imposed an interval of much-needed peace. Though an Arab by birth,

**Illustration 6.1**

**Relief from the Arch of Titus, Rome.** The relief shows the spoils taken from the capture of Jerusalem. The arch was erected after Titus's death, probably about A.D. 81, and commemorates the dual triumph celebrated by Vespasian and Titus in A.D. 71 after their victory over the Jews and the destruction of the Temple. Note the menorah at center left. The seven-branched candelabra first became a symbol of the Jewish people during this era.

Herod practiced Judaism and generally favored the more numerous Pharisees over their opponents. His realms extended north to the borders of Syria and east into Transjordan and provided the revenues for an extensive building campaign, the jewel of which was the reconstruction of the Temple at Jerusalem. Some of its huge stones are still visible at the base of the Western Wall. None of this endeared him to the more observant Jews, but they accepted his rule.

When Herod died, he divided his kingdom into three tetrarchies, each ruled by a son. Archelaus, the Tetrarch of Judaea, so offended his Jewish subjects that they asked Augustus to replace him with a Roman procurator. Augustus agreed to do so, but the experiment was a failure. In theory, the procurators were supposed to look out for Roman interests while leaving internal matters to the Jewish court known as the Sanhedrin, but, if the Jewish historian Josephus (c. 37–c. 100) may be believed, each procurator found new ways of insulting Jewish religious and political sensibilities. By A.D. 7 a group known as the Zealots had dedicated themselves to the overthrow of Roman rule.

After this, the turmoil in Jerusalem was broken only by the short reign of Herod Agrippa, a Jewish prince who governed Judaea from A.D. 41 to 44 under Roman protection. Riots and protests accompanied a growing belief in the coming of the Messiah, who would deliver the Jews from their enemies and restore the world. False messiahs appeared with predictable regularity and caused great concern among the Romans who feared that one of them might organize a general revolt. Finally, in A.D. 66 the emperor Nero dispatched an army under Vespasian to restore order. The Zealots and most of the population resisted, and Jerusalem fell to the Romans only after a long and terrible siege (see illustration 6.1).

Exasperated by his inability to come to terms with the Jews even after their defeat, Vespasian, who had by this time succeeded Nero as emperor, ordered the Temple destroyed and the Jews scattered to the far corners of the empire in A.D. 70. They retained their freedom to worship and the exemption from sacrificing to the state cult that had been granted them by Julius Caesar, but the new exile or diaspora changed the character of Judaism. The destruction of the Temple forced the abandonment of sacrifices and other temple rites, for it was thought that the Temple could be restored only by the coming of the Messiah. The role of the priesthood diminished. Religious guidance was provided by rabbis, or teachers, who interpreted the law to the far-flung congregations. The more distinguished of their opinions helped form the Talmud, the vast collection of scriptural commentaries that is the basis of Jewish learning and of modern Judaism. Only a handful of Jews remained in Judaea. A band of perhaps nine hundred Zealots held out in the great desert fortress of Masada until A.D. 73 when they committed mass suicide instead of surrendering to the Romans. Sixty years later, another small group of Jews launched a futile rebellion under Bar Kochva, but nearly two thousand years would pass before the establishment of another Jewish state.

## Jesus of Nazareth

Jesus lived in the midst of this chronic turbulence. He was probably born at Bethlehem in Judaea, between 7 and 4 B.C. Both the year and date of his birth are now regarded as the products of later calculation and tradition. A precise chronology is impossible because the Gospels provide no dates. The four Gospels are the most important sources dealing with his life and ministry. Though written by different authors more than a generation after his death (Mark, the earliest, was written about A.D. 70; John, the latest, shortly before 100), their accounts, though different in important ways, are in broad general agreement.

They describe the circumstances of Jesus's birth and of an appearance at the Temple when he was about twelve but remain silent about his activities until the age of thirty, the point at which he began to attract a following as an itinerant rabbi. Accompanied by twelve close associates or disciples, he preached throughout the Judaean countryside to ever-increasing crowds. His message was directed primarily against the Pharisees. Jesus felt that their rigid observance of the Law was an obstacle to faith and that it could largely be superseded by the simple commandment to "love thy neighbor as thyself." At the same time, his preaching left no doubt that he regarded himself as the Messiah (the Greek word for which is *christos*, or Christ). By this he did not mean the traditional Messiah who would lead the Jews to earthly glory, but the Son of God who brought them eternal salvation. His kingdom, he said, was "not of this world," and those who believed in him "would not perish but have eternal life."

This message enraged the Pharisees but attracted many, especially among the poor. When he entered Jerusalem at Passover accompanied by symbols attributed to the Messiah by prophetic tradition, Jesus provoked a crisis. The Sanhedrin demanded his arrest. The Roman procurator, Pontius Pilate, agreed, fearing that his presence would provoke further disorders when virtually the entire country had come to town for the festival. Jesus was tried by the Sanhedrin for blasphemy

and by Pilate for treason, though both trials as described by the Gospels were of dubious legality. Everyone responsible seems to have been motivated by political expediency, and Jesus was crucified with uncommon haste to avoid the possibility of demonstrations. After his execution, his followers reported that he had returned from the dead and ascended into Heaven after promising to return on the Day of Judgment.

## The Spread of Christianity

The story of Jesus's death and resurrection solidified his followers into a new Jewish sect, but someone who had never heard him preach spread his teachings throughout the Roman world. Saul of Tarsus was a Pharisee who had originally persecuted the followers of Jesus. After a dramatic conversion to the faith of his opponents, he began to use his Roman name, Paul, and devoted the rest of his life to the task of converting Jews and non-Jews alike. Though a Pharisee, Paul's early education had been cosmopolitan and strongly influenced by Hellenism. To him, the teachings of Jesus were universal. With some difficulty, he persuaded the more conservative disciples to accept converts without forcing them to observe the Jewish dietary laws or be circumcised. Had he not done so, Christianity probably would never have become a universal church. By emphasizing faith over the minute observance of the law, Paul influenced the theology of the growing church as well.

In his letters, Paul portrayed himself as small of stature and physically weak, but his efforts on behalf of the faith were heroic. While Jesus was still alive, his teachings had begun to spread through the Jewish communities of the Roman Empire. Opposition from the Jewish leadership could not prevent the formation of small, usually secret, congregations that became the organizational basis of Paul's efforts. Traveling incessantly, he moved from one to the other, prevailing upon them to accept non-Jews as converts, preaching to the gentiles, and helping individual churches with matters of belief and practice. By so doing, he not only gained converts but also provided stability and a vital link between isolated communities that might otherwise have lost contact with one another and drifted into confusion.

When he could not visit the churches in person, Paul communicated with them by letters that he seems to have composed in answer to specific questions. These Epistles, written in Greek, form an important part of the New Testament. In some, he deals with theological questions; in others, with morality, ethics, and church organization. For issues not addressed by Jesus, Paul's Epistles—logical, fervent, and rooted solidly in

Illustration 6.2

**The Catacomb of San Callisto, Rome.** Unlike pagans, who generally cremated their dead, Christians insisted on burial, often in underground vaults known as catacombs. In times of persecution, they held religious services in these tombs to avoid detection. This one, the so-called Chapel of the Popes, is unusually elaborate and dates from c. 250.

Scripture—became the basis of later church doctrine. Through his efforts and those of the other disciples, the Christian church grew rapidly.

In the beginning, Christianity appealed largely to women, slaves, and other people of modest social standing, for it was universal in the sense that it accepted converts regardless of gender or background. Salvation was open to all, though Paul objected strongly to women preaching and church offices were apparently restricted to men. Its high ethical standards appealed to a generation that seems to have been increasingly repelled by pagan vice, and its ceremonies were neither as terrifying nor expensive as those of the mystery cults. The most important were baptism with water—not bull's blood, as in the rites of Mithra—and a love feast or *agape* in which the entire congregation joined. After a common meal, the Christians celebrated communion in bread and wine. By 153 the love feast had been abandoned in favor of communion alone, which was preceded by a service that included preaching and the singing of hymns.

Though humble, the early church was remarkably well organized. Each congregation was governed by a committee of presbyters or elders, who were assisted by deacons, readers, and exorcists. Bishops were elected by their congregations to lead worship services and administer the community's finances. The extent of their power in earliest times has been the subject of much debate, but its expansion was clearly assisted by the doctrine of apostolic succession. This teaching, which holds that episcopal authority derives from powers given by Jesus to the disciple Peter, was generally accepted by the end of the second century.

Organization helped the young church to survive persecution, for the Christians were hated. Persecution came from two sources. Many Jews felt that Christianity divided and weakened their communities and were quick to denounce Christians to the authorities. The authorities, whether Roman or provincial, had other motives. Like the Jews, Christians refused to sacrifice to the Roman gods. The Jews were exempt from this requirement by their status as a separate nation whose customs were honored by Roman law, but Christianity was not. Many Romans feared that Christian exclusiveness masked a certain hostility to the state. Their suspicions were fed by the low social status of the Christians and, ironically, by the secrecy they had adopted for their protection. To avoid detection, Christians met in private houses or in the underground burial places known as catacombs (see illustration 6.2). Rumors of cannibalism, based upon a misunderstanding of communion, only made matters worse.

Christians, in short, were unpopular and lacked the protection of powerful individuals who might otherwise have intervened on their behalf. They made ideal scapegoats. Nero, for example, blamed them for the great fire at Rome and launched the first wave of executions that claimed the life of Paul in A.D. 64 (see document 6.1). Persecutions by later emperors caused great loss of life until well into the third century. They were chronicled in horrific detail by Eusebius of Caesarea (c. 260–c. 340) in his *History of the Church*, but to the annoyance of the pagans, "the blood of martyrs" was, as Tertullian had put it, "the seed of the church." Too many Christians died bravely. Their cheerful heroism, even as they were torn

### ◆ DOCUMENT 6.1 ◆

## Tacitus: Nero's Persecution of Christians

*Tacitus (c. A.D. 56–120) is the best known of the ancient Roman historians. He was born to a patrician family in Gaul, educated at Rome, and rose to the Senate and then to become consul under Nerva in A.D. 97. Tacitus produced two long histories,* The Annals *(covering A.D. 14–68) and* The Histories *(covering A.D. 68–96). Together they provide the best record of the early Principate. The Annals, from which the following excerpt is taken, is one of the few contemporary sources to mention Jesus of Nazareth.*

A disaster followed, whether accidental or treacherously contrived by the Emperor is uncertain, as authors have given both accounts; a fire—worse, and more dreadful than any which have ever happened to this city—broke out amid the shops containing inflammable wares, and instantly became fierce and rapid from the wind. . . . It devastated everyplace below the hills, outstripping all preventive measures; the city, with the narrow winding passages and irregular streets that characterized old Rome, was at its mercy. . . .

All human efforts, all the lavish gifts of the Emperor, all attempts to placate the Gods, did not dispel the infamous suspicion the fire had been started at someone's command. To quiet the rumor, Nero blamed and ingeniously tortured a people popularly called Christians, hated for their abominations [including their prediction

that the world would soon end in a conflagration marking the second coming]. Christus, from whom the cult had its origin, suffered the extreme penalty during the reign of Tiberius, at the hands of one of our procurators, Pontius Pilate, but this noxious superstition [Christianity], suppressed for a moment, broke out again not only in Judea, where it began, but in Rome itself, where all things hideous and shameful from every part of the world become popular.

Nero first arrested all who confessed [to being Christians]; then, upon their testimony, a vast multitude was convicted not so much of arson as of hatred of the human race. Mockery of every sort was added to their deaths. They were sewn in the skins of beasts and torn to pieces by dogs. Many died nailed on crosses or burned at the stake to illuminate the night. Nero gave his gardens for the spectacle and put on a circus, mingling with the crowd in the costume of a charioteer. . . . Thus, even though the victims deserved the severest penalty, a feeling of compassion arose on the ground that they suffered not for the public good but to glut the cruelty of one man.

Tacitus. *The Annals*, book 15, chaps. 38, 44, trans. A. J. Church and W. J. Brodribb. New York: Macmillan, 1906.

---

apart by wild beasts, impressed spectators and powerfully endorsed the concept of eternal life. Many pagans converted in spite of the obvious danger. Admittedly, had the persecutions been consistent they might have succeeded, but not all emperors were anti-Christian. Each persecution was followed by a generation or more in which the numbers of the faithful could be replaced and even grow.

Though persecution backfired, Christianity needed to explain itself to the educated elite to gain general acceptance. Moreover, as the movement spread, differences of opinion began to develop within it. During the second and third centuries, a growing number of writers addressed themselves both to the task of defining Christian doctrine and explaining it in terms acceptable to those who had received a Greco-Roman philosophical education. These men, who eventually became known as the Fathers of the Church, included the apologist Justin Martyr and theologians such as Tertullian, Origen, and Clement of Alexandria. Together, they be-

gan the process of forging a new intellectual tradition based upon faith as well as reason.

By the end of the third century, perhaps 10 percent of the empire was Christian. Most of the followers were concentrated in the east or in Africa. More significant, the Fathers had done their work: Converts were coming increasingly from the upper classes. In cities in Syria and Asia Minor, Christians had become a majority and even the leading families had accepted the faith. The last, and one of the most terrible, of the persecutions occurred under Diocletian in 303, but by then the church was too strong to be destroyed (see chronology 6.1).

◆

## The Crisis of the Later Roman Empire

In 1776, Edward Gibbon described the fall of Rome as "the triumph of Christianity and barbarism." Though his *The Decline and Fall of the Roman Empire* is one of the

## The Important Roman Emperors

| | |
|---|---|
| 27 B.C.–A.D.14 | Augustus |
| A.D. 14–37 | Tiberius |
| 37–41 | Caligula |
| 41–54 | Claudius |
| 54–68 | Nero* |
| 68–69 | The year of the four emperors |
| 69–79 | Vespasian |
| 79–81 | Titus |
| 81–96 | Domitian* |
| 96–98 | Nerva |
| 98–117 | Trajan |
| 117–138 | Hadrian |
| 138–161 | Antoninus Pius |
| 161–180 | Marcus Aurelius* |
| 180–192 | Commodus |
| 193–211 | Septimius Severus |
| 211–217 | Caracalla |
| 218–222 | Elagabalus |
| 222–235 | Severus Alexander |
| 249–251 | Decius* |
| 253–260 | Valerian* |
| 253–268 | Gallienus |
| 268–270 | Claudius II Gothicus |
| 270–275 | Aurelian |
| 284–305 | Diocletian* |
| 306–337 | Constantine |
| 337–361 | Constantius II |
| 361–363 | Julian the Apostate |
| 364–375 | Valentinian |
| 364–378 | Valens |
| 379–395 | Theodosius |

*Launched major persecutions of the Christians.

The true cause of imperial decline was instead a generalized crisis whose basic outlines had become apparent as early as the second century. When Marcus Aurelius died in A.D. 180, an army of more than a half million men patrolled a border of several thousand miles. Within that border the *pax romana* was broken only by occasional riots, but beyond it, powerful forces were gathering. Germanic tribes—Franks, Alemanni, Burgundians, and others in the west; Visigoths and Ostrogoths to the east—pressed against the Rhine and Danube frontiers. For reasons that remain unclear, their populations had grown beyond the available food supply in central Europe. Behind them, on the eastern steppes, other peoples with similar problems pushed westward into the German tribal lands. Population movements on this scale created intolerable pressure when they came up against settled borders. The Germans did not hate Rome. They sought only to settle within it. They were hard, determined fighters whose grasp of strategy was anything but primitive. In fighting them, Marcus Aurelius faced unpredictable attacks in force delivered along a perimeter too extensive to be manned completely by the legions. His bitter struggle with the tribes was an inkling of things to come.

To the east, the Romans faced a more conventional foe. The Parthian Empire was a sophisticated territorial state based, like Rome, on taxes and tribute. It fought until it exhausted its resources and then made peace until its economy could recover. The pressure it exerted on the eastern borders was therefore sporadic rather than constant, but it was nevertheless severe. Rome defeated the Parthians in A.D. 198 and briefly annexed Mesopotamia. This success was followed by a change of dynasty in the eastern kingdom. An Iranian prince, Ardashir I, overthrew the Parthians and established the Sassanid dynasty, which lasted until the Arab conquests of the seventh century. Determined to recapture Mesopotamia, he and his successors launched a series of wars that further depleted the Roman treasury, weakened the eastern provinces, and ended in 260 with the capture of the emperor Valerian.

The Roman economy could not sustain this level of military commitment, and the third century was one of almost unrelieved crisis. The prosperity of Augustan times had been in some respects artificial. Much of it was based on the exploitation of new wealth derived from imperial expansion. When the expansion stopped, that wealth was not replaced. Beneath the glittering surface of the early empire, the economy remained stagnant. The mass of slaves, tenant farmers, and unemployed citizens consumed little. Their productivity was

great masterworks of history, he was at best only half right. Neither Christianity nor pagan immorality contributed to the catastrophe that befell the western empire in the fifth century A.D. While the "barbarians" clearly played a major role, they were little more barbaric than some of the emperors they replaced.

low, and they had no incentive to improve efficiency to encourage growth. Without growth, the number of rich could not increase, and it was only they who, in the Roman system, could provide a market for luxuries and craft goods.

Arguably, had the Roman economy been able to expand, the empire might have been able to meet its military obligations. Instead, the imperial government was forced to extract more and more resources from an economy that may already have been shrinking. Taxes and forced requisitions to support the army consumed capital, reduced the expenditures of the rich, and drove ordinary people to destitution. Basic industries such as the trade in earthenware vanished, and food shortages became common as harvests were diverted to feed the troops. Trade languished.

Economic decline, though general, did not affect all regions of the empire equally. Those provinces closest to the front suffered the most because they were subject to requisitions of food, draft animals, and equipment and because governors could extract forced loans from citizens who found themselves in harm's way. Both east and west suffered, but the strain was greater in the west because the Germans exerted a steady, unrelenting pressure while the cyclical nature of the struggle with Persia allowed time for the eastern provinces to recover between wars. Africa and Egypt, far from the battlefields, were troubled only by the same ruinous taxes that afflicted everyone.

The crisis fed upon itself in an unending spiral of decline. The imperial government became more brutal and authoritarian in its efforts to extract resources from an ever-narrowing economic base, and with each exaction, poverty increased. The social consequences were appalling. A steady decline in population is evident from the mid-second century onward, which inhibited recruitment for the army and reduced the tax base even further (see table 6.1). Growing poverty and political helplessness blurred social distinctions and encouraged resistance that, in turn, forced the government to adopt even sterner measures.

Much of this new authoritarianism was the legacy of Septimius Severus, emperor from 193 to 211. Having commanded legions on the Danube, he believed that the full human and economic resources of the state had to be mobilized to meet the German threat. He introduced laws that imposed forced labor on the poor and trapped the decurions (officials who served as an urban elite) in an inescapable web of obligations. The army, meanwhile, was showered with favors. Severus doubled the soldier's pay—the first increase in more than two hundred years—and allowed officers to wear the gold

## TABLE 6.1

### The Population of the Roman Empire, A.D. 1–600

These estimates (in millions) of the population of the Roman Empire are necessarily imprecise, but they show dramatic population declines in every region of the empire after about A.D. 200. The Balkan figures include Illyria, Pannonia, Dacia, Macedonia, and Thrace. The dramatic decline around 400 marks the loss of Dacia. Note that, even at its peak, the population of the empire remained small relative to the size of the army it was forced to maintain.

| Region | A.D. 1 | 200 | 400 | 600 |
|---|---|---|---|---|
| Africa | 3.75 | 4.0 | 3.5 | 2.75 |
| Asia Minor | 6.0 | 7.0 | 6.0 | 5.0 |
| Balkans | 2.8 | 3.25 | 1.75 | 1.25 |
| Britain | a | 1.75 | a | a |
| Egypt | 4.75 | 4.75 | 4.0 | 3.25 |
| Gaul | 5.75 | 7.5 | 5.75 | 4.75 |
| Greece | 2.0 | 2.0 | 1.5 | .8 |
| Italy | 7.0 | 7.0 | 5.0 | 3.5 |
| Spain | 4.5 | 5.0 | 4.5 | 3.5 |
| Syria and Palestine | 2.25 | 2.25 | 1.75 | 1.5 |
| Total | 38.8 | 44.5 | 33.75 | 26.3 |

Source: Figures derived from C. McEvedy and R. Jones, *Atlas of World Population History* (Harmondsworth: Penguin Books, 1978).
aBritain was not part of the empire.

ring that signified membership in the equestrian order. Such measures improved morale, but they were not enough. Hard terms of service and the declining population of the interior provinces continued to make recruitment difficult. To compensate, Severus opened even the highest ranks to men from the border provinces and, for the first time since the days of Marius, allowed soldiers to marry.

These reforms, though rational and probably necessary, widened the gap between soldiers and civilians. The post-Severan army, composed largely of men with only the slightest exposure to Roman culture, was privileged as well as self-perpetuating. Children raised in the camps usually followed their father's profession. When they did not, they remained part of a garrison community whose political and economic interests were in conflict with those of the society it protected.

Because the soldiers, now half-barbarian themselves, continued to make emperors, the implications of this change were potentially disasterous. Severus was an African, whose family members had long been senators and were thoroughly romanized. His wife, Julia Domna, was a gifted administrator and a patron of Greek and Latin intellectuals who worked tirelessly for cultural unity. The emperors who followed were of a different sort. The tyrannical son of Severus and Julia, Caracalla, was followed by men whose only common characteristic was the support of a faction within the army. Most were poorly educated provincials who seemed like foreigners to a majority of their subjects. A few were eccentrics or even children, and their average tenure in office was short. All, however, tried to follow the deathbed advice of Severus: "Stay on good terms, enrich the soldiers, and don't take much notice of anything else." He had been nothing if not a realist.

## Imperial Efforts at Reform from Septimius Severus to Diocletian

As the third century progressed, "enriching the soldiers" grew more difficult. Both the economy and the population continued to decline. The rate of conception slowed, in part because people felt that they could no longer afford to raise families. Furthermore, malnutrition and disease contributed to the population loss. The first great epidemic struck in the reign of Marcus Aurelius. It was followed by others, whose exact nature is unknown.

Defense costs could not be reduced. The middle years of the third century saw a renewal of the Persian wars and the invasion of the Goths, a Germanic people who forced the Romans to abandon their provinces north of the Danube (the area now known as Romania) and threatened the interior as well. Imperial politics alone demanded enormous expenditures as regional commanders struggled against one another for the throne. Of the twenty-six emperors who ruled between A.D. 235 and 283, only one died of natural causes. All were forced to bribe the legions for their support; some even bribed the enemy. Large sums were expended to buy peace from both the Sassanids and the Goths. Such efforts predictably failed.

Emperors beginning with Caracalla tried to deal with these problems by reducing the precious metal content of their coinage, a practice that did little more than add inflation to the empire's list of economic woes. Taxation and forced requisitions had long since reached the limits of productivity. Decurions and tenant farmers, impoverished by an insatiable bureaucracy, abandoned their properties in favor of begging, banditry, and piracy. The emperors, distracted by war and by the

**Illustration 6.3**

%% **The Tetrarchs, St. Mark's Venice.** The sculpture shows Diocletian and his colleagues as an inseparable unit for purposes of propaganda.

requirements of personal survival, could do little about it. Whole regions fell under the control of men who were, in effect, warlords. In the east, Zenobia, queen of the caravan city of Palmyra, managed briefly to gain control of Syria, Egypt, and much of Asia Minor.

The emperors Claudius II Gothicus and Aurelian brought the military situation under control between 268 and 275. However, major reforms were necessary. Diocletian, who came to the throne in 284, embarked upon a reorganization of the entire empire. To enlarge the army without increasing its potential for anarchy, he divided the empire into two halves, each ruled by an augustus. Each augustus then adopted a caesar to serve as his subordinate and successor.

Diocletian created four emperors, for each caesar had primary responsibility for a region of his own (see illustration 6.3). His colleague Maximian was

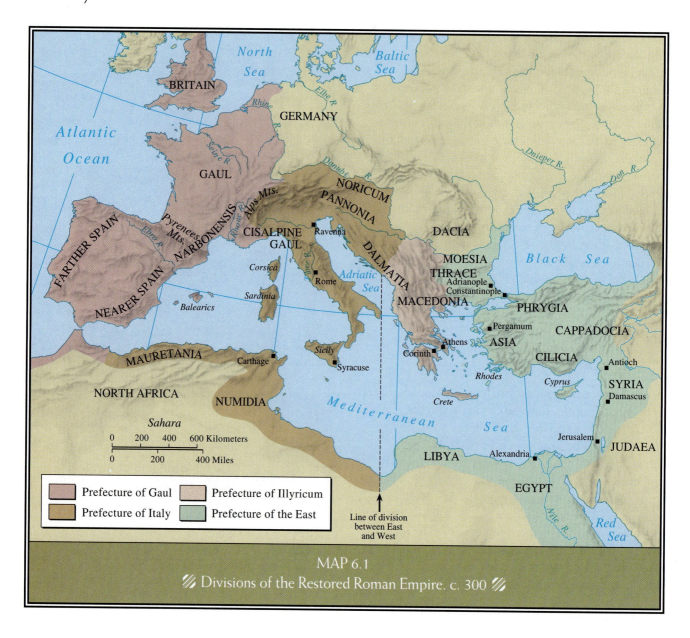

MAP 6.1
Divisions of the Restored Roman Empire. c. 300

given responsibility for the west, with another, Constantius, serving as caesar in Gaul and Britain. In recognition of its greater wealth and importance, Diocletian took the east for himself and established his headquarters at Nicomedia in Asia Minor. His trusted lieutenant Galerius was made caesar with special responsibility for Syria and Egypt.

Decentralization worked well as long as the authority of Diocletian remained intact (see map 6.1). He was probably right in assuming that no one man could effectively govern so vast and beleaguered an empire. If Maximian and the two caesars remained loyal, they could respond more quickly to crises without losing control of an army that numbered more than 650,000 men. To ensure even quicker response, the army was divided into

permanent garrisons and mobile expeditionary forces. The latter, reinforced with heavily armored cavalry (cataphracti) on an unprecedented scale, were capable of moving rapidly to threatened sectors of the frontier.

To separate military from civilian authority, Diocletian assigned each augustus and caesar a praetorian prefect with broad judicial and administrative powers. He then subdivided the existing provinces, increased the civil powers of their governors, and grouped the new, smaller units into dioceses supervised by imperial vicars. The vicars reported to the praetorian prefects.

The new administrative system would be the model for the later empire—and for the Christian church when it eventually achieved official status. Diocletian used it primarily to implement economic reforms. To him, and to his successors, only a command economy in which the government regulated nearly every aspect of economic life could provide the resources needed to maintain both the army and a newly expanded bureaucracy. All pretense of a free market was abandoned. Diocletian attempted to solve the labor shortage by forbidding workers to leave their trades and by binding tenants to the great estates for life. In later years, these provisions were made hereditary, but they did nothing to retard economic stagnation. In the long run, restricting the free movement of labor probably made matters worse, as did continued tax increases and a new, more efficient system of forced requisitions that he introduced early in his reign.

The long-term effect of these changes was obscured by peace, which enabled the economy to recover somewhat in spite of them, but Diocletian's effort to control inflation failed quickly and visibly (see table 6.2). He restored the metal content of silver and gold coins, devalued under his predecessors, but could not issue enough of them to meet demand. Silver-washed copper coins known as *nummi* remained the most common money in circulation and depreciated even faster in relation to the new coinage. Prices continued to rise. In 301, Diocletian responded by placing a ceiling on wages and prices. Like all such measures, the edict proved impossible to enforce. Riots and black marketeering greeted its introduction in the more commercial east, while the agricultural west seems to have ignored it altogether. The program was abandoned after a year.

Whatever their shortcomings, the reforms of Diocletian were perhaps the best answer that administrative genius alone could apply to the problems of the later empire. Little else could have been done within the constraints imposed by Rome's defensive needs. To preserve his achievements, Diocletian abdicated in 305 and retired to the magnificent fortified palace he constructed on the shores of the Adriatic (see illustration 6.4). Though many of his reforms endured, all plans for an orderly succession collapsed long before he died in 313.

## The Age of Constantine

Even had Diocletian's colleagues been fully willing to accept his settlement, their sons were not. Maximian, the western augustus, abdicated in favor of his caesar, Constantius, but when the latter died in 306, his son Constantine was proclaimed augustus by the troops and Maximian's son, Maxentius, rebelled against him. In

### TABLE 6.2
### Diocletian: Edict of Maximum Prices, A.D. 301

*The emperor Diocletian's reforms included an important effort to control the inflation of prices. His edict stated the maximum permissible price of wages in many jobs, of many commodities, and of transportation. Although the edict was often circumvented, it provides a remarkable portrait of daily life in the Roman Empire.*

For one *modius* (c. 2 gallons):

| | |
|---|---|
| Wheat | 100 *denarii* |
| Rye | 60 |
| Millet | 50 |
| Beans | 60 |
| Rice | 200 |
| Salt | 100 |

For 1 *sextarius* (approx. 16 ounces):

| | | | |
|---|---|---|---|
| Wine | 30 *denarii* | Honey | 40 |
| Ordinary wine | 8 | 1 pheasant | 250 *denarii* |
| Beer | 4 | 2 chickens | 60 |
| Egyptian beer | 2 | 10 sparrows | 16 |
| | | 100 oysters | 100 |
| | | 12 oz. pork | 12 |
| Olive oil | 40 | 12 oz. fish | 24 |

For daily labor:

| | |
|---|---|
| Farm laborer | 25 *denarii* |
| Carpenter | 50 |
| Painter | 75 |
| Baker | 50 |
| Shipwright | 60 |
| Camel driver | 25 |
| Shepherd | 20 |
| Sewer cleaner | 25 |
| For lawyer, simple case | 1,000 |

For skilled wages:

| | |
|---|---|
| Scribe, per 100 lines | 25 |
| Notary, per document | 10 |
| Tailor, cutting one cloak | 60 |
| Tailor, for breeches | 20 |
| Monthly scale for teachers, per pupil | |
| Elementary teacher | 50 |
| Arithmetic teacher | 75 |
| Teacher of Greek | 200 |
| Rhetoric teacher | 250 |

*Transactions of the American Philological Association*, 71 (1940), 157.

312 Constantine defeated Maxentius at the battle of the Milvian bridge and became undisputed augustus of the west. In the east, Licinius, who governed the dioceses on the Danube frontier, eventually succeeded Galerius and made an uneasy alliance with Constantine that ended, after much maneuvering, with the defeat and execution of Licinius in 324. Constantine, known thereafter as "the Great," had reunited the empire under his personal rule.

Constantine, like Diocletian and the rest of his imperial colleagues, came from the provinces along the lower Danube and had only an approximate acquaintance with traditional Roman culture. In administrative

**Illustration 6.4**

**Model of Diocletian's Palace at Split.** The emperor built this palace on the Dalmatian Coast after A.D. 293 for his retire-ment. The concern for security indicates the limited success of his reforms and a certain distrust of his fellow tetrarchs.

matters, he continued the policies of his predecessor and surpassed him in ritualizing the imperial office. All trace of republican values were abandoned. Under Constantine, the emperor became a godlike figure sur-rounded by eastern rituals who spoke to all but the most privileged of his subjects from behind a screen (see illustration 6.5).

Eastern ritual was appropriate because the empire's center of gravity had long since shifted to the east. The constant military pressure exerted by the Germans had drained the west of much of its wealth. What little re-mained tended to flow eastward, as westerners contin-ued to purchase craft and luxury items from the more advanced cities of Syria and Asia Minor. More than ever, the west had become a land of vast, self-sufficient latifundia, worked by tenants and isolated from the shrinking towns whose chief remaining function was to house a bloated imperial administration. Constantine, who had spent most of his adult life in the west, knew this all too well. That was why, in 324, he established a new capital at Byzantium on the shores of the Bosporus. Rome, the city, had declined in importance. Most of the emperors since Marcus Aurelius had passed their reigns closer to the military frontiers, and some had never vis-ited the ancient capital. Constantine's move was there-fore an acknowledgment of existing realities. Byzantium, renamed Constantinople in honor of himself, was at the strategic and economic center of the empire. Rome, though still a great city, was becoming a museum.

Moving the imperial capital from Rome to Con-stantinople hastened the decline of the west, but it was only one of several steps taken by Constantine that re-vealed the shape of the future. The most important was his personal acceptance of the Christian religion. His reasons for doing so are not entirely clear. Constantine's mother, Helen, was a Christian, but he grew up a vir-tual hostage at the pagan court of Diocletian. It was not until the battle of the Milvian Bridge in 312 that he had his troops paint Christian symbols on their shields. Af-terward, he claimed that a flaming cross in the sky had led them to victory. Constantine's grasp of Christian principles remained weak to the end, and he may have converted simply because he thought that the magic of the Christians was stronger. An element of political cal-culation probably also entered into his decision.

**Illustration 6.5**

⧆ **Monumental Head of the Emperor Constantine.** Originally part of a much larger seated statue, the head alone is more than eight feet tall and is meant to convey a godlike impression.

In the course of the third century, the Christians had become a political force in the eastern half of the empire. No longer a church of the weak and helpless, it included people of great influence in Diocletian's administration, some of whom were thought capable of fraud and violence. In 303 Diocletian became convinced that they were plotting against him and launched the last and most savage of the persecutions. He was encouraged in this by Galerius, whose tenure in the east had convinced him that the Christians were a menace to imperial government as a whole. When Diocletian abdicated, Galerius continued to pursue anti-Christian policies until his own death in 311 and bequeathed them to his successor, Maximin Daia. Constantine perhaps adopted Christianity because he and

his then-ally Licinius needed Christian support in their successful struggle with Maximin Daia. However, no direct evidence of this is available, and little reason exists to suppose that Christian support affected the final outcome of these imperial struggles.

In any case, Constantine's adoption of Christianity changed the basic character of the church. Though paganism continued to be tolerated, Christianity now had many of the characteristics of an official religion. Homes and catacombs were abandoned as centers of worship in favor of the basilica, an oblong structure of the sort used for Roman public assemblies (see illustration 6.6). The new construction—and the clergy itself—was funded in part with imperial monies, and membership was both a mark of status and essential for those who wished to reach the highest levels of the imperial service.

Converts poured in, and Christian principles became the basis for a mass of legislation. Even before his final victory in 324, Constantine moved to limit the brutality of official punishments and to expand poor relief. To provide poor women with an alternative to infanticide, the most common and effective method of birth control in ancient times, arrangements were made for the care of foundlings. Most measures were benign, but the sterner side of Christian morality was reflected in new and savage penalties for adultery, prostitution, and premarital sex.

Constantine might not have understood the intricacies of Christian theology. As a practical ruler, however, he knew that doctrinal disputes could lead to political disorder. He sought from the beginning of his reign to end the heresies that disturbed the church.

The most important of these involved the Trinity. By 260 a majority of Christians believed that there was one God, but that God had three persons—the Father, the Son (Christ), and the Holy Spirit. In the reign of Constantine, an Alexandrian priest named Arius advanced the view that Christ was a created being, neither fully God nor fully man. This called the nature of Christ's sacrifice into question, for, if he were not both fully man and fully God, how could his suffering on the cross have atoned for the sins of humankind?

The popular interest aroused by this argument is hard to imagine today, but trinitarian disputes became a fruitful source of riots and other violence in the cities of the empire. Arianism may have masked political and regional grievances that owed little to religion. In any case, Constantine was forced to call another general meeting of the church. In 325 the Council of Nicaea decreed that Christ was both fully man and fully God,

**Illustration 6.6**

The Basilica of Santa Maria Maggiore, Rome. The basilica, with its columned side isles and flat roof, was adapted from earlier Roman architectural practice and became the standard for Christian church construction in the west after Constantine's conversion. This example was built between 432 and 440.

and this formula was defined even more carefully by the Council of Chalcedon in 451 (see document 6.2). It eventually became the orthodox position in both the eastern and the western churches, but, for many, the question remained unsettled.

## The Final Division of the Empire and the Decline of the West

In retrospect, the reign of Constantine seemed to many a golden age. People saw the reunification of the empire, the establishment of a new capital, and the acceptance of Christianity as extraordinary achievements whose luster was enhanced by the godlike ritual that surrounded the emperor and by the overall competence of his administration. Yet for all his apparent brilliance, Constantine failed to solve the basic problems that were tearing apart the empire. He did nothing to limit the political influence of the army or to develop an orderly process of imperial succession. Though he was lucky enough to escape a major crisis along his northern and western borders, the underlying military and economic weakness of the west remained (see map 6.2). By shifting the center of government from west to east, he may have accelerated the west's decline.

Constantine's death in 337 was followed by a bitter struggle between his sons that ended with the victory of the Arian Constantius II (d. 361). Constantius's successor, Julian, known as the Apostate, rejected Christianity altogether. His effort to restore paganism died with him in 363 on a remote Mesopotamian battlefield. Imperial unity died as well. To western Germans such as the Franks and Alemanni, Julian's ill-fated attempt to destroy the Sassanid Empire provided them with an opportunity for renewed attacks along the Rhine and upper Danube. Realizing that the German threat would require all of his attention, the new emperor, Valentinian (reigned 364–375), established himself at Milan in northern Italy and left the eastern half of the empire to his brother Valens (reigned 364–378). The brothers maintained separate courts and administrations—the one Latin-speaking, the other Greek. The division between east and west, which had slowed at least outwardly under Constantine, accelerated.

Valentinian neutralized the Germans on the Rhine. Upon his death in 375, he left the western half of the empire to his son, Gratian. The next year a more serious crisis developed in the Balkans. The Huns, an Asiatic people of uncertain origin, conquered the Ostrogothic kingdom north of the Black Sea and pressed westward against the Visigoths who inhabited the lower Danube. The Visigoths asked and received permission to seek refuge within the empire. They repaid Valen's generosity by looting the Balkan provinces. The emperor was forced to break off yet another war with the Persians to confront them. The result was dis-

## DOCUMENT 6.2

### The Council of Chalcedon: The Nature of Christ

*The formula devised by the Council of Chalcedon in 451 defines the nature of Christ in such a way as to leave no room for Arian, Monophysite, or other interpretations of the Trinity. That is the reason for its precise, legalistic, and inelegant language.*

Following the holy fathers we teach with one voice that the Son [of God] and our Lord Jesus Christ is to be confessed as one and the same [Person], that he is perfect in manhood, very God and very man, of a reasonable soul and [human] body consisting consubstantial with the Father as touching his Godhead, and with us as touching his manhood; made in all things like unto us, sin only excepted; begotten of his Father before the worlds according to his Godhead; but in these last days for us men and for our salvation born of the Virgin Mary, the Mother of God according to his manhood. This one and the same Jesus Christ, the only begotten Son [of God] must be confessed to be in two natures, unconfusedly, immutably, indivisibly, inseparably, and that without the distinction of natures being taken away by such union, but rather the peculiar property of each nature being preserved and being united in one Person and subsistence, not separated or divided into two persons, but one and the same Son and only-begotten, God the Word, our Lord Jesus Christ.

Chalcedon, in P. Schaff and H. Wace, eds. *A Select Library of Nicene and Post-Nicene Fathers of the Christian Church,* vol. 14, 2d series. New York: 1899–1900.

cavalry, he reduced the role of the legions and made heavily armored *cataphracti* the dominant element in a reorganized Roman army. It was a major step in the development of medieval warfare. The importance of cavalry had been growing steadily since the military reforms of Diocletian.

His religious policies were equally important. Theodosius made Christianity the official religion of the empire and actively suppressed not only the pagans but also Arianism. Paganism remained more firmly entrenched in the west than in the east, especially among the educated upper classes. When Gratian's successor, Valentinian II, died in 392, Theodosius became sole emperor after suppressing a revolt in the west that had been inspired at least partially by paganism. Nicaean Christianity was imposed upon the west, and for two brief years the empire was once again united.

The final division came in 395, when the dying Theodosius left the empire to his two sons. The eastern half went on as before, an empire in its own right that, though Greek in language, continued to evolve according to Roman legal and administrative precedents. The west, as a political entity, ceased to exist within two generations. Long before the reign of Theodosius it had begun to exhibit the economic, political, and religious decentralization that is thought of today as medieval. As trade and the circulation of money decreased, the great estates grew larger and more self-sufficient. Their powerful owners, anxious to protect their workforce, prevented their tenants from joining the army. This, together with a slow but persistent decline in population, forced the emperors to recruit barbarians by offering them land within the empire. Barbarian chiefs or commanders sometimes acquired latifundia as a reward for their services, and by the end of the fourth century, the line between Roman and barbarian had become blurred, especially in Gaul.

Few of these men understood, or accepted, Roman ideas of law and culture. The persistence of old tribal or personal allegiances, in addition to conflict between Romans and barbarians, led to internal violence that the imperial government could rarely control. Faced with increasing disorder in the countryside, the latifundia developed small armies of their own, while peasants—both Roman and barbarian—were forced to seek protection by becoming their tenants. Those whose situation was truly desperate were accepted only under the harshest of terms and became little more than serfs.

Even the church did little to promote unity. It remained essentially an urban institution. The term *pagani*, or pagans, was originally Latin slang for rustics,

aster. In 378 the Visigothic cavalry destroyed Valens and his army at Adrianople (now Edirne in European Turkey), a strategic site that controls the land approaches to Constantinople. Gratian, as the surviving augustus, appointed the Spanish general Theodosius (347–395) to succeed his uncle as emperor in the east.

Theodosius was in many respects a remarkable character. He restored order in the Balkans by allowing the Visigoths to set up an independent, though allied, Germanic state on imperial soil. Believing that the battle of Adrianople had demonstrated the superiority of

MAP 6.2
Migration and Invasion Routes

and Christianity had long found penetrating the rural world difficult. That world was dominated by the estate owners, some of whom were still attached to the values of ancient Rome. Others, especially those of German origin, were Christian but remained Arians until well into the seventh century.

The church was more powerful in the western towns. It maintained a degree of independence that contrasted sharply with attitudes prevalent in the east. There, the imperial office retained some of the religious character it had inherited from paganism. The emperor normally controlled the appointment of eastern bishops and, in later years, would acquire the right to define dogma. Western bishops, meanwhile, were elected, sometimes by public acclamation. They often

controlled their city governments and were beginning to formulate the idea of separation between church and state. St. Ambrose (c. 339–397), as bishop of Milan, once imposed a public penance on Theodosius for ordering the massacre of rebels and told him on another occasion: "[D]o not burden your conscience with the thought that you have any right as Emperor over sacred things."

A society so burdened by poverty and decentralization could not defend itself against the renewed onslaughts of the barbarians (see documents 6.3 and 6.4). After 406 a Germanic people known as the Vandals marched through Gaul and Spain to establish themselves in Africa. In 410 an army of Visigoths sacked Rome. Attila the Hun invaded Italy between

## ◈ DOCUMENT 6.3 ◈

### St. Jerome: Conditions in the Early Fifth Century

*St. Jerome (c. 347–c. 420) is best known as the translator of the Bible into Latin. He was also deeply attached to Roman culture. This fragment from his letters is dramatic evidence of his dismay as well as of his skill as a rhetorician.*

Nations innumerable and most savage have invaded all Gaul. The whole region between the Alps and the Pyrenees, the Ocean and the Rhine, has been devastated by the Quadi, the Vandals, the Sarmati, the Alani, the Gepidae, the hostile Heruli, the Saxons, the Burgundians, the Alemanni, and the Pannonians. O wretched Empire. Mayence, formerly so noble a city, has been taken and ruined, and in the church many thousands of men have been massacred. Worms has been destroyed after a long siege. Rheims, that powerful city, Amiens, Arras, Speyer, Strasbourg—all have seen their citizens led away captive into Germany. Aquitaine and the provinces of Lyon and Narbonne, all save a few towns, have been depopulated; and these the sword threatens from without, while hunger ravages within. I cannot speak without tears of Toulouse, which the merits of the holy Bishop Exuperius have prevailed so far to preserve from destruction. Spain, even, is in daily terror lest it perish, remembering the invasion of the Cimbri; and whatsoever the other provinces have suffered once, they continue to suffer in their fear.

I will keep silence concerning the rest, lest I seem to despair of the mercy of God. For a long time, from the Black Sea to the Julian Alps, those things which are ours have not been ours; and for thirty years, since the Danube boundary was broken, war has been waged in the very midst of the Roman Empire. Our tears are dried by old age. Except for a few old men, all were born in captivity and siege, and do not desire the liberty they never knew. Who could believe this? How could the whole tale be worthily told?

Robinson, James Harvey, eds. *Readings in European History,* vol. 1. Boston: Ginn, 1904.

## ◈ DOCUMENT 6.4 ◈

### Roman Acceptance of Barbarian Rule

*Salvianus (c. 400–480) saw the fall of Rome as God's judgment on those who had oppressed the poor. His view is a valuable correction to that of St. Jerome and explains clearly why most Romans accepted barbarian rule without serious protest.*

But what else can these wretched people wish for, they who suffer the incessant and even continuous destruction of public tax levies. To them there is always imminent a heavy and relentless proscription. They desert their homes, lest they be tortured in their very homes. They seek exile, lest they suffer torture. The enemy is more lenient to them than the tax collectors. This is proved by this very fact, that they flee to the enemy in order to avoid the full force of the heavy tax levy. This very tax levying, although hard and inhuman, would nevertheless be less heavy and harsh if all would bear it equally and in common. Taxation is made more shameful and burdensome because all do not bear the burden of all. They extort tribute from the poor man for the taxes of the rich, and the weaker carry the load for the stronger. There is no other reason that they cannot bear all the taxation except that the burden imposed on the wretched is greater than their resources.

*The Writing of Salvian the Presbyter,* trans. J. F. O'Sullivan. Washington, DC: Catholic University of America Press, 1947.

451 and his death in 453. In 455 Rome was sacked again, this time by Vandals. Lacking an effective army of their own, the emperors were forced to rely upon barbarian chieftains for protection. As the barbarians soon realized, the emperor had become largely irrelevant.

The wars of the fifth century were struggles between various barbarian armies for control over the remains of the western empire. In 476 the Ostrogothic general Odoacer (c. 433–493) deposed the emperor Romulus Augustulus and was recognized by the eastern emperor as his viceroy. This event is known conventionally as "the fall of Rome," but the western empire had long since ceased to exist. Vandals ruled Africa, Visigoths governed Spain, and Gaul was now divided into a variety of jurisdictions ruled by Franks, Burgundians, and other tribes. Italy was given over to the Ostrogoths, but their rule was not destined to last.

In one final effort to reunite the empire, the eastern emperor Justinian "the Great" (reigned 527–565) conquered North Africa from the Vandals and mounted a campaign for the recovery of Italy. Assisted by his wife, Theodora (c. 497–548), a former actress and prostitute who was his equal in political skill and his superior in courage, Justinian sought to rebuild the empire of Constantine. He accomplished much, including the building of the great church of St. Sophia at Constantinople and the long overdue codification of Roman law, but his attempts at reunification failed. He was the first of the Byzantine emperors.

In 552, after seventeen years of warfare, an army under his eunuch general Narses defeated the Ostrogoths. The resources of the peninsula were by now depleted. Byzantine war taxes, together with forced requisitions and looting by both sides, destroyed the basis of subsistence while terrible plagues, spread by the passage of armies, killed tens of thousands who had survived the war. Some parts of Italy were reduced to a mere seventh of their former population.

Devastated by war and by years of economic decline, the country became easy prey for yet another wave of Germanic invaders, the Lombards. These fierce people quickly seized most of northern Italy. Unlike the Ostrogoths, they preferred to kill the remaining Roman landholders and confiscate their estates. The successors of Justinian, impoverished by his ambitious policies, could do little to stop them. By the end of the seventh century, Byzantine control was limited to the coastal regions along the Adriatic. The exarch or military governor who ruled this territory did so from Ravenna, a city built on a sandbar and protected from the armies of the mainland by a broad lagoon.

## The Evolution of the Western Church (A.D. 306–529)

In the midst of political turmoil, the church in the west continued to expand. As St. Augustine (354–430) pointed out in his book *The City of God*, no essential connection existed between the kingdom of Heaven and any earthly power, and Christians should leave politics alone if they valued their souls. Augustine was bishop of Hippo, near Carthage, and his view grew naturally from the suspicion of political authority that had been characteristic of the African church. He was also

the friend and convert of St. Ambrose. *The City of God*, completed in 426, was written in response to the first sack of Rome. In it, Augustine argued that "two cities have been formed by two loves: the earthly by love of self, even to the contempt of God; the heavenly by the love of God, even to the contempt of self." The earthly city must inevitably pass away as the city of God grows. In practical terms, this implied that the authority of the church must eventually supersede that of the state, though ideally church and state should cooperate for the greater protection of the faithful.

Augustine's work lies at the root of medieval political thought and reflects the growing gap between western and eastern concepts of the church's role. That gap was further widened by the evolution of the papacy. The early church recognized four patriarchs—bishops whose authority exceeded that of the others. They ruled the dioceses (ecclesiastical districts) of Rome, Constantinople, Alexandria, and Antioch. Of these, the bishop of Rome was most venerated, though veneration did not necessarily imply obedience. The erosion of political authority in the west and the removal of the capital to Constantinople caused the popes, notably Innocent I (served 402–417) and Leo I (served 440–461), to claim universal jurisdiction over the church and to base their claims more firmly upon the doctrine of apostolic succession (see document 6.5).

Such claims were contested, and the Council of Chalcedon greatly annoyed Leo by granting the patriarch of Constantinople primacy in the east, but papal claims were based to some extent on political reality. Throughout the dark years of the fifth century, the popes often provided leadership when the imperial office failed.

Intellectually, too, the western church continued to flourish. In addition to *The City of God*, St. Augustine elaborated on a concept of sin and grace that was to have a long-lasting impact on Western thought. He was moved to write on this subject by the teachings of Pelagius, a Briton who believed in unlimited free will. Pelagius argued that a Christian could achieve salvation simply by choosing to live a godly life. Augustine, whose early struggles with sin are chronicled in his *Confessions*, claimed that human nature was so corrupted by its Fall from the Garden of Eden that salvation was impossible without God's grace and that grace is given selectively. God, in other words, predestines some to salvation and some to punishment. In 529, long after both men were dead, the Synod of Orange rejected Pelagianism but did not officially endorse the Augustinian view, which remained an undercurrent in medieval theology, only to surface again with renewed vigor in

## ◆ DOCUMENT 6.5 ◆

# The Petrine Theory

*One of the clearest expositions of the Petrine theory or doctrine of the apostolic succession was by Pope Leo I "the Great" who claimed universal authority over the Christian church because as bishop of Rome he was the successor to St. Peter and in Matthew 16:18 Jesus had said: "Thou art Peter, and upon this rock I will build my church; and the gates of hell shall not prevail against it."*

Our Lord Jesus Christ, the Saviour of the world, caused his truth to be promulgated through the apostles. And while this duty was placed on all of the apostles, the Lord made St. Peter the head of them all, that from him as from their head his gifts should flow out into all the body. So that if anyone separates himself from St. Peter he should know that he has no share in the Divine blessing. . . . Constantinople has its own glory and by the mercy of God has become the seat of the empire. But secular matters are based on one thing, ecclesiastical matters on another. For nothing will stand which is not built on the rock [Peter] which the Lord laid in the foundation [Matt. 16:18]. . . . Your city is royal, but you cannot make it apostolic.

Thatcher, O. J., and McNeal, E. H., eds. *A Source Book of Medieval History.* New York: Scribner's, 1905.

the Protestant Reformation of the sixteenth century. The rest of Augustine's thought was less controversial. His concept of the church, its sacraments, and even his view of history were widely accepted in the Middle Ages and remain influential among Christians today.

Though not an original theologian, Augustine's older contemporary St. Jerome (c. 347–c. 420) was an outstanding scholar and Latin stylist who supported Augustine in the Pelagian controversy and continued the history of the church begun by Eusebius. His most important contribution, however, was the Latin translation of the Bible known as the Vulgate, which remained the standard for western Christendom until the sixteenth century.

Perhaps the most striking feature of Christian life in the later Roman Empire was the spread of monasticism. Most of the world's great religions have produced, at one time or another, men and women who dedicate

themselves to a life of religious devotion away from the distractions of the secular world. In Christianity, this impulse first surfaced when the church began to change from a persecuted congregation of believers to a universal faith. In 291 a young Egyptian named Anthony took to heart the words of Jesus: "If you will be perfect, go sell all thou hast and give to the poor, and come, follow me." He retired to a cave in the desert and became the first of many hermits who followed his example.

Within only a few years, another Egyptian, Pachomius (c. 290–346), realized that the isolated life of the hermit placed demands upon the mind and body that only the strongest could survive. Ordinary mortals, however devout, needed the support and discipline of a community that shared their goals. He therefore organized the first formal congregations of hermits and gave them a rule that became the basis of all subsequent monastic institutions in the west. The monks were to live in common and divide their time between work and prayer. Poverty and chastity were assumed as essential to a life lived in imitation of Christ, and obedience was regarded as a natural part of communal living.

During the age of Constantine, monasteries, some of them with congregations numbering in the thousands, sprang up throughout Egypt, Palestine, and Syria. Women were as attracted to the movement as men. Athanasius (c. 293–373), bishop of Alexandria and energetic opponent of the Arians, spread the gospel of monasticism during his travels in the west, and by the end of the fourth century, the institution was solidly established in every part of Europe. Augustine practiced communal living as a matter of course, and Jerome established a convent of saintly women at Jerusalem.

The chaos of the fifth century may have enhanced the attractions of monastic life, but monasteries were not as isolated from the world as their inmates might have wished. Many, if not most, houses were established in rural areas whose populations were imperfectly Christianized. Monks surrounded by pagans were obligated to attempt their conversion, and the monasteries became centers for the spreading of the faith. Each community, moreover, had to be supported economically. Peasants attached themselves to nearby convents and monasteries in much the same way that they became tenants of the great secular estates—and for many of the same reasons. The larger foundations became latifundia in their own right. Abbots and abbesses mastered the art of administration and exerted a substantial influence on regional politics. But monasticism made its greatest contributions in the intellectual realm. In a world of declining literacy, monasteries remained the chief purveyors of education and the heart of whatever intellectual life remained. Their libraries preserved the Latin classics for a later, more appreciative age.

The heart of monastic life was the rule that governed the lives of monks or nuns. In the west, the rule of St. Benedict of Nursia (c. 480–c. 547) was universally accepted for nearly six centuries and remains the basis of daily life in many religious orders today (see document 6.6). Benedict was abbott of the great monastery at Monte Cassino, north of Naples. His rule, though not wholly original, was brief, moderate, and wise in its understanding of human nature. He based it on the ideal of *mens sano en corpore sano,* a healthy mind in a healthy body. Work, prayer, and study were stressed equally in an atmosphere governed by loving discipline. The Benedictine rule prescribes an ordered, pious life well suited to the development of one of medieval Europe's most powerful institutions.

The growing importance of monasticism was only one of the ways in which late Roman society began to foreshadow that of the Middle Ages. It was above all increasingly Christian, though the western church had long since begun to diverge in organization and practice from its eastern counterpart. It was also agrarian and generally poor. Though small freeholds continued to exist in Italy, Frankish Gaul, and elsewhere, much of the countryside was dominated by self-sufficient estates worked by tenants and defended by bands of armed retainers. An increasing number of these estates supported monasteries. For reasons that are as yet poorly understood, crop yields rarely rose above the subsistence level. Western cities, reduced to a fraction of their former size, were often little more than large agricultural villages whose inhabitants tilled their fields by day and retreated within the walls at night. Ruled in many cases by their bishops, they retained something of their Roman character, but lack of specie and the violence endemic in the countryside limited trade and communications. Contacts with the eastern empire, though never entirely abandoned, became rare. By the end of the fifth century, the Mediterranean unity forged by Rome had ceased to exist. A distinctively European society, formed of Roman, Celtic, and Germanic elements, was beginning to emerge.

## ◆ DOCUMENT 6.6 ◆

### The Rule of St. Benedict

*The following sections capture St. Benedict's view that monks should live a disciplined but balanced life dedicated to apostolic poverty.*

Chapter 33—The sin of owning private property should be entirely eradicated from the monastery. No one shall presume to give or receive anything except by order of the abbot; no one shall possess anything of his own, books, paper, pens, or anything else, for monks are not to own even their own bodies and wills to be used at their own desire, but are to look to the father of the monastery for everything.

Chapter 48—Idleness is the great enemy of the soul, therefore monks should always be occupied, either in manual labor or in holy reading. The hours for these occupations should be arranged according to the seasons, as follows: From Easter to the first of October, the monks shall go to work at the first hour and labor until the fourth hour, and the time from the fourth to the sixth hour shall be spent in reading. After dinner, which comes at the sixth hour, they shall lie down and rest in silence; but anyone who wishes may read, if he does it so as not to disturb anyone else. Nones shall be observed a little earlier, about the middle of the eighth hour, and the monks shall go back to work, laboring until vespers. But if the conditions of the locality or the needs of the monastery, such as may occur at harvest time, should make it necessary to labor longer hours, they shall not feel themselves ill-used, for true monks should live by the labor of their own hands, as did the apostles and the holy fathers.

"*Regula Monchorum.*" in O. J. Thatcher and E. H. McNeal, eds., *A Source Book of Medieval History.* New York: Scribner's, 1905.

## CHAPTER 7

# ROME'S SUCCESSORS: BYZANTIUM, ISLAM, AND THE GERMANIC WEST

## CHAPTER OUTLINE

T he fall of Rome conventionally marks the beginning of European history, but Europe did not develop wholly in isolation. It was one of three great societies that emerged after the breakup of Mediterranean civilization. Byzantium and the world of Islam, were, like medieval Europe, heirs to the broader culture that had been consolidated and refined by centuries of Roman rule. They developed along radically different lines, but each exerted a powerful influence on Western civilization.

## The Byzantine Empire and Its Government

The reforms of Diocletian and Constantine established the institutional framework of the Byzantine Empire long before the separation of east and west. The system they created evolved without interruption until 1453, though the empire had been reduced in size by the conquests of Islam in the seventh century and weakened after 1100 by the impact of the Crusades.

The heart of that system remained the person of the emperor. Though he was usually the designated heir of his predecessor, he had to be acclaimed by the Senate, the army, and the people of Constantinople before he could be crowned. The empress, who might be the emperor's wife, sister, mother, or aunt, often exerted substantial power of her own and could rule independently if the emperor were incapacitated or a minor. Once in office, the emperor's power was theoretically absolute. As the vicar of God on Earth, he held the lives and property of every subject in his hands and could punish or confiscate without appeal. In practice, law and common sense limited the exercise of this arbitrary power. Any of the electoral groups—usually the army—could proclaim a successor if an emperor proved unsatisfactory. The choice then had to be confirmed by the Senate and the people before the usurpation was

## ◆ DOCUMENT 7.1 ◆

# Justinian: Institutes on Justice and the Law

*The Institutes is the shortest of the four parts of the Corpus Iuris Civilis, and it provides a framework for the entire Corpus. The first section of the first book of the Institutes opens with a preamble on the nature of justice and law, and the best means of teaching it to students. The discussion then moves to general categories in the law ranging from the law of persons to penalties for overeager litigants. The section on disinheriting children reflects partibility as the basis of inheritance in Roman law; that is, children must normally inherit equally.*

1.1   JUSTICE AND LAW. Justice is an unswerving and perpetual determination to acknowledge all men's rights. 1. Learning in the law entails knowledge of God and man, and mastery of the difference between justice and injustice. 2. As we embark on the exposition of Roman law after these general statements, the best plan will be to give brief, straightforward accounts of each topics. The denser detail must be kept till later. Any other approach would mean making students take in a huge number of distinctions right at the start while their minds were still untrained and short of stamina. Half of them would give up. Or else they would lose their self-confidence—a frequent source of discouragement for the young—and at the cost of toil and tears would in the end reach the very standard they could have attained earlier and without overwork or self-doubt if they had been taken along an easier road. 3. The commandments of the law are these: live honorably; harm nobody; give everyone his due.

1.3   THE LAW OF PERSONS. The main classification in the law of persons is this: all men are either free or slaves. 1. Liberty—the Latin *libertas* give us *liberi*, free men—denotes a man's natural ability to do what he wants as long as the law or some other force does not prevent him. 2. Slavery, on the other hand, is an institution of the law of all peoples; it makes a man the property of another, contrary to the law of nature.

2.13   DISINHERITING CHILDREN. Someone with a son within his authority must be sure to appoint him heir or to disinherit him specifically. If he passes over him in silence, his will becomes a nullity. . . . However, the old rules did not apply with the same rigour to daughters or to other male or female members of the family descended through the male line. If they were neither appointed heirs nor disinherited the will was not wholly invalidated. Instead they had a right to come in for their proper shares. The head of the family was also not obliged to disinherit them by name but could do it by a general clause.

4.16   PENALTIES FOR OVER-EAGER LITIGANTS. We should notice what pains the guardians of the law have taken to see that people do not turn lightly to litigation. This is our concern as well. The main checks on the eagerness of plaintiffs and defendants are money penalties, oaths to bind the conscience, and the fear of disgrace.

*Justinian's Institutes*, pp. 37–39, ed. and trans. Peter Birks and Grant MacLeod. Ithaca, NY: Cornell University Press, 1987.

---

complete. The voice of the people was normally expressed by the crowd at the Hippodrome, the great racetrack that lay next to the imperial palace at the heart of the city. Chariot racing remained a dominant passion in Byzantine life, and as many as 100,000 spectators would gather to cheer on the Blues or the Greens, racing teams that were also political factions. The possibility of being deposed and blinded by rival generals, or perhaps dismembered by the mob, preserved a measure of imperial accountability. Only about half of the Byzantine emperors died a natural death in office.

The Roman legal tradition acted as a further restraint on arbitrary behavior. The emperor Justinian, who came to the throne in A.D. 527 and reigned for nearly forty years before dying at age eighty-three,

saved the body of Roman law that has reached modern times. The distillation of Roman law and commentaries on it, compiled by Justinian and his advisers and collectively known as the *Corpus Iuris Civilis* (Body of the Civil Law) were published at Constantinople in A.D. 533. (see document 7.1). They filled three large volumes that became one of the most influential law books ever written. Ironically, the *Codex, Digest,* and *Institutes* produced under Justinian may have been more important in the west than in the east. In the west, Roman law was largely replaced by Germanic traditions and had to be revived in the twelfth century, a process that would have been impossible without accessible texts. In contrast, eastern courts maintained Roman law without interruption, modifying it on occasion to reflect Christian values. Respect for the tradition was universal, and though the emperor had the power to appoint and re-move judges, he rarely if ever ignored their opinions.

A massive bureaucracy, established originally by Diocletian and greatly expanded in the centuries after his death, carried out the imperial commands. It regu-lated every aspect of economic, political, and religious life. Prices and wages were fixed by law, and movement within the empire was controlled by a system of inter-nal passports designed to prevent people from leaving their homes or hereditary occupations. An effective po-lice system unlike anything in the medieval west main-tained order in town and countryside, while a fleet of galleys patrolled the seas to keep them free of pirates. Other officials managed state-owned factories, the mines, and the distribution of water.

Many of these people, especially at the higher lev-els of the bureaucracy, were eunuchs—men who had been castrated in youth. Eunuchs were excluded from the imperial office by law, and their inability to produce heirs prevented the establishment of administrative dy-nasties, much less the kind of hereditary aristocracy that encouraged political decentralization in the me-dieval west. Emperors thus trusted them, and their em-ployment made a substantial contribution to Byzantine stability. Ambitious parents sometimes had their sons castrated to advance their careers, not only in the church or civil service, but also in the army.

The Byzantine military, like the civil service, evolved from Roman precedents modified by experi-ence in the east. The army was composed of heavy ar-mored cavalry (*cataphracti*) supported by archers and by a heavy infantry armed with shields and swords or axes. "Greek fire," a kind of napalm whose composition re-mains secret to this day, was used on both land and sea, and siegecraft was a highly developed art. Though the Byzantines prided themselves on their superior grasp of strategy, they preferred whenever possible to rely upon negotiation. Their diplomacy was known for its sub-tlety as well as for its lavishness. They believed that even massive subsidies were cheaper than a war. Mag-nificent gifts were given to prospective enemies, and if such people chose to call it tribute, what else could one expect from barbarians?

The Byzantines paid heavily for all of this security and regulation. A land tax fell upon every property in the empire, including monasteries and the imperial es-tates. Reassessment took place every fifteen years. If a farmer could not pay, his obligation had to be assumed by his neighbors under a system known as *epiboli*. A head tax also was imposed. Levies on farm animals, business inventories, imports, and exports were supple-mented by surtaxes in times of special need.

Few governments have been more efficient in their extraction of surplus wealth, but some of the proceeds were spent on alleviating poverty. Though regular dis-tributions of grain to the poor stopped at the beginning of the seventh century, officials were expected to pro-vide food in times of scarcity and to administer a host of orphanages and other charities. The heavy taxes may have permitted only a few to rise above the poverty level, but fewer still were destitute.

## The Economic and Social Structures of Byzantine Society

In time, the autocratic and intrusive character of the Byzantine state produced a social structure that had few parallels in the medieval world. Asia Minor and the Balkan Peninsula formed the heartland of the Byzantine Empire even before the Muslims took Syria, Egypt, and North Africa in the seventh century. Both are rugged lands whose narrow valleys and small plateaus are cut off from one another because of geography and because their inhabitants come from different ethnic groups with long histories of mutual conflict. It would be hard to imagine a site less likely to encourage social equality and weak kinship ties, but that is what happened.

In the face of overwhelming imperial power, social distinctions receded. Below the throne, everyone was equal. Variations were seen in wealth, but Byzantine so-ciety had absorbed Christian teachings so that it did not regard money as a measure of virtue. Prestige de-pended primarily upon bureaucratic rank, and rank de-pended upon merit or on the bureaucrat's usefulness to the emperor. The widespread employment of eunuchs and the principle that all wealth could be appropriated to the service of the state inhibited the growth of those elaborate social hierarchies characteristic of the me-dieval west. As a result, social distinctions were fluid and relatively minor. The empress Theodora was not the only great personage to come from the lowest lev-els of society (see illustration 7.1).

Even ethnic distinctions became largely irrelevant. The Byzantines were remarkably free of prejudice, though they sometimes persecuted Jews on religious grounds and may, in the early years, have looked down upon the Germans who were found in disproportionate numbers among their slaves and household servants. The imperial court embraced Greeks, Serbs, Bulgars, Armenians, Cappadocians, and a score of other ethnic groups without distinction; the ordinary citizen could do no less.

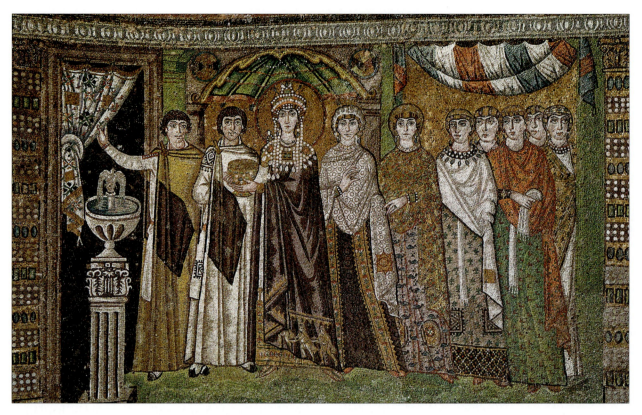

**Illustration 7.1**

**Empress Theodora and Her Attendants.** This mosaic from the church of San Vitale, Ravenna, Italy, is one of a pair; the other shows Theodora's husband, Justinian, with his own entourage in a similar pose.

The same conditions that promoted social equality may have discouraged the growth of extended families. A few great clans attached themselves to the imperial court, often for several generations, but the western development of lineages—extended families who took their names and social identities from their estates—had no parallel in the east until the tenth or eleventh century. Instead, the Byzantines lived overwhelmingly in tight-knit nuclear families, often maintaining a certain distance in their dealings with others. Some writers warned against friendship because it might arouse the suspicions of the state. Most people, encouraged perhaps by the *epiboli*, acknowledged the obligation to help one's neighbors. However, Byzantine society, for all its outward regimentation, remained on the personal level individualistic, self-seeking, and often cynical in its relationships.

Roman law reinforced these tendencies to some extent by ensuring the equal division of property among heirs and by favoring the preservation of freehold tenures. Most Byzantines were small farmers who owned their own land. Some were serfs or tenants on the estates of the emperor or his more important servants, and some were slaves, though the incidence of slavery declined throughout the Byzantine era and by the eleventh century had attracted the opposition of the church on moral grounds. Commerce centered in the great city of Constantinople, which, until the Crusades, dominated the trade between Asia and the west. With its population of more than 400,000 it dwarfed the other towns of the empire. Provincial cities declined steadily in importance throughout the Byzantine centuries as bureaucracy and centralization strangled the ancient Greek municipal tradition.

Christianity, not civic ideals, formed the moral and intellectual center of Byzantine life. Even the Byzantines sometimes complained that buying a piece of fruit in the market was impossible without becoming immersed in a discussion of the Trinity, but religion to them was more than a mental exercise; it was the conceptual framework of their lives. Religious disputes thus played an important role in Byzantine politics. The struggle between the orthodox and the Monophysites, who held that Christ's nature was fully human but that

**Illustration 7.2**

🎵 **Mosaic of Christ Pancrator, Daphni, Greece.** In Byzantine art, Jesus is normally portrayed as Christ Almighty, who mediates between God and humankind, and images such as this one are placed in the central dome or the main apse of eastern churches. In contrast, western church art tends to emphasize the crucifixion.

it had been transformed by the divine, convulsed the empire for nearly four centuries. The Iconoclastic Controversy over the use of religious images or icons generated revolts and persecutions from 726 to 843.

Though the Greek and Latin churches did not divide formally until 1054, they followed different lines of development almost from the first. In the east, church organization continued to parallel that of the imperial bureaucracy. Its higher officials—patriarchs, bishops, and metropolitans—were monks appointed by the emperor. They were expected to be celibate, if not eunuchs. Village priests, however, were normally married, in part because popular wisdom held that this would protect them from sexual temptation.

Like Byzantine society as a whole, eastern Christianity maintained a high degree of individualism within its rigidly hierarchical framework. It emphasized the inner transformation of the believer rather than sin and redemption. Its icons, or religious paintings, portray God as *Pantocrator* or ruler of the universe and virtually ignore Christ the crucified redeemer until late in

the empire's history (see illustration 7.2). The saints are abstract figures whose holiness is indicated by the golden aura of sanctity that surrounds them, not by individual features. Western legalism—the tendency to enumerate sins and prescribe penances—was almost wholly absent, and even monasteries encouraged individual development at the expense of communal living. Saintly hermits remained the most revered figures in Byzantium, advising emperors from their caves or from the top of pillars where they lived exposed to the elements, often for decades.

Before the death of Constantine, this faith had transformed the Greek way of life beyond recognition. The preoccupation with personal salvation, as well as the vast weight of the imperial bureaucracy, rendered the old idea of community meaningless. The ancient preoccupation with the human body vanished. The Byzantines wore long brocaded robes and heavy makeup that disguised the body's natural outlines and, like westerners, gradually abandoned the practice of bathing because the church thought of it as self-indulgent. For medieval Christians, the "odor of sanctity" was no mere figure of speech. In deportment, solemnity became the ideal even for children, who, like their elders, were supposed to mimic the icons that gazed down serenely from the domes of churches.

## Byzantium and the Slavs

At the height of its power, the Byzantine Empire exerted only a minor influence on the development of western Europe. It maintained contact with the west through the irregular correspondence of churchmen and through the remaining Byzantine possessions in southern Italy. Western poverty imposed severe limitations on trade as a medium of cultural exchange. The greatest impact of Byzantium on the west came later, through the Crusades and through the cultural borrowings transmitted by Slavs and Muslims. Byzantine influence on eastern Europe was, however, profound.

The Slavs came originally from central Asia and, by 2000 B.C., had settled a broad arc of territory from the shores of the Black Sea northwestward into what is now Poland. They appear to have weathered the passage of Celts and Germans, but the collapse of the Hunnish Empire after A.D. 455 started another cycle of population movements in eastern Europe. Slavic peoples from the valley of the Dnieper moved northward into Russia, while those from the Vistula and Oder valleys moved westward as far as the river Elbe in eastern Germany and south into Bohemia, Moravia, and what is now Hungary. By the middle of the sixth century, they had penetrated deep into the Balkan Peninsula. The Serbs, Bulgars, and Vlachs then became involved in a long and fruitful interaction with the Byzantine Empire. The northern shores of the Black Sea, long the granary of Greece and Asia Minor, remained a vital focus of Byzantine diplomacy as well, and here, too, relations were quickly established.

Contacts were not always peaceful, but the ties between Slavs and Byzantines were ultimately those of economic self-interest. War, trade, and diplomacy brought the Slavs within the larger orbit of Byzantium. With their usual indifference to ethnicity, the Byzantines accepted many of these people into the empire. By the ninth century a number of emperors had been of slavic origin, and Slavs of many sorts were firmly entrenched in the bureaucracy.

The churches, both eastern and western, made every effort to convert those Slavs who lived outside imperial territory. A bitter competition broke out between the Greeks and the Germans over whether the Greek or Latin rites should triumph. In the end, the Serbs and Bulgars were converted to the Greek rite by Sts. Cyril and Methodius in the middle of the ninth century. The Croats, Slovenes, Poles, and Czechs, among others, accepted the Latin church. In each case, the acceptance of Christianity appears to have been part of a movement toward political consolidation. During the ninth and tenth centuries Bohemia, Serbia, and Croatia emerged as independent states, and Bulgaria, which had existed in rudimentary form since the seventh century, evolved into an empire that became a serious threat to Byzantine power until the Byzantines destroyed it in 1014.

Finally, at the end of the tenth century, Byzantine missionaries converted Vladimir "the Saint," ruler of Kiev. Located on the Dnieper river, Kiev was the center of a trading network that connected the Baltic and Black seas and drew furs, amber, and wood from the forests of central Russia. Scandinavian adventurers had gained control of the city a century before. By Vladimir's time, Kiev was again thoroughly Slavic in language and culture and the center of the first great Russian state. The conversion of Kievan Rus ensured that the eastern Slavs would adopt not only Greek Christianity, but also the Greek alphabet and many elements of Byzantine culture. The connections forged in these centuries between the Byzantine Greeks and the Serbs, Bulgars, and Russians remain a powerful cultural bond to this day.

## Muhammad the Prophet and the Origins of Islam

Islam is the other great society whose interaction with Byzantium was to have profound consequences (see, map 7.1). Islam is a religion, a civilization, and a way of life. The word means submission, in this case to the will of Allah, and the followers of Islam are known as Muslims. Both the religion and the civilization based upon it grew from the revelation granted to one man.

Muhammad, the founder of Islam, was born about 570 in the Arabian caravan town of Mecca. He married a wealthy widow named Khadija and became a merchant. As he entered middle age he formed the habit of going into the mountains to meditate and pray. There, in about the year 610, the first of the teachings that make up the Koran were revealed to him by the angel Gabriel. Three years later, with his wife's encouragement, he began to preach, but Mecca was the center of an important pagan cult, and the townspeople saw his activities as a threat to their livelihood. In 622 he and his followers fled to the nearby city of Medina. This *hejira*, or immigration, marks the beginning date of the Muslim calendar. After a series of battles and negotiations, the Prophet and his followers returned and Mecca became once again the spiritual center of the movement.

The Koran is the scriptural basis of Islam, which, to Muslims, supersedes the earlier revelations found in the Jewish and Christian Bibles. It is supplemented by the *sunna*, or tradition of the prophet, a collection of sayings attributed to Muhammad that are not thought to be divinely revealed. The distinction is important because Islam is uncompromisingly monotheistic. As the *shahada* or profession of faith says: "There is no God but God, and Mohammed is his prophet." That is to say, Muhammad is not regarded as divine but only as the man through whom God's will was revealed. That revelation, embodied in the Koran, provides the Muslim with a comprehensive guide to life and thought that has the force of divine law.

Islam, like every other great world religion, eventually developed elaborate theologies, heresies, and schisms, but its essence is simple. Its creed demands belief in the one God, the angels, the revealed books, the prophets, and the Day of Judgment. The Five Pillars, or obligatory duties, are to recite the profession of faith; pray five times daily; pay the *zakat* or purification tax for the benefit of the poor; fast during the month of Ramadan, which commemorates the time in which the Koran was "sent down"; and make a pilgrimage to Mecca if wealth and family duties permit.

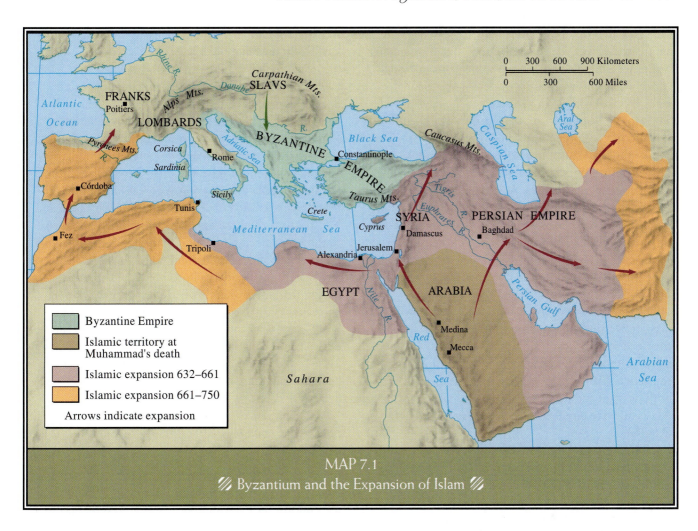

MAP 7.1

Byzantium and the Expansion of Islam

These are the basic requirements of Islam, but the goal of pious Muslims is to live according to *shari`a*, a way of life totally commanded by God. The guides to that life are the Koran, the tradition, and reason; no mysteries are required. Islam, like Judaism, is essentially a religion of the law. Based firmly on the Arabic of the Koran, which in theory cannot be translated, Islam has always been committed to the conversion of all peoples. This universality, together with the clarity of its ethical and theological demands, made the Muslim faith attractive to millions. By the time Muhammad died in 632, Islam had conquered most of the Arabian peninsula. Within the space of another generation, it had spread throughout the Middle East.

### The Expansion of Islam

From the beginning, Islam spread largely through military conquest. Muhammad had been a capable commander, and his caliphs or successors followed in his footsteps. The first Muslim attack on the Byzantine

Empire occurred in 629, while Muhammad was still alive. In 635 Arab armies seized Damascus for the first time. Recently converted Syrians took Mesopotamia in 638–639, and Egypt fell to an Arab army in 640. The motives behind this expansion were not entirely religious. Some Muslims regarded the conquests as a *jibad*, or holy war, and believed that they could attain paradise through death on the battlefield. Not all of the conquerors were religious, however, and some were not even Muslim. For such men, the Arabic tradition of raiding and the hope of booty would have been reason enough. Because Islam prohibits war against fellow Muslims, the raiding impulse tended to be directed outward, at least in the early years when the memory of the Prophet was still fresh.

The terrifying speed of the Arab conquests was in part a measure of Byzantine weakness. The emperor Heraclius (c. 575–641) had been engaged from 603 to 628 in a bitter struggle with the Persian Empire during which parts of Syria and Palestine had been ruined or occupied. At the same time he was forced to deal with

Lombard attacks on Byzantine Italy, increased activity among the Slavs on the Danube border, and incursions by Berber tribesmen against the settlements in North Africa. Heraclius was an able general—the first emperor to take the field in person since the days of Theodosius—but a war on four fronts was more than the resources of his empire could bear.

Without adequate manpower in Syria and Palestine, the Byzantines resorted to a mobile defense-in-depth conducted in part by Arab mercenaries. That is, they tried to draw the enemy into the interior, disrupting his communications and defeating his smaller contingents in detail. The size and speed of the Muslim attack coupled with an almost complete lack of intelligence about Arab intentions rendered this strategy futile. The Muslims overwhelmed their Byzantine opponents and then consolidated their victory with mass conversions in the conquered territories. By 640 they had seized Syria, Palestine, Mesopotamia, and Egypt, often without encountering significant local resistance. Many of the empire's subjects disliked both its taxes and its insistence upon religious orthodoxy and were unprepared to exert themselves in its defense.

The Sassanid Empire of Persia proved a more difficult target, but it, too, had been weakened by its long war with Byzantium. Attacked by several Arab contingents from Mesopotamia, the Persians maintained a heroic struggle until their last armies were overwhelmed in 651. In only twenty years, Islam had conquered everything from the Nile to Afghanistan.

But the death of the Caliph Omar in 644 marked the beginning of disputes over who should succeed him, and for another twenty years the newborn world of Islam was convulsed by civil wars. The eventual triumph of Mu'awia (ruled 661–680), founder of the Ommayad dynasty, led to Islam's first and greatest schism. His rival, Muhammad's son-in-law Ali, was murdered in 661, but his supporters refused to recognize Mu'awia and became the first Shi'ites. Most of these people were Persians who may have resented Arab dominance even after their conversion to Islam. In the centuries to come they would develop their own system of law; their own version of the *Hadith*, or tradition; and a number of ideas borrowed from Zoroastrian and other sources. Though a minority among Muslims as a whole, Shi'ites became the dominant Islamic sect in Iran and what is now Pakistan. The majority of western Muslims remained loyal to the *sunna* and are called Sunni Muslims to this day. In 681 a Sunni army marched from Egypt to the Atlantic Ocean and added North Africa to the house of Islam. From there, a mixed army of Berbers and Arabs crossed

the Strait of Gibraltar in 711, defeated the Visigothic king Rodrigo, and by 713 had seized all of Spain with the exception of its northern coast.

Islam may have been spread by conquest, but it does not sanction forced conversions. The attractive qualities of the faith aside, Islamic triumphs in the Middle East appear to have resulted in part from anti-Byzantine sentiment among populations long persecuted for Monophysite and other heresies and from the shrewd policy of offering tax breaks and other preferred treatment to converts. In such areas as Spain and North Africa the invaders may have seemed less alien to the Romanized population than their Germanic rulers. Their faith was different, but the Muslims generally shared the broader cultural values of the Mediterranean world. Nowhere was an attempt made to persecute Christians or Jews, the other "peoples of the book." Christian and Jewish communities lived peacefully within the Islamic world until Muslim intolerance arose in the twentieth century as a response to European colonialism.

## Social and Economic Structures in the Islamic World

The Arab warriors who conquered the world from the Indus to the Pyrenees came from a society that was still largely tribal in its organization. Lacking governmental institutions, they retained those of the Byzantines or Persians, modifying them when necessary to conform with Islamic law. Roman law was abandoned.

In theory, the caliphs, or successors to the Prophet, ruled the entire Islamic world as the executors of God's law, which they interpreted with the assistance of a body of religious scholars known as the *ulama*. The Abbasid dynasty, which claimed descent from the Prophet's uncle Abbas, displaced the Omayyads in 749 after a bitter struggle and occupied the office with declining effectiveness until 1538. After the reign of al-Mansūr from 754 to 775, they made their capital in the magnificent, newly founded city of Baghdad and administered their decrees through bureaucratic departments or *diwans* supervised by a *vizier* or prime minister. In practice, local governors enjoyed the independent powers conferred by distance. By the middle of the ninth century political decentralization was far advanced, and by 1200 the power of the Abbasids had become largely honorific. The Muslim world was ruled by local dynasties, which pursued their own policies while nominally acknowledging the authority of the caliph. Spain, which had never accepted the Abbasids, retained an Omayyad caliphate of its own. Though the caliph at Baghdad might call himself "the shadow of God on Earth," the dream of a politically united Islam proved as elusive as that of reviving the Roman Empire in the west.

The world of Islam was immense. Its geographic extent and its many different ethnic and religious groups ensured that it would be no more monolithic, politically or socially, than Catholic Europe. What unity it possessed derived from the fact that, though Jews and Christians continued to make valuable contributions to its culture, a majority of its peoples accepted the teachings of the Koran.

Generalizing about social structure in the Muslim world is difficult because of this diversity. In theory, Islam is wholly indifferent to race or class. However, the first Arab conquerors inevitably became a kind of urban aristocracy that superimposed itself on the older societies of the countryside without changing their economic structures. Systems of land tenure varied widely. Slavery was common in all parts of the Muslim world but was rarely the basis of anything except narrowly defined regional economies. It provided domestic servants and, in a development almost unique to Islam, soldiers. In the days of the great conquests, every male had the duty to defend the faith in battle. The Abbasid caliphs soon introduced the practice of purchasing slaves on the central Asian frontier, converting them to Islam, and training them in the martial arts. These *Mamluks* were mainly of Turkic origin and became the backbone of Islamic armies until well into the nineteenth century. When they enjoyed a local monopoly of military force, they sometimes usurped political power and established regional governments of their own.

Muslim clerics never became a privileged class like their Christian counterparts in the west. The scholars of the *ulama* were revered on the basis of their piety and wisdom, and some engaged in preaching, but no Muslim equivalent existed of the Christian sacraments, and any male Muslim can participate equally in prayers. The mosque, or Muslim place of worship, admits no hierarchies, and monasticism was unknown. Consequently, institutionalized religion based on the Christian model did not develop, though pious Muslims often established *waqfs* or religious endowments for charitable and other purposes.

Another unusual feature of Islamic society, at least by Western standards, was its treatment of women. The Koran permits Muslims to have as many as four wives, provided they are treated justly. In the Muslim past, practical considerations restricted polygamy largely to the rich; in modern times it has vanished almost entirely. Though shocking to Western sensibilities, this limited form of polygyny was a major improvement over the customs of pagan Arabia, which seems to have permitted unlimited numbers of wives and unlimited freedom in divorcing them. Under Islamic law, divorce remained far easier than in contemporary Christian codes. The Prophet's clear distaste for what he called "repudiation" has influenced subsequent legislation and made divorce more difficult in modern times. Another improvement was the Koranic injunction that permitted daughters to inherit property, albeit at half of the amount allotted to their brothers.

As in all such matters, the intent of the Koran was to protect women and encourage domestic morality, but the ultimate responsibility for their welfare was placed firmly in the hands of men (see document 7.2). Moreover, a number of customs that are regarded as typically Muslim have no Koranic basis.

For example, the common practice of having women wear a veil in public was not based directly on the Koran, which says only that "women should not make an exhibition of their beauty." The custom seems to have arisen in the eighth century when Muslim conquerors found themselves among people whose behaviour seemed dangerously immoral. They covered the faces of their wives to protect their virtue in what was perceived as an alien and dangerous environment.

## Islamic Culture, Science, and the Arts

Intellectually, the first few centuries after the Muslim conquests were a kind of golden age. Drawing from Greek, Persian, and Indian sources, Muslim thinkers made broad advances in mathematics, astronomy, and medicine that would eventually be adopted by the west (see document 7.3). The use of Arabic numerals and the Arabic names of the stars are examples of this influence. Western medicine, too, was based largely on the translation of Arabic texts until the "anatomical" revolution of the sixteenth century.

Philosophy reached its highest development later, between the ninth and the twelfth centuries. Muslim thinkers had better access to Greek sources than their western counterparts, and the works of such men as al-Kindi or Ibn Sina (Avicenna) were rooted firmly in the Aristotelian tradition. When they were translated into Latin in the twelfth century, their impact forced a major transformation in western thought (see chapter 9).

The arts also flourished. The Arab elite cultivated an image of sophisticated refinement that is reflected in their poetry and in the elegant calligraphy that dominated the visual arts. The Koran forbids the

◆ DOCUMENT 7.2 ◆

## The Koran on Wives and Orphans

*Sûrah 4, An-Nisâ (Women), is one of the longest sections in the Koran and is thought to have been revealed shortly after the battle of Uhud, in which many Muslims were killed. This brief extract is the basis of the Islamic toleration of polygyny and reveals the underlying concern for widows and orphans that was its inspiration.*

*In the Name of Allah, the Compassionate, the Merciful*

Men, have fear of your Lord, who created you from a single soul. From that soul He created its mate, and through them He bestrewed the earth with countless men and women.

Fear Allah, in whose name you plead with one another, and honour the mothers who bore you. Allah is ever watching over you.

Give orphans the property which belongs to them. Do not exchange their valuables for worthless things or cheat them of their possession; for this would surely be a great sin. If you fear that you cannot treat orphans [girls] with fairness, then you may marry other women who seem good to you: two, three, or four of them. But if you fear that you cannot maintain equality among them, marry one only or any slave-girls you may own. This will make it easier for you to avoid injustice.

Give women their dowry as a free gift; but if they choose to make over to you a part of it, you may regard it as lawfully yours.

Do not give the feeble-minded the property with which Allah has entrusted you for their support; but maintain and clothe them with its proceeds, and give them good advice.

Take care of orphans until they reach a marriageable age. If you find them capable of sound judgement, hand over to them their property, and do not deprive them of it by squandering it before they come of age.

Let the rich guardian not touch the property of his orphan ward; and let him who is poor use no more than a fair portion of it for his own advantage.

When you hand over to them their property, Allah takes sufficient account of all your actions.

representation of human or animal figures. Muslim artists excelled in calligraphic, geometrical, and floral decorations that were an integral part of both architecture and illuminated manuscripts (see illustration 7.3). Muslim architecture, based ultimately on late Roman and Byzantine technology but with a character all its own, was a great achievement that influenced builders in Spain, Italy, the Balkans, and Central Europe. The pointed arch favored by Muslim builders became a standard feature of gothic architecture in places as far away as England.

Throughout most of the Middle Ages, the Islamic world was richer and more sophisticated than the Christian west. Its technology, military and otherwise, was generally superior. While not escaping the limitations imposed by epidemic disease, marginal food supplies, and the other miseries of life before the industrial revolution, it probably offered a more comfortable standard of living as well. Yet westerners perceived that world as implacably hostile and tended to define themselves in opposition to its religious and cultural values.

They knew little or nothing about either, while Muslims, if they thought about westerners at all, regarded them as ignorant barbarians useful primarily as slaves.

From the eleventh century onward, the economic and military balance between the two cultures began to shift slowly in favor of the west. The advent of the Crusades and the revival of western trade increased contact between the two civilizations at every level, but the hostility remained. Europeans borrowed Muslim ideas, Muslim technologies, and Muslim tastes while waging war against Islam on land and sea. These borrowings were rarely acknowledged even though they became an important component of western culture.

◆

## Social and Economic Structures in the Post-Roman West

After the fifth century, Europe was dominated by the Germanic peoples whose migrations had brought about

## DOCUMENT 7.3

### Al-Ghazzali: Science and Religion

*Al-Ghazzali (1058–1111) was a leading defender of Islamic orthodoxy, but he understood clearly the difference between religion and science. In this passage he demonstrates the attitudes that encouraged mathematical and scientific studies in the Islamic world.*

Mathematics comprises the knowledge of calculation, geometry, and cosmography; it has no connection with the religious sciences, and proves nothing for or against religion; it rests on a foundation of proofs which, once known and understood, cannot be refuted. . . .

It is therefore a great injury to religion to suppose that the defense of Islam involves the condemnation of the exact sciences. The religious law contains nothing which approves them or condemns them, and in their turn they make no attack on religion. The words of the Prophet: "The sun and the moon are two signs of the power of God; they are not eclipsed for the birth or death of any one; when you see these signs take refuge in prayer and invoke the name of God"—these words, I say, do not in any way condemn the astronomical calculations which define the orbits of these two bodies, their conjunction and opposition according to particular laws.

*The Confession of Al-Ghazzali*, pp. 33–34, trans. Claud Field, London: John Murray, 1908.

the fall of Rome. Visigoths (West Goths) ruled Spain, and Vandals controlled the ancient province of Africa until they were supplanted in the eighth century by the Muslims. In Italy, Lombards superseded the Ostrogoths (East Goths) and maintained a violent and precarious frontier with the Byzantine Greeks. Gaul was divided among Visigoths in the southwest, Burgundians in the east, and Franks in the north. Most of these groups were themselves divided into subtribes with chieftains of their own.

Beyond the Rhine were the Alamanni, the Bavarians, and the Saxons. Slower to accept Christianity than their western cousins, they served as a barrier between the lands of what had once been the empire and the non-Germanic peoples to the east. Of these, the most important were the Slavs and the Avars, an Asiatic tribe related to the Huns who had seized control of the middle Danube valley.

Most of Britain fell to Germanic conquerors in the course of the sixth century. Small bands of Angles, Saxons, Jutes, and Frisians obtained a foothold on the eastern coast before the year 500. They seem to have made few efforts to preserve their tribal identities, and the large-scale migration that followed resulted in the establishment of seven small kingdoms that covered virtually the entire island from the English Channel to the Firth of Forth. Wales and West Wales (Cornwall) remained Celtic strongholds as did western Scotland and the Highlands, but England proper had become Anglo-Saxon. A society of Germanic warriors had once again superimposed itself on a larger body of partially romanized Celts. Anglo-Saxon cultural values are portrayed in

Illustration 7.3

🔳 **The Dome of the Rock, Jerusalem.** This superb example of early Islamic architecture was built on the site of Solomon's temple in 687–691. Though Byzantine influence is clear, the structure is a new departure. It encloses the rock formation from which Muhammad, led by the angel Gabriel, ascended into Heaven. The site remains a fertile source of controversy between Muslims and Israelis to this day. Note the Arabic calligraphy that encircles the entire cornice.

## ◆ DOCUMENT 7.4 ◆

## Rape and Murder in Frankish Law

*These excerpts from the law of the Salian Franks show how the assessment of fines was based not only upon the presumed seriousness of the crime but also upon the status of the victim. Note that while rape was taken more lightly than murder, the murder of a pregnant woman was regarded as far more serious than that of a free man. The value of a woman was related almost solely to her fertility. The higher fines for concealment may reflect a presumption of premeditation.*

### Title XIII. Concerning Rape Committed by Freemen

1. If three men carry off a free born girl, they shall be compelled to pay 30 shillings.
2. If there are more than three, each shall pay 5 shillings.
4. But those who commit rape shall be compelled to pay 2500 denars, which makes 63 shillings.

### Title XXIV. Concerning the Killing of Little Children and Women

1. If any have slain a boy under 10 years . . . and it shall have been proved on him, he shall be sentenced to 24,000 denars, which is 600 shillings.
3. If any one have hit a free woman who is pregnant, and she dies, he shall be sentenced to 28,000 denars, which make 700 shillings.
6. If any one shall have killed a free woman after she has begun bearing children, he shall be sentenced to 24,000 denars, which make 600 shillings.

7. After she can have no more children, he who kills her shall be sentenced to 8000 denars, which make 200 shillings.

### Title XLI. Concerning the Murder of Freemen

1. If any one shall have killed a free Frank, or a barbarian living under the Salic Law, and it have been proved on him, he shall be sentenced to 8000 denars.
2. But if he shall have thrown him into a well or into the water, or shall have covered him with branches or anything else to conceal him, he shall be sentenced to 24,000 denars, which make 600 shillings.
3. But if any one has slain a man who is in the service of the king, he shall be sentenced to 24,000 denars, which make 600 shillings.
4. But if he have put him in the water or in a well, and covered him with anything to conceal him, he shall be sentenced to 72,000 denars, which make 1800 shillings.
5. If any one have slain a Roman who eats at the king's palace, and it be proved on him, he shall be sentenced to 12000 denars, which make 300 shillings.
6. But if the Roman shall not have been a landed proprietor and table companion of the king, he who killed him shall be sentenced to 4000 denars, which make 100 shillings.

Henderson, E. F. *Select Historical Documents of the Middle Ages,* pp. 176–189. London: G. Bell & Sons, 1892.

the great epic *Beowulf* (first written down about the year 1000), while Anglo-Saxon conversion to Christianity was ably chronicled in the *Ecclesiastical History of the English People* by Bede (d. 735).

Though politically fragmented, the Germanic world was unified by its social and cultural similarities. War chiefs provided leadership in battle and divided the spoils among the *comites*, or warriors sworn to their support. The more prominent leaders acquired landed estates through conquest or through intermarriage with older, non-Germanic families. In time they formed the nucleus of an ethnically mixed aristocracy. The estates continued to be farmed by *coloni* or tenants, almost all of whom were drawn from the original, preinvasion, populations.

Poorer tribesmen held small *allods* or freehold properties, which they worked with their nuclear families and perhaps a slave or two. During the summer fighting

season, the women typically managed the farms. This gave them a measure of independence unknown to their Byzantine or Muslim sisters, but marriage laws were loose and concubinage common. Kings and tribal chieftains often remained openly polygamous even while claiming to be Christian. The church devoted some of its best efforts to modifying these customs but had only modest success until the great religious revivals of the eleventh and twelfth centuries.

Clerical attempts to restrain violence were even less successful. Endemic warfare among the tribes and subtribes reflected a society based firmly on the vendetta or feud. As a result, Germanic legal codes developed an elaborate system of fines as punishment for acts of violence. Their purpose had nothing to do with justice but was intended to prevent feuds by compensating the families of those who were killed or injured (see document 7.4). Though this worked often enough within the framework of the tribe, it was almost useless when applied to outsiders. Each of the Germanic peoples "lived its own law," even when on foreign territory. That is, a crime committed by a Frank against a Burgundian on Burgundian land could be resolved only by a duel—if the parties could agree upon terms—or by war. The only common feature of these Germanic codes, apart from their reliance upon fines, was that they were customary: Judges based their decisions upon the resolution of similar cases in the past. Precedent was supposed to reflect the accumulated wisdom of the people, or "folk," and formed the basis of "common" as opposed to Roman law.

Taking their cue from the Romans, historians have characterized these people as barbarians and the period from the fifth to the eighth century as the Dark Ages. It is, like most such characterizations, exaggerated, but material life in these years reached a level far lower than it had been or than it was later to become. Intellectually and artistically, the glories of antiquity dimmed and for a time almost vanished, while those of the Middle Ages were as yet only beginning to emerge.

Learning flourished primarily in far-off Ireland, a Celtic society that had been spared the turbulence of the continent. Though not unlike the Germanic lands in its social and political organization, the Christianization of the island in the early fifth century had released extraordinary energies. St. Patrick, who is generally credited with converting the Irish, had little interest in monasticism, but by the seventh century a rich monastic culture had evolved that stressed knowledge of the Latin classics—religious and secular—as well as a strict personal discipline. Irish monks transmitted Christianity to many parts of northern Europe, often at great personal risk. They also preserved much of Latin learning, ornamenting it with manuscript illuminations based on a rich artistic heritage. The eighth-century Book of Kells is a superb example of their work (see illustration 7.4).

## Frankish Society and Politics

The development of a Frankish kingdom that would by the eighth century impose political unity on much of continental Europe began with the reign of Clovis (c. 466–511), a chief of the Salian or "salty" Franks whose center was at Tournai in what is now Belgium. With skill and ferocity he consolidated his power over other branches of the Franks and seized all of Gaul north of the Loire River. He then routed an invasion by the Alamanni, conquered the Burgundians, and drove the Visigoths out of Aquitaine. When he died at what

**Illustration 7.4**

Page from the Book of Kells. The Book of Kells is perhaps the greatest monument to the art and scholarship of the Irish golden age. This illumination forms the first word of the Gospel of St. Luke.

was, for a Frank, the ripe old age of forty-five, Clovis was master of everything from the North Sea coast to the borders of Septimania, the province that extended along the Mediterranean coast from Provence to the Pyrenees. To his biographer, the Gallo-Roman bishop Gregory of Tours (c. 539–c. 595), he was a new Constantine because he converted to Catholic Christianity under the influence of his wife, Clotilda, probably in the year 506. His subjects therefore became Catholics, unlike the Arian Burgundians and Visigoths. To traditional historians, Clovis was the first king of France and founder of the Merovingian dynasty.

The Frankish kings regarded the monarchy as their private possession. They divided its lands and privileges equally among their sons when they died and seemed to have no sense of obligation toward their subjects. Personal interest dictated policy. Their subjects in turn felt no special loyalty to the king and served him only in return for benefices or gifts. These might take the form of land, grants of revenue, or other valuables. Unlike the benefices of later—feudal—times, such gifts implied no long-term obligation or relationship. Each new service demanded a new favor.

All of this was typical Germanic practice. The major difference between the Frankish idea of kingship and that of the other Germanic peoples was that Frankish kings from the time of Clovis onward were invested by the church with a sacred quality that other chieftains lacked. A bishop anointed the king with oil at his coronation to indicate that he ruled by God's grace. Such an endorsement could not always save the life of an individual, but it helped to stabilize the position of the dynasty.

Economically, Francia or Frankish Gaul had changed little since the days of the Roman Empire. Most of its people were non-Frankish tenants on estates owned either by members of the old Gallo-Roman aristocracy or by Frankish warriors. The poorer Franks and a few Gallo-Romans owned smaller farms, but life even for the freeholder remained a struggle. Yields were far lower than in Roman times—one-and-a-half grains for each grain planted seems to have been the rule. Coins were rarely seen by any but the rich, who tended to hoard them or convert them into jewelry, which became one of the dominant art forms of the day (see illustration 7.5).

In any case, little was available to buy. Every landowner, great or small, tried to be self-sufficient. When necessary, bartering for necessities was possible at a town fair, but towns were few and poor and often far away. A handful of Jews and Syrians managed the remnants of the long-distance trade in which metalwork was the chief Frankish export. The superbly crafted iron tools and weapons of the Franks found a market in nearly every part of Europe.

Better weapons may have given the Franks a small advantage over their neighbors, for their military organization remained no better than that of any other Germanic tribe. Every male Frank, as opposed to the Gallo-Romans and other non-Frankish inhabitants of the realm, was expected to answer the king's call to arms and to support himself for the duration of the campaign. Most Franks fought on foot, armed with a short sword and the small throwing axe that served as an emblem of their tribe. Unlike their ancestors who fought the legions of Rome, they seem to have been wholly innocent of strategy or of tactics that went much beyond the straightforward brawl, but this impression may reflect only the inadequacy of historical sources. Literacy had declined during the years of

Illustration 7.5

Jewelled Cover of the Lindau Gospels.  This book cover, from the ninth century, is an example of Carolingian jewel work.

imperial collapse, and written records in this period are few and incomplete.

The Merovingian dynasty began to decline almost immediately after the death of its founder. The Frankish custom of dividing even a kingdom equally among heirs ensured that each generation would be involved in bitter feuds that often ended in murder if not civil war. Many of the kings appeared to suffer from physical or mental problems and left the political direction of their realms to their queens. Fredegund (d. 597) and Brunhilda (d. 613) were especially notable for their cunning and forcefulness.

After the death of Dagobert I in 639 the dynasty sank into utter incompetence. War leadership as well as the administration of the royal properties fell into the hands of the mayor of the palace. This official was usually one of the Arnulfings, a powerful clan whose wealth derived from estates in the same region from which Clovis had sprung. Originally no more than the majordomo of the royal household, the mayor had, by the end of the seventh century, become the de facto ruler of Francia. Only the sacred character of Merovingian kingship, derived ultimately from the sanctions of the church, prevented the Arnulfings from claiming the throne for themselves.

Eventually, they were able to do just that. The Arnulfing mayors of the palace were capable men whose military exploits brought them respect. One of them, Charles Martel (Charles the Hammer), united the Frankish realms that had long been divided among various Merovingian heirs and won special glory in 732 by defeating a Muslim raiding party near Poitiers in central France. Though not perhaps as decisive an encounter as was sometimes claimed, this battle marked the furthest penetration of Islam in Europe and caught the imagination of the Franks. Finally, Charles's son, Pepin the Short, used the growing prestige of his family and his close relations with the church to depose the last Merovingian. With the full support of Rome he had himself crowned king of the Franks in the winter of 751–752.

## The Empire of Charlemagne

The dynasty founded by Pepin is called Carolingian after its greatest member: Charles the Great, or Charlemagne (c. 742–814). In forty-seven years he brought most of what is now France, Germany, and northern Italy under his rule, had himself crowned Roman emperor, and either reformed or created a host of institutions both secular and religious. To the historians of a generation ago he stood at the beginning of European history. To Einhard, his biographer and a contemporary (see document 7.5), Charlemagne held out the promise of a new Roman empire. But few of the emperor's achievements survived his death, and even fewer were the product of a grand and systematic historical vision.

The great king was above all a warlord who, like his father, allied himself with the church to further his interests. Pepin had left him western and northern France and the Frankish territories along the lower Rhine. A brother, Carloman, took the rest of France and parts of southwest Germany including the western Alps. When Carloman died in 771, Charlemagne annexed his brother's kingdom, forcing his wife and children to take refuge among the Lombards of northern Italy who had for some time been hostile to Charlemagne. Realizing that the Lombards were a threat to the papal territories, and perhaps to Rome itself, Pope Adrian I allied himself with Charlemagne. After two years of hard fighting, Charlemagne defeated the Lombards in 774 and annexed their kingdom. North Germany, too, required attention. The region

---

### ◆ DOCUMENT 7.5 ◆

## Einhard: Description of Charlemagne

*This brief passage from Einhard's biography of Charlemagne is both vivid and unusual in that it provides personal details often omitted by the authors of the day.*

Charles had a big and powerful body and was tall but well-proportioned. That his height was seven times the length of his own feet is well known. [He seems to have been about 6′3″ or more than a foot taller than the average man of his day.] He had a round head, his eyes were unusually large and lively, his nose a little longer than average, his gray hair attractive, and his face cheerful and friendly. Whether he was standing or sitting his appearance was always impressive and dignified. His neck was somewhat short and thick and his stomach protruded a little, but this was rendered inconspicuous by the good proportions of the rest of his body. He walked firmly and his carriage was manly, yet his voice, though clear, was not as strong as one might have expected from someone his size. His health was always excellent, except during the last four years of his life, when he frequently suffered from attacks of fever. And at the end he also limped with one foot. All the same, he continued to rely on his own judgment more than on that of his physicians, whom he almost hated because they ordered him to give up his customary roast meat and eat only boiled meat instead.

Einhard. *The Life of Charlemagne*, p. 87, trans. Evelyn Scherabon Firchow and Edwin H. Zeydel. Coral Gables: University of Miami Press, 1972.

---

between the Rhine and the Elbe was inhabited mainly by pagan Saxons who raided Frankish settlements in the Rhineland and murdered the missionaries sent to convert them. Treaties and agreements were useless because the Saxons acknowledged no political authority beyond that of the individual war band, and each chieftain felt free to act on his own.

Characteristically, Charlemagne's strategy focused on religion. In 772 he raided deep into Saxon territory and destroyed the Irminsul, the great tree that formed the heart of one of their most sacred shrines. He apparently thought that by doing so he would demonstrate the stronger magic of the Christian God, but the

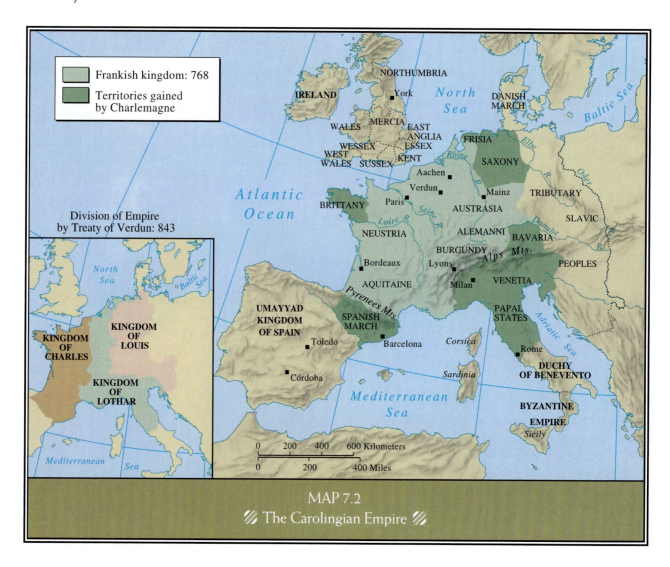

Frankish kingdom: 768

Territories gained by Charlemagne

**Division of Empire by Treaty of Verdun: 843**

**MAP 7.2**
〽 The Carolingian Empire 〽

outrage marked the beginning of a long and bloody struggle. The Saxons destroyed Christian settlements and monasteries. The Franks resorted to wholesale massacre and deportations and the Saxons were at last converted and incorporated into the empire in 797. Charlemagne did not shrink from converting people at swordspoint.

The rest of Germany fell into his hands when he deposed the ruler of Bavaria, who was not only a Christian but also a nominal tributary of the Franks. Then, to secure his borders, he defeated the Avars in 791 and 803, pressing into Croatia, which was partially resettled with Slavic and German immigrants. In the west, he repelled a Muslim raid on Narbonne and seized Catalonia, which after 811 became a Christian enclave in Muslim Spain. When he died three years later Charlemagne ruled everything from Catalonia to the Baltic and from the Netherlands to the middle Danube (see map 7.2).

To govern this vast territory, he relied upon counts, dukes, and bishops who supposedly acted on his behalf

in their own regions and who transmitted his decrees to their subjects. These men were bound to him by personal allegiance fortified with powerful oaths, but distance, poverty, and primitive communications left them with a great deal of independence. Though imperial administration remained fragmentary, communication was maintained through *missi dominici,* officials who traveled constantly from place to place on the ruler's business (see document 7.6). Charlemagne did, however, establish the principle that law was to be administered on a territorial instead of a tribal basis. That is, if a Frank committed a crime in Burgundian territory he was to be tried under Burgundian, not Frankish, law. This change represented a greater advance than it seems, for law was no longer paralyzed by jurisdictional disputes.

Everywhere, Charlemagne relied heavily upon the church to support his policies. In return, he strengthened its financial and institutional base. Monasteries established by royal grants on the fringes of the empire converted, and in some cases civilized, new subjects.

## ❖ DOCUMENT 7.6 ❖

# The Missi Dominici

*The following instructions are taken from one of Charlemagne's capitularies (decrees) dealing with official conduct. Like most such documents, it describes an ideal, not actual practice.*

And let the *missi* themselves make a diligent investigation whenever any man claims that an injustice has been done him by any one, just as they desire to deserve the grace of an omnipotent God and to keep their fidelity pledged to him, so that in all cases, everywhere, they shall, in accordance with the will and fear of God, administer the law fully and justly in the case of the holy churches of God and of the poor, of wards and widows, and of the whole people. And if there should be anything of such a nature that they, together with the provincial courts, are not able of themselves to correct it and do justice concerning it, they shall, without any reservations, refer this, together with their reports, to the judgment of the emperor. The straight path of justice shall not be impeded by any one on account of flattery or gifts, or on account of any relationship, or from fear of the powerful.

Robinson, James Harvey, ed. *Readings in European History*, vol. 1. Boston: Ginn, 1904.

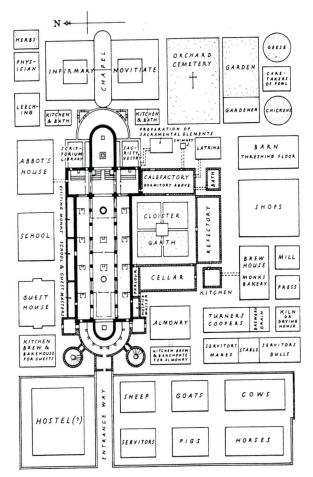

**Illustration 7.6**

Plan for the Monastery of St. Gall. This is a modernized and redrawn version of a plan devised late in the reign of Charlemagne. The original, which still exists, was apparently a monk-architect's vision of an ideal monastic facility. Though the great Swiss monastery of St. Gall was not rebuilt precisely along these lines, the drawing reflects, on a grand scale, the basic layout favored by the Benedictine monks. It also indicates something of the size and scope of monastic ambitions in the Carolingian age.

Many of these foundations were unparalleled in their size and magnificence (see illustration 7.6). The parish system, long established among the Franks to provide spiritual care in rural areas, was extended throughout Europe, and parish priests were firmly subordinated to their bishops. Bishops, in turn, were forced to obey the pope. To further secure the work of conversion he established new dioceses, reformed old ones, and introduced a compulsory tithe for their support. His efforts, though not always popular, became the model for the medieval church.

None of these measures could have been imposed by religious authority alone. They required the threat of military force wielded by a ruthless and dedicated monarch. Charlemagne had become the chief supporter of the papacy and the mainstay of its efforts to convert the Slavs and Germans. His assumption of the imperial title at the hands of Pope Leo III on Christmas

Day in 800 reflected only what had become obvious to many: He, not the pope, was the true leader of western Christendom. In spite of this, the motives and conduct of everyone involved in the coronation have been the subject of controversy, and even its practical consequences remain unclear. It seems to have meant little to the governing of Charlemagne's empire or to his relations with other princes. Even the Byzantine emperor, after initial protests, acknowledged the title in 811.

Regardless of its impressive achievements, the empire of Charlemagne rested in the last analysis on the personal authority of its ruler. The Frankish custom of divided or partible inheritance ensured that his

**Illustration 7.7**

〰 **Carolingian Minuscule.** Carolingian minuscule is the basis of modern writing. This example is from Bede's *Expositio in Lucam,* copied at Tours c. 820.

arrangements would not long survive him. Even had his son and grandsons been willing to ignore the ancient Salic law, the difficulties they faced would have been insurmountable. The empire's weak subsistence economy and poor communications could not sustain the development of institutions that might have saved it. For all its Roman and ecclesiastical trappings, the Carolingian Empire remained a Germanic chieftainship, different from its predecessors primarily in scale.

Charlemagne's interest in the church went beyond mere political calculation. Though he used the church—and the papacy—to further his interests, his personal piety and dedication to the conversion of pagans cannot be questioned. In addition to the essentially administrative reforms instituted, he took a lively interest in matters that might in other circumstances have been left to the pope. He also tried, with some success, to reintroduce the Gregorian chant and to encourage the practice of auricular confession in which the laity confess their sins, not to one another, but to a priest.

A major obstacle to the adoption of these reforms was the ignorance of the clergy. To correct their defi-

ciencies, he established a school at his palace in Aachen and staffed it largely with Irish and English scholars, the most famous of whom was Alcuin of York (c. 732–804). Charlemagne intended these men to raise the intellectual level of his court and to educate his sons. Under the king's patronage, his scholars began the task of recovering the classics, especially the religious ones, and copying them accurately in the beautiful, standardized hand known today as carolingian minuscule (see illustration 7.7). It is the basis of all modern systems of handwriting.

The major purpose of this activity was to provide a body of texts that could serve the needs of clerical education. Gathering the best minds of Europe together in a common enterprise paid other dividends as well. The courts of Charlemagne and his son, Louis the Pious, would serve as an intellectual beacon in the dark days to come. To be sure, the achievements of the Carolingian Renaissance were in some cases forgotten if not obliterated in the chaos of the ninth century. At no time did their volume or importance equal that of later classical revivals, but Charlemagne's scholars laid the foundations of medieval learning.

# CHAPTER 8
# THE BEGINNINGS OF THE FEUDAL AGE

The empire of Charlemagne did not long survive his death. As his grandsons divided their vast inheritance, Europe was attacked from all sides by ferocious warriors. Political decentralization aggravated by devastating raids threatened to destroy the fabric of society. New forms of military and social organization arose to combat the threat and gradually hardened into the system known as feudalism. Feudalism rested upon the far older social and economic system known as manorialism, which, though it had existed in Roman times, adapted to feudal circumstances and expanded enormously during the dark years of the ninth and tenth centuries. Together, feudalism and manorialism became the dominant institutions of medieval Europe and profoundly influenced the development of politics and social attitudes until well into modern times. Although feudalism pervaded most of what had been the Carolingian Empire and spread eventually to England and southern Italy, many parts of the subcontinent escaped its grasp.

## The Great Raids of the Ninth and Tenth Centuries

Even before the death of Charlemagne, reports reached him that trouble was brewing along the borders of his empire. Muslim raiders, sailing out of their North African ports in search of slaves and booty, had begun to harry the Mediterranean coasts. In the north the dragon prows of Viking longships made an unwelcome appearance in seacoast villages. The northmen came to trade if a village were well defended and to loot if it were not. By the middle of the ninth century these first tentative incursions had become massive raiding expeditions that threatened the survival of European life. Some years later the Magyars, a nation of horsemen whose origins lay in the steppes of central Asia, pastured their herds on the rich grasses of the

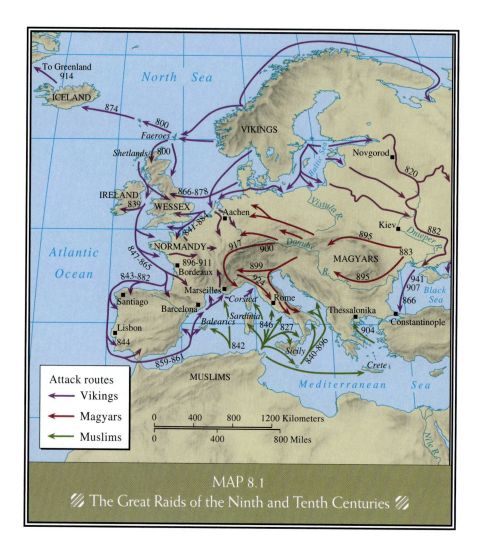

MAP 8.1
The Great Raids of the Ninth and Tenth Centuries

Danube Valley and began to plunder their neighbors to the west (see map 8.1).

The motives behind this activity varied. For many Muslims, the Christian west represented a backward society that could be pillaged at will. A wealthier, more technologically advanced society usually attempts to exploit a poorer one in close proximity. In fast sailing vessels using the triangular lateen rig of the Arab dhows, the North Africans raided extensively along the coasts, primarily to acquire slaves. An advanced base was established in the Balearic Islands. By 842 they had infested the Camargue, a marshy region on the European mainland, and were raiding in the valley of the Rhone as far as Arles. A half-century later they established themselves in an impregnable position at Freinet near the present site of Saint-Tropez. From these European bases they could devastate the countryside in a systematic way. By the middle of the tenth century detachments of Muslims had raided villages and monasteries as far afield as St. Gall in the Swiss Alps. In Italy, the raider's task was simplified by the Muslim conquest

of Sicily. Palermo fell to the North Africans in 831, but more than seventy years of warfare, enlivened by native revolts against both Greeks and Muslims, were required to gain control of the island. The last Byzantine garrison was not expelled until 965. Long before this, western Sicily had become a staging point for raids on the Italian mainland. Muslim slavers were still encountered as far north as the environs of Rome at the beginning of the eleventh century.

The Magyars had been driven westward across the Carpathians by another of those population movements characteristic of the central Asian heartland. Organized into seven hordes, they probably numbered no more than twenty-five thousand people, but they were formidable warriors and had little trouble in moving into the power vacuum created by Charlemagne's defeat of the Avars. Their raids, which extended as far west as the Meuse, were an extension of their nomadic tradition. The Magyars moved rapidly in fairly large numbers and were at first willing to meet western armies on equal terms. Later, they became more cautious and relied upon speed and evasion to make good their escapes.

The Vikings were perhaps the most formidable raiders of all. The name is generic and refers to all of those Scandinavians—Danish, Norwegian, and Swedish—who terrorized the coasts of Europe between 800 and 1050. Their society bore a marked resemblance to that of the early Germanic tribes. Scandinavia was a world of small farmers and fishermen who lived in widely scattered communities connected primarily by the sea. The heart of such communities was their market and their Thing, the assembly of free men that met, usually on market days, to discuss matters of public concern. These gatherings also ratified the selection of kings, who were in the beginning little more than regional warlords. Drawn mostly from the ranks of a hereditary aristocracy, these chieftains relied upon personal loyalties, the fellowship of the chief's great hall where warriors drank and celebrated, and the distribution of loot to organize war parties of free farmers and craftsmen. The leisure for such pursuits was provided by a large population of slaves, or thralls. Even the smallest farms might have at least three, and the need to replenish their numbers was an important incentive for the raids. In the summers while the men raided, the women managed the farms, the slaves, and the continued production of craft goods and services. Following the pattern of other maritime communities before and since, Scandinavian women tended to be far more independent and economically active than their inland sisters.

Warfare and raiding was endemic in the region long before the dawn of the Viking age, as was an extensive trading network that helps to explain the cultural similarities of the Scandinavian peoples. Danes, Swedes, and Norwegians spoke related languages, shared the system of formal writing known as runes, and enjoyed a common tradition of oral literature that was finally committed to writing in the thirteenth century. Its characteristic form was the saga, a mixture of historical fact and legend that reached its highest development in Iceland. Scandinavian religion was polytheistic and bore a close resemblance to that of other Germanic peoples.

Viking burial customs reveal much about Scandinavian art and technology. Dead chiefs were sometimes surrounded by their possessions and buried in their boats, a practice that left behind rich hordes of artifacts including exquisite carvings and jewelry. The boats were an extraordinary technical achievement. The typical Viking longship was about sixty-five feet in length, open-decked, and double ended (see illustration 8.1). It could be propelled by oars at speeds up to ten knots or

by a single square sail and was strongly built of overlapping planks that carried the structural load of the hull. Such vessels could cross oceans. Because their draft was rarely more than three feet they could also be beached without damage or rowed far into the interior on the shallowest of rivers. With a crew of forty to sixty men and no decks for shelter they cannot have been comfortable, but they provided the ultimate in operational flexibility.

The reasons for the Viking incursions are unclear. The Scandinavian population presumably had begun to exceed the available supply of food, perhaps because the cold, wet weather that troubled the rest of Europe in this period reduced northern harvests to an untenable level. Charlemagne's conquest of the Saxons may also have roused the suspicions of their Danish neighbors. In any case, the Northmen grew more aggressive with the passage of time. In the early years of the ninth century they contented themselves with lightning raids on coastal settlements, stealing what they could and putting out to sea before the inhabitants could call for reinforcements. Within a generation they had adopted the Muslim tactic of establishing bases from which they could loot the surrounding countryside. By midcentury they were establishing permanent colonies on the European mainland.

Their range was enormous. In 844 Vikings raided the Atlantic ports of Spain. In the following year they sacked Paris, and in 859–860 they reached Italy, penetrating the Val d'Arno almost to the outskirts of Florence. Fortunately for the Italians they did not return. In the north the Vikings soon learned how to extend their range by traveling on stolen horses when their ships reached the limits of navigation. Nothing seemed beyond their reach.

The establishment of permanent settlements grew from the habit of wintering in England or on the Continent in preparation for the next raiding season. Given that the dangers of this practice were minimal, Vikings brought their wives and families. In the decades after 851 they occupied all of northeastern England from Essex to the further limits of Yorkshire. The region came to be known as the Danelaw because the legal autonomy granted to the Danes by Saxon kings survived until the thirteenth century. From 1014 to 1042 England was ruled by a Danish dynasty. In 1066 it was conquered by the Normans, who as their name indicates, were also of Viking origin. They were the inhabitants of the great Norse state established around the mouth of the Seine at the beginning of the tenth century.

At the opposite end of Europe, Viking traders penetrated the Russian heartland by following the great

**Illustration 8.1**

**Viking Longship.** This Viking longship has elegant, and sea-worthy, lines. The general impression is one of both beauty and menace.

rivers. From the western branch of the Dvina, which flows into the Baltic at Riga, they were able to reach the headwaters of both the Dnieper and the Volga and to float from there to the gates of Constantinople. In the process they founded Novgorod and established themselves as the ruling aristocracy at Kiev, but they had little impact upon what was to remain a thoroughly slavic culture. Somewhat ironically, they gave Russia its name: "Rus" or "Rhos" was the slavic word for Viking.

The establishment of these Viking enclaves, like the contemporary colonization of Iceland and Greenland and the exploration of the North American coast by Bjarni Herjolfsson (c. 986) and Leif Ericsson (c. 1000), indicates that hunger for arable land was an important reason for the great raids. In the two centuries between 850 and 1050 the North Sea became the center of a cosmopolitan society in which interaction between Scandinavian and non-Scandinavian cultures grew increasingly complex. The Norsemen were even-

tually assimilated as the medieval kingdoms of France and England evolved, but their incursions had helped to provoke a reorganization of European society.

## The Emergence of Feudal Institutions

The great raids, whether Muslim, Magyar, or Viking, brought something like anarchy to most of Europe. The normal bonds of social interaction were submerged in an orgy of violence. No one's person or property was safe. Agricultural production fell, and the tenuous lines of trade and communication that held the empire together were virtually severed (see document 8.1).

The raids were inflicted on a political order that was in the process of disintegration. The empire of Charlemagne had been doomed from the start by poverty and by the problem of distance. Little surplus wealth was available to support either war or governance. Harvests, never abundant in the Carolingian age, may have declined even before the destructive effects of the raids were felt. The European climate had entered one of its cold, damp cycles, and yields of one-

◈ DOCUMENT 8.1 ◈

## The Great Raids

*The following is extracted from the Annals of Xanten, a chronicle thought to have been written in the archdiocese of Cologne at about the time of the events it describes. The year is 846, with the final sentence coming from the entry for 847. Frisia includes most of the northern Netherlands and the coastal region of northwest Germany. Lothaire was the grandson of Charlemagne who ruled the middle part of his empire known as Lotharingia. The passage reveals the sense of helplessness and isolation induced by disasters on every front.*

According to their custom the Northmen plundered Eastern and Western Frisia and burned the town of Dordrecht with two other villages, before the eyes of Lothaire, who was then in the castle of Nimwegen, but could not punish the crime. The Northmen, with their boats filled with immense booty, including both men and goods, returned to their own country.

At the same time, as no one can mention or hear without great sadness, the mother of all churches, the basilica of the apostle Peter, was taken and plundered by the Moors or Saracens, who had already occupied the region of Beneventum. The Saracens, moreover, slaughtered all the Christians whom they found outside the walls of Rome, either within or without this church. They also carried men and women away prisoners. They tore down, among many others, the altar of the blessed Peter, and their crimes from day to day bring sorrow to Christians. Pope Sergius departed life this year.

After the death of Sergius no mention of the apostolic see has come in any way to our ears.

Robinson, James Harvey, ed. *Readings in European History,* vol. 1. Boston: Ginn, 1904.

Charlemagne's son Louis the Pious (reigned 814–840) had hoped to pass on the empire intact, though the Salic law required that it be split equally among his heirs. He had three sons by his first marriage: Lothair, Pepin, and Louis "the German." A fourth son, Charles "the Bald," was born to his second wife, Judith of Bavaria, in 823. Lothair was the intended heir, but Judith instigated a civil war among the brothers in the hope of securing a kingdom for her son. After the emperor's death in 840, the surviving heirs divided his lands by the Treaty of Verdun (843). Lothair took the central portion including Italy, the Rhineland, and the Low Countries. Charles (d. 877) held most of what is now France, and Louis (d. 875) was given Bavaria, Austria, and the eastern part of Germany. Pepin had died in 838. When Lothair died in 855 the middle kingdom was divided again among his three sons and quickly ceased to be a major factor in European politics. By 870 transalpine Europe was divided into a West Frankish kingdom (France) under Charles, and an East Frankish kingdom (Germany) under Louis, while Italy became the playground of regional factions and Byzantine generals.

None of these states possessed the resources to mount a credible defense against the raiders. Cash remained scarce, and the kings that followed Charles the Bald and Louis the German were not always inspiring leaders. Militarily, the problem was not unlike that faced by the Roman emperors in the second and third centuries, but its scale was far greater and complicated by the decentralization of political power within the empire. Each of the successor kingdoms faced attacks along borders that extended for thousands of miles. The attacks might come by land or by sea. Their objective was unknown, and the size of the forces involved could not be anticipated. Post-Carolingian Europe was poor and sparsely settled. Peasant communities could not defend themselves against such formidable enemies as the Vikings, and the old Frankish system of levies was slow and cumbersome. By the time infantry was mobilized and marched to the point of contact, the enemy would be gone. Fortunately for the Europeans, Scandinavians and North Africans tended to fight on foot without benefit of the massed infantry tactics known to antiquity. The Magyars were a typical nomadic light cavalry. If they could be intercepted, all of these foes were vulnerable to attack by heavily armed and armored horsemen, the prototypes of the medieval knight.

From the technological point of view, the knight and his way of fighting was enhanced by

and-a-half grains for every seed planted were probably normal. Distances were huge and major population centers were connected, as they would be for centuries to come, by primitive tracks. Local magnates and local loyalties began to assert themselves while Charlemagne was still alive. Neither his lines of communication nor his military resources were able to hold them fully in check. After his death the division of the empire among his three grandsons only made matters worse.

**Illustration 8.2**

**A Knight and His Equipment.** This manuscript illumination shows a knight wearing the conical helmet and long coat of chain mail or birney typical of the feudal period. He is shown at the charge with lance in hand. The high saddle made him difficult to unhorse, while the stirrups allowed him to stand up for greater impact.

two innovations: the iron horseshoe and the stirrup. Neither were in common use before the ninth century. The iron shoe permitted a horse to carry heavy weights over bad ground without splitting its hooves. The stirrup allowed an armored man to brace himself and even to stand in the saddle, which made it easier to wield a heavy lance, shield, and double-edged sword on horseback. The new system produced an increase in offensive power over that available to ancient or nomadic cavalry, while a heavy chain mail coat offered an effective defense against most edged weapons (see illustration 8.2). The Franks, with their skill in ironwork, could easily fashion the necessary equipment.

A defensive system evolved that was based on mobile detachments of heavy cavalry garrisoned in scattered strongholds or castles and supported directly by the people they were intended to protect. In theory, a band of horsemen could reach the site of a raid within hours or, at worst, a day or two. As hundreds of smoking villages continued to attest, this solution was not perfect, but it forced the marauders to pay a higher cost in blood than they might otherwise have done. With time and practice the knights became a reasonably effective deterrent.

The new system was also used in disputes that had nothing to do with the raids. The division of the em-

pire encouraged territorial disputes that continued even in the face of external threats. Armored knights could be used to harry the lands of a hostile neighbor. Other knights could be sent out to oppose them, but castles provided the more effective defense. The presence of a castle filled with armed men posed a serious threat to any invading force, and operations had to be suspended until that threat could be eliminated. For this reason sieges were perhaps more common in medieval warfare than pitched battles between mounted knights. Knights directed the sieges and played a prominent role in the fighting. The hard work of digging, undermining the walls, and manning the rams or catapults fell to peasants levied for the occasion.

A major defect of this kind of warfare was its expense. The cost of a horse and armor was roughly equivalent to that of two dozen cattle, and few could afford it. Charlemagne had begun to encourage the development of heavy cavalry, but the tiny elite that served him had to be supplemented under his successors by the enlistment of nearly everyone who was rich enough and strong enough to fight on horseback. Moreover, the kind of warfare in which they were engaged demanded constant readiness and a level of skill that was difficult to acquire and could be maintained only through constant practice. The construction and maintenance of castles required vast reserves of labor and materials. Even those who were able to afford the initial outlay could not be expected to support themselves indefinitely. In an age chronically short of cash, the most practical, and perhaps the only, solution was to provide these men with grants of land that could be set aside for their use in return for military service.

The term *feudalism* refers to the social institutions that arose from this exchange of land for military service. In its simplest form, a feudal bond was created when a fighting man placed his hands between those of his lord or liege and vowed to support him on the battlefield in return for a grant of land known as a benefice or fief. By so doing he became the lord's man, or vassal. The terms of such contracts varied widely and were the subject of much negotiation, but the basic principle of mutual obligation remained constant. A vassal was to support his lord and do nothing contrary to his interest; the lord was obligated to provide his vassal with personal and legal protection as well as material support. "Money fiefs," in which cash was provided in return for military service, existed, but in a virtually cashless society they were rare.

The precedents for such arrangements were ancient. In principle, feudalism is a form of clientage that has been given sanction in law. In practice, the idea probably dates back to the oaths taken by members of a Germanic *conitatus* or war band (see document 8.2). The great men of Visigothic Spain and Merovingian Gaul had maintained bodies of armed companions who were pledged to them by oath. Some of them were free, but others were *vassi* who had entered into contractual relationships of dependency. Under the early Carolingians, the term began to lose its humble connotations. Charles Martel and his successors sometimes granted land to their retainers, who often became great lords in their own right. Charlemagne tried to make such arrangements legally binding, but the legal union of vassalage and benefice was achieved only in the reign of his son, Louis the Pious. By this time, the term *vassal* had lost all taint of servility.

In the dark years after Louis's death, feudalism spread throughout the Frankish kingdoms. Vassal homage was extended not only to household companions but also to regional magnates whose military assistance was valued. Bishops and abbots, though they were not supposed to shed blood, became vassals as well because for most purposes little difference existed between secular and ecclesiastical lordships. Monasteries and episcopal sees had long been endowed with "temporalities" or grants of land that in difficult times required the protection of armed men. A prominent churchman might therefore command a substantial force. In some cases, including most of those that involved the church, land was surrendered to the liege in return for his protection and then returned to the vassal after the oath of fealty had been taken. In most cases, the vassal received a new estate ranging in size from a few acres to an entire county, which might or might not contain a castle. The vassal was expected to make some provision for the security of his fief. When a fief was very large, this could be done only through subinfeudation. The vassal would recruit his own contingent of fighting men by offering them portions of his fief in return for their oaths of fealty. In this way the number of feudal jurisdictions increased rapidly within a few short years.

This decentralization of military force worked as well as could be expected. Its chief virtue was flexibility. Units of heavy cavalry based upon fortified strongholds were usually able to break up minor raids or at least to impose unacceptable casualties on the raiders. The building of castles, many of which were little more than halls surrounded by wooden palisades, was often a deterrent. Greater threats could be met by a general levy, which gathered the war bands of many vassals into a

---

### ◆ DOCUMENT 8.2 ◆

## The Act of Homage

*Galbert of Bruges described this act of homage in 1127. The form is thought to have changed little since the beginning of the feudal age.*

On Thursday, the seventh of the ides of April [April 7, 1127], acts of homage were again made before the count, which were brought to a conclusion through this method of giving faith and assurance. First, they performed the homage in this fashion: the count inquired if [the prospective vassal] wished completely to become his man. He replied, "I do wish it," and with his hands joined and covered by the hands of the count, the two were united by a kiss. Second, he who had done the homage gave faith to the representative of the count in these words: "I promise in my faith that I shall henceforth be faithful to count William, and I shall fully observe the homage owed him against all men, in good faith and without deceit." Third, he took an oath on the relics of the saints. Then the count, with the rod which he had in his hand, gave investiture to all those who by this promise had given assurance and due homage to the count, and had taken the oath.

Galbert of Bruges. "*Histoire du meurtre de Charles Bon comte de Flandre*," trans. David Herlihy. In David Herlihy, ed., *The History of Feudalism*, p. 98. New York: Walker, 1970.

---

great host. Such an army, organized by Otto the Great (912–973), met and defeated the Magyars at the battle of the Lechfeld in 955.

Otto's victory ended the last major incursion from the east. His reign as king of the East Franks—he was crowned Holy Roman emperor in 962—marked the turning of the tide. The Muslims were driven from Freinet in 972, and the number of Viking raids began to decline even in the west. They ceased entirely after about 1030.

How much of this resulted from the new military organization and how much from other factors is hard to determine. The Magyars were clearly discouraged by Otto the Great, but they had already begun to turn away from raiding as they discovered the rich agricultural possibilities of the Hungarian plain. After 950 the

Muslims were increasingly distracted by a series of civil wars. The hard work of dislodging them from their bases in Spain and the Balearics was for the most part undertaken by naval forces based on the Italian towns, not by feudal levies. Relative security was achieved in the western Mediterranean only by the end of the eleventh century.

The Vikings, too, may have returned home for reasons of their own. Even as they raided, the Scandinavian chiefs fought for hegemony among themselves. Much of the treasure they seized was used to buy influence and hire mercenaries for their dynastic quarrels. By the beginning of the eleventh century, this process had created the kingdoms of Denmark, Norway, and Sweden. The new rulers sought divine sanction by adopting Christianity and did everything in their power to monopolize the use of military force. Freebooting was actively discouraged because it led to the creation of alternative centers of power. The church condemned freebooting because it was directed against Christians. In the meantime, agricultural productivity seems to have improved, allowing reformed Vikings to accept the new policy without too much hardship.

## The Consolidation of Feudalism: Subinfeudation and the Heritability of Fiefs

Feudalism did not guarantee the salvation of Europe, but in much of the subcontinent it altered the structure of society beyond recognition. An expedient adopted in a time of poverty and dire peril evolved into a complex of social and economic relationships that survived for half a millennium.

The process began with subinfeudation, which increased political decentralization and weakened the power of kings (see document 8.3). The bonds of homage and fealty were entirely personal. A vassal who held his benefice from a count owed nothing to the king. If a tenant-in-chief (a lord who held land directly from the sovereign) chose not to honor his obligations under the feudal contract, all of his subtenants could be expected to follow suit. Moreover, fiefs commonly were accumulated from more than one lord. Conflicts of loyalty were therefore inevitable, and some of the greater vassals used them to build a power base of their own. The counts of Flanders, for example, held lands from the kings of both East Francia and West Francia. They easily played one against the other to create what amounted to an independent state by the end of the ninth century.

Because feudal tenures were theoretically based on service and good only for the lifetime of the vassal, de-

---

### ◆ DOCUMENT 8.3 ◆

### Subinfeudation

*This declaration of homage indicates some of the problems caused by subinfeudation as well as the kind of compromise that might, in theory, alleviate them.*

I, John of Toul, make known that I am the liege man of the lady Beatrice, countess of Troyes, and of her son, Theobald, count of Champagne, against every creature, living or dead, saving my allegiance to Enjourand of Coucy, lord John of Arcis, and the count of Grandpré. If it should happen that the count of Grandpré should be at war with the countess and count of Champagne on his own quarrel, I will aid the count of Grandpré in my own person, and will send to the count and countess of Champagne the knights whose service I owe to them for the fief which I hold of them. But if the count of Grandpré shall make war on the countess and the count of Champagne on behalf of his friends and not by his own quarrel, I will aid in my own person the countess and count of Champagne, and will send one knight to the count of Grandpré for the service which I owe him for the fief which I hold of him, but I will not go myself into the territory of the count of Grandpré to make war on him.

Thatcher, O. J., and McNeal, E. H., eds. *A Source Book of Medieval History.* New York: Scribner's, 1905.

---

priving a disloyal tenant of his benefice should have been easy, but this was not the case. By granting their lands in fief, kings reduced their military force to a household guard that might be no more numerous than the companions of any major tenant-in-chief. Deprivation of one important vassal therefore required the assistance of others, and most were reluctant to participate in an action that could one day be applied to them.

Political pressures were moving strongly in the opposite direction. As the decentralization of military force increased, kings were forced to offer better terms in return for support. Fiefs inevitably became heritable. Vassals wished to provide for the security of their families, and the right to pass lands on to their children was demanded with increasing frequency in negotiating feudal contracts. Rulers were reluctant to impoverish the widows and orphans of loyal vassals. The inheritance of fiefs was already common in France and Italy by the end of the ninth century and became universal in the eleventh. In Germany, heritability was at first applied only to the more important benefices. By the end of the twelfth century fiefs for life had become a rarity even there.

Heirs were supposed to renew their father's oaths and be capable of fulfilling them. In the early days, women were therefore denied the right of succession because they could not provide military service. Neither of these rules survived the first feudal age. Heirs frequently failed to appear before their liege but retained possession of their benefices. Women were inheriting fiefs in southern France before the end of the tenth century, and the practice spread quickly throughout the feudal world. Lords tried to ensure that the service aspects of the contract were fulfilled in these cases by a representative, usually the woman's husband, and used this as an excuse to intervene in the marriage plans of their female vassals. Such claims were frequently ignored. Matilda of Tuscany (c. 1046–1115) did not remarry after the death of her husband and became a dominant figure in Italian politics for almost forty years.

Alienation of fiefs for cash or other considerations was far more difficult to achieve than heritability, but it had become common by the twelfth century. Permission of the lord was still necessary if a fief changed hands, but the increasing frequency of such transactions indicates that the long process of transition to private property and a cash-based economy had already begun.

Private jurisdiction, or the establishment by vassals of feudal and manorial courts, was another matter. The practice of allowing great men to maintain their own law courts dates back to the latter days of the Roman Empire. Feudalism extended this benefit to nearly every vassal with subjects of his or her own. The right to preside over one's own court was commonly demanded by prospective vassals, and princes and tenants-in-chief were willing to accept it because their own courts could not cope with the proliferation of local disputes. Feudal society was contentious. A distinction was maintained between minor and major causes, the latter being reserved for royal or county jurisdictions. The proliferation of feudal and manorial courts inevitably weakened what threads of central authority remained.

Within a few short generations, feudalism had created a political system based upon decentralization and hereditary privilege. Though at first confined within

the limits of the old Carolingian Empire, feudal institutions were extended to England in 1066 and after 1072 to Sicily and southern Italy by the Norman expansion. In all of these regions, the permanence of the system was ensured by a tangled web of legal contracts and by the diffusion of military power among what had become a warrior caste.

The values and attitudes of that caste were increasingly defined by adherence to the ideals of chivalry. The term is derived from the French word for horse and reflects the self-conscious superiority of the mounted warrior. In the centuries to come the chivalric code would grow increasingly elaborate and its rituals would be fixed by a vast literature. Ceremonial initiations, designed to set the warrior apart from society as a whole, marked the creation of knights from the beginning of feudalism. They are not to be confused with the ceremony of vassalage but were the culmination of a long period of training and preparation. Boys of ten or twelve were usually sent by their fathers to serve as pages in the household of another lord. There they were trained in the art of war, including horsemanship and the use of lance, shield, and sword. Physical training was intense and consumed much of their time. The pages also learned fortification and enough physics to construct siege engines and other military devices.

Their first exposure to warfare was as squires who attended a knight on the battlefield, tended his horses and weapons, and protected him if he fell. When and if this apprenticeship was successfully completed the squire was dubbed a knight. In the early days the ceremony could be performed by any other knight and was usually concluded with a blow to the head or shoulders. Touching with the flat of a sword came later. In the Germanic world, the new knight was girded with his sword, a practice that probably dates from the knighting of Louis the Pious by his father, Charlemagne. Religious elements began to creep into these initiations by the middle of the tenth century and symbolized the growing sense that knights, like priests, had a divinely established vocation.

## Feudalism and the Manor

A fief could support a fighting man only if someone were available to work it. As a general rule, knights did not till the soil even in the days before their status became too great to permit physical labor. They were on call whenever danger threatened, and their training normally required several hours of practice and exercise each day. Even hunting, which was their primary recreation and which they always pursued on horseback, was a form of military exercise. The provision of labor was therefore a problem from the start, and the manorial system that was adapted to provide it grew hand in hand with the feudal institutions of the new aristocracy.

Manorialism as a means of securing scarce labor had existed since ancient times and would survive in eastern Europe until the nineteenth century. The basis of the medieval system was the manorial tenure, which in some respects paralleled the feudal tenures of the knights. In its simplest form, a peasant would surrender his allod or freehold to a lord in return for the lord's protection. The lord would then grant it back to him as a tenement with stipulations that made the tenant the legal subject of the lord. Those who possessed little or no land could also request protection, but their poverty placed them at a disadvantage in negotiating the terms.

The nature of manorial tenures varied widely. Although a tenant could remain technically free, in most cases tenancy involved a descent into serfdom. Serfs were unlike slaves in that they could not be sold and were entitled to hold property. They could also, within certain limits, negotiate contracts, undertake obligations, and testify in court. Both their land and their personal rights were contractually encumbered. Once they had placed themselves under a lord's protection, they were bound to their tenement for life and were often forbidden to marry anyone other than a subject of the same lord. Because they were legally subject to another person, they lost all political rights including the right to sue a free man in court.

Economically, the tenant was further obligated to return a portion of his annual crop to the lord or provide labor on the lord's lands for a fixed number of days per year or both (see document 8.4). Labor services might also involve maintenance work on the lord's castle or on the infrastructure of the manor, including roads, ditches, and other facilities. In some cases, military service was required, usually for a maximum of forty days per year between planting and harvest. Peasant troops were ineffective in a military environment dominated by heavy cavalry, but they could provide logistical support, dig trenches, and guard the baggage.

Another feature of these agreements involved services that could be provided only by the lord. The tenant accepted the jurisdiction of the lord's court and agreed to use only the lord's mill or the lord's animals at stud in return for payments in kind. Sometimes stipulations were made about access to orchards, woodlands, or streams. The right of tenants to hunt, fish, or gather fallen wood for fuel was strictly regulated. In return, the lord agreed to protect the tenant and his property both physically and in law. Though manorial tenures were usually heritable, an investiture fee was commonly required from the heirs when a tenement changed hands.

Women rarely had the right to make such agreements in the first instance. If they were married, their legal rights were largely subsumed under those of their husbands and even their testimony in a peasant court was acceptable only in limited circumstances. They could, however, inherit tenements. In such cases military and labor obligations were fulfilled by substitutes who were usually paid in goods or services instead of in cash.

The sum of these burdens could be great or relatively small and might be compounded by tithes or other obligations owed to the parish church. Rents calculated as a portion of the total harvest were better from the peasant's point of view than those expressed in fixed amounts. Miller's fees and similar charges would have to have been paid in any case and involved only a theoretical loss of freedom because transporting grain or livestock to distant villages for milling or stud services was impractical. Labor services, meanwhile, could be onerous and were often deeply resented. In a society that was still largely illiterate, these contracts were not written down, and the precise terms of each tenure were submerged in the "custom of the manor." In later years the margin of survival for a peasant family often depended upon the negotiating skills of their ancestors.

The bargains struck between lords and peasants were unequal, but the harshness of the system was modified to some extent by the ideal of mutual obligation. In feudal Europe, land—the basis of nearly all wealth—was no longer regarded as private property. Peasants held their tenements from lords, who held their fiefs from the king, who held his kingdom ultimately from God. The terms by which land was occupied were spelled out in law and custom, and they could rarely be changed or abrogated without difficulty. Fiefs could not be sold at will, and tenants could not be dispossessed without cause. Moreover, lords were obligated to protect their subjects' property as well as their persons. Some were wise enough to take a paternalistic interest in the well-being of those who inhabited their estates. Whether a lord was good or bad, tenants enjoyed a measure of security that the wage laborers of a later day would never know. If the lot of a medieval peasant was hard, it was in part because the margin of subsistence was small and the contribution of any of it was more than most people could afford.

Generally, manorial tenures were accepted voluntarily. A peasant without protection was at the mercy of

## ◆ DOCUMENT 8.4 ◆

## Manorial Obligations

*John Cayworth was one of the larger tenants on the English manor of Bernholme in 1307. His obligations were correspondingly great and may be compared with the data in tables 11.1 and 11.2. This excerpt from the* Custumals of Battle Abbey *provides a good example of how manorial tenures worked. Such agreements were almost never written down before the end of the thirteenth century, and it is doubtful if the monetary value of the obligations would have been calculated in this way before the widespread commutation of services for cash.*

They say, moreover, that John Cayworth holds a house and 30 acres of land, and owes yearly 2s. at Easter and Michaelmas; and he owes a cock and two hens at Christmas, of the value of 4d.

And he ought to harrow for two days at the Lenten sowing with one man and his own horse and his own harrow, the value of the work being 4d.; and he is to receive from the lord on each day 3 meals, of the value of 5d.; and then the lord will be at a loss of 1d. . . .

And he ought to carry the manure of the lord for 2 days with 1 cart, with his own 2 oxen, the value of the work being 8d.; and he is to receive from the lord each day 3 meals of the price as above, and thus the service is worth 3d. clear.

And he shall find 1 man for two days for mowing on the meadow of the lord, who can mow, by estimation 1 acre and a half, the value of the mowing of an acre being 6d.; the sum is therefore 9d.; and he is to receive each day 3 meals of the value given above; and thus the mowing is worth 4d. clear. And he ought to gather and carry

that same hay which he has cut, the price of the work being 3d. . . .

And he ought to carry wood from the woods of the lord as far as the manor [house] for two days in summer with a cart and 3 animals of his own, the value of the work being 9d. And he shall receive from the lord each day 3 meals of the price given above; and thus the work is worth 4d. clear.

And he ought to find a man for 2 days to cut heath, the value of the work being 4d., and he shall have 3 meals each day of the value given above; and thus the lord will lose, if he receives the service, 3d.

And he ought to carry the heath which he has cut, the value of the work being 5d., and he shall receive from the lord 3 meals at the price of 2 1/2d., and thus the work will be worth 2 1/2d. clear.

And he ought to carry to Battle twice in the summer season, each time half a load of grain, the value of the service being 4d. And he shall receive in the manor each time 1 meal of the value of 2d. And thus the work is worth 2d. clear.

The total of the rents with the value of the hens is 2s. 4d.

The total of the value of the works is 2s., 3 1/2d., owed from the said John yearly.

"Custumals of Battle Abbey." In Edward P. Cheyney, ed., *Pennsylvania Translations and Reprints,* vol. 3, no. 5, p. 30. Philadelphia: University of Pennsylvania Press, 1902.

---

all sorts of armed marauders, including neighboring lords whose behavior was often no better than the Vikings'. Faced with the prospect of unending, uncontrolled violence, most people accepted their loss of freedom as a necessity. Instances of coercion by prospective lords were apparently rare and sometimes subtle. The manorial system was, like its feudal counterpart, a necessary adaptation to a world gone mad.

In physical terms, no two manors were exactly alike. Their character differed widely according to topography, agricultural practices, and local custom (see illustration 8.3). Some constituted entire villages of peasant huts with their household gardens and perhaps a church. Not every manor boasted a lord in residence, and the church sometimes served as a fortified refuge in

case of attack. Paths radiating out from the village provided access to fields, which might be divided from one another by narrow balks of turf. Where the iron plow (see chapter 10) was in use, the fields were laid out in long strips to facilitate plowing with draft animals. They were often worked in common because not everyone could afford a plow or a team. In lands cultivated by the old Roman plow, fields might be irregular in shape and worked only by the peasant family or its servants.

The lands of an individual tenement were not necessarily contiguous. The equivalent of between thirty and forty acres was the maximum that could be cultivated by a peasant family. Many plots were far smaller. With the passage of time and the vagaries of inheritance, farmers might find themselves holding

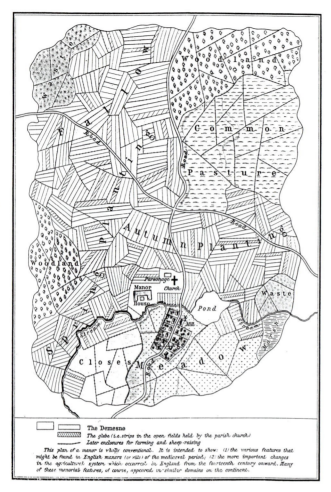

**Illustration 8.3**

🗺 **Plan of a Medieval Manor.** The drawing shows how a typical English manor might have been laid out. Not all manors were single villages of this kind in which all the inhabitants were subjects of the same lord.

fragments of land scattered over several square miles. Parcels of arable land might also be set aside for the lord and for the priest if there was one. Most communities also possessed common land that was available for allocation by the village elders.

Collection of the lord's dues and the maintenance of his property was typically in the hands of an appointed steward. The steward (reeve, *maire*, or *Bauermeister*) was originally a capable peasant who received lands, exemptions, or special privileges for his work on the lord's behalf. Such men almost invariably became wealthy, and in the later Middle Ages some of them were able to transcend the limitations of peasant status and acquire a coat of arms. Together with the *ministeriales*, the household officials who served the immediate needs of the lord and his castle, the stewards constituted an intermediate social class of some importance.

Few, however, were popular. Some were petty tyrants who extorted goods and favors from the peasants while embezzling from their lord. Even the best of them were powerful figures who had to be placated at every turn. In some regions they not only collected rents and dues, but also served as judges in peasant courts and determined the boundaries of tenements in case of dispute. In other, happier, places, these latter functions were assumed by the villagers.

Manors that contained one or more entire villages were the ideal because they were easier to administer and defend. In practice a manor was often spread through several villages with each village containing the subjects of more than one lord. This situation arose in Germany and parts of France because, in the beginning at least, peasants could sometimes commend themselves to the lord of their choice. In Italy and southern France the situation was further complicated by the survival of allodial holdings amidst the feudal and manorial tenures. A villager might own some of his land outright and hold the rest as a tenement from his lord. Only in England was the village manor almost universal.

Manorialism, defined as any system in which the tenants of an estate are the legal subjects of their lord, could exist without feudalism. Where manorialism and feudalism were combined, they produced a social and political system that was highly resistant to change. The knights had achieved a monopoly of both economic and military power and thus could impose the values of their class upon society as a whole.

## Social and Economic Structures in Nonfeudal Europe

By the middle of the tenth century feudal institutions were dominant in what had been the Carolingian Empire. Another, nonfeudal Europe successfully resisted the new social order. Scandinavia, untroubled by raids or invasions, preserved the main features of its social structure and system of land tenure until well into the early modern period. Individual farmsteads, often located at a distance from the nearest village and worked by the owner's family and its servants, continued to be common. Slavery declined and eventually disappeared under the influence of Christianity. The houses, built of logs and connected to their outbuildings for protection against the winter, retained the sturdy simplicity of Viking days.

Until the Norman invasion of 1066 (see illustration 8.4) the Anglo-Saxons, too, were able to function

**Illustration 8.4**

**Detail from the Bayeux Tapestry.**
The Bayeux Tapestry commemorates the Norman invasion of England in narrative form. It was designed to run clockwise around the entire nave of the Cathedral of Bayeux (consecrated 1077) and was originally 230 feet long and twenty inches high. It is an embroidery, not a true, woven tapestry. The work was probably done by the women of the court, who seem to have known a great deal about war and seafaring. In this segment, the Normans are beaching their Viking-style longboats and disembarking horses on the English coast for the invasion.

within the limits of their traditional social order, though the basis of land tenure changed dramatically. The Anglo-Saxon *ceorl* (churl), or peasant, was typically a freeholder who paid taxes for the support of his king's household and served in the *fyrd,* a kind of militia whose tactics resembled those of the Frankish hosts. As in other Germanic cultures, the kings were further served by a *comitatus* of fighting men, known as *gesiths. Gesiths* sometimes received land as a reward when they retired. They were usually supported during their fighting careers by the bounty of the king's hall and by the sharing of treasure.

On the eve of the Viking invasions, England was divided into seven kingdoms: East Anglia, Essex, Kent, Mercia, Northumberland, Sussex, and Wessex. Their small size made a decentralized mobile defense unnecessary, and feudal institutions did not develop, but the chaos of the mid-ninth century forced large numbers of hitherto independent *ceorls* to seek the protection of manorial relationships. Manorialism was firmly established and may have been the dominant form of English economic organization when Alfred the Great of Wessex (reigned 871–899) began the process of uniting the country into a single kingdom.

In Alfred's view, the achievement of political unity depended in part upon the revival of learning and of a sense of common cultural identity. He arranged for the translation of religious classics into Old English and commissioned the *Anglo-Saxon Chronicle,* one version of which was updated continuously until 1154. His policies bore fruit in the reign of Edgar, from 959 to 974, when political unity was achieved and the rich body of Anglo-Saxon poetry was compiled into four great

books, the most important of which was the epic *Beowulf.* The political failure of the succeeding years should not obscure the vibrant, functional society that fell to the Normans in 1066.

The Celtic world, though also subject to the full fury of the Norsemen, resisted the temptation to exchange land for military service until forced to do so in the twelfth and thirteenth centuries. Even then, the penetration of feudalism was far from complete. Ireland was ravaged from end to end by the Vikings, and Viking enclaves were established in the vicinity of Dublin and elsewhere. However, the old system of clans and kings survived. Feudalism was introduced only to those portions of the island that were conquered by Henry II of England in 1171–72, and even some of this territory was lost in the Irish revival of the fourteenth century.

The fate of Wales was similar. A kind of manorialism had been established in the more exposed coastal areas at the height of the raids. It was dominated by traditional chieftains instead of by feudal lords. The upland areas, rugged and inaccessible, remained free. After 1093 Norman adventurers tried to impose feudal tenures on certain parts of South Wales and Pembrokeshire. These efforts were partial and usually contested. Even in the areas of greatest Norman penetration, traditional institutions stood side by side with the new until well into the modern age.

The Welsh owed much of their independence to the ruggedness of their native land. In general, upland areas even in the heart of continental Europe stood a good chance of escaping feudal domination. Peasant communities in the Alps and the Pyrenees were remote as well as poor. Their inhabitants lived by herding and subsistence agriculture supplemented by hunting and gathering. Because they produced no surplus and were prohibited by geography from engaging in large-scale monoculture, they tempted neither the raiders nor the lords. They were also easily defended. Mounted knights were at a disadvantage in a largely vertical landscape, and narrow gorges were ideal sites for an ambush. Peasants of the high valleys found retaining their ancient freedoms relatively easy.

A rugged landscape also protected the remnants of Christian Spain. The situation in Cantabria and on the southern slopes of the Pyrenees was unique. The tiny states that survived the Muslim advance found themselves on a turbulent military frontier. Frankish influence brought feudalism to Cataluña, but the system that evolved in the northwest reflects a society that had begun, however tentatively, to take the offensive against *al Islam*. In the ninth and tenth centuries the kingdoms of Asturias, León, and Castile began to expand slowly at the expense of their Muslim neighbors, drawing back if the opposition became too intense, moving forward when a target of opportunity arose. Virtually the entire male population was militarized because warfare against the Muslims involved infantry and light cavalry as well as armored knights.

Advances were often achieved by individual nobles who were then free to keep the territory they conquered and rule it as they saw fit. Kings, however, reserved the right to grant and revoke titles at will. Feudal tenures were unknown, and private jurisdiction was strictly limited. Nobles placed themselves in *encomienda*, or commendation, to the crown, a term that was to have a different meaning in later centuries. Small landholders, who in this frontier society were usually free men and fighters, placed themselves in a similar relationship to the nobles. It was an exchange of military service for protection that might or might not involve a grant of land. More commonly it involved dues and services that created a *de facto* manor without the surrender of allodial property or of personal freedom. The *señorios* or lordships created by these arrangements were often vast. They were based upon a legal and political system unlike that of feudal Europe.

Spanish towns also played an important role in territorial expansion. Urban militias were established in the early ninth century and had become an important component of the Christian military effort by the tenth century. Whether they fought on their own behalf or under the direct orders of the king, towns were rewarded with booty and with royal grants whose provisions resembled those of the *señorios*. Large tracts of land

and many villages came under their control as peasants commended themselves to towns instead of to secular or ecclesiastical lords.

In northern Italy, towns were more effective as a barrier to feudal institutions, but for different reasons. Larger and richer than their Spanish counterparts, they could offer credible protection to their neighbors from the beginning of the feudal age. A patchwork of tenures developed in which allods, feudal manors, and urban jurisdictions might exist side by side in a relatively restricted space. The situation in some ways resembled that of southern France. The feudal component remained smaller, in part because the region was generally immune to large-scale raids. The south had been a region of large estates since Roman times. When Norman rulers imposed feudalism at the end of the eleventh century they substituted one set of lords for another while changing the legal basis of their holdings.

## The Feudal Monarchies

This rapid survey of nonfeudal Europe reveals that, though feudalism was not universal, the disorders of the ninth and tenth centuries led to the growth of manorialism or other systems of collective security in all but the most isolated sections of Europe. A majority of Europeans were forced to renounce personal and economic freedom as the price of survival. Peasants who had formerly been free, slave, or *coloni* shared a common servility.

The impact of this change on everyday life should not be exaggerated. The correlation between personal freedom and political or social influence has always been inexact. The free Anglo-Saxon or Frankish peasant had often been subordinated as effectively by debt and by the threat of personal force as his descendants were by the custom of the manor, and he was subjected to taxes and demands for military service that could be as onerous as the feudal dues of a later period. Women had never been free in the sense that they remained the legal subjects of their fathers or husbands.

Moreover, the world that emerged from the aftermath of the great raids retained many distinctions of wealth and status, even among peasants. Servility was not incompatible with a secure and even comfortable life, while freedom could mean a hardscrabble existence on marginal lands. Those who remained free often did so because they inhabited malarial swamps or mountain crags unwanted by either knights or Vikings.

The conversion to feudal and manorial tenures seems more dramatic when seen in relation to its effect on social institutions and attitudes—the ties that bound society together. After the great raids, the gap between the vast majority of the population and the aristocracy that ruled them widened perceptibly. Social mobility was not only difficult to achieve but also generally condemned. Chivalric and ecclesiastical writers maintained that people should not attempt to rise above their class. Permanence and stability were valued by a society that had just emerged from two centuries of near-anarchy, but the longevity of feudal institutions was based only in part on the conservatism of those who had suffered much.

The apparent success of heavy cavalry in dealing with the crises of the ninth and tenth centuries had created a powerful myth of class superiority. The medieval knight believed in it and made it the basis of an entire way of life. His education, leisure activities, and ultimately the moral and aesthetic values of his class were grounded in the perception of himself as the armed and mounted protector of society—a perception that also gave him his chief claim to social privilege. By the end of the tenth century the conditions that created the knights had largely disappeared, but the knights were now in possession of the bulk of society's resources and could be neither displaced nor effectively controlled. Class divisions would henceforth widen and acquire a more elaborate ideological basis than they had formerly possessed. A system of military tactics that was not suitable for all occasions would be preserved until long after it had outlived its usefulness. Above all, the creation of a dominant social class whose power was based upon widely scattered estates would perpetuate the decentralization of political authority for centuries to come.

An immediate consequence of this decentralization was feudal warfare, disruptive and endemic, though not as devastating as the great raids. The warrior's sense of vocation, the development of a code of conduct based upon the ideals of honor and courage, and the emphasis on individual and corporate rights characteristic of feudal law all encouraged the lords to fight one another in defense of what they considered their honor and their right. The church sought to restrain these tendencies by encouraging the "Peace of God" movement. Councils or bishops issued decrees against wanton violence and tried to limit the fighting to certain days of the week. Such measures could achieve little. The political history of the age became in large measure an attempt to control the centrifugal tendencies of feudalism in the interests of public order.

## France and Norman England

In northwestern Europe a protracted struggle between the kings of France and England was the legacy of Norman expansion. England fell to the Normans when Edward the Confessor died without heirs. There were three claimants to the throne: Edward's first cousin, William, duke of Normandy (c. 1028–87); Harald Hardrada, king of Norway; and the Saxon Harold Godwinsson. When the English Witan, or council, chose Harold Godwinsson, the new king found himself under attack on two fronts. He defeated the Norwegians at Stamford Bridge on September 23, 1066, and rushed south to meet William, who had landed near Hastings on the same day. Exhausted by the battle and by a march of almost three hundred miles, the Saxon army was crushed on October 14.

William was no friend of feudal decentralization. The fiefs he established in England were composed of manors in different parts of the country to prevent a concentration of power. He retained the Saxon office of sheriff or shire reeve, who collected taxes, administered the royal domains, and presided over the shire courts. In 1086 his officials produced a comprehensive survey of all English properties known as the Domesday Book (see document 8.5). Norman England was perhaps the most tightly administered monarchy of the central Middle Ages, but William's conquest gave birth to a political anomaly: The king of England was still duke of Normandy and vassal to the king of France for one of the richest provinces on the Continent.

The situation became critical in the reign of Henry II from 1154 to 1189. The development of the French monarchy had been slow and painful. In 987 the great French feudatories had elected Hugh Capet king, primarily because his small holdings in the region of Paris made it unlikely that he would ever pose a threat to their interests. The area was a hotbed of feudal anarchy, and the Capetian kings took more than a century to establish control. When Louis VI "the Fat" died in 1137, he left a small but powerful state in the Ile de France to his son Louis VII. Guided by his chief adviser, Suger, abbot of St. Denis, Louis VII tried to double his holdings by marrying Eleanor of Aquitaine (c. 1122–1204), the heir to vast estates in southwestern France (see illustration 8.5). The marriage was a disaster. Louis was pious and ascetic; Eleanor was attractive, witty, and a patron of troubadours. She apparently took the adulterous conventions of chivalric love too seriously, and the marriage was annulled in 1152 amid charges of infidelity with one of her cousins. The couple had two

## ◈ DOCUMENT 8.5 ◈

# The Domesday Book: Description of a Manor

*This description of the manor of Hecham, Essex, in 1086 illustrates the care with which William the Conqueror's administrators catalogued the wealth of England. It also provides a sense of what a medium-sized manor was like and of the dramatic changes brought by the conquest. A hide is a measure of land that varied between eighty and one hundred modern acres. A bordar was the lowest rank of villein, who performed menial service in return for a cottage.*

Peter de Valence holds in domain Hecham, which Haldane a freeman held in the time of King Edward, as a manor, and as 5 hides. There have always been 2 ploughs in the demesne, 4 ploughs of the men. At that time there were 8 villeins, now 10; then there were 2 bordars, now 3; at both times 4 *servi*, woods for 300 swine, 18 acres of meadow. Then there were 2 fish ponds and a half, now there are none. At that time there was 1 ox, now there are 15 cattle and 1 small horse and 18 swine and 2 hives of bees. At that time it was worth 69s., now 4£10s. When he received this manor he found only 1 ox and 1 acre planted. Of those 5 hides spoken of above, one was held in the time of King Edward by 2 freemen, and it was added to the manor in the time of King William. It was worth in the time of King Edward 10s., now 22s., and William holds this from Peter de Valence.

"Domesday Book," II, 78b. In *Translations and Reprints from the Original Sources of European History,* vol. 3, no. 5, pp. 3–4. Philadelphia: University of Pennsylvania, 1896.

**Illustration 8.5**

**Funeral Effigy of Eleanor of Aquitaine.** Eleanor, who had been both queen of France and queen of England, was a major political figure of the twelfth century as well as a great patron of troubadours and chivalric literature. This carving is from her tomb at the abbey of Fontrevault in France.

Becket, archbishop of Canterbury, who was killed by his henchmen in a dispute over the independence of ecclesiastical courts—he left the country far stronger than he had found it.

Unfortunately, his marriage to Eleanor of Aquitaine left Henry in possession of half of France. To Louis VII it was a personal affront as well as a threat to his sovereignty. For the next three hundred years the primary goal of French policy was to secure either the obedience or the expulsion of the English (see map 8.2). It was not at first an ethnic issue, for the English court was culturally and linguistically French. But the situation raised questions that went to the heart of feudal relationships: Could a sovereign prince be the vassal of another? What happened to ties of dependence when the vassal was richer and more powerful than his lord? The issue had been brought up in a somewhat different form by the powerful counts of Flanders and would be revived in later years by the growth of Burgundy. The dispute between France and England remained the

daughters but no son. Eleanor soon married Henry II of England, her junior by ten years.

Henry was a man of boundless energy and ambition. He was responsible, among other things, for the establishment of itinerant courts (the "justices in eyre") that offered sworn inquests and juries as an alternative to the duels and ordeals of the baronial courts and whose decisions became the basis of English common law. He also strengthened the Exchequer, or treasury, so called because calculations were made by moving counters on a checkered tabletop. Though Henry made mistakes—the worst being the murder of St. Thomas à

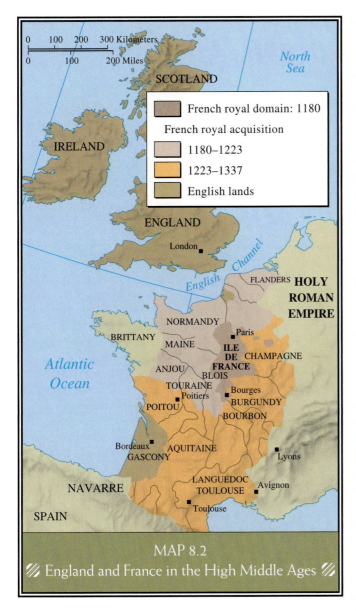

**MAP 8.2**
England and France in the High Middle Ages

Map legend:
- French royal domain: 1180
- French royal acquisition
  - 1180–1223
  - 1223–1337
- English lands

Labels on map: North Sea, SCOTLAND, IRELAND, ENGLAND, London, English Channel, FLANDERS, HOLY ROMAN EMPIRE, NORMANDY, Paris, BRITTANY, MAINE, ILE DE FRANCE, CHAMPAGNE, ANJOU, BLOIS, TOURAINE, Poitiers, Bourges, POITOU, BURGUNDY, BOURBON, Atlantic Ocean, Bordeaux, AQUITAINE, Lyons, GASCONY, NAVARRE, LANGUEDOC, TOULOUSE, Avignon, SPAIN, Toulouse

an unsuccessful rebellion against their father. Two of these sons, Richard I Lion-Heart (reigned 1189–99) and John (reigned 1199–1216), would, as kings of England, bring ruin to Henry's cause.

Richard spent most of his reign crusading in the Holy Land at ruinous expense. On his return he was captured by the emperor Henry VI and forced to pay an enormous ransom that pushed the English to the brink of revolt. His brother John compounded the folly with a series of catastrophic mistakes. In 1200 he married a woman who was already engaged to a vassal of Philip Augustus. The vassal appealed to his lord, and Philip called upon John, as duke of Normandy, to present himself so that the case could be judged. It was the normal way of dealing with disputes between vassals of the same lord, but John, acting in his capacity as king of England, refused to submit to the justice of another sovereign. Philip responded by confiscating Normandy in 1204.

John's attempts to recover his lost duchy forced him to extreme financial measures that further alienated his subjects and brought him into conflict with the church. He was excommunicated in 1209, and England was placed under an interdict, a papal decree that forbade the administration of the sacraments. To lift it, John had to declare England a papal fief and renounce the royal appointment of bishops. The final blow occurred at Bouvines in 1214 when Philip Augustus defeated John's Anglo-Flemish-Imperial coalition in battle. Disgusted, a coalition of English barons rebelled and forced John to accept the Magna Carta (Great Charter). Though the Magna Carta (see document 8.6) is widely regarded as a landmark in the development of Anglo-Saxon constitutional thought, it was primarily an affirmation of feudal privileges. It did nothing for ordinary men and women and was largely ignored by John's successors. A later age would see it as a bulwark of individual rights against the claims of the state.

The failures of King John left Philip Augustus the most powerful figure in western Europe. By 1204 he had already added Artois and the Vermandois to his realms. The struggle with John brought him Normandy, Maine, Anjou, and Touraine. Bouvines brought him Flanders. To govern his new estates he appointed royal officials known as *baillis* or *seneschals*. Their function was like that of an English sheriff, but they were usually lawyers with no prior connection to the territories in which they served. They were therefore dependent upon the king and had no opportunity to build a power base of their own. This would be the pattern of French administration until 1789: Provinces retained

central issue of west European politics until the fifteenth century.

The establishment of Henry II's Angevin Empire inspired a reorganization of the French monarchy. Begun by Louis VII, the work was completed by his son, Philip II Augustus (reigned 1179–1223). Louis created an effective royal army and, on the diplomatic front, concluded an improbable alliance with his ex-wife, Eleanor of Aquitaine. After sixteen years of marriage and eight children, Eleanor decided that she would no longer tolerate Henry's infidelity or his increasingly abusive behavior. She retired to Poitiers with her daughter, Mary, countess of Champagne, and established a court that was to become a veritable school of chivalry. In 1173 she and Louis encouraged her sons in

### ◈ DOCUMENT 8.6 ◈

## Magna Carta

*The following sections from the Magna Carta show that it was primarily intended to confirm and extend the privileges of the barons, but some of the provisions, such as number thirty-nine, had broader implications. Taken as a whole, the Great Charter set clear limits on the authority of the crown, and it is easy to understand why English revolutionaries of the seventeenth century regarded the document as one of the foundations of English liberty. Sections two and three restrict the crown's ability to extort fees from its vassals when a fief is inherited. Scutage in number twelve was a fee paid by a tenant in lieu of military service. John and some of his predecessors had begun to levy it for other purposes.*

1. In the first place we have granted to God, and by this our present charter confirmed, for us and our heirs forever, that the English church shall be free, and shall hold its rights entire and its liberties uninjured.

2. If any of our earls or barons, or others holding from us in chief by military service shall have died, and when he had died his heir shall be of full age and owe relief, he shall have his inheritance by the ancient relief; that is to say, the heir or heirs of an earl for the whole barony of an earl a hundred pounds; the heir or heirs of a baron for a whole barony a hundred pounds; the heir or heirs of a knight, for a whole knight's fee, a hundred shillings at most; and who owes less let him give less according to the ancient custom of fiefs.

3. If, moreover, the heir of any one of such shall be under age, and shall be in wardship, when he comes of age he shall have his inheritance without relief and without a fine. . . .

12. No scutage or aid shall be imposed in our kingdom except by the common council of our kingdom, except for the ransoming of our own body, for the making of our oldest son a knight, and for the once marrying of our oldest daughter, and for these purposes it shall be only a reasonable aid.

13. And the city of London shall have all its ancient liberties and free customs, as well by land as by water. Moreover, we will and grant that all other cities and boroughs and villages and ports shall have all their liberties and free customs.

39. No free man shall be taken or imprisoned or dispossessed, or outlawed, or banished, or in any way destroyed, nor will we go upon him, nor send upon him, except by the legal judgments of his peers or by the law of the land.

"Magna Carta." *Pennsylvania Translations and Reprints*, pp. 6–16, trans. Edward P. Cheyney. Philadelphia: University of Pennsylvania Press, 1897.

---

their institutions, which were controlled by officers of the crown. By the end of the thirteenth century, Philip's successors had acquired Languedoc, Toulouse, Poitou, and Champagne. Only English Aquitaine and Gascony remained outside their grasp.

### The Ottonian Empire

France and England would remain the archetypical feudal monarchies. In the German-speaking lands to the east, an effort to revive the empire along feudal lines was begun by Otto I the Great (reigned 936–973), the victor at the Lechfeld (see map 8.3). Otto was a self-conscious imitator of Charlemagne, though he never sought to extend his rule over West Francia. Like Charlemagne, he enlisted the church in his behalf, drawing both his administrators and many of his feudal

levies from the great ecclesiastical estates. In 962 Pope John XII crowned him emperor at Aachen in return for his help against an Italian enemy, Berengar of Friuli, and Otto agreed to protect the territorial integrity of the papal states. The price for all this was imperial control over ecclesiastical appointments. When John objected, he was deposed and his successor was forced to take an oath of allegiance to Otto.

These events were recorded in detail because Otto, like Charlemagne, knew the value of a good biographer. Hroswitha of Gandersheim (c. 935–1000) was one of the great literary figures of the age. In addition to the *Deeds of Otto* she wrote a history of her convent, some religious poems, and six comedies based on the works of Terence. They are thought to be the first dramas written in medieval times. Hroswitha did not write in isolation but was part of a broader flowering of literary culture and manuscript illumination among

MAP 8.3
◢◢ The Holy Roman Empire ◢◢

**Legend:** Kingdom of Sicily · Republic of Venice · Holy Roman Empire

women in religious orders in the Ottonian Empire (see illustration 8.6). Abbesses of great convents such as Uta of Niedermünster seem to have been even more powerful in Germany than elsewhere, and they took the responsibilities of patronage seriously. One of the extraordinary figures to emerge from this tradition was Hildegard of Bingen (1098–1179). The *Scivias*, a powerful record of her mystical visions, remains a classic of devotional and apocalyptic literature. She also wrote a treatise on medicine, at least one play, and the *Physica*, a categorical description of the natural world.

Otto's involvement with the papacy drew him and his successors more deeply into the quagmire of Italian politics. Their efforts to limit the growing power of the north Italian towns and their bitter struggle with the papacy over the issue of lay investiture (the imperial appointment of bishops) were among the most important political conflicts of the Middle Ages (see chapter 9).

The issues were intertwined, and both required massive investments of political and military capital. Emperors could easily neglect German affairs or subordinate them to the needs of their Italian policy. German nobles and ultimately the German towns found it equally easy to preserve their autonomy and to resist the development of a feudal monarchy on the French or English model. Germany, with its hundreds of small states, remained a stronghold of feudal particularism until the beginning of the modern age.

At their strongest, feudal monarchies such as England and France could command impressive resources. Their power was nevertheless limited. As long as fighting men were supported with land or by payments in kind, feudal lords could raise private armies and threaten the integrity of the realm. Kings had prestige and the legal advantages of sovereignty—their courts took theoretical precedence over all others, they could declare

**Illustration 8.6**

**Illumination from the Uta Codex.** This magnificent example of Romanesque manuscript illumination was commissioned by Uta, abbess of the convent at Niedermünster, and completed between 1002 and 1025, probably by the nuns in her own scriptorium. Uta, who appears in the upper right-hand corner, was one of many powerful abbesses in the Ottonian Empire. Women frequently served as manuscript illuminators. The subject here is "Saint Erhard Celebrating Mass."

war, and they could coin money—but feudal kingdoms were inherently unstable because the crown held no monopoly on the use of force. Such a monopoly could be achieved only by eroding the foundations of feudalism itself. Until then, good governance would be largely a matter of personal character and good luck. For most of the Middle Ages, Europe would remain politically fragmented while retaining a social structure that conserved feudal privilege long after its original justification had passed.

# CHAPTER 9

# MEDIEVAL RELIGION AND THOUGHT

The Latin church survived the fall of the Roman Empire in the west to become the major unifying element in European society.

Though it suffered from episodes of fragmentation and disorder throughout the early Middle Ages, it provided western Europeans with a common set of values and, through its universality and the preservation of the Latin language, with a measure of diplomatic and intellectual communication. With the passing of the great raids, the church gradually evolved into something more: a vast, institutionalized bureaucracy headed by popes who claimed full authority over a subordinate clergy as well as secular rulers. That authority was vehemently contested by the emperor and other princes, but all agreed that Europe, for all its divisions, was a Christian commonwealth ruled in theory by divine law.

The church of the High Middle Ages possessed vast wealth, political influence, and a virtual monopoly of thought and education, but its importance cannot be understood in purely institutional terms. Its values, sacraments, and holidays defined the lives of ordinary people in ways that are almost inconceivable today. While medieval people were neither excessively good nor moral, their personal identities and habits of thought were formed by near total emersion in Christian practices and categories of thought. The sacraments, from baptism to extreme unction, defined the stages of people's lives. They measured time by reference to the canonical hours and holidays of the church. They bound themselves by religious oaths that, to their minds, carried with them the real threat of eternal damnation, and they explained everything from politics to natural phenomena as an expression of God's will. In more concrete terms the church building was both the physical and social center of their communities and the most visible expression of communal or civic pride. Priests, monks, and nuns organized the distribution of charity, cared for the sick, and provided lodging for travelers in the great monasteries that dotted the countryside. Chapter 9 describes how the church evolved from the dark days of the tenth century to the glories of the twelfth and thirteenth centuries—the great age of cathedrals and crusades, of the founding of universities, and of scholasticism, a system of thought that retains its influence today.

## Monastic Revival and Papal Reform

The disorder created by the great raids profoundly weakened the western church. Cut off from contact with each other and from Rome, bishoprics and monasteries fell under the control of secular rulers who could protect them. These lords then appointed political henchmen or their own younger sons to episcopal rank with little regard for spiritual qualities. Monasteries suffered the same fate. Even when a monastery retained its independence, isolation and the absence of supervision often led to relaxations of the rule. Lay people, who in this age tended to believe that their chances of salvation depended on the prayers of those holier than themselves, were scandalized and frightened.

The papacy shared in the general decline. As bishop of Rome, the pope was both spiritual and secular ruler of the city. From the deposition of Pope Nicholas the Great in 867 to the appointment of Clement II in 1046, a generalized state of anarchy permitted the great Roman families to vie for control of the office with only an occasional nod to religious priorities or to the wishes of the emperors. To the laity and to pious churchmen alike, the situation was intolerable.

A reform movement that would transform both the papacy and the medieval church began in the Burgundian monastery of Cluny. Founded in 910 by William the Pious, duke of Aquitaine, its community followed a strict version of the Benedictine rule that emphasized liturgy and vocal prayer. In the decades that followed its establishment the Cluniac ideal attracted those who sought a more spiritual and disciplined religious life. The original foundation became the mother house to nearly fifteen hundred affiliated monasteries.

The agenda of the Cluniac monks included more than prayer. They saw themselves as the vanguard of a broader reform that would enhance the spirituality of the church and free it forever from secular control. To achieve this, they sought to create an independent, reformed papacy and to restore episcopal subordination as a first step to rooting out corruption among parish priests and monks.

The reformer's first step was to gain the support of the emperor Henry III (1017–56), who agreed with many of their ideas and saw in them an opportunity to expand his own political influence. Henry entered Italy in 1046, deposed the three existing popes, and suppressed the Roman political factions that had supported them. He then used his authority to appoint a series of popes, the most important of whom was the Cluniac reformer Leo IX (served 1049–54). Leo condemned simony, or the sale of church offices, called for the enforcement of clerical celibacy, and brought with him to Rome a number of young men who shared his convictions.

Henry's actions brought improvement, but to the monks, a papacy under imperial control was only slightly better than one controlled by Roman politicians. In the confusion that followed Henry's death, the reformers achieved something like full independence for the papacy. Taking advantage of the minority of Henry's young son, Henry IV (1050–1106), Pope Nicholas II placed the election of all future popes in the hands of the College of Cardinals, an advisory body composed of the most important, or cardinal, priests of the Roman diocese. The first such election took place in 1061, and the basic procedure used on that occasion has remained more or less intact to this day.

### The Investiture Controversy and Its Aftermath

The next step was to achieve papal control over the appointment of bishops. With the establishment of feudalism, bishops came to hold fiefs over which they exercised civil as well as ecclesiastical authority. The secular rulers whose vassals they became usurped the right to invest, or formally install, them as bishops. When Hildebrand of Soana, one of the men who had come to Rome with Leo IX, was elected Pope Gregory VII in 1073 he made the abolition of lay investiture his chief priority. The emperor, like all other secular authorities, was forbidden to invest bishops with ring and crozier, the symbols of their office, on pain of excommunication. To Henry IV, this edict was a serious threat, not only because it seemed to question the religious basis of imperial power but also because bishops were the temporal as well as spiritual lords over much of Germany. All hope of imperial consolidation, to say nothing of good governance, would be thwarted if such men were appointed by an outsider. To the pope, lay investiture prevented him from exercising full control over the church and seemed to guarantee that its highest offices would be occupied by political hacks incapable of furthering the work of reform. At a more fundamental level, the quarrel was about the nature of political power itself (see document 9.1). Pope and emperor agreed that all authority derived from God's grace, but was that grace transmitted directly to the ruler or through the agency of the church?

The political crisis that resulted was known as the Investiture Controversy, and it set the stage for generations of conflict between the emperors and the popes. Henry called upon his bishops to reject Gregory VII (see document 9.2). Gregory responded by excommunicating him and absolving his subjects of their allegiance. The entire empire chose sides. Because most of the imperial princes and many of the growing towns felt that they would profit from a weakening of imperial authority, a revolt led by the dukes of Saxony placed the emperor in dire peril. In a clever move, Henry decided to ask absolution of the pope. Gregory could not deny absolution to a legitimate penitent. At the castle of Canossa in the Italian Alps he supposedly forced the emperor to stand barefoot in the snow for three days before readmitting him to the fellowship of the church. Whatever satisfaction Gregory may have found in humiliating his rival did not compensate for being outmaneuvered. The revolt, deprived of its legitimacy, was over. Henry quickly reestablished his authority over the princes and in 1084 drove Gregory into exile.

The dispute over investiture was finally resolved in 1122 by the Concordat of Worms. Henry V (1086–1125) and Calixtus II (served 1119–24) reached a compromise by which Henry renounced his right to appoint bishops but retained the power to grant them fiefs and other temporal benefits. In theory, the freedom of the church from secular interference was securely established. In practice, episcopal appointments were still heavily influenced by the emperor who could withhold the income of a bishop who displeased him.

Whatever its importance for the evolution of church-state relationships, the investiture struggle marked the birth of a more assertive papacy that would one day claim *dominium* over the secular state. Gregory VII thought of the church as a body capable of giving law to all of Christendom and carefully fostered a growing interest in the study of canon or church law. This movement, which sparked a parallel revival of Roman civil law, reached its peak with the publication of Gratian's *Decretals* (c. 1140), an authoritative collection of papal and conciliar rulings supplemented by thirty-six *causae* or sample cases. Subsequent popes and

## ❖ DOCUMENT 9.1 ❖

### *Dictatus Papae*

*The* Dictatus Papae *appears to be an internal memorandum produced by the circle of churchmen around Gregory VII. Though he did not in all probability write it himself, it sets forth his concept of papal rights and prerogatives under twenty-seven headings, the most important of which are listed below.*

1. That the Roman church was established by God alone.
2. That the Roman pontiff alone is rightly called universal.
3. That he alone has the power to depose and reinstate bishops.
8. That he alone may use the imperial insignia.
9. That all princes shall kiss the foot of the pope alone.
10. That his name alone is to be recited in the churches.
12. That he has the power to depose emperors.
16. That no general synod may be called without his order.
17. That no action of a synod and no book shall be regarded as canonical without his authority.
18. That his decree can be annulled by no one, and that he can annul the decrees of anyone.
19. That he can be judged by no one.
20. That no one shall dare to condemn a person who has appealed to the apostolic seat.
22. That the Roman church has never erred and will never err to all eternity, according to the testimony of the holy scriptures.
24. That by his command or permission subjects may accuse their rulers.
25. That he can depose and reinstate bishops without calling a synod.
26. That no one can be regarded as catholic who does not agree with the Roman church.
27. That he has the power to absolve subjects from their oath of fidelity to wicked rulers.

"*Ordericus Vitalis*" (1119), trans. T. Forester. In *Ecclesiastical History*. London: Bohn, 1853–1856. Reprinted in James Bruce Ross and Mary Martin McLaughlin, eds., *The Portable Medieval Reader*. New York: Viking, 1949.

## ❖ DOCUMENT 9.2 ❖

### Henry IV to Gregory VII

*This excerpt is from a letter sent by the emperor Henry IV to Pope Gregory VII in 1076. It sets out the basis of Henry's case and, in its mastery of invective, shows something of the heat generated by the argument over papal authority.*

Henry, king not through usurpation but through the holy ordination of God, to Hildebrand, at present not pope but false monk. Such greeting as this hast though merited through thy disturbances, inasmuch as there is no grade in the church which thou hast omitted to make a partaker not of honor but of confusion, not of benediction, but of malediction. For, to mention few and special cases out of many, not only hast thou not feared to lay hands upon the rulers of the holy church, the anointed of the Lord—the archbishops, namely bishops and priests—but thou hast trodden them underfoot like slaves ignorant of what their master is doing. . . . As if we had received our kingdom from thee! As if the kingdom and the empire were in thine and not in God's hands! And this although our Lord Jesus Christ did call us to this kingdom, did not, however, call thee to the priesthood. For thou has ascended by the following steps. By wiles, namely, which the profession of monk abhors, thou hast achieved money; by money, favor; by the sword, the throne of peace. And from the throne of peace thou hast disturbed peace. . . . Let another ascend the throne of St. Peter, who shall not practice violence under the cloak of religion, but shall teach the sound doctrine of St. Peter. I Henry, king by the grace of God, do say unto thee, together with all our bishops: Descend, descend, to be damned throughout all the ages.

"Dictatus Papae." In O. J. Thatcher, and E. H. McNeal, eds. *A Source Book of Medieval History,* pp. 136–137. New York: Scribner's, 1905.

councils legislated so profusely that five new compilations were added in less than a century.

By the pontificate of Innocent III (served 1198–1216) the papacy had established itself as the legal arbiter of all matters, a *speculator* or overseer working in the best interests of the entire Christian common-

wealth. The church had developed a legal bureaucracy that was the envy of secular princes. Appeals from both secular and ecclesiastical authorities were referred to the Papal Tribunal, which included the Penitentiary (for matters of faith and morals) and the Court of the Sacred Palace. Cases were prepared by a corps of Auditors who in 1322 were organized into the *Rota Romana* with appellate jurisdiction of its own. Difficult or important issues were referred to the pope, who might choose to decide them in consultation with the cardinals. Their role was purely advisory, for no earthly power exceeded his own. Papal decisions were then handed down as decretals that formed the evolving basis of canon law. In theory, popes could overrule legal precedent, though they rarely did so.

The claims of the papacy had reached their peak. Innocent, like his predecessors, believed that all earthly power was based upon God's grace and that grace was administered by the church. When he argued that a pope could dethrone those who were ruling improperly, he did no more than carry the ideas of Gregory VII to their logical conclusion. Such theories were often difficult to implement, but the case of King John of England showed that he was fully prepared to intervene in the affairs of a sovereign kingdom.

### The New Monastic Orders and the Building of the Great Cathedrals

Though dramatic and politically controversial, the exalted notion of papal authority did not define the Cluniac program or the Hildebrandine or Gregorian reformation that arose from it. At the heart of the movement was a profound attachment to the monastic ideal and the belief that celibacy was essential to a truly Christian life. For this reason the reformers were suspicious of priests who lived in the world without monastic vows. The distinction between the "secular" clergy who serve bishops and parishes and the "regular" or monastic clergy dates from this period, with the regulars quickly gaining an advantage in the pursuit of high ecclesiastical office. This inevitably caused resentment among the seculars, but the monastic ideal continued to spread. Several new orders of both men and women were created, including the Carthusians in 1084 and the Premonstratensians in 1134. The Cistercians, founded in 1119, expanded under the leadership of St. Bernard of Clairvaux (1090–1153) to include 338 monasteries at the time of his death. Secular priests were also forced for the first time to take a vow of

## ◈ DOCUMENT 9.3 ◈

### The Cluniac Reformers and Clerical Celibacy

*The reforms of Pope Leo IX spread slowly in Western Christendom, and fifty years later, archbishops were still trying to impose a celibate life on priests. The following document is an account by Ordericus Vitalis in 1119 of how one French archbishop tried to enforce Leo's reforms.*

Geoffrey, the archbishop, having returned to Rouen from attending the church council at Reims, held a synod of priests in the third week in November. Stirred up by the late papal decrees, he dealt sharply and rigorously with the priests of his diocese. Among other canons of the council which he promulgated was that which interdicted them from commerce with females of any description, and against such transgressors he launched the terrible sentence of excommunication. As the priests shrunk from submitting to this grievous burden, and in loud mutterings among themselves vented their complaints of the struggle between the flesh and the spirit to which they were subjected, the archbishop ordered one Albert, a man of free speech, who had used some offensive words, I know not what, to be arrested on the spot, and he was presently thrust into the common prison.

This prelate was a Breton and guilty of many indiscretions, warm and obstinate in temper, and severe in his aspect and manner, harsh in his censures, and withal, indiscreet and a great talker. The other priests, witnessing this extraordinary proceeding, were utterly confounded; and when they saw that, without being charged with any crime or undergoing any legal examination, a priest was dragged, like a thief, from a church to a dungeon, they became so exceedingly terrified that they knew not how to act, doubting whether they had best defend themselves or take flight.

William of Malmesbury. *Chronicle*, trans. J. A. Giles. London: Bohn, 1847. Reprinted in James Bruce Ross and Mary Martin McLaughlin, eds. *The Portable Medieval Reader*, pp. 57–58. New York: Viking, 1949.

**Illustration 9.1**

The Romanesque Church of the Abbey of St. Léger at Merbach, Alsace. A typical Romanesque exterior has square towers and round arches. The structure was built between 1134 and 1155.

celibacy. The policy was first adopted by Leo IX, but implementation was gradual because it left concubines without support and because the laity was often suspicious of priests who lacked a woman of their own (see document 9.3).

The reformers were, in other words, triumphalists who believed that their monastic ideals should dominate the church and that the church should be the dominant institution in a Christian society. The visible symbols of that dominance were the great churches constructed during the eleventh and twelfth centuries in what has become known as the Romanesque style (see illustration 9.1). Abandoning the basilica with its

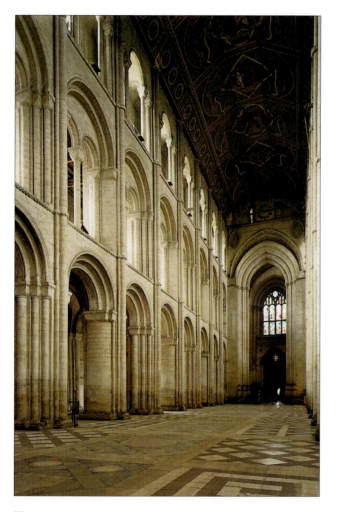

**Illustration 9.2**

🅰 **A Romanesque Interior.** The nave and choir of St.-Sernin at Toulouse, France, shows the round arches, simple barrel vaulting, and massive piers typical of Romanesque churches.

wooden roof, the builders covered the nave, or central isle of the church, with a massive barrel vault that rested upon a clerestory. The clerestory, with its arched windows, rested upon round arches reinforced by side aisles that served as buttresses (see illustration 9.2). The new style consumed vast quantities of cut stone, producing an overwhelming impression of power and serenity.

In the course of the twelfth century, a new style evolved based upon ribbed groin vaults and pointed arches. Flying buttresses were developed to support the weight of the vaulting, and the size of windows was increased until, in the High Gothic style of the thirteenth and fourteenth centuries, interiors were illuminated by vast sheets of stained glass that portrayed

episodes from the Scriptures so that even the illiterate might absorb the teachings of the church (see illustration 9.3 and 9.4).

The construction of cathedrals required enormous commitments of time and money. Some required centuries to build, and most were embellished with painting, sculpture, and stained glass on a grand scale. Such aesthetic achievements were made possible by the improved collection of tithes and the more efficient management of church estates. Medieval society was prepared to invest much of its meager economic surplus in religious buildings. However, not everyone viewed this development with enthusiasm. The glories of Durham or Palermo, Chartres or Amiens, were ultimately paid for by the labor of peasants. Some complained that such magnificence was inappropriate for the worship of a simple carpenter from Galilee, but the reformers were inspired by a vision of divine grandeur that demanded tangible expression on Earth.

Unfortunately, this vision could not comprehend dissent. The faith born originally of the Cluniac revival would inspire intellectual and artistic achievement for years to come. It would also provoke the Crusades and the virtual expulsion of the Jews from western Europe.

## The Crusades: The Reconquest of Muslim Europe

The Crusades were both an expression of religious militancy and the first of several European attempts to expand geographically at the expense of non-Christians. For the inhabitants of northern Europe, the Crusades provided their first sustained encounter with Islam, a society that was still in many ways more advanced than their own.

The model for Christian expansionism was provided by the beginnings of the Spanish *reconquista*, or reconquest. In 1031 the caliph of Córdoba was deposed during a prolonged civil war and Muslim Spain disintegrated into petty principalities based on the major towns. Their number reached as high as twenty-three. These small states, wealthy but militarily weak, offered a tempting opportunity to the Christian kingdoms. Taking advantage of Muslim disunity, the kings of León and Castile began extending their realms southward and received special privileges and plenary indulgences (remissions of the punishment for sins

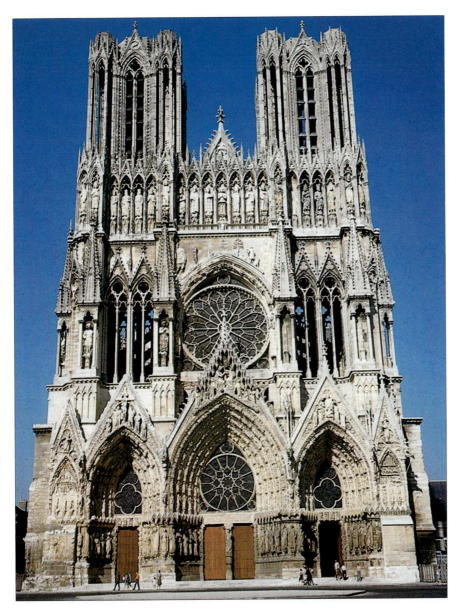

**Illustration 9.3**

**Reims Cathedral.** Begun about 1200, Reims is a superb example of High Gothic cathedral building.

committed on behalf of the faith) from the papacy as an encouragement.

The reconquest was not, however, a unified movement. Muslim Spain was reunited in 1086 under the Almoravides, a religious reform movement originating in North Africa, and again in 1172 by an even more puritanical group, the Almohades. Christian gains were made in the intervals between periods of Muslim strength. In the meantime, the Christian princes continued to fight among themselves, which led to the creation of the kingdom of Portugal in 1143. The age is best symbolized by the career of Rodrigo Díaz de Vivar, known as "El Cid" (c. 1043–99). El Cid fought for both Christian and Muslim potentates, changing

sides as his interest required, until he acquired the kingdom of Valencia in 1092. His ruthless cynicism did not prevent him from becoming the hero of chivalric romances.

Medieval Spain was a multicultural society in which Muslims, Christians, and Jews lived in uneasy balance. Religious tolerance was for the most part maintained out of necessity and gave birth to a rich philosophical and scientific tradition that flourished in spite of war and occasional outbreaks of religious violence. The balance was tipped in 1212 when Alfonso VIII of Castile defeated the Almohades at the battle of Las Navas de Tolosa. The Muslim towns fell one by one until in 1248 Sevilla surrendered to the Christians,

Illustration 9.4

The Cathedral of Saint-Pierre, Beauvais. Beauvais is in some ways an extreme example of Gothic architectural ambition. The choir was the tallest in Europe until it collapsed in 1284.

leaving the kingdom of Granada as the only Muslim enclave in Christian Europe (see map 9.1).

Christendom was also on the advance in Sicily. One problem with feudalism was that increases in the population of the knightly class rapidly produced more men trained in the profession of arms than could be supported by existing fiefs. An expansion of their opportunities, like the Norman invasion of England, could be seen as essential to social peace. Another group of Norman adventurers, including the twelve sons of the minor feudatory Tancred of Hauteville, had established themselves in Italy by 1050. Pope Leo IX regarded

them as a threat. Later popes, realizing that the Normans could be useful allies in the investiture crisis, supported one of Tancred's sons, Robert Guiscard (d. 1085), in his attempt to seize control of the Italian south. Robert drove the Byzantine Greeks from Calabria but left the conquest of Muslim Sicily to his brother Roger (d. 1101). The process was completed in 1092. Roger's son, Roger II, used his inheritance to create a powerful feudal kingdom on the Anglo-Norman model. Its superior resources and his qualities as a general enabled Roger to conquer all of southern Italy before his death in 1154.

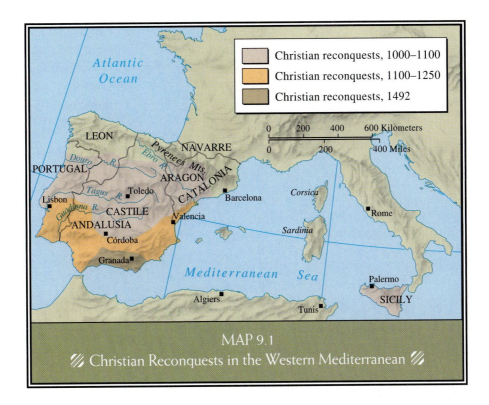

MAP 9.1
⚅ Christian Reconquests in the Western Mediterranean ⚅

## The Struggle for the Holy Land

Christian successes in Spain and Sicily were greeted with enthusiasm throughout Europe. When added to the great wave of piety unleashed by the Cluniac reforms, they raised the prospect of a general offensive against the Muslim infidel. In 1095 Pope Urban II proclaimed a crusade to free Jerusalem and the Holy Land from Muslim control. The privileges and indulgences were similar to those granted earlier in Spain (see document 9.4), but Urban's decision was rooted in the complexities of Middle Eastern politics.

Turkish tribes, most of them converts to Islam, were beginning their long migration from the steppes of central Asia into the lands of the Greek empire. One such group, called the Seljuks after the name of their ruling family, defeated the armies of Byzantium and seized control of eastern Anatolia at the battle of Manzikert in 1071. Alarmed, the Byzantine emperors hinted delicately at the reunification of the eastern and western churches if only the west would come to their aid.

Twenty years later, the death of the Abbasid sultan of Baghdad, Malek Shah, inaugurated a civil war among his emirs in Syria and Palestine. The disorder was such that Christian pilgrims could no longer visit the Holy Land in safety. This was intolerable, especially when Islam seemed elsewhere in retreat. The disintegration of the Caliphate of Córdoba, the expulsion of the Mus-

lims from the Balearic Islands in 1087, and the chaos in Syria could only encourage the dream of liberating Jerusalem and perhaps of uniting all Christendom under papal rule.

The proclamation of the First Crusade was met with more enthusiasm than the pope had anticipated. Thousands of European men and women were prepared to leave their homes and travel to fight in an unknown and hostile land. Their motives were in large part pious, but they had other reasons as well. The social pressures that had produced the Norman expansion were still at work throughout the feudal world. Younger sons hoped to claim Middle Eastern lands as their own, and an increasing number of landless peasants were happy to accompany them. Princes in turn were happy to see them go. The martial enthusiasm of the feudal classes had produced an alarming number of local wars. The church tried unsuccessfully to restrain them by proclaiming the Truce of God, which attempted to restrict fighting to certain days of the week. The Crusades provided an acceptable outlet for these energies. In a broader sense they justified the continuing privileges of a feudal class that no longer had an external threat to combat.

Though the Christian command was deeply divided, Jerusalem fell to the Christians on July 15, 1099. The Muslim and Jewish population of the city was

## ◆ DOCUMENT 9.4 ◆

### The Privileges of the Crusaders

*These privileges, granted to prospective crusaders by Pope Eugenius III in 1146, demonstrate some of the spiritual and material advantages that induced men to go to the Holy Land.*

Moreover, by the authority vested by God in us, we who with paternal care provide for your safety and the needs of the church, have promised and granted to those who from a spirit of devotion have decided to enter upon and accomplish such a holy and necessary undertaking and task, that remission of sins which our predecessor Pope Urban instituted. We have also commanded that their wives and children, their property and possessions, shall be under the protection of the holy church, of ourselves, of the archbishops, bishops and other prelates of the church of God. Moreover, we ordain by our apostolic authority that until their return or death is full proven, no law suit shall be instituted hereafter in regard to any property of which they were in peaceful possession when they took the cross.

Those who with pure hearts enter upon such a sacred journey and who are in debt shall pay no interest. And if they or others for them are bound by oath or promise to pay interest, we free them by our apostolic authority. And after they have sought aid of their relatives or lords of whom they hold their fiefs, and the latter are unable or unwilling to advance them money, we allow them freely to mortgage their lands and other possessions to churches, ecclesiastics, or other Christians, and their lords shall have no redress.

Otto of Freising. *Gesta Federici*, I, 35. *Pennsylvania Translations and Reprints*, p. 13, trans. Edward P. Cheyney. Philadelphia: University of Pennsylvania Press, 1897.

military orders were established—the Knights of the Hospital of St. John of Jerusalem (1113) and the Knights Templars (1119). Religious orders of fighting men, sworn to celibacy and dedicated to the protection of the holy places, the Knights were a model for later orders that sought to expand the frontiers of Christendom in Spain and Germany.

In spite of these efforts, Edessa fell in 1144, and a Second Crusade was launched in retaliation. It accomplished little. In 1187 Jerusalem was taken by the Kurdish general Saladin (c. 1137–93). The Third Crusade (1189–92) was a fiasco. The emperor Frederick Barbarossa (c. 1123–90) drowned in a stream, weighed down by his body armor. Richard I Lion-Heart, king of England, quarreled with Philip Augustus, who abandoned the siege of Jerusalem and returned to confiscate Richard's fiefs in France. Richard, trying to return home, was captured and held for ransom by the emperor Henry VI.

Subsequent crusades were even less edifying. The Fourth Crusade (1202–1204) foundered when the crusaders failed to provide for the cost of their passage in Venetian ships. The Venetians demanded that they seize Zara in payment and then inveigled them into attacking Constantinople. Constantinople fell in July 1203. The Venetians eventually abandoned their conquest after extorting more favorable trade privileges from the Greeks in return for the city. In 1228 the emperor Frederick II was excommunicated for abandoning the Sixth Crusade, ostensibly because of seasickness. He acquired Jerusalem by negotiation in the following year. The pope, who thought that he should have taken the city by force, was not pleased. The Muslims recovered it in 1244. Two more crusades by St. Louis IX of France accomplished nothing, and by 1291 the last Christian strongholds in the Levant had fallen to the Muslims (see map 9.2).

### The Impact of the Crusades upon Europe

The first attempt at European expansion had mixed results. Only in Spain and Portugal was new territory added to Christendom, but a precedent was set for the more sustained efforts of the fifteenth and sixteenth centuries. In the meantime, the effort to convert non-Christian populations by the sword—a notion hardly envisioned by the fathers of the church—poisoned relations with the Islamic world and probably strengthened the forces of intolerance and rigidity within Islam. European Jews suffered as well. The militant attitude deliberately fostered by a reformed papacy led to perse-

massacred, and the region as a whole was divided into the County of Tripoli and three kingdoms organized on the feudal model: Jerusalem, Edessa, and Antioch. All four were papal fiefs that provided new lands for ambitious knights and churchmen. In reality they were fragile enclaves surrounded by a population that despised the Christians as barbarians. To protect them, fortifications based upon the more sophisticated engineering techniques of the Muslims were constructed and two

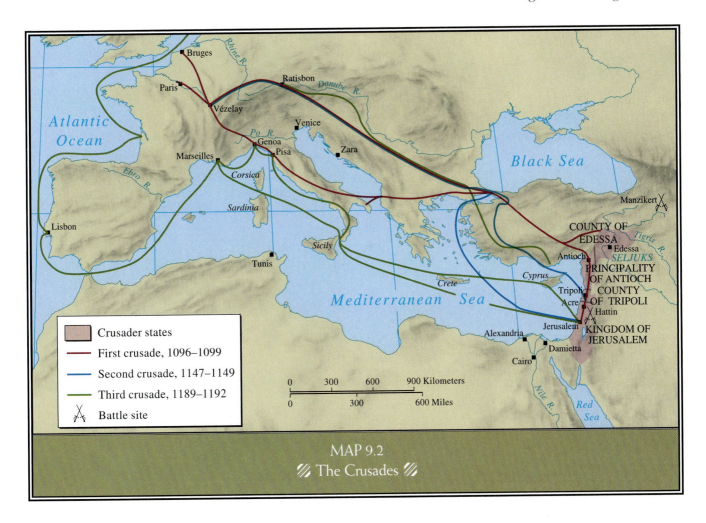

MAP 9.2

The Crusades

cutions, most of which were based on the blood libel that Jews sacrificed Christian children as part of their rituals (see document 9.5). It was no accident that such crusading princes as Richard Lion-Heart and St. Louis IX supported the expulsion of Jews from their lands.

The general climate of intolerance may also have affected the treatment of homosexuals. Though formally condemned by church doctrine, homosexuality appears to have been tolerated until the mid-thirteenth century. A substantial literature on homosexual love had been created by clerical writers in the great days of the Hildebrandine reform. After 1250, for reasons that are not clear, virtually every region of Europe passed laws making homosexual activity a capital crime. These laws, and the sentiments they reflected, remained in effect until well into modern times.

In personal terms, few of the crusaders gained the wealth and status they sought, but for western women of the upper classes the Crusades were probably beneficial. Many accompanied their husbands to the Middle East where they astonished the Muslims with their freespo-

ken manners. Those who stayed home often assumed the role of managers and defenders of the family's estates. In either case their independence and economic value were often enhanced. At the level of international politics the Crusades were the beginning of the end for the Byzantine Empire. Fatally weakened by the Fourth Crusade, the Greeks continued to lose ground until they were at last overwhelmed by Turkish expansion in 1453. The Venetians, as the architect of Greek misfortunes, benefited for a time by establishing a series of colonies on Greek soil. In the end these, too, were lost to the Turks.

Of more permanent value was the increase of trade in Eastern luxury goods. The Crusades, by bringing western Europeans into contact with a more technologically advanced civilization, fueled their growing taste for spices, silks, damascus cutlery, and similar items. The Eastern trade not only broadened cultural perspectives, at least in a material sense, but also encouraged capital accumulation, especially in the Italian towns. A related benefit was the improved knowledge of engineering, stonemasonry, and fortification that was

### ❖ DOCUMENT 9.5 ❖

## Pope Gregory X Denounces the Blood Libel

*A succession of popes inveighed against the blood libel with varying degrees of success. This letter by Gregory X (served 1271–76) is similar in tone to earlier letters by Innocent III and Innocent IV. The expulsions reveal that papal good sense had little impact on some of Europe's monarchs and their subjects.*

Since it happens occasionally that some Christians lose their Christian children, the Jews are accused by their enemies of secretly carrying off and killing these same Christian children and of making sacrifices of the heart and blood of these very children. It happens, too, that parents of these children or some other Christian enemies of these Jews, secretly hide these very children in order that they may be able to injure these Jews, and in order that they may be able to extort from them a certain amount of money by redeeming them from their straits.

And most falsely do these Christians claim that the Jews have secretly and furtively carried away these children and killed them, and that the Jews offer sacrifice from the heart and blood of these children, since their law in this matter precisely and expressly forbids Jews to sacrifice, eat, or drink, the blood, or to eat the flesh of animals having claws. This has been demonstrated many times at our court by Jews converted to the Christian faith; nevertheless very many Jews are often seized and detained unjustly because of this.

We decree, therefore, that Christians need not be obeyed against Jews in a case or situation of this type, and we order that Jews seized under such a silly pretext be freed from imprisonment, and that they shall not be arrested henceforth on such a miserable pretext, unless—which we do not believe—they be caught in the commission of the crime. We decree that no Christian shall stir up anything new against them, but that they should be maintained in that status and position in which they were in the time of our predecessors, from antiquity till now.

Marcus, Jacob R. *The Jew in the Medieval World*, p. 154. New York: Atheneum, 1972.

**Illustration 9.5**

〽 **The Mausoleum of Bohemond, Prince of Taranto.** This mausoleum at Canossa di Puglia illustrates the powerful influence of Islamic culture on the crusaders. Bohemond eventually became king of Antioch in Syria but was buried on his ancestral estates in Italy. His tomb combines Romanesque and Muslim styles and is meant to resemble a *turbeh*, the shrine of a Muslim holy man. It was probably built by Muslim craftsmen.

acquired through the observation of Arab models (see illustration 9.5).

Unfortunately, the nature of the crusading enterprise severely limited exchanges at the intellectual level. The glories of Arab philosophy, mathematics, astronomy, and medicine were viewed with deep suspicion by the average crusader. When they were eventually introduced—not by crusaders but by scholars working in the free atmosphere of multicultural Spain—the church reacted defensively. Arab poetry, mysticism, and religious thought were ignored.

## The Intellectual Crisis of the Twelfth Century

By the beginning of the twelfth century the Latin church was the dominant institution and chief unifying force of western and central Europe. Though feudal monarchies did not always acknowledge its political pretensions, they were usually prepared to accept its spiritual direction and to heed its calls for crusades or other actions on behalf of the faith. Religiously and intellectually it had no rivals.

As a result neither theology nor speculative philosophy was highly developed. Creative thought rarely evolves in an atmosphere of unanimity, and the teachings of the church had not been seriously challenged since the patristic era. The monastic and cathedral schools, which educated the priesthood, were able to avoid major controversies until the middle of the eleventh century. After that, whatever intellectual complacency Christians may have felt began to erode, and by 1200 it was entirely shattered.

Around 1050 a heated controversy developed over the ideas of Berengar of Tours (d. 1080). Arguing from logic, he rejected the doctrine of transubstantiation, which explained how, in the miracle of the mass, the bread and wine were transformed into the body and blood of Jesus Christ. Transubstantiation was not yet a dogma of the church, but his writings created a furor.

The dispute opened up two issues that were to perplex the church for centuries. The first was over the use of reason itself. St. Peter Damian espoused Tertullian's argument that faith required no support from logic; revelation was enough. Others, including St. Anselm of Canterbury (1033–1109), argued that reason could only illuminate faith and improve understanding.

Though the advocates of formal logic would triumph, at least in the schools, a third group distrusted them for other reasons. Led by John of Salisbury (d. 1180) and centered at the cathedral school of Chartres, these scholars feared that an excessive concentration on reason might narrow the scope of learned inquiry. They developed an interest in the secular literature of ancient Rome. Their efforts have been called the "Renaissance of the Twelfth Century" because modern historians thought that they foreshadowed the Renaissance of the fourteenth and fifteenth centuries.

The second issue was that of universals, which had first been raised by the sixth-century Christian philosopher Boethius and was implicit in the arguments of Berengar of Tours. The question, central to virtually all medieval thought, is: Are ideas or qualities objectively real? Does such a thing as "redness," for example, exist apart from any physical object that is "red"? "Realists" held that such universals were real and that they constituted the "substance" of things. The physical manifestation of a substance was its "accident." "Nominalists" believed that universals are merely *nomina*, or names that reflect little more than arbitrary linguistic convention. No distinction could be made between substance and accident.

Christian doctrines such as the Trinity and transubstantiation were usually explained in language that implied the reality of universals. In the miracle of the mass, the substance of the bread and wine in communion is changed or transubstantiated into the substance of the body and blood of Christ; the accidents remain unchanged. If, like Berengar, one did not believe in the distinction between substance and accident, this was difficult to accept. A partial solution to the problem was proposed by Pierre Abelard (1079–1142), who argued that a universal was a logical term related to both things and concepts. The controversy, however, was only beginning.

While Abelard avoided the extremes of either realism or nominalism, his career as a whole intensified the growing spirit of contention. He is best known outside theological circles for his affair with Heloise, the brilliant niece of Canon Fulbert of Chartres. Their relationship produced a child and some memorable letters before her relatives had him castrated. He thereupon became a monk and she a nun, but his penchant for making enemies was not yet satisfied. Abelard was determined to provide a rational basis for Christian doctrine, and his provocative writings—including *Sic et Non*, a list of apparently contradictory passages from the Fathers—set the agenda for much of what would one day be called Scholasticism .

To Abelard, Anselm, and the other philosophers of the cathedral schools, reason meant the logic of Aristotle as embodied in those parts of the *Organon* that had been translated into Latin by Boethius. They had no direct access to Aristotle's works and their knowledge of his thought was largely derived from the commentaries of his translator, but they were convinced that God's world must necessarily operate on logical principles. They also believed that Aristotle and other virtuous pagans would have accepted Christianity had they not been born before the time of Christ. It was in many ways an age of innocence.

That innocence was shattered after the mid-twelfth century by the discovery that Aristotle was far better known in Baghdad and Cairo than he was in the west and that his logic had been employed for centuries by thinkers who were not Christian, but Muslim or Jewish. A group of scholars, established themselves in the Spanish frontier city of Toledo and began to translate the works of Aristotle, Galen, Ptolemy, and other Greeks from Arabic into Latin. They then produced Latin editions of Arabic writers. Many of these works were on science or medicine. The medical treatises revolutionized the thinking of western physicians, but works on logic and speculative philosophy were received with greater caution.

A new world of philosophical sophistication was revealed, and it was not a reassuring place. Al-Kindi (d. circa 870) and Ibn-Sina (Avicenna, 980–1037) were more or less orthodox Muslims. Abu Bakr al-Razi (c. 865–c. 923) was an enemy of all religion, and Maimonides (1135–1204) was a pious Jew. Ibn-Rushd (Averroës, 1126–98) was perhaps the most influential. The greatest of the commentators on Aristotle, he believed as firmly as Anselm or Abelard that the logic of the Philosopher could be used to uphold revelation, but in his case, the revelation was that of the Koran. For the first time since antiquity, the church was faced with an intellectual challenge of threatening proportions.

Before a counterattack could be fully mounted, an even more serious challenge to orthodoxy appeared. Formal heresies attracting thousands of adherents surfaced, not in the newly converted regions of the north and west, but in the earliest established centers of Western Christendom: northern Italy and the south of France. To some extent these movements were a reaction against what was perceived as the greed and arrogance of a triumphant clergy. The newly exalted claims of the papacy, the cost of church buildings, and the more rigorous collection of the tithe led to demands for a return to apostolic poverty. This was the primary concern of the Waldensians, named after their apparent founder Waldes of Lyon, later known as Peter Waldo (fl. 1170–79). Their condemnation by the orthodox eventually led them to reject papal authority. Like the Protestants of the sixteenth century, the Waldensians regarded Scripture as the sole source of religious truth and translated the Bible into the vernacular. They also rejected several of the church's sacraments.

A far larger movement, the Cathars (sometimes known as Albigensians after the southern French town of Albi that served as one of their centers), went further. They embraced a dualistic system reminiscent of Zoroastrianism or the ancient Manichees. The physical world and the God of the Old Testament who had created it were evil. Spirit, as exemplified in Christ, whose own physical body was an illusion, was good. They had no clergy. *Parfaits* or perfects of both sexes administered the rite of *consolamentum* that guaranteed passage into Heaven. After consolation, one became a *parfait*. It was then forbidden to own property, to have sex, or to eat anything that was the product of a sexual union: meat, fish, eggs, or cheese. The meager necessities that remained were provided by begging. Some new converts deliberately starved themselves to death, but for the ordinary believer, Albigensianism held few terrors. Those who died without receiving the *consolamentum* would merely be reincarnated into a new life on Earth. The church, its hierarchy, its sacraments, and its monetary levies were categorically rejected. By the year 1200 the Cathar faith had attracted tens of thousands of adherents in southern France. It enjoyed the support of powerful political figures and even of priests, who retained their ecclesiastical rank while openly assisting the heretics. Once again, the church was on the defensive.

## Repression and Renewal (1215–92)

The official response to these challenges was crafted largely by Innocent III, who was not the man to shrink from repressive measures. The church's first reaction to the heretics had been gentle. Preachers, including Bernard of Clairvaux, were sent to reconvert the Albigensians, but their eloquence had little effect. In 1209 Innocent, infuriated by the murder of a papal legate, proclaimed a crusade. Under the leadership of Simon de Montfort, an army composed largely of knights from northern France embarked on a campaign of massacre and atrocity. The worst slaughter of the Albigensian Crusade happened near the Pyrenees Mountains in the town of Béziers. The people of Béziers refused to surrender some two hundred Cathars living there, so the crusaders stormed the town and killed twenty thousand of its inhabitants indiscriminately, following the exhortation of the abbot of Cîteau: "Kill them all; God will know his own." Like their compatriots who went to the Holy Land, the crusaders were inspired by the hope of acquiring new lands as well as salvation.

By 1212 most of Languedoc was in their hands, but the Cathars and the southern lords who supported them took refuge in remote castles and waged guerrilla warfare until 1226. A decisive campaign then was launched by Louis VIII of France. He saw the crusade as an opportunity to expand his royal domain and forced the southerners to surrender in 1229. The last great Cathar stronghold, a mountain-top castle known as Montségur, finally fell in 1244. More than two hundred Cathars refused to abjure their faith and were burned together on a huge pyre. Great cathedrals were built at Albi and Narbonne to proclaim the triumph of the faith, but Cathar communities flourished in secret until after 1300.

The papal Inquisition was established to ferret them out. An inquisition is basically a court established to investigate and root out heresy. Bishops had begun organizing inquisitions at the diocesan level in the mid-twelfth century. These episcopal inquisitions proved ineffective in the Albigensian heartland where heresy permeated entire communities. Even bishops who were themselves untainted by error might be reluctant to proceed against prominent individuals or members of their own families. By placing the Inquisition under papal control, Innocent III was able to secure a measure of impartiality. Legates responsible only to him were dispatched as needed, making it more difficult for heretics to take refuge behind local privilege. To believers, heresy was a terrible crime because it brought about the eternal damnation of those who accepted it. Inquisitors therefore felt justified in using every means available, including torture, to secure a confession. If none were forthcoming, or if the heretic confessed but would not repent, he or she would be turned over to the secular authorities and burned alive, the standard penalty for heresy in both canon and civil law.

After 1233 Gregory IX introduced the tribunal to the south of France on a systematic basis. As many as five thousand heretics were burned there by the end of the century. The Inquisition had other interests as well. Anyone, including academic theorists who overstepped the bounds of theological propriety, was subject to its jurisdiction. If the church of the early Middle Ages had been absorbed in its missionary role and relatively indifferent to the definition of orthodoxy, those days were gone.

The new order was solidified by the Fourth Lateran Council. Called by Innocent III in 1215, it was designed to resemble the great councils of the early church. Not only bishops, abbots, and the heads of religious and military orders, but also princes and municipal authorities from all over the Latin west were invited to consider a carefully prepared agenda. In only three days of formal meetings, the delegates adopted a confession of faith that specifically rejected Albigensian beliefs, defined the seven sacraments, and enshrined

transubstantiation as dogma. All Christians were ordered to confess and receive communion at least once a year, and a wide variety of reforms aimed at the purification of ecclesiastical life were adopted. In terms of its influence on both doctrine and practice, it was the most important council of the Middle Ages.

The organization of mendicant orders, the Dominicans and the Franciscans, must also be seen as a response to the crisis of the twelfth century. Among those who had hoped to convert the Albigensians by peaceful means was the Castilian preacher Domingo de Guzmán, or St. Dominic (c. 1170–1221). After several years among the heretics, he came to believe that, if the teachings of the church were presented by competent preachers who lived a life of apostolic poverty, heresy could not survive. In 1207 he organized a convent of women who had recently converted. In 1216 he secured papal confirmation of an order of men dedicated to preaching and living a life of austerity equal to that of the *parfaits*. Popularly known as the Dominicans, they stressed the intellectual formation of their members and lived by begging. Within a generation they had taken their place among the intellectual leaders of the church.

A second order, founded by Dominic's contemporary St. Francis of Assisi (c. 1181–1226), was not directly concerned with the problem of heresy but embraced the idea of evangelical poverty with even greater fervor (see illustration 9.6). The son of a wealthy merchant, Francis was inspired by a series of visions to abandon his family and retire to the town of Assisi where he began to preach, though still a layman. He had no intention of forming a religious order in the conventional sense, but his preaching and the holiness of his life attracted disciples. In 1209 he went to Rome with eleven others and secured Innocent III's approval of a new rule dedicated to the imitation of Christ.

The Franciscans, as they were called, met a contemporary need. Their dedication to absolute poverty and the attractive spirit of their founder endeared them to the laity, and they soon became the largest of the mendicant orders. The Second Order of St. Francis, sometimes known as the Poor Clares, was created for women.

Two smaller mendicant orders, the Carmelites and the Augustinians, were created in the same period. The friars, as the mendicants were called, emerged as the leaders of the great intellectual revival already under way in response to the challenges of the twelfth century.

**Illustration 9.6**

🌊 **St. Francis.** In this fresco by Italian master Giotto (1266?–1337), St. Francis renounces his patrimony. The decision to abandon all worldly goods to live in poverty marked the beginning of his ministry to the poor.

## The Founding of the Universities

The locus of that revival was a new institution: the university. The first universities emerged from the same regularizing impulses that inspired the consolidation of feudal states and the reforms of Innocent III. The twelfth century revival of learning had led to a proliferation of competing schools in such centers as Paris and Bologna. Church and municipal authorities became alarmed at the potential for disorder, and the masters soon recognized the need for an organization that could both protect their interests and ensure that new masters were properly trained. By the mid-twelfth century, a rudimentary guild system was beginning to evolve.

At Paris, the scholars soon found themselves in conflict with the cathedral chapter of Notre Dame, which tried to control them, and the townspeople, who were trying to protect their lives and property against the students (see document 9.6). The students were for the most part adolescent males who lived without supervision and were capable of rape, theft, and murder. They in turn complained of gouging by landlords and tavern keepers. Such grievances were ignored, while at-

---

◈ **DOCUMENT 9.6** ◈

### Privileges of the Students at Paris

*The following privilege was granted to the students at Paris by King Philip Augustus in 1200. It seeks to protect academic freedom by ensuring that students accused of crimes are tried only by ecclesiastical courts.*

Neither our provost nor our judges shall lay hands on a student for any offense whatever; nor shall they place him in our prison, unless such a crime has been committed by the student that he ought to be arrested. And in that case, our judge shall arrest him on the spot, without striking him at all, unless he resists, and shall hand him over to the ecclesiastical judge, who ought to guard him in order to satisfy us and the one suffering the injury. . . . But if the students are arrested by our count at such an hour that the ecclesiastical judge cannot be found and be present at once, our provost shall cause the culprits to be guarded in some student's house without any ill-treatment as is said above, until they are delivered to the ecclesiastical judge. . . . In order, moreover, that these decrees may be kept more carefully and be established by a fixed law, we have decided that our present provost and the people of Paris shall affirm by an oath, in the presence of the scholars, that they will carry out in good faith all the above-mentioned points.

Philip Augustus. "Privileges of the Students at Paris." *Pennsylvania Translations and Reprints,* vol. 2, pp. 5–7, trans. Edward P. Cheyney. Philadelphia: University of Pennsylvania Press, 1897.

---

tempts to arrest student criminals often led to bloody riots. Each new outrage brought a flood of appeals to the pope or the king. Between 1215 and 1231 a series of statutes and charters were issued that established the privileges of the university in both civil and canon law.

The situation at Oxford was not much different. The English masters had gathered in a market town that had no cathedral or other ecclesiastical organization against which to rebel, but their relations with the townsfolk were as envenomed as those at Paris. In 1209, after a violent riot, teaching was suspended and many of the scholars departed for Cambridge to found a separate university. Oxford's privileges were guaranteed only by the papal humiliation of King John in 1214. John had supported the town against what he perceived as clerical privilege, and Innocent III not only sided with the masters but also forced the municipality to provide an annual subsidy for impoverished students.

If the origins of Bologna were less violent, it was because its faculty emphasized the study of law instead of theology or the liberal arts. The students tended to be older men of considerable influence who were adept at securing imperial and papal privileges without knife-play. They were also unwilling to be ruled by their teachers. Bologna and the Italian universities based upon its model were dominated by the students, who hired the faculty and determined the curriculum.

As the idea of universities grew popular, a number were founded by royal or papal edict. By 1500, Spain and every region of Germany, including Switzerland and the Low Countries, had its own university. Most of them were princely foundations, while some, including Erfurt and Cologne, were established by clerics with the help of city governments.

Medical schools were at first unrelated to the universities and, in at least two cases, predated them. Salerno, in the kingdom of Sicily, was a center of medical studies in the eleventh century, well before the introduction of Arabic learning. The interference of the state in the person of Frederick II reduced its vitality, and it was largely superseded by Montpellier after 1231. Montpellier, in southern France, had been founded before 1140 and was a center of Arabic learning from the start. It gradually evolved during the thirteenth century into the major university that it is today. Other medical faculties were incorporated into universities at an early date, with Bologna and Paris achieving particular renown.

Organizationally, the heart of Paris, Oxford, and Cambridge was the faculty of liberal arts. The masters of arts had secured the independence of the universities. The theologians, though important, had been compromised by their obedience to ecclesiastical authority. The arts curriculum included the *trivium* (grammar, dialectic, and rhetoric) and the *quadrivium* (geometry, arithmetic, astronomy, and music). Dialectic meant the logic of Aristotle; rhetoric was largely the science by which one could unravel figures of speech. Those who received the master of arts were licensed to teach these subjects.

A course of the liberal arts had to be completed before being admitted to the schools of theology, which by midcentury were dominated by the mendicant friars. Their curriculum was based heavily on the *Sentences* of Peter Lombard (c. 1100–60), a collection of theological

**Illustration 9.7**

A University Lecture. In this illumination from fourteenth-century Germany, a master lectures to his class by reading from a text and explaining its meaning. The students are of different ages and a few are sound asleep.

arguments and propositions that was first published about 1150. Legal education was based on Gratian's *Decretals*. Because books were handwritten and expensive, teaching methods were the essence of simplicity: The master read the text and explained its meaning (see illustration 9.7). Formal disputations between masters were a welcome alternative to the lectures and often drew large crowds.

The students were under the control of the masters, at least in their academic lives. Both enjoyed full clerical immunity as part of their university charters. They could be tried only in ecclesiastical courts, even if they committed civil crimes. The university as a whole was governed by its rector who was elected for a term of no more than three months. The only administrator in the modern sense was the beadle, or "common servant of the scholars," who collected funds and tried to enforce the regulations.

By the end of the thirteenth century, universities had become powerful corporations whose independence guaranteed them a certain freedom of thought. This freedom, though not unconditional, brought a great breadth and vigor to Western culture.

## Scholastic Thought

The term *scholasticism* is generally used to describe the thought of the medieval universities. It was not an "ism" in the modern sense—that is, an ideology or system of belief—but a method for dealing with a wide range of questions in theology, philosophy, ethics, and the natural sciences. It relied almost exclusively on the system of linguistic logic adopted from Aristotle and, by the mid-thirteenth century, had evolved a standard form of argumentation. A question was posed, an answer was suggested, and all possible objections to the answers were analyzed before a final resolution was achieved. Authorities were cited in support of theses and objections alike. The final appeal was to reason unless a clear statement on the issue could be drawn from Scripture or the authority of the church. Even then, some of the more radical thinkers were prepared to venture forward on the basis of logic alone. It was a method of extraordinary power, and in the universities of thirteenth-century Europe it created an unparalleled flowering of creative thought.

Much of this effort was initially based on the need to confute the followers of Averroes. Some of them, such as Siger of Brabant (d.c. 1281), held that faith could not be supported by reason and adopted a view that was essentially skeptical. Others developed ideas that could be described as pantheistic.

Early attempts to suppress the Arabic commentators failed, though the teachings of the Averroists were finally condemned by the University of Paris in 1269–70. In the meantime, an effective synthesis of Aristotelianism and Christian doctrine was developed by two Dominicans, Albertus Magnus (c. 1200–1280) and his pupil St. Thomas Aquinas (c. 1225–74). Aquinas is generally regarded as one of the world's greatest thinkers. His approach to philosophy and theology, known as Thomism, has had a profound influence on Western thought and underlies much of Roman Catholic theology to this day. At the same time, he was a man of his times. His condemnation of Jews and homosexuals and his belief in the natural inferiority of women, though commonplace in the thirteenth century, had a disproportionate effect on Western attitudes as well.

Born to a noble family in the marches between Naples and Rome, Thomas spent most of his life at the University of Paris and at Rome, where he was theological adviser to the papal curia. In his student days his massive physique and natural reticence caused him to be nicknamed "the dumb ox," but his gentleness and courtesy, unique among the cantankerous academics of his day, endeared him even to opponents. His best known works, the *Summa contra Gentiles* and the unfinished *Summa Theologica*, reveal his purpose. They are comprehensive summations on practically every subject of contemporary theological and philosophical interest, and for all his insistence that learning is done even from errors, their intent is polemical.

An Aristotelian to his fingertips, Aquinas believed that God's universe was both rational and intelligible. On the question of universals he was a moderate realist whose views were reminiscent of Abelard's. Knowledge must be based on the experience of the senses; thought enables the universal to be isolated in the particular. Both substance and accident are real, but substance provides the limits within which accidents may exist. This position was the basis of equally moderate conclusions on subjects ranging from the nature of the soul to the origins of evil and the problem of time, and it sets Aquinas firmly in the tradition of Aristotelian humanism. The intellect, though sustained by God, is a part of every human being. The soul is the form or essence of the body, of sensation, and of thought. In thinking, the soul transcends this form and becomes independent of matter.

These ideas were eventually adopted by a majority of Aquinas's fellow Dominicans. They were disputed by the Franciscans, including his friend St. Bonaventura (c. 1217–74). Franciscan thought generally followed the tradition of St. Augustine and emphasized the importance of love and will as opposed to intellect. The gulf that separates human beings from God cannot be minimized or forgotten, and the intellect should not be identified too closely with the soul.

Several aspects of this Franciscan approach crystallized in the work of John Duns Scotus (1265–1308). A Scot who studied and taught at Paris, Oxford, Cambridge, and Cologne, he sought to preserve the concerns of St. Bonaventura without doing violence to Aristotle. To Scotus, everything had a reality of its own that existed independently of any universal. Universals existed only in the mind. This view enabled him to emphasize the uniqueness both of God and of individuals, but by denying the connection between human and divine intellect, he opened a gulf so vast that it could be bridged only by extraordinary means. To Scotus and many of his contemporaries, the majesty and isolation of God were so great that special intercession was required. It could be provided only by the Virgin Mary, whose veneration became a central feature of their piety. The Marian cult that emerged around the beginning of the fourteenth century would have a profound influence on Catholic spirituality. Scotus was its early advocate and one of the first to formulate the doctrine of the Immaculate Conception, which holds that Mary was preserved from all taint of original sin when she was conceived.

Scotus never saw himself as an opponent of Aquinas. He did not question the usefulness of reason in illuminating faith. That task was left to another Franciscan, William of Ockham (c. 1285–c. 1349). Ockham carried the ideas of Scotus a step further and declared that only individuals are real and that the object of the senses and of the intellect are the same. Universals are no more than mental patterns created by recurring similarities of experience. Although a subtle difference, it meant that God was unknowable, at least to the intellect.

Ockham was a Spiritual Franciscan who opposed the papacy after the condemnation of 1322. He was not a heretic. When his conclusions were questioned, he insisted that the doctrines of the church must be accepted in their entirety as revealed truth. His followers, known as nominalists because they supposedly believed that universals were only *nomina*, or names, became one of the three dominant philosophical schools of the later Middle Ages and by the fifteenth century were a majority on most university faculties. Some, such as Nicholas of Autrecourt (fl. 1340), went further than their master and declared that not even the existence of the material world could be demonstrated by rational means. Each person knows only his or her own soul. Though Thomism and Scotism continued to attract adherents, the Ockhamist critique of reason was highly corrosive. It presumed a dichotomy with faith that made formal thought virtually irrelevant. When such views became widespread, the creative age of scholasticism was over.

CHAPTER 10

# ECONOMIC DEVELOPMENT AND URBAN GROWTH IN THE HIGH MIDDLE AGES

## CHAPTER OUTLINE

◆◆◆◆◆◆◆◆◆◆◆◆◆◆◆◆◆◆◆◆◆

Two centuries of relative peace and prosperity after the end of the great raids permitted a general increase in agricultural production. This growth in productivity increased real wealth and allowed the population of Europe to double during the same period. It also encouraged agricultural specialization, which led to the development of a widespread trade in bulk agricultural commodities. Eventually, new wealth and the influence of the Crusades created a long-distance trade in luxury goods as well.

The chief beneficiaries of this new commercial activity were the towns. From about 1000 to 1250 they experienced rapid growth—in size, wealth, and power. As popes and princes grew more dependent upon their resources, the towns used their wealth to free themselves from feudal or ecclesiastical rule and to negotiate new privileges that made them bastions of civic freedom in the midst of feudal Europe. Some became sovereign states. Rich, free, and self-confident, the towns of medieval Europe began the great tradition of urban culture that would eventually leaven the whole of Western society.

◆

## Medieval Technology: Energy, Tools, and Transport

Medieval technology, like that of the Romans, was based on wood and iron. Its primary energy source remained the muscle power of humans or animals, though by the eleventh century water mills were universally employed for the grinding of grain. The water wheel had been used in Anatolia as early as the first century, but it was apparently unknown in the west until the brewers of Picardy adopted it around 820. By the mid-thirteenth century water power was also used in the fulling of cloth and to drive the hammers and bellows of forges. Wind provided assistance for ships at sea, but windmills, a Persian invention introduced to Europe at the end of the twelfth century, did not become common until the fifteenth century.

Fuel was limited almost entirely to wood and charcoal and was rarely used to generate power. Wood was burned for cooking and to supply heat. In western Europe, interior heating was usually accomplished, if at all, with residual heat from cooking. Charcoal, an expensive commodity, was used primarily in the smelting and forging of metals, while coal, first mentioned in European sources around the year 1200, did not come into general use for another four hundred years. This was largely because mining techniques remained primitive. In the absence of effective pumps the pits could not be kept dry, and the development of effective pumps depended upon metallurgical techniques that were as yet unknown. Mine pumps also require a cheap, reliable source of power because they must be worked continuously. Windmills, used from the fifteenth century onward to drain the tidal wetlands of Holland, were a possible solution, but they proved ineffective in hilly country or in regions where wind strength was inconstant. None of these problems was fully solved until the age of steam. In the meantime, coal and ores could be mined only from shallow pits, and transportation costs ensured that coal would be used only in the immediate vicinity of the mines. The scarcity of metals made ore worth transporting, but it was always best if deposits were located near abundant sources of charcoal so that smelting might occur on the spot.

Tools tended to be made of wood or of wood tipped with iron. Alloy steel was unknown, and the handwrought carbon steel used in knives and edged weapons was expensive. The process required great skill and enormous quantities of fuel. Even implements made from lower grades of iron represented a major capital outlay for farmers and artisans.

The high cost of iron resulted in part from the limitations of mining technology, but skilled iron workers were few in number, and the making of charcoal for use in the forges consumed large quantities of wood. Wood had long been scarce in the Mediterranean basin. By the end of the Middle Ages its availability was limited in northwest Europe as well. Only in the Baltic regions and in eastern Europe was timber plentiful, and even there prices increased steadily throughout the Middle Ages in response to increased demand from other regions. Given that wood was a primary building material as well as the major source of fuel, this is hardly surprising.

Ships were built almost entirely of wood and consumed vast quantities of the best timber. Their keels and frames demanded rare, naturally curved compass timbers, and their masts required tall, straight trees with few branches. Planking was almost invariably of the best available oak. However high the quality of planking, constant immersion in water and the ravages of marine organisms ensured a maximum life of seven or eight years before a ship's timbers had to be replaced. Given the hazards of navigation, many ships went to the bottom long before such repairs could be made, with even higher replacement costs as a result.

On land, most buildings were at least framed in wood. Fully wooden structures had once been common in northern Europe. By the twelfth century they were already becoming rare outside of Scandinavia and the Baltic. The growing cost of lumber was forcing builders to construct walls out of cob, wattle and daub, or some other combination of earth mixed with straw. Roofs were usually thatched and floors were of earth or clay. Only public buildings and the homes of the very rich were built of stone and roofed with slate or tile. Masonry construction was more common in the Mediterranean basin, although precious wood was used for joists and roof beams.

The high cost of iron and wood was symptomatic not only of scarcity but also of the problem of distance. They were heavy and expensive to ship. Owing to political fragmentation and the decay of the Roman highway system, transportation was more arduous and expensive than in antiquity. Besides raising shipping costs in general, this made compensating for local shortages or crop failures by importing goods from other regions difficult. Shipping grain overland for two hundred miles might raise its price by a factor of seven, making it unaffordable to the poor even if they were starving.

Land transport was generally conducted over roads that were little more than tracks, choked with dust in dry weather and mired axle-deep in mud when it rained. If the mud froze, ruts made the highways impassable for wheeled vehicles. For this reason, people traveled on foot or on horseback, and pack animals were generally preferred to ox-driven carts except in optimum conditions.

Water transport, if available, was more efficient (see illustration 10.1). Many European rivers are navigable for much of their length. Boats, rafts, and barges became increasingly important with the passage of time. The sea remained the greatest highway of all, uniting the peoples who lived along its shores. The Baltic, the North Sea, and the Atlantic coasts were served by a wide variety of ship types whose chief common feature was the use of a square sail set amidships. This rig was easy to handle and provided excellent performance

Illustration 10.1

⚡ **Unloading Wine at Paris.** The commercial revolution began with the bulk trade in such agricultural commodities as wine. Wine was always shipped in barrels, as bottling was unknown. Given the condition of the roads, shipping by river boat was almost always cheaper and faster. Here boatmen are delivering their casks at the port of Paris on the river Seine.

downwind. It was virtually useless in other conditions. Many of the smaller craft were therefore assisted by oars or sweeps and could penetrate coastal estuaries as had the Viking longships on which they were often modeled.

In the Mediterranean, many ships carried the triangular lateen sail, invented by Arab sailors in the Indian Ocean and introduced to Europe by the Byzantine Greeks. It permitted a ship to sail close to the wind and was used on both galleys and the larger round ships that were propelled by sails alone. The round ship, broad-beamed and steered by long oars slung from the stern quarters, was sturdy, capacious, and very slow. It was the bulk carrier of the Middle Ages. Galleys were still used for warfare and for cargos that were either perishable or whose value-to-weight ratio was high. Fast and maneuverable, they were as dependent on the land as their ancient counterparts and too fragile for extensive use in the open Atlantic.

These generalizations, referring as they do to a period of more than a thousand years, imply that little technological change was evident in the Middle Ages. This is not true, but by modern standards the rate of change was relatively slow. The medieval economy remained basically agricultural, with more than 90 percent of the population directly engaged in the production of food. Cash remained scarce, and the surplus of goods and services beyond those needed for mere subsistence was small. The accumulation of capital for investment in new technologies was therefore difficult, and the demand for innovations was slight because most people had little or no discretionary income.

## The Agricultural Revolution of the Eleventh and Twelfth Centuries

The rate of technological change, though slow by modern standards, did not prevent Europe from doubling its agricultural productivity between the years 1000 and 1250. Population doubled as well (see table 10.1). Climatological evidence suggests that a general warming trend extended the growing season and permitted the extension of cultivation to more northern regions and to higher elevations. No major famines occurred during this period, and crises of subsistence tended to be local and of short duration. However, changes in the climate alone cannot account for such an unprecedented expansion.

The return of more-or-less settled conditions after the great raids of the ninth and tenth centuries was certainly a factor. The annual loss of food, tools, livestock, and seed grain to the marauders had been substantial. When augmented by forced requisitions and by the depredations of local feudatories its impact on subsistence must have been great. A number of technical innovations increased productivity, though some were dependent upon a preexistent improvement in conditions for their success. The extension of the three-field system through much of northwest Europe is an example. By leaving only one-third of the land fallow in any given year, as opposed to half under the earlier system, peasants were able to increase their yields without seriously diminishing the fertility of their land. They typically planted a winter crop in one

**Illustration 10.2**

**The Mediterranean "Scratch" Plow.** The Mediterranean scratch plow preceded the heavy wheeled plow and had been used throughout the Roman Empire. It remained popular in dry regions until modern times because it did not turn over the furrows and therefore helped to preserve moisture in the soil.

field and a summer crop in another while leaving the third free to regenerate itself.

The success of this scheme depended upon the quality of the soil and the availability of adequate rainfall. Northwestern Europe, though at the same latitude as Newfoundland or Labrador, is mild and moist. Its weather is moderated by the Atlantic Ocean and, in particular, by the Gulf Stream, a warm water current that rises in the Caribbean and washes the shores of England and France. Pleasant summers with temperatures that usually do not exceed 80 degrees Fahrenheit follow long, wet winters in which prolonged freezes are rare. The prevailing winds are westerly, bringing abundant rainfall even in the summer months as Atlantic squalls, forced northward by high pressure over the Iberian Peninsula, drop their moisture on the land. In much of the Mediterranean basin, where little or no rain falls to support summer crops, the two-field system remained dominant; in the harsh, dry tablelands of Castile, seven-field systems in which only one-seventh of the land was cultivated at a time was common.

Production was further increased by the introduction of the heavy iron plow, or *carruca*, and the complex technology that surrounded it. This device was apparently of Slavic origin. Mounted on wheels, it consisted of a horizontal plowshare and an angled mould-board that turned the sliced earth aside. Cutting a deeper furrow than its Roman predecessor (see illustration 10.2), the iron plow made the seed less vulnerable to late frosts and to the depredations of birds and rodents. This increased yields and extended the limits of cultivation by allowing the seed to survive in colder climates. Heavy clay soils that were impervious to the scratchings of ancient plowmen could now be utilized for the first time, and the clearing of virgin land was greatly simplified (see illustration 10.3).

Iron plows were expensive. They also required the increased use of draft animals if their full potential was to be realized. The old Roman plow required, at the most, a single team of oxen and in light soils could often be pulled by a pair of human beings. The heavy plow might require as many as eight beasts. The increasing use of three- and four-yoke teams from the ninth century onward was responsible for a reorganization of labor on more cooperative lines. It was also an indication of greater prosperity, as was the innovation of plowing with horses. Horses are not as strong in absolute terms as draft oxen, but they are much faster. Horse plowing increases the amount of land that can be cultivated in a day by more than 30 percent. This represented a great increase in efficiency. However, horses are more inclined to sickness and injury than oxen, and their diet must be supplemented by feed grains. Oxen, for the most part, need only to graze. The introduction of horse plowing was therefore limited to those regions

**Illustration 10.3**

🌾 **The Heavy Wheeled Plow.** This illustration from an early sixteenth-century prayer book shows a typical wheeled plow in operation. It is not much different from those introduced in the ninth and tenth centuries. Note the arrangement of the harnesses on the team of horses.

that already enjoyed a considerable surplus of grain. It also required the development of a new type of harness. Horses cannot be yoked like oxen without constricting their windpipes, and attaching the plow to their withers or tail is not only cruel but also woefully ineffective. The modern harness, without which a draft horse is virtually useless, appears to have been developed in Asia and introduced to Europe around the year 800.

A fringe benefit associated with the increased use of draft animals was the greater availability of manure. Medieval peasants knew that manure greatly increased the fertility of soils, just as they knew that marl could be used to reduce soil acidity and that soils could be mixed to improve workability or drainage. All of these techniques were labor-intensive. Substantial quantities of manure were required to fertilize even a moderately sized field, and though draft animals were numerous af-

ter 1100, livestock production for meat remained modest until the second half of the fourteenth century.

Perhaps the most important advance in this area was the Frankish invention of the scythe, which largely replaced the sickle and permitted large-scale haying and the stall feeding of cattle. The cattle were kept for meat and dairy products, and their manure was carefully collected and spread on the fields. However, stockraising is a fundamentally inefficient use of land. Vegetable crops suited for direct human consumption fed more people from the same acreage. In marginal economies where even intensive cultivation provides modest yields, animal protein is a luxury. Supplies of manure, though improved, were therefore limited and were probably applied most frequently to household gardens and other small plots. The use of human waste as fertilizer, though common in Asia, was apparently rare in the West.

Larger fields could retain their productivity only by being left fallow or through crop rotation. Yields by modern standards remained poor, but they were a great improvement over those of Charlemagne's time. Whereas harvesting one-and-a-half grains for every grain planted was once common, harvesting four or five became possible. Theoretically, the maximum yield of wheat from an unfertilized field is about twelve bushels per acre. Peasants in the thirteenth century probably averaged about half this amount from fields that today produce sixty bushels per acre or more, but five to seven bushels per acre was a substantial improvement over times past (see table 10.2).

The improvement of yields, the extension of cultivation into new areas, and the reduction in the amount of labor required to produce a given quantity of food produced consistent surpluses of crops in those areas where they grew best. This in turn led to agricultural specialization. The Beauvaisis or the Ile de France, for example, were ideal for the cultivation of wheat but produced only small quantities of inferior wine. Parts of Burgundy produced excellent wine but relatively meager stands of wheat. Landholders found that they could improve their revenues as well as their standard of living by selling off surpluses and using the profits to purchase commodities that grew poorly, if at all, on their own manors. In time, whole regions were devoted to the cultivation of grains, while others specialized in wine, olives, or other commodities. The great wine-growing areas were planted for the most part in the twelfth century, usually along navigable rivers such as the Loire, the Rhone, or the Rhine. Corking and bottling had not yet been invented, so wine was shipped in casks that were too heavy to transport easily on land.

## TABLE 10.2

### Medieval Grain Yields

The following range of grain yields is taken from harvest records on the estates of the bishops of Winchester (England) between 1209 and 1349, a relatively fertile area that enjoyed good management. The figures are therefore probably higher than those for medieval Europe as a whole, but far below what can be achieved with modern technology. Yields of wheat on similar lands today have been known to reach seventy to eighty bushels per acre. The difference goes far to explain the insufficiency of medieval diets.

| Grain | Yield in grains per grain planted Maximum | Minimum | Yield in bushels per acre Maximum | Minimum |
|---|---|---|---|---|
| Barley | 5.6 | 2.8 | 27.6 | 11.0 |
| Oats | 3.4 | 1.8 | 16.0 | 7.5 |
| Wheat | 5.3 | 2.6 | 13.6 | 5.8 |

Source: J. Z. Titow, *Winchester Yields* (Cambridge: Cambridge University Press, 1972), p. 14.

For peasants, specialization was a mixed blessing. Monoculture left them more vulnerable to crop failures than were the subsistence farmers who grew a little bit of everything. Some evidence is available that diets deteriorated as more and more land was devoted to the cash crop. But from the standpoint of the European economy as a whole, specialization improved efficiency. It increased the overall production of commodities because land was not wasted on unsuitable crops, and it probably improved their quality as well. It also, by definition, created the basis for a trade in bulk agricultural commodities that grew into a full-blown commercial revolution.

## The Commercial Revolution

In the early Middle Ages most trading was local and conducted through barter. With the growth of agricultural specialization, this form of commerce expanded without changing its essential principles. Villagers brought their surplus goods to weekly markets held in a nearby town and exchanged them for clothing, tools, or agricultural products that they could not produce efficiently themselves. Larger transactions were con-

ducted at great annual fairs, such as the one at Champagne that attracted merchants from all over Europe until well into modern times.

At first, long-distance commerce was largely in the hands of Jews. Though Jews were not invariably barred from holding land, Christian hostility kept them socially peripheral and reinforced the natural cosmopolitanism of a people in exile. Their wide-ranging contacts, reinforced by strong kinship ties, gave them a powerful advantage when virtually everyone else was bound by interest and circumstance to the locality of their birth. This situation began to change in the eleventh century. The increased volume, safety, and profitability of trade began to make it more attractive to Christian entrepreneurs who were able to squeeze out their Jewish competitors by securing favored treatment from Christian authorities. The anti-Semitic persecutions that began in the twelfth century arose primarily from the crusading impulse, but they coincided with a perceived decline in the economic usefulness of the Jews.

The most aggressive of the new traders were the inhabitants of the Italian coastal towns. By the beginning of the eleventh century, a number of Italian cities had outgrown their local food supplies and emerged as net importers of agricultural commodities. Grain, oil, and other commodities had to be purchased abroad, usually in Spain or Sicily. Ports such as Pisa, Amalfi, and Genoa possessed the maritime skills necessary for this trade and were often forced to engage in it for their own survival. Only the threat of Muslim piracy stood in their way. By combining their fleets and taking advantage of political disorder in North Africa, the three cities were able to drive the Muslims from their bases in Sardinia, Corsica, and the Balearic Islands by 1088.

Venice, the greatest trading city of them all, had no *contado* or agricultural land of its own. It produced little more than glass and sea salt, but being located at the head of the Adriatic, it was the perfect center for trade between the eastern Mediterranean and central Europe. Dependent upon commerce almost from its beginnings, Venice, like other Italian ports, owed its eventual success to sheer necessity, maritime skill, and location. By the beginning of the twelfth century, the Italians were dominant in the Mediterranean carrying trade and were beginning to extend their routes northward.

The Crusades expanded Italian trade and greatly increased its value. Those crusaders who wished to go to the Holy Land by sea went for the most part in Italian ships and paid dearly for the privilege. When they arrived, they found a civilization that was in many ways more sophisticated than their own. They quickly developed a taste for silks, for spices from India, and for the superior cutlery of Damascus, to name a few of the items that by 1250 had become the components of an immense commerce. Those who returned to Europe brought their new tastes with them and created a fashion for Eastern luxuries that the Italians were well positioned to fill. Each shipload of crusaders offered its master the opportunity to make commercial contacts along the route, and elaborate trading networks soon developed between the Italians and their merchant counterparts in Greece, the Aegean, Anatolia, and the Levant.

The demand for Eastern luxuries was possible only because the real wealth of the west had increased since Carolingian times. The agricultural revolution was primarily responsible for this phenomenon. The return of settled conditions also permitted gold and silver that had been hoarded during the bad old days to be released into circulation. This, together with the slow but steady increase in European mining during the eleventh and twelfth centuries, increased the amount of specie available for trade. Copper coinage remained the standard in everyday transactions. Silver became more common, and in the mid-thirteenth century gold was introduced for the first time on a large scale.

From the Italian point of view, the Eastern trade was ideal. Luxuries from the East possessed a far higher ratio of value to weight than did agricultural products and could generate greater profits. The risks were correspondingly high. But, as in the case of the spice trade, a single voyage could make a trader's fortune. Spices, the most important of which were black pepper, nutmeg, and cinnamon, originated in India or in what is now Indonesia and were transported across the Indian Ocean in the dhows of Arab merchants. They were then transshipped by caravan to the Mediterranean ports where they were purchased by Italian traders who carried them home by ship. Other merchants carried them overland to consumers beyond the Alps. At each stage of this journey except the last, profits might amount to several hundred percent on invested capital. However, ships were frequently lost to pirates, bad weather, or the unpredictable fortunes of war and politics.

Risky ventures of this kind were often supported by a *commenda* contract (see document 10.1). An investor, usually an older man or a woman, would finance the voyage of a younger merchant in return for half of the total profits. After two or three such voyages, the younger man could then retire and become an investor in his own right. The Eastern trade never equaled bulk commodities either in volume or in total value, but as a means of capital accumulation it was

## ◆ DOCUMENT 10.1 ◆

### A Commenda from Venice, 1073

*This is a fairly standard example of a commenda contract from the early period of the commercial revolution.*

In the name of the Lord God and of our Savior, Jesus Christ. In the year of the Incarnation of the same Redeemer 1073, in the month of August, eleventh indiction, at Rialto, I, Giovanni Lissado of Luprio, together with my heirs, have received in partnership from you, Sevasto Orefice, son of Ser Trudimondo, and from your heirs, this amount: £200 Venetian. And I myself have invested £100 in it. And with this capital we have aquired two shares of the ship in which Gosmiro da Molina is captain. And I am under obligation to bring all of this with me on a commercial voyage to Thebes in the ship which the aforesaid Gosmiro da Molino sails as captain. Indeed, by this agreement and understanding of ours I promise to put to work this entire capital and to strive the best way I can. Then if the capital is saved, we are to divide whatever profit the Lord may grant us from it by exact halves, without fraud and evil device. And whatever I can gain with these goods from any source, I am under obligation to invest all of it in the partnership. And if all these goods are lost because of the sea or of hostile people, and this is proved—may this be averted—neither party ought to ask any of them from the other; if, however, some of them remain, in proportion as we invested, so shall we share. Let this partnership exist between us so long as our wills are fully agreed.

But if I do not observe everything just as is stated above, I, together with my heirs, then promise to give and to return to you and your heirs everything in the double, both capital and profit, out of my land and my house or out of anything that I am known to have in this world.

Lopez, Robert S., and Raymond, Irving W. *Medieval Trade in the Mediterrean World.* New York: Columbia University Press, 1955.

not surpassed. Many Italians became enormously rich. Much of this wealth was then reinvested in banking, which soon became international in scope. Banking began when traders sought to deposit their cash with goldsmiths or moneychangers who had the facilities for storing it safely. A fee was normally charged for this service. As the number of customers grew, the likelihood that they would try to redeem their deposits at the same time decreased. As long as the banker maintained an adequate reserve, a portion of his deposits could be loaned out to other businessmen at a profit.

Aware that a stable coinage was essential to a trading community, Venice and Florence established the ducat and the florin, respectively, at fixed values that made them the currency of choice throughout Europe and much of the Middle East. The rulers of other countries often reduced the precious metal content of their coins so that they might pay off their debts in depreciated money. Investors preferred currencies that protected them from this inflationary practice and, wherever possible, deposited their money with the Italians. To facilitate this, and to take advantage of the need for capital in other, less developed parts of Europe, Florentine, Venetian, and Milanese bankers established branches in leading centers of trade throughout the subcontinent.

By the thirteenth century, Italian bankers were the dominant force in international moneylending. Though in theory Christians could not loan money at interest, the Italians used their branch banks and the natural variations in exchange rates at different locations to avoid the church's ban. Bills of exchange would be issued at the Venetian rate, for example, and redeemed after a fixed period or usance at the higher London rate (see document 10.2). The difference between the two exchange rates would reflect the cost of the loan. Many churchmen probably were not fooled by this, but the technical requirements of theology were satisfied.

Additional Italian wealth was invested in manufacturing. A major problem with the eastern trade was that at first the East had little or no interest in Western merchandise and tended to demand payment for its goods in cash. A real chance existed that the trade would be destroyed by balance of payment problems similar to those that had beset the later Roman Empire. Many of the wiser merchants began to invest in the creation of products that would attract Eastern consumers. Among them were fine finished cloths based on merino wool from Spain, which were dyed and woven according to specialized techniques in Italy. Florence took an early lead in this trade, as it did in the production of fine leather goods. Silk, too, became an important Italian export when it was discovered that the mulberry trees on which silk worms grew could survive in southern Italy. The technique of spinning and weaving silk was

---

### ◆ DOCUMENT 10.2 ◆

## A Bill of Exchange

*This sample bill of exchange demonstrates how the system worked. Barna, in Avignon, orders his correspondents, the Bartoli of Pisa, to pay off a loan of 4.5 percent from Tancredi Bonagiunta and partners. Landuccio Busdraghi and compagni (partners) were Bonagiunta's correspondents in Lucca, which is only a few miles from Pisa. Several copies of such documents were usually sent to avoid accidental loss in transit. This one is marked "First" as the original.*

Avignon, October 5, 1339

In the name of God, amen. To Bartolo and partners [*compagni*], Barna of Lucca and partners [send] greetings from Avignon.

You shall pay by this letter on November 20 [1]339, to Landuccio Busdraghi and partners of Lucca, gold florins three hundred twelve and three fourths for the exchange [*per cambio*] of gold florins three hundred, because I have received such money today from Tancredi Bonagiunta and partners at the rate [*raxione*] of 4 1/2 per 100 to their advantage. And charge [it] to our account. Done on October 5 [1]339.

Francesco Falconetti has ordered us to pay in your behalf 230 gold *scudi* to the Acciajuoli *compagnia*.

[Address on outside:]

To Bartolo Casini and Partners, in Pisa    First.

Lopez, Robert S., and Raymond, Irving W. *Medieval Trade in the Mediterranean World*. New York: Columbia University Press, 1955.

---

mastered, and though the primary market for this commodity remained European, imports from the east were reduced and a highly profitable sideline was developed (see map 10.1).

As a result of these activities, Italy was perhaps fifty years ahead of the rest of Europe in economic development, but other areas enjoyed remarkable growth as well. The Catalans were formidable competitors in the Mediterranean trade. In the Baltic, German traders achieved a commanding position after the decline of their Scandinavian rivals in the tenth and eleventh centuries. The north German towns, of which Lübeck was the most important, dealt in salt herring, furs, amber,

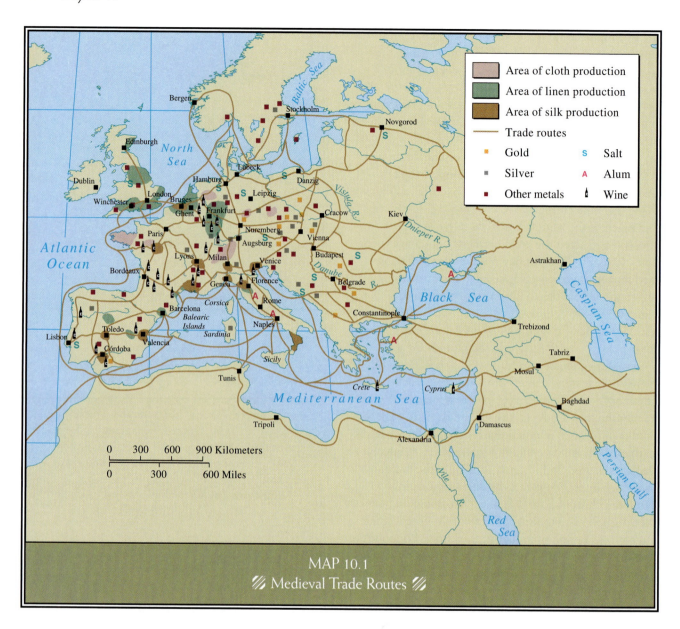

MAP 10.1

Medieval Trade Routes

wax, timber, pitch, tar, iron, and all the other products of the northern world. Organized into *hansas*, or merchant leagues, they prospered greatly throughout the High Middle Ages.

Ghent, Bruges, Ypres, and the other Flemish cities concentrated primarily on the manufacture of cloth. Their position near the mouths of the Meuse and Rhine made them natural ports that connected the European interior with England, Scandinavia, and northern Spain. Some of them also rivaled the Hanse in the salt trade, which was vital because salt was the primary means of preserving food. By the end of the thirteenth century, the Low Countries had become a highly urbanized center of wealth that rivaled Italy in commercial importance. Other, smaller, centers of trade and

manufacturing developed along the main trade routes or wherever a local product achieved some level of renown.

Manufacturing in the Middle Ages did not normally employ elaborate machinery or the techniques of mass production and cannot, therefore, be described as truly industrial, though some of the larger wool shops in Italy or Flanders employed as many as 150 workers. Goods were produced by artisans who, after the tenth century, were typically organized into guilds or associations that attempted to regulate price and quality in a particular trade. Because they included not only journeymen but also the masters who owned the shops and the apprentices who would one day be admitted to full membership, guilds combined a variety of functions.

## ❖ DOCUMENT 10.3 ❖

### The Guilds and Social Welfare

*This excerpt is from the "customs" of the Guild of the Holy Trinity at Lynn, England, dating from the late fourteenth century. Customs illustrate the degree to which guilds provided for the security and social welfare of member families.*

If any of the aforesaid brethren shall die in the said town or elsewhere, as soon as the knowledge thereof shall come to the alderman, the said alderman shall order solemn mass to be celebrated for him, at which every brother of the said guild that is in town shall make his offering; and further, the alderman shall cause every chaplain of the said guild, immediately on the death of any brother, to say thirty masses for the deceased.

The aldermen and skevins [from the French *echevin*—essentially the same as an alderman; in this case both terms refer to the guild's governing board] of the said guild are by duty obliged to visit four times a year all the infirm, all that are in want, need, or poverty, and to minister to and relieve all such out of the alms of the said guild.

If any brother shall become poor and needy, he shall be supported in food and clothing, according to his exigency, out of the profits of the lands and tenements, goods and chattels of the said guild.

The Guilds and Social Welfare. From *Pennsylvania Translations and Reprints,* vol. 2. trans. Edward P. Cheyney. Philadelphia: University of Pennsylvania Press, 1897.

They set wages and prices as far as market forces would permit. They supervised the training of apprentices and tried to guarantee a quality product through inspections and the use of such devices as the masterpiece, a work whose acknowledged excellence permitted its creator to be enrolled as a master in the guild. Because mechanisms for social support were few, guilds often attempted to provide for the welfare of widows, orphans, and those members who could no longer work (see document 10.3). They sponsored banquets and drinking parties, and they inevitably became the vehicle through which their members exerted political influence in the community. For the town-dwelling artisan family, the guild was the center of social, political, and economic life.

## The Growth of Towns

The commercial revolution brought a revival of the urban life that had been largely dormant since the fall of Rome. Trade inevitably centered on the towns. As trade increased, towns grew into cities and some of those cities became sovereign states. Many of the more important medieval towns, including Paris, London, Florence, Milan, and Naples, had existed in Roman times, but others were relatively new or had grown from humble beginnings. Venice was founded by refugees fleeing from the Lombard invasion. Other communities grew up around the castles of bishops or secular lords. Still others grew up at river crossings or heads of navigation, or near natural harbors.

The pattern of urban growth in frontier areas was different. Dozens of Spanish towns in New Castile and Extremadura were built on lands captured from the Muslims during the twelfth and thirteenth centuries. Laid out geometrically around a central plaza, they were apparently modeled on the Roman *colonia* whose function had been much the same. Along the Baltic coasts, in Silesia, and eastward into Poland and the Ukraine, German towns were founded throughout this period, often by princely fiat, to secure newly acquired regions or to protect existing borders. Because Germany remained politically decentralized and because territories changed hands frequently owing to the vagaries of partible inheritance, princely foundations of this kind were common there as well. Though most were intended to be garrisons, market towns, or princely residences, a few were located with an eye to commercial development.

Whatever their origins, towns soon became a magnet for the unemployed, the ambitious, and the malcontent. The rapid increase in population after the tenth century coupled with more efficient agricultural methods tended to displace villagers whose labor was redundant and for whom no new land was available. These workers were "freed from the soil," an economist's euphemism for becoming unemployed, and moved to the towns in the hope of finding work as laborers. Some succeeded. If they survived, their descendants eventually became citizens and, in a few cases, grew rich. The Medici, arguably the greatest of Renaissance families, were descended from humble immigrants who came down from the Mugello during the thirteenth century to work as laborers in the wool shops of Florence.

Most immigrants, however, simply died. The rapid growth of medieval and early modern towns was almost

## TABLE 10.3

### Urban Populations Before the Black Death

Estimated populations of various European cities are given below for the period 1250–1300. This was, for most of them, a peak not reached again until the later sixteenth century, but none of them probably had more than 100,000 people. As the numbers indicate, Italy was by far the most urbanized region of medieval Europe. Most German cities had fewer than 20,000 people. All figures are approximate.

| Population | City |
| --- | --- |
| 100,000 | Milan, Italy |
| | Venice, Italy |
| | Florence, Italy |
| 80,000 | Paris, France |
| 50,000 | Barcelona, Cataluña |
| | Bologna, Italy |
| | Cologne, Germany |
| | Córdoba, Spain |
| | Ghent, Low Countries |
| | London, England |
| | Palermo, Sicily |
| 30,000–40,000 | Bruges, Low Countries |
| | Hamburg, Germany |
| | Lübeck, Germany |
| | Montpellier, France |
| | Padua, Italy |
| | Pisa, Italy |
| | Naples, Italy |
| | Rome, Italy |
| | Sevilla, Spain |
| | Toledo, Spain |
| 20,000 | Nuremburg, Germany |
| | Strasburg, Germany |

Source: Estimates compiled by the authors from various sources.

Illustration 10.4

Medieval Italian Tower Houses. This view of San Gimignano, Tuscany, shows a cluster of typical medieval tower houses. Their survival is a tribute to San Gimignano's relative isolation from the troubles of the thirteenth century.

longer effective. Town life was not just becoming more complex. An increasingly wealthy and educated class of merchants, rentiers, and artisans was growing more assertive and less willing to have its affairs controlled by traditional authorities whose knowledge of commerce was deficient and whose interests were not always those of the business community. From an early date, these people began organizing themselves into what became communes or representative town governments.

The basis of the communes varied widely. The more substantial townspeople had long been members of occupational organizations such as the guilds or of neighborhood organizations that dealt with problems too minor to concern the bishop or lord. These neighborhood organizations might be based on the parish, the gate company (a volunteer organization created to maintain and defend one of the city's gates or a portion of its walls), or, as in Italy, the tower association, a group of citizens whose tower homes (see illustration 10.4) stood in close proximity to one another, usually around a single piazza, and whose members were usually related to one another by blood or clientage.

In times of crisis, such as an attack on the city, representatives of these groups would gather together to concert a common policy. As the meetings of these ad hoc committees became more frequent they gradually evolved into town councils or permanent *signorie*, which increasingly challenged the political and judicial authority of their nominal lords. They succeeded in this primarily because the nascent communes represented wealth and manpower that the lords desperately

purely a function of inward migration, for urban death rates greatly exceeded live births until the eighteenth century. Yet for some cities, including Venice, Florence, and Milan, populations reached 100,000 or more by the mid-thirteenth century, and several others topped 50,000 (see table 10.3).

Rapid increases in population and commercial activity mandated sweeping changes in town government. The old system of rule by a bishop or secular lord assisted only by a handful of administrators was no

## ◆ DOCUMENT 10.4 ◆

### The Liberties of Toulouse, 1147

*The following is a typical, if somewhat abbreviated, example of the liberties granted by princes and noblemen to towns in the High Middle Ages.*

Let it be known to all men living and to be born that I, Alphonse, Count of Toulouse, proclaim, recognize, and grant that in no way do I have tallage or tolls in the city of Toulouse, nor in the suburb of St. Sernin, nor against the men and women living there or who will live there, nor shall I have in the city the right to summon the militia to campaign unless war be waged against me in Toulouse, nor shall I make any loan there unless it should be the lender's wish. Wherefore I confirm and commend to all citizens of Toulouse and its suburb, present and future, all their good customs and privileges, those they now enjoy and which I may give and allow to them. All this, as it is written above, Raymond of St. Gilles, son of the said count, approves and grants.

Mundy, John H., and Riesenberg, Peter, eds. *The Medieval Town.* Princeton, NJ: Van Nostrand, 1958.

needed. Negotiations were rarely high-minded. A lord or bishop would request money to meet a crisis, and the commune would grant it on condition that he surrender a coveted right (see document 10.4). In time, a substantial measure of self-government was achieved even by cities such as London that were located in powerful kingdoms. In regions such as Italy or north Germany where conflicting ecclesiastical or feudal authorities created a power vacuum, cities might easily evolve into sovereign states.

### Italy and the Emergence of the City-States

In Italy, this process was set in motion by the Investiture Controversy. Communes apparently arose as a response to military threats posed by the struggle between pope and emperor. Once established, they were courted by both parties in the hope of securing their material support. The townsmen were happy to oblige in return for privileges that escalated as the crisis became more dire, and something like a bidding war de-

veloped between political authorities who supported the pope and those who supported the emperor. By the time the investiture issue was settled by the Concordat of Worms (1122), most Italian cities had achieved full sovereignty as a result of charters granted by one side or the other. They now had the right to coin money, declare war, and govern their own affairs without limitations of any kind. They immediately used these powers to secure control over the surrounding countryside or *contado* and to pursue policies of aggression against neighboring towns. Control over the *contado* was essential to stabilizing food supplies that were inadequate. Landholders were given the opportunity to become citizens of the commune. If they refused, the city militia would annex their estates and drive them into exile, whereupon they typically complained to their liege lord, the emperor, who was obliged by feudal agreement to support them.

The whole process was attended by bloodshed and disorder. The violent conflicts between cities were worse. Localism in Italy was intensified by trade rivalries and by disputes over the control of scarce agricultural land. This had been evident even in the throes of the investiture crisis. Because Florence supported the pope and had received its charter from his ally Matilda of Tuscany, neighboring towns such as Siena or Pisa were inevitably pro-imperial and received their charters from Henry IV. Once free of political constraints, they pursued their vendettas with enthusiasm. The resulting wars were unnecessarily bloody and accompanied by the wholesale destruction of vines, crops, and olive groves. Pressured by dispossessed vassals and hoping to profit from Italian disunity, the emperor Frederick Barbarossa (c. 1123–90) decided to intervene.

Pope Alexander III responded by organizing the Lombard League, which defeated Frederick at the battle of Legnano in 1176. At the Peace of Constance in 1183, Frederick confirmed the sovereign rights of the Lombard towns. The Tuscans had refused to join the league out of hatred for their northern neighbors and were specifically excluded from the settlement. An imperial *podestà* or governor was installed at San Miniato, a town on the road between Florence and Pisa that was known thereafter as San Miniato del Tedesco (San Miniato of the German). The Tuscans destroyed the place when they regained their freedom in 1197, after the premature death of Henry VII.

Internally, the Italian cities were beset from the start by factionalism. Clientage and kinship ties often proved stronger than allegiance to the commune, and by the beginning of the thirteenth century, civil strife was universal. Constitutional remedies such as elections

**Illustration 10.5**

The Condottiere. The mercenary lived apart from the communal values of the Italian city-state. In this painting from 1328, Simone Martini shows the Sienese commander Guidoriccio da Fogliano riding in splendid isolation across a war-torn landscape.

by lot or the institution of the *podestà*, an administrative judge who was by law a foreigner, proved relatively ineffective. The emperor Frederick II (1194–1250) tried to use this situation to restore imperial authority in northern Italy, but the papacy proved as effective an obstacle to his designs as it had to those of his grandfather. The son of Henry VI and Constance, daughter of Roger II of Sicily, Frederick inherited a powerful, well-organized kingdom in southern Italy that, together with his imperial election in Izzo, made him a genuine threat both to the freedom of the Italian towns and to papal autonomy. When a political faction, hard-pressed by its rivals, sought his support, its enemies invariably turned to the pope. In this way two great "parties," the Guelfs and the Ghibellines, were born. In theory, Guelfs supported the pope and Ghibellines the emperor, but ideological and even class differences were minimal. The real issue was which faction among the richer citizens would control the city.

The Guelf-Ghibelline struggles led to the breakdown of civil government in many Italian cities. Fearful of their own citizens, governments began the practice of hiring *condottiere* or mercenaries to defend them against their neighbors (see illustration 10.5). In so doing they created another mortal danger to their independence. Victorious captains proved capable of

seizing the town when the danger had passed. By the end of the thirteenth century, an exhausted citizenry was prepared to accept almost any remedy, and nearly all of the towns fell under the rule of despots. In some cases, as in Milan, the despot was the leader of a faction that finally triumphed over its rivals. In others, desperate citizens sought or accepted the rule of a prominent local family, a mercenary captain, or a popular *podestà*. They abandoned their cherished republican constitutions in return for the right to pursue business and personal interests in relative peace. It was not always a good bargain. Whatever their titles, despots were absolute rulers whose survival demanded a certain ruthlessness. Some were competent and relatively benign; a few were bloodthirsty psychopaths; but none was prepared to encourage the rich culture of civic participation that would one day produce the Renaissance.

That task was left to Florence and Venice, two cities that escaped the soft trap of despotism. In Florence, the Guelf triumph of 1266 paved the way for a guild-based democracy that survived, in theory at least, until the end of the fifteenth century. Social and economic tensions were expressed in the long struggle over whether or not the major guilds, which were dominated by the great bankers, should control the electoral process and therefore the *signoria*. The issue was revolved in favor of the major guilds in 1382, but in 1434 a clientage group headed by the banker-statesman Cosimo de' Medici gained control of the machinery of government. Though republican institutions were ostensibly maintained, the Medici and their friends were able to manipulate the constitution for their own purposes until 1494.

Venice, settled only in 568 and located among the desolate islands at the head of the Adriatic, had never been part of the Holy Roman Empire. Its development was therefore unlike that of any other Italian town. Several small refugee settlements coalesced during the ninth century into a single city ruled by an elective doge, or duke. Isolated from the imperial struggles on the mainland and interested primarily in the development of trade and an overseas empire, the Venetians evolved a system of government that has been called both a model republic and a class despotism.

Like other cities, Venice was troubled by clientage groups headed by prominent merchant families. To prevent any one family from gaining control of the state, the monarchical powers of the doge were eliminated between 1140 and 1160, and legislative power was vested in an elected Great Council with forty-five members. A Minor Council was established to assist the doge in his new role as administrator. The system was given its final form between 1290 and 1310 when a series of mishaps and scandals raised the specter of social revolution. The Great Council was expanded and then closed to anyone who did not have an ancestor sitting on it in 1297. A geneological registry was kept to establish pedigrees, and the membership hovered thereafter between twelve hundred and fourteen hundred certifiable members of the Venetian aristocracy. The Great Council elected the doge, whose role became largely ceremonial; his counsellors; and the Senate, a 160-man body that controlled the state. The Great Council was thus both the electorate and the pool from which officeholders were drawn. Only a direct appeal to the people could alter this closed system, and the chances of such an appeal succeeding were greatly diminished by the Council of Ten. This was a committee on state security, elected by the Great Council for one-year, nonrenewable terms, and granted almost unlimited power to deal with threats to the Venetian state at home or abroad. The constitution remained in effect until 1798.

Broad-based participation in public affairs, at least among the upper classes, is thought to have produced a civic culture of unusual vitality in both Florence and Venice. Though the government of the Medici has been called a family despotism, Cosimo made every effort to draw everyone of importance into his web of clientage. In Venice, a fairly numerous aristocracy had no alternative to participation in civic life, whereas in a true depotism, participation was restricted to the ruler and his immediate entourage. This level of civic activity contributed to the cultural and intellectual movement known as the Renaissance, but from the standpoint of social history, the Renaissance as a historical period has little meaning. The underlying realities of daily life in the Italian towns changed little between 1200 and 1500, and most generalizations that can be made about urban society, whether in Italy or elsewhere, are good for the Middle Ages as well as much of the early modern period.

## The Cities of Northern Europe

Beyond the Alps only a relative handful of cities achieved anything like full sovereignty. Most were in Germany. In the period of imperial disintegration that followed the death of Frederick II, free cities and those that owed their allegiance to the emperor were generally able to expand their privileges. The larger, richer communities, such as Nürnberg or Lübeck, were virtually city-states on the Italian model, though they retained their allegiance to the empire. Others were less secure, as emperors had been known to pledge them to neighboring princes in return for support or in the settlement of disputes.

Though almost all German towns, including those that had been founded by princes, enjoyed a wide measure of freedom guaranteed by charter, the threat of noble encroachment and the uncertainties of imperial politics favored the formation of leagues. The various Hansas of north Germany had political and economic purposes. The Rhenish League (1254) and the Swabian League (1376) provide further examples, while the Swiss Confederation, founded in 1291, evolved with relatively minor changes into the Switzerland of today. The original nucleus of three small forest cantons—Uri, Schwyz, and Unterwalden—was joined by larger communities when it demonstrated its ability to defend itself against the Habsburgs at Morgarten (1315). The process of confederation culminated only with the admission of Basel in 1501 and Geneva in 1536. Each canton governed itself as an independent unit and sent representatives to the Swiss Diet when presenting a united front became necessary. Though in many ways typical of late medieval leagues, the Swiss survived through sheer military prowess and the democratic character of their cantonal governments, which tended to limit social strife.

In those areas that possessed a strong monarchy, urban development took a somewhat different form. In Spain, France, and England, the king retained a large measure of control over the towns. London achieved substantial autonomy in the chaotic reigns of Richard I and John. Urban privileges, when they were granted, were usually the fruit of royal weakness.

In the Low Countries, cities enjoyed more independence than their French or English counterparts because the counts of Flanders and Holland and the dukes of Brabant were rarely able to bring them to full obedience. With the consolidation of a powerful Burgundian state in the fifteenth century, some of their freedoms were curtailed. However, they retained more independence than royal towns whose government was influenced at every stage by the presence of a royal bailiff.

Even in France or England the towns enjoyed a freedom unknown in the countryside. In matters of taxation, public works, social policy, sanitation, and the regulation of trades, the elected town councils were remarkably autonomous. The decisions of city courts were honored except when they came into conflict with the king's justice. In France the towns were represented both in the provincial estates and the Estates General. Royal taxes were normally collected by city officials who compounded with the crown for a specified amount and then made the assessments themselves. Citizens had the opportunity to participate in their own governance and were exempt from feudal dues and obligations. Though royal authority might be strong, the German saying held true: *Stadtluft macht frei* (city air makes one free). Personal freedom and the demands of civic responsibility made medieval cities, though they held less than 10 percent of Europe's population, its primary agents of cultural and intellectual change.

## Town Life in the Middle Ages

The freedom of a medieval town was a matter of personal status; the life lived within it was by most modern standards highly regulated and even claustrophobic (see illustration 10.6). The town walls defined a world of perpetual shade—a constricted maze of narrow, winding streets broken only occasionally by the open spaces of a churchyard or market. Because space within the walls was scarce and expensive, houses tended to be narrow, deep, and high, with upper stories that often overhung the street below until they nearly touched their neighbors. Light and ventilation were usually

poor, and privacy nonexistent. Much of the intensity of town life came from everyone knowing everyone else's business.

Crowding, together with the virtual absence of sanitary facilities, account for the extreme susceptibility of urban populations to epidemic disease. Regulations were established against dumping human waste into the streets, but piling it in courtyards, sometimes in close proximity to wells, was common. Travelers could smell a town long before it came into view. Town councils made valiant, if usually futile, efforts to keep the streets clean and to ensure the purity of the water supply. In the absence of a germ theory, this usually meant prohibitions on washing wool in the public fountains or orders restricting tanneries to locations downstream if not necessarily downwind. Death rates predictably exceeded birth rates in almost every European city.

Other regulations tried to preserve order as well as public health. Virtually every occupation had to be licensed. Business hours and practices were narrowly defined in the hope of protecting the consumer and reducing conflict between trades. Market women were the object of special scrutiny because their activities often threatened the prerogatives of the guilds. Standards of quality, enforced by official inspections, were laid down for the cloth industry and the victualing trades. The age and condition of meat or fish, the often dubious contents of sausages, and the conditions under which perishables of all kinds were prepared and sold were concerns, as was the integrity of weights and measures. Efforts were made to prevent the adulteration of grain or flour by adding sand or other substances to increase its weight. Every aspect of the operation of taverns, inns, wineshops, and bathhouses was minutely regulated. City ordinances and court records are a rich catalog of ingenious frauds and entrepreneurial excess.

After disease, the other great curse of medieval towns was fire. Fire companies were organized and regulations were proposed to prevent the most hazardous practices, but the combination of wood or wood frame construction and gross overcrowding could still turn ordinary kitchen mishaps into holocausts that threatened the entire community.

The city's walls not only defined the space in which townspeople lived, but also symbolized their attitude toward the outside world. For all their far-flung interests, medieval towns were intensely parochial. Carnival plays and masks are a useful key to a people's deepest fears. In cities such as late medieval Nürnberg, the citizens' nightmares seem to have revolved around nobles, Jews, peasants, and Turks. The fear of Jews and Turks

**Illustration 10.6**

🟊 **An Urban Street Scene in Fourteenth-Century Siena.** The mules are carrying wool and wood. On the left, a teacher conducts a class.

was the fear of infidels, and the nobles were everywhere a threat to the freedoms of the town. Peasants were seen as deceitful, sexually promiscuous, and vio-

lent. In even the largest cities, the countryside was never more than a few minutes' walk away, and the urban economy could not have existed without its rural suppliers. However, mutual distrust was universal. The city's gates were locked every evening, and all visitors had to secure permission to enter even in broad daylight. Jews and foreigners were commonly restricted to ghettos, often for their own protection. The word *ghetto* is of Venetian origin and refers to the section of the city reserved for Jews, but London had its Steelyard, where the Hansa merchants locked themselves up at night, and a Lombard Street where Italians were supposed to reside and operate their businesses. The outside world was perceived as threatening and only the citizen could be fully trusted.

Citizenship was a coveted honor and often difficult to achieve. With the exception of certain Swiss towns where the franchise was unusually broad, only a minority of the male residents in most cities enjoyed the right to participate in public affairs. For the most part that right was hereditary. Citizenship could be earned by those who performed extraordinary services for the commune or who had achieved substantial wealth in a respectable trade. Town councils tended to be stingy in granting citizenship, which carried with it status and responsibility. The citizen was relied upon to vote, hold office, perform public service without pay, and contribute to special assessments in time of need. Full participation in the life of the commune could be expensive and required a certain stability and firmness of character.

The distinction between citizen and noncitizen was the primary social division in the medieval town, but there were others. In most cities economic and political power rested in the hands of the richest citizens: bankers, long-distance traders, or their descendants who lived from rents and investments. Their wealth and leisure enabled them to dominate political life. They were also jealous of their prerogatives and resistant to the claims of other social groups. Serving the patricians, and sometimes related to them by blood, was a professional class composed of lawyers, notaries, and the higher ranks of the local clergy.

The men of this class frequently enjoyed close relations with princes and nobles and served as representatives of their cities to the outside world. In the later Middle Ages their contribution to the world of literature and scholarship would be disproportionate to their numbers. The women of the urban patriciate, however, were probably more isolated from society and more economically dependent than the women of any other social class. As wives, their economic role was negligible. Even housework and the care of children were usually entrusted to servants. As widows, however, they could inherit property, enter into contracts, and in some cities, sue on their own behalf in court. These rights allowed patrician widows to become investors, though, unlike the women of the artisan class, their direct involvement in management was rare.

Compared with the patricians and rentiers, artisans were a large and varied group not all of whom were cre-

ated equal. The social gap between a goldsmith and a tanner was vast, but their lives bore certain similarities. Artisans were skilled workers who processed or manufactured goods and who belonged to the guild appropriate to their trade. Patricians were rarely guild members except in such towns as Florence where guild membership was a prerequisite for public office. The masters of a given trade owned their own workshops, which doubled as retail salesrooms and typically occupied the ground floor of their homes. They sometimes worked alone but more often employed journeymen to assist them. These skilled workers had served their apprenticeships but did not own their own shops and usually lived in rented quarters elsewhere. Because the master had demonstrated his competence with a masterpiece that had been accepted by the other masters of his guild, he was also expected to train apprentices. These young men, often the sons of other guild members, learned the trade by working in the master's shop and living in his household. Apprenticeships typically began around the age of twelve and continued for seven years in northern Europe and three or four in Italy.

Artisan households were often large, complex units. Their management and the management of the family business were usually entrusted to the artisan's wife. While her husband concentrated on production and training, she dealt with marketing, purchasing, and finance. If the artisan died, she often continued the enterprise, using hired journeymen in his place or doing the work herself, for many women had learned their father's trade as children. In some cities, widows were admitted to guilds, though not without restrictions.

Women's work was therefore crucial to the medieval town economy. According to the *Livre des Métiers*, written by Etienne Boileau in the thirteenth century, women were active in eighty-six of the one hundred occupations listed for contemporary Paris. Six *métiers* or trades, all of which would today be called part of the fashion industry, were exclusively female (see document 10.5). In addition, women everywhere played an important part in the victualing trades (brewing, butchering, fishmongering, and so on) and in the manufacture of small metal objects including needles, pins, buckles, knives, and jewelry.

Women also played an important role as street peddlars. Operating from makeshift booths or simply spreading their goods on the ground, the market women sold everything from trinkets to used clothing, household implements, and food. After the expulsion of the Jews, many women became pawnbrokers. Their central role in retail distribution, their aggressive sales techniques, and their propensity to engage (like their

### ◆ DOCUMENT 10.5 ◆

## Women in the Paris Silk Industry

*Silk spinning in thirteenth-century Paris was a woman's trade. The women owned their own spindles and could take apprentices. Paris, however, lacked the freedom of the Italian and German towns. Like other métiers in this era, the spinsters had no true guild organization. Craft ordinances were proclaimed and enforced in the king's name by the provost of Paris, and the spun silk was purchased by merchants operating on the "putting-out" system. Those ordinances listed below were compiled between 1254 and 1271 and offer a glimpse of the conditions under which medieval tradeswomen worked.*

Any woman who wishes to be a silk spinster on large spindles in the city of Paris—i.e. reeling, spinning, doubling, and retwisting—may freely do so, provided she observe the following usages and customs of the craft:

No spinster on large spindles may have more than three apprentices, unless they be her own or her husband's children born in true wedlock; nor may she contract with them for an apprenticeship of less than seven years or for a fee of less than 20 Parisian sols to be paid to her, their mistress. The apprenticeship shall be for eight years if there is no fee, but she may accept more years and money if she can get them. . . .

No woman of the said craft may hire an apprentice or work-girl who has not completed her years of service with the mistress to whom she was apprenticed. If a spinster has assumed an apprentice, she may not take on another before the first has completed her seven years unless the apprentice die or foreswear the craft forever. If an apprentice spinster buy her freedom before serving the said seven years, she may not herself take an apprentice until she has practiced the craft seven years. . . .

If a working woman comes from outside Paris and wishes to practice the said craft in the city, she must swear before two guardians of the craft that she will practice it well and loyally and conform to its customs and usages.

If anyone give a woman of the said craft silk to be spun and the woman pawn it, and the owner complains, the fine shall be 5 sols.

No workwoman shall farm out another's silk to be worked upon outside her own house.

The said craft has as guardians two men of integrity sworn in the king's name but appointed and charged at the will of the provost of Paris. Taking an oath in the provost's presence, they shall swear to guard the craft truly, loyally, and to their utmost, and to inform him or his agents of all malpractices discovered therein.

Boileau, Etienne. *"Livres de Métiers."* In Julia O'Faolain and Lauro Martines, *Not in God's Image: Women in History from the Greeks to the Victorians.* New York: HarperCollins, 1973.

---

male counterparts) in monopolies and restrictive trading practices brought them into frequent conflict with the guilds and with the authorities who tried, often in vain, to regulate their activities.

Many market women were the wives or daughters of journeymen; most probably came from a lower echelon of urban society—the semiskilled or unskilled laborers who served as porters, construction helpers, wool carders, or any one of a hundred menial occupations. Such people were rarely guild members or citizens, and their existence was often precarious.

Employment tended to be sporadic. A laborer's wage was sometimes capable of supporting a bachelor but rarely a family, and everyone had to work to survive. In cloth towns, women often worked in the wool shops along with the men. For the aggressive and quick-witted, the street market was a viable alternative. Domestic service was another and provided employment for a substantial number of both men and women.

These respectable, if disenfranchised, workers were probably the most numerous group in any city. An underclass also was present of beggars, prostitutes, criminals, and people who for one reason or another were dependent on charity for their survival. In theory, the poor were the responsibility of the church or of pious individuals who contributed to their welfare. Town governments tended to see poverty, like criminality, as a question of social control, though by the later Middle Ages, some communities had begun to follow the lead of Venice in establishing hospitals and regular distributions of food to the needy. Even when they were established with government funds, these institutions were staffed mainly by the religious orders. Begging in many places was licensed, as was prostitution. The latter could be an important source of revenue, and most towns, such as Nürnberg, preferred to localize the trade in official brothels whose profits could be taxed.

Crime was more difficult to control. The intimacy of town life encouraged theft, and the labyrinth of streets and alleys provided robbers with multiple escape routes. No police force existed. Most towns had a watch for night patrols and a militia that could intervene in riots and other disturbances, but competent thieves were rarely caught and interpersonal violence, which was fairly common, aroused little concern. If an encounter stopped short of murder or serious disfigurement the authorities were inclined to look the other way. They were far more concerned with maintaining the social and economic order and with public health. Politically, even this was by no means easy. The close proximity between rich and poor and the exclusivity of most town governments made social tension inevitable. Laborers, the urban poor, and even some of the journeymen lived in grinding poverty. Entire families often occupied a single, unheated room and subsisted on inadequate diets while the urban rich lived with an ostentation that even the feudal aristocracy could rarely equal. The contrast was a fertile source of discontent. Though riots and revolts were not always led by the poor but by prosperous malcontents who had been excluded from leadership in the commune, such people found it easy to play upon the bitter resentments of those who had nothing to lose but their lives.

Civil disturbances would reach a peak in the years after the Black Death, but urban patriciates had long been fearful of popular revolts. Disgruntled weavers and other cloth workers in the towns of thirteenth-century Flanders launched revolts based openly on class warfare. Everywhere the apprentices, who shared the violent impulses of most adolescent males, were available on call to reinforce the social and economic demands of the artisans. Riots were common, and rebellion was suppressed with extreme brutality.

In southern Europe, social tensions were muted though not eliminated by clientage. The factions that dominated city politics had tentacles that reached down to the artisan and the laboring classes. Mutual obligation, though unequal in its benefits, tended to moderate class feeling and reduce the social isolation of the patriciate, which, in Flemish and German towns, was far more extreme. In spite of this, Venice faced the specter of revolution in the late thirteenth century, and the political life of fourteenth-century Florence was dominated by a struggle between the major and minor guilds that revealed deep social divisions. Where city governments were backed by the authority of a strong monarchy, as in France, England, and Castile, discontent was easier to control.

The commercial revolution of the Middle Ages marked a turning point in the history of the West. The years of relative isolation were over. By the mid-thirteenth century, even the most remote European villages were touched, at least peripherally, by an economy that spanned the known world. Trading connections gave Europeans access to the gold and ivory of Africa, the furs and amber of Russia, and the spices of the Far East. Even China, at the end of the long Silk Road across central Asia, was within reach, and a few Europeans, among whom the Venetian Marco Polo (1254–1324) is the most famous, traveled there. Few rural communities were in any sense dependent upon long distance trade and most were still largely self-sustaining, but their horizons had been broadened immeasureably.

The towns, themselves the products of trade, were the connecting links between the agrarian hinterland in which most Europeans lived, and the great world outside. They were also the cultural and intellectual catalysts for society as a whole. The requirements of business and of participation in government demanded literacy. The intensity of urban life encouraged vigorous debate. Some measure of intellectual life therefore flourished within the city walls. At the same time the tendency of surplus wealth to concentrate in cities permitted an investment in culture that was far beyond the capacity of even the greatest agricultural estates. Much of that investment was inspired by civic pride. If funds were available, city councils were prepared to support the building and decoration of churches or other public buildings and to lay out substantial sums for festivals and celebrations whose chief purpose was to demonstrate the superiority of their town over its neighbors. The absurd competition over the height of church towers may have been unproductive and at times hazardous, but it symbolized a spirit that produced much of medieval art and architecture.

Even the strife endemic to medieval towns had its positive side. Resistance to social injustice reflected the vitality of ancient ideals. Ordinary people continued to believe that the town was, or should be, a refuge for those seeking personal freedom and economic opportunity. They demonstrated by their actions that the Greco-Roman ideal of civic participation was far from dead. Medieval cities may often have been deficient and even brutal in their social arrangements, but they preserved important values that had no place in the feudal countryside. As the institutional matrix for creating, preserving, and disseminating the Western cultural tradition, the town had, by the thirteenth century, replaced the monastery.

# CHAPTER 11

# MATERIAL AND SOCIAL LIFE
# IN THE MIDDLE AGES

## CHAPTER OUTLINE

Though towns had become important, more than 90 percent of all medieval Europeans still lived in the countryside. Because society was organized along rigidly hierarchical lines, family and behavioral norms varied greatly according to class (see tables 11.1 and 11.2). Peasants and their feudal overlords, in effect, inhabited different worlds. In some cases, they spoke different languages even though they lived on the same land. A useful comparison between these two styles of life must take into consideration not only their physical environments, but also the impact of chivalric values on the feudal class and the wide variety of social and economic strategies adopted by peasants to ensure an often precarious survival.

## The Ecology of Medieval Life: The Medieval Diet

The material life of medieval Europe was not unlike that of antiquity in several important respects and would remain substantially unchanged until the industrial revolution. The biological regime established by the Neolithic revolution remained in effect. Grain remained the basic food. Wheat was preferred, but millet, spelt, barley, oats, and rye were also staples, especially among the poor. Ground into flour and then baked as bread or served in the form of gruels and porridges, grains were the staff of life and provided most of the calories in the average person's diet.

Bread was commonly baked outside the home because medieval ovens were large brick affairs that consumed great quantities of fuel. Several hours were required to heat them to the proper temperature, and economies of scale demanded that many loaves be baked at the same time. Only the households of the very rich, with their dozens of servants and retainers, required ovens of their own or could afford to dispense

## TABLE 11.1

### Wages and Earnings in Thirteenth-Century England

The relationship between earnings and prices is an important measure of living standards. This table provides estimated average earnings for several occupations in medieval England. Women, then as now, earned far less than men for the same work. The annual wage of a mason reflects the fact that bad weather shortened the number of days he could work. For the same reason, a carpenter doing outdoor work would make less than the amount noted below. There were twelve pennies (d.) in a shilling (s.) and twenty shillings in a pound (£). The wages for skilled laborers increased by 40 to 50 percent after the Black Death.

| Occupation | Per day | Per year |
|---|---|---|
| | | **Estimated earnings** |
| Agricultural laborer | | |
| Boy | 1/2d. | |
| Female | 1d. | £1.7s. 3d. |
| Male | 2d. | £2.14s.6d. |
| Carpenter | 3d.–3 1/2d. | £4 |
| Mason | 5d.–6d. | £4. 8s.5d. |
| Peasant family with 20 acres | | £4 |
| Royal huntsman | 7 1/2d. | |
| Rural priest | | £5–£15 |
| Sawyer | 3 1/2d.–4d. | £5 |
| Stonecutter | 4d. | £5. 8s. |
| Thatcher's assistant (female) | 1d. | £1.7s. 3d. |
| Town priest | | £75–100 |
| Unskilled laborer | 2d. | £2.14s.6d. |

Source: Figures abstracted from John Burnett, *A History of the Cost of Living* (Harmondsworth: Pelican Books, 1969), pp. 17–54.

## TABLE 11.2

### Prices in Thirteenth-Century England

The prices listed below are averages only. In reality, the medieval family had to contend with wild fluctuations according to the harvests.

| Product | Average price |
|---|---|
| Ale (per gallon) | 1/4d.–3/4d. |
| Bread (per loaf, weight varied) | 1/4d.–1/2d. |
| Candle wax (per pound) | 4d.–5d. |
| Capons (each, fully fattened) | 2d.–3d. |
| Eggs (per 100) | 4d. |
| Hens (per 1) | 1/2d. |
| Pears (per 100) | 3 1/2d. |
| Pepper (per pound) | 10d.2s. |
| Pike (per 1) | 6s.8d. |
| Salt herrings (per 10) | 1d. |
| Second-quality malt—2 quarters (1 year supply of ale for 4) | 7s. 7d. |
| Sugar (per pound) | 1s.–2d. |
| Wine (per quart) | £1.3s. 6d. |
| Wheat—4 quarters (sufficient for a family of 4 for 1 year) | 1d. |

Source: Figures taken from John Burnett, *A History of the Cost of Living* (Harmondsworth: Pelican Books), 1969, pp. 17–54.

with the services of the village baker. Many different kinds of bread existed, ranging from the fine white loaves and cakes prized by the nobles and high-ranking clergy to coarse breads made of rye or of oats and mixed grains. An important consideration in the grading of bread was the proportion of bran left in the flour. This created a strange paradox: The lower grades of bread consumed by the poor were often higher in nutritional quality than was the bread of the rich with its bleached, highly refined, wheaten flour. Another oddity of the baker's trade was that in many countries the price of a loaf of bread was fixed by law or custom but the size

was not. A ha'penny loaf in England always cost 1/2 d., but its weight might vary radically according to the price of grain. The shape and appearance of loaves was a matter of local preference and differed widely from region to region. Whatever its form or content, baked bread was often too expensive for the very poor, especially on a regular basis. Unbaked bread, or gruel, could be cooked at home and was commonly eaten by all classes for its economy and ease of preparation.

Baked or unbaked, bread accounted for at least 50 percent of a rich family's diet and for more than 80 percent of the calories consumed by poor people. The price and availability of grain was therefore a valid measure of living standards because few substitutes were available and a bad harvest brought widespread misery. Rice was expensive and little known outside parts of Spain and the Middle East until the fifteenth century. It seems to have been consumed largely by wealthy invalids. In some upland areas, chestnuts were ground and baked into a coarse but nutritious bread. In most areas the best insurance against hunger was to grow several kinds of grain at different seasons.

A diet of bread was monotonous and poor in virtually every nutritional element save carbohydrates. Whenever possible, people tried to supplement it with other foods, but their choices were limited. Protein was provided mainly by dried peas, beans, lentils, or chickpeas that were cooked into a wide variety of soups and stews. Meat was rare except on the tables of the feudal aristocracy. Their chief leisure pastime was hunting, and they tended to consume vast quantities of game, seasoned after the twelfth century with powerful spices from the East and washed down with great drafts of wine or beer. Many peasants could not afford to keep animals at all, though ducks and chickens were raised for their eggs and stewed or made into soup when they had passed their prime. Those with capital or excess land might have some hogs or a cow. Even for them, meat was likely to be a seasonal delicacy. The cost of feeding livestock over the winter was high, and even the wealthier peasants slaughtered their animals in the fall, eating some and preserving the rest by smoking or salting. By Lent, this had been consumed, which probably meant that the prohibition against eating flesh in the holy season caused little hardship.

Hunting and fishing provided other dietary supplements, though in many areas both fish and game belonged to the lord and poaching was discouraged by ferocious penalties. Even the gathering of nuts in the forest might be prohibited. Other sources of protein were milk and cheese, and salted herring became increasingly important as an item of commerce in the thirteenth century. Owing to the widespread use of salt as a preservative and to the general monotony of diets, scholars believe that medieval people consumed many times the quantity of salt that Westerners are accustomed to eating today.

Fresh fruits and vegetables were also rare. Those who possessed a kitchen garden might have a fruit tree or a cabbage patch, but many of today's most common vegetables were either unknown or raised, such as lettuce, for medicinal purposes. Onions and garlic, however, were common, as were indigenous spices such as thyme, rosemary, basil, and marjoram. Honey was the primary sweetener. Sugar was largely unknown and remained prohibitively expensive until the seventeenth century when it could be imported in quantity from the New World.

A wide variety of fermented beverages completed the medieval diet. Wine was rarely produced north of the forty-ninth parallel (roughly the latitude of Paris), though it was consumed everywhere, especially by the rich. North of the wine districts, the popularity of mead, a drink made from fermented honey, declined during the Middle Ages while that of cider appears to have increased. Beer, or "liquid bread," was an important food supplement throughout all of central and northern Europe. Properly speaking, medieval beer was a form of ale. It was brewed from malted grain, preferably barley, using the top fermentation process. Hops were sometimes used on the continent but never in the British Isles. The result was a dark, rather sweet concoction that resembled the stouts and Scotch ales of today. Bottom fermentation, which produces lager or pilsner beers, was invented by the Germans in the fifteenth century. Brewing was usually done in the home and, like other aspects of the beverage trade, was dominated by women. It was an important economic sideline for those families who could afford the vats and other equipment. A skilled woman who was otherwise housebound by small children could manage the process. Tea, coffee, and tobacco were as yet unknown in the West, while alcohol, distilled in alembics on a small scale, was used primarily for medicinal purposes. Water was regarded with suspicion because it was thought to cause an imbalance of humors, an impression no doubt created by the effects of drinking from polluted sources.

The nutritional value of medieval diets is difficult to determine. It varied widely according to region and social class and tended to fluctuate with the seasons. Autumn, when trees bore their fruit and animals were killed for the winter, was usually a time of relative abundance, while spring, for all its promise of harvests to come, was the leanest of seasons. Important as they were, even these variables were overridden by considerations of price and availability. Fluctuations based on the relative scarcity or abundance of different commodities were dramatic and often terrifying, especially for the poor who had limited opportunities to store food. The failure of a single harvest could lead to hunger for those who were economically marginal.

The best balance between protein, fats, and carbohydrates was probably found in pastoral villages and on the tables of rich townsfolk. Urban laborers and peasants on manors whose primary crop was grain suffered chronic deficiencies of everything except carbohydrates. Everyone else fell somewhere in between, though the feudal aristocracy may be suspected of eating too much animal protein. The concept of vitamins was unknown. The general scarcity of fresh fruits and vegetables ensured that minimum daily requirements would rarely have been met by anyone and deficiencies were probably common. The poor in particular were often deformed by rickets or goiter and likely were physically smaller than those with better access to protein in youth. The average height of an adult male was probably not much above five feet, though this differed widely by class and region.

◆
## Disease and Demography

Inadequate nutrition continued to affect population rates in several ways. The number of live births is determined in large part by the rate of conception and by maternal nutrition, both of which are directly related to diet. A third factor, obstetrical technique, is also important but changed little until the revolutionary developments of the nineteenth and twentieth centuries.

Rates of conception in a given population are determined in part by the total number of childbearing years available to a woman. Malnutrition, obstetrical accidents, and epidemic disease shortened life expectancy and reduced the childbearing years dramatically. They were also reduced by a far higher age of first menstruation than is now common. Though marriages were sometimes contracted at an early age, especially among the upper classes, medieval women are thought to have reached puberty at an average age of seventeen as opposed to today's average of 12.4. Nutrition is usually blamed for the difference. Inadequate nutrition can also prevent ovulation in mature women, which probably reduced conception rates even further.

After conception, poor maternal diet led to a high rate of stillbirths and complications during pregnancy. If a child were brought to term it then faced the hazards of childbirth. Babies were normally delivered at home in unsanitary conditions. The midwives who delivered babies were often experienced, but they knew nothing of sterilization and lacked the most elementary equipment (see illustration 11.1). Forceps, for example, were not invented until the middle of the eighteenth century. Though Trotula, a woman physician, taught at the University of Salerno in the thirteenth century and published a treatise on obstetrics, most medieval physicians were men and knew no more than a competent midwife. They were, in any case, available only to the rich.

Infants who survived the obstetrical techniques of the day then faced the possibility that their mothers would be unable to nurse. Malnutrition interferes with lactation as does the stress of poverty, exposure to war, and other forms of physical and mental insecurity. The problem could be solved by turning the child over to a wet nurse, but this was not always a satisfactory solution. The wet nurse was normally another woman in the village who had milk to spare because she had recently lost

**Illustration 11.1**

⁄⁄⁄ **Midwives at Work.** Midwives, or perhaps a midwife assisted by relatives, are trying to hasten a birth by shaking the mother up and down. Such obstetric techniques ensured a high rate of mortality for infants and mothers alike.

her own baby. She had to be paid—a serious problem for a poor woman—and did not always care for the child as she might have cared for her own. Babies put out for nursing had a higher mortality rate than those who remained at home. Either way, the children of poorly nourished mothers were often weak and susceptible to disease. The birthrate was therefore by modern standards low and the rate of infant mortality high. Valid statistics are unavailable for medieval times, but deaths presumably ranged from 30 to 70 percent in the first two years of life, depending upon such variables as current food supply and the presence or absence of epidemics.

In hard times, personal decisions hindered population growth as well. Those whose own survival was in doubt abstained from sex, used the primitive means of contraception then available (notably *coitus interruptus*), or, when all else failed, resorted to infanticide. Abortion, though not unknown, was extremely dangerous, and most women preferred to carry a child to term even if they could not afford to keep it. Infanticide may

## TABLE 11.3

### Life Expectancy in the Middle Ages

The figures below represent the estimated life expectancy of male landholders in medieval England. They are arranged by dates of birth and demonstrate the substantial changes in mortality that occurred over time. Life expectancy for women was probably somewhat shorter owing to the dangers of childbirth.

| Age | 1200–76 | 1276–1301 | 1301–26 | 1326–48 | 1348–76 | 1376–1401 | 1401–25 | 1425–50 |
|-----|---------|-----------|---------|---------|---------|-----------|---------|---------|
| 0   | 35.3    | 31.3      | 29.8    | 27.2    | 17.3    | 20.5      | 23.8    | 32.8    |
| 10  | 36.3    | 32.2      | 31.0    | 28.1    | 25.1    | 24.5      | 29.7    | 34.5    |
| 20  | 28.7    | 25.2      | 23.8    | 22.1    | 23.9    | 21.4      | 29.4    | 27.7    |
| 30  | 22.8    | 21.8      | 20.0    | 21.1    | 22.0    | 22.3      | 25.0    | 24.1    |
| 40  | 17.8    | 16.6      | 15.7    | 17.7    | 18.1    | 19.2      | 19.3    | 20.4    |
| 60  | 9.4     | 8.3       | 9.3     | 10.8    | 10.9    | 10.0      | 10.5    | 13.7    |
| 80  | 5.2     | 3.8       | 4.5     | 6.0     | 4.7     | 3.1       | 4.8     | 7.9     |

Source: Carlo Cipolla, *The Middle Ages*, Fontana Economic History of Europe (London: Colliers, 1973), p. 47. Used by permission of HarperCollins Publishers Ltd.

have been emotionally devastating to the mother and murder in the eyes of the law, but it was easy to conceal in a world where infant mortality was common and doctors scarce. Its incidence in the Middle Ages is therefore a matter of controversy. Contemporary religious and civil authorities thought it was common, and many an old folk tale recalls its horrors.

Abandonment, the most common alternative to infanticide, appears to have declined sharply in the prosperous years of the eleventh and twelfth centuries. It became more frequent as population pressures increased during the thirteenth century and revived between the famines of 1315–17 and the Black Death. As in ancient times, estimating how many of these abandoned children survived is impossible. If hard times persisted, less dramatic forms of birth control came into play. People simply refused to marry and remained celibate, sometimes for life. The marriage rate almost invariably declined during periods of economic stress.

Those who survived infancy still faced heavy odds. Medieval life expectancy was probably in the low thirties at birth (see table 11.3). Averages, however, can be deceiving. Many people lived into their fifties, and the proportionate number of individuals over the age of eighty-five was probably not much smaller than it is today. The primary causes of early death remained disease, often complicated by malnutrition, and the inadequate treatment of wounds and injuries.

The spread of disease was encouraged by crowding and by a widespread indifference to personal hygiene. In the absence of a germ theory, personal cleanliness was a matter of aesthetics, and bathing was regarded with suspicion by Christian thinkers who associated it with pagan luxury or with Jewish and Muslim rituals. Its alternative was difficult and expensive to achieve. By the twelfth century, firewood, like timber, had become scarce and expensive everywhere in western and central Europe. Bathing in cold water in an unheated room was unattractive. Most people had better uses for their limited supplies of precious firewood. Rashes and skin infections were therefore common. Crowding, often for warmth, and the custom of keeping livestock and pets in the home added to the problem by ensuring that many Europeans would play host to a variety of insect pests. This encouraged the spread of epidemics because lice and fleas carried infectious diseases including typhus and, later, plague.

Contaminated drinking water accounted for another group of deadly ailments, while airborne viruses and bacteria were as numerous as they are today. Here, too, the absence of a germ theory rendered public health measures ineffective. Water that looked clean was thought to be safe, and indoor air was purified by scenting it with perfumes and herbs. Malaria, endemic in southern Europe, was thought to be caused by breathing miasmas, or foul air. It is actually spread by mosquitoes. The offending parasite remains in the bloodstream for life, causing recurring attacks of chills and fever even if it fails to kill its victim outright. Those weakened by malnutrition or other ailments were the most likely to succumb.

## ◆ DOCUMENT 11.1 ◆

## The Treatment of Disease

*The following remedies are taken from a standard medical text,* Rosa Anglica practica medicine a capite ad pedes *(The Rose of England, the Practice of Medicine from the Head to the Feet), by John of Gaddesden (1280–1361), a graduate of Oxford and of the medical school at Montpellier. The treatments he prescribes are a typical mixture of common sense and natural magic.*

**For smallpox:** [I]n the case of the noble son of the English king, when he was infected with this disease . . . I made everything around the bed to be red.

**For tuberculosis:** 1). Keep in check the catarrh and the rheumata; 2). cleanse the body; 3). divert and draw away the matter [of the disease] to a different part; 4). strengthen the chest and head so that they do not take up the matter, and that it there multiply; 5). cleanse and dry up the ulcers and expel the matter from them; 6). consolidate them; 7). restrain and cure the cough by using demulcent drinks with ointments and stupes; 8). assist the patient to sleep; 9). strengthen and bring back the appetite; 10). keep in check the spitting of blood; 11). do what can be done to make the breathing more easy and to remove the asthma and the hoarseness; 12). regulate the way of life so far as the six non-naturals; 13). cure the putrid or hectic fever which goes with the disease. As to food, the best is the milk of a young brunette with her first child, which should be a boy; the young woman should be well-favored and should eat and drink in moderation.

**For toothache:** Again, write these words on the jaw of the patient: In the name of the Father, the Son, and the Holy Ghost, Amen. +Rex+Pax+Nax+ in Christo Filio, and the pain will cease at once as I have often seen. . . . Again, some say that the beak of a magpie hung from the neck cures pain in the teeth and the uvula and the quinsy. Again, when the gospel for Sunday is read in the mass, let the man hearing mass sign his tooth and head with the sign of the holy Cross and say a pater noster and an ave for the souls of the father and mother of St. Philip, and this without stopping; it will keep them from pain in the future and will cure that which may be present, so say trustworthy authorities.

Clendening, L., ed. *A Source Book of Medical History,* pp. 83–85. New York: Dover, 1960.

Some medieval diseases appear to have no modern counterparts, a tribute to the rapidity with which viruses and bacteria can evolve. Others, such as measles and chicken pox, the great killers of late antiquity, were now restricted largely to children. The population had acquired an hereditary immunity. But even childhood diseases were capable of carrying off the weak or poorly nourished. In general, malnutrition weakened resistance to every ailment and, like crowding, was a silent partner in the high rate of mortality. Towns may have been more dangerous than the countryside, but poverty, whatever its location, was likely to prove fatal.

Death by injury or misadventure was also common. Upper-class males were likely to destroy themselves in battle or in hunting accidents. Villagers were exposed to the inevitable hazards of agricultural life. Infants fell into fires, crawled into the path of carts, or were mauled by hogs. Adults fell out of trees while picking fruit or gathering firewood or toppled into wells while drawing water. They severed limbs and arteries with their scythes or accidentally brained each other with their flails. Drink and the absence of illumination by night also took its toll. Happy harvesters fell off their carts and were run over while people returning from late-night drinking bouts drowned in ditches or passed out and froze to death in the road.

Against this formidable array of human ills, doctors were as helpless as they had been in antiquity. Their theories and the remedies available to them had changed little. By the thirteenth century many physicians were university-trained, but they tended to concentrate on diagnosis and the prescription of drugs, most of which were of dubious value (see document 11.1). The surgeons who, unlike physicians, performed medical procedures were educated by apprenticeship. They operated without sterilization and without anesthetics. Broken bones could sometimes be set, but wounds were likely to become infected with fatal results. In any case, most people had no access to either physicians or surgeons and relied upon folk remedies about which little is known. They were probably as effective as the nostrums advocated by learned doctors. Survival still depended upon good luck, heredity, and the recuperative powers of the patient.

All of these things affected the distribution of population. Medieval people were younger and had far shorter working lives than their modern counterparts. Their reproductive lifetimes were also shorter. For people of mature years (aged thirty to fifty), men may have outnumbered women, primarily because so many women died in childbirth. At the same time, population levels were more closely related to epidemics and to fluctuations in the food supply than they have been since the industrial revolution. The doubling of the European population between the eleventh and the thirteenth centuries was a direct consequence of increased agricultural production, but because that increase was proportionate, nutrition did not improve. Instead, population densities, though still low by modern standards, had begun by the end of the thirteenth century to push against the limits of available land. Events would prove that when production and population were so closely balanced, epidemic disease or a series of failed harvests could serve as a corrective to demographic growth.

## The Rural Upper Classes

Knightly families made up only a small part of Europe's population. Most villages had no lord in residence, but such was the legal and economic power of the feudal class that the castle or manor house cast a figurative shadow over the entire countryside.

The symbol of feudal authority, the castle underwent an architectural metamorphosis during the eleventh and twelfth centuries. Kings and the greater vassals had always tried to build in stone. As society's wealth increased, the practice was extended to relatively modest structures. Wooden palisades gave way to stone curtains with towers spaced at regular intervals on the Roman model. The keep, or central stronghold, became more liveable, if not luxurious. Windows, side aisles, and even fireplaces were added to the hall. Separate kitchens and chapels became commonplace, while private chambers were built for the use of the lord and his immediate family. This tended to remove them from the life of the hall and introduced the revolutionary idea of personal privacy. In politically secure areas, stone manor houses were built on the same model without troubling about walls. Setting the hall above a raised ground floor and entering it by a staircase was protection enough.

Illustration 11.2

The Moat and Gatehouse of the Bishop's Palace, Wells, England. The fortifications were built in 1340 to protect the bishop from his tenants.

These developments reflected a basic change, not only in the function of the castle, but also in the feudal class as a whole. With the passing of the great raids, society no longer needed the protection of the knights and the purely military function of the castles was minimized. Castle building declined at the end of the twelfth century. Its revival, at the beginning of the thirteenth century, was primarily a response to growing social unrest (see illustration 11.2). Some structures, such as the great Welsh castles of Edward I, were intended to hold territory newly annexed by an expanding monarchy. Both purposes involved an element of political theater. The castles built to protect country gentlemen against their tenants, like those built to overawe the Welsh, were stronger and more sophisticated than any attack that was likely to be made against them (see illustration 11.3).

Illustration 11.3

Harlech Castle, Wales. Built by Edward I of England between 1283 and 1289, Harlech Castle's chief purpose was to serve as a visible symbol of English power. The Welsh were not rich, numerous, or threatening to a far weaker structure.

## The Evolution of the Chivalric Ideal

The knights, too, became more decorative and theatrical with the passage of time. As the importance of their original function began to diminish, the concept of nobility began to evolve in its place. The qualities of courage, loyalty, strength, and courtesy came to be regarded as hereditary attributes. The process began with the introduction of dubbing to knighthood in the late eleventh century. Knights were then regarded, in the language of the church, as an *ordo* or order in their own right, a social institution instead of a mere body of fighting men. Before long a priest customarily blessed the knight's arms and invested him with them in a rite reminiscent of ordination. This was perhaps inevitable when crusades were becoming the last legitimate outlet for military virtues. Finally, in the century after 1130, knighthood was transformed into a hereditary privilege. In 1140, Roger II of Sicily declared that only the descendants of knights would be admitted to knighthood. By 1187, it had become illegal to knight a peasant in the empire, and peasants were prohibited from carrying a sword or lance. Similar provisions were found in almost every European kingdom by the second half of the twelfth century.

Such prohibitions were not airtight. Members of the urban patriciate were sometimes able to achieve knightly rank, but their elevation was neither cheap nor easy. In a reversal of earlier practice, peasants were excluded from knighthood almost by definition. To forestall the proliferation of titles, kings achieved a statutory monopoly over the granting of knighthoods and forbade the ancient custom whereby any knight could make another. At the same time, they created a profusion of counts and barons to distinguish between their greater and lesser vassals. This process reached a peak in the empire, where the status of noble families was eventually graded in exquisite detail. When the military revolution of the fourteenth century brought commoners back to the battlefield in great numbers, such policies had to be reversed. Kings retained the sole right to grant titles but bestowed them once again on people of humble origin. The feudal nobility, whose importance in war was by this time greatly diminished, regarded such creations as an outrageous betrayal of chivalry.

Legal developments went hand in hand with an expansion of the chivalric ideal. What had once been little more than a prescription for courage and loyalty evolved into an all-encompassing moral and esthetic code. The church, in its drive to influence all European institutions, bore partial responsibility for the change. Courtesy, clemency to a fallen enemy, and the respectful treatment of women became hallmarks of the knight, though such behavior was extended only to members of the noble class. Peasants could still be raped and murdered with impunity under the laws of war.

Along with these presumed virtues went a style of speech and personal carriage that clearly set the knight

**A Tournament.** The tournament provided knights with training, entertainment, and, in some cases, wealth. This illumination captures the pageantry and spectacle that fascinated onlookers and participants alike.

and his lady apart from the rest of society. It could not be easily imitated because peasants no longer associated with the nobility on a regular basis and had few opportunities to observe them. The speech, movements, and gestures of ordinary men and women were eventually stigmatized as uncouth and boorish.

Chivalric values were disseminated by the troubadours and by the kings of arms who presided over the conventions of heraldry and acted to some extent as arbiters of taste. As literacy spread, the oral tradition of the troubadours was written down and circulated in manuscript form as the romance. Five works based upon the legendary court of King Arthur were composed by Chrétien de Troyes sometime after 1164 and formed the basis of an entire literary genre. Many others of similar importance also existed. A body of lyric poetry that exalted chivalric love served as further reinforcement for the new values. The language of this literature was French, and French, which had spread from England to Sicily by the Normans, became the language of the chivalric class. Social separation was now virtually complete. In some regions, knights could no longer speak the language of their tenants.

Theoretically, war remained the center of noble life and the justification for its privileges. Males were still expected to master the profession of arms in youth and practice it until age, wounds, or ill health permitted a dignified retirement. In practice, this ideal was gravely weakened by the development of hereditary knighthood. In the first feudal age, men who lacked the requisite ability commonly remained squires for life. In the twelfth and thirteenth centuries they could expect to be knighted regardless of their achievements.

Relative peace was an even greater threat to the knightly ethos. In the absence of Vikings or Magyars, the Crusades became a useful outlet for martial talents. As the interval between crusades grew longer, tournaments gradually took the place of war as the central preoccupation of the feudal class. Tournaments were a stylized form of combat in which two mounted knights, generally separated by a barrier, attempted to unhorse one another with their lances (see illustration 11.4). They might then attempt to fight on foot with swords or other weapons. The rules were elaborate and varied widely according to the occasion. It was, in other words, a sport. The bouts were refereed; murder was not the primary object but serious injuries and fatal mishaps were unavoidable. Women, who participated only as spectators, were a powerful symbolic presence. A knight entered the lists as champion of a particular lady and wore her scarf or some more intimate garment as a token of her favor. Because the conventions of chivalric love encouraged adulterous flirtations, the lady was not ordinarily expected to be his wife.

For all its frivolity, the importance of the tournament as a social ritual should not be underestimated. Those who were good at it could expect great rewards. A penniless younger son and knight errant such as William the Marshall (d. 1219) could parlay his athletic talent into an advantageous marriage, an estate, and a remarkable political career that ended with his appointment as regent for the King of England.

This was the point of the whole system. Beneath the veneer of chivalry, the advancement of personal and family interests through the accumulation of estates was a compelling goal. A sense of lineage developed early in feudal families and was strengthened immeasurably by the concept of nobility. Kinship ties were therefore stronger among the feudal classes than in other segments of society. The possession of landed estates ensured that the extended family would be a relatively common form of household organization.

For the same reason, weddings were almost invariably arranged, often at an early age. The disposition of great properties could not be entrusted to the vagaries of youthful lust. This may help to account for the fascination with adultery that characterized chivalric literature. However, a surprising number of noble marriages appear to have been happy and mutually supportive. The women of the feudal class were often formidable personages, capable of managing an estate or defending their castle against a siege in the absence of their husbands. Some, such as Matilda of Tuscany or Eleanor of Aquitaine, were major political figures in their own right. Virtually all were at home in the world of political intrigue. Their survival and that of their children often depended upon it.

Clientage, of which feudalism was in some respects a formalized expression, was also highly developed at this level of society. Almost everyone sought the favor and protection of those more powerful than themselves and tried wherever possible to develop clients and retainers of their own. The importance of the castle and even of the manor house was measured less by the grandeur of the masonry than by the hospitality of its hall. The greater households often included not only the lord and his nuclear family but also a respectable number of collateral relatives, stewards, servants, knights, and other retainers who owed him their allegiance and lived at least partially from his bounty. This much, at least, had changed little, and as always, the cost was born by the peasant.

Ironically, these developments took place as the economic fortunes of the feudal class began to decline. The greater availability of specie in the twelfth century led to the widespread commutation of feudal obligations for cash. Landholders greeted this development with enthusiasm because it increased their liquidity, but they made the mistake of commuting payments hitherto made in labor or in kind for fixed sums of money. These sums, not the proportional values that had determined them, quickly became enshrined in law and precedent while their value was slowly consumed by inflation (see table 11.4). A consequent decline in the real value of rents was masked during the thirteenth century by a strong demand for

### ⊠ TABLE 11.4 ⊠
### The Expenses of the Rich

An earl's income in thirteenth-century England might range from £1000 per year to more than £5000. From this a nobleman or noblewoman was expected to maintain a large household of servants and spend huge sums on food, building, travel, and recreation. A single household, for example, might require forty horses and more than one hundred servants, and spices were consumed in large quantities. Some of the costs, few of which would ever have been incurred by a peasant, are given below.

| Household item | Cost |
| --- | --- |
| Bonnet | 16d. |
| Candlewax | 5d. per pound |
| Cloth cloak | 3s. 4d. |
| Fowler | 3s. 4d. per week |
| Fur coverlet | £20 |
| Hunting bow | 2s. 4d. |
| Hunting falcon | £5–10 |
| Huntsman | 7 1/2d. per day |
| Lady's gold girdle | £37. 12s. |
| Minstrel | 12d. per day |
| Pack of hounds | £100 per year |
| Saddle horse | £5–27 |
| Stockings | 4s. the pair |
| War horse | £40–80 |
| Spices and delicacies (per pound) | |
| Almonds (5 pounds) | 1s. |
| Anise | 3d. |
| Black pepper | 10d.–2s. |
| Cloves | 3d. |
| Cumin | 2d.–10d. |
| Ginger | 10d.–2s.6d. |
| Horseradish | 3d. |
| Nutmeg | 3d. |
| Pomegranates | 6d. each |
| Rice | 1 1/2d. |
| Saffron | 10s.–14s. |
| Sugar | 1s.–2s. |

Source: Figures abstracted from John Burnett, *A History of the Cost of Living* (Harmondsworth: Pelican Books, 1969), pp. 31, 34–35, 37.

land created by population growth. When harvest failures were followed by the demographic collapse of 1347–50, property values fell as well and social tensions became insupportable.

# Medieval Society: The Village

In the High Middle Ages, 90 percent of all Europeans lived in villages and engaged directly in agriculture. They were not exclusively occupied with farming; many people had special skills that brought in supplementary income. Most communities could boast millers, carpenters, brewers, seamstresses, harness makers, blacksmiths, midwives, and other specialists, but these people also worked in the fields as needed and frequently held land in their own right. The wealthier peasants were more likely to have a trade than were their poorer neighbors, for a trade required skills as well as a substantial investment in tools or equipment.

The physical environment of medieval villages varied widely. The heart of a larger village was the parish church, which by the twelfth century was almost always of masonry construction. Timber churches continued to survive in northwest England, parts of Germany, and Scandinavia, but their numbers were declining. Lords frequently built or improved village churches as an act of piety and to increase their family's prestige. Some of them were, and are, architectural gems. Their cost was borne ultimately by the peasants in the form of dues and tithes, but the church was at least a form of expenditure that the villagers could enjoy. It was usually the only substantial building in the community unless the lord maintained a residence there.

The character of domestic architecture was determined by the availability of building materials and by the structure of families. In southern Europe, where timber had been scarce since biblical times, brick or stone construction was the rule. Peasant houses were sometimes large, having been expanded at various times to accommodate an increase in family size. If the family subsequently grew smaller, the permanence of the building materials often precluded the demolition of all or part of the house. This helps to explain why Mediterranean villages often appear larger today than their census figures indicate. It may also have encouraged the formation of extended families by making free space available to newly married couples.

Thanks to their sturdy construction, many communities in Spain, Italy, and southern France have changed little since the Middle Ages. Existing knowledge of northern villages is the product of painstaking archeological reconstruction. The use of wattle and daub (interwoven twigs or rushes covered by mud) or other impermanent materials meant that peasant housing in England, northern France, the Low Countries, and north Germany was often good only for a generation or two. Entire villages sometimes moved to a different location for reasons of health or economic advantage, leaving nothing behind but rubble and the outlines of their foundations.

In the days of Charlemagne, many houses were made of solid wood or logs, a practice that became prohibitively expensive with the passage of time (see document 11.2). By the end of the eleventh century, a house in a northern village was typically framed in wood and composed of bays or sections added together, usually in a linear pattern (see illustration 11.5). Bays could be built or torn down as needed because the walls were so flimsy that thieves sometimes broke through them rather than bothering with the door. Such homes were inexpensive. Newlyweds had little difficulty in setting up a place of their own, and people often had cottages built for them in their old age to separate them from their grown children. Though some houses had lofts or attics, true second stories were rare. Windows were few, small, and covered with wooden shutters, while chimneys were introduced only at the end of the Middle Ages. At the center of the house was a raised hearth, the smoke from which typically exited through a hole in the thatched roof. Most people went to bed at nightfall and rose at dawn. Interior lighting was available in the form of candles if a family could afford them. As the floors were of swept earth covered with straw or rushes, the danger of fire was ever present.

In these circumstances, cleanliness was as hard to achieve as safety. The interior of a peasant home was inevitably dark and smoky. Though the marks of vigorously wielded medieval brooms are still visible in archaeological digs, housekeeping inevitably fell below modern standards. This was in part because people lived in close proximity with their livestock. Most peasant homes, north or south, possessed a yard or garden and even outbuildings. Animals were often housed in a separate bay or in an unused room of the house. In one-room cottages, livestock might share the living space with humans.

The yard, croft, or close was an integral part of the family's living space. It was basically a walled or fenced-in working area in which children and animals wandered at will, and great efforts were made to prevent its disorder from invading the sleeping quarters. Drainage ditches and thresholds were the best defense, but muddy feet and wandering livestock were an inevitable part of the farmer's world. Dusting, however, was not. Most homes contained no furniture beyond the pallets on which people slept; their blankets, which were sometimes used as wraps in winter; and their cooking

## ◆ DOCUMENT 11.2 ◆

### The Timber Problem in Medieval Europe

*In 1140 Suger, abbot of Saint-Denis (near Paris), decided to construct a new church that would require twelve thirty-five-foot beams. His experience in a landscape virtually denuded of large trees indicates how serious the problem of adequate timber supplies had become.*

On a certain night, when I had returned from Matins, I began to think in bed that I myself should go through all the forests of these parts. . . . Quickly disposing of all duties and hurrying up in the early morning, we hastened with our carpenters, and with the measurements of the beams, to the forest called Ivelines. When we traversed our possession in the Valley of Chevreuse we summoned . . . the keepers of our own forests as well as men who know about the other woods, and questioned them under oath whether we would find there, no matter with how much trouble, any timbers of that measure. At this they smiled, or rather would have laughed at us if they had dared; they wondered whether we were quite ignorant of the fact that nothing of the kind could be found in the entire region, especially since Milon, the Castellan of Chevreuse . . . had left nothing unimpaired or untouched that could be used for palisades and bulwarks while he was long subjected to wars both by our Lord the King and Amaury de Montfort. We however—scorning what they might say—began with the courage of our faith as it were, to search the woods; and toward the first hour we found one timber adequate to our measure. Why say more? By the ninth hour or sooner, we had, through the thickets, the depths of the forest and the dense, thorny tangles, marked down twelve timbers (for so many were necessary) to the astonishment of all.

Panovsky, Erwin, trans. and ed. *Abbot Suger, on the Abbey Church of St. Denis.* Princeton, NJ: Princeton University Press, 1973.

**Illustration 11.5**

🗫 **A Peasant Cottage in Winter.** This depiction of a peasant cottage is from the *Tres riches heures* of the Duc de Berry by Paul, Herman, and Jean Limbourg (1413–16). The beehives, the number of animals in the close, and even the dresses of the women indicate that this was a wealthy household. The magnificent prayer book from which this illustration comes was intended to provide an idealized view of rural life.

This material simplicity extended to purely personal possessions as well. Like the lord in his hall, the peasant ate with his fingers and a knife. Stews and gruels were served from a wooden bowl or straight from the pot and eaten with wooden spoons. Soups were often drunk. Among the rich, a piece of coarse bread served as a plate for meat and was ideally given to the poor after it had absorbed the juices of the meal. On special occasions, the wealthy might eat from wooden trenchers. Even at formal banquets, two people might be expected to share a plate, a custom that sometimes contributed violence to the day's entertainment.

Clothing, for the peasant, consisted of little more than a homespun smock, leggings, and perhaps a hat for men, and a simple smock or dress for women. Shoes were normally reserved for bad weather. Until the late fourteenth century, peasants who could afford to do otherwise appear to have ignored the dictates of fashion. Most people seem to have owned only one set of working clothes and another outfit of better quality for

utensils. Castles and manor houses might contain a bedstead for the lord and cupboards for the storage of leftovers. Chairs were rare enough to be considered symbols of royalty. Much of medieval life was lived on the floor.

## ◆ DOCUMENT 11.3 ◆

### A Peasant Family in the Fields

*The following excerpt from* Peres the Plowman's Crede, *a long English poem by William Langland (c. 1330–c. 1400), provides a heartbreaking glimpse of peasant life.*

And as I went by the way, weeping for sorrow
I saw a poor man o'er the plow bending,
His coat was of a cloth that cary was called
His hood was full of holes and his hair seen through it.
With his shoes so worn and patched very thick
His toes pushed through as the fields he trod.
His hose o'erhung his gaiters all about
And he dragged in the mud as the plow he followed.
Two mittens had he, skimpy, made of rags,
The fingers uncovered and coated with mud.
This poor creature, beslimed in the mud almost to the ankle,
Four oxen before him, that feeble had become,
One might count the ribs, so pitiful they were.
Beside him his wife, with a long goad.
In a cutted skirt, cutted full high;
Wrapped in a winnowing sheet, to guard her from weather,
Barefoot on bare ice, so that the blood flowed.
And at the field's end lay a little basket
And therein a little child, covered in rags,
And twins of two years old upon another side.
And they all sang a song that was sorrow to hear,
They all cried a cry, a note full of woe—
The poor man sighed sore, and said "Children be still!"

Langland, William. *Peres the Ploughman's Crede,* trans. D. Resnick. In L. F. Schaefer et al., eds., *The Shaping of Western Civilization.* New York: Holt, Rinehart, and Winston, 1970.

or hired laborers as needed. They were more likely than poorer peasants to own draft animals and to graze livestock on the village common. If they were careful in planning their marriages or were able to form a business relationship with the lord or his steward they could become as wealthy as minor nobles. Their families tended to be larger than those of the poor and their houses were often substantial.

Perhaps the largest group in any community were smallholders whose land was insufficient to support their families, but who supplemented their earnings by leasing additional fields, practicing a trade, or engaging in occasional labor in return for food or wages. They usually had their own house and garden, and they might keep poultry or a hog. Below them on the economic scale were landless laborers whose situation was often precarious. Numbering perhaps a quarter of the community, they were dependent upon charity in hard times and sometimes resorted to petty theft. Small-scale pilfering was a common income supplement for other classes as well. Slavery, though still common in the cities of southern Europe, disappeared in the north and in rural areas during the twelfth century.

Social movement was extremely limited. The evolution of nobility as a social ideal opened an unbridgeable gap between the peasantry and those who bore arms. Wealthier peasants were sometimes able to place one of their children in the church, but even in this, the most egalitarian of medieval institutions, humble birth was a grave barrier to advancement. Within the narrow world of the village, wealth and social status could be increased through careful management, good marriage strategies, and luck. Over time, many families and a few individuals did so, but the pinnacle of ambition remained a place on the manorial court, control of a mill, or an appointment as one of the lord's stewards. Generally, the medieval villager had no choice other than to accept the status into which he or she had been born. To do otherwise would not only have been fruitless, it also would have run counter to the most cherished prejudices of an age in which stability was a paramount social goal.

Though stratified by wealth, the medieval village was a powerful, tightly knit social organism whose survival into modern times testifies to its adaptability. In size, it typically numbered between 250 and 500 inhabitants, with smaller villages being the more common. Many of its inhabitants were interrelated. However, the ecclesiastical prohibition against marrying one's relatives worked steadily against the pressures of isolation and an endemic distrust of strangers. People identified strongly with their village and tended to see it for what

church or festive occasions (see document 11.3). Both were washed when possible. Workday garments were worn until they fell apart. Children, once they were out of swaddling clothes, dressed like their parents.

Village society was stratified by wealth instead of by social class. The wealthier peasants held tenements or other lands on secure contracts. Such properties were often larger than they could work themselves, and they either sublet portions of their property to others

it was: a community made up exclusively of peasants, which, after the family, was their chief protection against a hostile world.

Cooperation was therefore an essential feature of village life, though the relative wealth of individual peasants varied immensely. At the very least, villagers had to maintain a united front in negotiating with outside forces that might pose a threat to their prosperity—their lord, the church, a city, or a neighboring village whose inhabitants tried to encroach on their lands or rights. If peasants seemed wily, grasping, and suspicious to outsiders it was because the outsiders were often trying to detach the peasants from their wealth.

Internally, some measure of cooperation was essential to the peasants' daily pursuits. In villages where the open field system was practiced, agricultural operations from plowing to harvesting were usually undertaken in common for efficiency's sake. In grazing areas, the rounding up and shearing of sheep was, and for the most part still is, a cooperative effort involving the entire population of the village. If the village possessed common lands, their use had to be regulated to prevent overexploitation, either by individuals or by the community as a whole. Peasants tended to be keenly aware of the limits of their local ecology and took great care to limit the number of animals that could be grazed on a particular parcel or the quantity of wood, nuts, and other products that could be harvested from woodlots. If the commons were planted to row crops, the land had to be allocated fairly. This was sometimes done on a customary basis. In Spain and in many other places allocation was often by lot.

The maintenance of what today would be called the village's infrastructure was also a community affair. The construction and repair of roads, bridges, and ditches may have been mandated by feudal obligation and was typically discharged by teams of peasants working in common. Villages were also capable of undertaking public improvements on their own. Private projects such as the construction or modification of a house or the digging of a drainage ditch around the close were usually undertaken with the help of friends or relatives. Such help was intended to be reciprocal. Labor exchanges were central to the peasant economy and are in themselves an extension of communal bonds.

Peasant communities also tried to control the social behavior of their inhabitants. The more prosperous villagers often sat on manorial courts that judged minor disputes within the village. Where the influence of the lord was weak, such matters might be dealt with by a council of village elders. The selection of village lead-

ers, including those who supervised communal labor and the allocation of common lands, remains something of a mystery. Some may have been elected. In most places they seem to have been chosen through an informal process of consensus building that avoided the confrontation of a vote.

Criminals were apprehended by what the English called a hue and cry, in which every able-bodied man was supposed to give chase if a crime were committed. This could be dangerous and was uncommon. Most villages were relatively peaceful, in part because everyone knew everyone else's business. Privacy, as in the towns, was unknown and probably would have been impossible to achieve. If an individual's behavior ran counter to prevailing local standards, he or she would be subjected to ridicule and abuse that in extreme cases might make life insupportable. In general, public opinion was a more powerful instrument of social control than courts or the bailiff.

## The Peasant Family

The structure of medieval family life varied immensely according to location, social class, and individual preference. It also varied over time as individual households adjusted to economic change and to the life cycles of their members. As a general rule, wealthier households were larger than those of the poor.

In northern Europe, the nuclear family predominated, at least among peasants. A married couple and their children lived together, rarely sharing their space with other relatives. When children married, they left the home and established a household of their own. Old people tried to maintain their independence as long as they could. The wasting diseases of old age were not prolonged as they are today by the miracles of modern medicine. If someone grew feeble or senile, they sometimes moved in with one of their grown children. That the elderly often preferred to board with another villager is a tribute to the relative weakness of kinship ties. Such an arrangement usually involved the transfer of land or other payments.

The nuclear family was also the most common form of household organization in Mediterranean Europe, but extended families in which adult siblings and grandparents lived under the same roof were not unusual. Many others lived as nuclear units in close proximity to their relatives and acted in common with them when necessary. Such behavior indicates that kinship obligations were more broadly defined than they were in the north. The phenomenon is probably related to the concept of the *domus*, or house, as a basic component of family identity.

In the north, the idea of family as a lineage group associated with a particular estate was largely restricted to the feudal aristocracy. The continuing presence of allodial land and the relative weakness of feudal ties in Mediterranean society extended the concept to relatively humble folk, though rarely to the very poor. In its extreme forms—the Catalan *masia*, for example—the name of the family, the stone house in which it lived, and the property upon which it was located were the same. The prevalence of family names among the more prosperous peasants reveals the degree to which *domus* was associated with family in a given region. In Italy, family names were well established in the twelfth century, while in England they did not become common among ordinary folk until after the Black Death. Those who did not own their own land could have adopted the custom in imitation of their social superiors, and with it the concept of familial obligation that it implies.

To southern Europeans with modest property and a name, the extended family was likely to be seen as a source of economic and social support. This created a sense of mutual obligation that many chose to ignore but that could be of great value in difficult times for those who did not. For them, the family was both a refuge and a protection against a hostile world. Some no doubt went further and agreed with Peter Lombard that those outside the family were *inimici*, or enemies. This, however, was a notion that disturbed jurists and helps to explain why the villages of Spain and Italy were as troubled by faction and vendetta as their cities.

The organization of all European families was typically patriarchal. Households dominated by widows have been recorded, as have phratries in which two or more brothers with their own nuclear families inhabited the same house. Such variants probably were family strategies adopted to meet specific conditions. Otherwise, the authority of the husband or father was universally recognized in law and custom. It was not an absolute authority over life and death and was typically modified by familial love, an emotion fully recognized by medieval writers from Augustine to Albertus Magnus. In extended families, the problem of authority was more complex. Decisions might sometimes require consensus, but one individual, usually a mature male characterized by greater wealth or force of character than the others, was generally acknowledged as the family's leader. This pattern was also found in the clientage groups that developed, as they had done in antiquity, from the economic or political success of prominent families.

The laws of inheritance had less to do with family organization than might be supposed. They, too, exhibit wide regional variations, but two main types emerged—partible and impartible. Partible inheritance provides equally for all heirs. It was a fundamental principle in Roman law and was far more common than its alternative, especially in continental Europe. Its chief disadvantage is that a multiplicity of holdings eventually results that are too small to support a family. Impartible inheritance leaves everything to a single heir. This preserves a family's estate while reducing most of its members to penury. Primogeniture, or exclusive inheritance by the eldest son, is the best known form of impartible inheritance, but in some peasant societies leaving everything to the youngest was the rule.

Everyone knew that partibility could impoverish and eventually destroy a family, while impartibility was grossly unfair and tended to destroy the family's bonds of affection. Many people therefore adopted strategies to circumvent the law or regional custom. Much of England, Scandinavia, and northern France had adopted primogeniture by the twelfth century. Bequeathing the bulk of a family's land to a single heir and making other provisions for noninheriting children while the parents were still alive became customary. A couple could also make special legacies in their wills that partially subverted the law's intent.

Where partibility was preferred, strategies varied widely. In Italy and southern France, siblings entered into a variety of arrangements (*consorterie* in Italian) that helped to preserve the integrity of the estate. Some sold or leased their portion to an elder brother in return for monetary or other considerations. Others agreed not to marry and remained on the family property. Such arrangements worked best when there was an extended family structure or, at the very least, a strong sense of family identity. In Castile, the practice of entailing parts of an estate on behalf of a single heir began as early as the thirteenth century. The grim alternatives were illustrated in places such as Galicia and parts of southwest Germany where partibility was strictly enforced. The inexorable subdivision of the land caused widespread misery among the peasants, while among the princely families of the empire it led to a bewildering proliferation of petty states.

## Marriage

The proportion of married people in the medieval population was undoubtedly lower than it is today, but most people eventually married. In the peasant societies of

## ✠ TABLE 11.5 ✠

### Average Age of Women at First Marriage

Most of the statistics in the following table are taken from sixteenth- and seventeenth-century sources because data were not compiled outside of Italy in the Middle Ages. They are probably a reasonable approximation of medieval figures because the age at which women married does not seem to have changed substantially in the preindustrial period. It did, however, fluctuate according to economic conditions, as the figures from Colyton, Elversele, and Amsterdam demonstrate. Note the disparity between the Florentine data and that from northern Europe.

| Place | Time | Age |
|---|---|---|
| Amiens (France) | 1674–78 | 25 |
| Amsterdam | 1626–27 | 25 |
| | 1676–77 | 27 |
| Elversele (Flanders) | 1608–49 | 25 |
| | 1650–59 | 27 |
| England | 1575–1624 | 21 |
| Titled nobility | 1625–75 | 22 |
| Village of Colyton | 1560–1646 | 27 |
| | 1647–1719 | 30 |
| Florence | 1351–1400 | 18 |
| | 1401–50 | 17 |
| | 1451–75 | 19 |

Source: Adapted from Carlo Cipolla, *Before the Industrial Revolution*, 2d. ed. (New York, N.Y.: W. W. Norton, 1980), p. 154.

northern Europe, this normally happened in the early or mid-twenties for both men and women, a pattern now regarded as the Western norm (see table 11.5). In southern Europe and among the upper classes, the custom was different. In Italy, husbands were on average seven to ten years older than their wives, and women were often married in their teens to men already in their thirties or older. The most extreme disparities were found in royal and princely families where marriages were used to cement political alliances and might be arranged when the bride was a mere child. Thankfully, such unions were not immediately consummated.

Freedom to choose one's mate was greatest at the lower end of the social scale. Arranged marriages were almost unknown among the landless poor, slightly more common among established peasants, and virtually obligatory among the rich. However, the wishes of the couple were not invariably ignored and even peasants did not marry as a general rule without seeking their parents' blessing. Like almost everything else connected with the institution of marriage, a wedding was usually the product of delicate and informal negotiations involving the couple, both families, and the village opinion makers. The degree to which the couple controlled the process was determined by local custom and family attitudes and varied enormously within the same village or social class.

When a couple publicly announced their intention to marry, village opinion generally permitted them to begin living together immediately. This practice was officially confirmed by the church at the beginning of the thirteenth century. In villages without a resident priest, or when the costs of a wedding could not immediately be met, this was often essential. If a child was born before the sacrament of marriage could be officially celebrated, that child was legitimate. The assumption was that the couple would marry as soon as the opportunity arose. Townspeople, wealthy peasants, and the aristocracy could afford to be less relaxed about such matters and tended to celebrate their family weddings with as much ostentation as possible. Wedding feasts were as central to medieval social life and folklore as they are today.

When a medieval woman married, she was expected to present her husband with a dowry. The early medieval custom of giving the bride a husband's gift had largely disappeared by the end of the twelfth century. The dowry was normally returnable if the husband died first. While he lived, he controlled it and all of the other resources owned by the couple. In some regions, the return of the dowry was all that a widow could legally expect from her husband's estate. In others, she was entitled to at least a portion of his property. As in all other aspects of inheritance law, many husbands found ways to subvert the system and provide other legacies for her support.

The choice, though, was his. Married women had few legal rights. They could not hold property in their own name. Though they were not to be killed or permanently maimed they could be beaten with impunity, and domestic violence appears to have been even more frequent than it is today. In some jurisdictions, women could not testify in court. Where they could, their testimony was not equal to that of a man. However, legal status did not always reflect the balance of power in everyday life. No two relationships were, or are, the same, and medieval marriages ranged from the abusive to the happily companionate. Medieval people presumably did not enter into marriage with modern expectations. The idea of romantic love was not yet fully developed and, to the degree that it existed at all, was associated with the adulterous conventions of chivalry.

Practical considerations were more important in the selection of a mate. Property, strength, temperance, and, in the case of wives, the ability to bear children, were essential. The hope was that, given these virtues, *caritas* would find a place in the household and a genuine affection would develop with time.

Many of these ideas and practices were a departure from those of the early Middle Ages. The church had adopted marriage as its own in the days of the Cluniac and Hildebrandine reforms and, in spite of its own mysogynistic traditions, had greatly improved the condition of women as a result. Concubinage was condemned if not eradicated, as was feudal interference in the marriage of vassals and tenants. Divorce, a catastrophe for women who had no means of support, was virtually eliminated for all but the very rich. Canon law, confirmed by the Fourth Lateran Council of 1215, defined the terms under which a wedding might take place and spelled out the impediments that might prevent it. Most of them involved prohibited degrees of relationship or consanguinity, including godparenthood. As the regulations were strictly enforced by parish priests, they posed a considerable hardship for the inhabitants of remote villages.

These efforts can be seen as a positive step toward the development of patrilineal descent and companionate marriages, but they did not assure domestic bliss. Hostility between the sexes remained a common theme in medieval writings. Evidence is available that many women deeply resented their subordinate status. Beginning in the early thirteenth century, increasing numbers sought refuge in the convent, and widows frequently chose not to remarry. A woman who was past the age of childbearing and who could claim property of her own experienced an immediate change of status upon the death of her husband. With her legal and personal rights restored, she could become a powerful figure in the village community. Some, such as Chaucer's Wife of Bath, remarried, but they did so usually to a younger, poorer man who posed little threat to their independence. Companionship aside, only the poor suffered from widowhood. Without property, a woman might have to depend upon the kindness of her surviving children or become a semioutcast living on the charity of her neighbors.

## Childhood, Old Age, and Death

In the natural law theories favored by the scholastic philosophers, the birth of children was the justification for marriage. A medieval child was brought into the world by the village midwife and baptized as quickly as possible, lest the terrible infant mortality of the day carry it into Limbo before its salvation was assured. So deep was this concern that the sacrament could be administered by a layman if no priest were available. Godparents, usually family friends, were designated to support the child if its parents should die. In southern Europe this role was sometimes given to a powerful friend or patron of the father. The baby was typically named for one of the godparents, a favored relative, or a patron saint. This practice, together with the limited number of names in contemporary use, sometimes resulted in more than one sibling having the same name. In everyday life, such children were differentiated by the appellations major or minor or by nicknames.

If possible, most women preferred to nurse their own babies. Infants were typically swaddled during the day. At night they sometimes slept with their mothers, though this practice was frowned upon because the mother might roll over in her sleep and smother the child. By the end of the first year children were permitted to crawl about on their own.

Medieval parents did not sentimentalize childhood as a world of innocence, but they loved their children and were emotionally affected by their loss. This would seem self-evident, but it has been the subject of a scholarly controversy. Parents also permitted their children to develop in stages that were not unlike those of today. Young children spent most of their time playing. As they grew older and stronger they took on responsibility for various tasks until, in their mid-to-late teens, they began to do the work of adults. For most children, this kind of informal apprenticeship was the only education that they would receive. Few villages had a school, and lords often claimed a fee from the parents for sending their children away. Fearing that workers would be lost to the manor, they also sought agreements that forbade children to enter the church.

The little that is known about child rearing practices comes from the end of the Middle Ages and seems to indicate that discipline was very harsh. This may not be applicable to earlier times. The fourteenth and fifteenth centuries were characterized by a deep fear of social disintegration and the perceived decline of parental authority. Criminals were punished more savagely than they had been before. Children, too, may have been increasingly victimized by the frustrations of society as a whole.

As efforts to circumvent the laws of inheritance indicate, every attempt was made to provide for a child's future. This included the possibility of orphanhood, which was not uncommon in a world of high mortality. Godparents were nominally responsible for the care of children whose parents had died. The task was more often undertaken by aunts, uncles, or other relatives. Stepparenting was also common because men, at least, tended to remarry upon the death of their wives. This created a form of extended family that has once again become common as a result of divorce. Legends about wicked stepmothers indicate that the new relationships were often difficult for all concerned. However, stepparents who loved their spouse's children as their own were common enough to be accepted as the ideal.

Wardship in any form created problems because children were sometimes financially or sexually exploited by their guardians. A substantial body of case law developed around these issues. Orphanages as such were unknown until the fourteenth century when foundling hospitals were opened in several Italian towns. The work of these institutions is not to be confused with oblation, in which children were given to the church by placing them in monastic houses at an early age. Such placements required a substantial donation. For the rich it was an effective means of providing a living for children without encumbering the family estate. The practice fell into disfavor during the twelfth and thirteenth centuries when churchmen began to realize that those consigned to a monastery or convent at the age of seven did not necessarily have a secure vocation.

The available evidence seems to indicate that medieval attitudes toward children were not radically different from those of today. Noble families sent their sons to learn courtesy and the profession of arms in the household of a powerful friend or patron. Townsmen sent their children to be apprenticed, and those who could afford to do so offered them to the church at an early age. None of these practices implied indifference. They were in some ways analogous to sending a child to boarding school, and the normal expectation was that contact with the family would be maintained or, at least, resumed at some point in the future.

Medieval attitudes toward death are less familiar. They were conditioned by the realization that life was likely to be short and by the universal belief in a hereafter. Death was seen in Christian terms as a transition. The preservation of life, though an important value, was not the all-consuming passion that it was later to become, in part because the soul was meant to live eternally. This was why heresy was thought by most jurists to be worse than murder. It killed the soul, whereas murder killed only that which was destined in any case to perish.

People tried to live as long as possible, but they also hoped to make a "good death." They knew that the means of preserving life indefinitely in the face of disease or injury were severely limited, and they were deeply concerned for the future of their souls. When the end drew near, they prepared themselves with prayer, pious reflections, and the last rites of the church. Suffering was regarded as a trial sent by God, to be born with patience and Christian fortitude. Above all, they hoped to die with dignity, because death, like so many other aspects of medieval life, was a public affair. Medieval people wanted to die in their own beds, surrounded by family, friends, and neighbors who could ease their passage to a better world. Most of them appear to have succeeded. Hospitals were few and were intended for travelers, the homeless, and other unfortunates. The injured, if possible, were carried to their homes, and a priest was called if one were available. Not everyone died well, but edifying deathbed scenes were by no means uncommon and few people reached adulthood without having been present at a number of them. In a sense, death was a part of everyday experience.

Burial was in the churchyard. It, too, was a communal experience because space was limited and an understandable reluctance existed to use good agricultural land as cemeteries. Archaeological digs reveal that bodies were often buried several layers deep. The dead slept as they had lived, in close proximity to their friends and relatives with no monument to mark their passing. The wealthy, as in so many other things, were the exception. Their graves were marked, increasingly decorated by their effigies, and located indoors, either within the parish church or in a separate crypt. Husband and wife were typically portrayed together; he in his armor, she in court attire. In the later Middle Ages, humility of a sort set in and tombs were sometimes adorned with effigies of corpses or skeletons (see illustration 11.6), but the idea of the grave as a memorial to the deceased remained.

Medieval society differed in almost every respect from that of the modern industrial world. The basic conditions of material life had changed little since the Neolithic revolution and would remain relatively constant until the industrial revolution. Social behavior, however, was influenced by feudal and Christian values that had been unknown to the ancients. Those values achieved gradual acceptance in the early Middle Ages but would, at least among the privileged, undergo substantial modification in the centuries after the Black Death. The breakdown of the feudal system and the intellectual upheavals of the sixteenth and seventeenth

Illustration 11.6

A Cadaver Effigy of Sir John Go-
lafre (d. 1442) at Fyfield Church, England. Another fully clad effigy of Sir
John appears on the bier immediately
above the cadaver effigy pictured here.

centuries profoundly altered the behavior and self-image of the upper classes. The lives of peasants changed more slowly. Without mass communication to inform them of changes in learning or fashion, they remained immersed in the demands of an agricultural routine that was much the same in the eighteenth century as it had been five hundred years earlier. The castle, in other words, was eventually transformed, but the village remained largely intact until industrialization altered the material conditions on which it was based.

For some, conditions may have grown worse with the passage of time. The lives of most Europeans in the twelfth and thirteenth centuries were simple and, by modern standards, hard, but society was more secure than it had been for many centuries. Wars were either limited or far away, and famines were rare. The activi-

ties of ordinary men and women, like the great intellectual and architectural triumphs of the age, reveal a certain confidence in the world's predictability and a willingness to build for the future. Yet society in the later thirteenth century was beginning to show signs of stress. There seemed to be too many people. They still ate, but poverty and landlessness were increasing. Wealthy people began to build moats around their houses to protect them from their neighbors, while moralists lamented the passing of a golden age. The following century would show that the moralists were in a sense correct: The relative balance of social and economic forces that characterized the High Middle Ages was giving way to conditions that people of all classes would find profoundly troubling.

CHAPTER **12**

# PLAGUE, WAR, AND SOCIAL CHANGE IN THE "LONG" FOURTEENTH CENTURY

## CHAPTER OUTLINE

The transition from medieval to early modern times is generally thought to have begun in the fourteenth century when economic decline, plague, and endemic warfare weakened the bonds of feudal society and undermined its values. Great historical transformations rarely limit themselves to the confines of a single century, and this one was no exception. Thinking, therefore, in terms of a "long" fourteenth century is helpful; that is, of an extended period of demographic, social, and political stress that in some of its manifestations lasted until well into the fifteenth century and beyond.

## Famine, Economic Decline, and the Black Death (1315–50)

The fourteenth century was marked by a series of economic and demographic crises that had a profound effect on the social structure of Europe. Local crises of subsistence became common and, for the first time in two centuries, a large-scale famine struck northern Europe in 1315–17 (see document 12.1). Southern Europe suffered a similar catastrophe in 1339–40. Overpopulation was the underlying cause. By 1300 only the cultivation of marginal soils could feed the ever-growing populace. A succession of bad harvests brought on by unusually cold, wet weather made these lands virtually unusable and destroyed the ecological balance between the people and their food supply. The result was widespread misery and an end to population growth. Scarcity pushed the price of bread to levels that only the rich could afford. Desperate peasants ate their seed grain, thereby destroying all hope for a harvest in the year to come. Others ate leaves, bark, and rats. Though adult deaths from malnutrition were probably rare, the demographic impact of the famine was seen in a declining rate of conception and increased infant mortality.

◆ DOCUMENT 12.1 ◆

## The Famine of 1315 in England

*This dramatic account of the famine is from the English chronicler Johannes de Trokelowe. The prices may be compared with those given for the preceding century in document 11.1.*

Meat and eggs began to run out, capons and fowl could hardly be found, animals died of pest, swine could not be fed because of the excessive price of fodder. A quarter of wheat or beans or peas sold for twenty shillings, barley for a mark, oats for ten shillings. A quarter of salt was commonly sold for thirty-five shillings, which in former times was quite unheard of. The land was so oppressed with want that when the king came to St. Albans on the feast of St. Lawrence [August 10] it was hardly possible to find bread on sale to supply his immediate household. . . .

The dearth began in the month of May and lasted until the nativity of the Virgin [September 8]. The summer rains were so heavy that grain could not ripen. It could hardly be gathered and used to make bread down to the said feast day unless it was first put in vessels to dry. Around the end of autumn the dearth was mitigated in part, but toward Christmas it became as bad as before. Bread did not have its usual nourishing power and strength because the grain was not nourished by the warmth of summer sunshine. Hence those who had it, even in large quantities, were hungry again after a little while. There can be no doubt that the poor wasted away when even the rich were constantly hungry. . . .

Four pennies worth of coarse bread was not enough to feed a common man for one day. The usual kinds of meat, suitable for eating, were too scarce; horse meat was precious; plump dogs were stolen. And according to many reports, men and women in many places secretly ate their own children.

Trokelowe, Johannes. "*Annales,*" trans. Brian Tierney. In Brian Tierney, ed., *Sources of Medieval History,* 4th ed. New York: Knopf, 1983.

branch failed it created a domino effect that might bring down the entire structure. This happened in 1343 when the two leading Florentine banks—the Bardi and the Peruzzi—failed, setting off a widespread financial panic. The immediate cause of their failure was the repudiation of war debts by a major borrower, Edward III of England, but both banks had been gravely weakened before the final blow.

The Black Death struck in 1347–51. Endemic in Asia since the eleventh century, the disease first entered Europe through the Mediterranean ports and spread with terrifying speed throughout the subcontinent. Following the trade routes it reached Paris in the summer of 1348, Denmark and Norway in 1349, and Russia in 1351. Estimates are that within four years a third of the population of Europe died. It was the greatest demographic catastrophe in European history, and its ravages did not end with the first virulent outbreak. Subsequent epidemics occurred regularly in every decade until the beginning of the eighteenth century. Given that immunity apparently cannot be transmitted from generation to generation, the plague served as a long-term check on population growth, and most countries required more than two centuries to recover the population levels they had in 1300 (see table 12.1).

The relationship, if any, between the plague and poverty or malnutrition is unclear. In its most common form, bubonic plague is spread by fleas, which are carried by rats and other small mammals. A pneumonic form of the plague is spread by coughing. The onset of either form is rapid, and death usually comes within three days (see illustration 12.1). The mortality rate seems to have been about the same for all who contracted the disease, so that lowered resistance as a result of malnutrition likely did not play an important part in its spread. At the same time, death came most frequently to those who lived in crowded conditions. Soldiers, ship's crews, and the urban poor were at greatest risk, followed by those country folk whose poverty forced them to huddle together in their one-room cottages for warmth. The rich often escaped, either because they lived in more sanitary conditions or because, like the characters in Giovanni Boccaccio's *Decameron,* they had the means to flee from the centers of population (see document 12.2).

No one knew what caused the plague. Most probably believed that it was a visitation from God and took refuge in prayer and religious ceremonies. Flagellants paraded from town to town, beating each other with metal-tipped scourges in the hope of averting God's wrath, while preachers demanded the reform of the

Predictably, trade declined. Defaults on loans increased, and the banking system came under stress. The great international banks still controlled their branches directly and had unlimited liability for their losses. If a

## ❧ TABLE 12.1 ❧

### Indices of Population Increase in Europe, 1000–1950

The data presented in this table show the dramatic effects of the Black Death as well as the substantial increases in the European population between 1150 and 1250 and between 1400 and 1450. The indices are based on the figures for 100 (that is 1000 = 100). These figures are estimates only and have proved controversial.

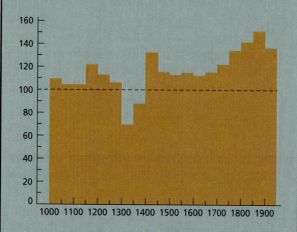

Indices per period of fifty years

| Period | Index | Period | Index |
|--------|-------|--------|-------|
| 1000–50 | 109.5 | 1500–50 | 113.0 |
| 1050–1100 | 104.3 | 1550–1600 | 114.1 |
| 1100–50 | 104.2 | 1600–50 | 112.4 |
| 1150–1200 | 122.0 | 1650–1700 | 115.0 |
| 1200–50 | 113.1 | 1700–50 | 121.7 |
| 1250–1300 | 105.8 | 1750–1800 | 134.3 |
| 1300–50 | 69.9 | 1800–50 | 141.5 |
| 1350–1400 | 88.2 | 1850–1900 | 150.8 |
| 1400–50 | 133.3 | 1900–50 | 136.7 |
| 1450–1500 | 115.0 | | |

Source: B. H. Slicher van Bath, *The Agrarian History of Western Europe, A.D. 500–1800*, trans. Olive Ordish (London: Edward Arnold, 1963), p. 79.

## ◆ DOCUMENT 12.2 ◆

### The Symptoms of the Plague

*A description of the Black Death survives from one of the greatest of the late medieval writers. In 1348–53 Giovanni Boccaccio, who would later become a founder of Renaissance humanism (see chapter 13), wrote the Decameron, a series of stories told in a villa outside Florence where a group of fashionable young people take refuge from the plague. The book begins with a description of the epidemic.*

In the year of our Lord 1348, there happened at Florence, the finest city in all Italy, a most terrible plague; which, whether owing to the influence of the planets, or that it was sent from God as a just punishment for our sins, had broken out some years before in the Levant, and after passing from place to place, and making incredible havoc all the way, had now reached the west. There, in spite of all the means that art and human foresight could suggest, such as keeping the city free from filth, the exclusion of all suspected persons, and the publication of copious instructions for the preservation of health; and not withstanding manifold humble supplications offered to God in processions and otherwise; it began to show itself in the aforesaid year, and in a sad and wonderful manner. Unlike what had been seen in the east, where bleeding from the nose is the fatal prognostic, here there appeared certain tumors in the groin or under the armpits, some as big as a small apple, others as an egg; and afterwards purple spots in most parts of the body; in some cases large and but few in number, in others smaller and more numerous—both sorts the usual messengers of death. To the cure of this malady, neither medical knowledge nor the power of drugs was of any effect; whether because the disease was in its own nature mortal, or that the physicians (the number of whom, taking quacks and women pretenders into the account, was grown very great) could form no just idea of the cause, nor consequently devise a true method of cure; whichever was the reason, few escaped; but nearly all died the third day from the first appearance of the symptoms, some sooner, some later, without any fever or accessory symptoms.

Boccaccio, Giovanni. "The Decameron." In *Stories of Boccaccio*, p. 1, trans. John Payne. London: The Bibliophilist Society, 1903.

**Illustration 12.1**

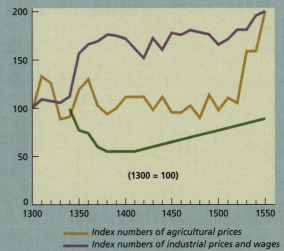 **The Burial of Plague Victims at Tournai, 1349.** Tournai is located in what is now Belgium. Similar scenes of mass burial were replayed throughout Europe during the plague years. As the death toll increased, attempts to provide coffins and individual funerals had to be abandoned. The overwhelmed survivors could only dump the bodies in mass graves.

church on the theory that its increasing interest in secular affairs had provoked divine retribution. Some have argued that the plague created a genuine and long-lasting demand for spiritual renewal. However, other, more sinister results were evident as well. In parts of Germany whole communities of Jews were burned alive because they were thought to have spread the disease by poisoning wells.

## The Economic Consequences of the Black Death

The psychological effects of the Black Death would have a profound impact on religious belief, but its material consequences were equally dramatic (see table 12.2). Demographic collapse relieved pressure on the land. Food prices dropped immediately. Land values and rents followed close behind, declining by 30 to 40 percent in most parts of Europe between 1350 and 1400. For landholders, both lay and religious, this was a serious loss; for ordinary men and women, it was a windfall. Stunned by the horror they had experienced, the survivors found not only that food was cheaper and land more abundant, but also that most of them had inherited varying amounts of property from their dead relatives.

The delicate ecological balance of the thirteenth century no longer existed. Acreage could be diverted to pursuits that were less efficient in purely nutritional terms, but more profitable and less labor intensive. Fields were converted to pasture for grazing sheep and cattle. Marginal lands in Germany and elsewhere reverted to forest where hogs could root at will and where the next generation of peasants could presumably find

---

**✄ TABLE 12.2 ✄**

### Population, Prices, and Wages in England, 1300–1500

The information presented in this graph shows the relationship of agricultural prices, industrial wages and prices, and population in the century and a half following the Black Death. After dramatic rises during the crises of 1315–17 and in the decade of the 1360s, agricultural prices remained fairly steady until the 1530s. The graph is much simplified, and the index numbers are based on prices, wages, and population in 1300.

(1300 = 100)

Index numbers of agricultural prices
Index numbers of industrial prices and wages
Index numbers of English population figures

Source: E. Perroy, "Les crises du XIVe siècle," *Annales,* vol. 4 (1949): pp. 167–82, as adapted in B. H. Slicher van Bath, *The Agrarian History of Western Europe, A.D. 500–1800,* trans. Olive Ordish (London: Edward Arnold, 1963), p. 139.

cheap firewood and building material. A larger percentage of the grain crop was devoted to the brewing of beer, and, in the south, vineyards spread over hillsides upon which in earlier times people had sought to grow food. If the prosperity of Europeans may be measured by their consumption of meat and alcohol, these were comfortable years. Some historians have referred to the period after the Black Death as the golden age of European peasantry. It did not last long.

For most people, calorie and protein consumption undoubtedly improved. Wages, too, increased, because the plague created a labor shortage of unprecedented severity. In Italy, employers tried to compensate by purchasing slaves from the Balkans or from dealers in the region of the Black Sea. This expedient was temporary and not successful. Before 1450 Turkish expansion brought an end to the trade, and although the Portuguese imported African slaves throughout the fifteenth century, they for the most part remained in Portugal. The handful of Africans who served the households of the very rich made no impact on the labor market. Wages remained high, and many people were able for the first time to leave their ancestral homes in search of better land or higher pay. Hundreds of communities were abandoned completely. Such movements cannot be accurately traced, but the century after 1350 appears to have been a time of extraordinary mobility in which the traditional isolation of village life diminished greatly.

These developments provoked a reaction from the propertied classes. Caught between rising wages and declining rents they faced a catastrophic reduction in their incomes. With the passage of time, some eased the situation by turning to such cash crops as wool or wine. Their initial response was to seek legislation that would freeze wages and restrict the movement of peasants. Between 1349 and 1351, virtually every European government tried to fix wages and prices (see document 12.3). For the most part, their efforts produced only resistance.

The failure of such measures led to strategies based upon the selective modification of feudal agreements. New restrictions were developed and long-forgotten obligations were revived. Southwest Germany provides some instructive examples. Peasants subject to one lord were often forbidden to marry the subject of another. If they did so, their tenures would revert to the husband's lord after the couple's death. As population movements had created a situation in which few subjects of the same lord inhabited the same village, this practically guaranteed the wholesale confiscation of peasant estates. At the same time, peasants were denied access to

## DOCUMENT 12.3

### The Statute of Laborers

*Issued by Edward III of England in 1351, this is a typical example of legislation designed to restrict the increase in labor costs created by the Black Death.*

The King to the sheriff of Kent, greetings: Because a great part of the people, and especially of working men and servants, have lately died of the pestilence, many seeing the necessity of masters and great scarcity of servants, will not serve unless they may receive excessive wages, and others preferring to beg in idleness rather than by labor to get their living; we, considering the grievous incommodities which of the lack especially of ploughmen and such laborers may hereafter become, have upon deliberation and treaty with the prelates and the nobles and the learned men assisting us, with their unanimous counsel ordained:

That every man and woman of our realm of England, of what condition he be, free or bond, able in body, and within the age of sixty years, not living in merchandise, nor exercising any craft, nor having of his own whereof he may live, nor land of his own about whose tillage he may occupy himself, and not serving any other; if he be required to serve in suitable service, his estate considered, he shall be bound to serve him which shall so require him; and take only the wages, livery, meed, or salary which were accustomed to be given in the places where he oweth to serve, the twentieth year of our reign of England [that is, in 1347], or five or six other common years next before.

The Statute of Laborers. From *Pennsylvania Translations and Reprints*, vol. 2, no. 5, trans. Edward P. Cheyney. Philadelphia: University of Pennsylvania Press, 1897.

the forests, whose game, wood, nuts, and berries were reserved for the landholders. These forest laws created enormous hardships and were similar in their effects to the enclosure of common lands by the English gentry a century later. Peasants who depended upon these resources for firewood and for a supplement to their diet might be driven from the land.

When such measures failed to raise enough money, landholders were often forced to sell part of their holdings to investors. If the land in question was held in fief, the permission of the liege lord was usually required and could be secured by a cash payment or in return for political favors. Some of the buyers were merchants, lawyers, or servants of the crown who wanted the status provided by a country estate. Others were simply landholders who sought to consolidate their holdings at bargain rates. In either case the purchase of land tended to eliminate feudal obligations in fact and sometimes in law. The new owners had no personal ties to the peasants on their newly acquired estates and felt free to exploit their property as efficiently as possible. The net effect was to accelerate the shift toward private ownership of land that had begun with the commutation of feudal dues in the twelfth and thirteenth centuries.

Princes, too, were affected by the drop in land values. Medieval rulers drew the bulk of their ordinary revenues from exploiting their domains. Domain revenue came from a variety of dues, rights, and privileges, as well as from rents, which were an important part of the whole. Most princes were happy to make common cause with the other great landholders or to compensate for their losses by levying new taxes.

## Social Disorder from the Jacqueries to the Bundschuh Revolts

Attempts to reverse the economic trends set in motion by the plague created widespread discontent. In 1358, much of northern France rose in a bloody revolt called the Jacquerie (Jacques Bonhomme being more-or-less the French equivalent of John Doe). Peasants attacked the castles of their lords in one of the worst outbreaks of social violence in centuries. There was no program, no plan—only violence born of sheer desperation. In this case peasant distress was greatly aggravated by that portion of the Hundred Years' War that had ended with the French defeat at Poitiers in 1356. The countryside was devastated, and the peasants were taxed to pay the ransoms of the king and his aristocratic followers who had been captured by the English on the battlefield.

Other revolts grew less from poverty than from the frustration of rising expectations. The English revolt of 1381, known as Wat Tyler's Rebellion in memory of one of its leaders, was triggered by the imposition of a poll or head tax on every individual. The rebels saw it as regressive, meaning it fell heavier on the poor than on the rich, and as a threat to the economic gains achieved since the plague. In Germany the exactions of princes and landholders, including the clergy, provoked a series of rebellions that flared periodically throughout the fifteenth century and culminated in the great Peas-

ant Revolt of 1524–25. These are generally referred to as the *bundschuh* revolts after the laced boots that served as a symbol of peasant unity.

Much urban unrest also was in evidence, but its relationship to the plague and its aftermath is unclear. The overall volume of European trade declined after 1350, which was offset to some extent by continuing strength in the market for manufactured and luxury items. A more equitable distribution of wealth broadened the demand for clothing, leather goods, and various furnishings, while the rich, in an apparent effort to maintain their status in the face of economic threats, indulged in luxuries on an unprecedented scale. The trade in manufactured articles, though smaller in total than it had been in the thirteenth century, was therefore larger in proportion to the trade in bulk agricultural commodities. It was also more profitable. Towns, now considerably smaller, seem to have enjoyed a certain measure of prosperity throughout the period.

Their political balance, however, was changed by the new importance of manufacturing. Craft guilds and the artisans they represented were generally strengthened at the expense of the urban patriciate, whose rents were greatly reduced in value. The process was not entirely new. The Flemish cloth towns of Ghent, Bruges, and Ypres had been the scene of periodic revolts for a century before 1350, and outbreaks continued for years thereafter. By 1345 the guilds had triumphed, at least in Flanders, but this in itself failed to create tranquility. The patriciate refused to accept exclusion from the government, and various factions among the guilds fought among themselves to achieve supremacy. Given the chronic discontent among the mass of laborers, most of whom were not guild members and therefore disenfranchised, riots were easy to incite almost regardless of the cause. The disturbances in the German towns of Braunschweig (1374) and Lübeck (1408) were apparently of similar origin. Political factions were able to mobilize popular discontent in the service of their own, decidedly nonpopular, interests.

The revolts of 1382 in Paris and Rouen appear to have been more spontaneous and closer in spirit to the rural uprisings of the same period, but the seizure of Rome by Cola di Rienzi in May 1347 was unique. Demanding a return to the ancient Roman form of government, he raised a great mob and held the city for seven months under the title of Tribune. The whole episode remains the subject of historical controversy. It was related to the absence of the pope at Avignon (see chapter 14). The departure of the papal court in 1305 had wrecked the Roman economy and placed the city's government in the hands of such old aristocratic families as the Orsini and the Colonna. Popular dissatisfaction kept the city in turmoil for several years even after Rienzi was forced into exile.

The revolt of the Florentine *Ciompi* in 1378 was the culmination of thirty years of civic strife. The depression of 1343 had led the *popolo grasso* (literally, fat people) to betray their city's republican traditions by introducing a despot who would, they hoped, control the population. The subsequent revolt led to a government dominated by the minor, craft-oriented guilds and to the incorporation of the semiskilled woolcarders (*ciompi*) into a guild of their own. In 1378 the Ciompi seized control of the city and introduced a popular and democratic form of government that lasted until the great merchants of the city hired a mercenary army to overthrow it in 1382.

Few of these rebellions, urban or rural, had clearly developed aims, and none of them resulted in permanent institutional changes beneficial to the rebels. For the most part, the privileged classes found them easy to suppress. The wealthy still possessed a near monopoly of military force and had little difficulty in presenting a united front. Their opponents, though numerous, were poor and usually disorganized. Communication among different groups of rebels was difficult, and outbreaks of violence tended to be as isolated as they were brief. These rebellions probably did not pose a fundamental threat to the existing social order, but they inspired fear. The chroniclers, who were by definition members of an educated elite, described appalling scenes of murder, rape, and cannibalism. They noted that women sometimes played a part in the agitation, and they regarded this as a monstrous perversion of nature. True or exaggerated, these accounts made it difficult for readers to sympathize with the rebels. The restoration of order was often followed by mass executions and sometimes by new burdens on the peasantry as a whole.

In general, the social disorders of the fourteenth century weakened whatever sense of mutual obligation had been retained from the age of feudalism and probably hastened the trend toward private ownership of land. Moreover they increased the fear and insecurity of the elite, who reacted by developing an attitude of increased social exclusivity. The division between popular and elite culture became dramatic at about this time. The tendency was to ridicule and suppress customs that had once belonged to rich and poor alike but were now regarded as loutish or wicked.

Meanwhile, an impulse that must have been largely unconscious led the upper classes into new extravagance and the elaboration of an extreme form of chivalric excess. The tournaments and banquets described in the *Chronicle* of Jean Froissart (c. 1333–c. 1400) surpassed anything that an earlier age could afford and were at least partially inspired by the flowering of chivalric romance as a literary form. Ironically, this "indian summer" of chivalry occurred not only amid social and economic insecurity but at a time when the feudal aristocracy was losing the remnants of its military function.

## The Transformation of Warfare: The Emergence of the Soldier

Fourteenth-century Europe suffered not only from famine and plague, but also from war. While the age was probably not more violent than others before or since, the scale and complexity of warfare was beginning to increase in highly visible ways. By 1500 the evidence was clear that the preceeding two hundred years had witnessed a military revolution.

Long before the Black Death, the feudal system of warfare had begun to break down. The warrior was becoming a soldier. The term *soldier* is used here in its original meaning: a fighting man who receives a cash payment or *solde* for his efforts as opposed to one who serves in return for land or in the discharge of some nonmonetary obligation. This was an important development, not only because it changed the way in which wars were fought, but also because it altered the structure of western European society.

The increase in real wealth and in the circulation of money between 1000 and 1250 allowed princes to alter the basis of military service. Their own revenues, which were based in part on import-export duties and occasional levies on movable goods, were augmented by the revival of trade. Beyond that the commutation of military and other services for cash helped to create substantial war revenues exclusive of taxes. Scutage, the payment of knight's fees, and similar arrangements by which even the feudal class could escape military service in return for cash payments are first noted in the mid-twelfth century. By 1250 they had become commonplace. In 1227 the emperor Frederick II demanded eight ounces of gold from every fief in his realms, but only one knight from every eight fiefs. A quarter-century later, the pope declared his preference for money over personal service from his vassals. The money was used to hire mercenaries or to pay knights to extend their service, often for an indefinite period. The case of Edward I of England is typical. His attempts to subjugate the Welsh and Scots could not be abandoned every autumn when his feudal levies went home. He therefore contracted with certain knights on a long-term basis, paying their wages from the proceeds of knight's fees and from the nine great levies on moveable property that he collected between 1297 and 1302.

The need for long-service troops and the superior professionalism of those who fought year in and year out for their livelihood were decisive. By 1340 unpaid feudal service was becoming rare in western Europe, though the crown was not yet the sole paymaster of its armies. Men from the great estates were still paid by the lords who employed them. Townsmen were paid by the towns. This changed by the mid-fifteenth century in England and France and by 1480 in Spain, though towns and nobles could be called upon to provide equipment. In Italy, the mercenary was dominant by 1300.

The major exceptions to this state of affairs were found in eastern Europe. In Poland a numerous class of small and middling gentry continued to perform unpaid military service throughout the fifteenth century. Those who account for this by pointing to the frontier character of Polish society would be wrong. In Hungary, Europe's most exposed frontier, even the *banderia*, a heavy cavalry unit composed of noblemen, was paid in cash at an early date, and the armies of János Hunyadi (c. 1407–56) and his son, Matthias I, were composed largely of mercenaries. Aside from such quasitribal survivals as the *szechely* of eastern Transylvania, the decision to pay or not to pay seems everywhere to have been governed by the availability of cash.

The first soldiers were probably poor knights or younger sons whose only inheritance was a sword, a horse, and a sound training in the profession of arms. They were soon joined by paid infantry, most of whom came from different social worlds. The fourteenth century also saw the evolution of infantry tactics that required either specialized skills or exceptional discipline and cohesion in battle. As those who possessed such training were rarely part of traditional feudal society, they, too, had to be paid in cash.

The skills were largely associated with the development of new or improved missile weapons. Archery had always been a factor in medieval warfare, but its effectiveness was diminished by improvements in personal armor. The introduction of the crossbow therefore marked the beginning of a major change. This weapon offered great accuracy and powers of penetration, though at a relatively slow rate of fire. Originating in the Mediterranean, it was first used as a naval weapon and found special favor among the shipmasters of

Genoa and Barcelona as a defense against pirates. Men selected and trained for this purpose had become numerous in the port cities of the western Mediterranean by 1300 and were willing to transfer their skills to land when the volume of maritime trade declined. The Genoese were especially noted for their service to France during the Hundred Years' War; natives of Barcelona and Marseilles were not far behind.

The advent of the crossbowmen marked an alien intrusion into the world of feudal warfare and was resented by many knights. Their world held little place for the urban poor. However, the involvement of marginal people with deviant forms of social organization was only beginning. The famous longbow was another case in point. Basically a poacher's weapon, it evolved beyond the edges of the feudal world in Wales and the English forests. Edward III introduced it in the Hundred Years' War with devastating effect. The longbow combined a high rate of fire with penetration and accuracy superior to that of early firearms. It required many years of training to be properly employed. As most of those who were expert in its use were marginal men in an economic and social sense they were usually happy to serve as mercenaries.

Handguns followed a similar pattern. First seen in Italy during the 1390s, they achieved importance in Bohemia during the Hussite wars. When peace returned, companies of handgun men found employment in Hungary and in the west.

All of these categories were overshadowed in the fifteenth century by the emergence of the pike as a primary battle weapon (see illustration 12.2). The pike was a spear, twelve to sixteen feet in length. It was used in a square formation similar to the Macedonian phalanx and could, if the pikemen stood their ground, stop a cavalry charge or clear the field of opposing infantry. Massed infantry formations of this kind had been neglected during most of the Middle Ages because such tactics were incompatible with feudalism as a social system. Infantry had to be highly motivated and carefully trained to meet a cavalry charge without flinching.

In medieval Europe, two main forms of social organization could meet this requirement: the city and the peasant league. Medieval towns were surrounded by enemies. In those areas where princely authority was weak (Italy, the Low Countries, and parts of Germany), they were forced to develop effective armies at a relatively early date. As most towns lacked either extensive territory or a large native nobility trained in the profession of arms, this meant that they had to rely on the creation of citizen militias supplemented on occasion

**Illlustration 12.2**

**Pikes in Action.**  This illustration of the opening of a battle between formations of pikemen shows the "fall" of pikes as the units come into action. It is a detail of *The Terrible Swiss War* by Albrecht Altdorfer, c. 1515.

by mercenaries. Those townsmen who could afford to, bought horse and armor and tried to fight like knights. The majority served with pike or halberd (a long-handled battle axe) and drilled on Sundays and holidays until they achieved a level of effectiveness far superior to that of peasant levies. The victory of the Flemish town militias over the chivalry of France at Courtrai in 1302 was a promise of things to come.

By 1422 pike tactics had been adopted by the Swiss Confederation, one of several peasant leagues formed in the later thirteenth century to preserve their independence from feudal demands. The successful defense of their liberties earned them a formidable military reputation, and after 1444 the Swiss were regularly employed as mercenaries by the French and by the pope. Their example was taken up by other poor peasants in south Germany who emulated their system of training and hired themselves out to the emperor and other princes. Pike squares remained a feature of European armies for two hundred years, and mercenary contracting became an important element in the Swiss and south German economies.

The emergence of paid troops, new missile weapons, and massed infantry tactics changed the character of European warfare. By the end of the fourteenth century, armies were larger and cavalry was declining in importance. The social consequences of these changes

were profound because they tended, among other things, to monetarize the costs of war. In the simplest form of feudal warfare, cash outlays were few. Men served without pay and normally provided their own food and equipment in the field. Feudal levies consumed resources in kind, but these costs rarely involved the state. This changed dramatically with the advent of the soldier, because only a sovereign state could coin money or raise taxes. As feudal nobles could rarely do either, they gradually lost their preeminent role as the organizers of war while the eclipse of cavalry reduced their presence on the battlefield. During the fifteenth century, many great feudal families began to withdraw from the traditional function as protectors of society, leaving the field to men who served the sovereign for pay and privileges. In the process, the state, too, was transformed. Where the feudal world had demanded little more than justice and military leadership from its kings, the new warfare demanded the collection and distribution of resources on an unprecedented scale. The monarchies of Europe were at first unprepared for such a task, and the difficulties they faced were compounded by a contemporary revolution in military technology.

The development of Western technology is often seen as a sporadic affair in which periods of innovation were interspersed with longer intervals of slow, almost imperceptible change. This is an illusion that comes from thinking of the inventions themselves instead of the complex process that created them, but periods certainly existed during which breakthroughs occurred at an accelerated rate. One of these was the later Middle Ages. Few of the changes had an immediate impact on everyday life, but their effects on war, trade, and government were great.

The development of artillery and portable firearms is a case in point. Evolution began with the invention of gunpowder. In Europe, saltpeter was first identified in the twelfth century. How or why it was combined with charcoal and sulphur is unknown, but the mixture was mentioned by Roger Bacon in 1248. A number of years passed before it was used as a propellent, and its first application probably was in mining. This, however, is uncertain. Only the obstacles to its use are fully documented. Saltpeter was scarce and expensive. Years of experimentation were needed to arrive at the proper ratio of ingredients and even longer to develop grains of the proper consistency. Mistakes were often fatal, for black powder was not totally safe or dependable in use, and its chemistry has only recently been understood. Nevertheless it presented fewer problems than the construction of the guns. Metallurgy, not powder milling, controlled the pace of artillery development.

The first guns, which appeared around the middle of the fourteenth century, were hand forged from wrought-iron bars and bound with iron hoops. They were heavy, expensive, and prone to bursting when fired. In spite of these drawbacks, they remained dominant until the middle of the fifteenth century when they were superseded by guns cast from bronze. The bronze used was approximately 80 percent copper and 20 percent tin. Large quantities of both metals were therefore required, and gun production on a large scale was prevented during the fourteenth century by the exhaustion of existing mines. Copper in particular was in short supply. In 1450 a new process was introduced that extracted copper from ores in which copper and silver were found together. Large, previously unusable deposits in Saxony, Hungary, and Slovakia thus could be exploited, and copper production increased dramatically.

The introduction of bronze cannons was further delayed by the lack of adequate furnaces and by an inability to deal with a physical property characteristic of bronze. Copper and tin tend to segregate as they cool, causing variations in the strength of the metal that might cause the guns to burst when fired (see illustration 12.3). Generations of experience were needed to

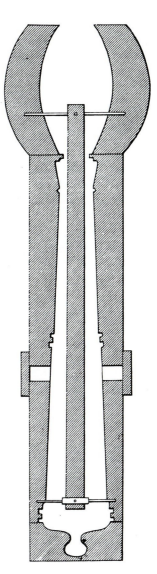

**Illustration 12.3**

⧼ **Gun-Casting Technique (after c. 1450).** The gun was cast around a core that was lowered into the mold and centered by an iron "cross" that was left in the casting. The pouring head at the top ensured that the mixture of tin and copper would not segregate during cooling and weaken the breach. The head was sawed off after the casting process was complete.

solve these problems. By the 1460s they were largely under control, and large numbers of bronze cannons were quickly added to European armories. Within a half-century, every existing fortress was obsolete, for the high, relatively thin walls of medieval fortifications could withstand no more than a few hours of battering by the big guns. Towns and strongholds in militarily exposed areas were forced to rebuild if they were to survive. Between 1500 and 1530, Italian engineers developed a system of fortifcation that set the pattern for defensive works until the nineteenth century. Walls were lowered and thickened to widths of forty feet or more. Bastions became wedge-shaped and were laid out geometrically so that every section of wall could be covered by the defender's guns. The works were then surrounded by a broad, steep-sided ditch that was usually faced with brick or stone.

The cost was enormous. The guns were expensive and required large numbers of skilled men and draft animals to maneuver. The new fortifications required less skill to construct than their medieval predecessors, but their scale was far larger and their expense proportionately high. The development of artillery had increased the already heavy burden of warfare on states and subjects alike.

The development of navies, though not taking place in earnest until the sixteenth century, was destined to have a similar effect. It rested upon changes in shipbuilding that by the fifteenth century had created vessels capable of crossing an ocean or using artillery in a ship-to-ship duel. The new ships were the result of a hybrid cross between two traditions of shipbuilding—the Mediterranean and the north European. The ships changed the world as few innovations have done before or since.

The dominant ship types in the medieval Mediterranean were the galley and the round ship. The galley was intended primarily for war. Long, narrow, and light, its chief virtues were speed and maneuverabilty independent of the wind. However, it was too fragile for use in the open Atlantic or for extended use in its home waters between October and May. It also lacked carrying capacity, and this, together with its high manpower requirements, limited its usefulness. Though galleys were sometimes used for commerce, especially by the Venetians, the preeminent Mediterranean cargo carrier was the round ship. As its name implies, it was double-ended and broad of beam with a high freeboard. Steered like a galley by side rudders located near the stern, it normally carried a two-masted rig with triangular lateen sails (see illustration 12.4). The round ship was not fast or graceful, but it was safe, roomy, and thanks to its high freeboard, relatively easy to defend against boarders. Its carvel type construction was typically Mediterranean. The hull planking was nailed or pegged edge on edge to a skeleton frame and then caulked to create a water-tight, non-load-bearing hull.

The ships of northern Europe were different. Most were clinker-built like the old Viking longships with overlapping planks fastened to each other by nails or rivets. Their variety was almost infinite. By the middle

Ilustration 12.4

The Evolution of Medieval Ship Types. These two ship models represent the best current thinking on the appearance and construction of medieval ships. (A) is a medieval round ship with a lateen sail and steering oars of the type used to carry crusaders. (B) is a model of the *Mary Rose*, Henry VIII's "great ship" that capsized in 1545. It may be regarded as an early galleon. Note the gunports.

of the thirteenth century, the cog had emerged as the preferred choice for long voyages over open water. Of Baltic origin, the cog was as high and beamy as the roundship. A long, straight keel and sternpost rudder made it different from and more controllable than its Mediterranean counterpart. The Genoese, in ships designed for their Atlantic trade, adapted carvel construction to this design to create a lighter, cheaper hull with greater carrying capacity.

The final step was the addition of multiple masts. Shipbuilders soon discovered that a divided rig reduced manning requirements because smaller sails were easier to handle. It also made possible the use of different sails—combined according to need, thereby increasing speed and maneuverability under a wider variety of conditions. With Portuguese, Dutch, and Basque innovators leading the way, a recognizably modern ship had evolved by 1500.

Given the military rivalry among states, a marriage between the new shipbuilding techniques and the cast bronze cannon was inevitable. The full tactical implications of this were not immediately apparent, but by the last quarter of the fifteenth century the major states were acquiring ships capable of mounting heavy guns. The competition to control the seas was on, and no state with maritime interests could afford to ignore it.

◆

## Centers of Conflict: The Eastern Frontiers

For much of the later Middle Ages, the great north European plain, where it made a borderless transition into Asia, was in turmoil. East of the Elbe, two great movements were under way. The first was the eastward expansion of the German-speaking peoples. Population growth in the twelfth and thirteenth centuries led to the establishment of German settlements in Poland, Lithuania, and the Baltic regions as well as in Transylvania and the Ukraine. The movement was not always peaceful, bringing the Germans into conflict with the Slavs who inhabited the region. Relations improved little with time, and the German "colonies" tended to remain isolated from their neighbors by linguistic barriers and mutual resentments. In its later phases, German expansion was led by the Teutonic Knights, a military order on the crusading model. From the mid-thirteenth century, the Knights attempted the large-scale conquest of Slavic as well as unclaimed land on which German peasants were then encouraged to settle (see map 12.1).

On its eastern fringes (see document 12.4) the Slavic world was under equal pressure from the Mongols, who conquered most of Russia and the Ukraine in 1240–42 and who raided as far west as Breslau in Silesia. The center of resistance to Mongol rule became the grand duchy of Moscow, founded by the son of the Russian hero, Alexander Nevsky. Nevsky had defeated

---

### ◆ DOCUMENT 12.4 ◆

## The Novgorod Chronicle

*Novgorod was an important trading city north of Moscow. This excerpt from its city chronicle provides a vivid picture of conditions on Europe's eastern frontier in the year 1224.*

A.D. 1224. Prince Vsevolod Gyurgevits came to Novgorod. The same year the Germans killed Prince Vyachko in Gyurgev and took the town. The same year, for our sins, this was not [all] the evil that happened: *Posadnik* [an elected official somewhat resembling a burgomaster or mayor] Fedor rode out with the men of Russia and fought with the Lithuanians; and they drove the men of Russia from their horses and took many horses, and killed Domazhir Torlinits and his son and of the men of Russa Boghsa and many others, and the rest they drove asunder into the forest. The same year, for our sins, unknown tribes came, whom no one exactly knows, who they are, nor whence they came out, nor what their language is, nor of what race they are, nor what their faith is, but they call them Tartars. . . . God alone knows who they are and whence they came out. Very wise men know them exactly, who understand books, but we do not know who they are, but have written of them here for the sake of the memory of the Russian princes and of the misfortune which came to them from them.

*The Chronicle of Novgorod, 1016–1471*, trans. Robert Michell and Nevill Forbes. Camden Society, 3d series, vol. 25. London: Camden Society Publications, 1914.

---

a Swedish incursion in 1238 and the Teutonic Knights in 1240. His descendants were forced to concern themselves almost exclusively with Asia. Though continuing to pay tribute to the Mongol khans, the Musovites engaged in sporadic warfare with them until 1480 when Ivan III refused payment and became, in effect, the first tsar. An early sign of the grand duchy's preeminence was the transfer of the Russian Orthodox patriarchate from Kiev to Moscow in 1299.

During the fourteenth century, Russian preoccupation with the Mongols encouraged the Teutonic Knights to step up their activities in the Baltic. Resistance was provided by the Catholic kingdom of

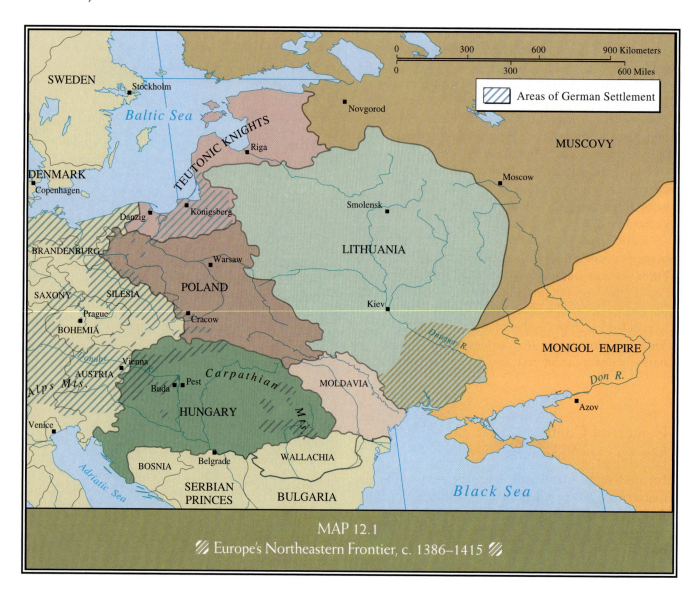

**MAP 12.1**

Europe's Northeastern Frontier, c. 1386–1415

Poland, established early in the eleventh century, and by a rapidly expanding Lithuanian state whose rulers were still pagan. In 1386 the two states merged for mutual defense. Under the leadership of the Lithuanian Jagiello, who converted to Catholicism and became king of Poland as well, the Knights were defeated at the battle of Tannenburg in 1410.

The Knights no longer existed as an aggressive force, but conflict did not end. Poland-Lithuania did not evolve into a centralized territorial state. It remained an aristocratic commonwealth with an elected king and few natural defenses. However, it was at this time a remarkably open society in which people of many faiths and languages could coexist. It even became the place of refuge for thousands of Jews. Driven from western Europe by the persecutions that followed the Black Death, they found that their capital and fi-

nancial skills were welcomed by the rulers of an underdeveloped frontier state. The parallels with the Iberian kingdoms are striking. By the mid-fifteenth century, Poland and Lithuania were the centers of a vigorous Jewish culture characterized by a powerful tradition of rabbinic learning and the use of Yiddish, a German dialect, as the language of everyday speech.

To the south, in the Balkan Peninsula, the fourteenth and fifteenth centuries marked the emergence of the Ottoman Empire as a threat to Christian Europe. By 1300 virtually all of the Byzantine lands in Anatolia had fallen under the control of *ghazi* principalities. The *ghazis*, of predominantly Turkish origin, were the Muslim equivalent of crusaders, pledged to the advancement of Islam. The last of their states to possess a common frontier with Byzantium was centered on the city of Bursa in northwest Anatolia. Under the aggressive leadership of Osman (1258–1324), it offered the opportunity for continued warfare to ambitious men from all over the Turkic world and a refuge to others who had fled from the Mongol advance in central Asia. With the population of the Ottoman state swelled by thousands of immigrants, the tiny emirate became the nucleus of the Ottoman Empire.

From the beginning, it was a serious threat to the Byzantine state revived by Michael Paleologus after the Fourth Crusade. Deprived of his Anatolian heartland and caught between the Ottomans on one side and the Serbian Empire of Stephen Dushan (d. 1355) on the other, the Greek emperor was only one of many regional princes striving for preeminence in the tangled world of Balkan politics. Taking advantage of divisions among the Christians, Osman's son, Orhan, ordered the first Turkish invasion of Europe in 1356. The best hope of expelling him lay in an alliance between the Serbians and the Bulgarians. A history of mutual distrust inhibited their cooperation, however, and the Serbian army was defeated in 1371. By 1389 the Turks had achieved military predominance in the peninsula.

The threat to Constantinople was now imminent, and the Greeks sent missions to Rome in the hope of enlisting western support against the Turks. Negotiations broke down over theological and other issues. The pope was reluctant to compromise, and some Greeks came to believe that the Latin church was a greater threat to the survival of their religion than Islam. From the standpoint of Western intellectual development, this contact between Greek and Latin scholar-diplomats would have far-reaching consequences, but politically it was a failure.

Meanwhile, southeastern Europe settled into a period of almost chronic warfare. The Serbs and Bulgarians were restless and unreliable tributaries of the Turks. The Byzantine emperor lacked a credible offensive force, but the Albanians remained a threat. In the northwest, the Hungarians were growing uneasy. Eventually a crusade was organized by János Hunyadi, the voivod of Transylvania who would one day become king of Hungary. His defeat at Varna in 1444 and again on the plain of Kossovo in 1448 left the Turks in control of virtually everything south of the Danube. Only the Albanian mountains and Constantinople remained free.

In 1453 the great city, now seriously depopulated, fell to Mehmet "the Conqueror" after a long siege. The Byzantine Empire had ceased to exist. The church of St. Sophia became a mosque, and the Greeks, together with the other Balkan peoples, became subjects of the Ottoman sultan. Their faith and much of their culture was preserved, for the Turks did not believe in forced conversions. They would not regain political independence until the nineteenth century.

## The Hundred Years' War in the West

The Hundred Years' War, though centered on France and England, was a generalized west European conflict that also involved the Low Countries and the Iberian kingdoms of Castile, Aragon, and Portugal. Because its active phases were interspersed with periods of relative peace, regarding it not as one war but as several whose underlying causes were related is probably best. The most immediate of these causes was the ongoing struggle over the status of English fiefs in France. The situation was complicated by dynastic instability and by the weakening of feudal institutions as a whole.

Of all the problems created by feudalism, none was more exasperating than the ambivalent situation of the kings of England. For two centuries they had struggled with their dual role as French vassals and as sovereign princes whose interests were frequently in conflict with those of France (see chapter 8). Every reign since that of Henry II had produced disputes over Guienne and Gascony. Another French attempt to confiscate these fiefs led to the outbreak of the Hundred Years' War in spring 1337 (see map 12.2).

This action by Philip VI of France came at the end of a long diplomatic crisis. Nearly a decade earlier, Philip had been proclaimed king when his cousin, Charles IV, died without male heirs. The claim of England's Edward III, son of Charles's sister, had been denied on the controversial premise that the Salic law forbade royal inheritance through the female line. Edward, young and beset with internal enemies, chose not to press the point. Relations gradually deteriorated when Philip began to pursue more aggressive policies on several fronts. In the year of his coronation he recaptured the county of Flanders from the urban rebels who had achieved independence from France at Courtrai in 1302. This represented a threat to the primary market for English wool, as Philip was now in a position to forbid its importation. Worst of all, he began to support Edward's enemies in Scotland.

By 1336 Edward was secure on his throne and began preparing for war. Papal attempts at mediation failed, and in May 1337, Philip ordered the confiscation of English fiefs in France, citing Edward's support for the Flemish rebels and other sins against feudal obligation as a pretext.

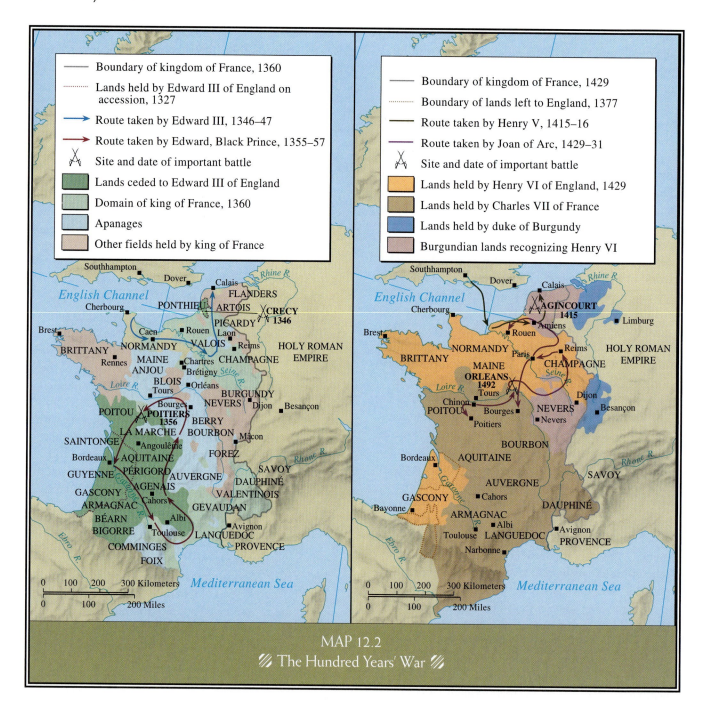

**Legend (left map):**
- Boundary of kingdom of France, 1360
- Lands held by Edward III of England on accession, 1327
- Route taken by Edward III, 1346–47
- Route taken by Edward, Black Prince, 1355–57
- Site and date of important battle
- Lands ceded to Edward III of England
- Domain of king of France, 1360
- Apanages
- Other fields held by king of France

**Legend (right map):**
- Boundary of kingdom of France, 1429
- Boundary of lands left to England, 1377
- Route taken by Henry V, 1415–16
- Route taken by Joan of Arc, 1429–31
- Site and date of important battle
- Lands held by Henry VI of England, 1429
- Lands held by Charles VII of France
- Lands held by duke of Burgundy
- Burgundian lands recognizing Henry VI

MAP 12.2
The Hundred Years' War

The first phase of the war went badly for France. This is at first sight surprising as England was by far the smaller and poorer of the two countries with a population only one-third that of her rival. The difference lay in superior leadership. Edward quickly proved to be not only an able commander, but also a master at extracting resources from Parliament. By defeating the French in a naval battle off Sluys in 1340, he secured control of the English Channel. Subsequent campaigns were fought on French soil, including the ones that culminated in the victories of Crécy (1346) and Poitiers (1356). In both cases, French cavalry employing traditional tactics were defeated by the imaginative use of longbows in massed formations.

The treaty of Bretigny (1360) secured a breathing space of seven years during which the locus of violence shifted to the Iberian Peninsula. Conflict there centered on the policies of Pedro of Castile, known to the Castilian aristocracy as "the Cruel" and to his other subjects as "the Just." Pedro's nicknames arose from his efforts to strengthen the crown against the landed nobility. When he became involved in a border war with Pedro "the Ceremonious" of Aragon, the latter encouraged an uprising of Castilian nobles under the leadership of Enrique of Trastámara, Pedro the Cruel's half-brother. Enrique and his Aragonese ally then sought assistance from France.

They received it in part because of a phenomenon that surfaced for the first time after the peace of Bretigny. The practice of paying troops had created a class of men whose only trade was war and who, after a generation of fighting, had no place in civilian society. For them peace was a catastrophe that forced them to become beggars or bandits. Most, understandably, chose the latter. Roaming the countryside, often in their original companies, they lived by systematic pillage and extortion reinforced by the threat of murder, arson, and rape.

The new French king, Charles V, was happy to dispatch a multinational contingent of these people to Spain under the command of Bertrand Duguesclin. Pedro of Castile responded by calling in the English under Edward of Woodstock, known as the Black Prince. The eldest son of Edward III and the winning commander at Poitiers, he repeated his triumph at Nájera in 1367. The Castilian war dragged on until 1398 when Enrique was able to kill Pedro with his own hands and gain the throne. Because Enrique had won with the aid of the Castilian aristocracy, he was forced to confirm and extend their privileges, thereby guaranteeing that his successors would be faced with internal disorder. His victory was a defeat, not only for Pedro, but also for the state-building ideals he represented.

An aftereffect of the Spanish war was the pretext for reviving Anglo-French hostilities. To pay for his Castilian adventure, the Black Prince so taxed his subjects in Guienne that they appealed to Charles V for help. The war that followed was far less dramatic than the first. Charles adopted a strategy of attrition, avoiding battle whenever possible and using the tactical skills of Duguesclin to harry and outmaneuver the English. By 1380 the English presence in France had been greatly reduced, but both kingdoms were at the limit of their resources. Fighting did not end completely. The next thirty-five years may be characterized as a period of military stalemate and internal disorder in both countries.

The last stage of the war began when Henry V of England invaded the continent in 1415. Ambitious and new to the throne, he sought to take advantage of the civil war then raging in France. The French king, Charles VI, had gone mad. His brother, the duke of Orleáns, was named regent, thereby arousing the envy

of John the Fearless, duke of Burgundy. Burgundy was perhaps the most powerful of the king's relatives. His appanage—estates granted to members of the ruling family—included the rich duchy of Burgundy and most of what is now Belgium and the Netherlands. He was probably wealthier than the king. John arranged the assassination of Orleáns in 1407 only to see another rival, Count Bertrand VII of Armagnac, installed in his place. In the struggle that followed, Burgundy tried to ally himself with England, drawing back when he perceived the extent of Henry's ambitions. The English king saw that John would do nothing to defend Charles VI or his Armagnac supporters.

The English invasion was an immediate success. Using a variant of the tactics developed at Crécy and Poitiers, Henry crushed the French at Agincourt on October 25, 1415. Alarmed by the magnitude of the French defeat, Burgundy began to rethink his position, but he, too, was assassinated in 1419 by soldiers in the pay of the Armagnacs. His son, Philip, whose nickname "the Good" belied a ferocious temper, sought revenge by allying Burgundy once again with England.

The French king was virtually isolated. In 1420 he was forced to ratify the treaty of Troyes, which disinherited his son, the future Charles VII, in favor of Henry V. When Charles VI and Henry both died in 1422, Henry's infant son, Henry VI of England, was proclaimed king of France with the English duke of Bedford as regent. The proclamation aroused great indignation in much of France where Charles of Valois was accepted as the rightful king. Charles, unfortunately, was not an inspiring figure. Inarticulate, physically unimpressive, and only nineteen years old, he retired with his supporters to Bourges where he quickly developed a reputation for lethargy and indecision. The task of galvanizing public opinion fell to an extraordinary woman, Joan of Arc.

Joan was an illiterate peasant from the remote border village of Domrémy. When she came to Charles in March 1429 she was probably no older than twenty but had already achieved local fame for her religious visions. She told him that "voices" had instructed her to raise the English siege of Orleáns, and Charles, who probably thought that he had little to lose, allowed her to go. The result was electrifying. By the time she arrived, the English had decided to give up, but the French did not know this. The apparently miraculous appearance of a young woman, dressed in armor and with her hair cut like a man's, was thought to have been the reason for the subsequent English retreat, and it created a sensation. The relief of Orleáns, which preserved the south of France for Charles, was followed by a string of victories that led to the repudiation of the treaty of Troyes and his coronation at Rheims in July. All of this was popularly attributed to Joan who was present throughout. She never commanded troops, but her inspiration gave them confidence, and even civilians, oppressed by a century of apparently pointless warfare, were roused to enthusiasm.

Unfortunately for Joan, Charles was not quite the fool he sometimes appeared to be. When she was captured by the English in 1430, he did nothing to secure her release or to prevent her from being tried at Rouen on charges of witchcraft and heresy. He no doubt preferred to take credit for his own victories and may have regarded her popularity as an embarrassment. The verdict was a foregone conclusion. Bedford was determined to discredit her as an agent of the devil, and she was burned at the stake on May 30, 1431. Her habit of dressing as a man was taken as evidence of diabolical intent. Twenty-five years later, in a gesture of belated gratitude, Charles VII reopened the case and had her declared innocent. The church made her a saint in 1920.

Joan's brief career offers a disquieting vision of fifteenth-century attitudes toward women, but it was a turning point for France. In 1435 Charles was reconciled with Philip the Good of Burgundy, and by 1453 the English had been driven out of France in a series of successful campaigns that left them with only the port of Calais as a continental base.

## Political Turbulence and Dynastic Collapse: France, Castile, and England

Dynastic failures played a major role in continuing and intensifying the Hundred Years' War. In a system based on heredity, the failure of a ruling dynasty to produce competent heirs in a timely manner meant either a disputed succession or a regency. The effect of a disputed succession may be seen in the origins of the war itself, in which the failure of all three of Philip IV's sons to produce heirs gave Edward III of England a pretext for his quarrel with Philip of Valois, or in Castile, where a similar failure by Pedro the Cruel encouraged the pretensions of his half-brother Enrique.

Regencies occurred when the legitimate heir could not govern by reason of youth or mental incapacity. An individual regent or a regency council might be designated in the will of a dying monarch or by agreement within the royal family, but these appointments were almost always contested. The reason lay in the struc-

ture of European elites. Each branch of the royal family and each of the great landholding clans were a center of wealth, power, and patronage to which other elements of society were drawn by interest or by hereditary obligation. Rivalries were inevitable, and the king's duty was to serve as a kind of referee, using his superior rank to ensure that no one became an "overmighty subject." Failure to perform this role in an adequate manner was often equated with bad governance.

By these standards, no regency could be good. Regents were usually either princes of the blood or connected with a particular faction of the royal family. They were partial almost by definition. Once installed, they were in a position to use the wealth and power of the crown to advance their factional interests while threatening the estates and the lives of their rivals. Those excluded from a regency often felt that they had no alternative but to rebel, though their rebellions were usually directed not at the semisacred person of the king, but at his "evil counselors." This happened in the struggle between John the Fearless and the Armagnacs. The result was a civil war and renewed English intervention in France.

Other forms of dynastic failure had similar effects. In some cases, adult, presumably functional, rulers behaved so foolishly that their subjects rebelled. Castile in particular suffered from this ailment throughout much of the fifteenth century. Juan II (1405–54) left the government in the hands of Alvaro de Luna, a powerful noble whose de facto regency factionalized the grandees, the highest rank of Spanish nobles who were not princes of the blood. Juan's son, Enrique IV "the Impotent" was generally despised for his homosexuality, his tendency to promote low-born lovers over the hereditary nobility, and his failure to maintain order. Faced with a monarchy they could neither support nor respect, the great landholding families raised private armies and kept the country in a state of near-anarchy until 1479.

In England, the regency appointed during the minority of Richard II was accepted largely because the social unrest that culminated in the revolt of 1381 forced the aristocracy to close ranks. When he came of age, the favoritism and ineptitude of the young king aroused such opposition that he was deposed and murdered in 1399. Reflecting contemporary attitudes, Richard, like Enrique IV of Castile, was accused of homosexuality. The reign of Henry VI—from 1422 to 1461 and 1470 to 1471—was even more chaotic than that of Richard II. Coming to the throne as an infant, Henry remained under the control of others throughout his life. Though respected for his piety, he was wholly incapable of governing and suffered a complete mental breakdown in 1453. His incapacity led to the War of the Roses, a nine-year struggle between the Lancastrian and Yorkist branches of the royal family that ended with a Yorkist victory at Tewksbury in 1471 and the murder of yet another English king (see chapter 13).

Whether the result of royal inbreeding or sheer bad luck, these dynastic failures retarded the development of western European states. The increasing cost of and sophistication of war were a powerful impetus to the growth of royal power, but these anarchic interludes tended to interfere with bureaucratic development and to strengthen local privilege, at least temporarily. Feudal nobles whose position was threatened by economic and military change often saw them as an opportunity to recover lost ground. Above all, they added to the sense of dislocation created by plague, war, and social change.

## Art and Literature: The Measure of Discontent

By the end of the fourteenth century, the accumulation of disasters was having an impact on the art and literature of Europe. The bonds of society seemed to be unraveling. Lords abandoned their ostensible function as the military protectors of society and compensated for declining rents by preying upon their tenants. Peasants responded when they could by abandoning their tenures. The idea of mutual obligation that lay at the heart of feudalism could no longer be sustained, and many, including the fourteenth-century author of the English poem *Piers Plowman*, came to believe that greed and self-interest were everywhere triumphant. Moralists complained that the simpler manners of an earlier day had given way to extravagance and debauchery. War was endemic and all the more intolerable because it did not end for the common people when a truce was signed. They still had to pay for it through taxes while trying to defend themselves against unemployed soldiers who often did more damage than the war itself. Plague, the conquests by the Turk, and the rule of imbecile kings were seen by many as signs of God's wrath.

The expression of these concerns varied. At one extreme was the upper-class tendency to take refuge in nostalgia for a largely fictional past. This took the form not only of chivalric fantasies, but also of the idyllic visions offered in the *Tres riches heures du Duc du Berry*, a

**Illustration 12.5**

**Nostalgia for a Past That Had Never Been.** Happy peasants toil beneath the walls of a fairy tale castle in this fifteenth-century illumination, which is from the *Très riches heures du Duc du Berry.*

magnificently illustrated prayer book in which happy peasants toil near palaces that seem to float on air (see illustration 12.5). At the other extreme was a fascination with the physical aspects of death (see document 12.5). The art of the period abounds with representations of skeletons and putrifying corpses. The Dance of Death in which corpses lead the living in a frenzied round that ends with the grave became a common motif in art and literature and was performed in costume on festive occasions. Popular sermons emphasized the brevity of life and the art of dying well, while series of popular woodcuts illustrated in horrifying detail how death would come to the knight, the scholar, the

◆ DOCUMENT 12.5 ◆

## The Vision of Death

*Georges Chastellain (c. 1415–75) was a Burgundian courtier best known for his* Chronicle, *but he also wrote poetry. The following excerpt is from a long poem entitled* Le Pas de la Mort (The Dance of Death). *It reveals an obsession with the physical aspects of death that was typical of the age.*

There is not a limb nor a form,
Which does not smell of putrefaction.
Before the soul is outside,
The heart which wants to burst the body
Raises and lifts the chest
Which nearly touches the backbone
—The face is discolored and pale,
And the eyes veiled in the head.
Speech fails him,
For the tongue cleaves to the palate.
The pulse trembles and he pants.
The bones are disjointed on all sides;
There is not a tendon which does not stretch as to burst.

Chastellain, Georges. "Les Pas de la Mort." In Johan Huizinga, *The Waning of the Middle Ages*, pp. 147–148. New York: Doubleday Anchor Books, 1949. Copyright © Johan Huizinga. Reprinted by permissoin of St. Martin's Press, Incorporated and Edward Arnold (Publisher) Limited.

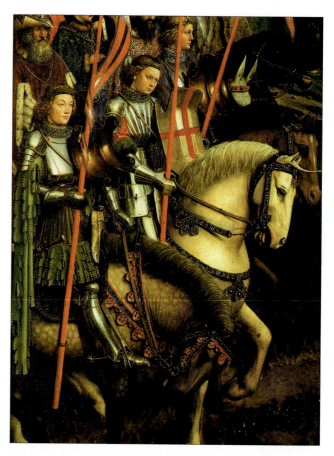

Ilustration 12.6

🖉 **Detail from the Ghent Alterpiece.** This panel, "The Knights of Christ," with its lovingly rendered costumes and harness is an example of fifteenth-century Flemish painter Jan van Eyck's preoccupation with the world of the senses.

beauty, and a whole host of other human stereotypes. Not surprisingly, the word *macabre* seems to have entered the French language at about this time.

Despair became fashionable, but it was not universal. In Brabant and Flanders artists such as Roger van der Weyden and the van Eycks developed techniques for portraying the beauties of the world with unprecedented mastery (see illustration 12.6). Their paintings, intended for display in churches and hospitals, dwelled lovingly on fine costumes, the brilliance of jewels, and the richness of everyday objects while portraying the hard, worldly faces of their owners with unflinching honesty. Regarding their work as an affirmative answer to the emphasis on death is tempting. Some certainly felt that because life was grim and short its pleasures should be enjoyed to the fullest. However, more exists to these paintings than meets the eye. Many of the

beautifully rendered objects they portray are also symbols of a moral or spiritual value whose meaning would have been clear to all who saw them. The medieval fondness for allegory survived the fourteenth century and may even have grown stronger with time.

The people of the later Middle Ages still used religious language and religious imagery to express themselves. They still thought in religious, traditional, and hierarchic terms, but their faith in traditional assumptions and values had been shaken badly by events they barely understood. They looked with dismay upon what had happened, but the transformation of their world had just begun.

# CHAPTER 13

# THE RENAISSANCE: POLITICAL RENEWAL AND INTELLECTUAL CHANGE

Changes in the conduct of warfare and the erosion of feudal institutions after 1300 created a new kind of state, administered by salaried bureaucrats and defended by paid soldiers. Though the policies of these states were governed by dynastic instead of national considerations and regional differences were accepted to a degree unimaginable today, the monarchies that emerged from this process in the later fifteenth century are the recognizable ancestors of the modern state.

At approximately the same time, a new intellectual movement began in the Italian city-states and, by the end of the fifteenth century, had spread throughout Europe. Under the influence of such writers as Petrarch and Boccaccio, Italians began to reinterpret the ancient Greco-Roman past and apply the lessons of that reimagined period to their own times. In the process, they transformed virtually all of the arts and sciences, gave birth to the modern study of politics and history, and created a model for liberal arts education that persisted, with some modifications, into the early twentieth century. They changed the way in which Westerners thought, not only about human affairs, but also about the physical sciences. This movement is known as the Renaissance, and the term has been used conventionally to describe the entire age in which Western learning moved away from medieval precedents and began to lay the foundations of the modern world.

## The Consolidation of the State (c. 1350–1500)

Medieval princes had worked, with varying degrees of success, to improve administration and strengthen royal authority. Most royal governments remained modest in size and centered firmly on the royal household until the later years of the thirteenth century. Under Henry

III of England (reigned 1234–72), for example, the royal budget hovered consistently in the range of £12,500 per annum. His son, Edward I, managed to spend more than £750,000 on war alone from 1297 to 1302, in part because he paid most of his fighting men in cash. Such figures indicate why the military revolution of the fourteenth and fifteenth centuries intensified the process of state building begun by such monarchs as Edward I and Philip the Fair. Faced with a massive increase in the cost of war, sovereign states had to maximize their incomes from every conceivable source to survive.

One way of achieving this was to expand the ruler's personal domain and to exploit it more efficiently. Domain revenues fell into two main categories. First, rents, fees, and other income were taken from lands held directly by the prince. The size of the domain could be increased by keeping property that reverted to the sovereign through confiscation or in default of heirs. In the feudal past such lands had often been given to other subjects almost as soon as they were received. By 1450 most states were trying to reverse this practice, and some were actively seeking new pretexts for confiscation. Second, other domain revenues came from the exercise of traditional rights that might include anything from the collection of customs duties to monopolies on such vital commodities as salt. The yield from these sources was regarded as the personal property of the crown and, like profits from the land, could be increased primarily through better administration.

Bureaucracies composed of "servants of the crown," paid in cash and serving at the pleasure of their ruler, were a legacy of the thirteenth century. They grew larger and more assertive with the passage of time. As the careers of the bureaucrats depended upon producing new revenue, they sought not only to improve efficiency but also to discover new rights for which few precedents often existed. Their efforts brought the state into conflict with privileges that had long been claimed by towns, guilds, private individuals, and the church. As such conflicts usually ended in the law courts, the state found strengthening its control over the legal system desirable. Manorial courts and other forms of private jurisdiction were therefore attacked for their independence as well as for the fines and court costs they levied that might otherwise go to the state. From the ruler's point of view, establishing courts by his or her own prerogative was far better, because a court in which the judge was a servant of the crown might deliver more favorable verdicts and bring in money that might otherwise be lost.

The expansion of prerogative courts, though controversial, was eased by the growing acceptance of Roman or civil law. The extensive development of canon law by the church during the eleventh and twelfth centuries had sparked a revival of interest in Justinian's code among laymen. By the thirteenth century, Roman legal principles had almost supplanted customary law in the empire and in Castile, where they formed the basis of the *Siete Partidas*, the great legal code adopted by Alfonso X (reigned 1252–84). In France and England, the principles of civil law tended instead to modify common law practice, but Roman law gained ground steadily through the fifteenth century. Everywhere, rulers—and the prerogative courts they established—preferred Roman procedures because the customary law, with its reliance on precedent and the use of juries, provided a stronger basis for resisting the claims of sovereignty. But these same virtues ensured that court proceedings would be long and therefore costly. People often asked that their cases be transferred to prerogative or civil law courts in the hope of a speedier judgment.

Though individuals might sometimes benefit from the state's activities, as a general rule, all attempts to increase domain revenue carried a high political cost. Only a strong, popular prince could overcome the entrenched resistance of powerful interests, which is why the dynastic failures of the late fourteenth and early fifteenth centuries delayed the extension of sovereignty even if they could not stop it completely.

The character of princes also affected their ability to impose taxes, the second route by which the power of the state might be increased. Taxes, unlike domain revenues, could be raised only with the consent of representative bodies. Late medieval assemblies generally voted taxes for a specified period of time, thereby forcing the princes to come back each year, hat in hand, to hear the complaints of their subjects. If the prince was popular, or if the taxes were needed to meet a genuine crisis, the sums involved might vastly exceed those generated from domain revenues, yet parliamentary bodies that held "the power of the purse" restricted the exercise of sovereignty. Most rulers no doubt preferred to "live of their own," but this was rarely possible in time of war.

The only solution to this dilemma was to convince hard-headed representatives of the landholding and merchant classes to grant at least some taxes on a perpetual basis on the theory that threats to the kingdom's integrity would never end. This was not easy, even in the interminable chaos of the Hundred Years' War, but the states that succeeded, notably France and Castile, became the great powers of the succeeding age. Not only did perpetual taxes make the revenues of these countries greater in real terms than those of their neighbors, but they also made them predictable. Budgeting for the long term became possible without the interference of elected bodies whose interests were not necessarily those of the prince. Above all, perpetual taxes made borrowing money easier because lenders could be guaranteed a return based on projected revenues.

Whether perpetual or temporary, late medieval and early modern taxes were usually levied on some form of moveable property. The governments of the day lacked the administrative technology to monitor personal incomes, and land, though it was the principle form of wealth, was usually tax exempt for a variety of political and historical reasons. The goods of merchants and artisans were fair game, as were the commodities offered for sale by peasants. Taxes on moveable property were regressive in the sense that wealthy landholders and rentiers could usually avoid them, but their impact on other social groups is hard to measure. Collection was never uniform and was rarely undertaken directly by the state. The most common practice was to negotiate the proposed yield from a tax with local authorities who would then be responsible for its collection. The rates collected were usually not those set by the legislation. Whatever their amount, late medieval taxes fell predominantly on the most economically active, if not the richest, segments of the population.

Governments knew this and attempted to encourage the transfer of resources from tax-exempt to taxable activities. This is one reason for their almost universal efforts to foster trade, mining, and manufacturing. It also helps to explain the policy, common to both England and Castile, of favoring sheepherders at the expense of those who cultivated the soil. Wool could be taxed; subsistence agriculture could not. Such policies clearly influenced economic development, but their overall impact on growth or on public well-being may have been negative. Taxes were ultimately paid by the consumer and were therefore a burden to be added to those already imposed by landholders in their efforts to compensate for falling rents.

Moreover, the maximization of tax yields often required changes in land use. Governments, through the decisions of their prerogative courts, tended to favor the extension of personal property rights over the claims of feudal privilege. An example was the English policy of encouraging landholders to enclose common lands for grazing. This practice, which reached a peak at the beginning of the sixteenth century, broke feudal

precedent and sometimes forced the expulsion of peasants who needed the marginal income provided by the commons for survival. As Sir Thomas More put it, "[I]n England, sheep eat men." This was perhaps an extreme case, and enclosures may not have been as common as More thought, but everywhere the extension of personal property rights to land had the immediate effect of favoring governments and landholders at the expense of peasants. Thus, the most insistent demand of German peasant revolutionaries was for a return to the "old law" that protected their feudal status.

If one part of state building was finding new revenues, the other was developing more efficient mechanisms by which they could be spent. Most late medieval states found this more difficult than locating the money in the first place. Bureaucracies whose purpose was to supply the needs of war grew like mushrooms but remained inefficient by modern standards until after the industrial revolution. They were inhibited in part by the same sense of corporate and personal privilege that resisted other aspects of state growth, but the underlying problem was structural. Communications were poor, and no precedent had been set for many basic administrative procedures. Archives, the basic tool of record keeping, were rare before the mid-sixteenth century. Censuses were unknown outside the Italian city-states, and how they might have been conducted in such kingdoms as France with their immense distances and isolated populations is hard to imagine. To make matters worse, the costs of war continued to grow more rapidly than the sources of revenue. Neither taxation nor the development of public credit kept pace, and money was often in desperately short supply. Because soldiers and officials were often paid poorly and at irregular intervals, governments were forced to tolerate high levels of what would today be called corruption. Bribery, the sale of offices, and the misappropriation of funds were common even in those states that prided themselves on their high administrative standards. The situation would improve under the "absolutist" regimes of the eighteenth century, but the improvements were relative.

No two states were alike. Though all were confronted with the need for consolidation and new revenues, they achieved their objectives in different ways according to their circumstances and traditions. The city-states of Italy evolved along lines of their own and have been considered separately in Chapter 10. The sovereign kingdoms and principalities must be examined individually or in regional groups if their development is to be understood.

## The Iberian Kingdoms: Ferdinand and Isabella

The Iberian Peninsula was in some ways an unlikely birthplace for two of the most successful early modern states. Difficult terrain and an average annual rainfall of twenty inches or less produced little surplus wealth. Ethnic, political, and religious differences were great. In 1400 no fewer than five kingdoms shared this rugged land. Portugal was probably the most homogeneous, though it possessed significant Muslim and Jewish minorities. Castile, comprising the two ancient kingdoms of León and Castile, contained not only Jews and Muslims, but also Basques and Galicians who, though devoutly Christian, possessed their own languages and cultures. The kingdom of Aragon had three separate regions: Aragon, Cataluña, and Valencia. Each of them had its own language and traditions, though the Aragonese spoke Castilian and some linguists regard Valencian as a dialect of Catalan. Finally, there was the kingdom of Granada, the last but still vigorous remnant of the Islamic Empire on European soil, and the tiny mountain kingdom of Navarre straddling the Pyrenees between Castile and France.

Portugal was the first European state to achieve consolidation, just as it would be the first to acquire an overseas empire. During most of the fourteenth century, it suffered like other monarchies from intrigue, dynastic failures, and ill-advised forays into the Hundred Years' War. In 1385 the Portuguese Cortes solved a succession crisis by crowning the late king's illegitimate son as John I. In the same year, John defeated the Castilians in a decisive battle at Aljubarrotta and suppressed most of the old feudal nobility, many of whom had supported the enemy. Under his descendants, the house of Avis, Portugal avoided the revolts and dynastic failures that troubled other states and evolved virtually without interruption until 1580.

Spain was another matter. Aragon and Castile had long been troubled by civil wars. Castile established a precedent for perpetual taxes in 1367, but the usurpation of Enrique of Trastámara left the crown dependent upon the nobles who had supported him. His successors, especially Juan II and Enrique IV "the Impotent," were incapable of maintaining order, in part because their favorites aroused the jealousy of the grandees. The accession of Enrique's half-sister Isabella and her marriage to Ferdinand of Aragon brought an end to the period of anarchy and led to the eventual union of the two kingdoms. Isabella and Ferdinand inherited their respective thrones in 1479, a decade after their marriage. Each ruled independently, but they cooperated on the broad outlines of policy, and an agreement was reached that their heirs would rule a united Spain by hereditary right.

The program of the Catholic kings, as they were called, was greatly assisted by the weariness brought on by decades of civil strife. The nobles of Castile were pacified by confirming their titles to all lands acquired by them, legally or illegally, before 1466 and by the judicious granting of *mayorazgos* or entails permitting them to exclude younger children from their inheritances. This was important because, under Spanish law, property was normally divided equally among the heirs, a practice that tended to deplete a family's wealth and influence over time. In return, the grandees agreed to give up all the land they had taken illegally after 1466 and to disband their private armies.

The towns, too, had suffered in the civil wars. Clientage and kinship ties were powerful in Castilian society, and many cities had fallen under the control of factions that persecuted their rivals mercilessly. At the Cortes of Toledo in 1480 the royal towns of Castile agreed to the appointment of *corregidores*, royal officials who would reside in the city, protect the interests of the crown, and supervise elections. This ensured a high degree of royal authority over city governments and over those who were elected to represent them in the Cortes. The consequent willingness of this body to support new taxes and other royal initiatives was to become an important cornerstone of Spanish power.

None of these measures applied to Aragon. To ensure domestic peace, Ferdinand was forced to confirm a series of rights and privileges granted by his father in 1472 at the height of the civil wars. These concessions, however, were less important than they might appear. The kingdom of Aragon was far smaller than Castile, and its most vital region, Cataluña, had been declining economically for more than a century. Castile was destined to be the dominant partner in this union of the crowns, and its dominance was only enhanced by its centralized institutions and higher level of taxation. In both kingdoms, administration was reformed and the crown's already extensive control over church appointments was strengthened.

With their realms at peace, the monarchs turned their attention to the kingdom of Granada. After ten years of bitter warfare, the Muslim state was conquered in 1492, the same year in which Columbus sailed for the New World. It was also the year in which the Jews were expelled from Spain, for the Catholic kings were committed to a policy of religious uniformity. Fanned by popular preachers, anti-Jewish sentiment had led to

MAP 13.1

〽️ Europe in the Renaissance 〽️

pogroms and a wave of forced conversions between 1390 and 1450. Many of these conversions were thought to be false, and the Spanish Inquisition, an organization wholly unrelated to the Papal Inquisition, was founded early in Ferdinand and Isabella's reign to root out *conversos* who had presumably returned to the faith of their ancestors. Large numbers of converts were executed or forced to do penance during the 1480s, and their property was confiscated to help finance the Granadan war. The Inquisition, as a church court, had jurisdiction over only those who had been baptized. The Jews who had escaped forced conversion were comparatively few and usually poor, but even a small minority was seen as a threat to the faith of the *conversos*. Those who still refused conversion were at last expelled. Some fled to Portugal, only to be expelled by the Portuguese as well in 1496. Others went to North

Africa or found refuge within the Turkish Empire, while a few eventually settled in the growing commercial cities of the Low Countries.

The war for Granada and the supplies of money guaranteed by the perpetual taxes and cooperative legislature of Castile enabled Ferdinand to create a formidable army that was put to almost constant use in the last years of the reign. Through bluff, diplomacy, and hard fighting, he restored Cerdanya and Rosseló to Cataluña and conquered the ancient kingdom of Navarre. When Charles VIII of France invaded Italy in 1495, Ferdinand used his actions as a pretext to intervene. This first phase of the Italian wars lasted until 1513. Under the command of Gonsalvo de Córdoba, "the Great Captain," Spanish armies devised a new method of combining pikes with shot that defeated the French and their Swiss mercenaries and drove them

## ❖ DOCUMENT 13.1 ❖

# Complaints of the French Estates General, 1484

*When the French Estates General brought together representatives of the clergy, the nobility, and the commons (or third estate), these representatives produced pamphlets known as cahiers, describing their grievances. The following excerpt from a cahier of 1484 gives a vivid complaint of the third estate against royal taxation.*

One cannot imagine the persecution, poverty, and misery that the little people have suffered, and still suffer in many ways.

First of all, no region has been safe from the continual coming and going of armies, living off the poor. . . . One should note with pity the injustice, the iniquity, suffered by the poor: the armies are hired to defend them, yet these armies oppress them the most. The poor laborer must hire the soldiers who beat him, evict him from his house, make him sleep on the ground, and consume his substance. . . . When the poor laborer has worked long, weary, sweaty days, when he has harvested those fruits of his labor from which he expects to live, they come to take a share of it from him, to pay the armed men who may come to beat him soon. . . . If God did not speak to the poor and give them patience, they would succumb in despair.

For the intolerable burden of the *taille*, and the taxes—which the poor people of this kingdom have not carried alone, to be sure, because that is impossible—the burden under which they have died from hunger and poverty, the mere description of these taxes would cause infinite sadness and woe, tears of woe and pity, great sighs and groans from sorrowful hearts. And that is not mentioning the enormous evils that followed, the injustice, the violence, and the extortion whereby these taxes were imposed and seized.

Bernier, A., ed. *Journal des états généraux de France tenus à Tours en 1484,* Paris: 1835. trans. Steven C. Hause.

from the peninsula. Spain added the kingdoms of Sicily and Naples to its growing empire and became the dominant power in Italian affairs at the expense of Italy's independence.

Isabella died in 1504; Ferdinand in 1516. So firm were the foundations they had built that the two crowns were able to survive the unpopular regency of Cardinal Francisco Jiménez (or Ximénez) de Cisneros in Castile. The cardinal not only preserved the authority of the crown, but also made substantial progress in reforming abuses in the Spanish church and in improving the education of the clergy. When the grandson of the Catholic kings, the emperor Charles V, ascended the two thrones and unified them in 1522, he inherited a realm that stretched from Italy to Mexico, the finest army in Europe, and a regular income from taxes that rested firmly on the shoulders of Castilian taxpayers.

## France: Charles VII and Louis XI

France, too, emerged from the Hundred Years' War with perpetual taxes that freed its monarchs from their dependence on representative institutions. The most important of these was the *taille*, a direct tax of feudal origin that was assigned exclusively to the crown in 1439. In a series of ordinances passed between 1445 and 1459, Charles VII made it perpetual and extended it throughout his realm. The *taille* became the largest and most predictable source of crown revenue and virtually eliminated the need for the Estates General, which met only once between 1484 and 1789. The meetings of the Estates General at Tours in 1484 redoubled the royal desire to avoid future meetings by producing loud complaints about the impoverishment of the people by royal taxes (see document 13.1). Charles also laid the goundwork for a professional army, a national administration, and a diplomatic corps.

His son, Louis XI (ruled 1461–83), went further. Most of Louis's reign was consumed by a bitter feud with the dukes of Burgundy, who had established a formidable, multilingual state along his eastern borders. Including Burgundy, the Franche-Comté, Artois, Picardy, the Boulonnais, and most of what is now Belgium and the Netherlands, it was almost certainly the wealthiest principality in Europe. Under Duke Philip "the Good" (d. 1467), it surpassed most kingdoms in courtly magnificence and in the richness of its musical and artistic life, but it was not a kingdom. Most of its territories were held in fief either from the Holy Roman

Empire or from France. To enhance his independence, Philip had supported the English and some discontented elements of the French nobility against Louis in the League of the Common Weal, which Louis defeated in 1465. Philip's son, Charles (known to some as "the Bold" and to others as "the Rash"), hoped to weld his holdings into a single territorial state stretching from the Alps to the North Sea. His ambitions brought him into conflict with the duke of Lorraine and with the Swiss, whose independence he seemed to threaten. These formidable opponents, richly subsidized by Louis, defeated and killed Charles at the battle of Nancy in 1477.

Charles died without male heirs. His daughter Mary was the wife of the Hapsburg archduke, Maximilian, who would become emperor in 1486. Under Louis's interpretation of the Salic law, she could not, as a woman, inherit her father's French fiefs. Maximilian was unable to defend his wife's claims, and in 1482 Burgundy, Picardy, and the Boulonnais reverted to the French crown.

The dismemberment of the Burgundian state was the capstone of Louis's career. It was accompanied by acquisitions of equal value. Louis may have been clever and ruthless, but he was also lucky. In 1480 René of Anjou died without heirs, leaving Anjou and the French segment of Bar to the crown. Maine and the kingdom of Provence were incorporated in the following year after the death of Duke Charles II, and the rights of succession to Brittany were purchased when it became apparent that its duke, too, would die without producing male heirs. When Louis died in 1483, he left a France whose borders were recognizably similar to those of today. Luck and a consistently antifemale interpretation of the laws of inheritance played their part, but he could not have done it without a superior army, fiscal independence, and great diplomatic skill. His immense resources permitted him to take advantage of the dynastic misfortunes of others.

## England: The Yorkists and Tudors

England was far smaller in land area and in population than either France or Spain. Its population was also more homogeneous, though regional differences were still important until well into the sixteenth century. Perhaps because it dominated an island whose integrity was rarely threatened by foreign enemies, it failed to develop perpetual taxes and its Parliament never lost "the power of the purse." England's development was therefore unlike that of the great continental powers,

and it remained a relatively minor player in international politics until late in the early modern period.

Henry VI (reigned 1422–61, 1470–71) came to the throne as an infant and suffered from protracted bouts of mental illness as an adult. He was never competent to rule in his own right. For the first thirty years of the reign, his regency council fought bitterly among themselves, brought the kingdom to the edge of bankruptcy, and lost the remaining English possessions in France with the exception of Calais. Eventually, Richard, duke of York claimed the throne with the support of a powerful segment of the nobility. Richard was descended from Edmund of Langley, the fourth surviving son of Edward III, while the king was the great grandson of Edward's third son, John of Gaunt, duke of Lancaster. The civil war that followed is called the War of the Roses because the heraldic symbol of the Yorkists was a white rose; that of the Lancastrians, a red.

In the first phase of the war (1455–61), the Lancastrians were led by Henry's formidable queen, Margaret of Anjou. She defeated the Yorkists at Wakefield and at St. Albans but failed to take London. Richard was killed at Wakefield. His son, an able commander, took advantage of her hesitation. He entered London and had himself proclaimed king as Edward IV. The struggle continued, but Edward retained the throne with one brief interruption until 1483. The last half of his reign was characterized by imaginative and energetic reforms in the administration of the royal domain. As customs duties were an important part of crown revenues, Edward used his extensive personal contacts in the London merchant community to encourage the growth of trade. He eventually became a major investor himself. The proceeds from these efforts, together with a pension extorted from Louis XI to prevent Edward from invading France, left him largely independent of Parliament. Some thought his methods unkingly, but when he died in 1483, he left behind an improved administration and an immense fortune.

He also left two young sons under the guardianship of his brother. The brother quickly had himself proclaimed king as Richard III, and the two little princes disappeared from the Tower of London, never to be seen again. This usurpation caused several of the leading Yorkists to make common cause with the Lancastrians, and in 1485, Henry Tudor, the last remaining Lancastrian claimant to the throne, defeated and killed Richard at the battle of Bosworth.

As Henry VII (reigned 1485–1509), Tudor followed the policies of Edward IV (see illustration 13.1). A subtle diplomat, he avoided war, intensified the

**Illustration 13.1**

🕅 **Henry VII of England.** This portrait by an unknown Flemish artist was painted c. 1505. Shrewd, cynical, and devoid of chivalric illusions, Henry was typical of a generation of monarchs who transformed their kingdoms into something resembling the modern state.

exploitation of his domain, and encouraged the development of trade. His Welsh connections—he had been born in Pembrokeshire and was partially of Welsh descent—secured him the cooperation of the principality and laid the groundwork for its eventual union with England in 1536.

The greatest threat to Henry's regime was the belligerence of the great nobles, many of whom continued to maintain private armies. He dealt with this menace through prerogative courts, including the Court of King's Bench and the Star Chamber, so called because it met in a room decorated with painted stars. Staffed by royal appointees, these bodies levied heavy fines for a variety of offenses against the crown that eventually destroyed the military power of the great families. Para-

doxically, Henry may have been aided by several pretenders to the throne who claimed to be one or another of the missing princes and who enjoyed the support of disgruntled Yorkists or other "over-mighty" subjects. The fines, confiscations, and executions imposed after each of these episodes added to the royal domain and further reduced the number of his enemies.

When Henry died in 1509, the treasury was full and the kingdom at peace. Many of the old feudal families were either impoverished or extinct, and a new elite composed largely of servants of the crown was beginning to develop. The authority of the crown, in other words, was great, but the state as a whole remained dependent upon domain revenues. The later Tudors would find this dependence limiting. The Stuarts would be destroyed by it.

### The Holy Roman Empire

The Holy Roman Empire of the later Middle Ages should be regarded as a confederation of cities and principalities instead of as a territorial state that failed. German parallels to the growth of Spain, France, or England may be found in states such as Brandenburg, Saxony, and Bavaria, not at the imperial level. Their rulers sought, with varying degrees of success, to enhance domain revenues, control representative bodies, and impose new taxes. The imperial office was an unlikely vehicle for this type of development because it was elective and because it lacked several of the more important attributes of sovereignty.

The century before the Black Death had been one of imperial paralysis and decentralization, caused in part by papal interference. The turning point came in 1355 when Charles IV renounced his Italian claims and turned his attention to reorganizing what would soon be called the Holy Roman Empire of the German Nation. The Golden Bull of 1356 regularized imperial elections by placing them in the hands of seven permanent electors: the archbishops of Trier, Mainz, and Cologne, the duke of Saxony, the margrave of Brandenburg, the count of Palatine, and the king of Bohemia. It further declared that the territory of these princes would be indivisible and that inheritance in the secular electorates would be by primogeniture.

These measures strengthened the electors and made consolidation of their territories easier, but they did little to create a more viable imperial government. No incentive existed to increase the power of the emperor, and the lesser states feared the growing influence of the electors. Efforts to create an electoral union or

## ◆ DOCUMENT 13.2 ◆

# The Twelve Articles of the German Peasants

*The Great Peasant War of 1524–25 was the last in a long series of revolts against the claims of lords, princes, and the church. Some of the Twelve Articles reflect the peasants' understanding of the Protestant Reformation. Most of them expressed grievances that had been accumulating for centuries. Those abridged below would have been as valid in 1424 as in 1524.*

The Third Article. It has been the custom hitherto for men to hold us as their own property, which is pitiable enough considering that Christ has redeemed and purchased us without exception, by the shedding of His precious blood, the lowly as well as the great. Accordingly, it is consistent with Scripture that we should be free and wish to be so. . . .

The Fourth Article. [I]t has been the custom heretofore that no poor man was allowed to catch venison or wild fowl, or fish in flowing water, which seems to us quite unseemly and unbrotherly. . . . Accordingly, it is our desire if a man holds possession of waters that he should prove from satisfactory documents that his right has been wittingly acquired by purchase.

The Fifth Article. [W]e are aggrieved in the matter of woodcutting, for our noble folk have appropriated all the woods to themselves alone. . . . It should be free to every member of the community to help himself to such firewood as he needs in his home.

The Eighth Article. [W]e are greatly burdened by holdings that cannot support the rent exacted from them. We ask that the lords may appoint persons of honor to inspect these holdings and fix a rent in accordance with justice.

The Ninth Article. [W]e are burdened with the great evil in the constant making of new laws. In our opinion we should be judged according to the old written law, so that the case shall be decided according to its merits and not with favors.

The Eleventh Article. [W]e will entirely abolish the custom called *Todfall* [death dues], and will no longer allow it, nor allow widows and orphans to be thus shamefully robbed against God's will.

"The Twelve Articles of the German Peasants." In Hans Hillerbrand, ed., *The Protestant Reformation*, pp. 65–66. New York: Harper Torchbooks, 1967.

*Kurfürstverein* with many of the powers of a central government were defeated in 1424, 1453, and 1500. The Common Penny, an imperial tax, was rejected by a majority of German states after it had been approved by their representatives in the Imperial Diet or *Reichstag*. The empire would remain an unstable grouping of eighty-nine free Imperial Cities together with more than two hundred independent principalities, most of which continued to divide and re-form according to the vagaries of partible inheritance. A few, such as Bavaria, achieved near-equality with the electoral states by introducing primogeniture. However, all sought to maximize their own power and to resist imperial and electoral encroachments.

In the process, German states—and cities—imitated the western monarchies by trying to increase revenues at the expense of traditional rights and privileges. The peasants, already squeezed by landholders trying to reverse the economic effects of a declining population, added the actions of the princes to their list of grievances and rebelled. The last and most serious of the *bundschuh* revolts was the Great Peasant War of

1524–25 that ended with the defeat of the peasant armies and the imposition of serfdom in many parts of the empire (see document 13.2). Serfs had no personal or legal rights and were usually transferred from one owner to another whenever the property on which they lived changed hands. Their status differed from that of slaves only in that they could not be sold as individuals. Serfdom was the final step in the destruction of peasant freedom.

### Central and Eastern Europe

Serfdom as an institution was also established in eastern Europe. In Bohemia, Hungary, and Poland-Lithuania, the growing power of aristocratic landholders deprived peasants of their traditional freedoms and blocked the development of western-style states. If western kings may be said to have tamed their nobles, in the east the nobles tamed their kings.

Bohemia and Hungary were in some ways politically similar, though Bohemia was part of the Holy

Roman Empire and Hungary was not. Both were elective monarchies whose powerful Diets or representative assemblies were dominated by the landed aristocracy. Rich mineral deposits provided a source of revenues for both crowns. Once elected, a capable monarch could use this wealth as the basis for administrative and military reforms, but his achievements were unlikely to survive him. By the late fifteenth century Diets customarily demanded concessions as the price of election, and as Diets were dominated by the great magnates, their demands invariably tended to weaken the authority of the crown and threaten the rights of common people.

Bohemia, though wealthy and cultured, was convulsed throughout the fifteenth century by the Hussite wars and their aftermath. The Czechs, deeply resentful of a powerful German minority, launched what was probably the first national movement in European history. It was anti-German, anti-empire, and under the leadership of Jan Hus, increasingly associated with demands for religious reform. Hus was burned as a heretic in 1415. After many years of civil war, the Czechs succeeded in placing the Hussite noble George of Podebrady (ruled 1458–71) on the throne. The king's ability and popularity were eventually seen as a threat to the great Bohemian landholders. When he died, the Diet elected Vladislav II (ruled 1471–1516), a member of the Polish Jagiello dynasty, on the promise that he would support their interests. Under Vladislav, the Bohemian nobles gained virtual control over the state, expelled the towns from the Diet, and introduced serfdom. The towns eventually achieved readmission, but the Bohemian peasantry did not recover its freedom until the eighteenth century.

The policies of Vladislav could only recommend him to the Hungarian nobility. During the long and brilliant reign of Matthias Corvinus (ruled 1458–90), the crown acquired unprecedented authority and supported a court that was admired even in Renaissance Italy. When Matthias died, the Hungarian Diet elected the more controllable Vladislav to succeed him. Vladislav and his son, Louis II, who was in turn elected king of both Hungary and Bohemia, reversed the achievements of Matthias and left the Diet free to promote repressive legislation. Driven to desperation, the peasants rebelled in 1514 only to be soundly defeated. After bloody reprisals, the Diet imposed "real and perpetual servitude" on the entire Hungarian peasant class.

By this time Hungary was on the edge of an abyss. The Turkish Empire, under the formidable Süleyman the Magnificent (reigned 1520–66), was preparing an

invasion, and Louis was crippled by the aristocratic independence he had done so much to encourage. Though king of Bohemia as well as Hungary, he was unable to gain the support of the Bohemians. The Hungarians were divided not only by rivalries among the leading clans, but also by an increasingly bitter feud between the magnates and the lesser nobility. Süleyman had little difficulty in annihilating a weak, divided, and badly led Hungarian army at Mohács in 1526. Louis, along with many great nobles and churchmen, was killed, and Hungary was partitioned into three sections. The center of the country would thereafter be ruled directly by the Turks. In the east, Transylvania became a Turkish client and tributary, while a narrow strip of territory in the west fell under Hapsburg rule.

After their union in 1386, Poland and Lithuania occupied an immense territory stretching from the borders of Baltic Prussia to the Black Sea. In spite of its ethnic and religious diversity and a substantial number of prosperous towns, it was primarily a land of great estates whose titled owners profited during this period from a rapidly expanding grain trade with the west. At the same time, the vast spaces of the north European plain and the Ukrainian steppe preserved the importance of cavalry and with it the military dominance of the knightly class.

The great magnates of both Poland and Lithuania negotiated their union after the death of Casimir the Great, and they continued to increase their power throughout the fifteenth century. The Jagiello dynasty survived mainly through capitulations. By 1500 Poland-Lithuania could be described as two aristocratic commonwealths joined by a largely ceremonial monarchy, not as a dynastic state. Serfdom was imposed in a series of edicts passed by the Polish *Sejm* or parliament between 1492 and 1501, and the crown, already elective in practice, became so in theory by 1572.

As in the case of Hungary, these aristocratic triumphs unfolded in the growing shadow of a menace to the east. Autocratic Russia, not the Polish-Lithuanian commonwealth, was destined to become the dominant power in eastern Europe, and by 1505 the borders of Lithuania were already shrinking. The process of transforming the grand duchy of Moscow into the Russian Empire began in earnest during the reign of Ivan III from 1462 to 1505. In the first thirteen years of his reign, Ivan was able to annex most of the independent Russian principalities and the city-states of Vyatka and Novgorod. In 1480 he refused to pay tribute to the Mongol khans and began to style himself "tsar of all Russia." Finally, in 1492, he invaded Lithuania and, in two successive campaigns, was able to annex much of Beloruss and the Ukraine.

Ivan was not a great field general. His son-in-law claimed rather sourly that "he increased his dominions while sitting at home and sleeping." But Ivan built an effective army and introduced the first usable artillery to eastern Europe. As most of his troops were cavalry, and therefore expensive to maintain, either he or his state secretary introduced the "service land" or *pomest'e* system, which granted land directly to cavalrymen instead of paying them in cash. It was an ideal way of supporting troops in a land that was still underpopulated and cash-poor. *Pomest'e* offered other dividends as well. It created an armed class that owed its prosperity directly to the tsar and permitted him to destroy local allegiances through the massive resettlement of populations. The annexation of Novgorod, for example, was followed by the removal of more than seven thousand citizens who were located elsewhere in Russia and replaced by Muscovites, many of whom were members of this service class.

The new service class cavalry were drawn primarily from the middle ranks of society and depended for their economic survival on peasant cultivators who worked their land. To ensure the stability of the labor force, they secured an edict in 1497 that restricted peasant movement. Thereafter, peasants were allowed to change employers only during a brief period centered on the feast of St. George (April 23). It was the first step toward serfdom. True serfdom on the Hungarian or Polish model did not become general until the end of the sixteenth century.

The Russia of Ivan III had little in common with western states or with its immediate neighbors. The tsar was an autocrat who ruled with little regard for representative institutions. The Orthodox church was implacably hostile to Latin christendom. The *pomest'e* system, like many other Russian institutions, derived from Turkish, Persian, and Byzantine precedents, and even daily life had an oriental flavor. Men wore beards and skirtlike garments that touched the ground while women were secluded and often veiled.

In the reign of Ivan's grandson, Ivan IV "the Terrible" (1530–84), the Russian state expanded eastward, adding Kazan and Astrakhan to its dominions. An effort to annex the areas now known as Latvia and Estonia was unsuccessful. Ivan attributed this failure to dissatisfaction among the *boyars*, or great nobles, and pretended to abdicate, returning only on the condition that he be allowed to establish an *oprichnina*. A bizarre

state within a state, the *oprichnina* was regarded as the tsar's private property. Land and even certain streets in Moscow were assigned to it, and the original owners were settled elsewhere. The purpose was to dismantle *boyar* estates as well as to provide income for Ivan's court and for a praetorian guard of six thousand men. Dressed in black and mounted upon black horses, these *oprichniki* carried a broom and the severed head of a dog as symbols of their primary mission: to root out "treason" and terrorize the enemies of the tsar. They succeeded admirably. Though disbanded in 1572, the *oprichniki* represented an institutionalization of autocracy and state terror that was unique in Europe.

Russia's size and military strength made it a great power, but its autocratic system of government ensured that political effectiveness would inevitably depend upon the personal qualities of the tsar. After Ivan IV, ability was conspicuously lacking. Russia turned inward for more than a hundred years, to emerge once again under the not-too-gentle guidance of Peter the Great at the beginning of the eighteenth century.

## The New Learning: Learned Culture in the Late Medieval Italian City-State

The social and political transformations of the late Middle Ages were accompanied, as great changes often are, by the development of new intellectual interests. The most important of these was the Renaissance, or, as it was sometimes called, the New Learning. The word *renaissance* means rebirth in French. It is often applied to the entire age that marked the end of the Middle Ages and the beginning of modern times, but its original meaning was more restricted. Beginning in the fourteenth century, a number of scholars became interested in the Greco-Roman past. They sought to recover the glories of classical literature because the learning of their own day seemed to them stagnant and largely irrelevant to their needs. A later generation saw the "renaissance" of classical antiquity that they created as the birth of modern times; more recent scholarship has emphasized its continuity with the medieval past. In its original form, the Renaissance was a direct outgrowth of life in the medieval Italian city-state, and its first proponents were Italian.

The status of medieval town dwellers was unclear. Even the richest were, by feudal standards, of humble origin, yet their wealth and literacy set them apart from the peasants. Chivalric literature affected to despise them, and ecclesiastical theorists found their activities dubious if not wicked. Trade, the lifeblood of any city, was often regarded as parasitic. The merchant bought low and sold high, profiting from the honest toil of the peasant and raising prices for everyone. The need for mechanisms of distribution was not always fully understood. Worse yet, the townsman was frequently a citizen (women, though they engaged in trade, had neither civic rights nor obligations). Under law he was compelled to vote and to hold public office if elected. Even before St. Augustine, western Christianity had been deeply suspicious of public life, regarding it as incompatible with concern for one's soul. In short, two of the most significant features of town life were either ignored by medieval writers or condemned by them outright.

A certain alienation from the norms of medieval culture was therefore to be expected among townsfolk even if it was not always fully conscious or easily articulated. This alienation was most intense in Italy. Italian town life had developed early. The acquisition of full sovereignty, rare in other parts of Europe, gave a peculiar intensity to political life in the Italian city-states while imposing heavy moral and intellectual responsibilities on their citizens. Extensive contact with the Muslim and Byzantine worlds may also have left the Italians more open to influences that came from outside the orbit of chivalric or scholastic ideas.

By the end of the thirteenth century, the intellectual life of the Italian towns was beginning to acquire a distinct flavor of its own. This was evident to some extent in the works of Dante Alighieri (1265–1321). His masterwork, *The Divine Comedy*, a brilliant evocation of hell, purgatory, and paradise written in the Tuscan vernacular (the basis of modern Italian), is arguably the greatest poem ever written by a European. It is filled with classical allusions and references to Florentine politics but remains essentially medieval in inspiration. The widening gap between Italian culture and that of the scholastic, chivalric north is far more striking in the city chronicles that were becoming popular with the urban elite. Unlike northern chronicles, which were often little more than a simple record of events, they increasingly sought to analyze the causes of political and economic phenomena to provide guidance for policy makers. On a less practical level, the *Decameron*, by the Florentine Giovanni Boccaccio (1313–75), was a collection of stories that portrayed the lives of city people with little reference to the conventions of chivalry.

That Boccaccio and another Florentine, Francesco Petrarca (or Petrarch, 1304–74), were among the first to develop a serious interest in the Roman past is no accident. Petrarch grew up in exile and spent most of his life at the papal court in Avignon, an existence that no doubt sharpened his personal sense of distance from chivalric and scholastic values. Believing, like other Italians, that he was descended from the ancient Romans, he began to seek out classical manuscripts and to compose works in Latin that demonstrated his affinity with the antique past. Among them were letters addressed to such ancient figures as Cicero and Livy and an epic poem, *Africa*, inspired by his reading of Virgil's *Aeniad*. His friend Boccaccio followed his lead in collecting manuscripts and compiled an encyclopedia of Greco-Roman mythology.

Petrarch is probably best known today for his sonnets written in the Tuscan vernacular, but classical studies consumed most of his working life. His efforts made an undeniably vital point. To Petrarch and to many of his readers, the society of ancient Rome had more in common with that of the Italian states than did the chivalric, scholastic world of transalpine Europe. The ancients had lived in cities and had believed that good citizenship was the highest of virtues. Accordingly, they had produced a vast body of literature on rhetoric, politics, history, and the other arts needed to produce effective citizens. Many Italians would eventually find these works to be of great practical value in the conduct of their lives.

Those who did so, and who made the study of antiquity their primary task, became known as humanists. The term was coined by Leonardo Bruni (c. 1370–1444) to describe those engaged in *studia humanitatis*, the study of secular letters as opposed to theology or divine letters. The movement became popular in Florence during the political crisis of 1392–1402 when Bruni and other publicists used classical examples of civic virtue to stir up the public against Giangaleazzo Visconti, despot of Milan, and his expansionist schemes. Even more important was the enthusiasm aroused by the arrival in Italy of Greek scholars who were seeking western aid against the Turks. Petrarch had known that Roman culture had Greek roots but could find no one to teach him classical Greek. Manuel Chrysaloras, Cardinal Bessarion, and other members of the Greek delegation were able to do this for Bruni's generation and, by so doing, opened up a great literary tradition that had been lost to the west for centuries. Spurred by these developments, humanism spread from Florence and

Rome to Venice and the other Italian states. By the mid-fifteenth century, it was attracting followers beyond the Alps.

## Humanism: Its Methods and Its Goals

Associating the early humanists with any fixed ideological or philosophical system is difficult. Most of them were either teachers of rhetoric or the editors of classical texts whose chief purpose was to study the classics and to apply ancient ideas and values to life in their own time. As such they might be found on almost any side of a given issue. But for all their variety, they shared certain presuppositions that defined them as a movement. Humanists by definition believed in the superiority of ancient culture. Errors, they said, were modern. Where medieval writers had seen their world as a historical extension of antiquity, the humanists saw a radical disjuncture between ancient and modern times, and they regarded the interval between the fall of Rome and their revival of antique ideals as a "middle age" of barbarity, ignorance, and above all, bad style. Immersed in the elegance of classical Latin, they were deeply concerned with form, sometimes, according to their critics, at the expense of substance.

Because they revered the classical past, they shared a preference for argument based on the authority of ancient sources and a suspicion of formal reason that bordered on contempt. The scholastics in particular were thought to be sterile and misguided, in part because of their bad Latin, but also because the nominalist rejection of reason as a support for faith had led the philosophers into pursuits that humanists regarded as trivial. Scholastics sometimes counterattacked by accusing them of irreligion. Though humanists were to be found among the critics of the church, few if any rejected conventional religious belief. The Renaissance moved Western society strongly toward secularism by reviving the ancient preoccupation with human beings and their social relationships. Writers such as Giovanni Pico della Mirandola asserted "the dignity of man" against preachers who saw humanity as wholly depraved (see document 13.3), but even Pico believed that human dignity derived largely from man's central place in a divinely established universe. Unbelief was not at issue. The humanists believed in perfecting their minds and bodies on Earth while preparing their souls for the hereafter.

Such a goal was fundamentally educational, and the humanists were predictably concerned with educational theory. Their purpose was to create *il uomo universale*, the universal man whose person combined intellectual and physical excellence and who was capable of functioning honorably in virtually any situation. It was the ancient Greco-Roman ideal, brought up-to-date and applied to life in the Italian city-state where the small size of the community forced citizens or courtiers to play many roles. Though most fully described in *The Courtier* by Baldassare Castiglione (published in 1528), it had long been present in the thinking of such educational theorists as Vittorino da Feltre (1386–1446) and Leon Battista Alberti (1404–72).

The heart of Renaissance education was ancient literature and history (see document 13.4). The classics were thought to provide both moral instruction and the deep understanding of human behavior without which correct action in the present is impossible. They were also a guide to style. The ability to communicate is essential to political life, and good writing comes largely from immersion in good literature. Humanists taught the art of persuasion through an exhaustive study of rhetoric based on the writings of Quintilian and Cicero.

Because citizens and courtiers would almost certainly participate in war, study was thought to be necessary in military history and theory, the art of fortification, and ballistics. Educators regarded proficiency with weapons and physical fitness as essential for war, furthermore, like the ancients, they regarded athletic skill as of value in its own right. The Renaissance man or woman was also expected to be good company. Sports were a social skill as was dancing, the ability to play musical instruments, and the possession of a trained singing voice. Art was useful, not merely for the sake of appreciation, but also as a tool of observation. Before the camera, only drawing or sketching could preserve a record of visual impressions—or accurately portray the fortifications of one's enemies. Other useful subjects included mathematics, accounting, medicine, and the natural sciences.

The preferred means of imparting this rather daunting quantity of knowledge was in small academies or by means of a tutor. The teacher was supposed to live with his students and be a moral example and friend as well as a purveyor of knowledge. Students were not to be beaten or threatened but induced to learn by arousing their interest in the subject at hand. These humanist theories, and the classical examples from which they came, remain the basis of today's liberal arts education. They have had an enormous impact on the formation of European youth and on the devel-

◆ DOCUMENT 13.4 ◆

## The Value of the Liberal Arts

*Peter Paul Vergerio (1370–1444) was a leading Renaissance educational theorist. The following is from a letter he wrote to another humanist, Ubertino of Carrara.*

For no wealth, no possible security against the future, can be compared with the gift of education in grave and liberal studies. By them a man may win distinction for the most modest name, and bring honor to the city of his birth however obscure it may be. . . .

We come now to the consideration of the various subjects which may rightly be included under the name of "Liberal Studies." Among these I accord the first place to History, on grounds both of its attractiveness and its utility, qualities which appeal equally to the scholar and to the statesman. Next in importance is Moral Philosphy, which indeed is, in a peculiar sense, a "Liberal Art" in that its purpose is to teach men the secret of true freedom. History, then, gives us the concrete examples of the precepts inculcated by philosophy. The one shows what men should do, the other what men have said and done in the past, and what lessons we may draw therefrom for the present day. I would indicate as the third main branch of study, Eloquence, which indeed holds a place of distinction among the refined Arts. By philosophy we learn the essential truth of things, which by eloquence we so exhibit in orderly adornment as to bring conviction to differing minds. And history provides the light of experience.

Vergirio, Peter Paul. Letter to Ubertino of Carrara. In W.H. Woodward, ed., *Vittorino da Feltre and Other Humanist Educators*, pp. 106–107. New York: Bureau of Publications, Teachers College, Columbia University, 1963.

opment of Western culture. However, humanist education was intended only for a relatively narrow social elite: the select group that participated in public life and exercised some degree of control over its own destiny. Even women were largely excluded, though humanists such as Leonardo Bruni, Juan Luis Vives, and Thomas More argued that women should be educated in much the same way as men (see document 13.5).

## ◆ DOCUMENT 13.5 ◆

## Louise Labé: The Education of Women

*Though the Renaissance ideal of education extended only to a minority of women, many saw even this as a liberating step forward in the development of women as a whole. One of them was Louise Labé (c. 1524–66), an important French poet whose ideas in some ways foreshadow modern feminism. The following is from a dedicatory preface written to a friend.*

Since a time has come, Mademoiselle, when the severe laws of men no longer prevent women from applying themselves to the sciences and other disciplines, it seems to me that those of us who can should use this long-craved freedom to study and to let men see how greatly they wronged us when depriving us of its honor and advantages. And if any woman becomes so proficient as to be able to write down her thoughts, let her do so and not despise the honor but rather flaunt it instead of fine clothes, necklaces, and rings. For these may be considered ours only by use, whereas the honor of being educated is ours entirely. . . . If the heavens had endowed me with sufficient wit to understand all I would have liked, I would serve in this as an example rather than an admonishment.

But having devoted part of my youth to musical exercises, and finding the time left too short for the crudeness of my understanding, I am unable in my own case, to achieve what I want for our sex, which is to see it outstrip men not only in beauty but in learning and virtue. All I can do is to beg our virtuous ladies to raise their minds somewhat above their distaffs and spindles and try to prove to the world that if we were not made to command, still we should not be disdained in domestic and public matters by those who govern and command obedience.

If there is anything to be recommended after honor and glory, anything to incite us to study, it is the pleasure which study affords. Study differs in this from all other recreations, of which all one can say, after enjoying them, is that one has passed the time. But study gives a more enduring sense of satisfaction. For the past delights us and serves more than the present.

Labé, Louise. Dedicatory preface. From J. Aynard, ed., *Les poétes lyonnais précurseurs de la Pléide.* In Julia O'Faolain and Lauro Martines, *Not in God's Image: Women in History from the Greeks to the Victorians,* pp. 184–185. London: Temple Smith, 1973.

Such women as Vitoria Colonna and More's daughter, Margaret Roper, developed a reputation for classical learning. But for the most part, the education of upper-class women continued to emphasize the domestic and social graces as it had done for centuries.

The usefulness of the Renaissance educational ideal was in part responsible for the spread of humanism beyond the Alps. The requirements of life as a courtier or servant of the crown in England, France, or Spain were not unlike those demanded of the upper-class Italian. Such people were among the first non-Italians to develop an interest in the classics, but they were quickly followed by their princes. Isabella of Castile, for example, imported Italian humanists to raise the educational standards of her court and administration. Lawyers, too, were intrigued by humanist methods. The development of philology and of the historical analysis of texts had been among the first achievements of humanist scholarship. The legal profession in France and Germany was soon divided between those who added the new tech-

niques to their arsenals and those who refused to do so. Above all, town councils were quick to recognize the usefulness of officials trained in the new learning. It became desirable, especially in the cities of the Holy Roman Empire, to have town clerks who could communicate with one another in classical Latin and who possessed the training to interpret and decipher old documents. Usefulness aside, the presence of learned humanists within a town or principality had become a matter of prestige.

The universities were in general more resistant to change. They remained the strongholds of Aristotelianism if for no other reason than that their traditional role had been the training of theologians. Some, however, such as John Colet at Oxford and Lefèvre d'Etaples at Paris, began to perceive the usefulness of humanism for the study of religious literature, which was another form of ancient text. Others, outside the universities, shared their concern. The most famous of those who turned humanist methods to the study of Scripture and

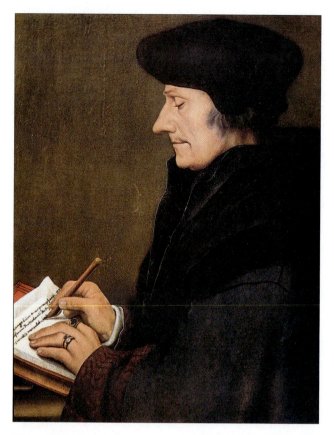

**Illustration 13.2**

🎨 **Erasmus of Rotterdam.** In this famous portrait by Hans Holbein, the greatest of the northern humanists is shown at his writing desk.

Cisneros, archbishop of Toledo, grand inquisitor, and ultimately regent of Castile, established the University of Alcalá de Henares in 1508 to provide humanist training for the Spanish clergy. Among its first products was the Complutensian Polyglot Bible, printed in Greek, Hebrew, and Latin.

## The Impact of Renaissance Humanism on the Arts and Sciences

By 1500 humanist methods and values had spread to virtually every part of Europe. Their impact on the arts and sciences was enormous, though not always what one might expect. The humanists developed classical studies as they are known today. They created the first standardized editions of classical works and distributed them widely after printing with moveable type was invented, probably by Johan Gutenberg, in the mid-fifteenth century. In the process, humanism gave birth to the disciplines of linguistics, philology (the study of words), and historical criticism.

In literature, however, humanist devotion to the classics retarded the development of vernacular writing for more than a century. Those with literary inclinations preferred to write in Latin, often in slavish imitation of the elaborate Roman style that had developed during the Augustan Age. When vernacular literature was revived in the sixteenth century by such figures as Tasso and Ariosto in Italy, Cervantes and Garcilaso de la Vega in Spain, Rabelais and Montaigne in France, and Marlowe and Shakespeare in England, it was transformed by classical themes and rules of composition. The fifteenth century, however, had been remarkably unproductive. Latin, in the meantime, was practically destroyed as a living language. Because the humanists insisted on weeding out all nonclassical usages, the language ceased to evolve as it had done throughout the Middle Ages when it was the day-to-day language of diplomacy and administration in both church and state. Ironically, by the middle of the sixteenth century, Latin had largely been supplanted by the various European vernaculars in every western government outside the papal states.

The contribution of humanism to the study of history and politics was far more positive. From the beginning, humanists had regarded history as essential to a political education. At the very least, it provided inspiring examples of civic virtue and cautionary tales that would help the citizen or courtier to avoid the mistakes of the past.

of the Fathers of the church was Erasmus of Rotterdam (1469–1536). Believing that corrupted texts had led to false interpretations, he devoted much of his extraordinarily busy and productive life to providing authoritative editions of religious texts. Best known today for his satirical attacks on ecclesiastical ignorance and for his bitter controversy with Martin Luther over the issue of free will, he was in many ways the epitome of the humanist whose chief interests were religious (see illustration 13.2). His English friend Sir Thomas More (1477–1535) combined religious with secular interests. A lawyer who ultimately became lord chancellor to Henry VIII, he is perhaps best known for *Utopia,* his vision of a perfect society that recalls Plato's *Republic.* More also applied humanist scholarship to the law and to religious questions before being martyred for his opposition to the Reformation. He was sainted by the Catholic Church in 1935. The value of humanist studies was recognized on occasion by even the most conservative churchmen. Cardinal Francisco Jiménez de

In the Middle Ages, the dominant form of history had been the chronicle. Outside the Italian cities, chroniclers tended to record events without troubling themselves greatly over causation or the objective accuracy of their sources. The cause of historical events was after all God's will. The Greeks and Romans had taken a different view. Beginning with Thucydides, the best of them had defined their topics as questions to be answered in causal terms because they believed that human nature was consistent and that history therefore repeated itself. If history was cyclical, it offered a priceless guide to action in the present, not so much because it was predictive in absolute terms, but because the process of historical causation could be understood and used by the educated to their own advantage.

The most effective exponent of this view during the Renaissance was the Florentine lawyer and some-time politician Niccolò Machiavelli (1469–1527). In works such as *The Prince* and *The Discourses on Livy* he attempted to establish rules for the conduct of political life based upon examples from the historical past. In the process, he freed political theory from the theological principles upon which it had long been based. While his name became a byword for cynicism and political manipulation, Machiavelli was in his own way an idealist. The Italian wars begun by Charles VIII of France in 1495 eventually destroyed the independence of the Italian cities with only Venice retaining full sovereignty. Machiavelli believed that this calamity could be understood and remedied only by looking with a clear eye at the way in which politics was conducted (see document 13.6).

His younger contemporary, Francesco Guicciardini (1483–1540), agreed but thought that governing oneself by the kind of rules proposed by Machiavelli was impossible. As he said in his *Ricordi*, a grim collection of musings on a variety of subjects, no two situations were the same; there were always exceptions. He seems to have believed that by studying history one absorbed what he called discretion: the ability to react intelligently to unforeseen contingencies. His *History of Italy*, which examines the loss of Italian freedom in the years after 1494, is probably the first modern historical work and remains a useful source for the political and military history of the age.

By comparison with its impact on politics and history, the humanist contribution to philosophy was indirect. The Renaissance was not a great age of formal speculation, but the course of modern philosophy would be hard to imagine without the recovery of classical works that had been lost during the Middle Ages.

---

◆ DOCUMENT 13.6 ◆

## The Political Philosophy of Machiavelli

*Niccolò Machiavelli's most famous book was* The Prince *in which he appears to favor despotic rule as a means of ridding Italy of its "barbarian" invaders. However, he was an ardent republican both in theory and in his own career as secretary to the second chancery of the Florentine republic. The following passage from* The Discourses *sets out what may be taken as his real view.*

And finally to sum up this matter, I say that both governments of princes and of the people have lasted a long time, but both require to be regulated by laws. For a prince who knows no other control but his own will is like a madman, and a people that can do as it pleases will hardly be wise. If now we compare a prince who is controlled by laws, and a people who is untrammeled by them, we shall find more virtue in the people than in the prince; and if we compare them when both are freed from such control, we shall see that the people are guilty of fewer excesses than the prince, and that the errors of the people are of less importance, and may therefore be more easily remedied. For a licentious and mutinous people can be brought back to good conduct by the influence and persuasion of a good man, but an evil-minded prince is not amenable to such influences, and there is therefore no other remedy against him but cold steel.

Macchiavelli, Nicoló, *The Discourses* I, 58, trans. Luigi Ricci, rev. E.R.P. Vincent. Modern Library Editions. New York: Random House, 1950.

---

Much of Aristotle, most of Plato and the Alexandrian Neoplatonists, the Pre-Socratics, and many of the Epicureans and Stoics were either unknown or had been studied with little regard to their historical and intellectual context. By recovering lost works and seeking a deeper understanding of the mental world that had produced them, the humanists immeasurably broadened philosophic discourse in the West. By attacking the scholastics, they opened the way for the acceptance of ideas that lay outside the Aristotelian tradition as it was then understood. They may have done little to exploit their own discoveries, but they made possible the great philosophical achievements of the seventeenth century. The impact of humanism on science was similar. Few humanists were scientists in the modern sense of the word. Many were devotees of what would now be called superstition, though the term is unhistorical. Believing that the wisdom of the ancients was superior, and aware that Greeks and Romans had believed in divination, sorcery, astrology, and natural magic, some humanists deliberately encouraged a revival of these practices. Notions that would have been regarded as absurd in the days of Aquinas were taken seriously. Nevertheless, in their zeal to recover every aspect of the ancient past, they found and edited works that would eventually revolutionize Western thought. Galen in medicine, Eratosthenes and Aristarchus of Samos in cosmology, Archimedes in physics, and a host of other writers were rediscovered, edited, and popularized.

The humanists also transmitted the idea, derived ultimately from Pythagoras, that the universe was based on number. This is the basic principle of numerology, now regarded as a pseudoscience, but it inspired such figures as Leonardo da Vinci (1452–1519) to explore the mathematization of physics. Leonardo is best known today as an artist and inventor whose ideas were far in advance of their time. Though Leonardo failed in his effort regarding physics, Galileo and others would eventually learn to express physical relationships in mathematical formulae, an important step in the development of modern science (see chapter 16).

Few of these achievements had an immediate impact on the life of ordinary Europeans. The recovery of classical antiquity was an intellectual movement created by and for a self-conscious elite, and many years would pass before it touched the consciousness of the general public. In one area, however, classical values intruded on material life, redefining the public spaces in which people moved and altering their visual perceptions of the world. Renaissance art, architecture, and city planning brought the aesthetic values of Greece and Rome down to street level. They eventually spread from the Italian towns to the farthest reaches of Europe and America.

Italian artists had turned to classical ruins for inspiration as early as the thirteenth century. With the emergence of humanism, ancient models became universal. The architect Filippo Brunelleschi (1377–1446) measured ancient ruins to determine their proportions. He then sketched their pediments, columns, and ornamentation with the intention of adapting Roman forms to

**Illustration 13.3**

**Leon Battista Alberti's Tempio Malatesta.** The unfinished church of San Francesco at Rimini was built about 1450. Rimini was a city in the papal states whose ruler, the infamous Sigismundo Malatesta, was a great admirer of all things Roman. At his request, Alberti transformed an existing church into a Roman temple whose facade resembles a triumphal arch. Sigismundo commissioned a statue of the Virgin Mary whose features were modeled on those of his mistress, Isotta degli Atti.

the purposes of his own day. Within a generation, churches were being built that resembled pagan temples (see illustration 13.3). New construction, private and public, sported columns, pilasters, and window treatments borrowed from the porticoes of Roman buildings. It was not mere antiquarianism because Brunelleschi and his successors—Alberti, Bramante, and the sixteenth-century master Palladio—knew that modern structures were different in function from those of the past. So successful were their adaptations that Roman forms and ornamentation remained a standard feature of Western architecture until the twentieth century.

The revival of classical taste in painting and sculpture was equally important. Medieval artists had illustrated classical themes, and some of them, such as Nicola Pisano (c. 1220–c. 1278), had successfully imitated classical forms, though only in portraying scenes from the Bible (see illustration 13.4). In medieval practice, tales from ancient history or mythology were normally portrayed in contemporary settings because they were intended as moral or religious allegories whose

**Illustration 13.4**

🎨 **The Anunciation, by Nicola Pisano.** This panel from the Baptistry at Pisa was completed in 1260. It demonstrates that classical models had come to influence Italian art long before the Renaissance took root as a literary movement.

**Illustration 13.5**

🎨 **St. James Led to Execution, by Andrea Mantegna.** Mantegna was one of the first Renaissance painters to use the laws of perspective discovered by the architect Filippo Brunelleschi. In this fresco from the Ovetari Chapel, Church of the Erimitani, Padua, painted c. 1454–57, the vanishing point is below the bottom of the picture. Note also the classicism of the triumphal arch.

message was often unlike that of their pagan originals. To the humanists, with their archaeological view of history, this was absurd. Classical forms were appropriate to classical subjects as well as to those derived from the Bible. The imitation of classical models and the use of classical settings therefore became almost universal. Ancient ideas of beauty and proportion were adopted, especially for the portrayal of the human body.

But Renaissance art was not an exercise in antiquarianism. The technique of painting with oils, developed in the Low Countries during the fifteenth century, was soon in general use. The effort to portray the world in three dimensions, begun with the use of *chiaroscuro* or shading by Giotto (c. 1266– c. 1337), was brought to a triumphal conclusion with Brunelleschi's discovery of the mathematical laws of perspective. Their application in the paintings of Andrea Mantegna (c. 1431–1506) inspired other artists, and the viewing public soon came to accept foreshortening and perspective as the norm (see illustration 13.5).

These techniques were new. Furthermore, Renaissance artists differed from the ancients in other ways. They were not pagans, and though they admired antiquity, they retained many of the ideas and symbols of the medieval past. Their art combined classical and Christian sensibilities in a new synthesis that shaped European aesthetic values until their vision was challenged by the rise of photography and nonrepresenta-

tional art in the nineteenth century. Eventually, artists such as Michelangelo Buonarroti (1475–1564) would transcend the rules of classical composition, distorting the proportions of the human body to express dramatic spiritual and emotional truths (see illustration 13.6). But even he and his Baroque followers in the seventeenth century remained well within the bounds of classical inspiration.

A century ago, most historians believed that the Renaissance marked the beginning of the modern world. As the full implications of the industrial revolution became clear, that conviction has dimmed and the distance between twentieth-century Westerners and the preoccupations of the humanists has widened. Few today believe that the Renaissance was a true rebirth of classical antiquity or as revolutionary as its more enthusiastic supporters claimed. There had been a Carolingian Renaissance and a Renaissance of the Twelfth

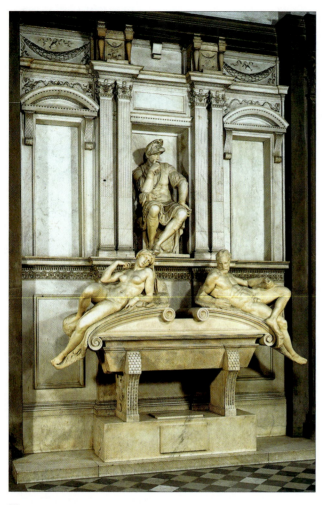

Century. Medieval scholars knew and quoted classical writers, but the Renaissance that began in Florence in the generation of the Black Death was far more than just another in a series of European infatuations with the antique past. By rediscovering the lost masterpieces of Greek and Roman literature, by reviving the ancient preoccupation with history, and by reexamining scientific theories ignored during the Middle Ages, the humanists redefined learning and transformed education. By the early fifteenth century, the new learning had become the dominant movement in European intellectual life. Directly or indirectly, it remade each of the arts and sciences in its own image and changed forever the way in which Westerners looked at their world.

**Illustration 13.6**

Tombs of Giuliano de' Medici, Duke of Nemours and Lorenzo de' Medici, Duke of Urbino, by Michelangelo. Michelangelo executed this magnificent group in the New Sacristy of San Lorenzo, Florence, between 1520 and 1534. The distorted poses of the heavily muscled reclining figures as well as the dramatic arrangement of the entire piece point away from classical balance and serenity while retaining a basically antique frame of reference.

# CHAPTER 14

# THE RELIGIOUS REFORMATIONS OF THE SIXTEENTH CENTURY

Much of Europe's religious life was transformed in the course of the sixteenth century. Scholars have called this period the Age of the Reformation, but this is somewhat misleading. There was more than one religious reformation. Several forms of piety arose that may be called Protestant, though their competing religious visions sometimes had little in common beyond opposition to the old church. Lutherans, Calvinists, Anabaptists, and a host of other groups distrusted and at times persecuted each other with un-Christian vigor. Others, such as the Antitrinitarians, were perhaps radical enough to require a classification of their own. Roman Catholicism was changed, in part by forces that had long been stirring within and in part by the church's need to defend itself against Protestantism.

All of these reformations arose from conflicts within the church and from its broader struggle with the claims of the state. Some of the issues were institutional and political. Others grew from changes in lay attitudes or from the influence of movements such as humanism and nominalism. Chapter 14 will examine the demands for church reform that arose during the later Middle Ages and describe how they grew into a series of religious movements that split western Christendom and transformed the old church even as they created new forms of religious belief.

◆

## Late Medieval Demands for Religious Reform

The new assertiveness of the secular states brought them almost immediately into conflict with the church over rights, privileges, and revenues. That this occurred when the laity and many clergy were demanding higher standards of spirituality than ever before was the church's misfortune. Plague, war, and the perception of social collapse had raised the overall level of spiritual anxiety. At the same time, higher literacy rates, already apparent in the fourteenth century, narrowed the intellectual gap between the clergy and their flocks and led to an increased sophistication in matters religious. When the church, beset with enemies and divided internally, failed to meet this revolution of rising spiritual expectations, the call for reform became strident and ultimately irresistible.

The role of the late medieval church was broader and more closely integrated with the secular world than it is today. The pope was responsible not only for the spiritual welfare of western Christians, but also for the administration and defense of the papal states, a territory that embraced much of central Italy. At the local level, bishops, parishes, monasteries, and other ecclesiastical foundations probably controlled 20 percent of the arable land in Europe. In less-settled areas such as the north of England the total may have approached 70 percent. Many Europeans therefore lived on estates held by the church or had regular business dealings with those who managed them. Such contacts often caused resentment and may at times have encouraged the appearance of corruption.

Social services, too, were the church's responsibility. Hospitals, the care of orphans, and the distribution of charity were commonly administered by clerics, as was formal education from the grammar school to the university. In an age when inns were few and wretched, monasteries often served as hotels, offering food and lodging to travelers in return for nominal donations.

Involvement with the world bred a certain worldliness. Because its practical responsibilities were great, the church was often forced to reward those in whom administrative skills were more developed than spirituality. Because the church offered one of the few available routes to upward social mobility, ambition or family interest caused many to become clerics without an adequate religious vocation. Some had little choice. Children were often destined for the priesthood at a tender age, while unmarriageable women or those who preferred a career other than that of wife and mother had only the convent as a refuge. For women of talent and ambition, the opportunity to govern an abbey or a charitable institution was a route to self-fulfillment and public service that was otherwise unavailable in medieval society.

Not all late medieval clerics were governed by worldly motives. Alongside spiritual indifference and corruption were extreme piety and asceticism. For many people the contrast may have been too painful in an era of great spiritual need. In any case the anticlericalism that had always been present in European life ran especially high in the fourteenth and fifteenth centuries. Though by no means universal—the ties between lay people and their parish priests often remained close—it was an underlying accompaniment to the events that convulsed the church throughout this period.

## Anticlericalism and the Decline of Papal Authority

Papal authority was one of the first casualties of the conflict between church and state and of the growing confusion over the temporal and spiritual roles of the clergy. A series of scandals beginning around 1300 gravely weakened the ability of the popes either to govern the church or to institute effective reforms in the face of popular demand.

In 1294 the saintly Celestine V resigned from the papacy in part because he feared that the exercise of its duties imperiled his soul. His successor, Boniface VIII, had no such concerns. A vigorous advocate of papal authority, Boniface came into conflict with both Edward I of England and Philip IV of France over the issue of clerical taxation. The two kings were at war with one another, and each sought to tax the clergy of their respective realms to pay for it. When the pope forbade the practice in the bull *Clericis Laicos*, Philip blocked the transmission of money from France to Rome. Boniface backed down, but Philip was not content with partial victories. In 1301, he convicted the papal legate of treason and demanded that Boniface ratify the decision of the French courts. This he could not do without sacrificing papal jurisdiction over the French church. When Boniface issued the decree *Unam Sanctam*, a bold assertion of papal authority over the secular state, Philip had him kidnapped at Anagni in 1303. Physically mistreated by his captors and furious over this unprecedented assault on papal dignity, Boniface died shortly thereafter.

After the brief pontificate of Benedict IX, French influence in the College of Cardinals secured the election of the bishop of Bordeaux, who became pope as Clement V (served 1305–14). The Roman populace was outraged. Riot and disorder convinced Clement that Rome would be an unhealthy place for a Frenchman. He decided to establish himself at Avignon, a papal territory in the south of France. The papacy would remain there for seventy-three years.

The stay of the popes at Avignon was called the Babylonian Captivity because the church appeared to have been taken captive by the French as the biblical children of Israel had been held at Babylon. It was an

**Illustration 14.1**

//// **The Papal Palace at Avignon.** The luxury and massive size of the papal residence built during the so-called Babylonian Captivity helps to explain why the Avignon popes developed a reputation for greed and spiritual indifference.

international scandal for several reasons. The pope was living outside his diocese, and absenteeism had long been considered an abuse by reformers. Worse yet, the pope seemed to be a mere agent of the French monarchy. This was not quite true. The Avignon popes were more independent than they appeared to be at the time, but their support of France against England in the later stages of the Hundred Years' War reinforced negative impressions. Their best efforts were devoted to strengthening papal finances and to the construction of a magnificent palace complex at Avignon (see illustration 14.1). Fiscal reforms backfired politically because most countries responded to it with legislation limiting papal jurisdiction and taxation within their borders. The palace was ostentatious and fostered the idea that the popes had no intention of returning to Rome. The overall impression was that the popes were subservient to France as well as greedy and luxurious.

Criticism mounted, and in 1377 Gregory XI returned the papacy to Rome. He died in the following year, and his Italian successor, Urban VI, was elected amid rioting by the Roman mob and dissension among the cardinals. Urban quickly alienated those who had elected him by his erratic behavior and by his demands for an immediate reform of the papal court. Thirteen cardinals, twelve of whom were French, left Rome. Claiming that the election had been held under duress, they elected an antipope, Clement VII. The Great Schism (1378–1417) had begun.

The church now had two popes. England, the Holy Roman Empire, Hungary, and Poland supported Urban VI. France, Castile, Aragon, Naples, and Scotland supported Clement. International and dynastic issues were involved, and neither claimant would step down. For nearly forty years each side elected its own successors while papal administration deteriorated and the prestige of the office sank to levels not seen since before the Cluniac reforms.

The most promising solution was to convene a general council of the church. In 1409 the Council of

◆ DOCUMENT 14.1 ◆

## The Decree *Sacrosancta*

*By issuing the decree Sacrosancta, the Council of Constance (1414–17) justified its deposition of three existing popes and the election of Martin V. Though repudiated by later popes, the decree helped to end the Great Schism and provided a concise statement of the conciliarist position for future generations.*

In the name of the Holy and indivisible Trinity; of the Father, Son, and Holy Ghost. Amen.

This holy synod of Constance, forming a general council for the extirpation of the present schism and the union and reformation, in head and members, of the church of God, legitimately assembled in the Holy Ghost, to the praise of Omnipotent God, in order that it may the more easily, safely, effectively, and freely bring about the union and reformation of the church of God, hereby determines, decrees, and declares what follows:

It first declares that this same council, legitimately assembled in the Holy Ghost, forming a general council and representing the Catholic Church militant, has its power immediately from Christ, and everyone, whatever his state or position, even if it be the Papal dignity itself, is bound to obey it in all those things which pertain to the faith and the healing of the said schism, and to the general reformation of the Church of God in head and members.

It further declares that anyone, whatever his condition, station or rank, even if it be the Papal, who shall contumaciously refuse to obey the mandates, decrees, ordinances or instructions which have been, or shall be issued by this holy council, or by any other general council, legitimately summoned, which concern, or in any way relate to the above mentioned subjects, shall, unless he repudiate his conduct, be subjected to condign penance and be suitably punished, having recourse, if necessary, to the other resources of the law.

Council of Constance. *"Sacrosancta."* In Edward P. Cheyney, ed., *Pennsylvania Translations and Reprints*, vol. 3, no. 6 Philadelphia: University of Pennsylvania Press, 1898.

---

Pisa elected Alexander V, who was generally accepted throughout Europe. However, the two prior claimants, arguing that the council had been called illegally by the cardinals instead of by a pope, refused to quit. There were now three popes. Finally, in 1413 Alexander's successor, John XXIII, called the Council of Constance, which declared itself superior to any pope (see document 14.1). John, who had in the meantime been found guilty of heresy, and the Avignon claimant Benedict XIII were deposed and Gregory XIII resigned. Martin V was elected to succeed Gregory, thereby preserving the legitimacy of the Roman line, which has since been regarded as official.

The Schism was over, but the papacy had been gravely weakened in both fact and theory. The actions of the council were supported by the work of three generations of thinkers who had come to believe that councils representing the entire body of the faithful had ultimate authority over the church and that the pope was little more than a symbol of unity. Made plausible by more than a century of papal scandals, conciliarism became a formidable obstacle to the governance of the church. Fifteenth-century popes feared with some justification that they might be deposed for

any controversial act, while councils, by their nature, found making everyday administrative decisions impossible. Legally, the issue was resolved in 1460 when Pius II forbade appeals to a council without papal authorization in the bull *Execrabilis*. The memory of conciliarism nevertheless would inhibit papal efforts at reform for years to come.

Conciliarism also served as a focus for criticisms of the papacy that had been simmering since the Babylonian Captivity. Other complaints against the papacy, some of which were adopted by the conciliarists, grew out of the possessionist controversy. By the end of the thirteenth century, the Franciscan order had split into two main factions: the Observant or Spiritual Franciscans, who insisted on a literal interpretation of the Rule of St. Francis, which prohibited the order from owning property; and the Conventuals, who believed that the work of the order could be done only if the brothers lived an orderly life in convents and possessed the material resources with which to perform their tasks. After much argument, the Observant position was condemned by John XXII. The Observant Franciscans responded with attacks on the validity of papal authority, many of which would be used by later critics of the church.

## The Struggle for the Transformation of Piety

The issue of church governance became entangled in a growing dispute over the forms of piety. This conflict, which was about two different ways of living a Christian life, had been present implicitly in the reform movements of the twelfth century. The dominant form of piety that had emerged from the early Middle Ages was forged by the monastic tradition. It saw the clergy as heroic champions whose chief function was to serve as intermediaries between the laity and a God of judgment. They did this primarily through the sacrament of communion (the Eucharist), which was considered a sacrifice, and through oral prayers of intercession. This view, with its necessary emphasis on the public repetition of formulae, was challenged in the eleventh and twelfth centuries by Bernard of Clairvaux and other monastic theorists who sought a more personal experience of God through private devotions and mental prayer. Their views were adopted by the Franciscans and eventually popularized by them, though the process was lengthy and incomplete. Personal piety was especially attractive to the Observant Franciscans, whose interpretation of the Rule of St. Francis made corporate devotions difficult.

To those who sought a transformation of their inner life through personal contact with God, the older forms of piety were unacceptable. They came to believe that excessive emphasis on the sacraments and on oral prayer encouraged complacency as well as contractualism, the habit of making deals with God in return for special favors. The point is arguable, but in their critique of popular piety they were on firmer ground. Much late medieval piety was mechanistic and involved practices that would today be regarded as abuses. The sale of indulgences, the misuse of pilgrimages, and the proliferation of masses for the dead were all symptoms of the popular obsession with death and purgatory that followed in the wake of the bubonic plague. Salvation was assured by the sacraments of the church, but every sin committed in life carried with it a sentence to be served in purgatory. As the pains of purgatory were like those of hell, without the curse of eternal separation from God, much effort was spent in avoiding them. A mass said for the soul of the dead reduced the penalty by a specified number of years. Henry VII of England, who seems to have had a bad conscience, left money in his will for ten thousand masses. Many priests survived entirely on the proceeds from such bequests and had no other duties. An indulgence was a remission of the "temporal" or purgatorial punishment for sins that could be granted by the pope out of the church's "treasury of merits." Its price, too, was related to the number of years it subtracted from the buyer's term in purgatory, and an indulgence sometimes could be purchased in advance for sins not yet committed.

Such practices were deeply rooted in the rich and varied piety of the Middle Ages. If some religious were scandalized by them, other priests were unwilling to condemn genuine expressions of religious feeling, and still others no doubt accepted them out of ignorance. No systematic education had been established for parish priests, and thanks to absenteeism, many parishes were served by vicars or substitutes whose qualifications were minimal at best. However, the church's critics did not reject pilgrimages, indulgences, the proper use of relics, or masses for the dead. They merely wished to ground these "works" in the faith and good intentions that would make them spiritually valid. They opposed simpleminded contractualism and "arithmetical" piety, but their concerns intensified their conflict with a church that remained immobilized by political and organizational difficulties.

Of those forms of piety that sought personal contact with God, the most ambitious was mysticism. The enormous popularity of mysticism in the later Middle Ages was in some respects a measure of the growing influence of women on religious life. Many of the great mystics were women. Others were men who became involved with the movement as confessors to convents of nuns. Mysticism may be defined as the effort to achieve spiritual union with God through ecstatic contemplation. Because the experience is highly personal, it had many variants, but most of them fell into two broad categories. The first, and probably the most common, was to experience visions or infusions of the Holy Spirit in the manner of St. Catherine of Siena (1347–80) or Julian of Norwich (1342–c. 1416). The second, best typified by Meister Eckhardt (c. 1260–1328) and the Rhineland mystics, was influenced by the Neoplatonic concept of ideas and aimed at a real union of the soul with God (see document 14.2). They sought to penetrate the divine intelligence and perceive the universe as God perceives it. Both views were rooted firmly in the medieval tradition of interior piety, but Eckhardt and those like him were suspected of heresy because they seemed to deny the vital distinction between the Creator and the human soul.

Neither form of experience was easy to achieve. Both involved a long process of mental and spiritual preparation that was described in an ever-growing literature. Manuals such as Walter Hilton's *Scale of Perfection* became extremely popular with lay people and were circulated in large numbers both before and after the invention of printing.

Though mysticism was essentially private, it influenced the development of a powerful corporate movement known as the *Devotio Moderna*, or modern devotion. Its founder was Gerhard Groote (1340–84) who organized a community of religious women at Deventer in the Netherlands. These Sisters of the Common Life were laywomen, not nuns. They pledged themselves to a communal life informed by contemplation but directed toward service in the world. A parallel group for men, the Brethren of the Common Life, was founded shortly thereafter by Groote's disciple Florens Radewijns. These two groups, together with the Augustinian Canons of the Windesheim Congregation, a fully monastic order also founded by Radewijns, formed the nucleus of a movement that spread rapidly through the Low Countries and western Germany. Catholic, but highly critical of the clergy, it emphasized charitable works, private devotion, and its own form of education. The goal of its adherents was the imitation of Christ. A book titled *The Imitation of Christ* by one of the Brethren, Thomas à Kempis, was a best-seller until well into the twentieth century and did much to popularize a style of piety that was the opposite of contractualism.

## The Heretics: Wycliffe and Hus

Other religious movements were less innocent, at least from the perspective of the church. Full-scale heresies emerged in England and Bohemia in response to the teachings of John Wycliffe (1330–84) and Jan Hus (c. 1372–1415). Wycliffe was a successful teacher of theology at Oxford who became involved with politics during the 1370s. England was attempting to follow the French lead in restricting papal rights of appointment and taxation, and Wycliffe became the chief spokesman for the anticlerical views of Edward III's son, John of Gaunt. At first Wycliffe restricted himself to the traditional arguments in favor of clerical poverty, but as his views began to attract criticism and as he came to realize that his personal ambitions would not be fulfilled, he drifted further into radicalism. In his last years, he rejected papal authority and declared that the Bible was the sole source of religious truth. Strongly influenced by St. Augustine and committed to an extreme form of philosophical realism, he supported predestination and ended by rejecting transubstantiation because it involved what he saw as the annihilation of the substance of the bread and wine. In his view, substance was by definition unchangeable, and the miracle of the mass was therefore an impossibility. This was heresy, as was his revival of the ancient Donatist idea that the value of the sacraments depended upon the personal virtue of the priest who administered them.

Though John of Gaunt discretely withdrew his support, Wycliffe died before the church could bring him to trial. By this time his ideas and the extraordinary violence of his attacks on the clergy had begun to attract popular attention. His followers, the Lollards, produced an English translation of the Bible and organized a march on London in 1413. Fearing that the egalitarian tendencies of the Lollards encouraged social disorder, Henry V suppressed the movement, but scattered communities preserved their traditions until the outbreak of the Protestant Reformation.

Because England and Bohemia were diplomatically aligned on the Great Schism, a number of Czech students left the University of Paris for Oxford after 1378. There they came in contact with the teachings of Wycliffe, and by 1400 his works were being openly debated at Prague. Wycliffe's ideas were popular because they seemed to coincide with an already well-developed reform movement. Czech preachers had long attacked the morality of the clergy and were now demanding a Czech translation of the Bible. Great resentment also existed over denying the communion to the laity in both kinds. Reserving both bread and wine for the priest while giving only bread to the laity was common throughout Europe. In Bohemia the practice was seen as an expression of clerical arrogance.

Though basically religious, these issues were hopelessly intertwined with the ethnic rivalry between Czechs and Germans that had troubled Bohemia for centuries. The Kingdom of Bohemia had a large population of Germans who were often resented by their Slavic neighbors. Moreover, the church held nearly 40 percent of the land, and many of the leading churchmen were German. To many, anticlericalism was therefore an expression of Czech national feeling as well as of frustrated piety, and this association quickly drew the reform movement into the arena of imperial politics.

The University of Prague found itself at the center of these controversies. In 1409 King Vaclav expelled the German students and faculty and appointed Jan Hus, a Czech professor, as rector. Hus had been attracted to Wycliffe's writings by their anticlericalism, but he also saw their extreme philosophical realism as a weapon against the German theologians, most of whom were nominalists. He did not, however, reject transubstantiation and was in general more conservative than Wycliffe on every issue save that of papal authority. Hus did not think of himself as a heretic, and in 1415 he accepted an invitation to defend his views before the Council of Constance. The invitation had been orchestrated by Sigismund who offered him a safe-conduct, but the promised guarantee was little more than a passport, and Hus was burned at the stake on July 6.

The burning of Hus provoked a national outcry in Bohemia. Taking the communion chalice as their sym-

bol, the Czechs broke with Rome and developed a liturgy in the Czech language. When their protector, Vaclav, died in 1419, he was succeeded by Sigismund. The Hussites, as they were now called, rose in armed revolt and resoundingly defeated the papal-imperial crusades against them in 1420, 1422, and 1431. Finally, in 1436 the Hussites secured a treaty that guaranteed them control over the Bohemian church and confirmed their earlier expropriation of church property.

## The Religious Impact of Nominalism, Humanism, and the Printing Press

The religious tensions and controversies of the later Middle Ages were heightened by intellectual movements that threatened the church's authority in more subtle ways. Nominalism (see chapter 9), which grew in popularity during the fourteenth and fifteenth centuries, tended to undermine the foundations of dogma by denying that they were susceptible to rational proof. Though never the dominant school in late medieval thought, it influenced many theologians including Martin Luther.

Humanism exerted an even stronger influence on religious issues. Humanists such as Erasmus criticized the moral shortcomings of the clergy and used their mastery of rhetoric to attack the scholastic philosophers. Their belief in the superiority of ancient over modern texts contributed to the idea that scripture alone was the ultimate source of religious truth. Though many humanists, including Erasmus, remained within the old church, this concept of *sola scriptura* would be central to the teachings of the reformers. Many of them, including Zwingli, Calvin, and Melanchthon had been trained as humanists. They used humanist methodology in their analysis of sacred texts. Humanist respect for antiquity may also have influenced the growing belief that the practices of the early church most closely approximated the intentions of Christ and that subsequent developments, including the rise of the papacy, were modern corruptions.

The reform movements that destroyed the unity of western Christendom in the sixteenth century may therefore be seen as the products of a generalized dissatisfaction with the church. The development of printing, which made the writings of the reformers available to thousands of people, and the conjunction of religious reform with the political needs of certain states and cities transformed that dissatisfaction into what is usually called the Protestant Reformation.

## Martin Luther and the Outbreak of the Protestant Reformation

The first and in many ways the most influential of these movements was the one created in Germany by Martin Luther (1483–1546). A monk of the Augustinian Observant order and professor of the New Testament at the University of Wittenberg in electoral Saxony, Luther experienced a profound spiritual crisis that eventually brought him into open conflict with the church (see illustration 14.2). Like many of his contemporaries, Luther was troubled by an overwhelming sense of sin and unworthiness for which the teachings of the church provided no relief. Neither the rigors of monastic life nor the sacrament of penance could provide him with assurance of salvation. In the course of his biblical studies, he gradually arrived at a solution. Based on his reading of Paul's Epistle to the Romans and on his growing admiration for the works of St. Augustine, he concluded that souls were not saved by religious ceremonies and good works but by faith alone. Human beings could never be righteous enough to merit God's forgiveness, but they could be saved if only they would believe and have faith in the righteousness of Christ.

Luther felt himself transformed by this insight. Even as he formulated it, he was confronted by the issue of indulgences. In 1517 a special indulgence was made available in the territories surrounding electoral Saxony. Its purpose was to raise money for the construction of St. Peter's basilica in Rome and to retire the debt incurred by Albrecht of Mainz in securing for himself through bribery the archbishoprics of Mainz and Magdeburg and the bishopric of Halberstadt. Albrecht had committed not only pluralism but also simony (the illegal purchase of church offices). To Luther, however, this was not the central issue. To him, as to many other clerics, the sale of indulgences was a symbol of the contractualism that beset medieval piety and blinded lay people to the true path of salvation. On October 31, 1517, he posted ninety-five theses condemning this practice to the door of Wittenberg's Castle Church.

His action was in no way unusual. It was the traditional means by which a professor offered to debate all comers on a particular issue, and the positions taken by Luther were not heretical. Furthermore, the sale of indulgences was later condemned by the Council of Trent. However, Luther's action unleashed a storm of controversy. Spread throughout Germany by the printing press, the theses were endorsed by advocates of reform and condemned by the pope, the Dominican

**Illustration 14.2**

**Martin Luther.** This portrait of Luther as a young monk was painted by Lucas Cranach the Elder about a year before the Diet of Worms and shows the reformer as he must have looked when he confronted the Imperial Diet.

order, the archbishop of Mainz, and the Fugger bank of Augsburg, which had loaned Albrecht the money for the elections.

In the debates that followed, Luther was forced to work out the broader implications of his teachings. At Leipzig in June 1519, he challenged the doctrinal authority of popes and councils and declared that Scripture took precedence over all other sources of religious truth. In 1520 he published three pamphlets that drew him at last into formal heresy. In his *Address to the Christian Nobility of the German Nation*, he encouraged the princes to demand reform (see document 14.3). *On the Babylonian Captivity of the Church* abolished five of the seven sacraments and declared that the efficacy of baptism and communion were dependent on the faith of the recipient, not the ordination of the priest. He also

## ◆ DOCUMENT 14.3 ◆

## Luther: Address to the German Nobility

*Martin Luther's primary concerns were always spiritual and theologi-cal, but he knew how to appeal to other emotions as well. These ex-tracts from his* Address to the Christian Nobility of the German Nation *are a relatively modest example of the rhetoric with which he attacked the authority of the Catholic Church.*

What is the use in Christendom of those who are called "cardinals"? I will tell you. In Italy and Germany there are many rich convents, endowments, holdings, and benefices; and as the best way of getting these into the hands of Rome they created cardinals, and gave to them the bishoprics, convents, and prelacies, and thus de-stroyed the service of God. That is why Italy is almost a desert now. . . . Why? Because the cardinals must have the wealth. The Turk himself could not have so desolated Italy and so overthrown the worship of God.

Now that Italy is sucked dry, they come to Germany. They begin in a quiet way, but we shall soon have Ger-many brought into the same state as Italy. We have a few cardinals already. What the Romanists really mean to do, the "drunken" Germans are not to see until they have lost everything . . . .

Now this devilish state of things is not only open rob-bery and deceit and the prevailing of the gates of hell, but it is destroying the very life and soul of Christianity; therefore we are bound to use all our diligence to ward off this misery and destruction. If we want to fight Turks, let us begin here—we cannot find worse ones. If we rightly hang thieves and robbers, why do we leave the greed of Rome unpunished? for Rome is the greatest thief and rob-ber that has ever appeared on earth, or ever will.

Luther, Martin. "Address to the Nobility of the German Nation," (1520), trans. Wace and Buckheim. In B.J. Kidd, *Documents Illustrative of the Continental Reformation*, No. 35. Oxford, England: Oxford University Press, 1911.

### Illustration 14.3

**The Lutheran Sacraments.** This al-tar painting from the Lutheran church at Thorslunde, Denmark, is intended as a graphic lesson in theology. Infant bap-tism is shown at the left. In the center, two communicants receive the sacra-ment in both kinds, while the preacher at the right emphasizes the importance of God's word.

rejected transubstantiation while arguing that Christ was nevertheless truly present in the Eucharist (see il-lustration 14.3). *The Freedom of a Christian* summarized Luther's doctrine of salvation by faith. Luther had not intended to break with the church, but his extraordi-nary skill as a writer and propagandist ignited anti-clerical and antipapal feeling throughout Germany.

Compromise was now impossible, and he was excommunicated on January 31, 1521.

The affair might have ended with Luther's trial and execution, but political considerations intervened. His own prince, Frederick "the Wise" of Saxony, arranged for him to defend his position before the Imperial Diet at Worms in April. The new emperor Charles V was unimpressed. He placed Luther under the Imperial Ban, and Frederick was forced to protect his monk by hiding him in the Wartburg Castle for nearly a year. Luther used this enforced period of leisure to translate the New Testament into German.

Frederick's motives and those of the other princes and city magistrates who eventually supported Luther's reformation varied widely. Some were inspired by genuine religious feeling or, like Frederick, by a proprietary responsibility for "their" churches that transcended loyalty to a distant and non-German papacy. Others, especially in the towns, responded to the public enthusiasm generated by Luther's writings. Regardless of personal feelings, everyone understood the practical advantages of breaking with Rome. Revenues could be increased by confiscating church property and by ending ecclesiastical immunity to taxation, while the control of church courts and ecclesiastical patronage were valuable prizes to those engaged in state building.

The emperor objected on both political and religious grounds. Charles V was a devout Catholic. He was also committed to the ideal of imperial unity, which was clearly threatened by anything that increased the power and revenues of the princes. Only twenty-one at the Diet of Worms, he was heir to an enormous accumulation of states including Austria, Spain, the Netherlands, and much of Italy (see chapter 15). In theory, only the Ottoman Empire could stand against him. When he abdicated and retired to a Spanish monastery in 1556, the Reformation was still intact. His power, though great, had not been equal to his responsibilities. Pressed on the Danube and in the Mediterranean by the Turks, forced to fight seven wars with France, and beset simultaneously by Protestant princes, urban revolutionaries, and popes who feared the extension of his influence in Italy, Charles failed utterly in his attempts to impose orthodoxy. The empire remained open to religious turmoil.

## Other Forms of Protestantism: The Radicals, Zwingli, and Calvin

Some of that turmoil began while Luther was still hidden in the Wartburg. The reformer had believed that, once the gospel was freely preached, congregations would follow it without the direction of an institutional church. He discovered that not all of the pope's enemies shared his interpretation of the Bible. Movements arose that rejected what he saw as the basic insight of the reformation: salvation by faith alone. To many ordi-

nary men and women, this doctrine weakened the ethical imperatives that lay at the heart of Christianity. They wanted a restoration of the primitive, apostolic church—a "gathered" community of Christians who lived by the letter of Scripture. Luther had not gone far enough. Luther in turn thought that they were *schwärmer,* or enthusiasts who wanted to return to the works righteousness of the medieval church. Faced with what he saw as a fundamental threat to reform, Luther turned to the state. In 1527 a system of visitations was instituted throughout Saxony that for all practical purposes placed temporal control of the church in the hands of the prince. It was to be the model for Lutheran Church discipline throughout Germany and Scandinavia, but it did not at first halt the spread of radicalism.

Because these radical movements were often popular in origin or had coalesced around the teachings of an individual preacher, they varied widely in character. Perhaps the most radical were the Antitrinitarians, who rejected the doctrine of the Trinity and argued for a piety based wholly upon good works. Under the leadership of two Italian brothers, Laelio and Fausto Sozzini, they found converts among the Polish nobility but had little influence on western Europe. The most numerous were the Anabaptists, a loosely affiliated group who were the spiritual ancestors of the modern Mennonites and Amish. Their name derives from the practice of adult baptism, which they saw not only as a sacrament, but also as the heart of the redemptive process. Baptism was the deliberate decision to follow Christ and could therefore be made only by a responsible adult acting in complete freedom of will. It signified entrance into a visible church of the saints that must, by definition, be separate from the world around it. Most Anabaptists were therefore pacifists who would accept no civic responsibilities, refusing even to take an oath in court (see document 14.4).

This rejection of civic responsibility was seen as a threat to the political order. Hatred of the Anabaptists was one issue on which Lutherans and Catholics could agree, and in 1529 an imperial edict made belief in adult baptism a capital offense. Hatred became something like panic when an atypically violent group of Anabaptists gained control of the city of Münster and proclaimed it the New Jerusalem, complete with polygamy and communal sharing of property. They were eventually dislodged and their leaders executed, but the episode, though unparalleled elsewhere, convinced political and ecclesiastical leaders that their suspicions had been correct. They executed tens of thousands of Anabaptists throughout Germany and the

### ❖ DOCUMENT 14.4 ❖

## The Anabaptists Reject Civic Life

*In 1527 a group of Anabaptists met at Schleitheim on the Swiss-German border to clarify issues connected with their teachings. The result was the Schleitheim Confession, a document widely accepted by later Anabaptists. In this excerpt, demands are made for separation from the world.*

Fourth. We are agreed as follows on separation: A separation shall be made from the evil and the wickedness which the devil planted in the world; in this manner, simply that we should not have fellowship with them, the wicked, and not run with them in the multitude of their abominations. This is the way it is: Since all who do not walk in the obedience of faith and have not united themselves with God so that they wish to do his will, are a great abomination before God, it is not possible for anything to grow or issue from them except abominable things. For truly all creatures are in but two classes, good and bad, believing and unbelieving, darkness and light, the world and those who have come out of the world, God's temple and idols, Christ and Belial; and none can have part with the other.

To us then the command of the Lord is clear when He calls us to separate from the evil and thus He will be our God and we shall be his sons and daughters.

He further admonishes us to withdraw from Babylon and the earthly Egypt that we may not be partakers of the pain and suffering which the Lord will bring upon them.

From all this we should learn that everything which is not united with our God and Christ cannot be other than an abomination which we should shun and flee from. By this is meant all popish and anti-popish works and church services, meetings and church attendance, drinking houses, civic affairs, the commitments made in unbelief [oaths] and other things of that kind, which are highly regarded by the world and yet carried on in flat contradiction to the command of God.

Therefore there will also unquestionably fall from us the un-Christian, devilish weapons of force—such as sword, armor and the like, and all their use for friends or against one's enemies.

"The Schleitheim Confession." In Hans Hillerbrand, ed., *The Protestant Reformation*, pp. 132–133. New York: Harper Torchbooks, 1967.

Low Countries, and by 1550 the movement had dwindled to a remnant. A group of survivors, afterwards known as Mennonites, were reorganized under the leadership of Menno Simons. Their moderation and emphasis on high ethical standards became a model for other dissenting groups.

Meanwhile, another kind of reform had emerged in Switzerland. Zürich, like other Swiss cantons, was a center of the mercenary industry. By 1518 a growing party of citizens had come to oppose what they called the exchange of blood for money. The innovations of Gonsalvo de Córdoba had cost the Swiss their tactical advantage on the battlefield, and their casualties during the latter part of the Italian wars had been very heavy. Moreover, the trade had enriched a few contractors who were now thought to exert undue influence on local politics while compromising the city's neutrality through their relations with France and the papacy. One of the leading spokesmen for the antimercenary forces was a priest, Huldrych Zwingli (1484–1531), who had been a chaplain to the troops in Italy. He had received a good humanist education and, like Luther,

was known for attacking indulgences and for sermons that relied heavily on the Scriptures. In 1519 the antimercenary party gained control of the Zürich city council and named Zwingli people's priest of the city's main church, a post from which he was able to guide the process of reform.

Zwingli's concept of reformation grew out of the democratic traditions of his native land. Believing that each congregation should determine its own policies under the guidance of the gospel, he saw no real distinction between the government of the church and that of the state. Both elected representatives to determine policy. Both should be guided by the law of God. He therefore proceeded to reform the city step by step, providing guidance and advice but leaving the implementation of reforms to the city council.

Like Luther, Zwingli was challenged at an early date by those who felt that his reforms were insufficiently thorough. In responding to such Anabaptist critics as Conrad Grebel and Georg Blaurock, Zwingli developed teachings that were at variance with Luther's as well. When the Anabaptists asked how a child could be baptized if the efficacy of the sacrament depended upon the faith of the recipient, Zwingli responded that the faith was that of the parent or guardian and that the sacrament was in effect a covenant to raise the child as a Christian. The rite was analogous to circumcision among the Jews. He also rejected Luther's doctrine of the Real Presence in communion and argued, after some hesitation, that for those with faith Christ was present in spirit though not in body.

Zwingli's ideas were theologically original and appealed strongly to other reformers, but Luther rejected them at the Marburg Colloquy in 1529. The failure of this meeting marked the beginning of a separation between the Lutheran and Reformed traditions that persists to this day. It also coincided with a vote by the Imperial Diet to enforce the Edict of Worms against all non-Catholics. Those who protested against this measure, Lutheran and Reformed, became known as Protestants. In the meantime, the efforts of Zürich to export its reformation to other parts of Switzerland led to conflict, and Zwingli was killed, sword in hand, at the battle of Kappel.

Among those influenced by Zwingli's teachings was John Calvin (1509–64). Calvin was born at Noyon in France, the son of a wealthy lawyer who for most of his career had been secretary to the local bishop. A brilliant student, Calvin was educated at Paris and at Orléans where he earned a law degree. His interests eventually turned to humanism and then to theology. In 1534 he adopted the reformed faith. His conversion bore immediate fruit in *The Institutes of the Christian Religion*, a more-or-less systematic explanation of reformed teachings. The first edition appeared in March 1536, and though Calvin continued to revise and expand it throughout his lifetime, this early effort contained the basic elements of his mature thought.

Calvin is best known for his uncompromising position on predestination, holding, like Zwingli, that God divides the elect from the reprobate by His own "dread decree" (see document 14.5). Luther, like St. Augustine, believed that God predestines certain individuals to salvation, but he had stopped short of declaring that some are predestined to hell. To Calvin, this seemed illogical. To select some is by definition to reject others. This doctrine of "double predestination," like many of his formulations on the sacraments and other issues, may be seen as refinements of ideas originally suggested by others, but Calvin was far more than a mere compiler. He made reformed doctrines more intelligible, educated a corps of pastors who spread his teachings to the farthest corners of Europe, and provided a model for

the governance of Christian communities that would be influential for generations to come.

The unlikely vehicle for these achievements was the small city of Geneva. When Calvin arrived there in July 1536, the city was emerging from a period of political and religious turmoil. It had long been governed by a bishop whose appointment was controlled by the neighboring dukes of Savoy. The belated development of civic institutions and dissatisfaction with Savoyard influence led to an alliance with the Swiss cantons of Bern and Fribourg and to the overthrow of the bishop. The Bernese, who had accepted the Reformation while remaining nominally Catholic for diplomatic reasons,

## ◆ DOCUMENT 14.5 ◆

## John Calvin: Predestination

*The importance of John Calvin's doctrine of predestination has probably been overstated. It was neither unique to him nor the center of his own theology, which emphasized what he called the knowledge of God. Nevertheless, the power of this summary statement from the* Institutes of the Christian Religion *indicates why Calvin's teachings on predestination made an indelible impression.*

As Scripture, then, clearly shows, we say that God once established by his eternal and unchangeable plan those whom he long before determined once for all to receive into salvation and those whom, on the other hand, he would devote to destruction. We assert that, with respect to the elect, this plan was founded upon his freely given mercy, without regard to human worth; but by his just and irreprehensible judgment he has barred the door of life to those whom he has given over to damnation. Now among the elect we regard the call as a testimony of election. Then we hold justification [that is, acceptance by God] another sign of its manifestation, until they come into the glory in which the fulfillment of that election lies. But as the Lord seals his elect by call and justification, so, by shutting off the reprobate from knowledge of his name or from the sanctification of his Spirit, he, as it were, reveals by these marks what sort of judgment awaits them.

Calvin, John. *Institutes of the Christian Religion*, vol. 2, p. 931, ed. J.T. McNeill, trans. Ford Lewis Battles. Philadelphia: Westminster Press, 1960.

then dispatched a French refugee, Guillaume Farel, to convert the French-speaking Genevans. Farel was a fine preacher, but he realized that he was not the man to organize a church. When Calvin stopped at Geneva on his way from Ferrara to Strasburg, he prevailed upon the young scholar to stay and assist him in the task of reformation.

Calvin's first years in Geneva were full of turmoil. Though they had no love for the pope, the Genevans resisted Calvin's attempts to reform their morals. He established the kind of godly commonwealth he sought only with great difficulty. His opponents finally discredited themselves by supporting Miguel Servetus, an antitrinitarian executed by the Genevan city council as a heretic in 1553. This act, now regarded as an example of gross intolerance, was universally applauded by Catholics and Protestants and secured Calvin's position in the city until his death.

Calvin's Geneva has been called a theocracy, but Calvin believed in the separation of church and state. Neither he nor any other Genevan pastor could hold public office, and the temporal affairs of the Genevan church were guided by an elected committee or presbytery of laymen. The city continued to be governed by its two elected councils. These bodies were empowered, as in Zürich, to enforce conformity in faith and morals. A Consistory, composed of church elders and certain municipal officials, was responsible for defining both. Geneva soon became known as a center of the Reformed movement and as a refuge for those who were persecuted elsewhere. An academy was established to train pastors who were then dispatched to create missionary congregations in other parts of Europe. They were most successful in France, the Netherlands, and in those countries such as Hungary, Bohemia, and Poland where resistance to German culture inhibited the spread of Lutheranism. When the reformer died in 1564, Calvinism was already a major international movement.

## The English Reformation

England's revolt against the papacy was an example of reformation from the top. Henry VIII (reigned 1509–47; see illustration 14.4) and his chief minister, Cardinal Thomas Wolsey (c. 1475–1530), had little use for reformed doctrines. Henry had even earned the papal title "Defender of the Faith" for publishing an attack on Luther's view of the sacraments and would probably

**Illustration 14.4**

🕭 **Henry VIII of England.** This portrait by Hans Holbein shows the king as he looked at the time of the Reformation.

have been content to remain in the church had he not decided to divorce his queen, Catherine of Aragon.

Catherine had suffered a series of miscarriages and stillbirths. One child, Mary, survived, but Henry feared that without a male heir the succession would be endangered. He resolved to ask for a papal annulment and to marry Anne Boleyn, a court lady with whom he had fallen in love. His request posed serious difficulties for pope Clement VII. The emperor Charles V was Catherine's nephew. Charles vehemently opposed the divorce, and as his troops had recently sacked Rome (1527), albeit in the course of a mutiny, the pope was intimidated. Moreover, the basis of the request struck many canon lawyers as dubious. Catherine had originally been married to Henry's brother Arthur, who died before he could ascend the throne. To preserve the vital alliance with Catherine's father, Ferdinand of Aragon, Henry VII had quickly married her to his second son, but this had required a papal dispensation because marriage to the wife of one's brother is prohibited by Leviticus 18:16 and 20:21. Another biblical passage, Deuteronomy 25:5, specifically commands such marriages, but an annulment would involve repudiation of the earlier dispensation. Moreover, the fact that the marriage had endured for eighteen years raised what canon lawyers called "the impediment of public honesty."

Clement temporized. He appointed Cardinals Wolsey and Campeggio as legates to resolve the matter on the theory that their opinions would cancel each other out. Henry could not wait. In 1529 he deprived Wolsey of his secular offices and took Thomas Cromwell (1485–1540) and Thomas Cranmer (1489–1556) as his advisers. These two, a lawyer and a churchman, respectively, were sympathetic to reformed ideas and firm supporters of a strategy that would put pressure on the pope by attacking the privileges and immunities of the church in England.

This strategy was implemented primarily through the Reformation Parliament that sat from 1529 to 1536. Though its proceedings were managed to some extent by Cromwell, a consistent majority supported the crown throughout. Parliament passed a series of acts that restricted the dispatch of church revenues to Rome and placed the legal affairs of the clergy under royal jurisdiction. Finally, in 1532, Anne Boleyn became pregnant. To ensure the child's legitimacy, Cranmer married the couple in January 1533, and two months later he granted the king his divorce from Catherine. He was able to do so because William Warham, the archbishop of Canterbury and a wily opponent of the divorce, had died at last (he was at least ninety-eight), permitting Henry to appoint Cranmer in his place. In September Anne Boleyn gave birth to a daughter, Elizabeth, and in 1534 Parliament passed the Act of Supremacy, which declared that Henry was "the only supreme head of the Church in England."

Opposition was minimal. John Fisher, bishop of Rochester and Sir Thomas More, the great humanist who had been Henry's lord chancellor, were executed for their misgivings, but most of political England either supported the king or remained indifferent. The Lincolnshire rebellion and the northern revolt known as the Pilgrimage of Grace were localized reactions to Henry's proposed closing of the monasteries in 1536 and he suppressed them easily. The dissolution of the monasteries proceeded apace. Unfortunately for his successors, Henry chose to sell off the monastic properties at bargain basement prices. By doing so he enriched those who had supported him in the Reforma-

tion Parliament and satisfied his need for ready cash. His failure to incorporate these lands into the royal domain deprived the crown of renewable income.

Henry now ruled the English church. He closed the monasteries and convents and adopted Coverdale's English Bible, but other changes were minimal. The clergy remained celibate (with the exception of Cranmer, who had been secretly married before his appointment as archbishop of Canterbury), and the principles of Catholic theology were reaffirmed in the Six Articles of 1539. A visibly Protestant English church began to emerge only after Henry's death in 1547.

In 1536 Henry arranged the execution of Anne Boleyn on charges of adultery and had their marriage annulled. His third wife, Jane Seymour, gave him a male heir in 1537 but died in childbirth, and three subsequent wives failed to produce further children. Both Mary and Elizabeth were officially illegitimate. Jane Seymour's son, aged ten, ascended the throne as Edward VI under the regency of his uncle, Edward Seymour, duke of Somerset. Somerset was a convinced Protestant with close ties to Cranmer and to the continental reformers. He and the young king, "that right godly imp," lost little time in abolishing the Six Articles, encouraging clerical marriage, and imposing Cranmer's *Book of Common Prayer* as the standard liturgy for English churches. An Order in Council abolished images in an act of official iconoclasm that destroyed centuries of English art.

In 1550 Somerset was succeeded by the equally Protestant duke of Northumberland who imposed a revised edition of the new liturgy and adopted the Forty-Two Articles, also written by Cranmer, as an official confession of faith. The articles proclaimed salvation by faith, reduced the sacraments to two, and denied transubstantiation, though not the Real Presence. Though many lay people remained loyal to the old church, they found no effective way to express their views. Aside from a brief and unsuccessful rebellion in the west of England, little resistance emerged. In 1553 Edward died at the age of sixteen. His sister Mary assumed the crown and immediately restored Catholicism with the assent of Parliament, which demanded only that she not return the lands taken from the church.

Mary's reign was a failure. Her marriage to Philip II of Spain aroused fears of Spanish-papal domination even among those English who were still unfavorably disposed to Protestantism. Her persecution of the reformers, though hardly the bloodbath portrayed in John Foxe's *Acts and Monuments*, the great martyrology of the English reformation, deeply offended others and earned her the historical nickname "Bloody Mary." When her sister, Elizabeth, succeeded her in 1558 she was able to restore a moderate Protestantism leavened by virtual tolerance for all who would acknowledge the royal supremacy. The Elizabethan Settlement, as it is called, was the foundation on which modern Anglicanism would be built after years of effort and struggle.

## The Catholic Reformation

Not all reformations of the sixteenth century were anti-Catholic. The church transformed itself as well in a movement that is sometimes called the Counter Reformation, but not all reforms undertaken by Catholics in the sixteenth century were a response to the challenge of the reformers. Cardinal Francisco Jiménez de Cisneros had begun to reform the church in Spain long before Luther nailed his Ninety-Five Theses to the church door, and similar changes were introduced in France by Cardinal Georges d'Amboise between 1501 and his death in 1510. Even Wolsey had attempted to reform the English monasteries during the 1520s. The impetus behind these reforms arguably came from the secular authorities and were largely directed toward the revival of monastic life. However, each of these cardinals received broad legatine authority from several popes, and monastic reform was a central issue in the late medieval church.

Moreover, the reform of existing orders and the creation of new ones was often undertaken without secular involvement. The Theatines, confirmed by the pope in 1524, were an outgrowth of the Oratory of Divine Love whose origins date to 1494. The Barnabites (1533–35), Somaschi (1540), and the Capuchins, an order of reformed Franciscans, were all voluntary associations of churchmen pledged to the ideal of monastic reform. The female counterpart of the Capuchins was founded by Maria Laurentia Longo (d. 1542), and in 1535 Angela Merici (c. 1473–1540) founded the Ursulines, an order that would play a decisive role in the education of Catholic women for centuries. None of these foundations was related in any way to the Protestant threat. Most popes regarded the proliferation of religious orders with suspicion. Their rivalries had long been a fruitful source of trouble, and most reform-minded clerics believed in consolidation rather than in new confirmations.

Of all the religious orders founded or reformed during the sixteenth century, the Society of Jesus, or Jesuits, played the largest part in the struggle against

Protestantism, but they had been created for other purposes. Their founder, Ignatius of Loyola (1491–1556), was originally inspired by the idea of converting the Muslims. After a long period of educational and religious development that produced *The Spiritual Exercises*, a manual of meditation that remains the foundation of Jesuit discipline, he and nine companions formed their order in 1534. Their asceticism, vigor, and vow of unconditional obedience to the pope led to their confirmation in 1540.

Though the order did little to convert the Muslims, it achieved moderate success in Asia under the leadership of St. Francis Xavier (1506–52). In Europe, the Jesuits became the intellectual shock troops of the Counter Reformation. Their high standards in recruitment and education made them natural leaders to reconvert areas of Europe that had deserted to Protestantism. Jesuit missions helped to restore a Catholic majority in regions as diverse as Bavaria and Poland. An important means of achieving this was through education. Jesuit academies combining humanist educational principles with religious instruction spread through the subcontinent after 1555 and served much the same purpose for men that the Ursuline academies served for women.

Efforts of this sort were essentially spontaneous, arising from reform-minded elements within the church, but the papacy itself was not idle. Reform was difficult if not impossible until the ghost of conciliarism was laid to rest, and for this reason the popes proceeded with great caution. Clement VII, besieged by the mutinous troops of Charles V and the demands of Henry VIII, accomplished little. Paul III (reigned 1534–49) at first sought reconciliation by appointing a commission to investigate abuses within the church. Its report, a detailed analysis with recommendations for change, caused great embarrassment when the contents leaked to the public. Then an attempt to negotiate a settlement with the Lutherans broke down at the Regensburg Colloquy in 1541. These failures encouraged a policy of repression, and in 1542 the Roman Inquisition was revived under the direction of Gian Pietro Caraffa, an implacable conservative and one of the founders of the Theatine order. Later, as Pope Paul IV (served 1555–59), Caraffa would conduct a veritable reign of terror against those whom he regarded as corrupt or heretical. To protect the faithful from intellectual contamination, he also established the celebrated *Index Librorum Prohibitorum*, an ever-expanding list of books that Catholics were forbidden to read.

Repression alone could not solve the problems of the church. In spite of the obvious danger to papal

Illustration 14.5

The Final Session of the Council of Trent, 1563. Attributed to Titian, this painting shows the conclusion of the great council whose decrees inspired the Catholic Church until the 1960s.

authority, Paul III decided to convene a general council at Trent in 1542. Sessions were held from 1543 to 1549, in 1551–52, and in 1562–63 (see illustration 14.5). Much disagreement arose over goals and the meetings were often sparsely attended, but the Council of Trent was a conspicuous success.

Theologically, Trent marked the triumph of Thomism. Luther's ideas on justification, the sacraments, and the priesthood of all believers were specifically rejected. The medieval concept of the priestly office and the value of good works was reasserted, and at the organizational level efforts were made to correct most of the abuses that had been attacked by the reformers. These included not only the clerical sins of pluralism, absenteeism, nepotism, and simony, but also such distortions of popular piety as the sale of indulgences and the misuse of images. The strengthening of ecclesiastical discipline was one of the council's greatest achievements.

Knowing that many of the church's problems arose from ignorance, the delegates mandated the use of catechisms in instructing the laity and the establishment of diocesan seminaries for the education of priests. The Council of Trent, in short, marked the beginning of the modern Catholic Church. Its institutional principles and the forms of piety that it established were not substantially modified until Vatican II (1962–65).

## The Political, Economic, and Social Consequences of Reform

The impact of the sixteenth-century reformations has been the subject of much scholarly debate. The religious unity of western Christendom was clearly shattered, but this had always been more an ideal than a practical reality. Politically, cities and territorial states were the chief beneficiaries of reform, for Protestantism tended to increase their control over church patronage and revenues. Even Catholic states exhibited more independence because the papacy became more cautious in its claims than it had been in the Middle Ages. Though hardly decisive, reform was therefore an important influence on the development of the modern state.

The economic consequences of the Reformation are far less clear. The idea that Protestantism somehow liberated acquisitive instincts and paved the way for the development of capitalism is highly suspect if for no other reason than that capitalism existed long before the Reformation and that the economic growth of such Protestant states as England and the Netherlands can be explained adequately in other ways. In some areas, notably England, the alienation of church property may have accelerated the capitalization of land that had be-

### ◆ DOCUMENT 14.6 ◆

## A Protestant View of Marriage

*The reformer of Strasbourg, Martin Bucer (1491–1551), was more generous than most in his attitude toward women. Here, he argues that under certain circumstances a woman may leave her adulterous or abusive spouse and be free to remarry.*

For the Holy Spirit says that there is neither male nor female in Christ. In all things that pertain to salvation one should have as much regard for woman as for man. For though she is bound to keep her place, to put herself under the authority of her husband, just as the church does in relation to Christ, yet her subjection does not cancel the right of an honest woman, in accordance with the laws of God, to have recourse to and demand, by legitimate means, deliverance from a husband who hates her. For the Lord has certainly not made married woman subservient to have her polluted and tormented by the extortions and injuries of her husband, but rather so that she may receive discipline from him, as if from her master and savior, like the church from Christ. A wife is not so subject to her husband that she is bound to suffer anything he may impose upon her. Being free, she is joined to him in holy marriage that she may be loved, nourished, and maintained by him, as if she were his own flesh, just as the church is maintained by Christ. . . . Again, though a wife may be something less than her husband and subject to him, in order that they be rightly joined, the Holy Spirit has declared, through its apostle, that man and woman are equal before God in things pertaining to the alliance and mutual confederation of marriage. This is the meaning of the apostle's saying that a wife has power over the body of her husband, just as a husband has power over the body of his wife (1 Corinthians 7). . . . Hence, if wives feel that their association and cohabitation with their husbands is injurious to salvation as well of one as of the other, owing to the hardening and hatred on the part of their husbands, let them have recourse to the civil authority, which is enjoined by the Lord to help the afflicted.

Bucer, Martin. *"De Regno Christi,"* book 2, chap. 34. In Julia O'Faolain and Lauro Martines, *Not in God's Image: Women in History from the Greeks to the Victorians,* pp. 200–201. New York: HarperCollins, 1973.

gun in the years after the Black Death, but in others it served primarily to increase the domain revenues of the crown. In Denmark, for example, 40 percent of the arable land was under direct royal control by 1620, primarily because the crown retained church lands confiscated during the Reformation.

The reformers also sought to change the status of European women. Beginning with Luther and Zwingli, they rejected the ideal of clerical celibacy and declared that a Christian marriage was the ideal basis for a godly life. They specifically attacked medieval writings that either condemned women as temptresses or extolled virginity as the highest of female callings, and drew attractive and sentimental portraits of the virtuous wife. A chief virtue of that ideal woman was her willingness to submit to male authority, but the attachment of the reformers to traditional social hierarchies should not be misinterpreted. The companionate marriage in which wife and husband offered each other mutual support was the Reformation ideal (see document 14.6). If women were subordinate it was, as Calvin said, because women "by the very order of nature are bound to obey."

To him, other reformers, and Catholic theologians, the traditionally ordered family was both part and symbol of a divinely established hierarchy. To disrupt that hierarchy risked chaos.

The Reformation endorsement of women was qualified, but it increased the status of wife and mother and placed new demands upon men, who were encouraged to treat their wives with consideration. As early as the 1520s, some German towns permitted women to divorce husbands who were guilty of gross abuse. The reformers also encouraged female literacy, at least in the vernacular, because they wanted women to have access to the Scriptures. The impact of these prescriptions on the lives of real women may be questioned. On the negative side, the Protestant emphasis on marriage narrowed a woman's career choices to one. Catholic Europe continued to offer productive lives to women who chose not to marry, but Protestant women could rarely escape the dominance of men. If they did, it was through widowhood or divorce, and Protestant societies offered no institutional support for the unmarried. St. Teresa de Avila, Angelique Arnauld, Madame Acarie,

Illustration 14.6

🌼 A Village Wedding. In this painting, Pieter Bruegel the Younger illustrates the sort of peasant behavior that political and ecclesiastical authorities hoped to restrict in the later sixteenth century.

Jeanne de Chantal, and the other great female figures of post-Tridentine Catholicism had few Protestant counterparts.

From the standpoint of the reformers, whether Catholic or Protestant, such issues were of secondary importance. Their primary concern was the salvation of souls and the transformation of popular piety. Heroic efforts were made to catechize or otherwise educate the laity in most parts of Europe, and after about 1570 an increasing tendency was seen toward clerical interference in lay morals. Catholic church courts and Protestant consistories sought to eliminate such evils as brawling, public drunkenness, and sexual misbehavior. Inevitably the churchmen were forced to condemn the occasions on which such activity arose. The celebration of holidays and popular festivals came under scrutiny as did public performances of every kind from street jugglers to those of Shakespeare and his troop of actors. Dancing aroused special concern. No one worried about the stately measures trod by courtiers, but the rowdy and often sexually explicit dances of the peasants seemed, after years of familiarity, to induce shock (see illustration 14.6).

Civil authorities supported this attack on popular culture for practical reasons. The celebration of holidays and popular festivals encouraged disorder. When accompanied as they usually were by heavy drinking, public amusements could lead to violence and even riots. Moreover, like street theater, most celebrations contained seditious skits or pageants. They mocked the

privileged classes, satirized the great, and delighted in the reversal of social and gender roles. The triumph of a Lord of Misrule, even for a day, made magistrates nervous, and prudence demanded that such activities be regulated or prohibited outright. Popular beliefs and practices were attacked with equal vigor. The authorities rarely took action against academic magic, astrology, or alchemy—sciences that, though dubious, were widely accepted by the wealthy and educated—but they no longer tolerated folk magic. In some cases, official suspicion extended even to the traditional remedies used by midwives and village "wise women."

The epidemic of witch hunting that convulsed Europe in the late sixteenth and early seventeenth centuries may have been related to these concerns. In the century after 1550, Protestant and Catholic governments in virtually every part of Europe executed more than sixty thousand people for being witches or satanists. Medieval thinkers such as Thomas Aquinas had denied the power of witches, but a later age thought differently. Magistrates and learned men built theories of a vast satanic plot around their imperfect knowledge of folk beliefs. Their ideas crystallized in manuals for witch hunters, the most famous of which, the *Malleus Maleficarum* (Hammer of Witches) went through twenty-nine editions between 1495 and 1669. Its authors, like most people in early modern Europe, believed that in a providential world there could be no accidents; evil required an explanation. Otherwise unexplained disasters were caused by witches who gained extraordinary powers through worshipping the devil and used those powers to injure their neighbors. The community could be protected only by burning witches alive.

In this case, ordinary people shared the concerns of the intellectual elite. Accusations of witchcraft tended to multiply in waves of hysteria that convulsed entire regions. Many of those denounced were no doubt guilty of trying to cast spells or some other unsavory act, but the victims fit a profile that suggests a generalized hostility toward women and perhaps that the persecutions were in part a means of exerting social control. The great majority of those burned were single women, old and poor, who lived at the margins of their communities. The rest, whether male or female, tended to be people whose assertive or uncooperative behavior had aroused hostility.

The trials subsided after 1650, but not before other traditional beliefs had been discredited by their association with witchcraft. Some of these involved "white" magic, the normally harmless spells and preparations used to ensure good harvests or to cure disease. Others were "errors," or what the Spanish Inquisition called "propositions." This was a broad category that included everything from the popular notion that premarital sex was no sin to alternative cosmologies devised by imaginative peasants. Post-Tridentine Catholicism, no less than its Protestant rivals, discouraged uncontrolled speculation and was deeply suspicious of those forms of piety that lacked ecclesiastical sanction. Popular beliefs about the Virgin Mary, the saints, and miracles were scrutinized, while lay people claiming to have religious visions were ridiculed and sometimes prosecuted.

The efforts of the reformers, in other words, bore modest fruit. Drunkenness proved ineradicable, but some evidence is available that interpersonal violence decreased and that behavior in general became somewhat more sedate. Though lay morals and religious knowledge improved slowly if at all, the forms of piety were transformed in some cases beyond recognition. Many ideas and practices vanished so completely that historians of popular culture can recover their memory only with great difficulty. Devotion based upon personal contact with God through mental prayer became common in virtually all communions. Catholics abandoned the sale of indulgences and consciously sought to limit such abuses as the misuse of pilgrimages and relics. Protestants abandoned all three, together with Latin, vigils, the cult of the saints, masses for the dead, and mandatory fasts. By 1600, the religious landscape of Europe was transformed, and much of the richness, vitality, and cohesion of peasant life had been lost beyond all hope of recovery.

# CHAPTER 15

# OVERSEAS CONQUEST AND RELIGIOUS WAR TO 1648

## CHAPTER OUTLINE

◆◆◆◆◆◆◆◆◆◆◆◆◆◆◆◆◆◆◆◆◆

The age of the Renaissance and Reformation marked the beginning of European conquests overseas. Their purpose in the first instance was to expand the resources available to the emerging monarchies of western Europe. The conquests were therefore an extension of the state-building process, but a religious motive was evident, too, which at times recalled the Christian triumphalism of the Crusades. To say that European expansion overseas changed the world forever is an understatement. Though it laid the foundations of a world market and added much to Europe's store of wealth and knowledge, it did so at a terrible cost in human misery.

In Europe itself, the rivalries that encouraged overseas exploration fueled the imperial struggles of the early sixteenth century and the so-called Religious Wars of 1559–1648. The growing cost of warfare stretched the resources of princes to the breaking point. This led to massive unrest as subjects sought to recover rights and privileges lost to rulers who were desperate to pay for security. Both the subsequent revolts and the international conflict that helped to sustain them were complicated by religious issues that made them extremely difficult to resolve. In the end, the wars of what has been called the Iron Age brought much of Europe to the brink of political and economic disintegration.

◈

## The Portuguese Voyages to Africa, India, and Brazil

The process of overseas exploration began appropriately enough in Portugal, the first modern monarchy and the center of the fourteenth-century revolution in shipbuilding. The Portuguese state had been effectively consolidated by John I in 1385. Like other medieval rulers, he and his descendants hoped to maximize domain revenue by increasing taxable commerce. The gold and ivory of Africa were a tempting goal, but that

**Illustration 15.1**

**A Portuguese Caravel of the Fifteenth Century.** Though rarely more than seventy or eighty feet in length, these vessels were extremely seaworthy and formed the mainstay of Portugal's explorations along the coasts of Africa and in the Atlantic. This one is lateen rigged for better performance to windward, but some of them carried square sails as well, usually on the foremast.

trade was dominated by Moroccan intermediaries who shipped products from the African heartland by camel caravan and sold them to Europeans through such ports as Ceuta and Tangier. The Portuguese knew that enormous profits could be realized by sailing directly to the source of these commodities and bypassing the middlemen, who were in any case Muslims and their traditional enemies.

These considerations, and others of a more spiritual nature, inspired Prince Henry "the Navigator" (1394–1460) to establish a center for navigational development on the windswept bluffs of Sagres at the far southwestern tip of Europe. While Henry's cosmographers and mathematicians worked steadily to improve the quality of charts and navigational techniques, his captains sailed ever further along the African coast, returning with growing quantities of gold, ivory, pepper, and slaves, for the enslavement of Africans was part of the expansionist enterprise from the start. Their ships were fast, handy caravels that combined the best features of northern and Mediterranean construction (see illustration 15.1). Their instruments were improved versions of the compass, the quadrant, and the astrolabe. The compass had been introduced to the Mediterranean in the twelfth or thirteenth century, probably by the

Arabs. The quadrant and the astrolabe permitted the sailor to find his latitude based on the elevation of the sun above the horizon.

Before the death of Prince Henry, the Portuguese adopted the idea of sailing around the tip of Africa to India as their primary goal. By so doing they hoped to bypass the Italian-Arab monopoly and gain direct access to the spice trade. In May 1498, Vasco da Gama reached Calicut on the coast of India after a voyage of two years. His arrival disturbed political and commercial relationships that had endured for centuries. Indian and Arab merchants found the newcomers rude and barbaric and their trade goods of little interest. Though the voyages of da Gama and Cabral made a profit, only the judicious use of force could secure a major Portuguese share in the trade. After 1508 Afonso de Albuquerque (1453–1515) tried to gain control of the Indian Ocean by seizing its major ports. Aden and Ormuz eluded him, but Goa became the chief Portuguese base in India and the capture of Malacca (1511) opened the way to China. A Portuguese settlement was established there at Macao in 1556. Trade with Japan was initiated in 1543, and for seventy-five years thereafter ships from Macao brought luxury goods to Nagasaki in return for silver.

These achievements earned Portugal a modest place in Asian commerce. The Portuguese may have been the first people of any race to trade on a truly worldwide basis, but the total volume of spices exported to Europe did not immediately increase as a result of their activities. Furthermore, the Arab and Gujerati merchants of the Indian Ocean remained formidable competitors for more than a century.

## Columbus and the Opening of America

Meanwhile, the Spanish, by sailing west, had reached America. Isabella of Castile and Ferdinand of Aragon regarded the expansion of their Portuguese rivals with dismay and believed, as Prince Henry had done, that they were obligated by morality and the requirements of dynastic prestige to spread the Catholic faith. When a Genoese mariner named Christopher Columbus proposed to reach Asia by sailing across the Atlantic, they were prepared to listen.

In August 1492, Columbus set sail in the ship *Santa Maria* accompanied by two small caravels, the *Pinta* and the *Niña*. Their combined crews totaled about ninety men. Columbus sailed southwest to the Canary Islands and then westward across the Atlantic, taking

## The Hazards of a Long Voyage

*This extract is taken from a firsthand account of Fernando Magellan's voyage around the world by Antonio Pigafetta, but similar conditions might be expected on any sea journey if it lasted long enough. The disease described is scurvy, which results from a deficiency of vitamin C. It was a serious problem even on transatlantic voyages. The cause was not understood until the eighteenth century, but captains could usually predict the first date of its appearance in a ship's company with some accuracy.*

Wednesday, November 28, we debauched from that strait [since named after Magellan], engulfing ourselves in the Pacific Sea. We were three months and twenty days without getting any kind of fresh food. We ate biscuit, which was no longer biscuit, but powder of biscuits swarming with worms, for they had eaten the good. It stank strongly of the urine of rats. We drank yellow water that had been putrid for many days. We also ate some ox hides that covered the top of the mainyard to prevent the yard from chafing the shrouds, and which had become exceedingly hard because of the sun, rain, and wind. We left them in the sea for four or five days, and then placed them on top of the embers and so ate them; and we often ate sawdust from boards. Rats were sold for one-half ducat a piece, and even then we could not get them. But above all the other misfortunes the following was the worst. The gums of both the lower and upper teeth of some of our men swelled so that they could not eat under any circumstances and therefore died. Nineteen men died from that sickness. . . . Twenty-five or thirty men fell sick.

Pigafetta, Antonio. *Magellan's Voyage Around the World,* ed. and trans. J. A. Robertson. Cleveland: 1902.

by Europeans was left to others. One of them, a Florentine navigator named Amerigo Vespucci (1454–1512), gave it his name. The true dimensions of the "New World" became clearer in 1513 when Vasco Núñez de Balboa crossed the Isthmus of Panama on foot and became the first European to look upon the Pacific.

The achievement of Columbus has been somewhat diminished by his own failure to grasp its significance and by the fact that others had no doubt preceded him. The Vikings visited Newfoundland and may have explored the North American coast as far south as Cape Cod. Portuguese and Basque fishermen had almost certainly landed there in the course of their annual expeditions to the Grand Banks, but being fishermen, they kept their discoveries secret and these early contacts came to nothing.

The voyage of Columbus, however, set off a frenzy of exploration and conquest. By the Treaty of Tordesillas (1494), the Spanish and Portuguese agreed to a line of demarcation established in mid-Atlantic by the pope. Lands "discovered" to the east of that line belonged to Portugal; those to the west belonged to Spain. The inhabitants of those lands were not consulted. This left Brazil, Africa, and the route to India in Portuguese hands, but a line of demarcation in the Pacific was not defined. Much of Asia remained in dispute.

To establish a Spanish presence there, an expedition was dispatched in 1515 to reach the Moluccas by sailing west around the southern tip of South America. Its leader was Fernando Magellan, a Portuguese sailor in Spanish pay. Magellan crossed the Pacific only to be killed in the Moluccas by natives unimpressed with the benefits of Spanish sovereignty (see document 15.1). His navigator, Sebastian del Cano, became the first captain to circumnavigate the globe when he brought the expedition's only remaining ship back to Spain with fifteen survivors in 1522. The broad outlines of the world were now apparent (see map 15.1).

◆

## The First Colonial Empires: Portugal and Spain

Conquest and the imposition of European government accompanied exploration from the beginning. The Portuguese made no effort to impose their direct rule on large native populations, in part because they lacked the manpower to do so and in part because the primary purpose of Portuguese expansion was trade. Instead they established a series of merchant colonies to collect

advantage of winds and currents that he could not fully have understood. In spite of the season he encountered no hurricanes and, on October 12, sighted what he believed to be an island off the coast of Japan. It was one of the Bahamas.

Columbus made three more voyages before his death in 1506, insisting until the end that he had found the western passage to Asia. The realization that it was a continent whose existence had only been suspected

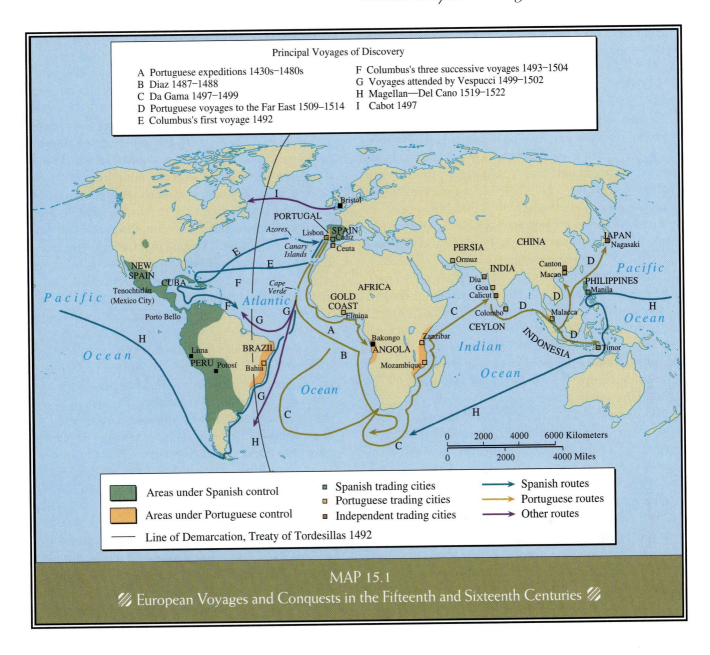

## Principal Voyages of Discovery

A Portuguese expeditions 1430s–1480s
B Diaz 1487–1488
C Da Gama 1497–1499
D Portuguese voyages to the Far East 1509–1514
E Columbus's first voyage 1492

F Columbus's three successive voyages 1493–1504
G Voyages attended by Vespucci 1499–1502
H Magellan—Del Cano 1519–1522
I Cabot 1497

Areas under Spanish control
Areas under Portuguese control
Line of Demarcation, Treaty of Tordesillas 1492
Spanish trading cities
Portuguese trading cities
Independent trading cities
Spanish routes
Portuguese routes
Other routes

MAP 15.1
European Voyages and Conquests in the Fifteenth and Sixteenth Centuries

goods from the African, Indian, or Asian interior for transshipment to Portugal in return for cash or European commodities. These colonies were rarely more than towns protected by a Portuguese garrison and governed by Portuguese law. They were not, for the most part, self-sustaining. To prosper, they had to maintain diplomatic and commercial relations with their neighbors while retaining the option of force, either for self-protection or to obtain a favorable market share in regional trade. Because Portugal's population was small, there was no question of large-scale immigration. Governors from Albuquerque onward sought to maintain colonial populations and to solidify Portuguese control by encouraging intermarriage with native peoples.

Communication between these far-flung stations and the mother country was maintained by the largest ships of the age, the thousand-ton carracks of the *Carreira da India*. The voyage around the tip of Africa took months and the mortality among crews was dreadful, but profit to the crown made it all seem worthwhile. To discourage smuggling, everything had to be shipped to and from a central point—the Guinea Mines House at Lagos, near Sagres—where royal officials could inspect the cargoes of spice and silks and assess the one-third share owed to the king. In return, the monarchy provided military and naval protection for the colonies and for the convoys that served them. Colonial governors, though appointed by the crown, enjoyed the freedom that comes from being far from home. Corruption flourished, but Portuguese rule was rarely harsh.

Where controlling large tracts of land became necessary, as in Brazil, the Portuguese established captaincies that were in fact proprietary colonies. Captains-general would be appointed in return for their promise to settle and develop their grants. The model was the settlement of Madeira. However, Brazil evolved into a society based upon African slavery. Its most valuable resources were dye woods and a climate ideal for growing sugar, a commodity for which Europeans had already begun to develop an insatiable craving.

The first Spanish attempts at colonization resembled the Portuguese experience in Brazil. Columbus had set a bad example by trying to enslave the native population of Hispaniola. Similar unsuccessful efforts were made at Cuba and elsewhere in the Caribbean. The Indians died of disease and overwork, fled to the mainland, or were killed while trying to resist. African slaves were then imported to work in the mines and sugar-cane fields. Royal efforts eventually were able to bring the situation under control, but in the meantime, the conquest of Mexico and Peru had changed the basic nature of Spanish colonial enterprise. For the first time, Europeans sought to impose their rule on societies as complex and populous as their own.

The various nations of central Mexico were grouped into political units that resembled city-states. Their combined population almost certainly exceeded that of Spain. By the fifteenth century, most of these peoples had become either subjects or tributaries of the warlike Aztecs whose capital, Tenochtitlán, was a vast city built in the midst of a lake where Mexico City now stands. With a force that originally numbered only six hundred men, Hernán Cortés seized control of this great empire in only two years (1519–21). He could not have done it without the assistance of the Aztecs' many native enemies, but his success left Spain with the problem of governing millions whose culture was wholly unlike that of Europeans.

The problem was compounded in Peru a decade later. In 1530 Francisco Pizarro landed at Tumbez on the Pacific coast with 180 men and set about the destruction of the Inca Empire. The Incas were the ruling dynasty of the Quechua people. From their capital at Cuzco they controlled a region nearly two thousand miles in length by means of an elaborate system of roads and military supply depots. More tightly organized than the Mexicans, Quechua society was based on communal landholding and a system of forced labor

that supported both the rulers and a complex religious establishment that did not, unlike that of the Aztecs, demand human sacrifice. Pizarro had the good fortune to arrive in the midst of a dynastic dispute that divided the Indians and virtually paralyzed resistance. By 1533 the Spanish, numbering about six hundred, had seized the capital and a vast golden treasure, but they soon began to fight among themselves. Pizarro was murdered in one of a series of civil wars that ended only in 1548.

The rapid conquest of two great empires forced the Spanish crown to confront basic issues of morality and governance. Tension between conquerors and the crown had begun with Columbus. His enslavement of the Indians and high-handed treatment of his own men led to his replacement as governor of Hispaniola. Balboa was executed for his misbehavior in Darien by officials sent from Spain. To regularize the situation, the *encomienda* system, an institution with deep medieval roots, was introduced after the conquests of Mexico and Peru. Conquistadores were to provide protection and religious instruction for a fixed number of Indians in return for a portion of their labor. The system failed. The conquistadores were for the most part desperadoes, members of a large class of otherwise unemployable military adventurers that had survived the wars of Granada or of Italy. They had braved great dangers to win what they thought of as a New World and had no intention of allowing priests and bureaucrats to deprive them of their rewards.

In the meantime, the Indians of the mainland had begun to die in enormous numbers like those of the islands before them. Though many were killed while trying to defend themselves, most fell victim to European diseases for which they had developed no immunities. Smallpox was probably the worst. Estimates of mortality by the end of the sixteenth century range as high as 90 percent, and though all figures from this period are open to question, the conquest clearly was responsible for the greatest demographic catastrophe in historical times (see table 15.1).

Given the state of medical knowledge, little could be done to control the epidemics, but church and state alike were determined to do something about the conquistadores. The Dominican friar Bartolomé de Las Casas (1474–1566) launched a vigorous propaganda campaign on behalf of the Indians that ended in a series of debates at the University of Salamanca. Las Casas won his point. Between 1542 and 1543, the emperor Charles V (1500–58) issued the so-called New Laws, forbidding Indian slavery and abolishing the encomienda system.

## ✴ TABLE 15.1 ✴
### Population Decline in Central Mexico

Little agreement exists on the size of Mexico's pre-Columbian population. These figures are more conservative than most but reflect a stunning rate of mortality.

| Region | Population in 1530–35 | Population in 1568 |
|---|---|---|
| Basin of Mexico (excluding Mexico City) | 589,070–743,337 | 294,535–297,335 |
| Mexico City | 218,546–273,183 | 109, 273 |
| Morelos | 460,797–614,396 | 153,599 |
| Southern Hidalgo | 257,442–321,802 | 128,721 |
| Tlaxcala | 140,000–165,000 | 140,000–165,000 |
| West Puebla | | |
| Above 2000 meters | 160,664–200,830 | 80,332 |
| Below 2000 meters | 152,412–190,515 | 38,103 |
| Total | 1,978,931–2,509,063 | 944,563–972,363 |

Source: Adapted from William T. Sanders, "The Population of the Central Mexican Symbiotic Region, the Basin of Mexico, and the Teotihuacán Valley in the Sixteenth Century," in *The Native Population of the Americas in 1492*, 2d ed., William M. Denevan (Madison, Wis.: University of Wisconsin Press, 1992), p. 128.

The edicts for the protection of the Indians met with powerful resistance (see document 15.2), and not until the reign of Philip II from 1556 to 1598 did a system of governance become fully implemented that would last throughout the colonial era. The basis of that system was the establishment of Mexico and Peru as kingdoms to be ruled by viceroys who were the personal representatives of the king. Like the Portuguese, Spain tried to limit access to its colonial trade. Foreigners were excluded, and all goods were to be shipped and received through the Casa de Contratación, a vast government establishment in Sevilla. From the middle of the sixteenth century, French and English adventurers sought to break this monopoly and eventually became a threat to Spanish shipping in both Caribbean and European waters. By this time, massive silver deposits had been discovered at Potosí in what is now Bolivia (1545) and at Zacatecas in Mexico (1548). Bullion shipments from the New World soon accounted for more than 20 percent of the empire's revenues, and a system of convoys or *flotas* was established for their protection.

## ◈ DOCUMENT 15.2 ◈
### Proclamation of the New Laws in Peru

*In 1544 a new viceroy, Blasco Nuñez Vela, introduced the New Laws to Peru. The popular outrage recounted here by Francisco López de Gómara led to a serious but unsuccessful revolt under the leadership of Gonzalo Pizarro, the conqueror's brother.*

Blasco Nuñez entered Trujillo amid great gloom on the part of the Spaniards; he publicly proclaimed the New Laws, regulating Indian tributes, freeing the Indians, and forbidding their use as carriers against their will and without pay. He told them, however, that if they had reason to complain of the ordinances they should take their case to the emperor; and that he would write to the king that he had been badly informed to order those laws.

When the citizens perceived the severity behind his soft words, they began to curse. [Some] said that they were ill-requited for their labor and services if in their declining years they were to have no one to serve them; these showed their teeth, decayed from eating roasted corn in the conquest of Peru; others displayed many wounds, bruises, and great lizard bites; the conquerors complained that after wasting their estates and shedding their blood in gaining Peru for the emperor, he was depriving them of the few vassals he had given them.

The priests and friars also declared that they could not support themselves nor serve their churches if they were deprived of their Indian towns; the one who spoke most shamelessly against the viceroy and even against the king was Fray Pedro Muñoz of the Mercedarian Order, saying . . . that the New Laws smelled of calculation rather than of saintliness, for the king was taking away the slaves that he had sold without returning the money received from them. . . . There was bad blood between this friar and the viceroy because the latter had stabbed the friar one evening in Málaga when the viceroy was *corregidor* there.

López de Gómara, Francisco. "*Historia de las Indias*," trans. B. Keen. In *Historiadores primitivos de las Indias*, vol. 1, p. 251. In *Latin American Civilization*, vol. 1, pp. 142–143. Boston: Houghton Mifflin, 1974.

# A Clash of Empires: The Ottoman Challenge and the Emperor Charles V

The wars that plagued sixteenth- and early seventeenth-century Europe were for the most part a continuation of old dynastic rivalries, complicated after 1560 by rebellion and civil war in nearly all of the major states. These struggles were pursued with unparalleled vigor even though most Europeans believed, or claimed to believe, that the survival of Christendom was threatened by Ottoman expansion.

The Turks first became a serious threat to western Europe in the reign of Süleyman I (the Magnificent, reigned 1520–66). In 1522 his fleet drove the Knights of St. John from their stronghold at Rhodes, thereby permitting unimpeded communications between Constantinople and Egypt. After defeating the Hungarians at Mohács in 1526, Süleyman established control of the central Hungarian plain. The Austrian Hapsburgs were able to claim a narrow strip of northwestern Hungary, but Transylvania under the voivod János Zapolya (d. 1540) became a Turkish tributary, Calvinist in religion, and bitterly hostile to the Catholic west. Then, in 1529 and again in 1532, Süleyman besieged Vienna. He failed on both occasions, largely because Vienna was beyond the effective limits of Ottoman logistics. But the effort made a profound impression. The Turk was at the gates.

In retrospect, the attacks on Vienna probably were intended only to prevent a Hapsburg reconquest of Hungary. They were not repeated until 1689. In 1533 a new Turkish offensive was launched at sea. Fleets under the command of Khair-ed-Din, a Christian convert to Islam known as "Barbarossa" for his flaming red beard, ravaged the coasts of Italy, Sicily, and Spain and threatened Christian commerce throughout the Mediterranean.

The brunt of these struggles ultimately fell upon the Spanish Empire. In 1517 Charles of Hapsburg (1500–58) ascended the thrones of Castile and Aragon to become Charles I, first king of a united Spain. He was the son of Juana "la Loca" (the Crazy), daughter of Ferdinand and Isabella, and Philip "the Handsome" (d. 1506), son of the emperor Maximilian I and Mary of Burgundy. His mother lived until 1555, but she was thought to be insane and had been excluded from the succession. From her, Charles inherited Spain, its possessions in the New World, and much of Italy, including Naples, Sicily, and Sardinia. On the death of his grandfather Maximilian in 1519, he gained the Haps-

burg lands in Austria and Germany and the remaining inheritance of the dukes of Burgundy including the seventeen provinces of the Netherlands. In 1521 he was elected Holy Roman emperor as Charles V (see illustration 15.2).

The massive accumulation of states and resources embroiled the young emperor in endless conflict. Though he had placed the Austrian lands under the rule of his brother Ferdinand, king of the Romans, Charles was forced to defend Vienna in person against the Turks. Because Turkish naval efforts were directed primarily against his possessions in Spain and Italy, he thought it necessary to invade Tunis in 1535 and Algiers in 1541. The Valois kings of France, seeing themselves surrounded by Charles's territories, fought seven wars with him in thirty years. This Hapsburg-Valois rivalry was in some ways a continuation of the Italian wars at the beginning of the century, but it was fought on three fronts: northern Italy, the Netherlands, and the Pyrenees. As a devout Catholic, the emperor also tried in 1546–47 and again in 1552–55 to bring the German Protestants to heel but received no help from the papacy. Paul III, fearing imperial domination of Italy, allied himself with the Most Christian King of France, who was in turn the ally of the major Protestant princes and of the Turks.

The empire of Charles V was multinational, but in time its center of gravity shifted toward Spain. Charles, born in the Low Countries and whose native tongue was French, became dependent upon the revenues of Castile, the only one of his realms in which permanent taxation had been established. Spanish soldiers, trained in the Italian wars, became the core of his army. Castilian administrators produced results, not endless complaints about the violation of traditional rights or procedures, and by 1545 his secretary, his chief military adviser, and his confessor were Spanish. Charles retired in 1556, sick and exhausted, to the remote monastery of Yuste in the heart of Spanish Extremadura. His son, Philip II (reigned 1556–98), was Spanish to his fingertips. His father's abdication left him Italy, the Netherlands, and the Spanish Empire, while the Hapsburg lands in central Europe were given to Charles's brother Ferdinand, who was elected emperor in 1558.

The war between France and Spain came to an end in 1559 with the treaty of Cateau-Cambrésis, but the underlying rivalry remained. Both sides were simply exhausted. Though Philip was forced to repudiate his father's debts, the predictability of Castilian revenues and a dramatic increase in wealth from the American mines

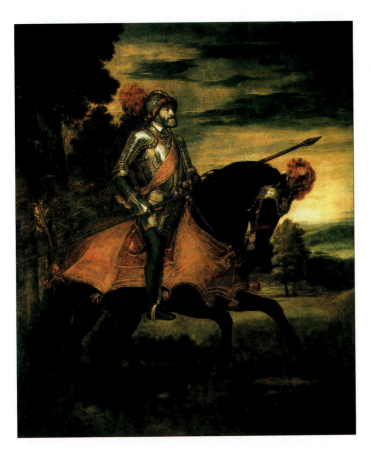

**Illustration 15.2**

**Charles V.** This portrait was painted by Titian after the battle of Mühlberg (1547) in which Charles defeated the Protestant princes of the Schmalkaldic League. It shows the emperor as he often was—on horseback and at war.

soon restored Spanish credit. The policies of the new king would be those of the late emperor: the containment of Islam and of Protestantism, and the neutralization of France.

## The Crisis of the Early Modern State

The wars and rebellions of the later sixteenth century must be understood in this context. Moreover, the cost of war had continued to grow, forcing the state to increase its claims upon the resources of its subjects. By midcentury, nobles, cities, and their elected representatives had begun to resist those claims with unprecedented vigor. Reassertions of ancient privilege were brought forth to counter demands for more money or for greater royal authority. This heightened resistance was based in part upon economics. A series of bad harvests, partially attributed to the Little Ice Age that lasted from the 1550s to well after 1650, worked together with monetary inflation to keep trade and land revenues stagnant. Real wealth was not increasing in proportion to the demands made upon it, and though European elites continued to prosper

by comparison with the poor, they grew ever more jealous of their prerogatives.

The controversies that arose in the wake of the Reformation made matters worse. Outside the Iberian Peninsula, the populations of most states were now bitterly divided along confessional as well as economic lines. Because nearly everyone believed that religious tolerance was incompatible with political order, each group sought to impose its views upon the others. This attitude was shared by many who were not fanatics. In a society that had always expressed political and economic grievances in religious language, the absence of a common faith made demonizing opponents easy, and reaching compromise difficult if not impossible.

In the light of these struggles, the evolution of dynastic states, for all its success, apparently had not resolved certain basic issues of sovereignty. The relationship of the crown to other elements of the governing elites was still open to question in France, England, and the Netherlands. In the Holy Roman Empire the role of the emperor was imperfectly defined, and many of the empire's constituent principalities were engaged in internal disputes. Underlying everything was the problem of dynastic continuity. The success of the early modern state still depended to an extraordinary degree upon the character and abilities of its ruler. Could its basic institutions continue to function if the prince were a child or an incompetent? Some even doubted that they could survive the accession of a woman.

## The French Wars of Religion and the Revolt of the Netherlands

The peace of Cateau-Cambrésis was sealed by the marriage of Isabel of Valois, daughter of Henry II of France, to Philip II of Spain. The celebrations included a tournament in which the athletic, if middle-aged, Henry died when a splinter from his opponent's lance entered the eye socket of his helmet. The new king, Francis II, was a sickly child of fifteen. The establishment of a regency under the leadership of the Guise family marked the beginning of a series of conflicts known as the Wars of Religion that lasted until 1598. The Guise were from Lorraine and unrelated to the royal family. Their ascendancy threatened the Bourbons, a clan descended from Louis IX and headed by the brothers Antoine, king of Navarre, and Louis, prince of Condé. It was also a threat to Henry's widow, Catherine de Médicis (1519–89), who hoped to retain power on behalf of her son Francis and his three brothers. Yet another faction, headed by Anne de Montmorency, constable of France, sought, like Catherine, to play the Guise against the Bourbons for their own advantage.

At one level the Wars of Religion were an old-fashioned struggle between court factions for control of the crown, but the Guise were also devout Catholics who intensified Henry II's policy of persecuting Protestants. Most French Protestants, or Huguenots, were followers of John Calvin. In 1559 they numbered no more than 5 or 10 percent of the population, but their geographic and social distribution made them a formidable minority. Heavily concentrated in the south and west, Calvinism appealed most to rural nobles and to the artisans of the towns, two groups with a long history of political, regional, and economic grievances (see document 15.3). The nobles were for the most part trained in the profession of arms; unhappy artisans could easily disrupt trade and city governments.

Searching for allies, the Bourbons found the Huguenots and converted to Protestantism. The conflict was now both religious and to a degree regional, as the Catholics of Paris and the northeast rallied to the house of Guise, who were secretly allied with Philip II of Spain. Francis II died in 1560, shortly after Condé and

◆ DOCUMENT 15.3 ◆

## The Defense of Liberty Against Tyrants

*In both France and the Netherlands, the Protestants had to justify their revolt against the monarchy. One of the most important theorists to do so was Philippe du Plessis-Mornay, a councillor to Henry of Navarre, the leader of the Bourbon faction who later became Henry IV. Plessis-Mornay based his argument on an early version of the social contract theory, which argued that all rulers received their power from the people. His ideas would have a powerful impact on the political thinkers of the Enlightenment and on the framers of the United States Constitution. This is an exerpt from his treatise,* Vindiciae contra tyrannos.

Thus, at the beginning all kings were elected. And even those who seem today to come to the throne by succession must first be inaugurated by the people. Furthermore, even if a people has customarily chosen its kings from a particular family because of its outstanding merits, that decision is not so unconditional that if the established line degenerates, the people may not select another.

We have shown . . . that kings receive their royal status from the people; that the whole people is greater than the king and is above him; that the king in his kingdom, the emperor in his empire, are supreme only as ministers and agents, while the people is the true proprietor. It follows, therefore, that a tyrant who commits felony against the people who is, as it were, the owner of his fief; that he commits *lèse majesté* [treason] against the kingdom or the empire; and that he is no better than any other rebel since he violates the same laws, although as king, he merits even graver punishment. And so . . . he may be either deposed by his superior or punished under the *lex Julia* [the Roman law on treason] for acts against the public majesty. But the superior here is the whole people or those who represent it. . . . And if things have gone so far that the tyrant cannot be expelled without resort to force, they may call the people to arms, recruit an army, and use force, strategy, and all the engines of war against him who is the declared enemy of the country and the commonwealth.

du Plessis-Mornay, Philippe. "*Vindiciae contra tyrannos.*" In *Constitutionalism and Resistance in the 16th Century,* trans. and ed. Julian H. Franklin. New York: Macmillan, 1969.

**Illustration 15.3**

///// **The Massacre of the Innocents.** In this work of art by Pieter Breughel the Younger, which is also a powerful propaganda piece, Spanish soldiers terrorize a Flemish village. The figure at the head of the troops bears a strong resemblence to the duke of Alba as he looked in 1567. To make a political point, Breughel the Younger may have repainted an earlier version of this work that had been done by his father.

the Huguenots tried unsuccessfully to kidnap him at Amboise. He was succeeded by his brother, Charles IX (reigned 1560–74), who was closely controlled by Catherine de Médicis, but the wars went on. Though the Huguenots were not at first successful on the battlefield, they gained limited religious toleration in 1570.

Meanwhile, the Netherlands had begun their long rebellion against the king of Spain. The seventeen provinces of the Low Countries were now the richest part of Europe, an urbanized region devoted to trade and intensive agriculture. Though divided by language (Dutch or Flemish was spoken in the north and west, French or Walloon in the south and east), they shared a common artistic and intellectual tradition and an easygoing tolerance for foreigners and heretics. Though a majority of the population remained Catholic, Lutherans and Calvinists flourished in the major cities. Government was decentralized and, from the Spanish point of view, woefully inefficient. Philip II was represented by a regent, his half-sister Margaret of Parma (1522–86), who presided over the privy council and the councils of finance and state. Seventeen provincial estates, all of which were represented in the States General, controlled taxes and legislation. A virulent localism based on the defense of historical privilege made agreement possible only on rare occasions. Taxes were usually defeated by squabbles over who should pay the largest share—nobles or townspeople. No common legal code existed, and a host of independent legal jurisdictions were controlled by nobles whose administration of justice was often corrupt.

None of this was acceptable to Philip II. He was determined to reorganize the government, reform the legal system, and root out heresy by reforming the church along the lines suggested by the Council of Trent. All of these proposals struck directly at the wealth and power of the Netherlandish nobles. Philip's plan to reorganize the governing councils weakened their authority, while legal reform would have eliminated the feudal courts from which many of the nobles drew large revenues. Though his reform of the church sought to increase the number of bishops, the king was determined to end the purchase of ecclesiastical offices and to appoint only clerics whose education and spirituality met the high standards imposed by the Council of Trent. The ancient custom by which nobles invested in church offices for the support of their younger sons was at an end.

Four years of accelerating protest by leading members of the aristocracy accomplished nothing. Finally, in 1566, a wave of iconoclasm brought matters to a head. The Protestants, acting in opposition to Philip's plan for ecclesiastical reform and encouraged by members of the higher nobility, removed the images from churches across the country. In some areas, iconoclasm was accompanied by rioting and violence. Though the regent's government was able to restore order, Philip responded in shock and anger. In 1567 he dispatched his leading general, the duke of Alba (1507–82), to put down what he saw as rebellion (see illustration 15.3). Though Alba was at first successful, the harshness of his government alienated virtually every segment of opinion. When he attempted to introduce a perpetual tax in 1572, most of the major cities declared their allegiance to William "the Silent," Prince of Orange (1533–84), the man who had emerged as leader of the revolt.

Though William was not yet a convert to Protestantism, he attempted to form an alliance with the French Huguenots, who, under the leadership of Gaspard de Coligny, had gained new influence with Charles IX. The situation was doubly perilous for Spain because Philip II, while maintaining Alba in the Netherlands, had renewed his father's struggles with the Turk. The Mediterranean war culminated in the great naval victory of Lepanto (October 7, 1571), but Philip's treasury was once again exhausted. French intervention in the Netherlands was averted only by the Massacre of St. Bartholomew (August 23–24, 1572) in which more than five thousand Protestants, Coligny included, were killed by Catholic mobs. The massacre revived the French civil wars and permitted Alba to retake many of the rebellious towns, but the duke was recalled in 1573 and his successors were unable to bring the revolt under control. Margaret's son, Alessandro Farnese, duke of Parma (1545–92), finally was able to reimpose Spanish rule on the ten southern provinces in 1585.

By this time, the seven northern provinces had organized into an independent state with William of Orange as stadtholder or chief executive. The United Netherlands was Dutch in language and culture. Enriched by trade, secure in its control of the sea, and defended by the heavily fortified "water line" of three broad rivers—the Rhine, the Maas, and the Waal—the new republic was almost invulnerable to Spanish attack. It was also Protestant. The government was dominated by Calvinists, and William converted to Protestantism before he was assassinated by a Spanish agent in 1584. Refugees from Spanish rule, most of them French-speaking Calvinists, poured into the north, while a number of Dutch Catholics headed south into what is now Belgium.

These developments critically altered the balance of power in northern Europe. Philip II was still determined to recover his lost provinces and to assist the Catholics of France in their battle against the Huguenots. The English, restored to Protestantism by Elizabeth I (ruled 1558–1603; see illustration 15.4), were equally determined to prevent a concentration of Spanish power on the coasts of the North Sea. When Parma took Antwerp, the largest and richest city in the Netherlands in 1584, they sent an expeditionary force to support the Dutch.

Illustration 15.4

Elizabeth I of England. This portrait from the workshop of Nicholas Hilliard dates from c. 1599, a time of great political difficulty for the queen. It is a propaganda piece intended to convey the wealth, majesty, and vigor of a ruler who was already in her sixty-sixth year.

Though a prosperous land of about three-and-a-half million people, Elizabethan England was no match for the Spanish Empire. It had the core of a fine navy but no army worthy of the name. Perpetual taxes were unknown, and the improvidence of Henry VIII had left his daughter with meager revenues from the royal domain. In the event of war, funds had to be sought from Parliament, and Parliament continually tried to interfere with the queen's policies. It was especially incensed at her refusal to marry, in part because it thought a woman incapable of governing on her own, and in part because it feared disorder if she died without an heir.

Parliament need not have worried about Elizabeth's ability, but this last concern, at least, was real. Catholics everywhere had rejected Henry VIII's divorce. To them, Elizabeth was illegitimate, and Mary Stuart, queen of Scots (1542–87), was the true queen of England. A devout Catholic, descended from Henry VII and connected on her mother's side to the house of Guise, Mary had been driven from Scotland in 1568 by a coalition of Protestants inspired by the

**Illustration 15.5**

🖎 **The Spanish Armada, 1588.** This painting by an unknown artist shows a critical moment in the defeat of the Spanish Armada. The Spanish fleet had anchored off Gravelines on the Flemish coast to support an invasion of England by the duke of Parma. The English sent fireships into the anchorage, forcing them to scatter and to abandon the invasion.

reformer John Knox and led by her kinsman the earl of Moray. Elizabeth offered her refuge but held her under house arrest for nineteen years before ordering her execution in 1587.

Mary was killed not only because she had plotted against Elizabeth, but also because the English queen was convinced that war with Spain was inevitable. Elizabeth wanted no rival to encourage the hopes of Philip II or of her own Catholic subjects. These fears, too, were realistic, because for more than twenty years Elizabeth had pursued a course of intermittent hostility toward Spain. She had encouraged her subjects, notably Sir John Hawkins and Sir Francis Drake, to raid Spanish colonies in the Caribbean and in 1586 sent an English force to assist the Dutch. From the Spanish point of view, the execution of Mary was the last straw. Philip responded by sending a fleet to invade England. The great Spanish Armada of 1588 failed (see illustration 15.5), but the disaster did not end the war. Philip rebuilt his navy and tried again without success in 1595, while Drake and the aged Hawkins made an-

other vain attempt on Havana and Cartagena de Indias in the same year.

By this time the Spanish were at war in France as well. In 1589 the Bourbon leader, Henry of Navarre, emerged from the "War of the Three Henrys" as the only surviving candidate for the throne. Henry of Guise and Henry III, the last surviving son of Catherine de Médicis, had been assassinated by each others' supporters. Philip thought that, if France were controlled by Huguenots, the Spanish Netherlands would be crushed between two Protestant enemies, and he sent Parma and his army into France. This expedition, too, was a costly failure, but Henry's interests turned out to be more political than religious. He converted to Catholicism in the interest of peace and ascended the throne as Henry IV (reigned 1589–1610). To protect the Huguenots he issued the Edict of Nantes (1598), which granted them freedom of worship and special judicial rights in a limited number of towns, most in the southwest. In some respects, a state within a state was created, but the ordeal of France was over.

## The Thirty Years' War

The resolution of the French wars and the death of Philip II in 1598 marked the end of a political cycle. The Netherlands continued to struggle under the leadership of William's son, Maurice of Nassau (1567–1625), until a ten years' truce was concluded in 1608, but it was a truce, not a treaty. Though Spain was financially exhausted, it still refused to recognize the Dutch state. War was expected to break out again when the truce expired in 1618. The war, when it came, was much more than a resumption of the Dutch Revolt. It involved all of the European states and turned central Europe into a battleground from 1618 to 1648.

The first phase of the Thirty Years' War began with a struggle for the crown of Bohemia. In 1555 the Peace of Augsburg had established the principle *cuius regio, eius religio;* that is, princes within the empire had the right to determine the religious beliefs of their subjects. Calvinists, however, were excluded from its provisions, and issues regarding the disposition of church properties and the conversion of bishops were left in dispute. Since then, two electoral principalities, the Palatinate and Brandenburg, had turned Calvinist, and several bishops had converted to Protestantism while retaining possession of their endowed lands. Violent quarrels arose over these issues and by 1610 the empire was divided into two armed camps: the Protestant Union and the Catholic League.

The Bohemian controversy arose because Matthias, king of Bohemia in 1618, was also Holy Roman emperor, a Catholic Hapsburg, and uncle of the future emperor Ferdinand II of Austria (1578–1637). Matthias was determined to preserve Bohemia for the faith and for his family, and in 1617 he secured the election of Ferdinand as his successor to the throne of Bohemia. This election was opposed by many of the Bohemian gentry and lesser nobility. They were, for the most part, Calvinists or Hussites and feared persecution from the devout Ferdinand and his Jesuit advisers. On May 23, 1618, an assembly of Bohemians threw three of the Hapsburg's regents from a window of the Hradschin palace, appointed a provisional government, and began to raise an army.

The "Defenestration of Prague" was an act of war. Revolt spread to the hereditary lands, threatening not only Bohemia but also the basic integrity of the Hapsburg state. Worse yet, the king of Bohemia was an elector of the empire. If the Bohemians elected a Protestant, the Protestants would have a majority of electors just as a new imperial election appeared imminent. Matthias was in poor health and Ferdinand hoped to succeed

him as king of Bohemia as well as emperor. Ferdinand needed time to muster support, but in June 1619 he invaded Bohemia with the army of the Catholic League, drawn largely from his ally, Bavaria. The Bohemians responded by offering the crown to a Calvinist prince, Frederick V (1596–1632), elector palatine and son-in-law of James I of England.

Frederick accepted, after the death of Matthias and the election of Ferdinand as emperor on August 28. It was a tragic mistake. He was supported by only a part of the Protestant Union. James I refused to help, and a diversionary attack on Hungary by Bethlen Gabor (1580–1629), the Calvinist prince of Transylvania, was eventually contained by the Hapsburgs. Finally, on November 8, 1620, Frederick and his Protestant allies were soundly defeated at the White Mountain near Prague. Frederick's cause was now hopeless. The Spanish truce with the Netherlands had expired, and the palatinate lay squarely across the route by which Spanish troops and supplies were sent to the Low Countries. While Frederick's forces fought to preserve his claim to Bohemia, a Spanish army invaded his ancestral lands.

A second phase of the war began in 1625 when Christian IV of Denmark (1577–1648) emerged briefly as the champion of Protestantism. Christian's Lutheranism was reinforced by his territorial ambitions in north Germany, but he was no match for the imperial generals. By 1629 he was out of the war. His place was taken by the formidable Gustav Adolph of Sweden (1594–1632). Since the reign of Erik XIV, from 1560 to 1568, Swedish policy had aimed at control of the Baltic. Wars with Russia and Poland had taught Gustav the art of war and given him all of Livonia, a territory roughly equal to present-day Estonia, Latvia, and Lithuania. He now sought to defend his fellow Protestants and to establish Swedish control over Mecklenburg and Pomerania on the north German coast. His brilliant campaigns, financed in part by France, came to an end when he died victorious on the battlefield at Lützen on November 16, 1632.

The last phase of the war (1535–1648) continued the Franco-Swedish alliance, but with France acting openly as the leader of the anti-imperial forces. Henry IV had died at the hands of an assassin in 1610, leaving the queen, Marie de Médicis, as regent for the nine-year-old Louis XIII (1601–43). Her regency was unpopular, but the disasters of 1560 were not repeated. Louis seized power from his mother in 1617 and, after 1624, entrusted much of his government to Armand de Plessis, cardinal duke of Richelieu (1585–1642). One of the ablest statesmen of the age, Richelieu was alarmed by the Spanish-Imperial alliance and returned

**MAP 15.2**
The Thirty Years' War

to the anti-Hapsburg policies of Francis I. He pursued the war through surrogates until the death of Gustav Adolph forced him into the open. The Spanish were by this time in irreversible decline, and their defeat by the French at Rocroi (1643) marked the end of their military power. Bavaria was ravaged by a Franco-Swedish force in 1648, and peace was at last concluded on October 24 of that year.

The Treaties of Westphalia brought the Thirty Years' War to an end, leaving France the dominant power in Europe (see map 15.2). The Netherlands, which had fought Spain in a series of bitter actions on land and sea, was at last recognized as an independent state, while the German principalities, many of which had been devastated, were restored to the boundaries of

1618. Bohemia reverted to the Hapsburgs, but imperial authority as a whole was weakened except in the Hapsburg lands of southeastern Europe. It was a meager return for three decades of unparalleled violence.

## The English Civil War

England did not participate in the Thirty Years' War because the early Stuart monarchs, James I (reigned 1603–25) and Charles I (reigned 1625–49), were caught in a political dilemma from which they could not escape. Like Denmark and Sweden, England was a "domain" state: the regular revenues of the crown came not from taxes, which could be levied only by Parliament, but from the royal domain. This was not necessarily a disadvantage. The Danish monarch held more than 40 percent of the arable land in Denmark and derived vast revenues from the Sound Tolls levied on every ship passing from the North Sea into the Baltic. The Swedish royal estate derived great wealth from export duties on copper and iron, the country's major exports. Both countries were therefore able to exert a political and military influence wholly disproportionate to their size.

England had no comparable sources of revenue. The failure of Henry VIII to retain monastic lands taken at the time of the Reformation left the crown without sufficient property to "live of its own." Even import and export duties, though technically part of the domain, had to be authorized by Parliament. The resulting poverty, already evident under Elizabeth, restricted the crown's ability to reward its supporters. Worse, it forced her Stuart successors to seek wealth in ways that profoundly offended their subjects (see document 15.4). Knights' fines, ship money, *quo warranto* proceedings, and the abuse of wardships struck directly at property rights and aroused a firestorm of opposition.

Much of this opposition was at first centered in the legal profession where such jurists as Sir Edward Coke (1552–1634) revived the common law as a protection against royal prerogatives, but in the end Parliament proved to be the crown's most formidable adversary. Between 1540 and 1640 the wealth and numbers of the landholding gentry, the professions, and the merchant community had increased enormously. These elements of the English elite dominated the House of Commons, which took the lead in opposing royal policies. The Stuarts feared their disaffection and would have preferred to rule without calling Parliament. Except for relatively short periods, this was impossible. Even the smallest of crises forced the crown to seek relief through parliamentary taxation.

The growing resentment in Parliament might have been better managed had it not been for the personalities of the Stuart kings. Neither James nor Charles was capable of inspiring great loyalty. James was awkward, personally dirty, and a homosexual at a time when homosexuality was universally condemned. His son was arrogant and generally distrusted, while the court as a whole was thought to be morally and financially corrupt. Though James, who annoyed his subjects with treatises on everything from the evils of tobacco to witchcraft, wrote eloquently in support of the divine right of kings, the legitimacy of his family's rule was continually undermined by his own behavior and by the devious policies of his son.

## ◆ DOCUMENT 15.4 ◆

### The English Petition of Right, 1628

*The 1628 Petition of Right summarized Parliament's grievances against Charles I, who was trying to solve his financial problems through illegal and arbitrary means. The objections are based largely upon perceived violations of the Magna Carta, also known as the Great Charter. The following are excerpts from a much longer document.*

And where also, by the statute called the Great Charter of the Liberties of England, it is declared and enacted that no freeman may be taken or imprisoned, or be disseised of his freehold or liberties or his free customs, or be outlawed or exiled or in any manner destroyed, but by the lawful judgment of his peers or by the law of the land. . . .

They do therefore humbly pray your most excellent majesty that no man hereafter be compelled to make or yield any gift, loan, benevolence, tax, or such like charge without common consent by act of parliament; and that none be called to make answer, or take such oath, or to give attendance, or be confined, or otherwise molested or disquieted concerning the same, or for refusal thereof; and that no freeman, in any such manner as is before mentioned, be imprisoned or detained; and that your majesty would be pleased to remove the said soldiers and mariners [who had been quartered in the counties to enforce the king's measures]; and that the foresaid commissions for proceeding by martial law may be revoked and annulled; and that hereafter no commissions of like nature may issue forth . . . lest by colour of them any of your majesty's subjects be destroyed or put to death, contrary to the laws and franchise of the land.

*Journals of the House of Lords, vol. 3.*

The religious question was more serious. Elizabeth, not wishing "to make windows into men's souls," had established a church that was Protestant but relatively tolerant. Some of her subjects had retained a fondness for the ideas and liturgical practices of the old church, while others, known as Puritans, followed Calvin with varying degrees of rigor. James was a Calvinist who commissioned the King James Bible in 1611 and established Protestant colonists in northern Ireland in the same year. He quarreled with the Puritans over church governance and other matters, but he managed to avoid an open breach as they grew more powerful over the course of his reign. Charles, however, supported the anti-Puritan reforms of Archbishop William Laud (1573–1645). Though Laud was no Catholic, Queen Henriette Marie (1609–1669) heard Mass regularly. She was the sister of Louis XIII and a strong personality who exerted great influence over her husband. The Puritans suspected that Charles meant to restore Catholicism. Faith, as well as liberty and property, was thought to be at risk.

Twenty years of increasingly bitter conflict between Parliament and the crown led to civil war in 1642. The Scots rebelled in 1638 when Charles tried to introduce the English *Book of Common Prayer* at Edinburgh. To pay for the Scottish war, he summoned what is called the Long Parliament because it met from 1640 to 1660. In response to his call for money, the Commons impeached Archbishop Laud and Charles's chief minister, Thomas Wentworth, earl of Strafford. They then abolished the prerogative courts of Star Chamber and High Commission. When Charles failed to impeach the parliamentary leaders he fled from London, and Parliament decided to raise an army in its own defense.

After three years of hard fighting, the royalists were defeated at Naseby (June 14, 1645), but serious divisions had appeared in the parliamentary ranks. The army was now dominated by Independents, who favored a congregational form of church government, while the Parliament they served was controlled by Presbyterians. The Independents refused to disband without guaranteed freedom of conscience and the removal of certain Presbyterians from Parliament. The Scots, fearing a threat to their own Presbyterian church order, were alarmed. Charles sought to capitalize on these strains by abolishing the Scottish episcopate in return for Presbyterian support, but the Scots and their English allies were defeated by the army at Preston (August 17–20, 1548). The victors now felt that compromise was impossible. In December the army captured Charles and purged the Commons of its Presbyterian members. A court appointed by the Rump, as the remnant of Parliament was now called, sentenced the king to death. He was beheaded at Whitehall on January 30, 1649.

For all practical purposes, England was governed by the army. A republican constitution had been established, but real power lay in the hands of Oliver Cromwell (1599–1658), the most successful of the parliamentary generals. In 1653 he was named lord protector of the Commonwealth of England, Scotland, and

Ireland. A radical Protestant, Cromwell attempted to reform English society along Puritan lines while following a vigorous policy abroad. After subduing the Scots, he fought a naval war with the Dutch (1552–54) and started another with Spain in 1656. The Irish Catholics, who had massacred thousands of Protestants in 1641, were ruthlessly suppressed.

Cromwell had refused to accept the crown when it was offered to him in 1657, but when he died in the following year he left the Protectorate to his son Richard. Richard's rule was brief and troubled. He was forced to resign after only nine months, and a Convention Parliament restored Charles II (1630–85), son of Charles I, on May 8, 1660. The English had tired of Puritanism and military rule.

## The Price of Conflict: Fiscal Crisis and Administrative Devolution

Surprisingly, this age of troubles was in many places a time of intellectual, literary, and artistic achievement. A distinction must be made between those regions that were combat zones, those that remained peaceful but were forced to assume heavy financial burdens, and those that were virtually untouched by the fighting. Even the most devastated regions experienced peace for at least a portion of the century between 1560 and 1660; their recovery was sometimes rapid.

In some cases the experience of war produced literary masterpieces. The age of the religious wars was not a golden one for France, but it produced the elegant and skeptical essays of Michel de Montaigne (1533–92), an antidote to sectarian madness. In Germany, the wreckage of the Thirty Years' War was nearly complete, but it was wryly chronicled in Grimmelshausen's *Simplicissimus*. *Don Quixote*, one of the greatest of all literary classics, was written by Miguel de Cervantes (1547–1616), who had lost an arm at Lepanto. It is, at least in part, a satire on his countrymen's fantastic dreams of glory.

Political turmoil gave birth to political theory. The English Civil War convinced Thomas Hobbes (1588–1679) that political salvation lay in *Leviathan*, an autocratic superstate, while *Oceana*, by James Harrington (1611–77) reflected the republican ideals of the Commonwealth. In *Paradise Lost*, Cromwell's Latin secretary, John Milton (1608–74), created a Puritan epic to rival the vision of Dante. Drama, too, flourished in the England of William Shakespeare (1564–1616) and in the Spain of Lope de Vega (1562–1635) and Calderón de la Barca (1600–81). The Netherlands, which after the 1590s enjoyed prosperity and internal peace in the midst of war, surpassed its own earlier achievements in the visual arts and became the center of a school of painting that influenced artists throughout northern Europe.

But if learning and the arts flourished, at least in some places, the struggles of the age were often highly destructive of political and economic life. This resulted primarily from the ways in which war was organized and fought. Armies had become vastly larger and more expensive in the course of the sixteenth century, and the wars were almost interminable. Given their political objectives, it could not have been otherwise. The French Wars of Religion were a struggle between two, and at times three, irreconcilable segments of the country's elite. Most of the battles were classic cavalry actions that resulted in a clear victory for one side or the other, but which could not end the war. Only the destruction of a major segment of the population could have prevented the losers from trying again.

In the Netherlands, the primary goal of both sides was to take and hold land or, conversely, to deny it to the enemy. After 1572 the war became a series of sieges that, thanks to the defensive value of the bastion trace, lasted months if not years. Both sides tended to avoid battles because their troops were, in the short term at least, irreplaceable. Sixteenth-century tactics demanded professional soldiers. The recruitment, training, and movement of replacements to the war zone took months, and positions under constant enemy pressure could not be left even partially defenseless.

If the war in the Netherlands was virtually static, the situation in Germany during the Thirty Years' War was too fluid. Central Europe had become a kind of power vacuum into which unpredictable forces were drawn. Bloody battles were fought only to see the victor confronted with yet another set of enemies. It is hard to imagine what, other than sheer exhaustion, might have ended the struggle. War, as Michael Roberts has said, "eternalized itself."

No early modern state could afford this. Even the wealthiest European monarchies lacked the ability to recruit and maintain full-scale standing armies. They relied instead on a core of subject troops (or, as in the French Wars of Religion, troops personally and ideologically committed to a cause), supplemented by a far larger number of mercenaries. The latter were usually recruited by contractors who commanded them in the field. If the mercenaries were not paid, they left; if they stayed, they had little incentive to risk their lives un-

necessarily. Their employers had little control over their actions, and even subject troops were capable of mutiny if they were left too long unpaid.

War, in other words, was a chaotic business. Rank in the modern sense meant little because officers sometimes refused to obey the orders of those who might have been their inferiors in civilian life. There were no uniforms, and weapons were not for the most part standardized. Logistics were a nightmare. An army might number anywhere from 30,000 to 100,000 combatants. The troops were housed either in makeshift field shelters or quartered on the civilian populations of the war zones, which meant that civilians might be forced to provide food and housing for months on end. The close contact between soldiers and civilians bred hostility and led to chronic breakdowns in military discipline. To complicate matters further, camp followers numbered at least three and often six for each combatant. These women and children were the support troops who made shelter, foraged for food, and nursed the sick and wounded. No army could function without them, but together with the men they made up a society that lived by its own rules with little concern for civilian norms.

The system reached a peak of absurdity during the Thirty Years' War when contractors such as the imperial general Albrecht von Wallenstein (1583–1634) offered recruits a month's pay—which they had to give back to pay for their arms and equipment—and then marched them so far from their homes that they could not easily return. From that point onward they were expected to live off the land. Such practices account for much of the dislocation caused by the German wars. It was safer to join an army with one's family than to remain at home to be robbed, raped, or killed by marauding soldiers (see document 15.5). Whole villages were depopulated only to reconstitute themselves wherever they found themselves when the war ended.

When a state tried to provide adequately for its troops, the costs were prohibitive and could lead to social breakdown. The fate of Spain is an example. In the 1570s Philip II was spending 140 percent of his annual revenues on warfare. The uncovered balance was provided by loans, often at high rates, from Italian or Dutch bankers. Not even American silver could long sustain this kind of expenditure, and in time the economy of Castile was badly damaged (see table 15.2). The other Spanish kingdoms were exempt from most forms of taxation, but in Castile taxes increased to the point that peasants were forced from the land and took refuge in the cities where the church periodically dis-

### ◆ DOCUMENT 15.5 ◆

## Soldiers Loot a German Farm

*The novel* Simplicissimus *by Hans von Grimmelshausen (c. 1622–74) was based in part on the author's own experiences in the Thirty Years' War. In these passages from the beginning of the book, the title character Simplicissimus, who is not as simple as he appears, describes the sack of his parent's farm. Like the hero, people took to the roads or joined the armies to avoid such horrors.*

The first thing these troopers did in the blackened room of my Dad was to stable their mounts. Thereafter, each fell to his appointed task, fraught in every case with ruin and destruction. For although some began to slaughter, cook, and roast, as if for a merry banquet, others stormed through the house from top to bottom, ransacking even the privy, as though they thought the Golden Fleece might be hidden there. Some packed great bundles of cloth, apparel, and household goods, as if to set up a stall for a jumble sale, but what they had no use for they smashed and destroyed. Some thrust their swords into the hay and straw as if they had not enough sheep and pigs to slaughter. Others emptied the feather-beds and pillows of their down, filling them instead with meat and other provender, as if that would make them more comfortable to sleep on. Others again smashed stoves and windows as if to herald an everlasting summer. They flattened copper and pewter utensils and packed up the bent and useless pieces; chests, tables, chairs, and benches they burnt, though in the yard they could have found many cords of firewood. Finally, they broke every dish and saucepan, either because they preferred their food roasted or because they intended to have no more than a single meal there.

And now they began to unscrew the flints from their pistols and to jam the peasant's thumbs into them, and to torture the poor lads as if they had been witches. Indeed, one of the captives had already been pushed into the bread oven and a fire lit under him, although he had confessed nothing. They put a sling around the head of another, twisting it tight with a piece of wood until the blood spurted from his mouth, nose, and ears. In short, each had his own device for torturing peasants, and each peasant received his individual torture. . . . Of the captured women, girls, and maidservants I have nothing in particular to tell, for the warriors would not let me see what they did with them. But this I do know: that from time to time one could hear pitiful screams coming from different parts of the house, and I don't suppose my Mum and Ursula fared any better than the others.

Grimmelshausen, H. J. C. von. *Adventures of a Simpleton*, pp. 8–9, trans. W. Wallich. New York: Ungar, 1963.

### ✳ TABLE 15.2 ✳

#### Crown Income and Debt in Castile

These figures (in millions of ducats) provide an idea of the financial burdens imposed on the Castilian economy by war. During most of this period, nonmilitary costs rarely rose above 10 percent of the annual budget.

| Year | Revenue | Debt | Interest on debt |
|------|---------|------|------------------|
| 1515 | 1.5 | 12 | 0.8 |
| 1560 | 5.3 | 35 | 2.0 |
| 1575 | 6.0 | 50 | 3.8 |
| 1598 | 9.7 | 85 | 4.6 |
| 1623 | 15.0 | 112 | 5.6 |
| 1667 | 36.0 | 130 | 9.1 |

Source: C. Wilson and G. Parker, eds., *An Introduction to the Sources of European Economic History* (Ithaca, N.Y.: Cornell University Press, 1977), p. 49.

tributed grain and oil to the poor. Commerce and industry were virtually destroyed. Declining production increased the country's dependence on imports, which lowered the value of Spanish money and worsened an inflation that had been fueled for years by silver from the Indies. When Philip II died in 1598, the population of Castile had been shrinking for nearly a decade.

Economic decline provoked a chain reaction that raised the costs of war by increasing the interest on government loans, while unfavorable exchange rates raised the cost of goods and services that Spain had to purchase in Germany or the Netherlands. Troops were often poorly supplied or left without pay for as much as three years at a time. This caused mutinies, which prolonged the wars and raised costs even higher. Similar problems arose in other countries, but they were far more serious in Spain because the military effort lasted for more than a century and a half. From the wars of Granada to the Peace of Westphalia, little opportunity existed for recovery.

Philip III (ruled 1598–1621) and his minister, the shrewd but lethargic duke of Lerma, tried to provide Spain with a much-needed respite from war but were unable to restrain the aggressive tendencies of their viceroys. When Philip IV's chief minister, the energetic count-duke of Olivares (1587–1645), tried to spread the burdens of taxation and recruitment to other Spanish realms, he faced rebellion. Portugal, which had been annexed by Philip II in 1580 after its king died without heirs, declared independence in 1640. Cataluña, on the other side of the peninsula, rebelled in the same year. The government of Olivares lacked the resources to stop them, and Portugal remains free to this day. Cataluña returned to the fold in 1652 after France emerged as a greater threat to its liberties than Castile.

Spain was in some respects a special case, but the condition of Europe as a whole after a century of war and rebellion was grim. Most of the German states were a shambles, while the emperor's role was much diminished outside his hereditary lands. Russia was still emerging from its "Time of Troubles," the period of anarchy that followed the death of Ivan the Terrible. The Romanov dynasty, established in 1613, had difficulty dealing with a series of Cossack rebellions and with the heresy of the Old Believers, a movement that rejected all innovation in the Russian church. Though Cromwellian England had briefly tapped the country's wealth in the service of the state, the restoration of Charles II revived many of the old conflicts between crown and Parliament and the king's wealth was once again severely limited. France with its enormous wealth was more resilient, but when the four-year-old Louis XIV ascended the throne under a regency, a series of aristocratic rebellions known as the Fronde (1648–52) revealed that the foundations of the monarchy were by no means fully secure. At midcentury only the Dutch Republic appeared strong and stable, and for Europe's monarchies the years of turmoil clearly had done little to resolve the problem of sovereignty.

# CHAPTER 16

# PREINDUSTRIAL EUROPE: SCIENCE, THE ECONOMY, AND POLITICAL REORGANIZATION

## CHAPTER OUTLINE

The political troubles of the late sixteenth and early seventeenth centuries did not preclude extraordinary developments in other areas. The scientific revolution changed the way Europeans thought about the physical universe. England, France, and above all the Netherlands challenged the Iberian powers and created substantial empires of their own. In the process they greatly expanded Europe's presence in world markets and accumulated capital in unprecedented amounts. The Netherlands emerged, however briefly, as a major power and a center of high culture. Eventually, states that had been nearly shattered by a century of war and revolution began to reconstruct themselves, reforming their governmental institutions, curbing the power of local elites, and gaining control over the armies and navies whose independence had threatened to engulf them. The model for many of these changes was the France of Louis XIV, but the rise of England as an economic and naval power would have an even greater influence on the age to come.

## Medieval Science and the Scientific Revolution

The scientific revolution of the late sixteenth and seventeenth centuries has no parallel among modern intellectual movements. Its impact was comparable to that made by the thinkers of ancient Greece because, like them, it changed not only ideas but also the process by which ideas are formulated. The Renaissance and the Reformation, for all their importance, were rooted in traditional patterns of thought. They could be understood without reordering the concepts that had permeated Western thinking for more than two thousand years. The development of modern science, though in some ways an outgrowth of these earlier movements, asked questions that were different from those that had been asked before and by so doing created a whole new way of looking at the universe. Modern science and the scientific method with which it is associated may be the one body of European ideas that has had a transforming effect on virtually every non-Western culture.

To appreciate the radicalism of the new views, examining what they replaced is useful. In 1500 the basic assumptions of science had changed little since the days of Pliny. The universe was thought to be organized according to rational principles. It was therefore open to human observation and deduction, but the principles of scientific inquiry were limited to those activities alone. As in other fields of thought, the logic of Aristotle, rooted firmly in language and in the meaning of words, was accepted as the most powerful tool of analysis. Scientific description therefore tended to be qualitative rather than quantitative. Accurate observation provided clues to the nature or essential quality of the object being observed. Reason could then determine the relationship of that object to other objects in the natural world.

This was important because ancient science believed that all parts of the universe were interrelated and that nothing could be studied in isolation. Today this idea is called holistic, or perhaps organic. It was stated expressly in Aristotle and, metaphorically, in the popular image of the individual human being as a microcosm of the universe as a whole. It formed the basis not only of academic science but also of the applied sciences of the day: medicine, natural magic, astrology, and alchemy. The last three were partially inspired by the Hermetic tradition, a body of occult literature that was supposedly derived from ancient Egypt. It was regarded with suspicion by the church because its practitioners were thought in various ways to interfere with Providence, but its theoretical assumptions did not conflict with those of the Aristotelians. Many, if not most, of the early scientists were as interested in astrology or alchemy as they were in physics and made no real distinction between the occult and what would today be regarded as more legitimate disciplines.

Whatever their interests, the learned agreed that the world was composed of the four elements—earth, air, fire, and water—and that the elements corresponded to the four humors that governed the body as well as the signs of the zodiac. Magic, "the chief power of all the sciences," sought to understand these and other relationships between natural objects and to manipulate them to achieve useful results. The causes of

natural phenomena were of academic but little practical interest and were generally explained teleologically. That is, they were understood in terms of the result they were intended to produce. Virtually everyone believed that the world had been created for a purpose and that the behavior of natural objects would necessarily be directed to that end. This preconception, together with the tendency to describe objects in qualitative terms, ensured that causation, too, would usually be explained in terms of the nature or qualities of the objects involved. It was a view that comported well with a providential understanding of the world.

Ideas of this kind are now found largely in the pages of supermarket tabloids, but they were once universally accepted by learned people. They provided a rational, comprehensive, and comforting vision of what might otherwise have been a terrifying universe. They have little in common with the principles of modern science, which substitutes measurement for qualitative description and attempts to express physical relationships in quantitative, mathematical terms. Because its vision of the world is mechanical instead of organic and providential, modern science concentrates heavily on the causes of physical and biological reactions and tries to reject teleological and qualitative explanations. It is more likely to ask "why?" than "what?" and has few compunctions about isolating a given problem to study it. Correspondences based upon qualitative or symbolic relationships are ignored.

## The Origins of Modern Scientific Thought: Physics from Copernicus to Newton

Methodologically, modern science seeks to create a hypothesis by reasoning logically from accurate observations. If possible, the hypothesis is then tested by experiment and a mathematical model is constructed that will be both explanatory and predictive. The scientist can then formulate general laws of physical behavior without becoming entangled in the emotional overtones of language. The scientific model of the universe tends to be mechanistic rather than organic, mythological, or poetic. It is not necessarily godless, but its predictability does away with the need for divine intervention on a regular basis.

An intellectual shift of this magnitude did not occur quickly. Its roots are found in several traditions that coexisted uneasily in late medieval and Renaissance thought: the Aristotelian, the experimentalist, and the humanistic. During the sixteenth century a process of fusion began as thinkers adopted elements of each in their attempts to solve an ever-growing list of problems. The problems arose mainly from the perception that old, accepted answers, however logical and comforting they may have been, did not square with observed reality. The answers, and the accumulation of methods by which they were achieved, laid the groundwork of modern science.

The Aristotelian tradition contributed a rigorous concern for accurate observation and a logical method for the construction of hypotheses. In the wake of Ockhamist criticism, many Aristotelians, especially in the Italian universities, had turned their attention to the physical sciences, often with impressive results. Their tradition remained vital in some places until the eighteenth century. Experimentalism, once the province of medieval Franciscans and Joachimites, was revived and popularized by Sir Francis Bacon (1561–1626), the lord chancellor of England. Like his predecessors, he accomplished little because his hypotheses were faulty, but the elegance of his prose inspired a host of followers. His contemporary Galileo Galilei (1564–1642) used experiment to greater effect, though many of his best demonstrations were designed but never performed. The humanist tradition contributed classical texts that reintroduced half-forgotten ideas, including the physics of Archimedes and the heliocentric theories of Eratosthenes and Aristarchus of Samos. It also encouraged quantification by reviving the numerological theories of Pythagoras.

The thinkers of the sixteenth and seventeenth centuries were interested in nearly everything, but they achieved their greatest breakthroughs in astronomy and physics. The Copernican theory, though by no means universally accepted, became their starting point. Copernicus had brought the traditional cosmology into question, but his system with its epicycles and circular orbits remained mathematically complex and virtually incomprehensible as a description of physical reality (see illustration 16.1).

A more plausible model of the cosmos was devised by Johannes Kepler (1571–1630), court astrologer to the emperor Rudolph II. Kepler's views were a fusion of organic and mechanistic ideas. He believed that the Earth had a soul, but as a follower of Pythagoras he thought that the universe was organized on geometrical principles. The Copernican epicycles offended his notions of mathematical harmony. He wanted to believe in circular orbits, but when he posited eccentric circles that did not center on the Sun, he was left with a minute discrepancy in his formulae. It was a terrible dilemma: The circle may have been the perfect geometric figure,

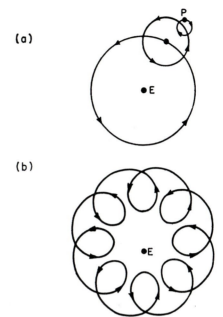

(a)

(b)

Illustration 16.1

The System of Epicycles as Used in Ptolemaic Cosmology. Epicycles were needed to predict the position of the planets, especially in the case of eccentrics and retrograde motions. These diagrams illustrate that the results were almost unimaginable. Drawing (a) shows an epicycle (P) on an epicycle, on a circular planetary orbit around the Earth (E). Drawing (b) shows the path a planet would have to take through space if this system of compound circles were taken literally. Copernicus and many of his contemporaries were dissatisfied with the Ptolemaic theory.

but he could not accept a universe founded on imperfect mathematics. In the end, he decided that planetary orbits had to be elliptical. This solution, which proved to be correct, was not generally accepted until long after his death, but Kepler did not mind. Like the number-mystic he was, he went on searching for other, more elusive cosmic harmonies that could be described in musical as well as mathematical terms.

Meanwhile, Galileo rejected the theory of elliptical orbits but provided important evidence that the planets rotated around the Sun. A professor at the University of Padua, Galileo was perhaps the first thinker to use something like the modern scientific method. He quarreled with the Aristotelians over their indifference to mathematical proofs and denounced their teleological obsession with final causes, but like them he was a careful observer. Unlike them, he tried to verify his hypotheses through experiment. From the Platonists and Pythagoreans, he adopted the view that the universe followed mathematical laws and expressed his theories

TVBVM OPTICVM VIDES GALILÆI INVENTVM ET OPVS QVO SOLIS MACVLAS
ET EXTIMOS LVNAE MONTES, ET IOVIS SATELLITES, ET NOVAM QVASI
RERVM VNIVERSITATE PRIMVS DISPEXIT A. MDCIX.

**Illustration 16.2**

〽 **Galileo's Telescopes** (c. 1610) With instruments like these Galileo discovered the moons of Jupiter and launched a new era in observational astronomy. He also gained support for his work by donating them to wealthy patrons.

in mathematical formulae that were intended to be predictive. His vision, however, was mechanistic, not mystical or organic.

Galileo's exploration of the planets was inspired by the invention of the telescope. The basic principles of optics had been discovered by the Aristotelians, and eyeglasses were introduced early in the sixteenth century. By 1608 Dutch and Flemish lens grinders were combining two lenses at fixed distances from one another to create the first telescopes. Using a perfected version of the telescope that he had built himself, Galileo turned it upon the heavens (see illustration 16.2). The results created a sensation. His discovery of the moons of Jupiter and the phases of Venus seemed to support the Copernican theory, while his study of

sunspots raised the unsettling possibility that the Sun rotated on its axis like the planets.

Perhaps because he was not interested in astrology, Galileo ignored the problems of planetary motion that obsessed Kepler. Instead he concentrated on the mechanics of motion. Kepler had established the position of the planets with his *Rudolphine Tables* of 1627 but had been unable to explain either the causes of their motion or what kept them in their orbits. The issue had perplexed the ancients because they believed that rest was the normal state of any object. The Aristotelians had argued that an object remains at rest unless a force is applied against it and that the velocity of that object is proportionate to the force exerted in moving it. As a result, finding an explanation for why a projectile continued to move after the impetus behind it had ceased was difficult. Galileo turned the problem on its head by proving that a body in motion will move forever unless it is slowed or deflected by an external force and that the application of uniform force results in acceleration instead of motion at a constant rate. Movement is therefore as natural a state as rest. Once it had been set in motion by its Creator, the universe could in theory go on forever without further intervention.

It was a profoundly disturbing vision. To Galileo, God was the Great Craftsman who created the world as a self-sustaining and predictable machine. To those who saw the universe as an organic entity upon which God still imposed His will, such a view was not only frightening but also blasphemous. It brought Galileo before the Papal Inquisition. He was tried because he defended the Copernican system and because his ideas undermined a worldview that had prevailed for nearly two thousand years. Yet the importance of this celebrated trial should not be exaggerated. Galileo's condemnation forced him to retire to his country villa; it did not prevent him or any other Italian from proceeding with research along the lines he had suggested. Galileo was arrogant and bad-tempered with patrons and opponents alike. He was also a brilliant writer and publicist (see document 16.1). Had his ability to attract enemies not equaled his genius, the episode might never have occurred.

The mechanistic view of the universe was destined to triumph over its predecessor, and the church would not again mount a frontal attack against it. René Descartes (1596–1650), the most influential philosopher of his day, developed a mechanistic vision that attempted to integrate philosophy, mathematics, and the sciences into a coherent, unified theory. He failed, but his efforts inspired others such as Pierre Gassendi (1592–1655), who attempted to revive the atomic the-

veloping theories about it. Many, including Boyle and Pascal, were also gifted writers whose work inspired others to emulate them. Science was becoming a movement, and it was only a matter of time until that movement was institutionalized. The English Royal Society and the French Academie des Sciences were founded in the 1660s, the latter under the patronage of Louis XIV's minister, Jean-Baptiste Colbert (1619–83). Colbert, like England's King Charles II, was quick to perceive the possible connection between the new science and improved technologies for war, agriculture, and manufacturing. Not all of the work performed was useful, and much of it remained tied to the earlier vision of an organic, providential universe, but mechanistic and mathematical views gained ground steadily throughout the century.

In physics, the movement culminated in the work of Isaac Newton (1642–1727). A professor at Cambridge and a member of the Royal Society, Newton was in some respects an odd character who spent at least as much time on alchemy and other occult speculations as he did on mathematics and physics. In spite of this, he formulated the laws of planetary motion and of gravity, thereby completing the work begun by Kepler and Galileo and establishing a cosmology that dominated Western thought until the publication of Einstein's theories in 1904.

In his *Principia,* or *Mathematical Principles of Natural Philosophy,* presented to the Royal Society in 1686, Newton formulated three laws of motion: (1) Every object remains either at rest or in motion along a straight line until it is deflected or resisted by another force (the law of inertia); (2) The rate of change in the motion of an object is proportionate to the force acting upon it; and (3) To every action there is an equal and opposite reaction. These formulations accounted not only for the behavior of moving objects on Earth, but also for the continuing movement of the planets. He then perfected Kepler's theories by demonstrating how the planets move through a vacuum in elliptical orbits under the influence of a force centered upon the Sun. That force was gravity, which he defined as the attractive force between two objects (see document 16.2). It is directly proportionate to the product of their masses and inversely proportionate to the square of the distances between them. To many, these theories explained the mysteries of a universe that acted like clockwork—smooth, mechanical, and eternal. Newton, who was a deeply religious man, would not have been pleased at the use to which his ideas would soon be put by the philosophers of the eighteenth-century Enlightenment.

## ◆ DOCUMENT 16.1 ◆

### Galileo: Scientific Proof

*In this excerpt from* The Assayer, *Galileo attacks an opponent for arguing in the traditional manner by compiling lists of authorities who support his position. It shows not only the gulf that separated scientific thinking from that of the traditionalists, but also provides some indication of how Galileo made enemies with his pen.*

Sarsi goes on to say that since this experiment of Aristotle's has failed to convince us, many other great men have also written things of the same sort. But it is news to me that any man would actually put the testimony of writers ahead of what experience shows him. To adduce more witnesses serves no purposes, Sarsi, for we have never denied that such things have been written and believed. We did say they are false, but so far as authority is concerned yours alone is as effective as an army's in rendering the events true or false. You take your stand on the authority of many poets against our experiments. I reply that if those poets could be present at our experiments they would change their views, and without disgrace they could say they had been writing hyperbolically—or even admit they had been wrong. . . .

I cannot but be astonished that Sarsi would persist in trying to prove by means of witnesses something that I may see for myself at any time by means of experiment.

Galilei, Galileo. "The Assayer," trans. Stillman Drake. In Stillman Drake, *Discoveries and Opinions of Galileo,* pp. 270–271. New York: Doubleday, 1957.

ories of the Epicureans. To do so, he was forced to posit the existence of a vacuum. The possibility of nothingness had been denied by virtually everyone from Aristotle to Descartes, but the results of barometric experiments by Toricelli and by Blaise Pascal (1623–62) could be explained in no other way. In 1650 Otto von Guericke ended the debate by constructing an air pump with which a vacuum could be created. These efforts in turn inspired Robert Boyle (1627–91) to formulate his laws about the behavior of gases.

Interest in scientific inquiry was assuming the proportions of a fad. All over Europe, men of leisure and education were examining the physical world and de-

## ◆ DOCUMENT 16.2 ◆

## Newton: Gravity

*In* The Mathematical Principles of Natural Philosophy, *Sir Isaac Newton describes his revolutionary concept of gravity and, in the process, sets forth some of his thoughts on scientific method.*

Hitherto, we have explained the phenomena of the heavens and of our sea by the power of gravity, but have not yet assigned the cause of this power. This is certain, that it must proceed from a cause that penetrates to the very centers of the sun and planets, without suffering the least diminution of its force; that operates not according to the quantity of the surfaces of the particles upon which it acts (as mechanical causes used to do) but according to the quantity of solid matter which they contain, and propagates its virtue on all sides to immense distances, decreasing always in the duplicate portion of the distances. . . .

Hitherto I have not been able to discover the cause of those properties of gravity from the phenomena, and I frame no hypothesis; for whatever is not deduced from phenomena is to be called an hypothesis; and hypothesis, whether metaphysical or physical, whether of occult qualities or mechanical, have no place in experimental philosophy. In this philosophy particular propositions are inferred from the phenomena, and afterward rendered general by induction. Thus it was the impenetrability, the mobility, and the impulsive force of bodies, and the laws of motion and gravitation were discovered. And to us it is enough that gravity does really exist, and acts according to the laws that we have explained, and abundantly serves to account for all the motions of the celestial bodies, and of our sea.

Newton, Isaac. *The Mathematical Principles of Natural Philosophy,* book 3, vol. 2, p. 310, trans. Andrew Motte. London, 1803, II.

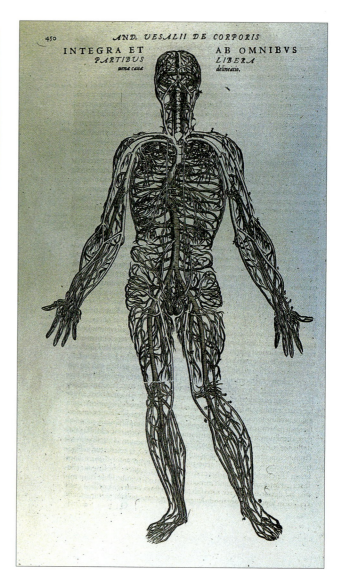

**Illustration 16.3**

*A Diagram of the Veins.* This diagram is from Andreas Vesalius (1514–64), *De humani corporis fabrica.* The venous system was especially important to physicians because drawing blood was the primary treatment for many ailments. As impressive as these drawings are, they contain anatomical errors. Vesalius did not understand the circulation of the blood and based some of his ideas on the dissection of animals (see the arrangement of veins at the base of the neck). However, his work, with its magnificent illustrations, is still a remarkable monument to the anatomical revolution.

## Medicine: From Galen to Harvey

Mechanistic views would also triumph in medicine, but the process by which they did so was more convoluted than it had been in physics. Physicians moved from mechanism to magic and back again in the course of the sixteenth century. The works of the ancient Greek anatomist Galen had long been known through Arabic commentaries and translations. Galen's views were mechanistic in the sense that he was careful to relate the form of organs to their function and had little use for magic or for alchemical cures. The recovery and

## William Harvey: Conception

*William Harvey (1578–1657) is best known as the physician who first described the circulation of the blood, but as this selection indicates, he was no more consistent in his application of scientific method than most of his contemporaries. Old modes of thinking had survived along with the new. In this description of conception he reverts to inadequate observation, metaphorical language, philosophical idealism, and sheer male vanity.*

[As] the substance of the uterus, when ready to conceive, is very like the structure of the brain, why should we not suppose that the function of both is similar, and that there is excited by coitus within the uterus something identical with, or at least analagous to, an "imagination" or a "desire" in the brain, whence comes the generation or procreation of the ovum? For the functions of both are termed "conceptions" and both, although the primary sources of every action throughout the body, are immaterial, the one of natural or organic, the other of animal actions; the one (viz., the uterus) the first cause and beginning of every action which conduces to the generation of the animal, the other (viz., the brain) of every action done for its preservation. And just as a "desire" arises from a conception of the brain, and this conception springs from some external object of desire, so also from the male, as being the more perfect animal, and as it were, the most natural object of desire, does the natural (organic) conception arise in the uterus, even as the animal conception does in the brain.

From this desire, or conception, it results that the female produces an offspring like its father. For just saw we, from the conception of the "form" or "idea" in the brain, fashion in our works a form resembling it, so, in like manner, the "idea" or "form" of the father existing in the uterus generates an offspring like himself with the help of the formative faculty, impressing, however, on its work its own immaterial form.

Harvey, William. "On Conception." In *The Works of William Harvey*, trans. R. Willis. London: 1847.

translation of original Galenic texts by the humanists popularized his teachings, and by the early sixteenth century his influence dominated academic medicine.

In response, a Swiss physician and alchemist who called himself Paracelsus (1493–1541) launched a frontal attack on the entire medical establishment. Declaring that "wise women" and barbers cured more patients than all of the Galenists put together, he proposed a medical philosophy based upon natural magic and alchemy. All natural phenomena were chemical interactions between the four elements and what he called the three principles: sulphur, mercury, and salt—the combustible, gaseous, and solid components of matter. Because the human body was a microcosm of the universe and because diseases were produced by chemical forces acting upon particular organs of the body, sickness could be cured by chemical antidotes.

This chemical philosophy was widely accepted. Its hermetic and neoplatonic overtones recommended it to many scholars, while those who practiced it may have killed fewer patients than their Galenist opponents. Paracelsus believed in administering drugs in small, carefully measured doses. He rejected bleeding, purges, and the treatment of wounds with poultices whose vile ingredients almost guaranteed the onset of infection. As a result, the bodies of his patients had a fighting chance to heal themselves and he was credited with miraculous cures.

The war between the Galenists and the Paracelsians raged throughout the mid-sixteenth century. In the end, the Galenists won. Their theories, though virtually useless for the treatment of disease, produced new insights while those of Paracelsus did not. Andreas Vesalius (1514–64) was shocked to discover that Galen's dissections had been carried out primarily on animals. Using Galenic principles, he retraced the master's steps using human cadavers and in 1543 published his *De humani corporis fabrica* (On the Structure of the Human Body). Though not without error, it was a vast improvement over earlier anatomy texts and a work of art in its own right that inspired others to correct and improve his work (see illustration 16.3). The long debate over the circulation of the blood, culminating in William Harvey's explanation of 1628 (see document 16.3), was also a Galenist enterprise that owed little or nothing to the chemical tradition.

By the time microscopes were invented in Holland at the beginning of the seventeenth century, the anatomists had seized the initiative. The new device strengthened their position by allowing for the examination of small structures such as capillaries. Blood corpuscles were described for the first time and bacteria were identified, though a full-fledged germ theory would not be verified until the nineteenth century. These discoveries made sustaining the ancient metaphor of the human body as a microcosm of the universe even more difficult. The body was beginning to look more like a machine within a machine.

## The Expansion of the Northern Powers: France, England, and the Netherlands

In the years when Galileo and others were transforming European thought, seafarers from France, England, and the Netherlands continued the work of mapping the globe and exploiting its economic resources. The centralized, closely controlled empires created by the Iberian powers had been resented from the first by northern Europeans who wished to engage in the American trade. French pirates and privateers were active in the Caribbean after the 1530s and sacked Havana in 1556. A colony of French Protestants was massacred by the Spanish near the present site of St. Augustine, Florida, in 1565. However, neither of these failures inhibited French, English, and Dutch captains from trying to enter the Caribbean market. The Englishman John Hawkins (1532–95) tried to break the Spanish-Portuguese monopoly by introducing cargoes of slaves in 1562 and again in 1567 but was caught by the incoming *flota* in 1567 and barely escaped with his life. One of his surviving captains, Francis Drake (c. 1543–96), raided Panama in 1572–73 and attacked Spanish shipping in the Pacific when he circumnavigated the globe in 1577–79.

To many in England these efforts, however inspiring, were no substitute for the establishment of permanent English colonies. Commercial interests and the growing political and religious rivalry with Spain demanded nothing less. The first English settlement in North America was planted on Roanoke Island, North Carolina, in 1585 but disappeared before it could be reinforced. Subsequent efforts at Jamestown (1603) and Plymouth (1620) were more successful. The Spanish claimed sovereignty over North America but lacked the resources to settle it or to protect it against interlopers. The native American population was, by comparison with that of Mexico or Peru, small, scattered, and politically disunited. The obstacles to settlement were there-

fore easy to overcome, and by 1650 the English were established at various locations along the entire Atlantic seaboard from Newfoundland to the Carolinas.

From the standpoint of global politics and immediate gain, these North American colonies were something of a disappointment. They produced no precious metals and offered England few strategic advantages. With the notable exception of tobacco from Virginia and Maryland, they had little of value to export and quickly became self-sufficient in everything but luxury items. In the meantime, the French had established themselves in the St. Lawrence valley and were developing an important trade in furs from the North American interior. English competition in the form of the Hudson's Bay Company did not emerge until 1670.

Expansion in the Caribbean remained a primary goal. An English colony was established on the uninhabited island of Barbados in 1624, and sugar was introduced in 1640. By 1660 its sugar exports made Barbados the most valuable of English colonies while its position to windward of the Spanish Main made it virtually invulnerable to Spanish attacks. Sugar colonies of equal wealth were established by the French on the nearby islands of Guadeloupe and Martinique. By this time, Spanish power was in decline. In 1656 an English fleet seized Jamaica. Eight years later the French West India Company took possession of some settlements that had been established years before by French buccaneers in the western part of Hispaniola and laid the foundations of St. Domingue, the rich slave colony that would one day become Haiti.

The French and English, like the Spanish and Portuguese, wanted their colonial systems to be self-contained and closed to outsiders, but in practice, this was as difficult to achieve as it had been for their rivals. Both France and England governed their possessions on the proprietary model, and neither developed anything like the elaborate colonial bureaucracy of Spain. Royal authority tended to be correspondingly weak. Distance, the limitations of sailing ship technology, and the perishability of certain cargos, notably slaves, encouraged smuggling and made it difficult to suppress. Planters and merchants had nothing to gain from dealing exclusively with their own countrymen when others might offer better prices or more rapid delivery. Cargos could always be landed secretly in remote coves, but much illegal activity was conducted in the open, for governors were under enormous pressure to look the other way.

Almost from the beginning, the chief beneficiaries of this illegal trade were the Dutch, whose maritime activities increased during their revolt against Spain. The Dutch had some ninety-eight thousand ships registered by 1598, but ships and skill were not enough. They needed bases from which to conduct their operations. Between 1621 and 1640 the newly formed Dutch West India Company seized Curaçao, St. Eustatius, St. Maarten, and Saba in the Caribbean and established a colony called New Amsterdam on the present site of New York. From 1624 to 1654 the Dutch controlled much of the Brazilian coast, and in 1637 they captured the African fortress and slave-trading station of Elmina from the Portuguese. Brazil and New Amsterdam were expensive ventures. The Dutch, like the Portuguese, lacked the manpower to impose their rule on large geographic areas, and when the English seized New Amsterdam in 1664 the West India Company settled down to a more modest, and in the end more profitable, career as a trading company based on Curaçao and St. Eustatius.

Only in the East did the Dutch manage to establish something like regional hegemony. Dutch traders first appeared in East Indian waters in 1595. Bypassing India, they sailed directly to the Spice Islands (Indonesia), rounding the Cape of Good Hope and running due east in the so-called roaring forties before turning north to Java or Sumatra. The fast but dangerous trip brought them directly to the sources of the Portuguese and Indian spice trade. To improve efficiency and minimize competition, the Dutch traders organized in 1602 into the East India Company.

Under the governor-generalship of Jan Pieterszoon Coen (1587–1629), the company's forces destroyed the Javan town of Djakarta and rebuilt it as Batavia, center of Dutch enterprise in the East. Local rulers were forced to restrict their trading activities to rice and other local necessities while European competition was violently discouraged. English traders especially had been active in Asian waters since 1591. They formed their own East India Company on Christmas Day in 1600 but lacked the ships and capital to match the Dutch. Coen expelled most of them from the region by 1620. His successors attacked the Portuguese colonies, seizing Malacca in 1641 and the Indian bases shortly thereafter, but Goa survived a Dutch blockade and remained in Portuguese hands until 1961. The Japanese trade fell into Dutch hands when the Portuguese were expelled in 1637, and for two centuries a Dutch trading station in Nagasaki harbor provided that country's only contact with the West.

By 1650 the Dutch had become the dominant force in Europe's Asian trade. More than one hundred Dutch ships sailed regularly to the East, exchanging German arms, armor, linens, and glass for spices and finished silks. Even the surviving Portuguese colonies were forced to deal largely through Dutch intermediaries. The major exception was Macao, which continued to export Chinese silks to Spain via Manila. This monopoly was successfully challenged in the eighteenth century by the revived British East India Company and to a lesser degree by the French, but the Dutch remained in control of Indonesia until the outbreak of World War II.

## The Golden Age in the Netherlands

Long-distance trade made the Netherlands an island of wealth and culture amidst the turmoil of the early seventeenth century (see illustration 16.4). A century before, the economy of the region had been dominated by Antwerp. Its merchants traded in wool from Spain and England, finished cloth from the towns of Brabant and Flanders, wine from the Iberian Peninsula, and a variety of products exported from Germany to England and Scandinavia. The city's prosperity, however, did not survive the Revolt of the Netherlands. Antwerp is located at the head of navigation on the Scheldt, a broad estuary whose western approaches are controlled by the Zeeland towns of Vlissingen (Flushing) and Middelburg. When the Zeelanders joined the Dutch revolt, they cut off Antwerp from the sea and destroyed its prosperity.

Amsterdam took its place. Set in the marshes where the Amstel River meets the IJ, an inlet of the Zuider Zee, the city was virtually impregnable to attack by sea or land. Already the center of the Baltic trade, it grew enormously after 1585 when southern refugees poured in, bringing their capital with them. When Maurits of Nassau took the lands east of the Ijssel from Spain between 1591 and 1597, contact with Germany improved and Amsterdam replaced Antwerp as the conduit through which goods flowed from the German interior to the Atlantic and North Sea. The repeated failure of Spanish and Sicilian harvests in the same years made Amsterdam a dominant force in the Mediterranean trade as well. Dutch merchants had established themselves in the Baltic ports of Riga and Gdansk (Danzig) at an early date. The Amsterdam exchange determined the price of wheat, and vast quantities were shipped southward in Dutch ships, together with timber, Swedish iron, and other northern products.

Shipbuilding, always a major industry in the ports of Holland and Zeeland, expanded with the growth of the carrying trade. Economies of scale, better access to Baltic naval stores, and the presence of a skilled maritime population enabled the Dutch to charge

**Illustration 16.4**

**The Amsterdam Bourse, or Stock Exchange.** This painting by Job Berckheyde shows the Bourse as it was in the seventeenth century. Though not the first such exchange in Europe, it was by far the largest and most important of the early modern period. Small shareholders and great capitalists traded shares in the East India Company and many smaller enterprises.

lower shipping rates than their competitors. With the founding of the East and West India companies, this advantage became global. The axis of the spice trade shifted from Lisbon to Amsterdam while Dutch skippers took advantage of the delays occasioned by the *flota* system and by a general shortage of Iberian shipping to intrude upon the commerce of the Americas. The profits from these sources generated investment capital, and Amsterdam soon became Europe's banking center as well as its commercial hub.

In these years, the modern city with its canals and high, narrow townhouses took shape. For all its wealth and beauty, however, Amsterdam was never more than the largest of several towns that supported and at times competed with each other in a variety of markets. The

Dutch republic was overwhelmingly urban. A network of canals linked its cities and provided cheap, efficient transportation. Agriculturally, though a few large estates remained, most of the land was divided into relatively small plots and cultivated intensively to grow produce and dairy products for the nearby towns. Most peasants were independent farmers and relatively prosperous. Pockets of urban misery existed, but no real industrial proletariat was evident outside the cloth towns of Haarlem and Leiden. Dutch society was therefore resolutely bourgeois. Hard work, thrift, and cleanliness were valued; ostentation was suspect.

A series of extraordinary painters provide a vivid picture of Dutch life in the seventeenth century. Jan Vermeer (1632–75) portrayed bright, spotless interiors and virtuous housewives at work in an idealized vision of domesticity that was central to Dutch notions of the good life. Rembrandt van Rijn (1606–69), Frans Hals (c. 1581–1666), and a host of others left brilliant portraits of city magistrates, corporate directors, and everyday drunks as well as grand illustrations of historical events. The brooding skies and placid landscapes of the Netherlands were painted by such masters as Ruisdael and van Goyen, while dozens of still lifes dwell lovingly on food, flowers, and other everyday objects.

The political and the social structure of the republic rested on the values of the late medieval city, preserved tenaciously through the long struggle against Spanish regalism. Each town elected a council, which in turn elected representatives to the Provincial Estates. The States General was elected by the provinces. The stadtholder, when there was one, was not a king, but a kind of "first citizen" with special responsibilities for the conduct of war on land. Five admiralties, each of which was nominally independent and each of which supplemented its own warships with vessels leased from the chartered companies, conducted war at sea.

Local privilege was built into the system at every level, and conflict among the various components of the body politic was normally intense. Fortunately, the leadership of the councils, states, directorships, and committees formed a kind of interlocking directorship. A great merchant, banker, or rentier might hold several elected offices in the course of a lifetime, as well as directorships in one or more of the chartered companies. The Dutch republic was an oligarchy, not a democracy, but the existence of a well-defined group of prominent citizens facilitated communication, dampened local rivalries, and helped to ensure a measure of continuity in what might otherwise have been a fragmented and overly decentralized system.

National policies were remarkably consistent. Trade, even with the enemy, was encouraged and the states supported freedom of the seas long before Hugo Grotius (1583–1645), attorney general of Holland, publicized the modern concept of international law. Though aggressive in its pursuit of new markets and the protection of old ones, Dutch foreign policy was otherwise defensive.

Tension between the governing elite and the stadtholders of the House of Orange dominated internal politics. At times the struggle took the form of religious antagonism between extreme Calvinists, who tended to be Orangists supported by the artisan class, and the more relaxed Arminians, who rejected predestination and were supported by the great merchants. Class feeling played a major part in these struggles, but

by comparison with other countries, both sides remained committed to religious toleration. Jewish settlement was actively encouraged and Catholics were generally protected from harassment. Holland became a refuge for the persecuted, many of whom, such as Descartes and the philosopher Baruch Spinoza (1632–77), a Sephardic Jew, added luster to its intellectual life. The Dutch republic was an oasis of tolerance as well as prosperity.

## The Reorganization of War and Government: France under Louis XIV

Most seventeenth-century states were not as fortunate as the Dutch. Between 1560 and 1648 France, Spain, England, and the German principalities all suffered in varying degrees from military stalemate and political disintegration. Public order, perhaps even dynastic survival, depended upon the reorganization of war and government. The restructuring of virtually every European state after 1660 has been called the triumph of absolutism (see document 16.4), but the term is in some ways misleading. No government before the industrial revolution could exert absolute control over the lives of its subjects. To do so even approximately requires modern transport and communications, but if by absolutism one means the theoretical subordination of all other elements of a country's power structure to the crown, the word is at least partially descriptive. The Spain of Philip II met this definition in the sixteenth century; after 1660 the model for all other states was the France of Louis XIV.

Louis XIV (ruled 1643–1715) came to the throne as a child of four. To the end of his life he harbored childhood memories of the Frondes and was determined to avoid further challenges from the French aristocracy at all costs. He knew that their influence derived from the networks of patronage that had long dominated rural life and used the fact that such networks are ultimately dependent upon favors to destroy them as independent bases of power. As king of a country in which perpetual taxation had long been established, Louis had more favors to hand out than anyone else. He developed the tactic of forcing aristocrats to remain at court as a condition of receiving the titles, grants, monopolies, offices, and commissions upon which their influence was based. By doing so he bound them to himself while cutting them off from their influence in the countryside.

This was the real purpose behind the construction of Versailles, a palace large enough to house the entire court while separating it from the mobs of Paris, twelve

## ◆ DOCUMENT 16.4 ◆

### Absolutism in Theory

*Jacques-Bénigne Bossuet, bishop of Meaux (1627–1704) was court preacher to Louis XIV and tutor to his son. In this passage, which reveals something of his power as a preacher, he describes the divine basis of royal absolutism in unmistakable terms.*

The royal power is absolute. . . . The prince need render account of his acts to no one. . . . Without this absolute authority the king could neither do good nor repress evil. It is necessary that his power be such that no one can escape him, and finally, the only protection of individuals against the public authority should be their innocence. This confirms the teaching of St. Paul: "Wilt thou not be afraid of the power? Do that which is good" [Rom. 13:3].

God is infinite, God is all. The prince, as prince, is not regarded as a private person: he is a public personage, all the state is in him. As all perfection and all strength are united in God, so all power of individuals is united in the person of the prince. What grandeur that a single man should embody so much!

Behold an immense people united in a single person; behold this holy power, paternal and absolute; behold the secret cause which governs the whole body of the state, contained in a single head: you see the image of God in the king, and you have the idea of royal majesty. God is holiness itself, goodness itself, and power itself. In these things lies the majesty of God. In the image of these things lies the majesty of the prince.

Bossuet, Jacques-Bénigne. "Politics Drawn from the Very Words of Holy Scripture." In J. H. Robinson, ed. *Readings in European History*, vol. 2. Boston: Ginn, 1906.

miles away (see illustration 16.5). To occupy his new courtiers, Louis developed an elaborate ritual centered around his own person. Every royal action was accompanied by great ceremony, and proud aristocrats contended for the honor of emptying the king's chamberpot or handing him his shirt (see illustration 16.6). The world of Versailles was cramped, artificial, and riddled with intrigue, but it was a world controlled in every particular by a king who knew what was happening under his own roof (see document 16.5). To stay

was to sacrifice one's independence; to leave was to lose all hope of honor or profit. By 1670 the French nobility had been domesticated.

The centralization implied by Versailles was extended to the royal administration, though in this case Louis followed precedents established by Henry IV and Richelieu. Richelieu in particular had worked to replace the old system of governing through councils with ministries, in which one man was responsible to the crown for each of the major functions of government. He had also brought royal authority to the provinces by introducing intendants, commissioners who supervised the collection of taxes and served as a constant check on local authorities. Louis expanded and perfected this system. Intendancies transcended provincial borders, further weakening the ties of local privilege. The ministers of war, finance, foreign affairs, and even of roads and bridges reported directly to the king who, unlike his father, served as his own prime minister. Louis may have been the Sun King, surrounded by ritual and devoted to the pleasures of the bed, the table, and the hunt, but he was a hard worker. At least six hours a day, seven days a week, were devoted to public business. Significantly, he usually drew his ministers from the *nobles de la robe*, the great legal dynasties of the French towns, not from the old nobility.

Because war was the primary function of the early modern state and accounted for the vast majority of its expenditures, every effort was made to bring the military under control. Louis instituted a series of reforms under the guidance of the war ministers Michel Le Tellier (1603–85) and his son, the Marquis de Louvois (1639–91). A tableau of ranks, comparable to that used by most modern armies, established a hierarchy of command that in theory superseded civilian titles. The cost of quartering troops was allocated to entire provinces instead of to specific towns, and, like military justice, financial arrangements were placed under the control of the intendants.

On the battlefield, the French army abandoned the old combination of pike and shot in favor of volleys of musket fire from ranks that were rarely more than three deep. Based on the innovations of Gustav Adolph, this tactic required regular drill and marching in step, practices that had first been introduced by Maurice of Nassau but generally ignored by other armies. To improve discipline and unit cohesion, barracks, uniforms, and standardized muskets were all adopted by 1691. Combined with the scientific principles of siege warfare perfected by Sebastian le Prestre de Vauban (1633–1707), the reforms of Le Tellier and Louvois created what

**Illustration 16.5**

⁂ **Versailles.** This view of the west front of Louis XIV's palace shows only a portion of the whole, but it provides a sense of the grandeur that Louis and his architects, Louis Le Vau and Jules Hardouin-Mansart, were attempting to convey as they created a magnificent stage set for the politics of the Sun King.

might be called the first modern army. It was given ample opportunity to prove itself.

In the early years of his reign, Louis's foreign policy was aggressive and, in the best French tradition, anti-Habsburg. His invasion of the Spanish Netherlands in 1667–68 brought him into conflict with the Dutch republic, which he tried to destroy in a bitter war that lasted from 1672 to 1679. Faced with almost certain destruction, the Dutch overthrew their government and made William III of Orange (1650–1702) stadtholder. Holland saved itself by flooding the countryside, and William's diplomacy brought Spain, Sweden, Brandenburg, and the Holy Roman Empire into the war. France fought them all to a standstill, but the alliance was a precursor of things to come.

Emboldened by the favorable terms he had negotiated at the Peace of Nijmegen (1679), Louis then tried to annex all territories that had ever belonged to France, whether in the Netherlands, Italy, the Pyrenees, or the Rhineland. Hostility to the Holy Roman Empire made him the only Christian prince to oppose the liberation of Hungary from the Turks (1682–99), though it was at last achieved with the assistance of Eugene of Savoy (1663–1736), a prince who had been raised at his court and who became one of his most formidable enemies. At the same time, Louis's revocation of the Edict of Nantes and expulsion of the Huguenots in 1685 alienated Europe's Protestants. Many believed that he aimed at nothing less than French hegemony, and by 1689 nearly all of Europe had turned against him. For the rest of his life he followed a basically defensive policy, but it was too late. In the War of the League of

Augsburg (1689–97), Louis fought a powerful Anglo-Dutch coalition while France suffered through one of the worst economic depressions in its history. In the War of the Spanish Succession (1701–14), his armies were consistently defeated by an allied army commanded by John Churchill, duke of Marlborough (1650–1722). Not even France could sustain such burdens indefinitely, and when the Sun King died in 1715, the country was in a severe, if temporary, decline.

## French Absolutism: A Model for Reform

The power of Louis XIV was not unlimited. Within France, his intentions were subject to modification by local privilege and by the rulings of the *parlements*, superior courts that could determine the validity of royal edicts under law. Moreover, neither he nor his successors were able to solve basic problems of credit and finance. Until the revolution of 1789, the kings of France were forced to borrow against tax revenues, which were then farmed out to the creditors. Tax farming by private individuals was not only inefficient but also woefully corrupt and left no room for the sophisticated financial practices being devised by Louis's Dutch and English rivals.

In spite of these shortcomings and of the uneven success of Louis's foreign policy, the France of Louis XIV became a model for other princes. From Spain to the Urals, they copied his court etiquette, his system of military and administrative organization, and even the architectural style of Versailles, which became the pattern for dozens of palaces and country estates. The last

**Illustration 16.6**

Louis XIV. This 1701 painting by Hyacinthe Rigaud is an example of art as political propaganda. This vision of the king's magnificence was painted on the eve of the War of the Spanish Succession. Even at sixty-three, Louis was proud of his legs and sensitive about his height, hence the elevator shoes.

Hapsburg king of Spain, Charles II "the Bewitched" died childless in 1700, and the final war of Louis's reign was waged to place a Bourbon on the Spanish throne. The new ruler, Philip V (reigned 1700–46), began a process of reform that by 1788 had created a near replica of French administration. Austrian archduke Charles (1685–1740), though he failed to gain the allegiance of the Spanish in the War of the Spanish Succession, received the Spanish Netherlands as a consolation prize at the Peace of Utrecht in 1713. This territory, the present-day Belgium, was incorporated into the Austrian Empire as Hungary had been in 1699. After his election as Charles VI in 1711, he began to reform the far-flung Austrian administration on French lines.

Most of the German princes followed suit, though it could be argued that Frederick Wilhelm I of Prussia (1688–1740) had already carried reform beyond anything achieved by Louis XIV. Set without geographic defenses in the midst of the North German plain, Brandenburg-Prussia had been devastated in the

## Louis XIV at Versailles

*The memoirs of Louis de Rouvroy, Duc de Saint-Simon (1675–1755) provide a detailed, if often venomous, picture of life at the court of Louis XIV. Here Saint-Simon, an aristocrat, describes the king's method of controlling the French aristocracy.*

The frequent fêtes, the private promenades at Versailles, the journeys, were means on which the King seized in order to distinguish or mortify the courtiers, and thus render them more assiduous in pleasing him. He felt that of real favors he had not enough to bestow; in order to keep up the spirit of devotion, he therefore unceasingly invented all sorts of ideal ones, little preferences and petty distinctions, which answered his purpose as well.

He was exceedingly jealous of the attention paid him. Not only did he notice the presence of the most distinguished courtiers, but those of inferior degree also. He looked to the right and the left, not only upon rising but upon going to bed, at his meals, in passing through his apartments, or his gardens of Versailles, where alone the courtiers were allowed to follow him; he saw and noticed everybody; not one escaped him, not even those who hoped to remain unnoticed. He marked well all the absentees from the court, found out the reason of their absence, and never lost an opportunity of acting towards them as the occasion might seem to justify. With some of the courtiers (the most distinguished), it was a demerit not to make the court their ordinary abode; with others, 'twas a fault to come but rarely; for those who never or scarcely ever came it was certain disgrace. When their names were in any way mentioned, "I do not know them," the King would reply haughtily. Those who presented themselves but seldom were thus characterized: "They are people I never see;" these decrees were irrevocable.

Saint-Simon [Louis de Rouvroy, Duc de Saint-Simon]. *The Memoirs of the Duke of Saint-Simon,* trans. Bayle St. John, vol. 2, p. 364, 8th ed. London: 1913.

**Illustration 16.7**

**Peter the Great.** The tsar is shown by a Dutch painter during his visit to the Netherlands in 1697.

Thirty Years' War and remained vulnerable to the shifts of central European politics. A veteran of the war of the Spanish Succession, Frederick Wilhelm resolved to turn his kingdom into a military power of the first rank and ended by making its administration subservient to the army. After 1723 his government was little more than a branch of the *kriegskommisariat* or war ministry, but his reforms laid the groundwork for Prussia's emergence as a major power.

Perhaps the most spectacular efforts at reform were undertaken by Peter I "the Great" of Russia (1672–1725). Like Louis XIV he had survived a turbulent regency in his youth and came to the throne determined to place his monarchy on a firmer basis (see illustration 16.7). Peter realized that to do so he would have to copy Western models, and he spent 1697–98 traveling incognito to France, England, and the Netherlands as part of what he called the Grand Embassy. When he returned, he immediately began to institute reforms that, though Western in inspiration, were carefully adapted to Russian conditions.

Using knowledge acquired firsthand in the ship-yards of Holland and England, Peter supervised the building of a navy that could control the Baltic. The *streltsy*, or palace guard that formed the core of the Russian army and had long been a fruitful source of plots against the tsars, was destroyed and replaced by an army organized on the French model. Peter, however, raised his troops through conscription for life, a method suggested by Louvois that could not be implemented in the less autocratic atmosphere of France. The new forces served him well. In the Great Northern War (1700–20), he broke the power of Sweden and established Russian control over Estonia, Karelia, and Livonia. To consolidate his gains and to provide Russia with an all-weather port, he built the modern city of St. Petersburg near the mouth of the Neva River and made it his capital.

Internally, Peter established a series of colleges or boards to supervise the work of thirteen new governmental departments and divided the country into fifty provinces, each with its own governor appointed by himself. He created a table of ranks for civilian officials and opened state service for the first time to men of middle-class origin. To compensate the hereditary nobility for its loss of state positions, Peter abandoned the distinction between *pomest'e* and hereditary lands, and he introduced primogeniture. In some cases he resorted to large-scale distributions of land and serfs. The condition of the latter predictably worsened, and peasant rebellions were put down with memorable savagery.

## The Emergence of England as a World Power

The system created by Peter the Great was more autocratic than its Western models—and more permanent. It lasted without major modifications into the nineteenth century. The situation in England was very different. Though Charles II reclaimed his father's throne in 1660, the fundamental issue of sovereignty had not been resolved. Like his predecessors, Charles was reluctant to call Parliament into session, and the taxpaying gentry were as unwilling as ever to provide adequate support for the crown. Shrewd, affable, and personally popular, the new king avoided open confrontations with his subjects, but his freedom of action was limited by poverty. For a time he even accepted a pension from Louis XIV, who hoped for English support against the Dutch. For this reason, England did not for some time develop the administrative structures that were being adopted on the continent.

Only in the creation of a modern navy could the English keep pace. Before 1660 England, like other countries, had possessed a handful of fighting ships that were supplemented in time of war by contracting with private owners who provided both ships and crews for the duration. No permanent officer corps existed, and fleets were typically commanded by men who owed their positions to civilian rank or to military experience on land. Administration was minimal, often temporary, and usually corrupt. The success of 1588 and the remarkable performance of the Commonwealth navies showed that such fleets could do well if they were properly motivated. But the system as a whole was analogous to military contracting on land: It was at best inefficient and at worst uncontrollable.

Both Charles II and his brother James, duke of York (1633–1701) were deeply interested in naval affairs, and their unswerving support of secretary of the Admiralty Samuel Pepys (1633–1703) enabled him to introduce reforms that, in effect, created the English navy. Pepys, who is probably best known today for his famous diary, created a permanent corps of naval officers who attained their rank by the passage of formal examinations. To ensure their availability when needed, they were kept on half-pay when not at sea. Provisioning and repair facilities were improved, and the number of royal ships increased under the command of a reformed Admiralty. By the end of the century, even tactics had been changed to permit better control of battle fleets.

But a reformed fleet was in itself no guarantor of world-power status. Colbert had introduced similar measures in France, only to have his plans abandoned during the fiscal crisis of the 1690s. Great ships, like great armies, need a consistent supply of money. Ironically, England achieved this only by overthrowing the men who had made the naval reforms possible. When Charles II died in 1685, his brother ascended the throne as James II. A convert to Roman Catholicism, James instituted policies that alienated virtually every segment of the English elite, and in the fall of 1688 he was deposed in favor of his daughter Mary and her husband, William of Orange. As stadtholder of the Netherlands and king of England, William III brought the island nation into the Grand Alliance against Louis XIV. The Glorious Revolution changed the basis of English politics. By overthrowing one king and effectively appointing another, Parliament and those it represented had at last resolved the issue of sovereignty. Parliament and not the king would rule England. Under William and again under his sister-in-law Anne

## ◆ DOCUMENT 16.6 ◆

### Dutch Trade in Decline

*The problem of maintaining Dutch trade reached a crisis during the War of the Spanish Succession (1702–13), when the conflict closed many traditional markets. The following memo was presented to the States General in 1706 by Adrianus Engelhard Helvetius, who points out that Holland's English allies were quick to take advantage of his countrymen's misfortunes.*

The commerce of the United Provinces in Europe has never been in worse condition than it is today. During the course of earlier wars, although Dutch vessels were also open to the attacks of privateers, at least they could take refuge in the Atlantic and in the Mediterranean ports under Spanish rule, which are now closed to them. Furthermore, even when they were completely barred from the trade of France, they still continued to ply both the Baltic trades, which they continue to enjoy, and the trades of Spain, the kingdoms of Naples and Sicily, and Spanish Flanders, which now they have good reason to miss. Not only is the market greatly reduced for their cloth, both of their own manufacture as well as that made in India and the Baltic, and for their other wares, spices, salt fish, etc., but they are also deprived of the profitable return trade in wool, wine, and necessary commodities. . . .

As a result, there are frequent bankruptcies, word of which scares people and discourages them from entrusting money to the merchants, whose own funds are limited, as they are in the habit of doing in peacetime. This decline even affects the domestic commerce of the country, which is suffering badly, especially thanks to the cunning manipulations of the English, who take advantage of the opportunity to raise themselves upon the ruins of their allies.

The English, a people as fierce as they are capable, being convinced that the States General need their help so badly that they would not dare dispute anything with them, follow the maxim of making the Dutch pay their auxiliary troops, even when they are engaged in battle. They supply them with goods of every kind, sending cloth and Indian fabrics which are forbidden in England, butter, tallow, even manufactured candles, grain, etc., and in this they manage to make a profit on the support of troops for which they ought to be paying themselves.

Helvetius. *"Mémoire sur l'état présent du Government des Provinces Unis."* In M. van der Bijl, ed., *Bijdragen en Mededeldingen van het Historisch Genootshap 80* (1966), 226–227, trans. Herbert H. Rowen, *The Low Countries in Early Modern Times. A Documentary History.* New York: Harper & Row, 1972.

(reigned 1702–14), Parliament showed an unprecedented willingness to open its purse and support massive outlays for war, knowing that a weakened monarchy could not use the money to subvert the freedoms of its subjects.

The wealth that underwrote England's command of the sea and financed the campaigns of Marlborough on land came from nearly a century of unparalleled economic growth. England's growing commercial strength was based in part on geographic advantage. Faced with the implacable hostility of Louis XIV, the Dutch were forced to spend much of their wealth defending their borders on land. England, an island, was spared this expense. Moreover, with their deep water ports and location to windward of the continent, the English could disrupt Dutch trade by blocking access via the English Channel. The Anglo-Dutch wars of 1652–53, 1665–66, and 1672–73 were fought over this issue. As George

Monk, the English general-at-sea in the Second Dutch War said: "[W]hat we want is more of the trade the Dutch now have." Dutch seamen acquitted themselves well, but the cost of battles in which more than a hundred ships might be engaged on each side, together with the need to provide convoys for trading vessels even in peacetime, gradually eroded their competitive advantage (see document 16.6).

Even favorable geography probably could not have given England a decisive lead had it not been for a system of credit and finance that became the envy of Europe. The revolution of 1688 paved the way for the land tax of 1692 and the extension of excise taxes to a wide range of consumer goods. England acquired the benefits of permanent taxation for the first time in its history. The Bank of England, established in 1694, then stabilized English finances by underwriting government war loans. In the eighteenth century it became the first of Europe's central banks, allowing private bankers to draw upon its gold reserves in periods of financial crisis.

Credit, backed by reliable taxation, paid for the fleet, Marlborough's armies, and the large subsidies that England paid to its continental allies. England, which became Great Britain when it merged with Scotland in 1707, was therefore able to expand its empire and protect its markets more easily than the Dutch, whose war fleet declined after 1673 and whose decentralized institutions blocked the formation of more effective credit mechanisms. English trade, which had been expanding steadily throughout the seventeenth century, became a flood during the War of the Spanish Succession when the British navy swept the seas of all rivals (see table 16.1). In time the enormous wealth derived largely from overseas markets would provide the capital for the industrial revolution and further strengthen English claims to great power status.

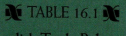

## TABLE 16.1

### English Trade Balances

The most active phase of the War of the Spanish Succession lasted from 1701 to 1711. During that period the English lost 1,061 merchant ships to enemy raiders, while the English balance of trade (surplus of exports over imports) increased enormously, owing primarily to increased exports of cloth and grain to Portugal, Holland, Germany, and Russia and to decreased imports from France and Spain. Because the increase in trade more than compensated for the subsidies sent to the continent for war, the British were, in mercantilist terms, net beneficiaries of the war.

| Year | Extra-European trade balance | Overall trade balance |
|---|---|---|
| 1699–1701 | £ 489,000 | £ 974,000 |
| 1702 | 233,000 | 971,000 |
| 1703 | 515,000 | 1,745,000 |
| 1704 | 968,000 | 1,519,000 |
| 1706 | 836,000 | 2,705,000 |
| 1707 | 672,000 | 2,024,000 |
| 1708 | 630,000 | 2,022,000 |
| 1709 | 271,000 | 2,111,000 |
| 1710 | 825,000 | 2,486,000 |
| 1711 | 969,000 | 2,731,000 |

Source: Adapted from D. W. Jones, *War and Economy in the Age of William III and Marlborough* (Oxford: Basil Blackwell, 1988), p. 220.

CHAPTER 17

# THE SOCIAL AND ECONOMIC STRUCTURE
# OF THE OLD REGIME

## CHAPTER OUTLINE

E uropean society before the political and industrial revolutions of the late eighteenth century is known as the Old Regime. For most people in the eighteenth century, life was little changed from the Middle Ages and closer in its essentials to that of ancient Rome than to the early twenty-first century. Though global commerce was growing and signs were seen of increased capital accumulation and preindustrial development, the vast majority of Europeans were still engaged in agriculture. Society reflected this by remaining hierarchical. A majority of the population worked the land but owned little or none of it, while most of the wealth continued to be held by a small landowning elite.

Chapter 17 examines the social and economic structure of the Old Regime. The chapter starts by looking at the population of Europe, then considers the social categories, called estates, into which people were divided. (The term *social class* is a product of nineteenth-century analysis.) The majority of Europeans lived in rural villages, so the chapter next surveys the rural economy, including preindustrial manufacturing. This leads to a detailed examination of three major social categories: the aristocracy, the peasantry, and town dwellers. The urban economy leads to a discussion of national economies, covering mercantilism, the dominant economic philosophy of the Old Regime, and the global economy.

◆

## The Population of Europe in the Old Regime

Historians do not know with certainty how many people lived in Europe in 1680, or even in 1780. Governments did not yet record births and deaths (churches usually documented them), and they did not

## TABLE 17.1

### Estimated Population of Europe in 1700

| Country | Population (in millions) |
| --- | --- |
| France | 19.3 |
| European Russia | 17.0 |
| German states | 13.5 |
| Prussia | 1.6 |
| Italian states | 13.0 |
| Austrian Empire | 11.0 |
| Poland | 9.0 |
| Spain | 7.5 |
| Great Britain | 6.4 |
| Turkish Empire | 6.4 |
| Ireland | 2.5 |
| Portugal | 2.0 |
| Holland | 1.9 |
| Sweden and Finland | 1.5 |

Source: B. R. Mitchell, ed., *European Historical Statistics, 1750–1970* (London: Macmillan, 1975), pp. 17ff; and Jack Babuscio and Richard M. Dunn, eds., *European Political Facts, 1648–1789* (London: Macmillan, 1984), pp. 335ff.

conduct a regular census. The first modern census in England, for example, was held in 1801. Isolated census data exist for the eighteenth century, such as a Swedish census of 1750 and the Spanish census of 1768–69, but most population figures are estimates based on fragmentary records, local case studies, and demographic analysis.

The best estimate is that Europe at the start of the eighteenth century had a total population of 120 to 130 million people (see table 17.1)—less than one-seventh of the count at the end of the twentieth century. Spain, the richest world power of the sixteenth century, had a population of 9.2 million in 1769. A good estimate of the population of Great Britain (England, Scotland, and Wales) at the beginning of the eighteenth century is 6.4 million—less than the population of London in 1998. The strength of France during the Old Regime can be seen in its estimated population of 19.3 million in 1700. In all countries, most people lived in small villages and on isolated farms. Even in a city-state such as the republic of Venice, more than 80 percent of the population was rural. In France, one of the most developed countries of the Old Regime, the figure was more than 75 percent.

## The Economic Structures of the Rural World

Most of Europe lived, as their ancestors had, in small villages surrounded by open fields. The land was parceled for farming in many ways, but the general pattern was consistent: Peasants and small farmers inhabited and worked land that belonged to aristocrats, the state, or the church. A typical village left some woodland standing (for gathering food and fuel), set aside some of the worst soil as wasteland (for grazing livestock), maintained some land as commonly owned, and left most of the land unfenced in open fields. Enclosed, or fenced in, fields were rare, but in some regions of western Europe—such as southwestern England, Brittany, and the Netherlands—the land was already subdivided by fences, stone walls, or hedgerows. Enclosure had occurred in some places to assist livestock farming and in others where peasants had been fortunate enough to acquire their own land. In most of Europe, however, the arable land was still farmed in the open field system. From the midlands of England to eastern Europe (especially the German states and Russia), open fields were divided into long rectangular strips of approximately one acre each, defined by grass pathways between them. A peasant family usually worked several strips scattered around the community, plus a kitchen garden near home. This was an inefficient system, but one that allowed the bad and good fields to be shared more equitably. In other regions of Europe (such as Spain, southern France, and Italy) the open fields were divided into small, irregular plots of land that peasant families farmed year after year.

Whatever system of land tenure was used, most plowland was planted with the grains on which the world lived—wheat, rye, barley, and oats. These crops were usually rotated annually, and each field laid fallow on a regular basis, normally every third year (see document 17.1). Leaving a field unplanted was needed for the replacement of nitrates in the soil because chemical fertilizers were unknown and animal manure was scarce. Fallow fields had the secondary advantage of providing additional pasture land for grazing.

Scientific agronomy—the study of field-crop production and soil management—was in its infancy in the Old Regime, but noteworthy changes were appearing. In Britain, the improvements suggested by the studies of Jethro Tull and the Viscount Charles Townshend significantly increased eighteenth-century harvests. Tull, a gentleman farmer and scientist introduced a new

❖ DOCUMENT 17.1 ❖

## An Eighteenth-Century Sharecropping Contract

*This list summarizes the chief points of a contract negotiated in southern France in 1779 on behalf of a great landowner. It was an agreement "at half fruits"—a 50/50 sharing of the crop between a marquis and the father and son who farmed his land. A study of this contract has estimated that this land would yield a harvest of 100 setiers of wheat. Thus, the peasant sharecroppers paid (1) 20 setiers off the top to the marquis; then (2) 10 setiers of wheat as the price of cutting and flailing the wheat, leaving a harvest of 70 setiers. They then paid (3) 35 setiers as "half fruits" and (4) 20 setiers for seed. The result was 55 setiers to the marquis, 15 setiers for the peasant family. A family of five ate 20 setiers of wheat per year.*

1. The lease shall be for one year, at "half fruits" and under the following conditions.
2. The lessees will furnish the seed.
3. Before the division of the harvest, the marquis will receive twenty setiers of wheat off the top.
4. The lessees will deliver the wheat already cut and flailed, at no cost to the marquis.
5. The lessees must use the "three field" system of planting—1/3 of the land planted to wheat, 1/3 to some other grain, and 1/3 left unplanted.
6. If the lessees do not leave 1/3 of the land fallow, they forfeit the entire harvest.
7. All livestock will be held in common with profits and losses equally shared.
8. If there is a shortage of hay and straw for the livestock, the lessees must pay half of the cost of buying forage.
9. The lessees must maintain the land, including making drains for water, cutting brush, pruning vines. . . etc.
10. In addition to sharing the crop, the lessees must pay a rent of 72 chickens, 36 capons, and 600 eggs.
11. The lessees must raise pigs, geese, ducks, and turkeys, to be divided evenly; they must purchase the young animals to raise at their own expense.
12. The lessees must make their own ploughs and pay for the blacksmith work themselves.

Forster, Robert, and Forster, Elborg, eds. *European Society in the Eighteenth Century,* New York: Harper & Row, 1969.

system of plowing and hoeing to pulverize the soil, and invented a seed drill that increased yields and decreased labor. Townshend advocated a planting system that eliminated the need for summer fallowing of plowland. His Norfolk, or four-course, system rotated plantings of a root crop, barley, clover, and wheat. Townshend championed the choice of turnips as the root crop so vigorously (because they provided both nitrogen fixation and fodder for livestock) that he became known as "Turnip Townshend." Ideas such as these, circulated by a growing periodical press, raised crop yields to the extent that England fed an increasing population and still exported grain in the early eighteenth century.

Most European agriculture was not so successful, and peasant families faced a struggle to survive. Their primary concern was a harvest large enough to pay their obligations to the landowning aristocracy, to the royal tax collector, and to the church in the form of a compulsory tithe as well as to provide seed grain for the next year, with food left over to sustain life for another year (see document 17.1). The yield per acre was higher in western Europe than in eastern Europe, which explains much of the comparative prosperity and strength of the west. Each grain sown in Russia and Poland yielded an average harvest of four grains, while Spanish and Italian peasants harvested six grains, and English and Dutch farmers averaged more than ten grains. Peasants typically supplemented their meager stock of grains with the produce of a small garden and the luxury of some livestock such as a few pigs or chickens. Surplus grain would be sold or bartered—a money economy was not yet the rule throughout the rural world—at the nearest market town to acquire necessities that could not be produced at home. Even when livestock were slaughtered, peasants rarely ate the entire animal; they generally sold the choicer cuts of pork and kept the fatty remnants for soups, stews, or bacon.

Home production was an essential feature of this rural economy and meant more than churning butter or making cheese at home. Domestic manufacturing often included making all of a family's clothing, so many peasants learned to spin yarn, weave cloth, or sew clothing. This part-time textile production sometimes led to the sale of excess household products, and in some textile regions domestic manufacturing evolved into a system of production known as cottage industry (see illustration 17.1) in which a peasant family purposely made goods for sale instead of for use in the home. Cottage industry sometimes grew into a handcraft form of industrial manufacture (often called

**Illustration 17.1**

🌾 **Cottage Industry.** The textile industry began in rural cottages, not great factories. This scene depicts a family textile shop for making knitwear. Note the sexual division of labor: Women spin and wind yarn while a man operates a knitting frame, making stockings.

protoindustrialization), when entrepreneurs negotiated contracts with peasant spinners and weavers. An entrepreneur might provide raw materials and pay peasant spinners to produce homespun threads; the yarn could then be delivered to a peasant weaver who also worked at home. This "putting out" system of textile manufacture stimulated later industrialization by developing manufacturing skills, marketing networks, and a class of prosperous provincial entrepreneurs. By some estimates 10 percent of the rural population of Old Regime Europe was engaged in cottage industry.

Domestic manufacturing, like farming, depended upon a family economy; that is, everyone worked. Peasant society generally followed a sexual division of labor in which, for example, men did most of the plowing and women played an important role in the harvest. In the production of textiles, women did most of the spinning and men were more likely to be weavers. However, the labor of every family member, including children, was needed if the family were to survive. As an old poem recalls:

Man, to the Plow
Wife, to the Cow
Girl, to the Yarn
Boy, to the Barn
And your Rent will be netted.

Working women were thus essential to the family economy long before industrialization and urbanization

transformed families and work. A study of peasant women in eighteenth-century Belgium, for example, has found that 45 percent of all married women were listed in government records as farmers and 27 percent were recorded as spinners; only 6 percent were listed without an occupation. Unmarried adults were at a disadvantage in this rural economy, and widows were often the poorest members of a rural community.

The rural community of peasant families was typically a village of fifty to a few hundred people. In parts of Europe, these villages had corporate structures with inherited rules and regulations. These might regulate weights and measures, or they might regulate morality and behavior such as the control of stray dogs or mandatory church attendance. Village assemblies, led by elders or by the heads of the households controlling most of the land, often held powers such as assigning land use (as they did in most German states and in Russia), dictating farming methods and crop rotation, settling disputes, collecting taxes, and even arranging marriages. Women were usually excluded from participation, though widows were sometimes accepted. Recent research has identified some exceptionally democratic villages in which women participated with full rights.

## Corporative Society and the *Ständestaat*

Europeans of the Old Regime lived in highly stratified societies and generally accepted their fixed place in the hierarchy. In two-thirds of Europe (France, Savoy, part of Switzerland, Denmark, the German states, Austria, Bohemia, Hungary, the Danubian provinces, Poland, and Russia), law and custom divided people into estates. The division of the population into such bodies, with separate rights, duties, and laws, is known as corporative society, or by its German name, the *Ständestaat*.

Corporative society was a legacy of the Middle Ages. In much of western Europe, the legal basis for it had disappeared, whereas eastern Europe remained caste-ridden. Everywhere, hierarchical ideas provided the foundations of society. The structure of corporative society resembled a pyramid. Most of the population (peasants and laborers) formed the base of the pyramid while a few privileged people (aristocrats and wealthy town dwellers) sat at the top, with a monarch at the pinnacle. Everyone was born to a position in the hierarchy, a position that, according to most churches, was divinely ordained, and little social mobility was evident from one order to another.

## TABLE 17.2
### The Social Structure of England in the Old Regime

The data in this table are based upon statistical calculations made by Gregory King in the last years of the seventeenth century, based upon a study of the tax rolls.

| Social group | Individuals on tax rolls | Population (with families) | Percentage of England |
|---|---|---|---|
| Aristocracy | 4,560 | 57,000 | 1.0 |
| Landowning gentry | 172,000 | 1,036,000 | 18.8 |
| Small farmers | 550,000 | 2,050,000 | 37.2 |
| Rural total | 726,560 | 3,143,000 | 57.0 |
| Merchants | 10,000 | 64,000 | 1.2 |
| Educated professions | 25,000 | 145,000 | 2.7 |
| Clergy | 10,020 | 52,520 | 0.9 |
| Government service | 10,000 | 70,000 | 1.3 |
| Urban trades | 110,000 | 465,000 | 8.5 |
| Laborers | 360,000 | 1,275,000 | 23.2 |
| Urban total | 525,020 | 2,101,520 | 38.3 |
| Military officers | 9,000 | 36,000 | 0.7 |
| Soldiers and sailors | 85,000 | 220,000 | 4.0 |
| Military total | 94,000 | 256,000 | 4.7 |

Historians have mostly studied corporative society in France, where the population was divided into three estates. The clergy, approximately 1 percent to 2 percent of the nation, comprised the first estate. The aristocracy, also less than 2 percent of the population, formed the second estate. The remaining 97 percent of France, from bankers to vagabonds, collectively made up the third estate. In central Europe, the *Ständestaat* often contained four orders (*Stände*) because Scandinavian and German law divided what the French called the third estate into two parts, an order of town dwellers and another of peasants. The constitutions of the Old Regime, such as the Swedish Constitution of 1720, retained the ideal of corporative society. German jurisprudence perpetuated this division of the population throughout the eighteenth century. A fifty-volume compendium published in the 1740s, reiterated the principles of the *Ständestaat*, and they were embodied in subsequent legal reforms, such as the Frederician Code in Prussia.

The society of the Old Regime was more complicated than simple legal categories suggest. In England, the legal distinctions among social groups were mostly abolished during the seventeenth century. The English aristocracy remained a privileged and dominant elite, but a new stratification based upon nonlanded wealth was also emerging (see table 17.2). In contrast, Russian fundamental laws perpetuated a rigid corporative society, and eighteenth-century reforms only tightened the system. In central Europe, yet another pattern developed where reformers known as cameralists refined the definitions of social categories. Austrian tax laws adopted in 1763, for example, divided the population into twenty-four distinct categories.

The composition and condition of each estate varied across Europe. The Polish aristocracy included 10 percent of the population compared with 1 percent in France; this meant that the Polish aristocracy included barefoot farmers who lived in simple homes with earthen floors. Only 1 percent of Poles lived in towns of ten thousand, compared with more than 15 percent of England and Wales. Sometimes, as in Spain, peasants lived in farming towns, but they were not part of an urban estate. But everywhere, peasants were the majority. In England, 65 percent of the population lived by farming; in France and Sweden, 75 percent of the population were peasants; in Poland, 85 percent.

The rights and duties of people in each estate also varied from country to country, with the most striking differences evident between eastern and western Europe. Historians frequently express this division of Europe by an imaginary line called the Elbe-Trieste line, running from the mouth of the Elbe River on the North Sea to the Adriatic Sea at the city of Trieste (see map 17.1). West of the Elbe-Trieste line (including Scandinavia), peasants could own farm land. French peasants, for example, owned between 30 percent and 40 percent of the arable land, although it was frequently of the poorest quality. East of the Elbe River, peasants lived in a form of legal servitude called serfdom. Millions of serfs were deprived of legal and civil rights, including the right to own land. Even those states that permitted peasant land ownership, however, saw little of it. Swedish peasants accounted for 75 percent of the population but owned only 31 percent of the land; the king and the aristocracy, less than 5 percent of the population, owned 69 percent of the land in 1700. Sweden, however, was far ahead of most of Europe in peasant land ownership. In Bohemia, one of the richest provinces of the Habsburg Empire, the monarch owned 5 percent of the land and the nobility owned 68.5 percent, while peasants owned less than 1 percent.

## The Aristocracy: Varieties of the Privileged Elite

The pinnacle of the social structure in rural communities was the aristocracy, who enjoyed a life of comparative ease. In most countries, aristocrats formed a separate legal caste, bound by different laws and traditions that gave them special privileges, such as tax exemptions and the right to unpaid labor by the peasantry. Nobility was considered a hereditary condition, which originated when a monarch granted noble status to a family through a document called a patent of nobility. In each generation, the eldest son would bear the title of nobility (such as duke or count) and other males in the family might bear lesser titles. Lesser aris-

tocratic status was typically shown by the aristocratic particule within a family name; this was usually the word *of* (*de* in French, *di* in Italian, *von* in German). Pretenders sometimes tried to copy this habit, but the nobility zealously guarded its privileged status. In Venice, a Golden Book recorded the names of the nobility; in the German states, an annual publication (the *Almanac of Gotha*) kept watch on aristocratic pedigrees.

The aristocracy was a small class, but it was not homogeneous. Gradations of status depended upon the length of time that a family had been noble, the means by which it had acquired its title, and the wealth and political influence that the family held. One of the distinctions frequently made in western Europe separated a "nobility of the sword" composed of families ennobled for centuries as a result of military service to the monarch from a "nobility of the robe" composed of families more recently ennobled through service to the government. In central and eastern Europe, important distinctions rested upon the number of serfs an aristocrat owned. The aristocracy might include an elite of less land and wealth, known as the gentry, although in some countries, such as Britain, the landowning gentry did not possess aristocratic titles. While the gentry enjoyed a comfortable existence, it was far removed from the wealth of great nobles (see table 17.3).

The highest nobles often emphasized the length of time their family had been noble. British history provides a good example. The leading figure in early eighteenth-century English politics, Sir Robert Walpole, was not born to a noble title, but for his accomplishments, he was ennobled as the first earl of Orford in 1742. One of Walpole's leading opponents, however, was the fourth duke and eighth earl of Bedford, heir to a pedigree nearly three hundred years old and a title that originated with the third son of King Henry IV, born in 1389. Thus, the earl of Bedford was unlikely to consider the earl of Orford his equal. And both of them yielded precedence to the earl of Norfolk, whose title dated back to the year 1070, shortly after the Norman conquest of England.

Many of the fine distinctions within the aristocracy were simply matters of pride within a caste that paid excruciating attention to comparative status. The aristocratic competition for precedence, however, involved real issues of power and wealth. Only the top 5 percent (perhaps less) of the aristocracy could hope to be presented at court and meet the royal family; fewer still were invited to live at the royal court, hunting with King Louis XV of France in the royal forests, sharing the evening tabagerie (a smoking and drinking session) with King Frederick William I of Prussia, or enjoying

## TABLE 17.3
### The Finances of a Great Noble in the Eighteenth Century

This table has excerpts from the financial records of a French noble family, the counts and countesses of Tavannes. The unit of measure is the livre, which had approximately the same value as an English shilling (one-twentieth of the pound sterling). Figures are given for mixed years because only partial records have survived.

| Income or expenses | Amount |
| --- | --- |
| **Income from land owned by the count** | |
| Rent for lands in region #1 (annual average, 1696–1730) | 5,000+ |
| Rent for lands in region #2 (annual average, 1699–1726) | 3,500+ |
| Rent for lands in region #3 (annual average, 1698–1723) | 8,700+ |
| Income from sale of wood from forest in region #3 (1788) | 40,000+ |
| Gross revenue from all land (after paying upkeep and wages) in 1788 | 86,269 |
| **Income from pensions given by the king** | |
| Total pensions for 1754 | 46,900 |
| Pension as commander of royal forces in Burgundy | 26,250 |
| **Income from seigneurial dues (obligations paid by peasants)** | |
| Total dues paid in 1788 | 26,986 |
| **Income from the inheritance of the countess (1725)** | |
| Income from four houses in Paris (value = 200,000) | 10,000 |
| Income from investments (value = 367,938) | 8,698 |
| Total capital inherited in 1725 | 803,924 |
| **Wages paid to the count's staff (1780–86)** | |
| Annual wages for the count's agent in Paris | 800 |
| Annual wages for a forest warden in Burgundy | 200 |
| Annual wages for a gardener or a maid in Burgundy | 70 |
| Annual wages for a chef in Paris | 945 |
| Annual wages for a coachman in Paris | 720 |
| **Personal expenses** | |
| Total personal expenses in 1788 | 62,000 |
| Expenses for clothing, jewelry, and gifts in 1788 | 20,000 |
| Expenses for the theater in 1788 | 2,000 |
| Monthly expenses for Roquefort cheese (January 1784) | 32 |
| Monthly expenses for cognac (January 1784) | 30 |
| Monthly expenses for cayenne coffee (January 1784) | 30 |

Source: Data from Robert Forster, *The House of Saulx-Tavannes: Versailles and Burgundy, 1700–1830* (Baltimore, Md.: Johns Hopkins University Press, 1971), passim.

the life of lavish dinners and balls. Yet a position at court was often the route to political office, military command, or perhaps a pension providing a lifetime income. Most provincial nobles lacked the opportunities for such advancement.

The provincial aristocracy, living on inherited lands in the rural world, encompassed a great range of social and economic conditions. The Spanish, for example, distinguished between grandees (a term for the greatest nobles, such as the dukes of Alba) who possessed immense estates and national influence, locally important aristocrats (called *caballeros*) who owned enough land to live as a privileged elite, and a comparatively poor gentry (called *hidalgos*) who were said to have more titles than shirts. Such distinctions existed across Europe. In the east, a few families of grand seigneurs owned most of the land (and the serfs on it) while thousands of aristocrats owned little or nothing. The Polish aristocracy, known collectively as the *szlachta*, included 700,000 to one million people, but only thirty to forty magnate families possessed the wealth and power normally associated with the nobility. Part of the *szlachta* worked on the estates of great nobles as bailiffs, stewards, or tenant farmers; most of this caste lived as small farmers on rented land, and many were so poor that they were known as the *golota*, a barefoot aristocracy.

## The Privileged Status of the Aristocracy

The wealth and power of the high nobility present one of the most vivid images of the corporative society of the Old Regime. Some aristocrats enjoyed dizzying wealth and a life of luxury. In the Austrian Netherlands (now Belgium), the duke of Arenberg had an annual income eighteen times the income of the richest merchant. In Poland, Prince Radziwill kept ten thousand retainers in his service. In England, the top four hundred noble families each owned estates of ten thousand to fifty thousand acres. In Russia, Empress Catherine the Great gave one of her discarded lovers a gift of thirty-seven thousand serfs, and Prince Menshikov owned 100,000 serfs. In Bohemia, one hundred noble families owned one-third of the entire province, and the poorer members of this group owned land encompassing thirty villages. In Spain, the count of Altamira owned the commercial city of Valencia.

Such wealth produced breathtaking inequality. The count of Tavannes in France paid a gardener or a maid on his provincial estates seventy livres per year, and the valued chef at his Paris residence earned 945 livres per year; yet the count lavished twenty thousand livres on clothing and jewelry. The count's monthly expenditure on coffee and cognac totaled nearly a year's wages for a servant, and his budget for theater tickets would have cost the total yearly earnings of twenty-eight servants. Sustaining a life of such extreme luxury led many lesser nobles into ruinous debt. Extravagance and debt became so typical of the nobility (including royalty) in the eighteenth century that some countries, such as Spain, made arresting aristocrats for their debts illegal.

In addition to enormous wealth, nobles held great power. They dominated offices of the state, both in the government and in the military. In some countries, notably Sweden, Prussia, and Russia, the concept of aristocratic service to the throne had led to an arrangement in which the aristocracy accepted compulsory state service and received in return a legal monopoly over certain positions. The eighteenth-century Russian Charter of the Nobility, for example, stated: "The title and privileges of the nobility . . . are acquired by service and work useful to the Empire." Therefore, it continued, whenever the emperor "needs the service of the nobility for the general well being, every nobleman is then obligated . . . to perform fully his duty." In return for this compulsory service, the Charter of the Nobility recognized the right of nobles to buy and sell villages, excluded nobles from some taxes that fell on commoners, gave nobles a monopoly of some positions, and spared nobles some of the punishments (such as flogging) specified in Russian law. In much of Europe, only aristocrats could become army officers. Nobles universally dominated the highest positions in government. At the beginning of the eighteenth century, the chief minister of the king of France was a marquis, the prime minister of the king of Prussia was a count, the head of the state council of the Habsburg Empire was a count, the chief minister of the tsar of Russia was a prince, and the chief adviser to the king of Spain was a cardinal. For the century before the French Revolution of 1789, the chief ministers of the kings of France were (in order): a marquis, a cardinal, a duke, a duke, a cardinal, a marquis, a count, a minor aristocrat, a duke, a duke, and a count.

In addition to personal wealth and powerful offices, aristocrats of the Old Regime usually held a privileged position in the law, exceptional rights on their landed estates, and great power over the people who lived on their land. In most countries, nobles were governed by substantially different laws than the rest of the population. Some countries had a separate legal code for aristocrats, some had legal charters detailing noble privileges, some simply adopted laws granting special treatment. Legal privileges took many forms. Exemption from the laws that applied to commoners was one of the most cherished. Aristocrats were exempted from most taxes that fell on peasants or town dwellers, and they tenaciously defended their exemptions even as the monarchy faced bankruptcy. In Hungary, the Magyar nobles were free from all direct taxes such as those on land or income; they guarded this privilege by giving regular contributions to the throne, but nobles controlled the process and the amount themselves. Aristocrats were exempt from the *corvée*, a labor tax by which peasants were obliged to maintain roads and bridges (see illustration 17.2). Penal codes usually exempted nobles from the corporal punishment common, such as flogging and branding.

**Illustration 17.2**

🏵 **The Corvée.** The highway system of eighteenth-century Europe required a great deal of labor to maintain it. In most of central and eastern Europe, where serfdom survived, monarchs expected great landowners to require roadwork as part of the *ro-* *bot* owed by serfs. In France, where serfdom had largely disappeared, peasants were required to pay a tax, called the *corvée*, by their labor, like the roadwork shown here.

Aristocratic privilege varied significantly from country to country. In Britain and the Netherlands, most exemptions were abolished by revolutions in the seventeenth century. Both countries made aristocrats and commoners equal before the law and allowed neither tax exemptions nor a monopoly on offices. Yet important privileges persisted there, too. English nobles held hereditary control of the upper house of Parliament, the House of Lords, and the right to be tried only by a jury of their peers.

The core of aristocratic privilege was found on their provincial estates. An aristocrat, as lord of the manor, held traditional manorial rights over the land and its inhabitants. These rights are also known as feudal rights, because many had survived from the feudal system of the Middle Ages, or seigneurial rights, because the lord of the manor was known as the seigneur. Manorial rights increased significantly as one passed from western Europe to eastern Europe, where peasants remained in the virtual slavery of serfdom. But even in regions where serfdom no longer existed, aristocratic

landowners were often entitled to feudal dues (payments in money or in kind), to unpaid labor by peasants in the seigneurial fields, or to both. Thus, peasants might be expected to harvest an aristocrat's crops before they could harvest their own and then to pay a percentage of their own crops to the same aristocrat.

Seigneurial rights in many countries (particularly in central and eastern Europe) also included the powers of local governance. The seigneur provided, or oversaw, the functions of the police, the judiciary, and civil government on his lands; a noble might thereby preside over the arrest, trial, and punishment of a peasant. Many aristocrats thus governed their provincial estates as self-sufficient, miniature kingdoms. A study of the Old Regime manors of Bohemia shows this vividly. Only the noble landowner was legally a citizen of the larger state (the Austrian Empire). The residents of the noble's villages and farmlands were completely under his jurisdiction. Peasants farmed their fields for him. He conscripted them for the *corvée*, selected them for service in the Austrian army, and collected their taxes for the Habsburg government. The same lord arrested draft evaders or tax delinquents and punished them, and peasants could not appeal his justice.

## Variations within the Peasantry: Serfdom

The majority of Europeans during the Old Regime were peasant farmers, but this peasantry, like the aristocracy, was not a homogeneous class. The foremost difference distinguished free peasants from those legally bound by virtual slavery. Outright slavery no longer existed in most of Europe by 1700, although European governments allowed slavery in their overseas colonies. Portugal (the only country to import African slaves into Europe), the Ottoman Empire, and the Danubian provinces (where 200,000 gypsies were enslaved) were exceptions.

Multitudes of European peasants still lived in the virtual slavery known as serfdom, a medieval institution that had survived into the Old Regime (and would last into the nineteenth century in parts of Europe). Serfdom was not slavery, but it resembled slavery in several ways. Serfs could not own land. They were bound to the soil, meaning that they could not choose to migrate from the land they farmed. In addition, serfs might be sold or given away, or gambled away. Entire villages could be abolished and relocated. Serfs might be subjected to corporal punishment such as flogging. One Russian count ordered the whipping of all serfs who did not attend church, and the penalty for missing Easter Communion was five thousand lashes. A Russian decree of 1767 summarized this situation simply: Serfs "owe their landlords proper submission and absolute obedience in all matters."

The distinction between serfdom and slavery was noteworthy. Unlike slaves, serfs were not chattel property (property other than real estate). Serfs were rarely sold without including the land that they farmed or without their families. Serfs enjoyed a few traditional legal rights. They could make a legal appeal to a village council or a seigneurial court. They could not press charges or give evidence against nobles or their bailiffs, so their legal rights protected them within the peasant community but not against their lords.

Serfdom survived in some portions of western Europe and became more common as one traveled east. East of the Elbe River, serfdom was the dominant social institution. In parts of France and the western German states, vestigial serfdom still restricted hundreds of thousands of people. In Prussia and Poland, approximately 20 percent of the peasants were free and 80 per-

cent serfs. In Hungary, only 2 percent of the peasants were free; in Denmark and in the Slavic provinces of the Austrian Empire (Bohemia and Silesia), perhaps 1 percent; in Russia, less than 1 percent.

Variations did exist within serfdom. In Russia, a peasant family typically belonged to a noble landowner, but 40 percent of the serfs were state serfs farming the imperial domains. These state serfs had been created by Peter the Great when he seized lands belonging to the Russian Orthodox Church. Those who labored for the nobility experienced conditions as diverse as did their seigneurs; more than 30 percent of landowners held small farms with fewer than ten serfs, while 16 percent of the Russian nobility owned estates large enough to encompass an entire village of one hundred or more serfs. The great nobility possessed so many souls that many served as house serfs, domestic servants whose life differed significantly from their counterparts who labored in the fields.

The basic legal obligation of serfs was compulsory, unpaid labor in the fields of landowners. This obligatory labor, called *robot* in much of central and eastern Europe, was defined by law but varied from region to region. In Prussia serfs owed the Junker aristocrats two or three days of unpaid labor every week and more during the harvest. Junkers, however, needed more labor than their serfs provided and therefore hired some free peasants. The feudal labor laws of Bohemia specified three days per week of *robot*, plus harvest labor "at the will" of a noble. A law of 1775 defined a day of labor as eight hours during the winter, twelve hours during the spring and summer, and fourteen hours during the harvest. Russian serfs commonly worked six days per week for a landowner (see document 17.2). In some regions, however, a different system applied: Serfs farmed an allotment of land and gave the landowners a large percentage of the harvest.

A study of the serfs in the Baltic provinces of Russia reveals how these obligations added up. A family of eight able-bodied peasants (including women) owed their master the following: two field workers for three days per week, every week of the year; ten to twelve days of miscellaneous labor such as livestock herding; four trips, totaling about fifty-six days of labor, carting goods for the seigneur; forty-two days of postal-relay services; and twenty-four days of spinning flax. In addition to such labor, European peasant families owed feudal payments in kind, such as grain, sheep, wool, chickens, and eggs. Even then they could not keep their remaining production. They had to guard 20 percent to 25 percent of a harvest as seed for the following year. Peasants also usually owed a compulsory tithe to

### ◆ DOCUMENT 17.2 ◆

## A Traveler Observes the Life of Russian Serfs

*One of the difficulties facing social historians is that the surviving records of the past were (by definition) written by literate, educated people. The illiterate masses could not record the conditions of their lives for posterity. Historians must therefore rely on the indirect evidence provided by observers (and their deductions from other sources). Alexander Radishchev (1749–1802) was a Russian writer who opposed serfdom and wrote about it, resulting in his exile to Siberia. The following excerpt is Radishchev's description of his meeting with a serf, as published in his* A Voyage from St. Petersburg to Moscow (1790).

The corduroy road tortured my body; I climbed out of the carriage and (walked). A few steps from the road I saw a peasant ploughing a field. The weather was hot. . . . It was now Sunday. . . . The peasant was ploughing very carefully. The field, of course, was not part of his master's land. He turned the plow with astonishing ease.

"God help you," I said, walking up to the ploughman. . . .

"Thank you sir," the ploughman said to me, shaking the earth off the ploughshare. . . .

"You must be a Dissenter, since you plough on a Sunday."

"No, sir, I make the true sign of the cross," he said, showing me the three fingers together. "And God is merciful and does not bid us starve to death, so long as we have strength and a family."

"Have you no time to work during the week, then, and can you not have any rest on Sundays, in the hottest part of the day, at that?"

"In a week, sir, there are six days, and we go six times a week to work on the master's fields; in the evening, if the weather is good, we haul to the master's house the hay that is left in the woods. . . . God grant that it rains this evening. If you have peasants of your own, sir, they are praying to God for the same thing."

". . . But how do you manage to get food enough, if you have only the holidays free?"

"Not only the holidays: the nights are ours, too. If a fellow isn't lazy, he won't starve to death."

Radischev, Alexander. *A Journey from St. Petersburg to Moscow.* Cambridge, MA: Harvard University Press, 1958.

an established church—approximately 10 percent of a harvest—and taxes to the government, which frequently took between 30 percent and 40 percent of the crop. Studies have found that serfs owed 73 percent of their produce in Bohemia, 75 percent in eastern France, 83 percent in Silesia, and 86 percent in parts of Galicia. Such figures changed from year to year, but the burden remained crushing.

### Variations within the Peasantry: Free Peasants

The free peasants of western and central Europe had been escaping from the burdens of serfdom since the fourteenth century. The evolution of a money economy reduced the importance of feudal services by enabling some peasants to commute *robot* or *corvée* with cash. To increase revenues from import and export tariffs, some governments had encouraged a shift to livestock production by allowing aristocrats to enclose their own, and sometimes their tenants', lands. As a result, the capitalization of land was far advanced in the west by

1700, though most families still owed at least some feudal obligations to the landowning aristocracy. Whereas eastern serfs were fortunate to keep 25 percent of their harvest, free peasants could expect to keep more than half. Two different studies of Old Regime France have found that peasants owed between 33 percent and 40 percent of their total production in feudal dues, taxes, and tithes.

The condition of free peasants varied according to the forms of land tenure. The most prosperous peasants were landowners themselves. Studies of the French free peasantry found that nearly four million peasants owned some land and their own home (see illustration 17.3) in the eighteenth century, though most families owned so little land that they could not afford to market any of their harvest. Although most free peasants were landless, one group of them found relatively comfortable lives. The most successful of the landless French peasants were usually tenant farmers, about 10 percent to 20 percent of the landless population. Tenant farmers rented land, typically for a long term—such as nine years—for a fixed money payment, and

Illustration 17.3

The Home of a Successful Peasant Family. Eighteenth-century peasant homes often had only one room, which was used for all purposes, including housing animals. This Breton family from a village near Morbihan possessed considerable wealth in its horses, cattle, and pigs. Note the limited furnishings and the absence of windows.

they then made the best profit that they could after paying the rent. Such long-term contracts protected peasant families from eviction after a single bad harvest, and many aristocrats discovered the advantages of short-term contracts, which were typical in Spain. Other tenant farmers managed the rented lands but did not labor in the fields themselves, or they became wealthy by trading in grain or other commodities.

The other 80 percent to 90 percent of landless peasants were not as fortunate as the tenant farmers. The most secure group were usually sharecroppers, often called *métayers*. They produced most of the grain marketed in France by farming the estates of great landowners under contracts negotiated as free peasants. The sharecropping contract (see document 17.1) typically provided leased land in return for a large share of its yield. Sharecropping contracts provided these peasant families with the means of survival, but little more. Below the sharecroppers was a lower class of agricultural laborers. Some worked for wages, others, called cotters in many countries, worked for the use of a cottage. Some found only seasonal employment (working to harvest grapes in the autumn, for example), in some cases living as migrant laborers, traveling with the changing harvests. Thus, the peasantry included a range of conditions that saw some peasants employed as laborers (or even domestic servants) by other peasants.

## The Urban Population of the Old Regime

Urban Europe in the eighteenth century ranged from rural market towns of 2,000 people to great administra-

| ❧ TABLE 17.4 ❧ | |
|---|---|
| **The Great Cities of Europe in 1700** | |

Table shows all European cities with a population of 100,000 or more in 1700

| City | Population |
|---|---|
| Constantinople | 700,000 |
| London | 575,000 |
| Paris | 500,000 |
| Naples | 300,000 |
| Amsterdam | 200,000 |
| Lisbon | 180,000 |
| Madrid | 140,000 |
| Venice | 138,000 |
| Rome | 135,000 |
| Moscow | 130,000 |
| Milan | 125,000 |
| Vienna | 114,000 |
| Palermo | 100,000 |

tive and commercial capital cities of 500,000. Important regional towns—such as Heidelberg, Helsinki, and Liverpool—often had populations below ten thousand. A population of 100,000 constituted a great city, and only a few capital cities reached that level in the early eighteenth century (see table 17.4 and map 17.1). Berlin had fifty-five thousand people in 1700. St. Pe-

MAP 17.1

⚙️ Urban Europe in 1750 ⚙️

tersburg reached sixty-eight thousand in 1730. Buda and Pest were then separate towns with a combined total of seventeen thousand people. Many cities, such as Geneva, with a population of twenty-eight thousand in 1750, were so small that residents could easily walk their full width for an evening stroll.

The largest city in Europe sat on its southeastern edge: Constantinople had an estimated 700,000 persons. The two dominant cities in the development of modern European civilization, London and Paris, both exceeded 500,000 people, but no other cities rivaled them. Rome was smaller than it had been under the Caesars, with a population of 135,000 in 1700. Such large cities were the centers of western civilization, but they did not yet make it an urban civilization. If one defines *urban* as beginning at a population of ten thousand people, Europe was only 9.4 percent urban at the end of the eighteenth century; if the definition goes down to towns of five thousand people, Europe was

12.1 percent urban. Even if one counts small farming towns of two thousand people (which were different from manufacturing and commercial towns), Europe was still less than one-fourth urban, although some regions were one-third urban.

In legal terms, cities and towns of the Old Regime were corporate entities (hence the terms *incorporated* and *unincorporated* for towns). Towns held legal charters, often centuries old, from the government. Charters specified the rights of town dwellers—collectively called the bourgeoisie (from the French term *bourg*, for town) or burghers (from the similar German term)—rights that the rural population did not enjoy. As in the Middle Ages, the old German saying held true: "City air makes one free." The urban population thus formed a clearly defined estate, lacking many of the privileges of the aristocracy but freed from the obligations upon the peasantry. Hence, they came to be seen as a "middle" class. As a group, they possessed significant nonlanded wealth although they did not rival the wealth of landed nobles. Studies of wills probated during the Old Regime have shown that nobles possessed more than two-thirds of the wealth. A study of England in the 1740s has shown that the landowning aristocracy and upper gentry (a total of less than 3 percent of population) owned 95 percent of the national wealth.

Many countries, particularly those east of the Elbe-Trieste line, prohibited peasants from migrating to the towns and obtaining urban freedoms. Bavarian law, Austrian law, and the Prussian legal code, for example, all bound German peasants to stay on the soil. Even in western Europe, some town charters restricted residence and citizenship, usually to people who showed a means of support. Cities needed migration, however. Conditions were generally so unhealthy that the death rate exceeded the birthrate. Cities could only maintain their size or grow by attracting rural immigrants. Thus, restrictions on population mobility began to disappear during the Old Regime. London grew rapidly in the eighteenth century, yet recorded more deaths than births in every year of the century until 1790; in 1741, burials outnumbered baptisms by two to one.

## The Social and Economic Structure of Urban Europe

The towns of the eighteenth century varied in their function as well as their size. Capital cities formed a special category of large cities where government and finance were centered, and the population was so huge that it was a challenge just to feed them. The next range of major cities were usually manufacturing centers (such as Lyons and Granada) or great port-cities (such as Marseilles, Hamburg, and Liverpool). Important regional towns similarly varied, as centers of administration (both governmental and religious) and manufacturing. European towns were not yet characterized by the heavy industry or mass production associated with modern urban life. Economic historians have estimated that in 1750 Britain had attained only 10 percent of the industrialization that it would reach by 1900; France, the Italian states, and the German states were only at 7 percent to 9 percent. Manufacturing in the eighteenth century chiefly meant textiles. Combined textile manufacturing (wool, cotton, linen, and silk) accounted for 28 percent of all British manufacturing, whereas combined heavy industries (mining, metalworking, and construction) accounted for only 22 percent. Textiles similarly provided the traditional basis

of urban prosperity in many regions of continental Europe, such as northeastern France, Flanders, and the city-states of northern Italy.

The occupational structure of towns varied with the town's function. A study of Bayeux, a provincial administrative town in Normandy, found a working adult male population of twelve hundred. Their employment shows how an administrative town was different from the image of towns as manufacturing centers. Slightly more than 10 percent of the men of Bayeux were in the educated professions, mostly lawyers and officials or people trained in medical arts—physicians, surgeons, and apothecaries. An additional 1 percent were tax collectors (an independent occupation) for the monarch or the regional nobility. The prosperous great merchants (not shopkeepers) who traded in regional agricultural or manufactured goods constituted nearly 3 percent of the male population. At the opposite end of Bayeux's social spectrum, 10 percent of the population were urban laborers—a low number that shows that this was not a manufacturing town. Between the two extremes, approximately 75 percent of the male population were engaged in trades. Most of them worked in the production or distribution of food (grocers, butchers, and bakers), clothing (tailors, cobblers, and wig makers), and housing (hoteliers and innkeepers or the building trades). The remainder of the population practiced other trades characteristic of urban life: coopers, goldsmiths, clock makers, saddlers, cabinetmakers, drapers, dozens of other crafts whose practitioners were called artisans.

At the pinnacle of the urban social structure sat the wealthy patrician class of the big cities and great manufacturing towns—a bourgeoisie of banking and finance, of manufacturing and commerce (see illustration 17.4). This urban oligarchy lacked the hereditary titles and privileges of the aristocracy. They were not yet as wealthy as nobles, and they held much less political power. But many families possessed enough wealth to live nobly and aspired to aristocratic status. A few members of this urban elite might enter the aristocracy through state service, and some families married into the aristocracy by providing lavish dowries to daughters who married nobles in debt. This wealthy class lived handsomely, but they represented only a small percentage of urban population, just as aristocrats did in the rural world.

The typical town dweller in the Old Regime was an artisan, and the dominant feature of an artisan's life was the guild—yet another corporation (see illustration 17.5). Guilds had developed in Europe in the late Middle Ages (between the twelfth and fifteenth centuries) for the purpose of organizing craft production. They received statutes or charters specifying their rights from the monarch, making them corporations like the towns themselves. Guild charters were still being reaffirmed

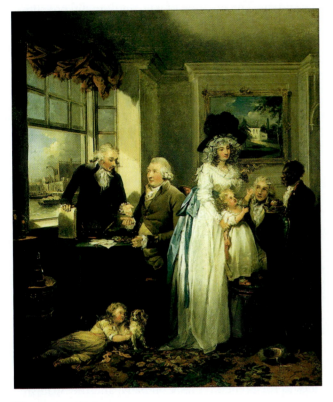

**Illustration 17.4**

⫻ **The Rising Middle Class.** The wealthy middle class of businessmen, merchants, manufacturers, and bankers became increasingly influential in the eighteenth century despite being largely excluded from aristocratic circles and institutions. In this painting, a prosperous British merchant flaunts his wealth: his docks and warehouses outside the window, his country estate in the painting, his gold on the table, and his richly dressed family.

by monarchs in the late eighteenth century, as the king of Saxony did in 1780. These corporate charters gave the guilds monopolistic control of manufacturing in their respective trades. Thus, only a member of the coopers' guild could make barrels. Such monopolies extended to all manufacturing for sale or for exchange, but not for home use, and this naturally caused some tension between urban guilds and rural domestic manufacturing. The men of an urban tailors' guild, for example, could fight against the sale of any goods produced by women who worked as seamstresses in the surrounding countryside. Guilds used their charters to regulate trade. They restricted access to, or training in, each occupation; defined the standards of quality; and regulated the right to sell goods.

Membership in a guild involved three stages of development: apprenticeship, when one learned the basic skills of a trade; journeyman, when one developed these skills as a paid employee; and master of a craft, when one obtained the full privilege of practicing it, including the right to train apprentices and hire journeymen. Children became apprentices, learning a trade from a master, at an early age. A study of the guilds of Venice, for example, shows that apprentice goldsmiths began at age seven, weavers at twelve; by age eighteen, one was too old to apprentice in most crafts. A child had to meet many requirements of the guild (such as proof of legitimate birth or practice of Christianity) and pay fees to both the guild and the master before becoming an apprentice. The children of masters had additional advantages. Guild regulations usually required masters to accept the children of other guild members as apprentices, to house them in their homes, and to provide them with adequate training and experience in a trade. Apprentices, in turn, were obliged to serve their masters for a fixed period of years (typically three or

**Illustration 17.5**

⫻ **Guild Labor in the Towns.** The larger towns of Europe were centers of skilled artisanal labor such as the German metalworkers depicted in this engraving. The master of such a shop would typically employ one or more journeymen; train children as apprentices in the trade; and entrust the business side of the shop to his wife, who oversaw sales and kept the records.

four, but often more) without pay. Upon the completion of their training, apprentices became journeymen and were expected to leave the town of their training and journey to work for wages with masters in other towns. The journeyman carried papers identifying him and his experience, signed by each of the masters for whom he had worked. Only after several years of such travels could a craftsman hope for acceptance as the master of a trade.

Master craftsmen were important figures in a town. They controlled the guilds and therefore most of the occupations. Masters were expected to marry and to lead respectable lives. They usually maintained their workroom, shop, and residence in the same building. Women were generally excluded from an independent role in a guild, but they were an integral part of the craftsman's family economy. The wife of a master usually handled sales in the shop, kept the accounts for her husband's business, and managed the household. If a master died, his widow had the right to keep their shop, to hire the journeymen to work in it, and to manage the business.

The lower rungs of the urban social structure were domestic servants and the laboring poor. At the beginning of the eighteenth century, domestic service was already becoming one of the largest sources of employment for the unskilled. Studies have found that 7 percent of the population of Ypres (Belgium), 15 percent of Münster (western Germany), and 20 percent of London were working as domestic servants. They lacked the independence and economic prospects of artisans, but they escaped from the poverty of unskilled labor while finding some comfort and security in the homes of their employers. For unmarried women, domestic service was often the only respectable employment available.

# National Economies: The Doctrine of Mercantilism

*Economics* is an ancient word whose derivation goes back to Aristotle's *Oikonomia*, but economics as a field of study and theory is a recent development. In the eighteenth century economics in the modern sense formed a small part of the study called moral philosophy. The first university professorship in political economy was created at the University of Naples in 1754, and the field of political economy (the precursor of modern economics) chiefly prospered in Scotland under the

leadership of theorists such as Adam Smith, the most important founder of modern capitalism.

Despite the limited study of political economics in the Old Regime, governments followed a well-developed economic philosophy known as the mercantile system. The doctrine of mercantilism did not stress the predominant feature of the economy of the Old Regime (agriculture) or the greatest form of wealth of that world (land). Instead, the mercantile system chiefly concerned manufactures, trade, wealth in gold and silver, and the role of the state in encouraging these. The basic principle of mercantilism was a concept called autarky—the idea that a state should be self-sufficient in producing manufactured goods and should import as few foreign goods as possible. Simultaneously, the state sought export markets for its own goods. To achieve a favorable balance of trade and the consequent accumulation of wealth in gold required government regulation of the economy.

An important aspect of the mercantilist regulation of the economy was state support for manufactures and commerce. Many governments of the Old Regime chartered monopolies on the models of the British East India Company and the Dutch East India Company. During the 1720s alone, the Austrians chartered the Ostend Company to control trade with the Indies, the French merged several trading monopolies as the French Indies Company, and the Spanish gave the Chartered Company of Guipuzcoa (Caracas) a monopoly of the American trade. The shareholders in these mercantilist monopolies usually became rich. The Ostend Company, for example, paid its investors 137 percent interest in its first seven years (nearly 20 percent per annum) while serving the emperor's interests by reviving the port of Ostend, stimulating Belgian business, and bringing Austria closer to self-sufficiency.

The mercantilist practice of creating chartered companies with protected privileges applied to much manufacturing in Europe. The French monarchy, for example, held a state monopoly in tapestries and porcelain, high-quality manufactures that could be profitably traded abroad. Prussia created a state tobacco monopoly and Russia held a state salt monopoly. Many countries followed the Dutch example by chartering a national bank similar to the Bank of Amsterdam (1609). These banks served many important functions, such as supplying the mint with metals for coinage or providing the trading monopolies with credit. Parliament chartered the Bank of England in 1694 and gave it the privilege of printing paper money in 1718. The French created a Banque royale in 1717; the Prussians, a Bank of Prussia in 1765.

Mercantilism encouraged manufacturing through direct aid and state regulation of business. Direct aid might include subsidies, interest-free loans, or bonuses to manufacturers. Regulation took the form of explicit legislation. The French monarchy, for example, regulated mines, iron works, glass factories, and paper mills. French law specified what type and quality of raw materials could be used, which equipment and manufacturing processes must be employed, and standards of quality for the finished product. The French then sent factory inspectors to visit manufacturing sites and guarantee compliance with the law. A decree of 1740 explained that this procedure would maintain the quality of French manufactures and protect French trade from "the negligence and bad faith of the manufacturers and merchants."

The most common mercantilist laws were tariffs and Navigation Acts. Tariffs placed taxes on goods entering a country to discourage imports (which produced an unfavorable balance of trade and drained gold from a country) and to protect domestic manufactures from foreign competition. Peter the Great of Russia, for example, levied heavy taxes on imported goods in 1724, even though Russians relied upon European manufactures and luxury goods. In 1767 Charles Townshend, the British chancellor of the exchequer (minister of finance), drafted one of the most famous tariffs of the Old Regime: a high tax on glass, lead, paints, paper, and tea imported into Britain's American colonies, which led to the Boston Tea Party. While governments imposed such restrictions upon imports, they simultaneously controlled trade through Navigation Acts requiring that goods shipped into (or out of) a country be carried only on ships of that country, or that goods shipped into a country's colonies must depart from a port in the mother country.

Mercantilism was not unchallenged. Governments in the early eighteenth century remained generally pleased with the successes of mercantilism (Britain and France both had very favorable balances of trade), but by midcentury mercantilist policies were drawing increasing criticism. A group of theorists called the Physiocrats began to suggest major changes in economic policy, and their ideas supplanted the mercantile system with the basic doctrines of capitalism. The Physiocrats, led by French theorist François Quesnay, believed in limiting the powers of government, especially the power to intervene in economic activities. Quesnay and others proposed the abolition of monopolies and special privileges, the replacement of these policies by open competition in an unregulated marketplace, and the substitution of free trade for tariffs. The physiocratic school did not win great influence with the monarchical governments of the eighteenth century, but it opened the debate that ended mercantilism. Adam Smith employed many of the ideas of the physiocrats in writing his *Inquiry into the Nature and Causes of the Wealth of Nations* (1776), the cornerstone of the new political economy.

## Global Economies: Slavery and the Triangular Trade

European world trade grew and changed significantly during the Old Regime. In the seventeenth century, global trade chiefly linked Europe to India and the Far East, as the chartering of the great east Indies companies indicates. This trade had originally concentrated upon the spice islands because great fortunes could be made by bringing pepper and other aromatic spices back to Europe, but the largest Asian trade evolved into competition for mainland markets such as India. During the seventeenth century, trade with the Indies might reward shareholders with more than 100 percent profits on their investment. By the eighteenth century, however, the focus of European global trade had turned to Africa and the Americas, where the profits had become larger.

The profits of eighteenth-century trade, and much of Europe's prosperity, depended upon slavery. The most profitable exploitation of slavery was a system called triangular trade, which began in the 1690s. The corners of this triangle were in Europe, Africa, and the Americas. British merchants were the most adept at the triangular trade, but it was practiced by slave traders from many countries. These slavers began their commerce by taking European manufactured goods (particularly textiles) to the western coast of Africa. These goods were sold or bartered for African slaves who were offered for sale by local African rulers, by rivals who had taken them prisoner, or by Moslem slave traders. In the second leg of the triangular trade, a ship filled with slaves made the Atlantic crossing to European colonies in the Americas. The British, for example, brought slaves to Caribbean colonies (where 85 percent of the population lived in slavery) such as Jamaica and Barbados or to the mainland colonies in North America (where 20 percent of the population

Illustration 17.6

/// **Slave Labor on a Caribbean Sugar Plantation.** The European craving for sugar created a growing slave economy in the West Indies. In this engraving, an armed white overseer (lower right) watches sugar making from harvesting sugarcane (center left edge) to milling it (upper right) and compressing it in molds.

lived in slavery). African slaves were then sold to plantation owners, and the revenue was used to buy the agricultural goods (chiefly tobacco in North America and sugar in the Caribbean), which slave labor had produced. On the third leg of the triangle, these goods were returned to England, where they were sold at huge profits.

All European states with American colonies (including Holland and Denmark), and a few states without colonies (notably Prussia), participated in the slave trade. The French triangular trade sent textiles, jewelry, and hardware to west Africa; then shipped slaves to Saint Domingue (Haiti), Guadeloupe, and Martinique in the Caribbean; and finally brought sugar and coffee back to France. The French amplified the British system by reexporting sugar to the rest of continental Europe. That sugar was the commodity upon which the Caribbean slave economy rested (see illustration 17.6). Sugarcane was not cultivated in Europe, and sugar was not yet extracted from beets. Slave-produced sugar from America sustained a growing European love of sweets. The European addiction to sugar cost humanity dearly: During the century 1690–1790, one African died for every ton of sugar shipped to Europe. When the consumption of Caribbean sugar reached its peak in 1801, the cost had become one dead slave to provide the sugar for every 250 consumers in Britain.

The scale of the slave trade was immense (see table 17.5). The British Board of Trade estimated in 1709 that British colonies needed twenty-five thousand additional slaves each year—four thousand for Barbados, five thousand for North America, and twelve thousand for Jamaica. When Britain obtained

the *Asiento*, the contract for supplying slaves to Spanish America, in 1713, English slave traders brought an additional five thousand slaves for Spanish colonies. The French delivered only four thousand slaves per year in the early eighteenth century, but that figure rose to an average of thirty-seven thousand slaves per year by the 1780s. Britain and France alone sold approximately 3.5 million African slaves in the Americas during the eighteenth century. An average of 10 percent to 20 percent of the slaves died during an Atlantic crossing (50 percent to 75 percent on voyages when scurvy or amoebic dysentery broke out on the ship), so the number of African slaves initially taken was closer to four million. Adding the Portuguese, Dutch, Danish, and Prussian slave trade, the grand total probably surpasses five million Africans. The demand for slaves was so high because the average life expectancy of a Caribbean slave was seven years after arrival.

During the eighteenth century, signs were evident that this economy would also change. Moral revulsion with slavery began to create antislavery opinion, both in Europe and the Americas. An American, Samuel Sewall, published an antislavery tract, *The Selling of Joseph*, as early as 1700. Two Portuguese Jesuits who served in Brazil, Jorge Benci and Giovanni Andreoni, published works in Europe attacking slavery. By 1727 the Society of Friends (widely known as the Quakers) had begun an abolitionist crusade. The moral arguments against slavery made slow progress because they faced powerful economic arguments that slavery was essential for both the colonial and the home economies. The Portuguese example illustrates both the progress and its slowness.

## TABLE 17.5
### Estimated Slave Population of European Colonies in the Americas, 1770

| Region | Total population | Slave population | Percentage in slavery |
|---|---|---|---|
| Spanish colonies | 12,144,000 | 290,000 | 2.4 |
|   Mainland | 12,000,000 | 240,000 | 2.0 |
|   Caribbean | 144,000 | 50,000 | 34.7 |
| British colonies | 2,600,000 | 878,000 | 33.8 |
|   Mainland | 2,100,000 | 450,000 | 21.4 |
|   Caribbean | 500,000 | 428,000 | 85.6 |
| Portuguese Brazil | 2,000,000 | 700,000 | 35.0 |
| French Caribbean | 430,000 | 379,000 | 88.1 |
| Dutch Caribbean | 90,000 | 75,000 | 83.3 |
| Danish Caribbean | 25,000 | 18,000 | 35.0 |
| Total, Mainland colonies | 16,100,000 | 1,390,000 | 8.6 |
| Total, Caribbean islands | 1,189,000 | 950,000 | 79.9 |

Source: Adapted from data in Robin Blackburn, *The Overthrow of Colonial Slavery, 1776–1848* (London: Verso, 1988), p. 5.

Royal decrees abolished the slavery of American Indians (1755) and Asians (1758), then freed any African slave brought into Portugal (1761), and finally emancipated all African slaves held in Portugal (1773). But these decrees permitted the continuance of the slave trade and the perpetuation of African slavery in the Portuguese colony of Brazil, where it continued until 1888.

# CHAPTER 18

# DAILY LIFE IN THE OLD REGIME

## CHAPTER OUTLINE

For most Europeans, the basic conditions of life in the eighteenth century had changed little since the agricultural revolution of Neolithic times. Chapter 18 describes those conditions and shows in dramatic terms how life at the end of the Old Regime differed from that of the present day. It begins by exploring the basic relationships between people and their environment, including the density of population in Europe and the barriers to speedy travel and communication. The chapter then examines the life of ordinary people, beginning with its most striking feature: low life expectancy. The factors that help to explain that high level of mortality, especially inadequate diet and the prevalence of epidemic disease, are then discussed. Finally, the life cycle of those who survived infancy is considered, including such topics as the dangers of childbirth; the Old Regime's understanding of childhood; and its attitudes toward marriage, the family, sexuality, and reproduction.

## People and Space: Population Density, Travel, and Communication

The majority of the people who lived in Europe during the Old Regime never saw a great city or even a town of twenty-five thousand people. Most stayed within a few miles of their home village and the neighboring market town. Studies of birth and death records show that more than 90 percent of the population of the eighteenth century died in the same region where they were born, passing their lives amid relatively few people. Powerful countries and great cities of the eighteenth century were small by twentieth-century standards (see population tables in chapter 17). Great Britain numbered an estimated 6.4 million people in 1700 (less than the state of Georgia today) and Vienna held 114,000 (roughly the size of Fullerton, California, or Tallahassee, Florida). People at the start of the twenty-first century are also accustomed to life in densely concentrated populations. New York City has a population density of more than fifty-five thousand people per square mile, and Maryland has a population density of nearly five hundred people per square mile. The eighteenth century did not know such crowding: Great Britain had a population density of fifty-five people per square mile; Sweden, six (see table 18.1).

## ✠ TABLE 18.1 ✠
### European Population Density

Population density is measured by the number of people per square mile.

| Country | Population density in 1700 | Population density in the 1990s |
| --- | --- | --- |
| Dutch republic (Netherlands) | 119 | 959 |
| Italian states (Italy) | 112 | 499 |
| German states (Germany) | 98 | 588 |
| France | 92 | 275 |
| Great Britain | 55 | 616 |
| Spain | 38 | 201 |
| Sweden | 6 | 50 |

Source: Jack Babuscio and Richard M. Dunn, eds., *European Political Facts, 1648–1789* (London: Macmillian, 1984), pp. 335–53; and *The World Almanac and Book of Facts 1995* (Mahwah, N.J.: World Almanac Books, 1994), pp. 740–839.

Life in a rural world of sparse population was also shaped by the difficulty of travel and communication. The upper classes enjoyed a life of relative mobility that included such pleasures as owning homes in both town and country or taking a "grand tour" of historic cities in Europe. Journeymen who sought experience in their trade, agricultural laborers who were obliged to migrate with seasonal harvests, and peasants who were conscripted into the army were all exceptions in a world of limited mobility. Geographic obstacles, poor roads, weather, and bandits made travel slow and risky. For most people, the pace of travel was walking beside a mule or ox-drawn cart. Only well-to-do people traveled on horseback, fewer still in horse-drawn carriages (see illustration 18.1). In 1705 the twenty-year-old Johann Sebastian Bach wished to hear the greatest organist of that era perform; Bach left his work for two weeks and walked two hundred miles to hear good music.

Travelers were at the mercy of the weather, which often rendered roads impassable because of flooding, mud, or snow. The upkeep of roads and bridges varied greatly. Governments maintained a few post roads, but other roads depended upon the conscription of local labor. An English law of 1691, for example, simply required each parish to maintain the local roads and bridges; if upkeep were poor, the government fined the parish. Brigands also hindered travel. These bandits might become heroes to the peasants who protected them as rebels against authority and as benefactors of the poor, much as Robin Hood is regarded in English

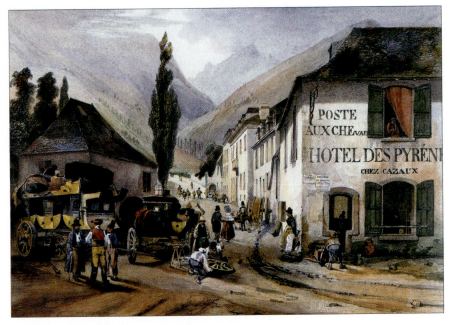

**Illustration 18.1**

✠ **Coach Travel.** Horse-drawn carriages and coaches remained the primary form of public transportation in Europe before the railroad age of the nineteenth century. Postal service, business, and government all relied upon a network of highways, stables, and coaching inns. In this illustration, travelers in the Pyrenees wait at a coaching station and hotel while a wheel is repaired.

folklore, but they made travel risky for the few who could afford it.

The fastest travel, for both people and goods, was often by water. Most cities had grown along rivers and coasts. Paris received the grain that sustained it by barges on the Seine; the timber that heated the city was floated down the river. The great transportation projects of the Old Regime were canals connecting these rivers. Travel on the open seas was normally fast, but it depended on fair weather. A voyager might be in England four hours after leaving France or trapped in port for days. If oceanic travel were involved, delays could reach remarkable lengths. In 1747 the electors of Portsmouth, England, selected Captain Edward Legge of the Royal Navy to represent them in Parliament; Legge, whose command had taken him to the Americas, had died eighty-seven days before his election but the news had not yet arrived in Portsmouth.

Travel and communication were agonizingly slow by twenty-first-century standards. In 1734 the coach trip between Edinburgh and London (372 miles) took twelve days; the royal mail along that route required forty-eight hours of constant travel by relay riders. The commercial leaders of Venice could send correspondence to Rome (more than 250 miles) in three to four days, if conditions were favorable; messages to Moscow (more than twelve hundred miles) required about four weeks. When King Louis XV of France died in 1774, this urgent news was rushed to the capitals of Europe via the fastest couriers: It arrived in Vienna and Rome three days later; Berlin, four days; and St. Petersburg, six days.

## Life Expectancy in the Old Regime

The living conditions of the average person during the Old Regime holds little appeal for people accustomed to twenty-first-century conveniences. A famous writer of the mid-eighteenth century, Samuel Johnson, described the life of the masses as "little to be enjoyed and much to be endured." The most dramatic illustration of Johnson's point is life expectancy data. Although the figures vary by social class or region, their message is grim. For everyone born during the Old Regime, the average age at death was close to thirty. Demographic studies of northern France at the end of the seventeenth century found that the average age at death was twenty. Data for Sweden in 1755 give an average life of thirty-three. A comprehensive study of villages in southern

England found a range between thirty-five and forty-five. These numbers are misleading because of infant mortality, but they contain many truths about life in the past.

Short life expectancy meant that few people knew their grandparents. Research on a village in central England found that a population of four hundred included only one instance of three generations alive in the same family. A study of Russian demography found more shocking results: Between 20 and 30 percent of all serfs under age fifteen had already lost both parents. Similarly, when the French philosopher Denis Diderot in 1759 returned to the village of his birth at age forty-six, he found that not a single person whom he knew from childhood had survived. Life expectancy was significantly higher for the rich than for the poor. Those who could afford fuel for winter fires, warm clothing, a superior diet, or multiple residences reduced many risks. The rich lived an estimated ten years longer than the average in most regions and seventeen years longer than the poor.

## Disease and the Biological Old Regime

Life expectancy averages were low because infant mortality was high, and death rates remained high throughout childhood. The study of northern France found that one-third of all children died each year and only 58 percent reached age fifteen. However, for those who survived infancy, life expectancy rose significantly. In a few healthier regions, especially where agriculture was strong, the people who lived through the terrors of childhood disease could expect to live nearly fifty more years.

The explanation for the shocking death rates and life expectancy figures of the Old Regime has been called the biological old regime, which suggests the natural restrictions created by chronic undernourishment, periodic famine, and unchecked disease. The first fact of existence in the eighteenth century was the probability of death from an infectious disease. Natural catastrophes (such as the Lisbon earthquake of 1755, which killed thirty thousand people) or the human violence of wartime (such as the battle of Blenheim in 1704, which took more than fifty thousand casualties in a single day) were terrible, but more people died from diseases. People who had the good fortune to survive natural and human catastrophe rarely died from heart disease or cancer, the great killers of the early twenty-

## TABLE 18.2

### The Causes of Death in the Eighteenth Century Compared with the Twentieth Century

| | Deaths in Edinburgh in 1740 | | Deaths in the United States in the 1990s | |
|------|-----------------------------------|------------|-------------------------|------------|
| Rank | Cause | Percentage | Cause | Percentage |
| 1 | Consumption (tuberculosis) | 22.4 | Heart disease | 32.6 |
| 2 | Smallpox | 22.1 | Cancer | 23.4 |
| 3 | Fevers (including typhus and typhoid) | 13.0 | Stroke | 6.6 |
| 4 | Old age | 8.2 | Pulmonary condition | 4.5 |
| 5 | Measles | 8.1 | Accident | 3.9 |

Source: Data for 1740 from John D. Post, *Food Shortage, Climatic Variability, and Epidemic Disease in Preindustrial Europe* (Ithaca, N.Y.: Cornell University Press, 1988), p. 241; data for the United States from *The World Almanac and Book of Facts 1995* (Mahwah, N.J.: World Almanac Books, 1994), p. 959.

first century. An examination of the 1740 death records for Edinburgh, for example, finds that the leading causes of death that year were tuberculosis and smallpox, which accounted for nearly half of all deaths (see table 18.2).

Some diseases were pandemic: The germs that spread them circulated throughout Europe at all times. The bacteria that attacked the lungs and caused tuberculosis (called consumption in the eighteenth century) were one such universal risk. Other diseases were endemic: They were a constant threat, but only in certain regions. Malaria, a febrile disease transmitted by mosquitoes, was endemic to warmer regions, especially where swamps or marshes were found. Rome and Venice were still in malarial regions in 1750; when Napoleon's army marched into Italy in 1796, his soldiers began to die from malaria before a single shot had been fired.

The most frightening diseases have always been epidemic diseases—waves of infection that periodically passed through a region. The worst epidemic disease of the Old Regime was smallpox. An epidemic of 1707 killed 36 percent of the population of Iceland. London lost three thousand people to smallpox in 1710, then experienced five more epidemics between 1719 and 1746. An epidemic decimated Berlin in 1740; another killed 6 percent of the population of Rome in 1746. Social historians have estimated that 95 percent of the population contracted smallpox, and 15 percent of all deaths in the eighteenth century can be attributed to it. Those who survived smallpox were immune thereafter, so it chiefly killed the young, accounting for one-third of all childhood deaths. In the eighty years between

1695 and 1775, smallpox killed a queen of England, a king of Austria, a king of Spain, a tsar of Russia, a queen of Sweden, and a king of France. Smallpox ravaged the Habsburgs, the royal family of Austria, and completely changed the history of their dynasty. Between 1654 and 1763, the disease killed nine immediate members of the royal family, causing the succession to the throne to shift four times. The death of Joseph I in 1711 cost the Habsburgs their claim to the throne of Spain, which would have gone to his younger brother Charles. When Charles accepted the Austrian throne, the Spanish crown (which he could not hold simultaneously) passed to a branch of the French royal family. The accession of Charles to the Austrian throne also meant that his daughter, Maria Theresa, would ultimately inherit it—an event that led to years of war.

Although smallpox was the greatest scourge of the eighteenth century, signs of a healthier future were evident. The Chinese and the Turks had already learned the benefits of intentionally infecting children with a mild case of smallpox to make them immune to the disease. A prominent English woman, Lady Mary Wortley Montagu, learned of the Turkish method of inoculating the young in 1717, and after it succeeded on her son, she became the first European champion of the procedure (see document 18.1). Inoculation (performed by opening a vein and introducing the disease) won acceptance slowly, often through royal patronage. Empress Maria Theresa had her family inoculated after she saw four of her children die of smallpox. Catherine the Great followed suit in 1768. But inoculation killed some people, and many feared it. The French outlawed the procedure in 1762, and the Vatican taught acceptance

## ❖ DOCUMENT 18.1 ❖

# Mary Montagu: The Turkish Smallpox Inoculation

*Lady Mary Wortley Montagu (1689–1762) was the wife of the British ambassador to the Ottoman Empire. While living in Constantinople, she observed the Turkish practice of inoculating children with small amounts of smallpox and was amazed at the Turkish ability to prevent the disease. The following excerpts are from a letter to a friend in which Montagu explains her discovery.*

Mary Montagu to Sarah Chiswell, 1 April 1717:

I am going to tell you a thing that I am sure will make you wish yourself here. The smallpox, so fatal and so general amonst us, is here entirely harmless [because of] the invention of "engrafting" (which is the term they give it). There is a set of old women who make it their business to perform the operation. Every autumn in the month of September, when the great heat is abated, people send to one another to know if any of their family has a mind to have the smallpox. They make parties for this purpose, and when they are met (commonly 15 or 16 together), the old woman comes with a nutshell full of the matter of the best sort of smallpox [the fluid from a smallpox infection] and asks what veins you please to have opened. She immediately rips open that which you offer to her with a large needle (which gives no more pain than a common scratch) and puts into the vein as much venom as can lie upon the head of her needle, and after binds up the little wound with a hollow bit of shell, and in this manner opens four or five veins. . . .

The children, or young patients, play together all the rest of the day and are in perfect health till the eighth day. Then the fever begins to seize them and they keep to their beds for two days, very seldom three days. They have very rarely above 20 or 30 [smallpox sores] on their faces, which never leave marks, and in eight days time they are as well as before their illness. . . .

Every year thousands undergo this operation . . . [and] there is no example of any one that has died of it. You may believe I am very well satisfied of the safety of the experiment since I intend to try it on my dear little son. I am a patriot enough to take pains to bring this useful invention into fashion in England. . . .

Montagu, Mary Wortley. *The Complete Letters of Lady Mary Wortley Montagu*, ed. Robert Halsband. 3 vols. Oxford, England: Clarendon Press, 1965.

---

of the disease as a "visitation of divine will." Nonetheless, the death of Louis XV led to the inoculation of his three sons.

While smallpox devastated all levels of society, some epidemic diseases chiefly killed the poor. Typhus, spread by the bite of body lice, was common in squalid urban housing, jails, and army camps. Typhoid fever, transmitted by contaminated food or water, was equally at home in the unsanitary homes that peasants shared with their animals.

The most famous epidemic disease in European history was the bubonic plague, the Black Death that killed millions of people in the fourteenth century. The plague, introduced by fleas borne on rodents, no longer ravaged Europe, but it killed tens of thousands in the eighteenth century and evoked a special cultural terror. Between 1708 and 1713, the plague spread from Poland across central and northern Europe. Half the city of Danzig died, and the death rate was only slightly lower in Prague, Copenhagen, and Stockholm. Another epidemic spread from Russia in 1719. It reached the port of Marseilles in 1720, and forty thousand people perished. Russia experienced another epidemic in 1771, killing fifty-seven thousand people in Moscow alone.

## Public Health before the Germ Theory

Ignorance and poverty compounded the dangers of the biological old regime. The germ theory of disease transmission—that invisible microorganisms such as bacteria and viruses spread diseases—had been suggested centuries earlier, but governments, scientists, and churches dismissed this theory until the late nineteenth century. Instead, the dominant theory was the miasma theory of contagion, holding that diseases spring from rotting matter in the earth. Acceptance of the miasma theory perpetuated dangerous conditions. Europeans did not understand the dangers of unsanitary housing, including royal palaces. Louis XIV's palace at Versailles was perhaps the greatest architectural ornament of an epoch, but human excrement accumulated in the corners and corridors of Versailles, just as it accumulated in dung-heaps alongside peasant cottages. One of the keenest observers of that age, the duke de Saint-Simon, noted that even the royal apartments at Versailles opened out "over the privies and other dark and evil smelling places."

The great cities of Europe were filthy. Few had more than rudimentary sewer systems. Gradually, enlightened monarchs realized that they must clean their capitals, as King Charles III (Don Carlos) ordered for Madrid in 1761. This Spanish decree required all households to install piping on their property to carry solid waste to a sewage pit, ordered the construction of tiled channels in the streets to carry liquid wastes, and committed the state to clean public places. Such public policies significantly improved urban sanitation, but they were partial steps, as the Spanish decree recognized, "until such time as it be possible to construct the underground sewage system." The worst sanitation was often found in public institutions. The standard French army barracks of the eighteenth century had rooms measuring sixteen feet by eighteen feet; each room accommodated thirteen to fifteen soldiers, sharing four or five beds and innumerable diseases. Prisons were worse yet.

Another dangerous characteristic of Old Regime housing was a lack of sufficient heat. During the eighteenth century the climatic condition known as the Little Ice Age persisted, with average temperatures a few degrees lower than the twentieth century experienced. Winters were longer and harder, summers and growing seasons were shorter. Glaciers advanced in the north, and timberlines receded on mountains. In European homes, the heat provided by open fires was so inadequate that even nobles saw their inkwells and wine freeze in severe weather. Among the urban poor, where many families occupied unheated rooms in the basement or attic, the chief source of warmth was body heat generated by the entire family sleeping together. Some town dwellers tried heating their garrets by burning coal, charcoal, or peat in open braziers, without chimneys or ventilation, creating a grim duel between freezing cold and poisonous air. Peasants found warmth by bringing their livestock indoors and sleeping with the animals, exacerbating the spread of disease.

In a world lacking a scientific explanation of epidemic disease, religious teaching exercised great influence over public health standards. Churches offered solace to the afflicted, but they also offered another explanation of disease: It was the scourge of God. This theory of disease, like the miasma theory, contributed to the inattention to public health. Many churches organized religious processions and ceremonies of expia-

tion in hopes of divine cures. Unfortunately, such public assemblies often spread disease by bringing healthy people into contact with the infected. Processions and ceremonies also prevented effective measures because they persuaded churches to oppose quarantines. Churches were not alone; merchants in most towns joined them in fighting quarantines.

## Medicine and the Biological Old Regime

Most Europeans during the Old Regime never received medical attention from trained physicians. Few doctors were found in rural areas. Peasants relied on folk medicine, consulted unlicensed healers, or allowed illness to run its course. Many town dwellers received their medical advice from apothecaries (druggists). The propertied classes could consult trained physicians, although this was often a mixed blessing. Many medical doctors were quacks, and even the educated often had minimal training. The best medical training in Europe was found at the University of Leiden in Holland, where Hermann Boerhaave pioneered clinical instruction at bedsides, and similar programs were created at the College of Physicians in Edinburgh in 1681 and in Vienna in 1745. Yet Jean-Paul Marat, one of the leaders of the French Revolution, received a medical degree at Edinburgh after staying there for a few weeks during the summer of 1774.

Medical science practiced curative medicine, following traditions that seem barbaric to later centuries. The pharmacopeia of medicinal preparations still favored ingredients such as unicorn's horn (ivory was usually used), crushed lice, incinerated toad, or ground shoe leather. One cherished medication, highly praised in the first edition of the *Encyclopaedia Britannica* (1771), was usnea, the moss scraped from the scalp of prisoners hung in irons. The medical profession also favored treatments such as bleeding (the intentional drawing of blood from a sick person) or purging the ill with emetics and enemas. The argument for bleeding was derived from the observation that if blood were drawn, the body temperature dropped. Because fevers accompanied most diseases, bleeding was employed to reduce the fever. This treatment often hastened death. King Louis XV of France was virtually bled to death by his physicians in 1774, although officially he succumbed to smallpox. As Baron von Leibnitz, a distinguished German philosopher and scientist, observed, "[A] great doctor kills more people than a great general."

The treatment given to King Charles II of England in 1685, as he died of an apparent embolism (a clot in

Illustration 18.2

💮 An Eighteenth-Century Hospital. This scene of a German hospital ward in Hamburg depicts many aspects of pre-modern medicine. Note the mixture of patients with all afflictions, the nonsterile conditions, the amputation of a leg on a conscious patient, the arrival of a daily ration of bread, and the administration of the last rites to a patient.

an artery), shows the state of learned medicine. A team of a dozen physicians first drew a pint of blood from his right arm. They then cut open his right shoulder and cupped it with a vacuum jar to draw more blood. Charles then received an emetic to induce vomiting, followed by a purgative, then a second purgative. Next came an enema of antimony and herbs, followed by a second enema and a third purgative. Physicians then shaved the king's head, blistered it with heated glass, intentionally broke the blisters, and smeared a powder into the wounds (to "strengthen his brain"). Next came a plaster of pitch and pigeon excrement. Death was probably a relief to the tortured patient.

Hospitals were also scarce in the Old Regime. Nearly half of the counties of England contained no hospital in 1710; by 1800, there were still only four thousand hospital beds in the entire country, half of them in London. Avoiding hospitals was generally safer in any case (see illustration 18.2). These institutions had typically been founded by monastic orders as refuges for the destitute sick, and most of them were still operated by churches in the eighteenth century. There were a few specialized hospitals (the first children's clinic was founded at London in 1779), and most hospitals typically mixed together poor patients with a variety of diseases that spread inside the hospital. Patients received a minimal diet and rudimentary care but little medical treatment. The history of surgery is even more frightening. In many regions, surgeons were still members of the barbers' guild. Because eighteenth-century physicians did not believe in the germ theory

of disease transmission, surgeons often cut people in squalid surroundings with no thought for basic cleanliness of their hands or their instruments. Without antisepsis, gangrene (then called hospital putrefaction) was a common result of surgery. No general anesthetics were available, so surgeons operated upon a fully conscious patient.

In these circumstances, opium became a favorite medication of well-to-do patients. It was typically taken as a tincture with alcohol known as laudanum, and it was available from apothecaries without a prescription. Laudanum drugged the patient, and it often addicted survivors to opium, but it reduced suffering. Many famous figures of the eighteenth and nineteenth centuries died, as did the artist Sir Joshua Reynolds in 1792, "all but speechless from laudanum."

◆

## Subsistence Diet and the Biological Old Regime

The second critical feature of the biological old regime was a dangerously inadequate food supply. In all regions of Europe, much of the population lived with chronic undernourishment, dreading the possibility of famine. A subsistence diet (one that barely met the minimum needed to sustain life) weakened the immune system, making people more vulnerable to contracting diseases and less able to withstand their ravages. Diet was thus a major factor in the Old Regime's high mortality rates and short life expectancies.

Most of Europe lived chiefly on starches. The biblical description of bread as "the staff of life" was true, and most people obtained 50 percent to 75 percent of their total calories from bread. Interruptions of the grain supply meant suffering and death. In good times, a peasant family ate several pounds of bread a day, up to three pounds per capita; in lean times, they might share one pound of bread. A study of the food supply in Belgium has shown that the nation consumed a per capita average of one-and-a-quarter pounds of cereal grains per day. A study of eastern Prussia has shown that the adult population lived on nearly three pounds of grain per day. Peasant labors there received their entire annual wages in starches; the quantity ranged from thirty-two bushels of grain (1694) to twenty-five bushels of grain and one of peas (1760).

Bread made from wheat was costly because wheat yielded few grains harvested per grain sown. As a result, peasants lived on coarser, but bountiful, grains. Their heavy, dark bread normally came from rye and barley. In some poor areas, such as Scotland, oats were the staple grain. To save valuable fuel, many villages baked bread in large loaves once a month, or even once a season. This created a hard bread that had to be broken with a hammer and soaked in liquid before it could be eaten. For variety, cereals could be mixed with liquid (usually water) without baking to create a porridge or gruel.

Supplements to the monotonous diet of starches varied from region to region, but meat was a rarity. In a world without canning or refrigeration, meat was consumed only when livestock were slaughtered, in a salted or smoked form of preservation, or in a rancid condition. A study of the food supply in Rome in the 1750s has shown that the average daily consumption of meat amounted to slightly more than two ounces. For the lower classes, that meant a few ounces of sausage or dried meat per week. In that same decade, Romans consumed bread at an average varying between one and two pounds per day. Fruits and fresh vegetables were seasonal and typically limited to those regions where they were cultivated. A fresh orange was thus a luxury to most Europeans, and a fresh pineapple was rare and expensive. Occasional dairy products plus some cooking fats and oils (chiefly lard in northern Europe and olive oil in the south) brought urban diets close to twenty-five hundred calories per day in good times. A study of Parisian workers in 1780 found that adult males engaged in physical labor averaged two thousand calories per day, mostly from bread. (Figures of thirty-five hundred to four thousand are common today

among males doing physical labor.) Urban workers often spent more than half of their wages for food, even when they just ate bread. A study of Berlin at the end of the eighteenth century showed that a working-class family might spend more than 70 percent of its income on food (see table 18.3). Peasants ate only the few vegetables grown in kitchen gardens that they could afford to keep out of grain production.

Beverages varied regionally. In many places, the water was unhealthy to drink and peasants avoided it without knowing the scientific explanation of their fears. Southern Europe produced and consumed large quantities of wine, and beer could be made anywhere that grain was grown. In 1777 King Frederick the Great of Prussia urged his people to drink beer, stating that he had been raised on it and believed that a nation "nourished on beer" could be "depended on to endure hardships." Such beers were often dark, thick, and heavy. When Benjamin Franklin arrived in England, he called the beer "as black as bull's blood and as thick as mustard."

Wine and beer were consumed as staples of the diet, and peasants and urban workers alike derived

### TABLE 18.3
### Food in the Budget of a Berlin Worker's Family, c. 1800

| Expense | Percentage |
| --- | --- |
| Food | |
| Bread | 45 |
| Other vegetable products | 12 |
| Animal products (meat and dairy) | 15 |
| Beverages | 2 |
| Total food | 74 |
| Nonfood | |
| Housing | 14 |
| Heating, lighting | 7 |
| Clothing, other expenses | 6 |
| Total Nonfood | 27 |

Note: Figures exceed 100 percent because of rounding.

Source: From data in Fernand Braudel, *The Structures of Everyday Life* (New York, N.Y.: Harper and Row, 1981), p. 132.

Illustration 18.3

🏇 **Alcohol.** Alcohol consumption rates during the eighteenth century were higher than they are today. Drinking to excess was one behavior pattern that cut across social classes, from the taverns in poor districts advertising "dead drunk for a penny" to the falling down drunks of the upper class depicted in Hogarth's "A Midnight Modern Conversation" here. Note that smoking pipes is nearly universal and that women are excluded from this event. See also the chamber pot in the lower right corner.

much of their calories and carbohydrates from them, partly because few nonalcoholic choices were available. The consumption of milk depended upon the local economy. Beverages infused in water (coffee, tea, cocoa) became popular in European cities when global trading made them affordable. The Spanish introduced the drinking of chocolate (which was only a beverage until the nineteenth century) but it long remained a costly drink. Coffee drinking was brought to Europe from the Middle East, and it became a great vogue after 1650, producing numerous urban coffeehouses. But infused beverages never replaced wine and beer in the diet. Some governments feared that coffeehouses were centers of subversion and restricted them more than the taverns. Others worried about the mercantilist implications of coffee and tea imports. English coffee imports, for example, sextupled between 1700 and 1785, leading the government to tax tea and coffee. The king of Sweden issued an edict denouncing coffee in 1746, and when that failed to control the national addiction, he decreed total prohibition in 1756. Coffee smuggling produced such criminal problems, however, that the king legalized the drink again in 1766 and collected a heavy excise tax on it. Even with such popularity, infused beverages did not curtail the remarkable rate of alcohol consumption (see illustration 18.3). In addition to wines and beer, eighteenth-century England drank an enormous amount of gin. Only a steep gin tax in 1736 and vigorous enforcement of a Tippling Act of 1751 reduced consumption from 8.5 million gallons of gin per year to 2.1 million gallons during the 1750s.

## The Columbian Exchange and the European Diet

The most important changes in the European diet of the Old Regime resulted from the gradual adoption of foods found in the Americas. In a reciprocal Columbian exchange of plants and animals unknown on the other continent, Europe and America both acquired new foods. No Italian tomato sauce or French fried potato existed before the Columbian exchange because the tomato and potato were plants native to the Americas and unknown in Europe. Similarly, the Columbian exchange introduced maize (American corn), peanuts, many peppers and beans, and cacao to Europe. The Americas had no wheat fields, grapevines, or melon patches; no horses, sheep, cattle, pigs, goats, or burros. In the second stage of this exchange, European plants established in the Americas began to flourish and yield exportation to Europe. The most historic example of this was the establishment of the sugarcane plantations in the Caribbean, where slave labor made sugar commonly available in Europe for the first time, but at a horrific human price (see map 18.1).

Europe's first benefit from the Columbian exchange came from the potato, which changed diets in the eighteenth century. The Spanish imported the potato in the sixteenth century after finding the Incas cultivating it in Peru, but Europeans initially refused to eat it because folk wisdom considered tubers dangerous. Churches opposed the potato because the Bible did not mention it. Potatoes, however, offer the tremendous advantage of yielding more calories per acre than grains do. In much of northern Europe, especially in western Ireland

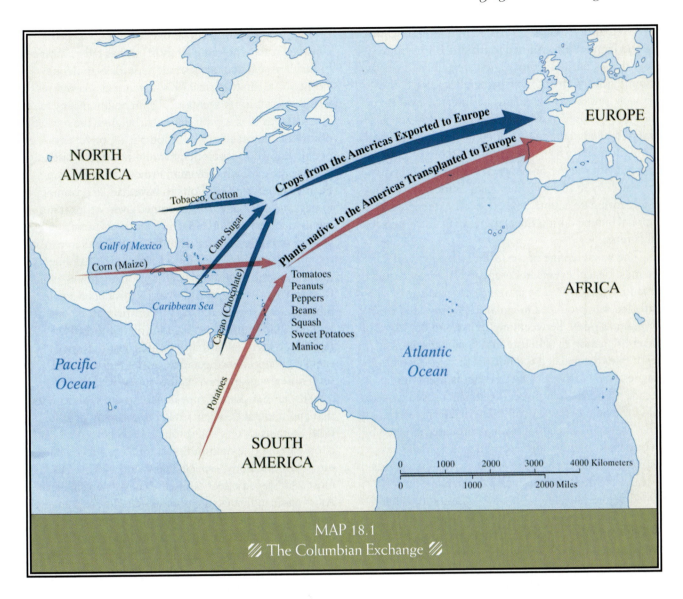

MAP 18.1
The Columbian Exchange

and northern Germany, short and rainy summer seasons severely limited the crops that could be grown and the population that could be supported. Irish peasants discovered that just one acre of potatoes, planted in soil that was poor for grains, could support a full family. German peasants learned that they could grow potatoes in their fallow fields during crop rotation, then discovered an acre of potatoes could feed as many people as four acres of the rye that they traditionally planted. Peasants soon found another of the advantages of the potato: It could be left in the ground all winter without harvesting it. Ripe grain must be harvested and stored, becoming an easy target for civilian tax collectors or military requisitioners. Potatoes could be left in the ground until the day they were eaten, thereby providing peasants with much greater security. The steady growth of German population compared with France during the eighteenth and nineteenth centuries (with

tremendous historic implications) is partly the result of this peasant decision and the educational work of agronomists such as Antoine Parmentier, who showed its merits in his *Treatise on the Uses of the Potato*. Just as the potato changed the history of Germany and Ireland, the introduction of maize changed other regions. Historians of the Balkans credit the nutritional advantages of maize with the population increase and better health that facilitated the Serbian and Greek struggles for independence.

## Famine in the Old Regime

Even after the introduction of the potato and maize, much of Europe lived on a subsistence diet. In bad times, the result was catastrophic. Famines, usually the result of two consecutive bad harvests, produced starvation. In such times, peasants ate their seed grain or harvested unripe grain and roasted it, prolonging both life and famine. They turned to making bread from ground chestnuts or acorns. They ate grass and weeds, cats and dogs, rodents, even human flesh. Such disasters were not rare. The records of Tuscany show that the three-hundred-year period between 1450 and 1750 included one hundred years of famine and sixteen years of bountiful harvests. Agriculture was more successful in England, but the period between 1660 and 1740 saw one bad harvest in every four years. France, an agriculturally fortunate country, experienced sixteen years of national famine during the eighteenth century, plus local famines.

The worst famine of the Old Regime, and one of the most deadly events in European history, occurred in Finland in 1696–97. The extreme cold weather of the Little Ice Age produced in Finland a summer too short for grain to ripen. Between one-fourth and one-third of the entire nation died before that famine passed—a death rate that equaled the horrors of the bubonic plague. The weather produced other famines in that decade. In northern Europe, excess rain caused crops to rot in the field before ripening. In Mediterranean Europe, especially in central Spain, a drought followed by an onslaught of grasshoppers produced a similar catastrophe. Hunger also followed seasonal fluctuations. In lean years, the previous year's grain might be consumed before July, when the new grain could be harvested. Late spring and early summer were consequently dangerous times when the food supply had political significance. Winter posed special threats for city dwellers. If the rivers and canals froze, the barges that supplied the cities could not move, and the water-powered mills could not grind flour.

Food supplies were such a concern in the Old Regime that marriage contracts and wills commonly provided food pensions. These pensions were intended to protect a wife or aged relatives by guaranteeing an annual supply of food. An examination of these pensions in southern France has shown that most of the food to be provided was in cereal grains. The typical form was a lifetime annuity intended to provide a supplement; the average grain given in wills provided fewer than fourteen hundred calories per day.

## Diet, Disease, and Appearance

Malnutrition, famine, and disease were manifested in human appearance. A diet so reliant on starches meant that people were short compared with later standards. For example, the average adult male of the eighteenth

century stood slightly above five feet tall. Napoleon, ridiculed today for being so short, was as tall as most of his soldiers. Meticulous records kept for Napoleon's Army of Italy in the late 1790s (a victorious army) reveal that conscripts averaged 5'2" in height. Many famous figures of the era had similar heights: the notorious Marquis de Sade stood 5'3". Conversely, people known for their height were not tall by later standards. A French diplomat, Prince Talleyrand, appears in letters and memoirs to have had an advantage in negotiations because he "loomed over" other statesmen. Talleyrand stood 5'8". The kings of Prussia recruited peasants considered to be "giants" to serve in the royal guards at Potsdam; a height of 6'0" defined a giant. Extreme height did occur in some families. The Russian royal family, the Romanovs, produced some monarchs nearly seven feet tall. For the masses, diet limited their height. The superior diet of the aristocracy made them taller than peasants, just as it gave them a greater life expectancy; aristocrats explained such differences by their natural superiority as a caste.

Just as diet shaped appearance, so did disease. Vitamin and mineral deficiencies led to a variety of afflictions, such as rickets and scrofula. Rickets marked people with bone deformities; scrofula produced hard tumors on the body, especially under the chin. The most widespread effect of disease came from smallpox. As its name indicates, the disease often left pockmarks on its victims, the result of scratching the sores, which itched terribly. Because 95 percent of the population contracted smallpox, pockmarked faces were common. The noted Anglo-Irish dramatist Oliver Goldsmith described this in 1760:

> Lo, the smallpox with horrid glare
> Levelled its terrors at the fair;
> And, rifling every youthful grace,
> Left but the remnant of a face.

Smallpox and diseases that discolored the skin such as jaundice, which left a yellow complexion, explain the eighteenth-century popularity of heavy makeup and artificial "beauty marks" (which could cover a pockmark) in the fashions of the wealthy. Other fashion trends of the age originated in poor public health. The vogue for wigs and powdered hair for men and women alike derived in part from infestation by lice. Head lice could be controlled by shaving the head and wearing a wig.

Dental disease marked people with missing or dark, rotting teeth. The absence of sugar in the diet delayed tooth decay, but oral hygiene scarcely existed because

## ✕ TABLE 18.4 ✕

### A Comparison of Life Cycles

| Life cycle characteristic | Sweden, 1778–82 | United States (1990 census) |
|---|---|---|
| Annual birthrate | 34.5 per 1,000 population | 15.6 per 1,000 population |
| Infant mortality (age 0–1) | 211.6 deaths per 1,000 live births | 9.2 deaths per 1,000 live births |
| Life expectancy at birth | | |
|   Male | 36 years | 71.8 years |
|   Female | 39 years | 78.8 years |
| Life expectancy at age 1 | | |
|   Male | 44 years longer (45 total years) | 72.3 years longer (73.3 total) |
|   Female | 46 years longer (47 total years) | 78.9 years longer (79.9 total) |
| Life expectancy at age 50 | | |
|   Male | 19 years longer (69 total years) | 26.7 years longer (76.7 total) |
|   Female | 20 years longer (70 total years) | 31.6 years longer (81.6 total) |
| Population distribution | ages 0–14 = 31.9% | ages 0–19 = 28.9% |
| | ages 15–64 = 63.2% | ages 20–64 = 58.7% |
| | ages 65+ = 4.9% | ages 65+ = 12.5% |
| Annual death rate | 25.9 deaths per 1,000 population | 8.5 deaths per 1,000 population |

Source: Swedish data from Carlo M. Cipolla, *Before the Industrial Revolution* (New York, N.Y.: Norton, 1976), pp. 286–87; U.S. data from *The World Almanac and Book of Fact, 1995* (Mahwah, N.J.: World Almanac Book, 1994), p. 957; and *Information Please Almanac, Atlas, and Yearbook 1994* (Boston, Mass.: Houghton Mifflin Co., 1993), pp. 829, 848, 850–52.

people did not know that bacteria caused their intense toothaches. Medical wisdom held that the pain came from a worm that bored into teeth. Anton van Leeuwenhoek, the Dutch naturalist who invented the microscope, had seen bacteria in dental tartar in the late seventeenth century, and Pierre Fauchard, a French physician considered the founder of modern dentistry, had denounced the worm theory, but their science did not persuade their colleagues. For brave urban dwellers, barber-surgeons offered the painful process of extraction. A simple, but excruciating, method involved inserting a whole peppercorn into a large cavity; the pepper expanded until the tooth shattered, facilitating extraction. More often, dental surgeons gripped the unanesthetized patient's head with their knees and used tongs to shake the tooth loose. Whether or not one faced such dreadful pain, dental disease left most people with only a partial set of teeth by their forties.

◆

## The Life Cycle: Birth

Consideration of the basic conditions of life provides a fundamental perspective on any period of the past. So-

cial historians also use another set of perspectives to examine the history of daily life: an examination of the life cycle from birth to old age (see table 18.4). Few experiences better illustrate the perils of the Old Regime than the process of entering it. Pregnancy and birth were extremely dangerous for mother and child. Malnutrition and poor prenatal care caused a high rate of miscarriages, stillbirths, and deformities. Childbirth was still an experience without anesthesia or antisepsis. The greatest menace to the mother was puerperal fever (child-bed fever), an acute infection of the genital tract resulting from the absence of aseptic methods. This disease swept Europe, particularly the few "laying-in" hospitals for women. An epidemic of puerperal fever in 1773 was so severe that folk memories in northern Italy recalled that not a single pregnant woman survived. Common diseases, such as rickets (from vitamin deficiency), made deliveries difficult and caused bone deformities in babies. No adequate treatment was available for hemorrhaging, which could cause death by bleeding or slower death by gangrene. Few ways existed to lower the risks of difficult deliveries. Surgical birth by a cesarean section gave the mother one chance in a thousand of surviving. Attempts to deliver a baby by using large forceps saved many lives but often produced horrifying injuries to the newborn or hemorrhaging in the mother. A delicate balance thus existed between the deep pride in bearing children and a deep fear of doing so. One of the most noted women of letters in early modern Europe, Madame de Sévigné, advised her daughter of two rules for survival: "Don't get pregnant and don't catch smallpox."

The established churches, backed by the medical profession, preached acceptance of the pain of childbirth by teaching that it represented the divine will. The explanation lay in the Bible. For "the sin of Eve" in succumbing to Satan and being "the devil's gateway" to Adam, God punished all women with the words: "I will greatly multiply thy sorrow and thy conception; in sorrow thou shalt bring forth children" (Gen. 3:16). Even when the means to diminish the pain of childbirth became available, this argument sustained opposition to it.

## The Life Cycle: Infancy and Childhood

Statistics show that surviving the first year of infancy was more difficult than surviving birth. All across Europe, between 20 percent and 30 percent of the babies born died before their first birthday (see table 18.5). An additional one-fourth of all children did not live to be eight, meaning that approximately half of the population died in infancy or early childhood. A noted scientist of the 1760s, Michael Lomonosev, calculated that half of the infants born in Russia died before the age of three. So frightful was this toll that many families did not name a child until its first birthday; others gave a cherished family name to more than one child in the hope that one of them would carry it to adulthood. Johann Sebastian Bach fathered twenty children in two marriages and reckoned himself fortunate that ten lived into adulthood. The greatest historian of the century, Edward Gibbon, was the only child of seven in his family to survive infancy.

The newborn were acutely vulnerable to the biological old regime. Intestinal infections killed many in the first months. Unheated housing claimed more. Epidemic diseases killed more infants and young children than adults because some diseases, such as measles and smallpox, left surviving adults immune to them. The dangers touched all social classes. Madame de Montespan, the mistress of King Louis XIV of France, had seven children with him; three were born crippled or deformed, three others died in childhood, and one reached adulthood in good health.

## TABLE 18.5
### Infant Mortality in the Eighteenth Century

Percentages represent deaths before the first birthday; they do not include stillbirths.

| Country | Period | Percentage of deaths before age 1 |
|---|---|---|
| England | pre-1750 | 18.7 |
| | 1740–90 | 16.1 |
| | 1780–1820 | 12.2 |
| France | pre-1750 | 25.2 |
| | 1740–90 | 21.3 |
| | 1780–1820 | 19.5 |
| German states | pre-1750 | 15.4 |
| | 1740–90 | 38.8 |
| | 1780–1820 | 23.6 |
| Spain | pre-1750 | 28.1 |
| | 1740–90 | 27.3 |
| | 1780–1820 | 22.0 |
| Sweden | pre-1750 | n.a. |
| | 1740–90 | 22.5 |
| | 1780–1820 | 18.7 |
| United States | 1995 | 0.8 |

Source: European data from Michael W. Flinn, *The European Demographic System, 1500–1820* (Baltimore, Md.: Johns Hopkins University Press, 1971), p.92; U.S. data from *The World Almanac and Book of Facts, 1997* (Mahwah, N.J.: World Almanac Books, 1996), p. 962. n.a. = Not available.

Eighteenth-century parents commonly killed unwanted infants (daughters more often than sons) before diseases did. Infanticide—frequently by smothering the baby, usually by abandoning an infant to the elements—has a long history in Western culture. The mythical founders of Rome depicted on many emblems of that city, Romulus and Remus, were abandoned infants who were raised by a wolf; the newborn Moses was abandoned to his fate on the Nile. Infanticide did not constitute murder in eighteenth-century British law (it was manslaughter) if done by the mother before the baby reached age one. In France, however, where infanticide was more common, Louis XIV ordered capital punishment for it, although few mothers were ever executed. The frequency of infanticide provoked instructions that all priests read the law in church in 1707 and again in 1731. A study of police records has found that more than 10 percent of all women arrested in Paris in the eighteenth century were nonetheless charged with infanticide. In central and eastern Europe, many mid-wives were also "killing nurses" who murdered babies for their parents.

A slightly more humane reaction to unwanted babies was to abandon them in public places in the hope that someone else would care for them. That happened so often that cities established hospitals for foundlings. The practice had begun at Rome in the late Middle Ages when Pope Innocent III found that he could seldom cross the Tiber River without seeing babies thrown into it. Paris established its foundling hospital in 1670. Thomas Coram opened the foundling hospital at London in 1739 because he could not endure the frequency with which he saw dying babies lying in the gutters and dead ones thrown onto dung-heaps. The London Foundling Hospital could scarcely handle all of the city's abandoned babies: In 1758, twenty-three hundred foundlings (under age one) were found abandoned in the streets of London. Abandonment increased in periods of famine and when the illegitimate birthrate rose (as it did during the eighteenth century). French data show that the famine of 1693–94 doubled the abandonment of children at Paris and tripled it at Lyon. Abandonments at Paris grew to an annual average of five thousand in the late eighteenth century, with a peak of 7,676 in 1772, which is a rate of twenty-one babies abandoned every day. Studies of foundlings in Italy have shown that 11 percent to 15 percent of all babies born at Milan between 1700 and 1729 were abandoned each year; at Venice, the figures ranged between 8 percent and 9 percent in 1756–87 (see illustration 18.4).

The abandonment of children at this rate overwhelmed the ability of church or state to help. With 390,000 abandonments at the Foundling Hospital of Paris between 1640 and 1789—with thirty abandonments on the single night of April 20, 1720—the prospects for these children were bleak. Finances were inadequate, partly because churches feared that fine facilities might encourage illicit sexuality, so the conditions in foundling homes stayed grim. Whereas 50 percent of the general population survived childhood, only 10 percent of abandoned children reached age ten. The infant (before age one) death rates for foundling homes in the late eighteenth century were 90 percent in Dublin, 80 percent in Paris, and only 52 percent in London (where infants were farmed out to wet nurses). Of 37,600 children admitted to the Foundling Hospital of Moscow between 1766 and 1786, more than thirty thousand died. The prospects of the survivors were poor, but one noteworthy exception was Jean d'Alembert, a mathematician and coeditor of the

**Illustration 18.4**

**Abandoned Children.** One of the most common forms of population control in the eighteenth century (and continuing through the nineteenth century) was the abandonment of newborn children. Because so many babies were left at churches and public buildings, and a shocking number were left to die outdoors, governments created foundling homes where babies could be abandoned. To encourage mothers to use foundling homes, many of them (such as this one in Italy) built revolving doors to the outside, allowing women to leave a baby without being seen or speaking to anyone.

*Encyclopédie*, who was discovered in a pine box at a Parisian church in 1717.

Young children were often separated from their parents for long periods of time. Immediately after birth, many were sent to wet nurses, foster mothers whose occupation was the breast feeding of infants. The studies of France show that more than 95 percent of the babies born in Paris in 1780 were nursed commercially, 75 percent going to wet nurses in the provinces. As breast feeding normally lasted twelve to eighteen months, only wealthy parents (who could hire a live-in wet nurse) or the poorest might see their infant children with any frequency. The great French novelist Honoré de Balzac was born in 1799 and immediately dispatched to a wet nurse; he bitterly remembered his infancy as being "neglected by my family for three years."

Infant care by rural wet nurses was not universal. It was most common in towns and cities, especially in social classes that could afford the service. The poor usually fed infants gruel—flour mixed in milk, or bread crumbs in water—by dipping a finger into it and letting the baby suck the finger. Upper-class families in England, France, and northern Italy chose wet-nursing; fewer did so in Central Europe. Every king of France, starting with Louis IX (Saint Louis), was nurtured by a succession of royal nurses; but mothers in the Habsburg royal family, including the empress Maria Theresa, were expected to nurse their own children.

Separation from parents remained a feature of life for young children after their weaning. Both Catholicism, which perceived early childhood as an age of innocence, and Protestantism, which held children to be marked by original sin, advocated the separation of the child from the corrupt world of adults. This meant the segregation of children from many parental activities as well as the segregation of boys and girls. Many extreme cases existed among the aristocracy. The Marquis de Lafayette, the hero of the American revolution, lost his father in infancy; his mother left the infant at the family's provincial estate while she resided in Paris and visited him during a brief vacation once a year. Balzac went straight from his wet nurse to a Catholic boarding school where the Oratorian Brothers allowed him no vacations and his mother visited him twice in six years.

Family structures were changing in early modern times, but most children grew up in patriarchal families. Modern parent-child relationships, with more emphasis upon affection than upon discipline, were beginning to appear. However, most children still lived with the emotional detachment of both parents and the stern discipline of a father whose authority had the sanction of law. The Russian novelist Sergei Aksakov recalled that, when his mother had rocked her infant daughter to sleep in the 1780s, relatives rebuked her for showing "such exaggerated love," which they considered contrary to good parenting and "a crime against God." Children in many countries heard the words of Martin Luther repeated: "I would rather have a dead son than a disobedient one."

Childhood had not yet become the distinct and separate phase of life that it later became. In many ways, children passed directly from a few years of infancy into treatment as virtual adults. Middle- and upper-class boys of the eighteenth century made a direct transition from wearing the gowns and frocks of infancy into wearing the pants and panoply (such as swords) of adulthood. This rite of passage, when boys went from the care of women to the care of men, normally happened at approximately age seven. European traditions and laws varied, but in most economic, legal, and religious ways, boys became adults between seven and fourteen. Peasant children became members of the household economy almost immediately, assuming such duties as tending to chickens or hoeing the kitchen garden. In the towns, a child seeking to learn a craft and enter a guild might begin with an apprenticeship (with another family) as early as age seven. Children of the elite were turned over to tutors or governesses, or they were sent away to receive their education at boarding schools. Children of all classes began to become adults by law at age seven. In English law seven was the adult age at which a child could be flogged or executed; the Spanish Inquisition withheld adult interrogation until age thirteen. Twelve was the most common adult age at which children could consent to marriage or to sexual relations.

Tradition and law treated girls differently from boys. In the Roman law tradition, prevalent across southern Europe and influential in most countries, girls never became adults in the legal sense of obtaining rights in their own name. Instead, a patriarchal social order expected fathers to exercise the rights of their daughters until they married; women's legal rights then passed to their husbands. Most legal systems contained other double standards for young men and women. The earliest age for sexual consent was typically younger for a girl than for a boy, although standards of respectable behavior were much stricter for young women than for young men. Economic considerations also created double standards: A family might send a daughter to the convent, for example, instead of providing her with a dowry.

## The Life Cycle: Marriage and the Family

Despite the early ages at which children entered the adult world, marriage was normally postponed until later in life. Royal or noble children might sometimes be married in childhood for political or economic reasons, but most of the population married at significantly older ages than those common in the twentieth century.

A study of seventeenth-century marriages in southern England has found that the average age of men at a first marriage was nearly twenty-seven; their brides averaged 23.6 years of age. Research on England in the eighteenth century shows that the age at marriage rose further. In rural Europe, men married at twenty-seven to twenty-eight years, women at twenty-five to twenty-six. Many variations were hidden within such averages. The most notable is the unique situation of firstborn sons. They would inherit the property, which would make marriage economically feasible and earlier marriage to perpetuate the family line desirable.

Most people had to postpone marriage until they could afford it. This typically meant waiting until they could acquire the property or position that would support a family. Younger sons often could not marry before age thirty. The average age at first marriage of all males among the nobility of Milan was 33.4 years in the period 1700–49; their wives averaged 21.2 years. Daughters might not marry until they had accumulated a dowry—land or money for the well-to-do, household goods in the lower classes—which would favor the economic circumstances of a family. Given the constraints of a limited life expectancy and a meager income, many people experienced marriage for only a few years, and others never married. A study of marriage patterns in eighteenth-century England suggests that 25 percent of the younger sons in well-to-do families never married. Another historian has estimated that fully 10 percent of the population of Europe was comprised of unmarried adult women. For the middle class of Geneva in 1700, 26 percent of the women who died at over age fifty had never married; the study of the Milanese nobility found that 35 percent of the women never married.

The pattern of selecting a mate changed somewhat during the eighteenth century. Earlier habits in which parents arranged marriages for children (especially if property was involved) were changing, and a prospective couple frequently claimed the right to veto their parents' arrangement. Although properted families often insisted upon arranged marriages (see document 18.2), it became more common during the eighteenth century for men and women to select their own partners, contingent upon parental vetoes. Marriages based upon the interests of the entire family line, and marriages based upon an economic alliance, yielded with increasing frequency to marriages based upon romantic attachment. However, marriage contracts remained common.

After a long scholarly debate, historians now agree that Western civilization had no single pattern of family structure, but a variety of arrangements. The most common pattern was not a large family, across more than two generations, living together; instead, the most frequent arrangement was the nuclear family in which parents and their children lived together (see illustration 18.5). Extended families, characterized by coresidence with grandparents or other kin—known by many names, such as the *Ganze Hauz* in German tradition or the *zadruga* in eastern Europe—were atypical. A study of British families has found that 70 percent were comprised of two generations, 24 percent were single-generation families, and only 6 percent fit the extended family pattern. Studies of southern and eastern Europe have found more complex, extended families. In Russia, 60 percent of peasant families fit this multigenerational pattern; in parts of Italy, 74 percent.

Family size also varied widely. Everywhere except France (where smaller families first became the norm), the average number of children born per family usually ranged between five and seven. Yet such averages hide many large families. For example, Brissot de Warville, a leader of the French Revolution, was born to a family of innkeepers who had seventeen children, seven of whom survived infancy; Mayer and Gutele Rothschild, whose sons created the House of Rothschild banks, had twenty children, ten of whom survived. The founder of Methodism, John Wesley, was the fifteenth of nineteen children. Households might also contain other people, such as servants, apprentices, and lodgers. Studies of eighteenth-century families in different regions have found a range between 13 percent and 50 percent of them containing servants. A survey of London in the 1690s estimated that 20 percent of the population lodged with nonrelatives.

One of the foremost characteristics of the early modern family was patriarchal authority. This trait was diminishing somewhat in western Europe in the eighteenth century, but it remained strong. A father exercised authority over the children; a husband exercised authority over his wife. A woman vowed to obey her husband in the wedding ceremony, following the Christian tradition based on the words of Saint Paul: "Wives, submit yourself unto your own husbands, as unto the Lord." The idea of masculine authority in marriage was deeply imbedded in popular culture. As a character in a play by Henry Fielding says to his wife, "Your person is mine. I bought it lawfully in church." The civil law in most countries enforced such patriarchy. In the greatest summary of English law, Sir William Blackstone's *Commentaries on the Law of England* (1765–69), this was stated

◆ DOCUMENT 18.2 ◆

## Arranged Marriages in the Eighteenth Century

*Richard Brinsley Sheridan (1751–1816) was an Irish dramatist who wrote comedies of manners for the London stage. One of his greatest plays, The Rivals (1775), made fun of the tradition of arranged marriages. In it, a wealthy aristocratic father, Sir Anthony Absolute, arranges a suitable marriage for his son, Captain Jack Absolute (who is in love with a beautiful young woman), without consulting him. In the following scene, Captain Absolute tries to refuse the marriage and Sir Anthony tries first to bribe him and then to coerce him.*

*Absolute:* Now, Jack, I am sensible that the income of your commission, and what I have hitherto allowed you, is but a small pittance for a lad of your spirit.

*Captain Jack:* Sir, you are very good.

*Absolute:* And it is my wish, while yet I live, to have my boy make some figure in the world. I have resolved, therefore, to fix you at once in a noble independence.

*Captain Jack:* Sir, your kindness overpowers me—such generosity makes the gratitude of reason more lively than the sensations even of filial affection.

*Absolute:* I am glad you are so sensible of my attention—and you shall be master of a large estate in a few weeks.

*Captain Jack:* Let my future life, sir, speak my gratitude; I cannot express the sense I have of your munificence. —Yet, sir, I presume you would not wish me to quit the army?

*Absolute:* Oh, that shall be as your wife chooses.

*Captain Jack:* My wife, sir!

*Absolute:* Ay, ay, settle that between you—settle that between you.

*Captain Jack:* A wife, sir, did you say?

*Absolute:* Ay, a wife—why, did I not mention her before?

*Captain Jack:* Not a word of her sir.

*Absolute:* Odd, so! I mus'n't forget her though. —Yes, Jack, the independence I was talking of is by marriage—the fortune is saddled with a wife—but I suppose that makes no difference.

*Captain Jack:* Sir! Sir! You amaze me!

*Absolute:* Why, what the devil's the matter with you, fool? Just now you were all gratitude and duty.

*Captain Jack:* I was, sir—you talked of independence and a fortune, but not a word of a wife!

*Absolute:* Why—what difference does that make? Odds life, sir! If you had an estate, you must take it with the live stock on it, as it stands!

*Captain Jack:* If my happiness is to be the price, I must beg leave to decline the purchase. Pray, sir, who is the lady?

*Absolute:* What's that to you, sir? Come, give me your promise to love, and to marry her directly.

*Captain Jack:* Sure, sir, this is not very reasonable. . . . You must excuse me, sir, if I tell you, once for all, that in this point I cannot obey you. . . .

*Absolute:* Sir, I won't hear a word—not one word! . . .

*Captain Jack:* What, sir, promise to link myself to some mass of ugliness!

*Absolute:* Zounds! Sirrah! The lady shall be as ugly as I choose: she shall have a hump on each shoulder; she shall be as crooked as the crescent; her one eye shall roll like the bull's in Cox's Museum; she shall have a skin like a mummy, and the beard of a Jew—she shall be all this, sirrah! Yet I will make you ogle her all day, and sit up all night to write sonnets on her beauty.

Sheridan, Richard. *The Rivals.* London: 1775.

bluntly: "The husband and wife are one, and the husband is that one." A compilation of Prussian law under Frederick the Great, the Frederician Code of 1750, was similar: "The husband is master of his own household, and head of his family. And as the wife enters into it of her own accord, she is in some measure subject to his power" (see document 18.3).

Few ways of dissolving a marriage existed in the eighteenth century. In Catholic countries, the church considered marriage a sacrament and neither civil marriage by the state nor legal divorce existed. The church permitted a few annulments, exclusively for the upper classes. Protestant countries accepted the principle of divorce on the grounds of adultery or desertion, but divorces remained rare, even when legalized. Geneva, the home of Calvinism, recorded an average of one divorce per year during the eighteenth century. Divorce became possible in Britain in the late seventeenth century, but it required an individual act of parliament for each divorce. Between 1670 and 1750, a total of 17 parliamentary divorces were granted in Britain, although the number rose to 114 between 1750 and 1799. Almost all divorces were granted to men of prominent social position who wished to marry again, normally to produce heirs.

**Illustration 18.5**

⁊⁊ **The Family.** Attitudes toward the family were beginning to change in the eighteenth century, as indicated by the increasing habit of the wealthy to commission paintings of the entire family. Note the subtle symbolism of this painting: The wife sits at the center of the family, with the husband somewhat in the background of family matters. The father relates to his eldest son and heir, but he is turned slightly away from his other children.

Where arranged marriages were still common, the alternative to divorce was separation. The civil laws in many countries provided for contracts of separation, by which the maintenance of both partners was guaranteed. Simpler alternatives to divorce evolved in the lower classes, such as desertion or bigamy. The most extraordinary method, practiced in parts of England well into the nineteenth century, was the custom of wife sale. Such sales were generally by mutual consent, but they nonetheless resembled cattle sales. Though the Old Regime was fundamentally an era of indissoluble, life-long marriage, this did not mean a couple lived together for long periods of time. Given an average age at marriage in the mid-twenties and an average age at death (for people who reached the mid-twenties) in the mid-forties, the typical marriage lasted for approximately twenty years.

## The Life Cycle: Sexuality and Reproduction

Ignorance about human sexuality was widespread during the Old Regime, and remarkable theories still circulated about human reproduction, many of them restatements of sex manuals inherited from the ancient world. Medical science held that the loss of one ounce of semen debilitated a man's body the same way that the loss of forty ounces of blood would and that a woman's menstruation could turn meat rancid. Consequently, physicians advised people to avoid all sex during the summer because a man's body would become dried out. Similarly, people were taught to avoid sex during menstruation because a child conceived then would be born diseased.

There were other disincentives to sexual activity. The strongest came from Christian moral injunctions. A Christian tradition regarding sex as unclean and chastity as a spiritual ideal, dated from St. Paul and St. Jerome. Only marital intercourse was permissible, and then only for procreation; other sexual activity was understood to be a violation of the Seventh Commandment forbidding adultery. Good Christians were expected to practice chastity during pregnancy (when conception was impossible), on Sundays, and during the forty days of Lent.

In addition to the disincentives of medical advice and Christian teaching, poor health, uncleanliness, fears of pregnancy or venereal disease, and repressive laws also restricted behavior. Laws varied regionally, but most sexual practices were against the law. Ecclesiastical courts in Catholic countries tried priests and laity alike for sexual offenses; secular courts acted in a similar manner in Protestant countries. A study of the archdiocesan tribunal at Cambrai (France) has found that 38 percent of the moral offenses involved unmarried sex, 32 percent adultery, and 11 percent incest. Punishments ranged from death (for incest between father and daughter) to providing a dowry (for seducing a virgin). Bestiality merited burning to death, for both the human and the animal. Pornography (broadly defined) often led to imprisonment, as it did for Denis Diderot. Sentences to a public pillory, a flogging, or being paraded through the streets with a shaved head were also common.

Homosexuality was universally illegal before the French Revolution (which legalized consenting adult relationships in 1791). Assessing its frequency is diffi-

## ❖ DOCUMENT 18.3 ❖

# The Husband in the Law: The Frederician Code of 1750

*The Frederician Code, adopted in Prussia under Frederick the Great, was one of the greatest efforts to reorganize a legal system during the eighteenth century. It was chiefly the work of the minister of justice, Samuel von Cocceji. He relied on the principles of Roman law but also drew ideas from Germanic customary law and from the "enlightened" philosophy of the eighteenth century. The following excerpt states the legal rights of a husband; a similar section specified the rights and privileges of the wife, without curtailing the authority of husband.*

1. As the domestic society, or family, is formed by the union of the husband and wife, we are to begin with enumerating the advantages and rights which result from this union.

2. The husband is by nature the head of his family. To be convinced of this, it is sufficient to consider, that the wife leaves her family to join herself to that of her husband; that she enters into his household, and into the habitation of which he is the master, with intention to have children by him to perpetuate the family.

3. Hence it follows, judging by the sole light of reason, that the husband is master of his own household, and head of his family. And as the wife enters into it of her own accord, she is in some measure subject to his power; whence flow several rights and privileges, which belong to the husband with regard to his wife.

For, (1) the husband has the liberty of prescribing laws and rules in his household, which the wife is to observe.

(2) If the wife be defective in her duty to her husband, and refuse to be subject, he is authorized to reduce her to her duty in a reasonable manner.

(3) The wife is bound, according to her quality, to assist her husband, to take upon her the care of the household affairs, according to his condition.

(4) The husband has the power over the wife's body, and she cannot refuse him the conjugal duty.

(5) As the husband and wife have promised not to leave each other during their lives, but to share the good and evil which may happen to them; the wife cannot, under pretext, for example, that her husband has lost his reason, leave him, without obtaining permission from the judge.

(6) For the same reason, the wife is obliged to follow her husband when he changes his habitation; unless, (a) it has been stipulated by the contract of marriage, or otherwise, that she shall not be bound to follow him if he should incline to settle elsewhere; or (b) unless it were for a crime that the husband changed his habitation, as if he had been banished from his country.

Bell, Susan G., and Offen, Karen M. eds. *Women, the Family, and Freedom: The Debate in Documents,* vol. 1. Stanford, Calif.: Stanford University Press, 1983.

---

cult. It had been a crime in England for centuries, normally punished by the pillory, and a public execution for homosexuality took place as late as 1772. Yet homosexuality was relatively open in England in the eighteenth century and gentlemen's clubs of homosexuals existed with impunity in London, though periodic arrests of sodomites (the term *homosexual* was not coined until the late nineteenth century) occurred, such as the police campaign of 1707. King Frederick William I of Prussia was horrified to discover that both of his sons—the future Frederick the Great and Prince Henry, whom the Continental Congress briefly considered as a constitutional king for the United States—were homosexuals. The double standard obscures the extent of lesbianism in the eighteenth century even more, but high society enjoyed widespread rumors about many prominent figures such as Queen Anne of England. Contemporary works such as Mary Wollstonecraft's

*Mary: A Fiction,* Diderot's *La Religieuse,* and Fielding's *The Female Husband* indicate that the subject was much discussed.

As the partial tolerance of homosexuality suggests, the eighteenth century was a period of comparatively relaxed sexual restrictions, especially compared with the more repressive sixteenth and seventeenth centuries. Some historians even describe the Old Regime as a period of sexual revolution. In Protestant countries, strict moral Puritanism weakened, and Catholicism repudiated its own version of Puritanism—Jansenism. In all countries, the ruling classes set an example of permissiveness. Most monarchs (who married for reasons of state, not for love) kept lovers, gently called favorites. Louis XV kept a small personal brothel and Catherine the Great had an equally long list of favorites. Augustus the Strong, king of Poland and elector of Saxony, fathered at least 365 children, only one of them legitimate.

The double standard remained a feature of the relaxed sexual standards. Tribunals assessing sex crimes typically gave harsher sentences to women, particularly for adultery. Women at the highest levels of society might act with some freedom if the legitimacy of heirs were certain. But European culture attached a value to female virginity and chastity and still associated a man's honor with the chastity of his female relations.

One of the foremost disincentives associated with eighteenth-century sexuality was the circulation of the venereal diseases (VD) syphilis and gonorrhea. These diseases, commonly called the pox, were rampant in the ruling classes and found in most of the royal families of Europe. Louis XIV, Louis XV, and Napoleon all had VD. Syphilis was not as fatal as when epidemics of it swept Europe in the fifteenth and sixteenth centuries, but it remained a debilitating disease. Gonorrhea was pandemic in urban Europe. The famous Venetian lover Giovanni Casanova contracted eleven cases of VD during his life although he survived until age seventy-three. James Boswell, the distinguished British writer, caught gonorrhea seventeen times. Physicians could provide only limited help; their favored cure was treatment with mercury, a dangerous poison.

Prostitution was one of the chief sources of the spread of venereal diseases. It was illegal but generally tolerated in public brothels. The open prostitution of the Middle Ages, with municipally operated (and even church-operated) brothels, no longer existed. Yet large numbers of prostitutes were found in all cities. King Frederick I of Prussia tried to end prostitution in Berlin by closing all brothels in 1690, causing an increase of prostitution practiced in taverns. When the Prussian government decided to tolerate brothels again, a survey of 1765 found that Berlin contained nearly nine thousand prostitutes in a population of approximately 120,000 people. The Parisian police estimated an even higher number of prostitutes there—between twenty thousand and thirty thousand, or one of every eight women of marriageable age. Even in the shadow of the Vatican, 2 percent of all adult women were officially registered prostitutes.

Draconian measures did not eliminate prostitution. The Austrian government sought to end it in Vienna in the 1720s with harsh treatment of prostitutes. After the failure of such punishments as the pillory or being made to sweep the streets with shaved heads, the government staged a public decapitation of a prostitute in 1723. Yet the empress Maria Theresa soon created a Chastity Commission to study the subject anew. Governments chose to control prostitution by limiting it to certain districts and keeping it off the streets or by reg-

istering prostitutes, thereby permitting some public health control and taxation. Governments were mostly concerned about the spread of disease (particularly to military garrisons) more than the condition of the women (frequently domestic servants who had been seduced or girls from the country who could not find employment) driven by economic necessity to prostitute themselves.

Another subject of social concern about eighteenth-century sexuality was the general increase in illegitimate births (see table 18.6). Illegitimacy had been relatively uncommon, particularly in rural areas, in the seventeenth century. The rate for rural France had been only 1 percent of all births. During the eighteenth century, and particularly after 1760, both illegitimate births and premarital conceptions increased significantly. The illegitimacy rate remained high because the practice of birth control was limited both by Christian moral injunctions and by slight knowledge of effective procedures. Tertullian had established the theological view of birth control in the third century, asserting that "to prevent a child being born is to commit homicide in advance." Religious opposition to birth control continued in the eighteenth century, even in Protestant Europe: It was the divine will that people "be fruitful and multiply." Despite Christian teaching, a significant percentage of the English upper classes and the general population of France practiced some forms of birth control in the eighteenth century, and both populations experienced a decline in their fertility rate compared with the rest of Europe. France had a birthrate of forty per one thousand population in the mid-eighteenth century, falling to thirty-three per one thousand at the end of the century, thirty per one thousand in some areas. Many people clearly had found economic advantages in smaller families and had chosen to put economic factors above religious ones.

Judging the extent to which knowledge about birth control circulated is difficult. Christianity offered one traditional method: abstinence. *Coitus interruptus* was practiced, but its extent is unknown. The French philosopher Jean-Jacques Rousseau discussed (with disapproval) that method of birth control ("cheating nature") in his *Discourse* of 1753 as well as many forms of nonreproductive sex, such as oral and manual sex. (Rousseau also fathered five illegitimate children and abandoned them to foundling homes.) Those who practiced birth control employed such methods. Condoms (made from animal membranes) had been virtually unknown in the seventeenth century but were available in late eighteenth-century London and Paris, although they were chiefly employed against VD, not

## TABLE 18.6
### Premarital Conception and Illegitimate Birth in the Old Regime

| Country | Period | Percentage of premarital conceptions | Percentage of illegitimate births |
|---|---|---|---|
| England | pre–1750 | 19.7 | 2.6 |
| | 1780–1820 | 34.5 | 5.9 |
| France | pre–1750 | 6.2 | 2.9 |
| | 1780–1820 | 13.7 | 4.7 |
| German states | pre–1750 | 13.8 | 2.5 |
| | 1780–1820 | 23.8 | 11.9 |
| Spain | pre–1750 | n.a. | 5.4 |
| | 1780–1820 | n.a. | 6.5 |
| United States | 1940 | n.a. | 3.5 |
| | 1990 | n.a. | 28.0 |

Sources: Data for the Old Regime from Michael W. Flinn, *The European Demographic System, 1500–1820* (Baltimore, Md.: Johns Hopkins University Press, 1971), p. 82; data for the United States from *Information Please Almanac Atlas and Yearbook 1989* (Boston, Mass.: Houghton Mifflin Co., 1989), p. 788 and 1994, p. 844.

for family planning. Knowledge about female means of control, such as douching, also began to circulate in that period.

Abortion was also used to terminate unwanted pregnancies during the Old Regime. A Christian tradition received from Aristotle and passed onward by Roman law held that a soul was implanted in the fetus at the time of "animation" or "the quickening." Though all abortions were illegal, both moral law and criminal law distinguished between those before and after "ensoulment." The means of attempting abortions were crude and dangerous. Folk knowledge circulated about supposed abortifacient drugs and vegetal or mineral poisons, however, and the learned reference work of the century, the French *Encyclopédie*, discussed them in detail.

### The Life Cycle: Old Age

Statistical averages showing the low life expectancies of the Old Regime should not produce the mistaken conclusion that older people were rare in the eighteenth century. Twenty percent of all newborns reached the age of fifty, and 10 percent lived until seventy. French demographic studies have found that, in the 1740s, 17 percent of men and 19 percent of women would reach age sixty; by the 1770s, this had risen to 24 percent for

men and 25 percent for women. The aged clearly represented a significant group in society. Once someone had survived to the age of fifty, his life expectancy was not greatly different than it would be in the twentieth century.

Thus, a large proportion of the powerful and famous individuals who are remembered from the eighteenth century had life spans typical of twentieth-century leaders. King Louis XIV of France lived to be seventy-seven (1638–1715); his successor, Louis XV, died at sixty-four (1710–74). The three Hanoverian kings of eighteenth-century England (George I, George II, and George III) died at an average age of seventy-five (sixty-seven, seventy-seven, and eighty-two, respectively). Empress Catherine II of Russia and King Frederick II of Prussia earned their appellation, "the Great," partly because they lived long enough to achieve greatness—Catherine died at sixty-seven, Frederick at seventy-four. And the eight popes of the eighteenth century, who were typically elected at an advanced age, died at an average age of nearly seventy-eight; four lived into their eighties. Similar life spans characterized many of the famous cultural figures of the Old Regime. Christopher Wren and Anton van Leeuwenhoek both lived into their nineties; Goethe, Goya, Kant, and Newton all lived into their eighties.

# SUGGESTED READINGS

◆◆◆◆◆◆◆◆◆◆◆◆◆◆◆◆◆◆◆◆◆◆

## Chapter 1

General histories of the ancient Near East include A. B. Knapp, *The History and Culture of Ancient Western Asia and Egypt* (1987), W. von Soden, *The Ancient Orient* (1994), and C. Burney, *The Ancient Near East* (1977).

On Mesopotamia, see A. L. Oppenheim, *Ancient Mesopotamia*, 2d. ed. (1977) and H. Crawford, *Sumer and the Sumerians* (1991). A leading authority on post-Sumerian Mesopotamia is H. W. F. Saggs. His works include *The Babylonians* (1995), *Everyday Life in Babylonia and Assyria* (1965), and *The Might That Was Assyria* (1984).

A general survey of the prehistoric world is provided by T. Champion, C. Gamble, S. Shennan, and A. Whittle, *Prehistoric Europe* (1984). The problem of human origins is discussed in R. Leakey, *The Making of Mankind* (1981) and in P. Mellars and C. Stringer, *The Human Revolution* (1989). M. Ehrenberg, *Women in Prehistory* (1989) and F. Dahlberg, ed., *Woman the Gatherer* (1981) describe the role of women in prehistoric society. For the Neolithic revolution, see N. Cohen, *The Food Crisis in Prehistory: Overpopulation and the Origins of Agriculture* (1977), G. Barker, *Prehistoric Farming in Europe* (1984), and A. Whittle, *Neolithic Europe: A Survey* (1985).

General surveys of ancient Egypt include C. Aldred, *The Egyptians* (1984), B. J. Kemp, *Ancient Egypt* (1989), and C. Hobson, *The World of the Pharaohs* (1987). An unusually rich literature also can be found on Egyptian social history. See B. G. Trigger, B. J. Kemp, D. O'Connor, and A. B. Lloyd, *Ancient Egypt, A Social History* (1983), G. Robins, *Women in Ancient Egypt* (1993), and J. White, *Everyday Life in Ancient Egypt* (1963). The best book on the pyramids is I. E. S. Edwards, *The Pyramids of Egypt*, rev. ed. (1974). On religion, see J. Cerney, *Ancient Egyptian Religion* (1979).

Several works deal with the other peoples of the eastern Mediterranean and Near East. G. Herm, *The Phoenicians: The Purple Empire of the Ancient World* (1975) emphasizes commerce and expansion, while the development of the alphabet is covered by D. Diringer, *The Alphabet* (1975).

Many histories of ancient Israel have been written. See the fundamental J. Bright, *A History of Israel*, 3d ed. (1981), J. M. Miller and J. H. Hayes, *A History of Ancient Israel and Judah* (1986), and M. Grant, *The History of Ancient Israel* (1984). Social history and institutions are covered by N. P. Lemche, *Ancient Israel: A New History of Israelite Society* (1988). The literature on religion is enormous, but the following are useful as general studies: Y. Kaufmann, *The Religion of Israel* (1960), H. Ringgren, *Israelite Religion* (1966), and D. R. Hillers, *Covenant: The History of a Biblical Idea* (1969).

## Chapter 2

J. B. Bury and R. Meiggs, *A History of Greece to the Death of Alexander the Great*, 4th ed. (1975) has held up well as the standard survey of Greek history, but N. G. L. Hammond, *A History of Greece to 322 B.C.*, 3d ed. (1986) is a venerable competitor.

On Minoan civilization, see S. Hood, *The Minoans: The Story of Bronze Age Crete* (1971). The best studies of Mycenaean Greece are L. W. Taylor, *The Mycenaeans*, rev. ed. (1983) and J. T. Hooker, *Mycenaean Greece* (1976), but several good surveys of early Greek history as a whole can be found, including M. I. Finley, *Early Greece: The Bronze and Archaic Ages*, 2d ed. (1982), and R. Drews, *The Coming of the Greeks* (1988), which describes the migrations. On Homer and the Homeric Age, see J. Griffin, *Homer* (1980). C. Starr, *The Economic and Social Growth of Early Greece, 800–500 B.C.* (1977) and C. Roebuck, *Economy and Society in the Early Greek World* (1984) are good on the early period. V. Hanson, *Warfare and Agriculture in Classical Greece* (1983) deals with hoplite warfare and and its purposes. Political development is described by W. G. Forest, *The Emergence of Greek Democracy* (1966). A. J. Graham, *Colony and Mother City in Ancient Greece*, rev. ed. (1984) describes the process of colonization.

W. Guthrie, *The Greeks and Their Gods* (1965) and W. Burkert, *Greek Religion* (1985) are general studies of Greek religious beliefs. The role of athletics in the Greek world is described by D. Sansone, *Greek Athletics and the Genesis of Sport* (1988).

Studies on politics are heavily weighted toward Athens. See A. Jones, *Athenian Democracy* (1975), and J. Ober, *The Athenian Revolution* (1996). R. Hopper, *Trade and Industry in Classical Greece* (1979) covers economic development. Social history, too, is based heavily on Athenian sources. See T. B. L. Webster, *Everyday Life in Classical Athens* (1969), and S. C. Humphreys, *The Family, Women, and Death* (1983). Slavery is covered in Y. Garlan, *Slavery in Ancient Greece* (1988). The best general work on Greek women is probably the early chapters of S. Pomeroy, *Goddesses, Whores, Wives, and Slaves* (1975), which also covers the Hellenistic and Roman periods. The complex issue of homosexuality is examined by K. Dover, *Greek Homosexuality* (1978) and E. Cantarella, *Bisexuality in the Ancient World* (1992).

The best studies of Sparta are P. Catledge, *Sparta and Laconia: A Regional History, 1300–362 B.C.* (1979) and W. Forrest, *A History of Sparta, 950–121 B.C.*, 2d ed. (1980).

Herodotus remains indispensible for the Persian War and for much else about the ancient world. A. Burn, *Persia and the Greeks: The Defense of the West*, rev. ed. (1984) is a fine modern study.

Any study of the Peloponnesian Wars must begin with Thucydides, but the modern works by D. Kagan are indispensable: *Outbreak of the Peloponnesian War* (1969), *The Archidamian War* (1974), *The Peace of Nicias and the Sicilian Expedition* (1981), and *The Fall of the Athenian Empire* (1987).

## Chapter 3

The standard survey of Greek literature is A. Lesky, *History of Greek Literature* (1966). For Greek drama, see A.W. Pickard-Cambridge, *The Dramatic Festivals of Athens*, 2d ed. (1968), and H.C. Baldry, *The Greek Tragic Theater* (1971). Studies on the development of historical writing include J. A. S. Evans, *Herodotus* (1982) and K. Dover, *Thucydides* (1973). Surveys of Greek art include M. Robertson, *A History of Greek Art*, 2 vols. (1975) and J. Boardman, *Greek Art* (1985) and A. W. Lawrence, *Greek Architecture*, rev. ed. (1983). W. K. C. Guthrie, *A History of Greek Philosophy*, 6 vols. (1962–81) is a comprehensive survey of the subject.

Substantial literature exists on politics after the Peloponnesian Wars. On Athens in the fourth century B.C., see J. Ober, *Mass and Elite in Democratic Athens* (1989) and J. Cargill, *The Second Athenian League* (1981); for Sparta, P. Cartledge, *Agesilaos and the Crisis of Sparta* (1987). The standard work on Thebes is J. Buckler, *The Theban Hegemony, 371–362 B.C.* (1980). For the rise of Macedon, see E. Borza, *In the Shadow of Olympus: The Emergence of Macedon* (1990), and R. Errington, *A History of Macedonia* (1990). The career of Philip II is covered in N. Hammond, *Philip of Macedon* (1994). Modern biographies of Alexander the Great include N. G. L. Hammond, *Alexander the Great* (1981), and Peter Green, *Alexander of Macedon* (1991).

The best general survey of Hellenistic civilization is probably F. W. Wallbank, *The Hellenistic World* (1993). Studies of individual kingdoms include N. G. L. Hammond and F. Wallbank, *A History of Macedonia*, vol. 3, 336–167 B.C. (1988), H. I. Bell, *Egypt from Alexander the Great to the Arab Conquest* (1948), and O. Morkholm, *Antiochus IV of Syria* (1966). B. Bar-Kochva, *The Seleucid Army* (1976) is the most current treatment of military affairs. The dislocation of the Greeks and their impact on Egypt is discussed in A. K. Bowman, *Egypt after the Pharaohs* (1986) and N. Lewis, *Greeks in Ptolemaic Egypt* (1986).

For Hellenistic social and economic history, begin with M. Rostovtzeff, *Social and Economic History of the Hellenistic World*, 3 vols., 2d ed. (1953), supplemented by M. I. Finley, *The Ancient Economy*, 2d ed. (1985). S. B. Pomeroy, *Women in Hellenistic Egypt* (1984) is a valuable study. For slavery, see the appropriate sections of W. L. Westerman, *The Slave Systems of Greek and Roman Antiquity* (1955).

Good surveys of Hellenistic higher culture include M. Hadas, *Hellenistic Culture: Fusion and Diffusion* (1959) and J. Onians, *Art and Thought in the Hellenistic Age* (1979). G. E. R. Lloyd, *Greek Science after Aristotle* (1973) is an outstanding survey. The best survey of Hellenistic art is J. J. Pollitt, *Art in the Hellenistic Age* (1986). A. A. Long, *Hellenistic Philosophy* (1974) is the standard survey in its field. L. Martin, *Hellenistic Religions: An Introduction* (1987) is a useful survey. Jewish resistance to hellenizing tendencies is discussed by V. Tcherikover, *Hellenistic Civilization and the Jews* (1959) and M. Hengel, *Judaism and Hellenism* (1974). B. Bar-Kochva, *Judas Maccabeus* (1988) deals with the Maccabean revolt.

## Chapter 4

The best surveys of Rome under the republic are H. H. Scullard, *History of the Roman World, 753–146 B.C.* (1978) and M. H. Crawford, *The Roman Republic*, 2d ed. (1993). For the Etruscans, see M. Pallottino, *The Etruscans*, rev. ed. (1975). Roman relations with and other early Italians are covered by J. C. Meyer, *Pre-Republican Rome* (1983). E. Salmon, *The Making of Roman Italy* (1985) examines Roman expansion in the peninsula. F. Adcock, *The Roman Art of War under the Republic*, rev. ed. (1963) describes the development of the Roman military system.

K. D. White, *Roman Farming* (1970) is a thorough treatment of this important subject. Many of the works on religious and social history cover both the republic and the empire; see J. Liebeschutz, *Continuity and Change in Roman Religion* (1979), J. Balsdon, *Life and Leisure in Ancient Rome* (1969), J. Balsdon, *Roman Women*, rev. ed. (1974), F. Dupont, *Daily Life in Ancient Rome* (1994), J. F. Gardner, *Women in Roman Law and Society* (1986), and S. Dixon, *The Roman Family* (1992). The struggle of the orders and the evolution of Roman law are covered by R. Mitchell, *Patricians and Plebians: The Origins of the Roman State* (1990), and H. Jolowicz and B. Nicholas, *Historical Introduction to Roman Law* (1972).

Roman expansion under the republic is described by R. M. Errington, *The Dawn of Empire: Rome's Rise to World Power* (1971), and W. V. Harris, *War and Imperialism in Republican Rome* (1979), while J. Lazenby, *Hannibal's War: A Military History of the Second Punic War* (1978) provides a detailed account of the most important of the Carthaginian wars. A broader treatment of the crisis is found in B. Caven, *The Punic Wars* (1980). The best works on Roman expansion in the east are E. S. Gruen, *The Hellenistic World and the Coming of Rome*, 2 vols. (1984) and A. N. Sherwin-White, *Roman Foreign Policy in the Near East* (1984). For Spain, see L. Curchin, *Roman Spain: Conquest and Assimilation* (1991). The Roman method of securing frontiers is dealt with by S. L. Dyson, *The Creation of the Roman Frontier* (1985).

## Chapter 5

The best general works on the crisis of the late republic are R. Syme, *The Roman Revolution*, rev. ed. (1960) and M. Beard and M. Crawford, *Rome and the Late Republic* (1985). For the underlying social crisis, see K. Hopkins, *Conquerors and Slaves* (1978), P. A. Brunt, *Social Conflicts in the Late Republic* (1971), and C. Nicolet, *The World of the Citizen in Republican Rome* (1980). D. Stockton, *The Gracchi* (1979) and A. H. Bernstein, *Tiberius Sempronius Gracchus: Tradition and Apostasy* (1978) are standard works on the reformers. A. Keaveney, *Sulla: The Last Republican* (1983) deals with a reformer of a different kind. A. Eckstein, *Senate and Generals* (1987) analyzes the role of the army in Roman domestic and foreign affairs. E. S. Gruen, *The Last Generation of the Roman Republic* (1971) provides an overview of the end. The best work on Caesar is M. Gelzer, *Caesar: Politician and Statesman* (1968). A. H. N. Jones, *Augustus* is a good short summary.

For surveys on the history of the early Roman Empire, see C. Wells, *The Roman Empire* (1984), P. Garnsey and R. Saller, *The Roman Empire: Economy, Society, and Culture* (1987), and J. Wacher, *The Roman Empire* (1987).

The most useful survey of Roman art is D. E. Strong, *Roman Art* (1976). On architecture, see J. B. Ward-Perkins, *Roman Imperial Architecture* (1981). R. M. Ogilvie, *Roman Literature and Society* (1980) offers a broad general survey.

The economy of the Roman Empire is covered by R. Duncan-Jones, *The Economy of the Roman Empire: Quantitative Studies*, 2d ed. (1982). T. Frank, *An Economic Survey of Ancient Rome*, vols. 2–5 (1933–40) is uneven but still useful. A number of excellent works are available on social history, including R. MacMullen, *Roman Social Relations, 50 B.C. to A.D. 284* (1981), P. Garnsey, *Social Status and Legal Privilege in the Roman Empire* (1970), R. P. Saller, *Personal Patronage under the Early Empire* (1982), and K. Bradley, *Slaves and Masters in the Roman Empire* (1988). Town life is memorably described by J. Carcoppino, *Daily Life in Ancient Rome*, rev. ed. (1975) and by T. Africa, *Rome of the Caesars* (1965).

## Chapter 6

J. Lebreton and J. Zeiller, *History of the Primitive Church*, 3 vols. (1962) is a survey of early church history from the Catholic point of view. H. Lietzmann, *History of the Early Church*, 2 vols. (1961) offers a Protestant point of view. Works on the origins and spread of Christianity include T. Barnes, *Christianity and the Roman Empire* (1984), S. Benko, *Pagan Rome and Early Christians* (1985), W. Frend, *The Rise of Christianity* (1984), and R. MacMullen, *Christianizing the Roman Empire* (1984). The lives of both Christian and pagan women are explored in G. Clark, *Women in Late Antiquity: Pagan and Christian Life Styles* (1993).

A rich literature exists on the Roman army and the problem of imperial defense. See L. Keppie, *The Making of the Roman Army* (1984), and J. B. Campbell, *The Emperor and the Roman Army* (1984). Strategy and policy are covered in E. Luttwak, *The Grand Strategy of the Roman Empire from the First Century A.D. to the Third* (1976), and S. L. Dyson, *The Creation of the Roman Frontier* (1985).

The broader subject of Rome's decline and the collapse of the west was first described in E. Gibbon, *The Decline and Fall of the Roman Empire* (1776). More modern surveys include A. H. M. Jones, *The Decline of the Ancient World* (1966), A. H. M. Jones, *The Later Roman Empire* (1964), F. Walbank, *The Awful Revolution* (1969), and A. Cameron, *The Later Roman Empire* (1993). On Diocletian's reforms, see S. Williams, *Diocletian and the Roman Recovery* (1985) and T. D. Barnes, *The New Empire of Diocletian and Constantine* (1982); for Constantine, R. MacMullan, *Constantine* (1969) and M. Grant, *Constantine the Great: The Man and His Times* (1993). The last years of the Roman west are described in E. A. Thompson, *Romans and Barbarians* (1982), and A. Ferrill, *The Fall of the Roman Empire: The Military Explanation* (1983).

The religious and intellectual life of the fourth and fifth centuries is described by P. Brown, *The World of Late Antiquity* (1971). His *Augustine of Hippo* (1969) is also the best biography of that central figure. On St. Benedict and the beginnings of western monasticism, see O. Chadwick, *The Making of the Benedictine Ideal* (1981).

## Chapter 7

Brief introductions to Byzantine history may be found in J. Norwich, *Byzantium: The Early Centuries* (1989), S. Runciman, *Byzantine Civilization* (1956), H. Haussig, *A History of Byzantine Civilization* (1971), and C. Mango, *Byzantium: The Empire of New Rome* (1980). R. Browning, *Justinian and Theodora*, 2d ed. (1987) is the standard treatment of the reign. For church history, see J. Hussey, *The Orthodox Church in the Byzantine Empire* (1986). The early history of the Slavs is covered by Z. Vana, *The World of the Ancient Slavs* (1983), and A. Vlasto, *The Entry of the Slavs into Christendom* (1970).

Surveys dealing with the early history of Islam include G. von Grunebaum, *Classical Islam: A History, 600–1250* (1970), H. Kennedy, *The Prophet and the Age of the Caliphates: The Islamic Near East from the Sixth to the Eleventh Centuries* (1986), and J. Saunders, *A History of Medieval Islam* (1965). For social history in the Islamic world, see E. Ashtor, *A Social and Economic History of the Near East in the Middle Ages* (1976) and M. Ahsan, *Social Life under the Abbasids* (1979). Islamic art and architecture are covered by O. Graber, *The Formation of Islamic Art*, 2d ed. (1987). The best introductions to Muslim thought are O. Leamon, *An Introduction to Medieval Islamic Philosophy* (1985) and M. Fakhry, *History of Islamic Philosophy*, 2d ed. (1983).

The best surveys of Europe in the early Middle Ages are R. Collins, *Early Medieval Europe, 300–1000* (1991), and J. Wallace-Hadrill, *The Barbarian West*, rev. ed. (1985). On the papacy in this period, see J. Richards, *The Popes and the Papacy in the Early Middle Ages* (1979). For the invasions and their impact, see L. Musset, *The German Invasions* (1975), W. Goffart, *Barbarians and Romans, A.D. 418–554: The Techniques of Accommodation* (1980), and P. Geary, *Before France and Germany* (1988). On England, F. Stanton, *Anglo-Saxon England*, rev. ed. (1947) is comprehensive. For Ireland as a center of missionary Christianity, see L. Bitel, *Isle of the Saints: Monastic Settlement and Christian Community in Early Ireland* (1990).

The standard surveys of Carolingian history are H. Fichtenau, *The Carolingian Empire* (1957), D. Bullough, *The Age of Charlemagne* (1966), and J. McKitterick, *The Frankish Kingdoms under the Carolingians, 751–987* (1983). For Charlemagne, see H. Loyn and R. Percival, *The Reign of Charlemagne* (1976). Carolingian society is described in P. Riché, *Daily Life in the World of Charlemagne* (1978) and in S. Wemple, *Women in Frankish Society: Marriage and the Cloister* (1981). The Carolingian Renaissance is described in P. Riché, *Education and Culture in the Barbarian West: From the Sixth through the Eighth Century* (1976).

## Chapter 8

The age of the great raids is surveyed by G. Barraclough, *The Crucible of Europe: The Ninth and Tenth Centuries in European History* (1976) and E. James, *The Origins of France: From Clovis to the Capetians* (1982). For the Vikings, see G. Jones, *A History of the Vikings*, rev. ed. (1984) and F. Logan, *The Vikings in History*, 2d ed. (1991). In P. Suger and others, *A History of Hungary* (1990), chapters 1–3 deal with the Magyars and early Hungary in general. Military issues are covered by P. Contamine, *War in the Middle Ages* (1984) and J. Beeler, *War in Feudal Europe* (1991). Three outstanding studies on the emergence of medieval institutions in general are R. W. Southern, *The Making of the Middle Ages*, rev. ed. (1973), M. Bloch, *Feudal Society* (1961), and G. Duby, *The Early Growth of the European Economy: Warriors and Peasants from the First to the Twelfth Century* (1974). For feudalism, see F. Ganshof, *Feudalism* (1952). More suggested readings on the evolution of feudalism and chivalry and readings on the life and work of a medieval manor are found in chapter 11.

The Celtic portion of the nonfeudal world is covered in D. Walker, *Medieval Wales* (1990), R. Davies, *Domination and Conquest: The Experience of Scotland and Wales* (1990), and A. Cosgrove, ed., *A New History of Ireland, 1169–1534*, vol. 2 (1993). The best work on medieval Spain is J. O'Callaghan, *Medieval Spain* (1975).

A vast literature can be found on the feudal monarchies. For England, see R. Brown, *The Normans and the Norman Conquest*, 2d ed. (1986), and R. Frame, *The Political Development of the British Isles, 1100–1400* (1990). W. L. Warren, *Henry II* (1973) is a good biography. D. C. Holt, *Magna Carta* (1965) deals with the circumstances surrounding that extraordinary document. R. Turner, *King John* (1994) provides a balanced view of a controversial figure. Developments in France are covered by J. Dunbabin, *France in the Making, 843–1180* (1985) and E. M. Hallam, *Capetian France, 987–1328* (1980). For feudalism in Germany, see B. Arnold, *German Knighthood 1050–1300* (1985). H. Fuhrmann, *Germany in the High Middle Ages c. 1050–1250* (1986) provides a good general account of feudal Germany. On Hildegard of Bingen, see S. Flanagan, *Hildegard of Bingen* (1989).

## Chapter 9

The Cluniac movement is covered by H. E. J. Cowdrey, *The Cluniacs and the Gregorian Reform* (1970). On the background of the investiture crisis, see K. Morrison, *Tradition and Authority in the Western Church 300–1140* (1969). A number of studies on the evolution of the medieval papacy are also useful, including C. Morris, *The Papal Monarchy* (1989), and I. Robinson, *The Papacy* (1990). For the issue of clerical celibacy, see A. Barstow, *Married Priests and the Reforming Papacy* (1982).

W. Ullman, *Law and Politics in the Middle Ages* (1975) discusses the development of canon law. Monastic reform is described in B. Bolton, *The Medieval Reformation* (1983). On the great cathedrals see G. Duby, *The Age of the Cathedrals: Art and Society, 980–1420* (1981).

Works that deal with the Iberian reconquest include G. Jackson, *The Making of Medieval Spain* (1971), and A. Mackay, *Spain in the Middle Ages* (1977). The Normans in Sicily and elsewhere are the subject of J. le Patourel, *The Norman Empire* (1976), D. Douglas, *The Norman Achievement* (1969), and R. Brown, *The Normans* (1983). The literature on the Crusades is rich. H. E. Mayer, *The Crusades* (1972) and J. Riley-Smith, *The Crusades: A Short History* (1987) are good surveys. There is also a multivolume work, edited by K. M. Setton, *A History of the Crusades* (1955–77). Medieval attitudes toward the Jews are covered by R. Chazan in *European Jewry and the First Crusade* (1987), *Church, State, and the Jew in the Middle Ages* (1980), and *Daggers of Faith: Thirteenth Century Christian Missionizing and Jewish Response* (1989). J. Marcus, *The Jew in the Medieval World* (1972) is a broad general survey. For attitudes toward homosexuals, see J. Boswell, *Christianity, Social Tolerance, and Homosexuality* (1980).

General surveys of medieval thought are provided by D. Knowles, *The Evolution of Medieval Thought* (1962) and A. Murray, *Reason and Society in the Middle Ages* (1978). For the intellectual re-

newal of the twelfth century and the crisis it provoked, see the classic by C. H. Haskins, *The Renaissance of the Twelfth Century* (1957). For the heresies of the twelfth century, see R. I. Moore, *The Origins of European Dissent* (1977), and J. Strayer, *The Albigensian Crusades* (1971). For the Inquisition, B. Hamilton, *The Medieval Inquisition* (1981), while the rise of the mendicant orders is described by R. Brooke, *The Coming of the Friars* (1975). The classic work on medieval universities is H. Rashdall, *The Universities of Europe in the Middle Ages*, 3 vols. (1936), but see also A. Cobban, *The Medieval Universities* (1975) and S. Ferruolo, *The Origin of the Universities* (1985). For scholasticism, see J. W. Baldwin, *The Scholastic Culture of the Middle Ages, 100–1300* (1971). The best analysis of Aquinas's thought is in F. Copleston, *Aquinas* (1965); whose *A History of Philosophy*, vols. 2 and 3 (1963) provide a useful analysis of the other scholastics including Scotus and Ockham.

## Chapter 10

For medieval technology, see L. White, *Medieval Technology and Social Change* (1962), J. Gimpel, *The Medieval Machine* (1976), and J. Langdon, *Horses, Oxen, and Technological Innovation* (1986). B. Slicher van Bath, *Agrarian History of Western Europe: A.D. 500–1850* (1963), C. Cipolla, *Before the Industrial Revolution: European Society and Economy, 1000–1700* (1976), G. Hodgett, *A Social and Economic History of Medieval Europe* (1974), and G. Duby, *The Early Growth of the European Economy: Warriors and Peasants from the Seventh to the Twelfth Century* (1978) provide broad general surveys of agricultural developments. The standard work on the revival of trade is R. S. Lopez, *The Commercial Revolution of the Middle Ages, 950–1350* (1970).

On the Italian cities, see J. K. Hyde, *Society and Politics in Medieval Italy, 1000–1350* (1973), D. Waley, *The Italian City Republics* (1969), D. Herlihy, *Cities and Society in Medieval Italy* (1980), and G. Tabacco, *The Struggle for Power in Medieval Italy, 400–1400* (1989).

Most studies of town life focus on the later Middle Ages and Renaissance when documentation became more consistent, but many of their conclusions are valid for earlier periods as well. The basic social structures had changed little since the thirteenth century. J. Gies and F. Gies, *Life in a Medieval City* (1969) offers a good, popular portrait of urban life. Among the better monographs are M. Howell, *Women, Production, and Patriarchy in Late Medieval Cities* (1986), D. Nicholas, *The Domestic Life of a Medieval City: Women, Children, and the Family in Fourteenth-Century Ghent* (1985), and a host of works on the Italian towns, including D. Herlihy, *The Family in Renaissance Italy* (1974), S. Cohn, *The Laboring Classes in Florence* (1980), F. Kent, *Neighbors and Neighborhoods in Renaissance Florence: The District of the Red Lion in the Fifteenth Century* (1982), and D. Romano, *Patricians and Popolani: The Social Foundations of the Venetian Renaissance State* (1987).

## Chapter 11

A basic work, J. C. Russell, *The Control of Late Ancient and Medieval Populations* (1985), covers diet, disease, and demography. For the role of epidemic disease, see W. H. McNeill, *Plagues and Peoples* (1976). S. Rubin, *Medieval English Medicine* (1974), B. Rowland, *Medieval Woman's Guide to Health* (1981).

For castles, see W. Anderson, *Castles in Europe* (1970), N. J. G. Pounds, *The Medieval Castle in England and Wales: A Social and Political History* (1990). Medieval concepts of the social order are studied in G. Duby, *The Three Orders: Feudal Society* (1980). An immense literature exists on chivalry and the life of the knightly classes. S. Reynolds, *Kingdoms and Communities in Western Europe, 900–1300* (1984), and G. Duby, *The Chivalrous Society* (1977). M. Keen, *Chivalry* (1984) is the standard work on the subject. On noble marriages, see G. Duby, *The Knight, the Lady, and the Priest* (1984); on tournaments, R. Barber and J. Barker, *Tournaments: Jousts, Chivalry and Pageants in the Middle Ages* (1988).

The rural economy and village life are described in G. Duby, *Rural Economy and Country Life in the Medieval West* (1968), G. Homans, *English Villagers in the Thirteenth Century* (1975), H. S. Bennett, *Life on an English Manor: A Study of Peasant Conditions* (1960), and the best-selling E. Le Roy Ladurie, *Montaillou* (1978). For the lowest levels of the social order, see M. Mollat, *The Poor in the Middle Ages* (1986). The standard work on family structure, marriage patterns, inheritance, and similar questions is D. Herlihy, *Medieval Households* (1985). B. Hanawalt, *The Ties That Bind: Peasant Families in Medieval England* (1986) provides a vivid and insightful picture of English peasant life. On women in various social settings, see M. Labarge, *A Small Sound of the Trumpet: Women in Medieval Life* (1986), and S. Shahar, *The Fourth Estate: A History of Women in the Middle Ages* (1983). On children, P. Ariés, *Centuries of Childhood* (1962) has proved controversial. See also D. Herlihy, "Medieval Children," in *Essays on Medieval Civilization*, ed. B. Lackner and K. Philip (1978). For the common practice of abandonment, see J. Boswell, *The Kindness of Strangers: The Abandonment of Children in Western Europe from Late Antiquity to the Renaissance* (1989).

## Chapter 12

Attempts to understand the later Middle Ages should begin with the classic J. Huizinga, *The Waning of the Middle Ages* (1949). B. Tuchman, *A Distant Mirror: The Calamitous Fourteenth Century* (1980) is a popular, best-selling, and memorable vision of the age. R. Gottfried, *The Black Death* (1983) is the most recent account of the plague. W. H. McNeill, *Plagues and Peoples* (1976) discusses the impact of epidemic disease in general. H. Miskimin, *The Economy of Early Renaissance Europe, 1300–1460* (1975) is the best study of economic matters, but see also J. Hatcher, *Plague, Population, and the English Economy, 1348–1550* (1977) and G. Huppert, *After the Black Death: A Social History of Early Modern Europe* (1986). M. Mollat and P. Wolff, *The Popular Revolutions of the Late Middle Ages* (1973) surveys both peasant and urban revolts.

A general work that covers military innovations in the later Middle Ages is P. Contamine, *War in the Middle Ages* (1984). On the evolution of the ship, see R. Unger, *The Ship in the Medieval Economy* (1980) and the profusely illustrated R. Gardner and others, eds., *Cogs, Caravels and Galleons* (1994).

For the tribulations of Russia, begin with D. Morgan, *The Mongols* (1986). I. Grey, *Ivan III and the Unification of Russia* (1964) is a brief biography of the founder of the Muscovite state. For Poland, see N. Davies, *Poland: God's Playground* (1981). The standard work on the Ottomans is H. Inalcik, *The Ottoman Empire: The Classical Age* (1973). S. Runciman, *The Fall of Constantinople 1435* (1965) is excellent.

The best accounts of the Hundred Years' War are E. Perroy, *The Hundred Years' War* (1951) and C. Allmand, *The Hundred Years'*

*War: England and France at War, c. 1300–1450* (1988). M. Warner, *Joan of Arc: The Image of Female Heroism* (1981) is the best study of "The Maid." On the Hundred Years' War in Spain, see the pertinent chapters of J. O'Callaghan, *Medieval Spain* (1975) and J. N. Hillgarth, *The Spanish Kingdoms, 1250–1516*, vol. 1 (1978).

## Chapter 13

The best survey of fifteenth-century Spain is J. Hillgarth, *The Spanish Kingdoms, 1250–1516*, vol. 2 (1978). See also P. Liss, *Isabella the Queen* (1992). Henry Kamen, *The Spanish Inquisition* (1997). On France, J. Major, *Representative Institutions in Renaissance France, 1421–1559* (1960) is an outstanding monograph. P. M. Kendall, *Louis XI: The Universal Spider* (1971) and R. Knecht, *Francis I* (1982) are good biographies. For Burgundy, see R. Vaughan, *Valois Burgundy* (1975). The best study of the War of the Roses is J. Gillingham, *The War of the Roses* (1981). *The Reign of Henry VI* (1981), *Edward IV* (1974), and *Richard III* (1982) by C. Ross are sound biographies as is S. Chrimes, *Henry VII* (1972). F. Boulay, *Germany in the Later Middle Ages* (1983) surveys the later empire. F. L. Carsten, *Princes and Parliaments in Germany: From the Fifteenth to the Eighteenth Century* (1963) is a classic study of representative institutions. For eastern Europe, see the collection of essays by A. Maczak and others, *East-Central Europe in Transition from the Fourteenth to the Seventeenth Century* (1986), and R. Crummey, *The Formation of Muscovy, 1304–1613* (1987).

L. Martines, *Power and Imagination: City-States in Renaissance Italy* (1988) is an excellent survey of the Italian cities and their cultural preoccupations; G. Brucker, *Renaissance Florence*, 2d ed. (1983) remains the best general treatment of Florence. Two outstanding introductions to Renaissance humanism are C. Nauert, *Humanism and the Culture of Renaissance Europe* (1995) and D. Kelley, *Renaissance Humanism* (1991).

Useful collections of essays on various aspects of the humanist program are found in A. Rabil, ed., *Renaissance Humanism: Foundations, Forms, and Legacy*, 3 vols. (1988) and C. Trinkhaus, *The Scope of Renaissance Humanism* (1983). Humanist ideas on rhetoric and education are explored by J. Siegel, *Rhetoric and Philosophy in Renaissance Humanism* (1968), P. Grendler, *Schooling in Renaissance Italy, 1300–1600* (1989), and A. Grafton and L. Jardine, *From Humanism to the Humanities: Education and the Liberal Arts in Fifteenth- and Sixteenth-Century Europe* (1988). See also M. King, *Women in the Renaissance* (1991). On the dissemination of humanism to northern Europe, see R. Weiss, *The Spread of Italian Humanism* (1964) and the collection of essays by A. Goodman and A. MacKay, *The Impact of Humanism on Western Europe* (1990). E. Eisenstein, *The Printing Press as an Agent of Change*, 2 vols. (1978) examines the impact of the printing press. On Erasmus, see R. Bainton, *Erasmus of Christendom* (1969) and J. Tracy, *Erasmus of the Low Countries* (1996).

E. Cochrane, *Historians and Historiography in the Italian Renaissance* (1981) is a good survey of an important topic. Among the immense literature on Machiavelli and Guicciardini, J. R. Hale, *Machiavelli and Renaissance Italy* (1960), F. Gilbert, *Machiavelli and Guicciardini* (1965) remain especially useful. F. Hartt, *History of Italian Renaissance Art* (1979) is an introductory survey to an immense topic. K. Clark, *The Art of Humanism* (1983) is a brief but provocative essay.

## Chapter 14

The problems of the late medieval church are best summarized in F. Oakley, *The Western Church in the Later Middle Ages* (1979). A study of the papacy at Avignon is Y. Renouard, *The Avignon Papacy, 1305–1403* (1970). On the Great Schism, see W. Ullmann, *Origins of the Great Schism* (1949). The conciliar movement is analyzed in F. Oakley, *Natural Law, Conciliarism, and Consent in the Late Middle Ages* (1984). A good survey of the papacy is J. A. F. Thompson, *Popes and Princes, 1417–1517: Politics and Polity in the Late Medieval Church* (1980). A. Kenny, *Wyclif* (1985) is a good introduction to the English heretic. For Hus and the Hussites, see M. Spinka, *John Hus: A Biography* (1979) and H. Kaminsky, *A History of the Hussite Revolution* (1967).

Good biographies of Luther include R. Bainton, *Here I Stand: A Life of Martin Luther* (1950), the more modern J. Kittelson, *Luther the Reformer* (1986), and the revisionist work by H. Oberman, *Luther: Man between God and Devil* (1992).

G. H. Williams, *The Radical Reformation* (1962, 1991) is a comprehensive account that covers Anabaptists, Spiritualists, and Antitrinitarians. See also the shorter M. Mullett, *Radical Religious Movements in Early Modern Europe* (1980). The most accessible biography of Zwingli is probably G. Potter, *Zwingli* (1976). A. McGrath, *A Life of John Calvin* (1990) is a good introduction. See also the brilliant, if somewhat difficult, study by W. Bousma, *John Calvin* (1988) and W. Monter, *Calvin's Geneva* (1967). On the English Reformation, the interpretation of G. Dickens, *The English Reformation* (1964) has been challenged, among others, by J. J. Scarisbricke, *The Reformation and the English People* (1984). The best biography of Henry VIII remains J. J. Scarisbricke, *Henry VIII* (1968); for Cranmer, see D. MacCulloch, *Thomas Cranmer* (1996). The most reliable study on Mary is by D. Loades, *The Reign of Mary Tudor* (1979).

Good surveys of the Catholic Reformation include G. Dickens, *The Counter Reformation* (1969), M. O'Connell, *The Counter Reformation, 1559–1610* (1974), and L. Chatellier, *The Europe of the Devout: The Catholic Reformation and the Formation of a New Society* (1989). See also the important revisionist interpretation of J. Delumeau, *Catholicism from Luther to Voltaire* (1977).

On the consequences of reform, G. Strauss, *Luther's House of Learning* (1978) has proved as controversial as the views of Delumeau. For the effect of the Reformation on women and the family, see S. Ozment, *When Father's Ruled: Family Life in Reformation Europe* (1983), M. Wiesner, *Working Women in Renaissance Germany* (1986), L. Roper, *Work, Marriage, and Sexuality: Women in Reformation Augsburg* (1985), and J. Irwin, *Womanhood in Radical Protestantism, 1525–1675* (1989). For popular culture and its struggles, see P. Burke, *Popular Culture in Early Modern Europe* (1978), and M. Mullett, *Popular Culture and Popular Protest in Late Medieval and Early Modern Europe* (1986). B. Levack, *The Witch-Hunt in Early Modern Europe* (1987) is a broad survey of the witch persecutions.

## Chapter 15

Standard introductions to the history of European expansion overseas are J. H. Parry, *The Age of Reconnaissance: Discovery, Exploration, and Settlement, 1450–1650* (1963, 1981) and G. Scammell,

*The World Encompassed: The First European Maritime Empires, c. 800–1650* (1981). Portuguese expansion is described in B. Diffie and G. Winius, *Foundations of the Portuguese Empire, 1415–1580* (1979) and C. R. Boxer, *The Portuguese Seaborne Empire, 1415–1825* (1969). Among the best biographies of Columbus are S. Morison, *Admiral of the Ocean Sea: A Life of Christopher Columbus* (1942) and F. Fernández-Armesto, *Columbus* (1991). The best overall descriptions of the Spanish imperial system are still C. H. Haring, *The Spanish Empire in America* (1947), and C. Gibson, *Spain in America* (1966).

The standard biography of Charles V is K. Brandi, *The Emperor Charles V* (1939). M. Rady, *The Emperor Charles V* (1988) is a brief, but useful, handbook. For good general histories of Spain in the sixteenth and seventeenth centuries, see J. H. Elliott, *Imperial Spain* (1963) and J. Lynch, *Spain under the Habsburgs*, vol. 1, 2d ed. (1981). Good studies of Philip II and his reign include H. Kamen, *Philip of Spain* (1997), P. Pierson, *Philip II of Spain* (1975), and G. Parker, *Philip II* (1978).

The best surveys of the French Wars of Religion are probably M. Holt, *The French Wars of Religion* (1993) and J. H. M. Salmon, *Society in Crisis: France in the Sixteenth Century* (1975). The best account of the revolt of the Netherlands is G. Parker, *The Dutch Revolt* (1977), but see also P. Geyl, *The Revolt of the Netherlands*, 2d ed. (1966) and A. Duke, *Reformation and Revolt in the Low Countries* (1990). English foreign policy in this era is described by R. B. Wernham, *Before the Armada* (1966). A vast literature exists on the Spanish Armada of 1588. The classic G. Mattingly, *The Armada* (1959) and C. Martin and G. Parker, *The Spanish Armada* (1988) are excellent. On Elizabeth I, see W. MacCaffrey, *Elizabeth I* (1993), and S. Bassnett, *Elizabeth I: A Feminist Perspective* (1988). The most reliable treatment of the Thirty Years' War is G. Parker, *The Thirty Years' War* (1984). For Gustav Adolph, see M. Roberts, *Gustavus Adolphus and the Rise of Sweden* (1975). The literature on the English civil wars is enormous. Begin with L. Stone, *The Causes of the English Revolution* (1972) and C. Russell, *The Causes of the English Civil War* (1990), then see R. Ashton, *The English Civil War: Conservatism and Revolution, 1604–1649* (1976) and M. Kishlansky: *The Rise of the New Model Army* (1979). Among the better works on Cromwell are C. Hill, *God's Englishman: Oliver Cromwell and the English Revolution* (1976), and R. Howell, *Cromwell* (1977).

To understand the military history of the sixteenth and seventeenth centuries, begin with J. R. Hale, *War and Society in Renaissance Europe, 1450–1620* (1985) and two enlightening special studies, G. Parker, *The Army of Flanders and the Spanish Road, 1567–1659* (1972) and J. Guilmartin, *Gunpowder and Galleys: Changing Technology and Mediterranean Warfare at Sea in the Sixteenth Century* (1975). G. Parker, *The Military Revolution: Military Innovation and the Rise of the West, 1500–1800* (1988) provides a global perspective.

## Chapter 16

Good surveys of the scientific revolution include A. R. Hall, *The Revolution in Science, 1500–1700* (1983), and A. Debus, *Man and Nature in the Renaissance* (1978). For the occult and hermetic traditions, see W. Shumaker, *The Occult Sciences in the Renaissance: A Study in Intellectual Patterns* (1985). Medieval ideas on cosmology may be found in P. Duhem, *Medieval Cosmology: Theories of Infinity, Place, Time, Void, and the Plurality of Worlds* (1985), a condensation of the ten-volume original. For astrology, see E. Garin, *Astrology in the Renaissance: The Zodiac of Life* (1983).

Copernicus stands at the beginning of modern cosmology. See E. Rosen, *Copernicus and the Scientific Revolution* (1984) and T. Kuhn, *The Copernican Revolution: Planetary Astronomy in the Development of Western Thought* (1971). A. Koestler, *The Sleepwalkers: A History of Man's Changing Vision of the Universe* (1959) is a broad, often ironic, survey. A vast literature exists on Galileo; the works of S. Drake, *Galileo at Work: His Scientific Biography* (1978), *Galileo* (1980), and *Galileo: Pioneer Scientist* (1990) are standards. On Newton, see R. Westfall, *The Life of Isaac Newton* (1993). The development of medicine is surveyed by W. Wightman, *The Emergence of Scientific Medicine* (1971). M. Jacobs, *The Cultural Meaning of the Scientific Revolution* (1988) and L. Schiebinger, *The Mind Has No Sex? Women in the Origins of Modern Science* (1989) are useful essays on science as an intellectual movement.

On the expansion of the northern powers, see C. R. Boxer, *The Dutch Seaborne Empire, 1600–1800* (1965) and R. Davis, *English Overseas Trade, 1500–1700* (1973). J. Israel, *The Dutch Republic: Its Rise, Greatness, and Fall, 1477–1806* (1995) is a monumental survey, and S. Schama, *The Embarrassment of Riches: An Intepretation of Dutch Culture in the Golden Age* (1987) is an ambitious study of Dutch culture.

J. Black describes military changes in *European Warfare, 1660–1815* (1994) and *A Military Revolution? Military Change and European Society, 1550–1800* (1991). On the reorganization of the state in France, see M. Greengrass, *France in the Age of Henri IV: The Struggle for Stability* (1984), and D. Parker, *The Making of French Absolutism* (1983). See also R. Knecht, *Richelieu* (1991), and the insightful essay by J. H. Elliott, *Richelieu and Olivares* (1984). J. Collum, *The State in Early Modern France* (1995) is a recent overview. J. B. Wolf, *Louis XIV* (1968) and O. Bernier, *Louis XIV* (1988) are good studies of the Sun King. For a survey of the German-speaking states, see M. Hughes, *Early Modern Germany, 1477–1806* (1992). The standard work on the Austrian Empire is R. J. W. Evans, *The Making of the Habsburg Monarchy, 1550–1700* (1979); on Prussia, see F. Carsten, *The Origins of Prussia* (1954)

and H. Rosenberg, *Bureaucracy, Aristocracy, and Autocracy: The Prussian Experience, 1660–1815* (1966). Good studies of Peter the Great include M. Anderson, *Peter the Great* (1978), and the popular R. Massie, *Peter the Great* (1980). For the English politics, see R. Hutton, *The Restoration: A Political and Religious History of England and Wales, 1658–1667* (1985) and J. R. Jones, *Country and Court: England, 1658–1714* (1978). R. Hutton, *Charles II* (1989) is a good biography.

## Chapter 17

For broad overviews of the eighteenth-century economy, see J. H. Clapham and others, eds., *The Cambridge Economic History of Europe*, 10 vols. (1941–89) and C. Cipolla, ed., *The Fontana Economic History of Europe*, 6 vols. (1972–76). Compare these with the more recent R. Floud and D. McCloskey, eds., *The Economic History of Britain since 1700*, 2 vols. (1993), which is highly statistical, and C. H. Lee, *The British Economy since 1700* (1986), which gives a broader view. R. Forster, ed., *European Society in the Eighteenth Century* (1967) is an exceptional collection of contemporary readings on both social and economic topics.

## Chapter 18

For a general social history of the Old Regime, the masterwork is F. Braudel, *Civilization and Capitalism, 15th–18th Century*, 3 vols., especially vol. 1, *The Structures of Everyday Life* (1985). For demographic studies and population, see M. W. Flinn, *The European Demographic System, 1500–1820* (1981), the standard work on western Europe; M. Anderson, *Population Change in Northwestern Europe, 1750–1850* (1988); For sickness and disease, see the pertinent chapters in W. McNeill, *Plagues and Peoples* (1976), the pioneering work in this field; For the history of the family, see M. Anderson, *Approaches to the History of the Western Family* (1980), an excellent introduction; The most helpful general works for the history of women included an excellent anthology by S. G. Bell and K. M. Offen, eds., *Women, the Family, and Freedom*, 2 vols. (1983), B. Anderson and J. Zinsser, *A History of Their Own: Women in Europe from Prehistory to the Present*, 2 vols. (1988).

# PHOTO CREDITS

◆◆◆◆◆◆◆◆◆◆◆◆◆◆◆◆◆◆◆◆

# GLOSSARY

◆◆◆◆◆◆◆◆◆◆◆◆◆◆◆◆◆◆◆◆

## Chapter 1

**Biological Old Regime.**   The natural restrictions on population size and living conditions in the age before the Industrial Revolution, such as widespread undernourishment, famine, and unchecked disease.

**Clientage.**   A system of mutual dependency in which a powerful individual protects the interests of others in return for their political or economic support. It may exist with or without legal sanction, and has long been a basic institution in many societies.

**Demography.**   The statistical study of populations through data such as birth and death rates, censuses, or marriage rates.

**Extended Family.**   A family unit containing not only the nuclear family, but other relatives (siblings, parents, etc.) living under the same roof.

**Matrilineal.**   Inheritance of property, and sometimes the family name, through the female line.

**Monotheism.**   Belief in the existence of only one god, as opposed to **Polytheism**, or the belief in many.

**Neolithic Revolution.**   The transition to the "new stone age" involving the domestication of animals, the development of agriculture, and the extensive use of basketry and pottery.

**Nuclear Family.**   The basic family unit of mother, father, and their children.

**Paleolithic.**   The "old stone age" before the invention of agriculture. Tools were made of stone and people lived by hunting and gathering.

**Slave.**   A person who is the chattel property of another and therefore without rights.

**Debt Slavery**   is the practice of enslaving someone to satisfy a debt, often for a fixed period of time.

## Chapter 2

**Democracy.**   Rule by the people. In Greek terms, this meant government by the entire body of male citizens as opposed to by a small group of wealthy aristocrats. Slaves, women, and resident aliens were excluded.

**Hoplites.**   Armored spearmen trained to fight shoulder to shoulder in a rectangular formation that was normally eight ranks deep.

**Polis.**   The Greek city-state, composed in theory of those who shared a common ancestry and worshipped the same gods. It was the basis of Greek life and values in the Classical Age.

**Trireme.**   The dominant warship of the Classical Age. It was propelled by three ranks of oars supplemented by square sails, and had a metal prow for ramming opponents.

**Tyrant.**   A ruler who, though sometimes legitimately elected, ignored the laws and institutions of his polis and governed as a dictator.

**Zoroastrianism.**   A Persian religion based upon the conflict between a god of good (Ahura Mazda) and a god of evil (Ahriman). Its duallism influenced later Christian thought.

## Chapter 3

**Epistemology.**   In philosophy, the study of how human knowledge is acquired.

**Hellenistic.**   The Greek culture of the fourth through the first centuries B.C., based not on the polis, but on the great empires founded by Alexander the Great's commanders.

**Pharisees.**   A Jewish sect that demanded strict observance of the religious laws and opposed the introduction of Greek customs and ideas by their rivals, the **Sadducees**.

**Platonic Idealism (Realism).**   Plato's theory that ideas or forms are real and intelligible, and that they exist independently of appearances discernible to the senses.

**Sophists.**   Teachers of rhetoric who held that individual experience, based primarily on the senses, was the only basis for knowledge, and that all teachings were therefore relative.

**Syllogism.**   A form of argument, common to much of western thought, that reasons: if all A is B, and all C is A, then all C must be B.

**Teleological.**   Relating to the assumption that things can best be understood in relation to their end or purpose. In ethics, the principle that actions must be judged in terms of the result they are intended to produce.

## Chapter 4

**Censor.**   The official responsible for conducting the **Census** which ranked each citizen's property qualifications. In later years the censor acquired substantial authority over public morals and religious observances as well.

**Consul.** The highest office in the Roman state. Consuls served one-year terms and could succeed themselves only after the passage of ten years. They commanded the army and, in civil matters, their edicts had the force of law.

*Familia.* In Roman Law, the entire household headed by a *Paterfamilias,* or father, including his nuclear family, dependent relatives, and slaves.

**Partible Inheritance.** The legal requirement that all property be distributed equally among an individual's heirs. It is the opposite of **Nonartible Inheritance**, which permits all of the property in an estate to be passed to a single heir, often the eldest son.

**Patricians.** The hereditary aristocracy of the Roman Republic. Only they could hold office as magistrates or serve in the Senate.

**Plebeians.** The lower class of Roman citizens. They could vote and, after the so-called struggle of the orders, served in the Plebeian Assembly and were represented to the Senate by Tribunes.

**Proconsul.** A consul whose authority was extended for the duration of a military campaign, normally in a distant province.

## Chapter 5

**Pax Romana.** The Roman Peace. A long period of peace within the empire established by Augustus. It did not preclude revolts within individual provinces or conflicts with the Germanic tribes and other outsiders.

**Latifundia.** Large, self-sufficient estates that dominated the economic life of the western Roman empire. In the late Republic they were usually worked by slaves, who were gradually replaced by tenants (*coloni*) under the empire.

**Codex.** A manuscript volume of pages, usually bound in leather. It began to replace the scroll in the first century A.D.

*Coloni.* Tenants on a Roman estate or *latifundia*. Under the early empire *coloni* were normally free citizens who leased their land and returned a percentage of their yield to the estate.

**Equestrians.** A new social class that emerged after the Punic Wars. Most were merchants or financiers who, while rich enough to fight on horseback (hence the term "equestrian"), lacked the political privileges of the Patricians.

*Imperator.* Originally a military title, it was adopted by Vespasian as a symbol of ultimate power. The origin of the title "emperor."

*Insulae.* The large, tenement-like apartment houses in which most urban Romans lived.

*Publicani,* or **Publicans.** Tax farmers who purchased the right to levy provincial taxes at auction in return for a percentage of the funds to be raised.

## Chapter 6

**Arianism.** The doctrine, advanced by Arius and accepted by many of the Germanic tribes, that Christ was a created being, neither fully God, nor fully man. The orthodox view in both the Eastern and Western churches is that Christ is both fully God and fully man.

*Cataphracti.* Armored heavy cavalry first commonly used under Diocletian. They became the dominant branch of the Roman army after the battle of Adrianople in 378.

**Command Economy.** An economic system in which the government sets wages and prices and attempts to regulate production.

**Decurians.** In the late Roman empire, members of the urban elite who monopolized most city offices, but who also paid many of the costs of government.

**Forced Requisitions.** The practice of confiscating food, draft animals, and other private property to support the army in a particular region.

**Monasticism.** The practice of living in a secluded community under the rule of religious vows.

**Paganism.** A generic term for all those who had not been converted to Christianity. It is derived from the Latin word *pagani*, a slang term for rustics.

**Predestination.** The doctrine, advanced by Augustine, that God selects those who will be saved. **Double Predestination** holds that God also selects those who will be damned. (see also Chapter Fourteen)

**Tetrarchy.** The system introduced by Diocletian under which the empire was ruled by two caesars and two augusti.

## Chapter 7

*Epiboli.* The Byzantine system whereby all of the members of a community were required to pay the taxes of those unable to do so.

**Iconoclasm.** The belief that images should be destroyed because they are contrary to God's commandment.

*Shahada.* The Muslim profession of faith: "There is no God but God and Mohammed is his prophet."

*Shar'ia.* A way of life wholly commanded by God. The religious goal of pious Muslims.

*Jihad.* A holy war fought against the enemies of *al-Islam.*

**Caliph.** The chief civil and religious ruler in Islamic society.

**Allod.** A freehold property, normally unencumbered by feudal dues or other obligations.

**Carolingian Minuscule.** A style of handwriting developed in the Carolingian renaissance that became the basis of most modern hands.

**Salic Law.** The law of the Salian, or "salty" Franks that became the basis of succession in the Frankish kingdoms and later in

France. It demanded partible inheritance and in later years was said to forbid the succession of women.

## Chapter 8

*Comitatus.*   The Latin term for a war band bound to their chieftain by oaths of loyalty.

**Custom of the Manor.**   The collective record of contractual obligations within a manor, including the dues and services owed by each tenant to the lord. It was usually preserved in the form of an oral tradition until the fourteenth century.

**Fief.**   The landed property granted to a warrior in return for his promise of military service. It was sometimes called a **Benefice**, but this term more commonly refers to property granted for the support of a cleric.

**Feudalism.**   A social and economic system based upon grants of land offered in exchange for military service.

**Homage.**   The formal expression of loyalty offered by a vassal to his lord.

**Private Jurisdiction.**   The right of a vassal to establish courts of law within his fief. It was normally granted by a lord as part of the feudal contract.

**Manor.**   An estate whose inhabitants are the legal subjects of its lord or owner. In most cases, manorialism involves some form of tenancy. Peasants hold land and a cottage in return for specified dues and services.

**Subinfeudation.**   The process by which vassals grant a portion of their fiefs to vassals of their own, thereby creating subtenants who owe homage to them rather than to the original tenant-in-chief.

**Tenement, or Tenure.**   Property held by a peasant within the manor.

**Vassal.**   The party to a feudal agreement who receives a fief in return for military service. Though subordinate to a lord, all vassals were by definition members of the feudal elite.

## Chapter 9

*Dominium.*   The theory that the church, and in particular the pope, has authority over secular rulers.

**Gothic.**   A style of medieval architecture characterized by pointed arches, extensive carving, and sometimes by flying buttresses.

**Hildebrandine Reformation.**   The movement for papal reform that grew out of the Cluniac movement, for which Hildebrand of Soana (Pope Gregory VII) has been given too much credit.

**Investiture.**   The process by which rank or office is bestowed. In the Middle Ages, **Lay Investiture** meant the granting of ecclesiastical rank or authority by lay people.

**Mendicant Orders.**   Religious societies, the first of which were founded in the thirteenth century. Their members were bound by vows and were expected to live by begging. Collectively called **Friars**, they included the Dominicans and the Franciscans.

**Nominalism.**   The theory that universals are not real, but *nomina* or "names" that reflect little more than linguistic convention.

**Romanesque.**   A style of architecture that featured massive vaulting and round arches. It generally preceeds the Gothic.

**Scholasticism.**   The thought of the medieval schools and universities. It attempted to solve theological and philosophical problems through the application of Aristotelian logic.

**Universals.**   Those qualities and categories held by philosophical realists to have objective reality of their own (e.g., redness, justice, beauty, etc.).

## Chapter 10

**Agricultural Specialization.**   The practice of cultivating those crops for which a given estate is best suited. It is the opposite of **Subsistence Farming**, which seeks to grow everything that the inhabitants of a farm or estate may need.

**Commune.**   A government of citizens and its institutions, as opposed to one controlled by a bishop or feudal lord. In some medieval towns the commune at first grew in parallel with the government of the lord and then supplanted it.

*Signorie.*   In some Italian cities, the name of the elected council that governed the town, combining legislative and executive authority.

**Ghetto.**   Part of a city in which members of a minority group live as a result of social, religious, or economic discrimination. Originally, the district of Venice to which Jews were confined.

**Guild.**   An association of craftsmen or merchants whose purpose was to guarantee quality, set prices, and provide for the general welfare of its members. In some cities, citizens had to be guild members.

**Hanse.**   In North Germany, a league of cities formed to protect their commercial and military interests.

**Militia.**   The citizen-soldiers of a medieval city.

**Monoculture.**   Primary reliance on a single crop by a farm or manor. The ultimate form of agricultural specialization.

**Rentiers.**   Townspeople who live primarily from the proceeds of rented or leased property. They were an important segment of the elite in most medieval towns.

**Vendetta.**   A feud or private war, usually between two clientage groups or factions within a town or among the landed nobility.

## Chapter 11

**Chivalric Romance.**   An epic, often recited in poetic or musical form by troubadours, which glorified the chivalric values of bravery, loyalty, and courtesy.

**Domus.** In southern Europe, an entity composed of the family (usually extended), the household, and the physical property from which both took their name.

**Entail.** A legal restriction placed upon an inheritance to prevent future generations of heirs from alienating or otherwise disposing of property against the wishes of the original holder.

**Lent.** The six-and-a half week period of fasting and penitence from Ash Wednesday to Easter during which Christians were supposed to refrain from eating meat.

**Lineage.** The concept of a family name and family identity handed down from generation to generation. More common in southern than in northern Europe, it was often based upon the *domus* or the possession of some other landed estate.

**Midwife.** A woman trained to assist in childbirth. In medieval and early modern times, university-trained physicians did not normally practice obstetrics.

**Primogeniture.** Inheritance of all or most of an estate by the eldest son.

**Tournament.** A contest between knights that attempted to mimic the conditions of feudal warfare in a controlled, ritualized setting.

**Wardship.** The placement of orphans (and their assets) under the guardianship of an individual or of the courts. In medieval and early modern times the practice was largely restricted to the wealthier classes.

## Chapter 12

**Bastion Trace.** A system of fortification based upon a series of bastions or projections connected by walls and manned by artillery. Ideally, every part of a bastion trace could be covered by defending fire.

**Bundschuh.** The peasant boot, bound with laces. German peasants took it as symbol of social revolt during the fifteenth century, hence the term **Bundschuh revolts.**

**Forest Laws.** Laws passed to prevent peasants from hunting, fishing, or gathering firewood in forests claimed by the lords

**Ghazis.** Muslim raiders, primarily of Turkish origin, who raided the Byzantine Empire and other Christian states. They were in some respects the Muslim equivalent of crusaders.

**Regency.** The period during which an individual or group of individuals is appointed to rule on behalf of a prince who is either a minor or incapacitated.

**Soldier.** A warrior who receives a cash payment or *solde* for fighting, as opposed to one who serves in return for land or in the discharge of some non-monetary obligation.

## Chapter 13

**Classicism.** The admiration (and emulation) of the styles, aesthetics, and thought of the "classical" civilization of ancient Greece and Rome.

**Domain.** Land, properties, rents, and income-producing rights that are the personal property of a ruler. **Domain Revenues** are those derived from the domain as opposed to those derived from taxation.

**Enclosure.** The process by which landowners deprived peasants of a village's common lands and seized them for their own use.

**Humanism.** The study of Greek and Roman classics with the intention of applying their teachings to life in the present.

**Neoplatonism.** A philosophical school founded originally in Hellenistic Alexandria and revived during the Renaissance. Its chief concern was achieve knowledge of the Platonic forms.

**Perpetual Taxes.** Taxes that may be collected each year without further permission from a representative body. In the medieval and early modern period, most taxes required a special and separate vote each time they were levied.

**Pomest'e System.** In Muscovy, the system by which the Tsar granted land directly to cavalrymen in return for military service, thereby creating a kind of "service nobility" that was separate from the traditional *boyars.*

**Serfdom.** A form of servitude in which tenants are regarded as the property of an estate. Unlike slaves, they cannot be sold as individuals, but they lack all other rights and may be sold as part of the property on which they live.

## Chapter 14

**Anticlericalism.** Opposition to the influence and special privileges of the clergy or to the existence of the clergy as an organized hierarchy.

**Conciliarism.** The theory that the rulings of a council of the church are superior to those of any pope, and that a council may depose an unworthy pope if necessary.

**Mysticism.** The effort to achieve personal union with God through ecstatic contemplation.

**Popular Culture.** The culture that springs from the interests, activities, and entertainments of the people rather than from the received traditions of the cultural elite.

**Possessionist Controversy.** The dispute between Spiritual or Observant Franciscans and Conventual Franciscans over whether it was permissible for the order to hold property.

**Transubstantiation.** The doctrine that the substance of the bread and wine in Communion are converted by consecration to the body and blood of Christ, though their appearance or "accidents" remains the same.

**Witchcraft.**   In the sixteenth century, a body of practices that included magic, the casting of spells, and usually Satanism, or devil-worship.

## Chapter 15

**Administrative Devolution.**   The process by which early modern rulers assigned military and administrative functions to private contractors in an attempt to save money.

**Cuius regio, eius religio.**   The principle that the religion of an area may be determined by its ruler.

**Encomienda.**   An institution in which Spanish kings placed newly converted subjects under the "protection" of a Christian lord who was supposed to defend them and see to their religious instruction in return for certain dues and payments.

**Military Contractors.**   Entrepreneurs who contracted to provide a fixed number of fully equipped troops, and sometimes to lead them, in return for pay. Ships were often contracted on a similar basis in time of war.

**Proprietary Colonies.**   Overseas colonies granted to a private individual (a Captain or Lord Proprietor) whose responsibility it was to settle and defend them.

**Puritans.**   A party of English Protestants which demanded simplicity in church ceremonies and a high standard of moral conduct.

## Chapter 16

**Absolutism.**   A political doctrine that asserts the unrestrained power of a monarch, who is usually considered to hold sovereignty by divine will.

**Chartered Companies.**   Companies of merchants chartered by the crown to conduct business in specified areas overseas (e.g. The East India Company). Such companies often maintained their own armies and fleets of warships.

**Cosmology.**   The study of the universe as an ordered whole.

**Experimentalism.**   The idea, supported by Francis Bacon, Galileo, and others that experiment can determine the validity of a scientific theory, and that, conversely, theories should be experimentally verifiable.

**Heliocentric Theory.**   The theory, originally developed by such ancient thinkers as Eratosthenes and Aristarchus of Samos, that the planets revolve around the sun. Revived by Copernicus in the sixteenth century it was accepted by Kepler and Galileo.

**Hermetic Tradition.**   A body of occult literature, supposedly derived from ancient Egypt, that concerned itself with natural magic, alchemy, and related subjects.

**Magic.**   A science or pseudo-science that attempts to manipulate the supposed relationships among phenomena or natural objects for the magician's ends.

**Oligarchy.**   A form of government in which power is in the hands of a relatively small group of people, usually wealthy ones.

## Chapter 17

**Corporative Society.**   Term to describe the highly stratified social structure of Europe during the Old Regime, with the population in most countries divided into separate legal bodies (most often called estates) each with separate rights, duties, and laws. Also called the *Ständestaat*.

**Elbe-Trieste Line.**   An imaginary diagonal line, drawn on the map of Europe between the mouth of the Elbe River on the North Sea and the town of Trieste at the head of the Adriatic Sea; used by historians as a general line separating western and eastern Europe.

**Gentry.**   A portion of the land-owning upper class, deemed people of "gentle" birth (gentlemen and women), holding a privileged position but not always part of the titled aristocracy (as in England).

**Mercantilism.**   The predominant economic theory of the Old Regime, holding that states should seek self-sufficiency in resources and manufactured goods and thus import little; to achieve this end, the state regulated trade, granting monopolies and regulating manufactures and trade.

**Nobility of the Robe.**   A branch of the nobility in many countries (especially France), composed of families who had recently acquired noble status through service to the monarch, typically as judges; in contrast to the older "nobility of the sword," ennobled for military service.

**Old Regime.**   Term used to describe the period before the French Revolution of 1789 – roughly the 17th and 18th centuries – and its institutional structure of monarchy, aristocracy, and state religions.

**Triangular Trade.**   A pattern of Old Regime commerce, following a triangle across the Atlantic Ocean: European manufactured goods were taken to Africa, slaves from Africa were shipped to the Americas, and American agricultural goods (especially sugar and tobacco) went to Europe.

## Chapter 18

**Columbian Exchange.**   The reciprocal introduction of unknown plants, animals, and microorganisms into Europe and the Americas following the voyages of Columbus, such as the arrival of the first potatoes in Europe or the first sheep in the Americas.

**Eendemic Disease.**   A disease located only in specific regions, such as malaria, which is native to warm, swampy regions.

**Foundlings.**   Unwanted newborn babies, abandoned by their parents at high rates during the Old Regime, sometimes in the open with the expectation of death, sometimes at churches or hospitals, with modest prospects of survival.

**Germ Theory.** The theory of disease transmission holding that invisible microorganisms such as bacteria and viruses spread disease.

**Inoculation.** A medical procedure which intentionally introduces a mild dose of a disease, such as smallpox, into a patient to build antibodies against that disease and acquire future immunity.

**Patriarchal Family.** The typical structure of families during the Old Regime, in which authority—domestic, legal, and economic authority—was vested in the husband/father and obedience was expected from the wife/children.

**Puerperal Fever.** The greatest cause of death among pregnant women during the Old Regime (also known as "child-bed fever") in which the absence of aseptic methods during delivery led to acute infections.

# INDEX

◆◆◆◆◆◆◆◆◆◆◆◆◆◆◆◆◆◆◆◆